PRODUCTIVITY TRENDS IN THE UNITED STATES

NATIONAL BUREAU OF ECONOMIC RESEARCH
NUMBER 71, GENERAL SERIES

Productivity Trends in the United States

BY JOHN W. KENDRICK

THE GEORGE WASHINGTON UNIVERSITY

ASSISTED BY MAUDE R. PECH

A STUDY BY THE

NATIONAL BUREAU OF ECONOMIC RESEARCH, NEW YORK

PUBLISHED BY

PRINCETON UNIVERSITY PRESS, PRINCETON

1961

Printed in the United States of America

This study, one of a series dealing with trends in wages and productivity in the United States during the past century, was made possible by funds granted by the Alfred P. Sloan Foundation. The Sloan Foundation is not, however, the author, publisher, or proprietor of this publication, and is not to be understood as approving or disapproving by virtue of its grant any of the statements made or views expressed herein.

Contents

CONTENTS

CONTENTS

CONTENTS

Tables

APPENDIX TEXT TABLES

APPENDIX BASIC TABLES

Charts

Acknowledgments

MY GREATEST debt for the successful completion of this volume is to Solomon Fabricant, Director of Research of the National Bureau of Economic Research. He provided the opportunity for me to undertake the study and has given me unfailing support and stimulus throughout.

In point of time, my first acknowledgment of indebtedness goes to George Jaszi, formerly Chief of the National Income Division, and now Assistant Director, Office of Business Economics, Department of Commerce. It was while employed in the Office of Business Economics that I was assigned to complete the work, which had been going on for several years, on deflation of the gross national product. Collaborating with Mr. Jaszi on this task, finished in early 1950, was a fruitful experience. Our many discussions taught me much concerning the conceptual and statistical problems involved in the estimation of real product. We also jointly prepared a paper on the productivity implications of the real-product estimates for the 1950 National Conference on Productivity, which helped awaken my interest in the productivity factor in economic growth.

I have also learned much from Gerhard Colm, who directed my doctoral dissertation at the George Washington University on the concept and measurement of national productivity. Dissatisfied with the current "output per manhour" measures, I attempted in the thesis to develop in some detail an operational concept of "total factor productivity." Dr. Colm also provided the opportunity for me to present an early summary of my thinking in a paper on "National Productivity and Its Long-term Projection" for the 1951 Conference on Research in Income and Wealth (subsequently published in Volume 16 of the National Bureau's *Studies in Income and Wealth*).

The present work, begun in late 1953, builds on previous National Bureau estimates of output, labor input, and capital stocks for various industries by extending and supplementing these series and coordinating them with productivity estimates for the economy as a whole. Resource limitations, however, have prevented me from providing much more than an introduction to the analysis and interpretation of these estimates. I hope that this study will, nonetheless, provide a basis for much more research into the dynamic economic processes of which productivity change is an integral part.

ACKNOWLEDGMENTS

Maude Remey Pech has been of invaluable assistance throughout the entire study. She was responsible for most of the calculations involved in the estimates and statistical analyses, and she was my frequent consultant on matters of methodology. She checked all numerical text references against basic tables and was largely responsible for coordinating the final stages of preparation of the finished manuscript.

In the basic work of estimation I had the assistance, for shorter or longer periods, of Lora Katz, John Myers, Lionel Epstein, Harry Campbell, Joseph Viladas, Radivoj Ristic, Howard Ross, and George Philip. The first four worked primarily on the manufacturing industries. Mr. Myers wrote the appendix section on manufacturing capital. Mr. Ristic completed the work, begun by Mr. Viladas, on the mining segment and wrote the first draft of Appendix C. Mr. Ross extended to 1953 the original estimates by Harold Barger of output and employment in the transportation industries. Mr. Phillip brought up to date the estimates for communications and public utilities and prepared an early draft of Appendix F.

I am also much indebted for valuable suggestions to the NBER staff reading committee: Milton Friedman, Thor Hultgren, and Warren Nutter; and to the Directors' committee: Stanley Ruttenberg, George Soule, and Jacob Viner. Further assistance and suggestions were received from other individuals and organizations, as noted to some extent in the appropriate parts of the volume.

I am especially grateful to my wife, Maxine, for her cooperation and understanding during the preparation of this manuscript, which has claimed many of my evening and week-end hours. Indeed, she has been my personal secretary, handling correspondence and filing, and typing many handwritten drafts.

The National Bureau's stenographic group, under the direction of Dorothy Chesterton, deserves commendation for competently typing innumerable pages of the manuscript in its various stages of preparation.

Ester Moskowitz gave the manuscript its final editorial polish, and the charts provide further evidence of H. Irving Forman's skill in graphic presentation.

All these people have my gratitude, as will the readers of this volume who share my appreciation of the key role of productivity in our past, and future, economic progress.

JOHN W. KENDRICK

Basic Facts on Productivity Change

AN INTRODUCTION BY SOLOMON FABRICANT

Importance of the Facts

PRODUCTIVITY has been much discussed in recent years, and too frequently misunderstood.

Productivity deserves the attention that it has received, for it is a measure of the efficiency with which resources are converted into the commodities and services that men want. Higher productivity is a means to better levels of economic well-being and greater national strength. Higher productivity is a major source of the increment in income over which men bargain and sometimes quarrel. And higher—or lower—productivity affects costs, prices, profits, output, employment, and investment, and thus plays a part in business fluctuations, in inflation, and in the rise and decline of industries.

Indeed, in one way or another, productivity enters virtually every broad economic problem, whatever current form or new name the problem takes—industrialization, or research and development, or automation, or tax reform, or cost-price squeeze, or improvement factor, or wage inflation, or foreign dollar shortage.

Despite its importance and the wide attention paid it, productivity is a subject surrounded by considerable confusion. For this there are a number of reasons. First, people employ the same term but mean different things. As a consequence, various figures on productivity change come into use, and these often differ in significant degree. Further, the rate of productivity change is not a fixed quantity. Professor Kendrick's figures show that it varies from one period to another. What the past or current rate of productivity change is depends on the particular period for which the calculation is made. If no reference is made to the period, and if the period varies considerably from one context to another, confusion results. In addition, the statistical information available for calculating productivity

NOTE. A longer version of this summary was published by the National Bureau in 1959 as Occasional Paper 63. Included here are also some paragraphs from a statement presented before the Joint Economic Committee of the United States Congress in April 1959.

John W. Kendrick and Thor Hultgren made helpful comments on a first draft, as did Moses Abramovitz, Jack Alterman, Gary S. Becker, Leon Greenberg, Oswald W. Knauth, Geoffrey H. Moore, and Theodore W. Schultz. The writer is deeply grateful also to Maude Pech.

indexes is deficient in various respects. Better or worse—or merely different—methods of meeting these deficiencies, enumerated below, often yield results that differ appreciably. Failure to specify the methods and the assumptions involved in the process of estimation, or failure to understand them, adds to the confusion.

As has been said, the questions into which productivity enters are important. They are also difficult. We all have far to go before any of us can claim to understand fully the process of productivity change, its causes, or its consequences, or to see clearly the way to deal with the issues involved. But surely the way to more effective policy would be clearer if the basic facts of productivity change were established and widely known.

Establishing important economic facts is an objective of the National Bureau. Because the facts bearing on productivity are important, the Bureau has for a long time devoted a portion of its efforts to their determination and analysis. Its completed studies of national income, capital formation, production trends, mechanization, employment, and productivity have contributed essential pieces of information.

Currently, the task of cultivating this significant area of economic knowledge is being undertaken at the National Bureau in a number of separate, though related, projects: a study of trends in wages and productivity; a study of trends in national product, capital formation, and the relation between capital and product; and a study of cycles in productivity, costs, and profits. Some of the results of these current investigations have already been published (the present report by Professor Kendrick is the latest to be issued); some are in press; others are in various stages of preparation.[1]

Like the other studies, Professor Kendrick's must be rather technical in character, devoted as it is to the examination of concepts, the sifting of evidence, the preparation of estimates, and the analysis of complex results.

[1] The reports already published and those soon forthcoming are as follows: John W. Kendrick, *Productivity Trends: Capital and Labor*, Occasional Paper 53, New York (NBER), 1956; Solomon Fabricant, *Basic Facts on Productivity Change*, Occasional Paper 63, New York (NBER), 1959; John W. Kendrick, *Productivity Trends in the United States* (the present volume); Clarence D. Long, *Wages and Earnings in the United States: 1860–1890*, Princeton University Press (for NBER), 1960; Albert Rees, *Real Wages in Manufacturing, 1890–1914*, Princeton University Press (for NBER), 1961; and Albert Rees, *New Measures of Wage-Earner Compensation in Manufacturing, 1914–57*, O.P. 75, New York (NBER), 1960.

Also, Simon Kuznets, *Capital in the American Economy: Its Formation and Financing*, Princeton University Press (for NBER), in press; Leo Grebler, David M. Blank, and Louis Winnick, *Capital Formation in Residential Real Estate: Trends and Prospects*, Princeton University Press (for NBER), 1956; Alvin S. Tostlebe, *Capital in Agriculture: Its Formation and Financing since 1870*, Princeton University Press (for NBER), 1957; Melville J. Ulmer, *Capital in Transportation, Communications, and Public Utilities: Its Formation and Financing*, Princeton University Press (for NBER), 1960; Daniel Creamer, Sergei P. Dobrovolsky, and Israel Borenstein, *Capital in Manufacturing and Mining: Its Formation and Financing*, Princeton University Press (for NBER), 1960 and Thor Hultgren, *Changes in Labor Cost During Cycles in Production and Business*, Occasional Paper 74, New York (NBER), 1960.

Readers who put Professor Kendrick's important findings to practical use will appreciate the care he has taken to expose to their scrutiny the evidence on which the findings are based.

The more general reader may wish to have a less technical summary of the main results of this substantial research effort. This introduction is for him.

Even a summary of facts will have to cover a good deal of territory. Something needs to be said about each of the following matters: the long-term average rate of growth of national productivity; the degree to which growth of productivity has experienced change in pace; productivity increase in relation to the rise in the nation's real output; and the extent to which increase of productivity has been the general experience of the various industries of the economy. To each of these subjects, therefore, a brief section is devoted, which lists the main facts and provides such discussion of concepts, data, alternative measurements and findings as is necessary to make the results intelligible. We begin with a capsule statement of the highlights.

The Facts in a Nutshell

The essential facts on productivity and economic growth in the United States can be put most briefly and simply as follows:

1. During the past three generations, the nation's real output per manhour of work done has been rising at a substantial average rate—between 2 and 2.5 per cent per annum, or about 25 per cent per decade. This upward movement shows no signs of slowing down. On the contrary, the trend witnessed by this generation has been higher than the trend witnessed by earlier generations. Indeed, during the most recent period—after World War II—national output per manhour rose at a rate of 3 to 3.5 per cent per annum, or 35 to 40 per cent per decade. This means, in absolute terms, that in ten years there has seen *added* to an already large output per hour of American labor an amount that is well in excess of the *total* output obtained per hour of work in most regions of the earth.

2. The increase in national output per manhour is the outcome, first, of a heavy investment in business and farm plant and equipment, in public improvements, and in other tangible capital goods. The volume of tangible capital per head of the population has increased at an average rate of over 1 per cent per annum, or 10 per cent per decade. A contribution has come, second, from investment in education and on-the-job training and from expenditures on research and development and other forms of intangible capital. No really adequate figures can yet be offered here, but the contribution has undoubtedly been significant. Third has been greatly improved efficiency in the use of the country's labor and tangible and intangible capital resources.

3. A growing fraction of the potential product offered by a higher and higher output per manhour has been given up by our people in order to enjoy more leisure. Normal weekly hours of work per employed person, for example, have been cut by 20 to 30 per cent, on the average, since the turn of the century; and the practice of paid vacations, and of longer vacations has beome more widespread. Another fraction of the rising output per manhour has been used to finance investment in private and public capital. This fraction, however, has not had to rise to bring the great expansion in capital per head of the population to which reference was made a moment ago. In fact, it may even have fallen a bit. Still another and growing fraction has been used to meet the increased needs of national security. Along with this, a much smaller fraction has gone into technical and military assistance and aid to other countries. The rest, the great bulk of the rise in output per manhour, has been used by our people to get the goods and services for which they have worked and saved —a larger volume and better quality of goods and services, and many new goods and services. National consumption per capita has grown at a rate somewhat lower than the rate of increase in output per manhour; but the rate has nevertheless been very substantial—something like 1.8 per cent per annum, or 20 per cent per decade, on the average.

4. The gains of productivity have been widely diffused among our people. Real hourly earnings, including fringe benefits of several sorts, have grown about as rapidly, on the average, as has output per manhour. Further, a roughly similar upward trend is visible in the real hourly earnings of each of the industries for which figures are available. The rate of return on capital has tended to remain roughly constant, on the average, but even this horizontal trend reflects a gain from productivity in an important sense, since the great increase in capital per worker already mentioned would probably have reduced the rate of return on capital had not productivity risen.

5. Increased productivity inevitably involves the growth of new industries and the relative, or even absolute, decline of old ones. So, too, for different occupations and regions, which also have grown at widely different rates. In some cases this has meant the painful and difficult adjustments that constitute one of the costs of economic progress.

To spell out some of these points, and present some of the significant details, let us now draw on the remarkable record provided by Professor Kendrick.

The Long-Term Rate of Increase in National Productivity

Over the seventy-year period since 1889—the period which has been examined most closely and for which presently available statistics are most adequate—the rate of increase in productivity has been as follows:

Physical output per manhour in the private economy has grown at an average rate that appears to be about 2.4 per cent per annum.

Comparing output with a measure of labor input in which a highly paid manhour of work counts for proportionately more than a low-wage manhour yields a measure of productivity for the private economy that grew at a significantly smaller rate—about 2.0 per cent per annum.

A measure of productivity for the private economy that compares output not only with labor input (determined as before) but also with tangible capital, each weighted by the market value of its services, grew still less rapidly—about 1.7 per cent per annum.

All these indexes of productivity in the private economy rose somewhat more rapidly than the corresponding indexes for the economy as a whole, including government, when the usual measurements of government output and input are utilized. For the total including government, productivity rose about 1.5 per cent per annum.

This list presents the main broad measures of long-term productivity increase that Professor Kendrick has calculated for the American economy. It is by no means complete. Kendrick goes to some trouble to provide still other measures that differ in definition of output or input, in the degree to which they cover the economy, or in details of estimation. However, these alternative calculations yield results similar to those just given (compare, for example, Tables 1, 2, and 3), and we may, therefore, concentrate on the above measures. They differ enough among themselves to raise a serious question about the meaning and measurement of productivity.

Which measure of productivity is appropriate in any case depends, of course, on the question in mind. Change in output per manhour, for example, shows the combined effect on the product obtained from an hour of labor of two groups of factors: first, those causing increases in efficiency; and, second, those causing changes in the volume of tangible and intangible capital available per manhour. This measure answers an important question. But if what is wanted is a measure of increase in efficiency alone —and it is efficiency on which we are concentrating here—the index of output per manhour is deficient. A better measure, for our purpose, is one that compares output with the combined use of *all* resources.

Information on all resources is not available, however. Until rather recently, economists interested in measuring the rate of increase in national productivity had to make shift with labor input alone—first in terms of number of workers, then in terms of manhours. This is still true for most individual industries, narrowly defined, even on a historical basis, and for both individual industries and the economy as a whole on a current basis.

For this reason, the most widely used index of productivity—the one cited first—is simply physical output per manhour. It is a useful index, if its limitations are recognized. Because in the economy at large and, as we shall see, in most—not all—individual industries, labor input is by far the most important type of input (measured by the fraction of income accruing to it), the index based on manhours alone is not often in serious error. It is a fair approximation to a more comprehensive index of efficiency. But as such it is usually subject to an upward bias, as the figures cited indicate.

The bias in output per manhour results not only from the omission of capital input. The usual index of output per manhour fails also to take into account change in the composition or quality of labor.[2] That is, manhours worked by persons of different skills, levels of education, and lengths of experience are treated as if equivalent, thus ignoring important forms of human capital that aid in production and contribute to wage and salary differentials. The index of output per weighted manhour—the second index cited—catches some of this intangible capital, for the labor in industries with high rates of pay is given a heavier weight than that in low-pay industries. However, the procedure of weighting is only a step in the right direction. All the labor within an industry is still assumed to be homogeneous. Perhaps more important, broad advances in education and the like, which improve the quality of labor in industries generally, are not taken into account. And differences in labor quality are imperfectly measured by pay differentials, since these are influenced by such other factors as the noneconomic advantages and disadvantages of particular occupations, differences in the cost of living, and uncompleted adjustments to changes in demand and supply. The figures previously given— the difference between the rate of increase in output per manhour and in output per unit of labor (weighted manhours), which is 0.4 per cent per annum—therefore indicate the direction, but not the degree of bias, arising from the neglect of changes in the quality of labor.

With respect to the volume of tangible capital, we are in a better position than with respect to the quality of labor. In recent years the available information on tangible capital has been broadened, worked

---

[2] If the index relates output to manhours of work done only by "production workers"— which is frequently the case for individual industries—there is a further source of error. In that case, the index will usually rise more rapidly than output per manhour of work done by all workers; for "nonproduction workers" have, over the years, generally increased in relative importance. Kendrick's indexes relate output to the work done by *all* workers, including proprietors, supervisory employees, and clerical workers, as well as wage earners.

over, pieced out, and put into usable form by Kuznets and his collaborators, and this has helped greatly to expand the coverage of inputs for productivity indexes. The data on tangible capital are still far from perfect. In calculating them, difficulties of all sorts are involved—the treatment of depreciation, the problem of allowing for changes in prices, and the proper valuation of land, among others. These problems have not been entirely solved, but we appear to be sufficiently close to a solution to warrant use of the data. With them, output per unit of tangible capital may be computed (as in Table 1). This is informative; but, like output per unit of labor, it is an incomplete index of productivity. It tells only part of the story.

Indexes of productivity based on the comparison of output with the input of both labor and tangible capital are better measures of efficiency than those based on labor input or capital input alone.

Indeed, the best currently available approximation to a measure of efficiency is such an index. As we have seen (it is the third index cited initially in the text), it indicates a rate of growth of productivity that is significantly below the rate for output in relation to labor input alone. That it is lower will not be a surprise, since it is well known that tangible capital has increased substantially more than the labor force: tangible capital per weighted manhour has risen at the average annual rate of 1.0 per cent. Because the services of labor have become more and more expensive relative to those of tangible capital, there has been a strong incentive for business firms and other producers to substitute capital for labor. Yet—and this may be surprising—capital increased less rapidly than did output. On net balance, output per unit of tangible capital rose by about 1 per cent per annum. Technological advance and the other means to improved efficiency have led to savings of capital as well as of labor.

Surprising, also, may be the fact that the difference between productivity measured in terms of labor and tangible capital combined and productivity measured in terms of labor alone is no more than the 0.4 per cent per annum that we have found. The reason is the relatively high weight given labor in combining it with tangible capital. Obviously, manhours cannot be combined with dollars of tangible capital without translating each of them into comparable units. The appropriate unit is a dollar's worth of services in a reference base period. If a manhour of labor commands $2 in the base period, and $100 of capital equipment commands $6 of net revenue per year (whether in rent, profits, or otherwise is immaterial), we count the $100 of equipment as equivalent to 3 manhours. Because, in production, use is made of many more manhours than of even hundreds of dollars of capital, labor as a whole gets a much greater weight than does capital. The weights for the private economy are currently as 8 to 2. The index of output per unit of labor and capital combined—

which rose at the rate of 1.7 per cent per annum in the private economy—is thus, in effect, a weighted average of the index of output per unit of labor—2.0 per cent per annum—and of the index of output per unit of capital—1.0 per cent.

This weighted index was called the best available approximation to the measure of efficiency that we seek. It is approximate for more reasons than those already given. One is the problem of measuring output, which involves combining into a meaningful aggregate a changing variety of old and new goods. A special difficulty arises in putting a figure on the quantity of services produced by government to meet collective wants. This accounts for the greater confidence most statisticians have in the estimate of productivity for the private economy, exclusive of government, and explains the plurality of estimates given in Table 2 for the economy inclusive of government.

A general deficiency of all the measures of output—and thus of productivity—is their failure to take adequate account of change in the quality of output. This, it is likely, subjects them to a downward bias. And to, repeat, the indexes of output per unit of labor and tangible capital combined, though broader than any other indexes now available, fail to cover adequately the investment in education, science, technology, and social organization that serves to increase production—a point to which we shall have to return.

The technical questions raised above (which have been selected from the host to which Kendrick pays attention) are, of course, matters primarily for the producer rather than the user of productivity statistics. But for the user it is important to be aware of the sharp differences made in the rate of growth of productivity by technical choices not always specified: whether output or input is defined in one way rather than another, or weights of components of output and input are determined by this rather than that method, or data are selected or estimated from one or another source.

Measured in any of the ways listed above, however, productivity in the United States has grown at a remarkable average rate over the past two-thirds of a century. The more comprehensive indexes, in which output is compared with both labor and capital input, indicate a doubling of efficiency every forty years. The index of output per unweighted manhour indicates a doubling even more frequently—every thirty years. Not many of the countries for which corresponding records might be constructed would show average rates as high or higher over so long a period. Over shorter periods, it is very likely, our long-term rate has been exceeded in various countries. This has happened here, as well as elsewhere, as we shall see in a moment. But it is safe to say that the United States long-term rate is not low in relation to the experience of other countries over comparable periods. It may appear low only in comparison with aspirations—the long-term rates dreamed of by countries embarked on ambitious programs of economic development, or the rates some of our own citizens believe we need to reach and maintain if we are to meet some of the urgent problems that confront us.

Fluctuations in the Rate of Productivity Increase

Productivity did not grow at an even rate. Its rate of growth was subject to a variety of changes, which may be characterized as follows:

A distinct change in trend appeared sometime after World War I. By each of our measures, productivity rose, on the average, more rapidly after World War I than before.

Over the whole period since 1889, productivity fluctuated with the state of business. Year-to-year rises in productivity were greater than the long-term rate when business was generally expanding, and less (or often, falling), when business was generally contracting.

The slow rates of increase (or decline) in productivity appear to have been largely concentrated in the first stages of business contraction. Productivity rose most rapidly, as a rule, towards the end of contraction and during the early stages of expansion.

Year-to-year changes in productivity were appreciably influenced also by random factors.

The change in trend that came after World War I is one of the most interesting facts before us. There is little question about it. It is visible not only in the indexes that Kendrick has compiled for the private domestic economy, to which Charts 3 and 4 are confined. It can be found also in his figures for the whole economy, including government, as well as in his estimates for the group of industries for which individual productivity indexes are available. Some readers of the charts might prefer to see in them not a sharp alteration of trend, but rather a gradual speeding up of the rate of growth over the period as a whole. The latter reading is not entirely out of the question, but it seems to fit the facts less well than the former. By either reading, it is clear, the rate of growth in productivity witnessed by the present generation has been substantially higher than the rate experienced in the quarter-century before World War I.

The numerical rates of increase that Kendrick gives in Table 1 help to sharpen the differences. Alternative choices of the boundary year (which is rather arbitrarily set at 1919), and of the technical method of calculating the average rate,[3] would not eliminate the difference between the two periods.

[3] Because productivity fluctuates cyclically and otherwise, it is usually somewhat better to derive rates of increase from averages for several years, rather than from the figures for single years. For the long periods covered in Table 1, the differences would be negligible, however.

The change in trend came in each of the indexes shown, and at about the same time in each—in output per unit of labor (weighted or unweighted), in output per unit of tangible capital, and in output per unit of labor and capital combined. There is this difference, however: the quickening of pace was greater for capital productivity than for labor productivity, though it was by no means negligible for the latter. For output per unit of labor and capital combined, the rate of growth since World War I has been as much as 50 per cent higher than during the earlier period.

The charts show also the cyclical pattern of change in productivity, insofar as this is revealed by annual figures. As a rule, whenever national output rose—which is virtually whenever business was generally expanding—productivity grew more rapidly than its trend rate; whenever output fell, productivity grew less rapidly than its trend rate, or actually declined.

It is obvious why this is so when input is measured by the resources available for use, as it is in the case of tangible capital. The total volume of tangible capital in existence seldom declines even during business contractions, for net additions to capital have rarely become negative in this country; nor does the volume of tangible capital rise nearly as rapidly as output during business expansion, for additions to capital are small relative to the existing stock. For similar reasons, the labor force—and even more so, the population of persons of working age—also is very stable. Output per unit of available resources, whether of labor, capital, or labor and capital combined, will therefore show pronounced cyclical fluctuations—as Kendrick illustrates in Chart 5.

Much less obvious is the cyclical fluctuation of output per unit of resources actually put to use, which can be measured for labor.[4] There were 47 year-to-year rises and 21 falls in general business. Accompanying these rises and falls in output were the changes in labor productivity shown in Table 3. The average of the rates of growth in output per weighted manhour during the years of expansion in output equaled 2.4 per cent. During the years of contraction in output, the average annual rate of growth of output per weighted manhour equaled only 1.3 per cent.

[4] It is not possible to construct an adequate measure of capital input that takes account of the rise and fall in the intensity with which capital is used as business improves or worsens. There is, at present, insufficient information on the opening up or shutting down of plants or production lines, the movement of stand-by equipment into and out of use, and the change in number of shifts per day. Nor would using the rate of employment of the labor force and of hours of work per employee to approximate the rate of use of tangible capital add anything to what the index of output per manhour tells us.

Even for labor, the measure of actual use leaves something to be desired in the case of salaried workers. The measure of output, too, probably has some cyclical bias, for a variety of reasons; for example, it does not cover some types of maintenance and repair to which workers can be diverted when business is slack.

Because Kendrick's annual indexes involve a great deal of estimation and the piecing out of scanty data, it is encouraging to find some confirmation of the results in a sample of individual industries (largely manufacturing) that has been compiled by Thor Hultgren for the period since 1933. In gathering these statistics, Hultgren made a special effort to obtain adequate and comparable data on output and the manhours worked by wage earners. His sample has the further advantage of providing information on a monthly basis, far more satisfactory for the study of cyclical fluctuations than annual data.

Hultgren's data, set forth in his *Changes in Labor Cost During Cycles in Production and Business*, point to a most striking fact, something that we miss in the annual figures. As was shown by Kendrick's annual data, interruption of the rise in output per manhour came mainly during contractions. But the monthly data suggest, further, that most of the interruption may have usually been concentrated in the first half of contraction. After contraction had been under way for a while, and well before general business revival, output per manhour as a rule resumed its upward march, and increased at a rate even greater than the rate of increase during the latter part of expansion.

Hultgren's results are not altogether consistent, and his sample of industries and cycles is narrow and needs to be broadened. But if confirmed, his findings have interesting implications for the causes and consequences of productivity change. For example, they suggest that the most rapid rates of increase in output per manhour appear during that portion of the business cycle—the last stages of contraction and the early stages of expansion—when replacement and increase of plant and equipment are proceeding most slowly, and that during the initial stages of contraction, decline in output per manhour joins with increase in wage rates to push unit labor costs up.

Beyond the cyclical fluctuations in the rate of growth of productivity, other changes may be noticed in Kendrick's charts. These include occasional spurts and slowdowns that extend over a period of years. Kendrick's estimates, and similar data compiled earlier by Kuznets and Abramovitz for the full period following the Civil War, suggest the existence of a long cycle in the rate of change of productivity.[5] High rates of increase in net national product per unit of total input came, it seems, during periods of a decade or more centered in the late 1870's, the late 1890's, the early 1920's, the late 1930's, and the late 1940's or early 1950's.

[5] See Moses Abramovitz, *Resource and Output Trends in the United States since 1870*, Occasional Paper 52, New York (NBER), 1956. A section of Kuznets's forthcoming *Capital in the American Economy* is devoted to long waves in output, capital, and the ratio of capital to output. Abramovitz is currently studying this class of phenomena and related factors; for progress reports see the *Thirty-eighth Annual Report* of the National Bureau, 1958, pp. 47–56, and the *Thirty-ninth Annual Report*, 1959, pp. 23–27.

Low rates of increase came during periods centered in the late 1880's, the late 1910's, the early 1930's, and the 1940's.[6]

Some of the irregular changes shown in Charts 3 and 4 undoubtedly reflect inadequacies of the figures. Productivity change is measured by the ratio of two indexes, each subject to error; and even slight errors in these will sometimes combine to produce considerable error in the ratio, just as they will sometimes cancel one another. We cannot be sure whether or not the change between any particular pair of years is the result simply of statistical error. On the other hand, that the errors are, on the whole, not overwhelming is suggested by the fairly systematic business cycle behavior that we have noticed. We know, also, that some of the irregularities reflect not statistical error but the impact of weather, strikes, and the other real random factors to which life is subject.

The picture emerging from the information gathered by Kendrick and Hultgren is one of a persistent and powerful tendency towards improvement in efficiency. Sometimes the outcome was a rapid, sometimes a slow, rate of growth in productivity. Sometimes the tendency was entirely offset for a while by cyclical and random factors. But only twice was the interruption long enough to prevent productivity from reaching a new high within five years.

Because the rate of increase in productivity has been far from uniform, the user of productivity figures must know the period to which they relate. Rates of productivity increase derived from one period will differ, sometimes considerably, from those derived from a longer, or shorter, or altogether different period. The same caution may be noted with regard to extrapolations of past trends into the future. These, the record suggests, will always be rather risky.

Productivity and the Increase in National Product

The nation's product or real income—the terms are interchangeable—may be said to have grown through increases in the volume of resources available for use in production, and through increases in productivity, or the efficiency with which these resources are turned into product. Measurement of these two sources of increase in product suggests their relative importance over the past sixty-eight years:

Each year's increase in productivity accounted, on the average, for almost half of the year's increase in product. The other half reflected, of course, an increase in resources—labor and tangible capital.

Productivity increase accounted for a larger fraction—about eight-tenths—of each year's increase in per capita product, with

[6] A word of caution: The dating is very rough; and the levels of peaks in rate of increase vary greatly among themselves, as do the levels of troughs.

the rise in per capita resources contributing the other two-tenths.

Prior to World War I, both per capita resources and productivity grew significantly, and thus both contributed to the rise in per capita product. Since World War I, per capita resources have fallen slightly; but productivity has risen even more rapidly than before—rapidly enough, in fact, to keep per capita product growing at an average rate not far below the rate for the earlier period.
The full set of statistics for the national economy is set forth in Charts 6 and 7.

These results—and the results presented earlier—can be properly understood only if certain qualifications are kept in mind.

It is evident, to begin with, that the relative contributions to growth of product, of productivity on the one hand and of resources on the other, that emerge from these and similar calculations, depend on what is included in product and what is included in resources. More exactly, they depend on the importance and relative growth of the borderline items that are or are not included in each of these. What is in fact included is in part influenced by convention and in part by the availability of statistical data.

With respect to output, we have already noticed the question of government services. Similar questions arise with respect to certain expenditures by families—trade union fees and costs of getting to work are examples; and with respect to certain expenditures by business—for example, subsidies to factory cafeterias, "expense accounts," and medical services provided employees.[7] The main problem, however, appears to be with respect to defense expenditures by government (which has reached large proportions), and for this reason Kendrick has presented estimates that differ in the treatment of these expenditures (Table 2; and Appendix A, "National Product as Estimated by Kuznets").

More important seems to be the definition of resources. Kendrick has measured these by weighted manhours of work done and tangible capital available, and has thus largely excluded intangible capital. This results in some understatement of the contribution of resources, for it is likely that intangible capital has risen in relation to the resources he includes. There is a corresponding overstatement of the rise of productivity. It is possible that the upward shift in the rate of growth of productivity after World War I, and the downward shift in the rate of growth in per capita tangible

---

[7] For recent discussions, see *A Critique of the United States Income and Product Accounts*, Studies in Income and Wealth, Volume 22, and *The National Economic Accounts of the United States: Review, Appraisal, and Recommendations*, both issued by the National Bureau in 1958.

capital at about the same time, reflect some substitution of investment in intangible capital for investment in tangible capital.

In an important sense, society's intangible capital includes all the improvements in basic science, technology, business administration, and education and training that aid in production—whether these result from deliberate individual or collective investments for economic gain or are incidental by-products of efforts to reach other goals. If intangible capital were so defined, it would probably follow that much (not all) of the increase in product would reflect increase in resources. But so wide a definition of intangible capital would get us no closer to determining the causes of increase in product.

With the statistics presently available we have been able to measure the direct effects on output of the increases in labor time and in volume of tangible capital. We have been forced to lump together under the heading of productivity, and to measure as a whole, the indirect effects of the increases in these resources and the effects of all other causes. The residue includes the contributions of the several forms of intangible capital mentioned; the economies resulting from increased specialization within and between industries, made possible by growth in the nation's resources and in its scale of operations generally; the improvement (or falling off) of efficiency in the use of resources resulting from changes in the degree of competition, in the volume, direction and character of governmental subsidies, in the nature of the tax system, and in other government activities and regulations; and the greater (or smaller) benefits resulting from changes in the volume, character, and freedom of commerce among nations.

The simple calculation presented above does no more than suggest the high relative importance of the factors grouped under productivity. But that is significant. It is, as Abramovitz has pointed out, a "measure of our ignorance" concerning the causes of economic growth, and an "indication of where we need to concentrate our attention."[8] It is well to know how far short we are of determining the sources of increase in national product.

Productivity in Individual Industries

The rate of growth in the entire economy's productivity is the prime fact with which we are concerned. The facts on productivity in individual industries, to which Kendrick has devoted his last two chapters, are important, however, because they help us to understand the process by which national productivity has been raised:

> Rise in productivity has been a general industrial phenomenon. Virtually every individual industry for which a reasonably adequate index can be calculated shows an upward trend in

[8] *Op. cit.*, p. 11.

output per manhour, and this was almost as universally true of output per unit of tangible capital and of output per unit of labor and capital combined.

Among individual industries, as for the economy as a whole, the rise in output per manhour—the index most commonly available—nearly always exceeded the rise in productivity with capital as well as labor taken into account. For some industries the difference between the two measures was considerable.

Though almost all industries showed rises in productivity, there was great variation among them in the average rate of rise. Also, as might be expected, individual industries usually experienced greater temporal variation in the rate of productivity increase than did the economy as a whole.

The industries whose productivity advanced more rapidly than productivity in industries generally were more often than not also those that expanded their output and employment of labor and capital more than industry at large. Industries in which productivity lagged usually had a smaller growth in output and employment of labor and capital than industry at large—or even declined.

The generality of rise in productivity is the outstanding fact that emerges when individual industries are studied. It is illustrated by the detailed figures for major divisions given in Chart 12, and by the changes between 1899 and 1953 in thirty-three industries or divisions given in Table 35.

It is true that the statistics relate to a limited number of industries. The thirty-three industries for which individual productivity indexes are available make up less than half the entire economy, measured either by output or input. These industries, some narrowly and some broadly defined, are largely from the commodity-producing sectors of the economy, and observations are for the period beginning with 1899. Lack of data prevents giving similar information for earlier years and for other industries—the service industries, construction, trade, and government, and even some individual manufacturing, mining, and utility industries.[9]

However, it is very likely that productivity has increased not only in the industries for which separate productivity indexes could be calculated, but also in the others, including the service industries. This is indicated by Kendrick's comparison of the productivity rise in the "covered" industries (Table A-XXV) with the rise in the economy as a whole (Table A-XIX). The implied rate of increase of productivity in the industries not covered is of the same order of magnitude as the rate for the

[9] Kendrick's index for manufacturing as a whole, like all such indexes, is based on a sample of manufacturing industries. This is also true, in greater or lesser degree, of the other industries he could cover.

aggregate of those covered. Since this estimate is subject to considerable error, it cannot be conclusive in itself. But what we know of technological developments and the other immediate causes of productivity change in the service industries, for example, supports the impression of a rise.[10] We know, too, that the factors that make for increasing efficiency in the use of resources are general in character and are felt everywhere in the economy. Virtually all industries use mechanical power and have reaped some advantages from broadened national markets. More fundamentally, no industry has been free of the drives that improve efficiency.

Since the indexes for individual industries are often put to specific use, it is well to recognize that they are often less reliable than the indexes for the economy at large. In part, the deficiency arises from the diversity of sources from which the data on output and input come. This causes discrepancies in the matching of output and input. And other statistical errors are imbedded, which tend to cancel out in the indexes for the economy as a whole.

Probably more important is the difficulty created by interindustry flows of materials, fuel, services, and semifabricated components. For a single industry, output is generally measured on a gross basis: that is, output is not only the value (at base-period prices) of work done by labor and tangible capital on the goods and services supplied by other industries, but also the sum of the value of the work done and the value (also at base-period prices) of these supplies from other industries.[11] Subtraction of these supplies from gross output to yield an index of net output (as is in effect done to get the economy-wide index of output) would solve the problem. But only a few attempts to measure the net output of individual industries have been made, and these (except possibly for agriculture) must be viewed as still largely experimental and subject to considerable error.[12] With output measured gross, the supplies from other industries constitute an input on a par with the services of the labor the industry employs and the services of the tangible (and intangible) capital it uses. Labor and tangible capital alone thus fall short of measuring total input— much more so than in the case of the private economy as a whole. The usual productivity index for an individual industry, even if broad enough to include capital in the measure of resources used, is therefore

[10] See, for example, the interesting discussion of developments in trade in Harold Barger's *Distribution's Place in the American Economy since 1869*, Princeton University Press (for NBER), 1955.

[11] Gross output in this sense is "grosser" than gross national product, which differs from net product only by the amount of depreciation and other capital consumption.

[12] This and other problems of measurement were discussed in a meeting of the Conference on Research in Income and Wealth (October 1958). The proceedings have been published as Volume 25, *Output, Input, and Productivity Measurement*, Princeton University Press (for NBER), 1961.

correspondingly deficient. For many industries, perhaps, the resulting error is small. But this is by no means always the case, as is indicated by Kendrick's figures for agriculture (Tables B-I and B-II).

There is good evidence, further, that improved efficiency in the use of materials, fuel, and the like had been significant in certain industries— for example, electric power plants—and for these, the index of productivity based on gross output relative to input of labor and capital alone will understate the rise of efficiency. On the other hand, industries have generally become more specialized, and many now purchase materials and services formerly produced on their own premises—power used in manufacturing is an example. This works in the other direction.

Connections of these sorts between individual industries and other industries not only create difficulties of productivity measurement, but point also to the sources of productivity increase and diffusion. The connections provide channels along which new or improved or lower-cost materials, fuel, power, services, and equipment, as well as ideas, flow in to improve efficiency. What happens in an industry is influenced by the diligence, enterprise, and ability of its workers, management, and investors. It is influenced also by the quality and quantity of what the industry obtains from the rest of the world, domestic and foreign.

The fact that most of the individual-industry indexes are subject to greater error than the national indexes partly accounts for the differences among industries in average rate of productivity increase. It also contributes to the greater temporal variability of the industry indexes as compared with the fluctuations of the over-all indexes. But these deficiencies can hardly account for all the variation in average rate or for all the differences in degree of fluctuation. Technological development and the other immediate factors that impinge on labor, capital, or total productivity often affect different industries at different times and in different degrees. Some of the time and space variation in rate of productivity increase must be "real."

Industry differences in the behavior of output per unit of tangible capital, are especially striking and deserve comment. We noticed earlier that progress in the economy at large has led to reductions in the quantity of capital used per unit of product, despite substitutions of capital for labor. Over the period as a whole the phenomenon has been a general one, but the exceptions have been many. For example, output per unit of capital fell in agriculture over the twenty years 1899–1919, and, more recently, during 1948–53; rose during most of the other years of the period 1899–1953; and remained unchanged on net balance between 1899 and 1953. In manufacturing industries, also, output per unit of capital fell rather generally during 1899–1919; and in a fair number of them this was true also for 1948–53; but for the period as a whole, there was a net rise in output per unit of capital in the great majority of manufacturing industries. In the case of the railroads and public utilities, the figures suggest rather clearly that increase in the scale of operations led to important economies in the use of fixed capital. The tendency may have been operating in other industries also, but if so, it was overshadowed by other developments.

Increased efficiency in the use of supplies, materials, fuel, or equipment, and substitution of one input for another, already mentioned, altered relations among industries and caused differences in rates of growth of output and input. Further, a better-than-average increase in an industry's productivity usually meant lower relative costs, lower relative prices (as we shall see later), and, therefore, a better-than-average increase in its output (Chart 22). Better-than-average increases in output were usually accompanied by better-than-average increases in employment of workers and tangible capital, despite the more rapid rise in productivity. Correspondingly, less-than-average increases in productivity were usually accompanied by less-than-average increases (or even decreases) in output and in the use of labor and capital resources.[13]

These relations do not exhaust the channels through which productivity and the forces back of it caused diversity in the growth of industries. The general increase in productivity and the increased income it brought per capita raised the demand for the output of industries that produce the goods and services on which people spend more freely as they grow richer, and thus helped push their output up more than that of other industries less favored—even when their productivity lagged behind that of other industries, and their costs and prices rose. The service industries are examples.

No one concerned with the rise and fall of industries, or—to single out a currently discussed problem—with the effects of "automation" on employment, may ignore these basic facts.

Although I have taken a good deal of space to introduce Professor Kendrick's study, I have not been able to include, or even refer to, many of his results that will interest even the general reader. For Professor Kendrick has provided us with what is, to the best of my knowledge, the most comprehensive survey of productivity trends in the United States ever made. It is a record that should find many uses.

[13] It should be noted that "better-than-average" in the text above refers to a comparison with the unweighted median of the thirty-three industry changes covered in the correlation, not to a comparison with the weighted average for the entire private domestic economy.

PART I

Introduction

CHAPTER 1

The Significance of Productivity Change : Introduction and Preview of Study

THE story of productivity, the ratio of output to input, is at heart the record of man's efforts to raise himself from poverty. The record for the United States begins mainly in the latter part of the nineteenth century. This is a relatively brief segment even of modern history, but it is a period and a setting in which efforts to raise productive efficiency were notably successful. Of the fourfold increase in real net national product per capita between 1889 and 1957, productivity advance accounted for about three-fourths. This meant not only a large gain in the plane of living, but an increase in the quality and variety of goods and an expansion of leisure time, while increasing provision was made for future growth and for national security. It is the purpose of this volume to describe these United States productivity trends and to indicate some interrelationships between productivity change and changes in economic aggregates and the economic structure.

The Growth of Interest in Productivity

Almost from the beginning of the modern scientific-technological era economists have been concerned with the effects of technological advance on economic development. It has only been in the last generation, however, that concern with productivity advance has become widespread.

Adam Smith gave classic expression to the role of productivity advance in national economic growth when he wrote:

> The annual produce of the land and labour of any nation can be increased in its value by no other means, but by increasing either the number of its productive labourers, or the productive powers of those labourers who had before been employed . . . in consequence either of some addition and improvement to those machines and instruments which facilitate and abridge labour; or of a more proper division and distribution of employment.[1]

---

[1] Adam Smith, *An Inquiry Into the Nature and Causes of the Wealth of Nations*, New York, Random House, 1937, p. 326. Various mercantilist writers before Smith had noted the importance of productivity in national economic growth (see E. A. Johnson, *Predecessors of Adam Smith*, New York, Prentice-Hall, 1937).

David Ricardo and John Stuart Mill, who dominated economic thought over much of the nineteenth century, likewise recognized the importance of productivity change in economic development, but did not share Smith's optimistic view of the future. They theorized that as population grew and pressed against limited natural resources, productivity in agriculture and mining would decline and offset any rise in industrial productivity, thus tending to check population growth. Ricardo recognized that the "stationary state" might be postponed by technological advance, but he held that over the long run the tendency towards a diminishing return in the extractive industries would prevail. Naturally, some economists disagreed with this dismal prognosis. Henry C. Carey, John Rae, and Henry George in America, for example, asserted that productivity advance rather than diminishing returns accompanies economic expansion. Even Marx clearly recognized the capitalist dynamic that promotes cost-reducing innovations, although he mistakenly predicted that workers would not share in productivity gains.[2]

In speculating about economic change, it is obvious that the theorists were badly handicapped or misled by lack of economic data. It became generally apparent by the latter part of the nineteenth century that the Ricardo-Mill thesis was wrong, at least for relevant time periods. As Henry Sidgwick judiciously concluded ". . . our evidence does not enable us to lay down any concrete law."[3]

With the development of marginal analysis, the focus of economics shifted to value theory which, with its assumptions of static technology, tastes, and resources, does not depend on economic time series for its content. Yet many economists continued to be intrigued by the "high theme of economic progress." Alfred Marshall himself, although one of the architects of static equilibrium theory, cautioned that "economic problems are imperfectly presented when they are treated as problems of statical equilibrium, and not of organic growth. For though the statical treatment alone can give us definiteness and precision of thought . . . it is yet only an introduction."[4] But major progress in the study of economic change had to await a new impetus that would spur the development of the body of economic statistics necessary for fruitful analysis.

That impetus came with the great depression of the 1930's and was heightened by subsequent events. Odd as it may seem to the postwar generation, interest in obtaining data on productivity and related economic

[2] "Capital must revolutionize the technical and social conditions of the labour process itself, before the productivity of labour can be increased." Karl Marx, *Capital*, trans. from 4th German edition, New York, International Publishers, 1929, p. 328.

[3] Henry Sidgwick, *Principles of Political Economy*, pp. 154–155 (quoted in Edmund Whittaker, *A History of Economic Ideas*, New York and London, Longmans, Green, 1940, p. 345).

[4] Alfred Marshall, *Principles of Economics*, 8th ed., London, Macmillan, 1920, p. 461.

variables arose out of concern with the labor-displacing role of technology and with the possibility of secular stagnation. With World War II and the postwar era, concern with technological unemployment and stagnation evaporated and interest in productivity shifted to its income-expanding aspect. Strong advances in productivity were recognized as necessary to increase output and national security potentials during both the war and the "cold war" that followed. Productivity gains were seen as vital for the reconstruction of war-torn nations and for the development of economically backward countries in which there was increasing pressure for economic growth. Productivity advances were also regarded as a means of mitigating the inflationary tendencies arising from the generally buoyant demand situation in the postwar era. Union leaders viewed productivity increase as a major argument for raising wage rates and as the chief means of increasing real labor income. The establishment of productivity centers in many countries of the world and the visits of "productivity teams" to the United States to study our practice are evidence of the degree to which productivity-mindedness has spread in the past decade.

Interacting with the growing consciousness of the important role of productivity advance in meeting major challenges of the period was the accelerated development of a body of economic statistics concerning output, inputs, productivity, and related variables. The obvious need in the 1930's for improved economic intelligence in order better to devise policies to combat depression led Congress to step up appropriations for the expansion of statistical work. Of potential importance for productivity estimation was the beginning of regular official national income estimates in 1932. The Department of Commerce was aided in this work by technicians from the National Bureau of Economic Research, which had begun national income studies more than a decade earlier and had expanded its own work in the field in the 1930's. The national income estimates were later transformed into the broad set of national economic accounts, including estimates of the real product of the economy and several major sectors, published in the 1950's. Price deflation of current values was made possible by expansion and improvement in the collection of price data by the Bureau of Labor Statistics, and by the Bureau's preparation of detailed index numbers of both wholesale and retail prices. The Bureau also improved its estimates of current employment and hours, while the employment data that emerged as a by-product of the social security programs provided a more reliable continuous basic record than was ever before available.

Direct studies of productivity trends and technological changes in many industries of the economy based on census data were undertaken by the National Research Project of the Works Progress Administration. Upon liquidation of that agency in 1940, the task of continuing the productivity estimates was turned over to the Bureau of Labor Statistics. The Bureau had made occasional studies previously, but the importance of continuing estimation and study of productivity change was recognized by the creation of a Division of Productivity and Technological Developments within the Bureau.

The National Research Project studies of farm productivity and technology were carried forward in the Department of Agriculture. The National Bureau of Economic Research also began in the 1930's studies of output, employment, and productivity in various industries of the economy; and after World War II, it expanded its earlier studies of capital formation to include real stocks. It is largely from previous National Bureau and federal government studies that the estimates underlying this volume were derived. This continuing cumulation of economic time series is providing the basis for a deeper understanding of the dynamic processes of economic growth.

The Productivity Concept

The term "productivity" is generally used rather broadly to denote the ratio of output to any or all associated inputs, in real terms. Ratios of output to particular inputs may be termed "partial productivity" measures, the most common of which is output per manhour. Partial productivity ratios, while useful for measuring the saving in particular inputs achieved over time, do not measure over-all changes in productive efficiency, since they are affected by changes in the composition of input, i.e., by factor substitutions. In order to measure net savings in all inputs and, thus, changes in productive efficiency as such, we have attempted to relate real product in the economy and in thirty-three major industry groups to total factor input, as well as to labor and to capital (including natural resources) separately. This and the following section will develop in more detail the concept and meaning of total factor productivity.

THE PRODUCTION FUNCTION

Underlying the estimation of output-input relations stands the concept of the production function, i.e., the notion that the physical volume of output depends on the quantities of productive services, or inputs, employed in the production process and the efficiency with which they are utilized. The output, or real product, of the economy as a whole is generally measured in terms of final products only. Intermediate goods and services consumed in the production process are netted out through consolidation of the accounts of individual producing units. This procedure yields an unduplicated total, for the value of the intermediate goods is already included in the value of the final products. The inputs associated with the national product reduce to the services of the factors of production, which can be usefully classified into the two broad groupings of human and non-human capital.

Industry output, however, is frequently measured gross, in that no deduction is made for purchases from other industries. In this case, the associated inputs are the basic factors plus the intermediate-product inputs. To be consistent with the economy real-product estimates, however, the purchased intermediate goods should be netted out of the real gross value of output in order to obtain the net output (value added) or real product originating in an industry. Then the associated inputs reduce to the services of the basic factors, as in the economy case.

Change in the "productiveness" of the services of tangible factors cannot be measured directly. It can only be indirectly estimated by relating real output to the time-flow of services of real tangible stocks taken *net* of changes in efficiency. The concepts and measures used for outputs and inputs are explained in greater detail in Chapter 2, since the meaning of the ratios is obviously influenced by the precise content of the constituent elements. At this point, however, it is apparent that the productivity measure reflects, to an important extent, the excluded input of the *intangible* capital accumulated in order to increase the efficiency, i.e., the productive capabilities, of the tangible factors. But this and other qualitative elements cannot be independently measured in a satisfactory way.

Another aspect of production theory that we must note, since it affects the interpretation of individual productivity ratios (and creates a weighting problem as well), is that the composition of inputs, as well as of outputs, varies over time. A given quantity of output, with given technical knowledge, can usually be produced with differing combinations of inputs. The actual combination used will tend to be the least-cost combination, at given relative input prices. The combinations are subject to change as a result of changing relative input prices, changing technical knowledge, or changing output (if returns to scale are not constant).

Changes in factor combinations mean that ratios of output to particular inputs, even to a major class of inputs such as labor, cannot be used as measures of changing productive efficiency. Such partial productivity ratios are revealing as measures of the saving achieved over time in the use of particular inputs per unit of output. This meaning is perhaps more clearly revealed by inverting the ratio to read "input per unit of output," in which case the decreasing unit real cost, or the saving in the use of the input, is indicated by a declining ratio. But changes in the partial productivity ratios are affected by factor substitutions reflected in changing input combinations, as well as by changes in productive efficiency generally. Output per manhour, for example, may go up as a result of the substitution of capital for labor (increased capital per manhour) as well as because of the increased efficiency of production generally.

To measure the *net* saving in factor inputs and thus the increase in over-all productive efficiency, it is necessary to relate output to *all* associated inputs. The effects of factor substitutions cancel out in the total productivity indexes. Output-labor ratios were more adequate measures of changing efficiency when capital was quantitatively less important than it has since become. The growth of the real stock of capital in relation to the labor force means that "labor productivity" measures have an upward bias as efficiency indexes. However, because capital per worker has grown in almost all industries, the measures of output per manhour tend to provide fairly accurate measures of the rankings of the various industries with respect to productivity change.[5] Increasingly in recent years, investigators have sought to estimate productivity change in terms of a complete production function. Although regression equations may be fitted to the output and input data to reveal the coefficient of technological progress, we have chosen to work in terms of productivity ratios, which provide greater flexibility for the analysis of movements and of relationships with other variables.[6]

WEIGHTING

In order to determine the changes in aggregate outputs and factor inputs, and thus productivity, it is necessary to combine unlike types of output and of input units by weights that indicate their relative importance for the purpose at hand. If all types of outputs, or of inputs, moved proportionately, weights would make no difference and partial productivity ratios would measure changes in efficiency. But this case is improbable. With changing output and input proportions, the extent, or even the direction, of productivity change cannot be determined without appropriate weights. As Tinbergen has written:

> Technical progress occurs when new combinations become possible that are cheaper than the cheapest combinations before, at the given level of prices. . . . The fact of technical progress can easily be established if there is a reduction in the use of each of the factors of production; sometimes, however, a decrease in the quantity of labor may be accompanied by an increase in the quantity of capital used. If the increase in capital represents less

[5] Cf. George J. Stigler, "Economic Problems in Measuring Changes in Productivity," *Output, Input, and Productivity Measurement*, Studies in Income and Wealth, Volume 25, Princeton University Press (for NBER), 1961.

[6] References to other works that use a total-productivity approach are contained in John W. Kendrick, *Productivity Trends: Capital and Labor*, Occasional Paper 53, New York (NBER), 1956. A fuller discussion of the theoretical basis of the total-productivity concept is contained in the author's doctoral dissertation, *The Meaning and Measurement of National Productivity*, George Washington University library, Washington, D.C., typescript, 1955.

sacrifice as measured by current prices than the decrease in the quantity of labor, there is a net reduction in sacrifice.[7]

Types of weights. It is generally held that for purposes of productivity analysis, outputs should be weighted by product prices at factor cost, and inputs should be weighted by unit factor compensation (factor price).[8] By this method the values of output and of input are equal in the base period; the unit values of the outputs are proportional to the values of the factor services required for their production; and the unit values of the inputs are proportional to the shares of the value of outputs which they obtain for their services. Under competitive conditions the prices of the factors represent the relative values of their marginal contributions to output, in equilibrium.

Market price differs from factor cost by the value of capital consumption and of indirect business taxes less government subsidies.[9] With factor cost weights, the relative importance of different goods is not necessarily proportional to their marginal utilities; rather it is proportional to the relative volume of embodied factor service.

Under competitive conditions, factor price may be interpreted as representing the marginal value products of the various types of factor inputs, on the one hand, and the relative marginal disutility of work or saving, on the other. The marginal products indicate what the producer can *afford* to pay for the quantities used, while the marginal disutilities indicate what he *has* to pay in order to induce people to work rather than to enjoy additional leisure, and to save and invest rather than to enjoy additional consumption or liquidity. Although productivity analysis has to do with physical volumes of output and input, we cannot get away from the psychological elements involved in the mutual determination of prices of both outputs and inputs since relative prices are necessary to aggregation.

The weight-base. Perhaps the most serious problem of measurement is introduced by variations in the relative prices of outputs and of inputs. Inputs in perfectly competitive factor markets are utilized up to the point at which the values of their marginal products are equal to their prices. So their prices indicate the ratios at which units of the inputs may be

---

[7] Jan Tinbergen and J. J. Polak, *The Dynamics of Business Cycles*, Chicago, University of Chicago Press, 1950, pp. 27–28.

[8] See J. R. Hicks, "The Valuation of the Social Income," *Economica*, May 1940, p. 105.

[9] In practice, we use market prices for combining the physical volumes of production of different commodities within the industry and the economy. This is done because of the statistical difficulties involved in estimating the factor cost of goods. But in the United States it is probable that for most goods and services relative market prices are not far different from relative factor costs. And in combining output indexes of industries (see the Appendixes) we have used value-added or national income originating weights, which approximate closely factor cost. See John W. Kendrick, "The Estimation of Real National Product," *A Critique of the United States Income and Product Accounts*, Studies in Income and Wealth, Volume 22, Princeton University Press (for NBER), 1958; and also Introduction to *Output, Input, and Productivity Measurement*, Studies in Income and Wealth, Volume 25, Princeton University Press (for NBER), 1961.

9

subsututed for one another at the margin. So long as the relative prices and marginal rates of substitution are constant, use of relative factor-price weights yields an unambiguous net change in the total volume of input. If relative prices change but factor proportions in real terms remain constant, a change in total input can also be measured precisely.

But if, as is generally the case, there occur relative changes in both factor prices and proportions and these are intercorrelated to any significant extent, the degree, or even the direction of change, in total input may be ambiguous. That is, it may not be clear whether production functions have shifted or whether producers have merely shifted position on a given isoquant, i.e., have changed factor proportions under existing technical knowledge. There is, of course, no ambiguity as to direction if the same or a larger volume of output is produced by a smaller quantity of one or more of the inputs, and no more of the others. But if one input decreases and another increases, while their relative prices change in inverse relation, the direction of movement may also differ depending on whether base-period or given-period price weights are used. The same problem is encountered in aggregating different types of output when there have been relative changes in quantities and prices.

At best, one can compare the changes in aggregate output and input in two periods using the prices of each as weights in order to bracket the range of uncertainty. In time-series comparisons, one might make alternative computations using the most extreme sets of weights. In order to simplify analysis, we have generally used average prices in the terminal years of the various subperiods as weights. By this method of periodically changing weights, productivity changes in each subperiod are made to reflect the concurrent economic structure. In practice, the differences in movement of the productivity ratios using alternative weights are not large relative to the total change, partly because both output and input are similarly affected by alternative weight-bases (see Chapter 2). But it should be kept in mind that proportionate changes in productivity cannot be measured uniquely, and the changes shown in this study are to some extent a function of the weighting conventions used.

The Meaning of Productivity Change

Total factor productivity may be thought of as the ratio of real product in the economy or in component industries (preferably at constant unit factor cost) to the associated real national income deflated by factor prices. That this ratio can be used to indicate changes in productive efficiency was observed by Morris Copeland at the first meeting of the Conference on Research in Income and Wealth in 1936:

> Income derived from an area may be deflated to show changes in the physical volume of services of labor and wealth

employed by the economic system from time to time. If we may neglect net income from abroad as relatively small, the deflated distributive shares may be compared with the deflated consumed and saved income to show changes in the efficiency of operation of the economic system.[10]

If standard output and input units of a given period (II) are weighted by the unit factor costs and unit factor compensations (prices), respectively, of a base period (I), then the meaning of changes in the ratio may be stated as follows. We are comparing what the outputs of II would have cost at the factor prices and unit factor requirements of I (real output) with what they did cost in constant I factor prices but at the II level of productive efficiency (real input). Alternatively, we are comparing the actual real output of II with what the output of the factors would have been in II had the productive efficiency of I (real input) prevailed.

Although we may define changes in total factor productivity as changes in "productive efficiency," this is a broad term which needs further clarification to give it more definite meaning. Productive efficiency may change as a result of technological innovation, changes in scale of output, and changes in the rate of utilization of capacity. It may also reflect changes in inputs of "intangible capital" designed to increase the quality of the input of the tangible factors, and such change is not readily susceptible to measurement. Mere *description* of the components of changing productive efficiency does not, of course, *explain* the causes of the changes.

For example, the volume of technological innovation designed to reduce costs is influenced by economic conditions in any given period. But over longer time periods, the volume of innovation depends essentially on the quantity and quality of resources devoted to increasing scientific and technical knowledge and developing commercial applications. Still more fundamentally, the relative volume of resources devoted to research, development, and innovation depends on the basic values and motivations of a people and on the efficacy of the rewards and penalties provided by prevailing institutions for success or failure in the efforts to improve productive efficiency.

Some innovations in the organization of production are made possible by growth in the scale of output of the industry and the economy. That is, as output increases, certain overhead-type inputs or activities do not need to be increased proportionately, and the growing specialization of plants or firms in various industries tends to lower real costs per unit of output.[11] Such "external economies" may be offset to some extent by a tendency

[10] Morris A. Copeland, "Concepts of National Income," *Studies in Income and Wealth, Volume 1*, New York (NBER), 1937, p. 31.

[11] See George J. Stigler, "The Division of Labor is Limited by the Extent of the Market," *Journal of Political Economy*, June 1951.

towards "diminishing return," in the extractive industries, as land and other proven natural resources are worked more intensively or as inferior natural resources are brought into production. Even in the extractive industries, however, tendencies towards rising unit costs may be countered by increasing returns from organizational improvements as well as from autonomous innovation. The productivity ratios for these industries, as for the whole economy, reflect the *net* effect of changes in scale as well as innovations that are not associated with changes in scale.

Changes in the volume of output are a rough measure of the opportunities afforded for organizational innovations; the associated productivity advance depends on managerial alertness and flexibility in adapting to the cost-reducing possibilities. Inevitably, some invention is induced when production is organized on a scale not previously experienced. It should also be noted that were it not for autonomous innovation, there would be a slower growth of output and, therefore, fewer attendant economies of scale. It is not readily feasible, however, to split a given change in productivity between the part resulting from innovations induced by changes in scale and the part resulting from autonomous innovation.

The rate of utilization of capacity chiefly affects productivity over the business cycle. In each plant there is some most efficient rate of utilization of the fixed capital. Substantial departures from this rate result in increasing costs per unit of output. Productivity in the industry and economy, as weighted averages of productivity indexes for individual plants, reflect the net effect of changes in rates of utilization of many plants. The net effect of this variable between years of high demand should not change significantly, assuming no great difference over time in entrepreneurial foresight in anticipating demand changes and planning capacity accordingly.

Our analysis of productivity trends is based largely on productivity estimates for "key years" of relatively high-level economic activity in order to minimize the effect of changing rates of utilization of capacity. The productivity trends over intermediate and longer time periods thus reflect primarily the impact of innovation on the organization and technology of production, including that induced by changes in scale. Cyclical fluctuations indirectly affect the secular productivity trend, however, since they affect the cumulative volume of investment in both tangible and intangible capital. The milder the fluctuations, the higher the growth rates are likely to be.

The Significance of Productivity Change: Preview and Plan of Study

Although informed people the world over are more productivity-minded today than ever before, the social and economic ramifications of productivity change are often not fully appreciated. We shall try to indicate the main ways in which productivity is related to other significant economic variables, reviewing briefly the areas treated in this study and summarizing some of the findings. This will be done in the same sequence as the material is developed in the rest of the volume in order to provide a guide for the reader.

In this chapter we have already discussed the productivity concept in general terms. But the movement of the productivity ratio will depend on the precise definitions given to its component output and input terms, the methods used to estimate the several variables, and the reliability of the underlying data. Chapter 2, which is a review of these matters, will be of primary interest to the technician. Although trend movements are more accurate than shorter-period changes, and estimates for recent decades are more reliable than those for earlier years, we believe that the estimates are good enough to support the general picture of productivity change presented in later chapters. This appraisal is more credible in that the over-all and relative productivity movements appear to be broadly consistent with the movements of related variables.

AGGREGATE ECONOMIC DEVELOPMENT

Part II is devoted to a description of productivity change in the economy as a whole and its interrelationship with aggregate economic growth. Chapter 3 is largely a description of productivity movements in the private domestic economy, since the estimates of real product and productivity for the private domestic economy are more reliable than those for the total economy including government.

Between 1889 and 1957 total factor productivity in the private domestic economy grew at an average annual rate of around 1.7 per cent. Output per unit of labor input rose considerably faster than the output-capital ratio, since capital per unit of labor input increased at an average rate of 1 per cent a year. It is nevertheless significant that savings in capital as well as in labor inputs were achieved—particularly after 1919.

There is some variability in the rates of change in total productivity from one decade to the next and much more variability in the annual changes that are shown to be associated with the business cycle. The variability in the movements of the two partial productivity ratios is greater than that of the total productivity measure. The most striking fact to emerge from the time series is a pronounced acceleration in productivity advance to an annual rate of 2.1 per cent beginning around the time of World War I.

What has been the contribution of productivity advance to aggregate economic growth, and what are some of the chief developments that have promoted the technological progress that underlies productivity gains? These questions are treated in Chapter 4. The contribution of productivity

13

to economic growth differs according to the growth measure employed. Thus, whereas productivity gains account for almost half the increase in real net national product between 1889 and 1953, they account for three-quarters of the increase in real product per capita. More complex measures of economic progress are also analyzed.

Examination of the composition of inputs and outputs yields evidence as to the causal forces at work in the process of productivity advance. Estimates are presented showing the marked rise in outlays designed to increase the quality of productive resources. Growing relative outlays for education and for health have increased the average productive powers of the population; and rising outlays for research and development have improved the organization, processes, and instruments of production. Consumption of basic materials per unit of output has declined significantly.

Rising productivity has meant that the prices of final goods and services have risen less than the prices (average unit compensations) of the factors of production. It is in this way that the fruits of productivity advance have been distributed to those who provided the factor services—the theme of Chapter 5. The relative shares of labor and capital in the productivity increment have depended on the relative price movements of these factors. Owing in part to the increase in capital per worker, the relative price of labor has risen, real average hourly labor compensation has grown at a somewhat higher rate than productivity, and the labor share of national income has increased.

CHANGES IN ECONOMIC STRUCTURE

In Part III we go behind the national average rate of productivity advance to look at the different rates of change experienced by major industries and the effect of these differential rates on the economic structure. The descriptive material of Chapter 6 makes it clear that there was considerable dispersion of industry rates of change in total productivity and in the partial productivity ratios, and that these rates have varied more over time than indexes for broader aggregates. This has been partly due to the differing relative amounts of resources devoted to research and development, to different rates of change in scale of output, to differing degrees of cyclical fluctuation, and to other factors too complex for complete analysis. But we should also recognize that almost all industries showed advances, which testifies to the strength of the basic forces in our economy conducive to material progress.

The differential rates of productivity advance by industry have had profound effects on the economic structure—the focus of Chapter 7. Those industries with larger than average productivity increases have generally shown relative price declines. Although relative price is only one of several factors influencing demand, the output of the more progressive industries has tended to rise more than the real national product as a whole—and enough more to provide for the absorption of an increasing proportion of the labor and capital available to the private economy.

Although we do not attempt to project productivity changes into the future, it is clear that the study is of relevance in this regard. We can be reasonably certain, for example, that short of the devastation of war, total factor productivity will continue to grow in the economy and most of its industries. Rates of growth will vary from one decade to another, but major acceleration or deceleration in economy rates of growth is unlikely unless there are major changes in basic forces not presently apparent. We can also be reasonably certain that future rates of productivity change will differ considerably from one industry to another (although narrowing of dispersion is not unlikely), and that the ranking of industries with respect to productivity change will differ from one period to another. As long as competition remains strong, we can expect the technologically more progressive industries as a whole to continue to grow more than the average and to continue to absorb an increasing share of available labor and capital resources.

Uses and Limitations of Productivity Estimates

Productivity estimates have proved useful in economic analyses and projections as a background for public and private policy decisions. However, they have also been used for purposes for which they are not appropriate, or without regard to their inherent limitations. In this concluding section, we discuss both the uses and possible abuses of the measures.

The measurement of productivity increases our understanding of an important aspect of the modern economy. But what "practical" use may be made of the estimates? The applications of important bodies of statistics develop slowly, and it is likely that new uses for productivity estimates will continue to evolve. However, we shall suggest some of the major types of application. These relate to productivity indexes as measures of performance and thus as a means of motivating improved efficiency; their use in the analysis of factors that promote productivity advance as a basis for prediction and policy formation; and their use in the analysis of dynamic economic relationships, again as a background for prediction and policy decisions. Increasing use is being made of productivity estimates at the company level, as well as at the industry and the total economy levels.

The existence of productivity estimates increases productivity-mindedness by inviting comparisons with the historical record or with the records of other countries or firms. Within the firm, productivity comparisons may be made of similar plants for use as a management tool. Intercompany comparisons may reveal unfavorable trends sooner than would the profit-and-loss statement and may suggest ways in which management can improve the techonological performance of the business. Comparisons of national economy and industry productivity trends with those of other countries may likewise prove the need and provide the motivation for improved performance. With an increasing body of estimates relating to other countries, international comparisons will become more important.

Understanding of the interrelationships between productivity and causal variables is necessary both to project productivity change and to take appropriate measures to influence it. Quantitative analysis is probably of limited applicability in this area, but it can be a useful supplement to qualitative analysis (see Chapter 6). Hitherto, productivity projections have largely been made by extending past trends, with reasonably good results.[12] But the forecaster should at least be aware of the complex of factors whose net effect he assumes will be the same in the future as in the past; he should also be alert for possible indications of significant changes in important causal factors.

Understanding of the interrelationships between productivity changes and changes in related economic variables is necessary for consistent prediction of the related variables, and for the selection of appropriate measures to influence one or more of the variables. In long-range, macroeconomic models, projections of productivity and factor supplies make possible projections of the real national product. National product projections are indispensable for national planning and policy purposes, and serve as a basis for projecting the sales and output of particular industries and firms. In short-range national projections, output is usually forecast on the basis of demand forces, and input requirements are derived as the quotient of the output and productivity projections. The same technique is used in long- as well as short-range industry and company projections. Here, the productivity projection is a means of estimating requirements for labor, capital, and materials.

Given projections of productivity and factor prices, the implied change in product prices can be derived. Or, given the productivity and product price projections (or objectives), the consistent change in factor prices can be derived. At the industry or company level, the projected relative price change is, of course, an element that must be taken into account in the sales and output projections.

[12] See James W. Knowles, "An Appraisal of Productivity Projections," *Journal of the American Statistical Association*, June 1959, p. 580.

LIMITATIONS

Certain limitations on the use of productivity measures must also be noted. Such measures are not precision tools of analysis, but are subject to unknown and probably not inconsequential margins of error. Their meaning must be interpreted carefully in the light of knowledge as to their construction. Their relationship with other variables must likewise be interpreted cautiously, particularly regarding inferences of causality. They are clearly not "all-purpose" indexes, but must be used in conjunction with other measures in order to assess progress in the broader realms of social and economic efficiency as contrasted with the narrower realm of technological efficiency.

The question as to the accuracy of productivity estimates is treated in the next chapter; all we need say here is that significance should not be attached to small changes or differences in productivity ratios. Our earlier analysis of the meaning of changes in productivity as it is now measured indicates clearly the complexity of the variable. Partly as a supplement to the earlier discussion, this section will point up some of the things that the indexes do *not* measure as a warning against some of the more common misinterpretations.

In the first place, it bears repeating that the *partial* productivity ratios, somewhat misleadingly labeled "labor productivity" or "capital productivity," do not measure changes in the efficiency of a particular resource nor changes in productive efficiency generally. They are influenced by the latter factor (of which the former is a part), but also by factor substitutions.

An even cruder fallacy is to confuse productivity with production or capacity measures. Total-productivity measures provide an index of efficiency in the use of resources, but do not allow for the degree of utilization of available resources. Productive efficiency may be rising, but if part of the output potential is lost by underutilization, this is an offset which must be taken into account in any over-all appraisal of the economic system. Actually, productivity indexes are affected by cyclical fluctuations, as noted earlier; but this is only part of the waste involved in lapses from relatively full employment of resources.

The productivity ratios cannot be used in any simple manner to indicate the degree to which average hourly labor compensation in the economy can rise consistent with a stable general price level. As a matter of fact, real average earnings of employees have risen proportionately more than total factor productivity over the period we have surveyed, and more than output per unit of labor input in some of the subperiods. The magnitude of noninflationary wage increases depends, of course, not only on productivity advance but also on the movement of the return on capital relative to changes in the output-capital ratio. Even if real product per unit of capital were constant, average hourly labor compensation could increase in proportion to real product per manhour and still provide a constant rate of return on capital. The complexities of these interrelationships are discussed in some detail in Chapter 5.[13]

Measures of productivity also *do not* provide an index of "economic efficiency" as such.[14] That is, we cannot tell from productivity measures whether or not the various types of resources are employed in their most productive uses at each given stage of technology, resource development, and wants. To the extent that there are monopolistic practices or impediments to the mobility of resources, the relative prices of products differ from those that would prevail under perfect competition; the allocation of the factors is somewhat distorted; and the factors do not receive the exact value of their marginal products. Changes in economic efficiency affect productivity measures only indirectly. Over long periods in a dynamic economy with as much economic freedom and mobility as prevails in the United States, the gains to be realized from tightening up economic efficiency are probably minor compared with those that accrue from the increases in technological efficiency, which are primarily reflected in the productivity measures. Nevertheless, a continuing appraisal of economic efficiency and the adoption of policies designed to promote it remain important objectives, particularly in less advanced economies.

The productivity index numbers likewise do not measure changes in economic welfare. As is demonstrated in Chapter 4, increases in real input per capita have proceeded at a slow rate in this century; so it is true that productivity gains have accounted for the bulk of the increases in real national product per capita. But real product per person cannot be construed as measuring changes in material welfare. In the first place, changing proportions of real product are devoted to consumption goods, the type of goods that bears most directly on welfare. It is true that investment is designed to promote future welfare and that both national security and capital outlays absorb resources that could be potentially transferred to the production of consumption goods. But real product per person, at best, gives only an indication of changes in the *potential* welfare of individuals.

Then there are the many reservations that attach to measures of real consumption expenditures per capita as indicators of welfare changes,

---

[13] See also John W. Kendrick, "The Wage-Price-Productivity Issue," *California Management Review*, Spring 1960.

[14] Tibor Scitovsky has contrasted economic efficiency with technological efficiency. He defines economic efficiency as production in "conformity with the community's wishes," while technological efficiency is "the achievement of the greatest possible output with given means or the achievement of a given output with the smallest means" (*Welfare and Competition*, Homewood, Ill., Irwin, 1951, p. 148).

which have been elaborated by welfare economists. Over time, there are changes in the composition of population, in income distribution, in tastes, technology, and relative prices, which make it impossible precisely to quantify changes in the economic welfare of the community—even if it were legitimate to make interpersonal comparisons of satisfactions.

Even if we could precisely measure changes in the levels of material welfare of the community, this would illuminate only one aspect of the welfare or well-being of people considered more broadly. It is not necessary to embroider the theme that the good life is not an automatic consequence of a life replete with material goods. It is true that broadening the material base of life has provided the *potential* for a better life for an increasing number and proportion of individuals. The realization of that potential is a supreme challenge. In at least one important respect, however, productivity indexes are an indicator of the health of a community, since rising productivity reflects the expression on the material plane of the creative forces of individuals.

Finally, it must be remembered that the technological changes upon which productivity gains rest are bound to have a more or less disruptive influence on individuals and institutions. The strains on the social fabric that occur as the limits of adaptability to technological change are approached may be great and may offset the material advantage of the last fraction of productivity gain. On the other hand, people and institutions can be very flexible. One of the important problems involved in accelerating productivity advance (when this becomes a social objective), is to increase the range of adaptation. This is a problem that requires continuing research and inventiveness by those in the social and behavioral sciences.

CHAPTER 2

The Concepts and Measurement of Output and Input

IN THE first chapter we saw that there are various productivity concepts and that the movements of the corresponding measures differ accordingly. Given the general definition of a particular productivity measure, its movement will again be affected by the precise definitions given to the output and input components of the productivity ratios. This forms the subject matter of the first part of the present chapter. With respect to national output—the real value of the final goods and services produced in the nation's economy—the scope and movement of the measure will depend on the precise operational meaning given to such key words of the definition as "final," "nation," and "economy." These questions have been debated at length by national income experts; but we should like to indicate the significance for productivity analysis of the major issues that are resolved somewhat differently in the several important sets of available real product estimates. Industry output measures are likewise conditioned by industry classifications and output definitions, particularly as regards the distinction between gross and net output. These points also will be discussed.

With respect to input, the labor productivity ratios differ depending on whether the input is defined and measured in terms of employment, or manhours, or manhours weighted by relative average hourly earnings in the various occupations or industries. Thus, output per manhour (un-weighted) generally rises more than output per unit of labor input (weighted manhours) since there has been a relative shift of manhours to higher-paying jobs.

Output per unit of capital input will vary in movement depending on whether capital input is assumed to move proportionately with real capital stocks or whether capital stocks are adjusted for changes in rates of utilization. Further, it makes a difference whether reproducible capital stocks are measured gross or net of depreciation allowances—the net measures rise less in periods of growth—and whether stocks in the several industries are separately weighted by the relevant rates of return.

Output per unit of total factor input will, of course, rise less rapidly than the labor productivity measures to the extent that capital input, as measured, rises more rapidly than labor input. The relative movements of the total and partial productivity measures will also vary depending on the weights accorded each of the major factor classes, a problem which will also be discussed later.

Once the operational concepts of output and input are defined, the reliability of the derived productivity estimates will depend on the quality of the basic data and will also be influenced by methodology. The second part of this chapter describes in brief the sources of the data and the methods used in preparing the economy and industry output and input estimates. This summarizes the material contained in the appendixes. An attempt is also made to appraise roughly the accuracy of the estimates and, thus, to point out the sources of possible weakness. For example, since the output and some of the input estimates are "benchmarked" on occasional comprehensive censuses, with estimates for intervening years interpolated by sample data, it is apparent that the productivity estimates more accurately portray intermediate and long-term trends than annual changes. For benchmark years, we have attempted to reconcile direct estimates of output and of inputs for the private domestic economy with aggregates of industry estimates. The relative closeness of the two sets of partially independent estimates attests to the consistency of the economy and industry figures, although it does not prove the accuracy of either, since they may have errors in common.

Methodology also affects the movement of the variables. Reference has already been made to weighting systems. Weights of more recent periods tend to produce smaller historical increases in aggregates than early-period weights, owing to a tendency of consumers and producers to shift their outlays to goods and services that are becoming relatively cheaper. Fortunately, the effects of alternative weight-bases on outputs and inputs tend to be partially offsetting with respect to the productivity ratios. Other methodological questions arise in connection with coverage adjustments, the choice of physical units, and the direct weighting of physical units as compared with the deflation of values by price indexes to obtain physical volume series. No one rule could be followed, but methods were chosen in particular cases which promised to give better results than alternatives.

The general reader may not wish to read the latter part of this chapter on sources and methods. The main point to remember is that the movement of the productivity measures depends not only on the definitions employed, but also on the data and methodology used to prepare the estimates. Since the basic data leave a good deal to be desired, the productivity estimates are not precision instruments in analytical work. Although they are probably good enough to indicate the general order of magnitude of trend rates of change, significance should not be attached to small changes or differences particularly over short periods. It is nonetheless encouraging that the relationships between the estimates of productivity and of associated variables, discussed subsequently, seem broadly reasonable.

Operational Concepts of Output or Real Product

In this and the following section we shall describe the concepts of the physical volume of output and of the factor inputs *as measured for this study*. Reference will be made to some ways in which the operational concepts may depart from ideal measures or from possible alternative definitions.

OUTPUT OR REAL PRODUCT

In estimating the physical volume of final output (real product) of the economy or its various sectors and industries, it is important first to define the scope of the measure. This means identifying "final" goods as contrasted with intermediate products, which must be excluded to avoid double counting; delineating the scope of economic activity; and drawing the boundaries of the geographical area covered and its component sectors. Then, there are the problems involved in specifying the dimensions of the physical units of goods and services constituting national or industry outputs and defining the unit values in terms of which the physical units may be aggregated or the total values deflated to eliminate the influence of price change.

Scope of the National or Domestic Product Estimates

Although there are wide areas of agreement, there are also differences of opinion among national income specialists as to the proper concepts and definitions to use to guide empirical work.[1] It is not our purpose intensively to review national income theory. Rather, we shall indicate several of the chief conceptual bases of national product estimates, and the main differences between the product estimates of the Commerce Department and those of Professor Simon Kuznets, both used in this study.[2] Several different versions of these basic sets of estimates are useful for productivity estimates and will be described. A few other alternative treatments of national product will be alluded to in passing, although they have not been implemented statistically. The point will be clear that there is no unique, definitive set of national product estimates. The selection depends on the theoretical predilections of the estimator, the analytical purpose of

[1] For literature on concepts, see *Bibliography on Income and Wealth, 1937–1947*, International Association for Research in Income and Wealth, Cambridge, England: Bowes and Bowes, 1952; recent volumes of *Studies in Income and Wealth*, Princeton University Press (for NBER), particularly Volume 22 (1958); and the several volumes of *Income and Wealth*, International Association for Research in Income and Wealth, London, Bowes and Bowes.

[2] *National Income Supplement, 1954, Survey of Current Business*, Dept. of Commerce; Simon Kuznets, *National Income and Its Composition, 1919–1938*, New York (NBER), 1941.

the user, and the availability of data. Each of the alternatives used here has somewhat different productivity implications, which will be pointed up in the following discussion and quantified in Chapter 3.

"Net" or final output. The most important judgment underlying the measurement of national product has to do with the goals of economic activity, on the basis of which net output is distinguished from gross, or final product from the "intermediate" products consumed in the process of producing final goods and services. Economists are not interested in production without regard to use, and we judge efficiency in terms of the inputs required to produce outputs that are desired for their own sake by the community. Obviously, the definition of the final product affects estimated productivity change, since with a given change in inputs the resulting change in output depends in part on its definition.

Kuznets distinguishes final products on the basis of individualistic, welfare criteria, assuming that "the goal of economic activity is to satisfy wants of individual consumers who are members of the nation, present and future."[3] "If by social welfare we mean a positive contribution to some socially determined set of goals, it is clear that "net product" is an approximation to net additions to social welfare. I don't mean to imply that national income can be an accurate measure of social welfare; but it must be viewed as an approximation to it. . . . Without final goals there is no final or ultimate consumer. . . ."[4]

The Department of Commerce and its spokesmen have not elucidated the conceptual basis of their national product series so explicitly as has Kuznets. They have, rather, relied more heavily on operational rules of measurement defined as follows: "An effective criterion for distinguishing between final and intermediate products can be established by reference to business practices followed in the production of goods and services. There emerges a working definition of final product as a purchase that is not resold, and of intermediate product as one that is resold. . . . A final product is a purchase that is not charged to current cost whereas an intermediate product is one that is so charged."[5]

The practical effect of these approaches is to give quite similar content to private purchases of goods and services, consisting of consumption expenditures and capital formation, as estimated by Kuznets and Commerce; the major difference appears in the composition of government output discussed below. A few minor differences between Kuznets and Commerce on the content of private purchases are noted in Appendix A. It should, nevertheless, be pointed out that a different application of their

[3] Simon Kuznets, "Government Product and National Income," *Income and Wealth, Series I,* p. 180.
[4] *Ibid.,* p. 179.
[5] *National Income Supplement, 1954,* p. 30.

criteria could result in larger differences. Thus, expenditures incurred by individuals primarily on account of their work could be excluded, while expenditures by business concerns designed to promote the welfare of their employees, which are only indirectly a business "cost," might be included in the flow of goods to consumers. Expenditures by individuals necessary to offset industrial nuisances might also be deducted. Further, consumer outlays for durable goods could be classed as capital formation, with an imputed rental (service) value including depreciation counted in consumption expenditures, as is done with owner-occupied dwellings. These alternative treatments have not been adopted, partly for statistical reasons; the movement of existing aggregates would be affected only insofar as the adjustments were not offsetting.

In the area of capital formation, the chief differences relate to the treatment of the consumption of fixed capital. Kuznets presents estimates, both gross and net of capital consumption, in current and in constant dollars, of capital formation and of national product. Commerce presents only gross national product (i.e., gross of capital consumption but net of intermediate products) in constant dollars, while estimates of capital consumption are shown in a mixture of current dollars and original cost.

Theoretically, the most meaningful basis for long-run comparisons is net national product, including only net capital formation. Net additions to capital stock may be measured after provision is made in each period for the decline in the productive powers of existing assets. The net additions alone, and not outlays which offset capital erosion, can be devoted to consumption "without creating an expectation of being worse off at the end of the period than at the beginning of it."[6] We have adjusted the Kuznets estimates of real capital consumption to the Commerce basis, in order to present net as well as gross national product estimates in real terms.

National product and capital formation estimates that are gross of capital consumption continue to be made and used for several reasons. Gross capital formation can be estimated unambiguously, whereas serious theoretical and statistical problems are involved in estimating capital consumption. Moreover, resources devoted to offsetting capital consumption are available for final consumption in the short run in a way that intermediate products are not.[7] We also need gross national product estimates for purposes of comparison with industry output estimates similarly gross of capital consumption. From a welfare standpoint, however, it is clear that net national product estimates are conceptually preferable.

---

[6] This definition of the net national income has been used by Richard Stone in "Functions and Criteria of a System of Social Accounting," *Income and Wealth, Series I*, p. 3.
[7] Cf. Kuznets, *National Product in Wartime*, New York (NBER), 1945, pp. 20–24.

Apart from the fact that Kuznets lumps public and private capital formation together, whereas Commerce includes the former in government purchases, the two sets of investment estimates are virtually identical. As in the case of consumption outlays, however, alternative treatments are possible. For example, research and development outlays could be classed as capital formation rather than intermediate product since they are designed to increase the future income stream. Here, again, statistical problems would be great.

The chief conceptual difference between the Commerce and the Kuznets series, and the area of greatest controversy generally, arises with respect to government output. In his long-term series, Kuznets counts the cost of government activities as final output only insofar as these conduce directly to the ultimate satisfaction of individuals as consumers, or as they result in durable capital formation (including defense items). The range of government activities designed to promote the productivity of the business economy or maintain the social framework generally (including nondurable national security outlays) are considered to be intermediate products, the costs of which are excluded from final product.

As an analytical tool for use during World War II, Kuznets introduced his "wartime concept" of national product, in which total national security outlays are included. This he justified by placing the goal of national survival during war on a par with the basic goal of satisfaction of consumers wants by the economy. By a simple extension of this reasoning one can maintain that national security is *at all times* a prime objective of economic organization—on these grounds we have seen fit to present a "national security version" of the Kuznets series that includes national security outlays in all years.

National security outlays may also be thought of as representing potential output of consumer goods, since the resources devoted to security could be shifted to consumption if conditions permitted. This is also true of net capital formation, but not of intermediate products proper, of which the production is technically a function of the output of final goods. A great advantage of the national security version is that national product and the derived productivity estimates are not directly affected in significant degree by changes in the proportion of national output devoted to the goal of national security. The national security version thus accords with a basic principle of national income measurement—invariance to institutional changes, if this term be construed to cover changes in international relations and the resulting changes in the relative emphasis on welfare and security objectives within the nation. Actually, the two versions of the Kuznets national product estimates differ but little except in wartime and in the situation of high security outlays that have characterized the recent years of "cold war."

In contrast to Kuznets (either version), the Department of Commerce includes in national product the cost of *all* government purchases as representing the value of public services. This procedure is justified by reference to the "rule," since purchases of goods and services by general government are not resold in a market sense. Thus, the Commerce estimators treat as final those "goods and services provided on behalf of the community as a whole, which it has been found better to secure collectively rather than individually."[8] In practice, the Commerce estimates and the national security version of the Kuznets estimates show much the same broad movements. They differ only to the small degree that the portion of civilian government purchases judged by Kuznets to be intermediate has changed relative to the total national product. The movement of the several aggregate real product and productivity series are compared and interpreted further in Chapter 3.

The economy. In developed countries, national income and product estimates have been closely associated with the relevant purchase and sale transactions of the market place plus the value (at cost) of the services of general government and of private nonprofit institutions. While the market criterion is basic for distinguishing between economic and other activities, certain imputations have traditionally been made in order to value and include in the national product several productive activities that do not involve bilateral transactions but have significant market analogues. The major imputations in both the Commerce and Kuznets estimates are for the food produced and consumed on farms, the rental value of owner-occupied houses, and certain payments in kind. Commerce also imputes a value to the unpaid services of financial intermediaries, which gives rise to a discrepancy between the Commerce and Kuznets consumer service estimates (see Appendix A).

It might be possible to go considerably further in the direction of imputations for nonmarket activity. Thus, a value could be attached to the services of housewives, as well as of domestic employees, and to all the other productive activities adjudged to be economic by some broader criterion than that of appearance on organized markets.

The advantage of a broad measure of economic output is that temporal or spatial comparisons are less affected by institutional changes or differences than is the case with a predominantly market measure. Over the long run, there has been a considerable shift of production from households for own-consumption to business firms for sale in markets.[9] This means that national product has an upward bias as a measure of total production. The bias is less in the case of the productivity measures, however, since the

---

[8] *National Income Supplement, 1954*, p. 38.

[9] Cf. George J. Stigler, *Trends in Output and Employment*, New York (NBER), 1947, pp. 13–15.

inputs are restricted to the same sectors covered by the output measures. Bias enters the productivity measures only to the extent that productivity in the uncovered area moves differently from that in the covered (largely market) area. It seems reasonable to suppose that productivity in household production has increased less than that in the business sector. So the national productivity estimates as constructed have some upward bias, but to a progressively lesser degree as the uncovered sector shrinks in relative importance. In other words, a total-economy productivity measure, if we had one, would show a lesser rate of increase than the existing measures; but the discrepancy would diminish over time.

The disadvantage of an inclusive measure is the difficulty of defining economic activity apart from market criteria[10] and of estimating the magnitudes involved, which is crucial when the objective is productivity measurement. Aside from the problem of valuing predominantly non-market activities, it would be impracticable in most cases to make estimates of the output, as distinct from the inputs, on the basis of existing data. Measures of output tied predominantly to the market criterion thus give us more accurate productivity indexes than would broader measures. The important thing is that the estimates of output and of input cover essentially the same activities.

From the standpoint of accuracy, there are some advantages in taking even narrower measures of output than the existing estimates of national product provide. There is a particular advantage in analyzing the private economy apart from the output originating in general government because of the difficulties in measuring output of the public sector. We therefore estimate real private (domestic) product and productivity, derived from the Commerce series, as the basis for detailed examination of productivity changes.

Perhaps the most meaningful aggregate from the standpoint of relatively reliable productivity estimates would be the real product of the business economy alone. This sector excludes the areas of households and non-profit institutions, which also present serious problems of definition and measurement of output, as well as government. We have not used such an aggregate; but the possibility is mentioned in order to illustrate further that the "economy" taken for study may be defined in a broader or a narrower way, depending on the objectives at hand and the requirements of accuracy as opposed to those of comprehensiveness. The narrower measures cannot, however, be taken as substitutes for the broader measures.

The nation or domestic geographical area. Both Kuznets and Commerce delimit their product estimates geographically with reference to the income

---

[10] See Irving B. Kravis, "The Scope of Economic Activity in International Income Comparisons," *Problems in the International Comparison of Economic Accounts*, Studies in Income and Wealth, Volume 20, Princeton University Press (for NBER), 1957.

produced by the factors whose owners reside in the continental United States.[11] Another possibility is to measure product with reference to the location of the factors themselves: income paid on the foreign investments of American residents is excluded, and only the income and product of factors located here counted, regardless of the residence of their owners. We have estimated the latter alternative, "domestic product," by making appropriate adjustments as described in Appendix A to the available national product estimates. This variant is recommended in the United Nations Studies in Method No. 2, *A System of National Accounts and Supporting Tables*.[12] It is more appropriate to productivity analysis as such and to comparisons of economy with industry output and productivity measures.

Scope of the Industry Measures

In theory, we should like to identify industries by meaningful collections of products. In practice, even when data are collected from relatively similar establishments, the range of goods produced is often quite heterogeneous. It is possible to define an industry in terms of certain groups of goods or services which are "primary" to it, in that they are primarily produced in a certain group of establishments. However, these products may also be produced in other groups of establishments which primarily produce other products, and the given industry may also produce "secondary" products which are primarily produced elsewhere. So the industry is a matter of classification, and while the concept aids in arranging establishment data in an orderly way, the operational concept is seldom clean-cut.

Not only is there some heterogeneity in industry output, but the boundaries of an industry may change over time both as the functions of establishments change and as industry definitions change in recognition of changing industrial structure. For example, the farm industry formerly produced much of its capital in the form of horses and mules, but now purchases mechanical tractive equipment from other industries. With this shift has come a corresponding increase in purchases of motor fuel relative to the growing of feed. Similarly, whereas farms used to supply most of their feed and seed directly, they now purchase much of these commercially.

In manufacturing, many industries at one time had to produce their own specialized equipment and intermediate products; but with the growth in scale of output, specialized industries have grown up supplying these goods. This development has increased the efficiency of production,

[11] It would also be possible to define the nation in terms of its customs area, for example, by including the territories and possessions. The resulting product and productivity estimates would be somewhat less reliable than those presently available.

[12] Dept. of Economic Affairs, Statistical Office, New York, 1953.

but not the efficiency of measurement. Also, as new products have been developed, these either have increased the range of products characterizing existing industries, or, if their production warranted it, have given rise to new industry classifications.

Thus, industry product and productivity statistics may relate to a somewhat changing range of activities over time. The analyst can live with this situation so long as inputs and outputs are consistent, recognizing that average productivity movements in the industry are affected when efficiency changes in divested activities differ from those in the industrial "core." Real temporal discontinuities in the productivity measures are introduced, however, if the range of intermediate products produced and consumed in the industry changes, since this affects input requirements but not the amount of gross output. The problem may be serious for certain minor industry classes, but becomes less important as the industry grouping is widened to include more of the intermediate product output. The difficulty disappears in productivity measures for the economy as a whole.

This problem is overcome in principle if industry output is conceived of as real value added or product originating. By this concept, the real value of the purchased intermediate products consumed is deducted from the real value of the final output of an industry. If the production of a particular intermediate product is shifted to a different industry, the real value added in the given industry is reduced by the extent of the additional real purchases. Since factor input would be correspondingly reduced, industry productivity would not appear to increase merely as a result of a shift in the scope of industry activity.

Dimensions of Output Units

The physical volume of output may relate to the final goods and services entering national product or to the intermediate products that are the outputs of some industries and the inputs of others. In either case, it is necessary to define the product units in terms of which physical volumes are measured. It is easy to define types of products broadly; but, strictly speaking, each quality of a given type of product should be distinguished if its physical characteristics and price differ at all from those of other members of the product family.

Specification of most goods and services is generally feasible. In some cases it may be difficult to visualize the unit underlying the payments for certain types of services, particularly in the financial area, but close analysis can usually produce working definitions. In other instances, the product may not be standardized if produced to the order or requirements of particular customers, as in residential construction. In this situation, hypothetical bids can be taken on a standard item in order to reveal what the price would have been had the product been standard and price deflation of the value of production resorted to. Or, if both standard and custom-built goods are produced by an industry, such as the machinery industry, the value of the custom-built product can be deflated by the average price of similar standard items. In these cases, it is apparent that the physical volume of output is of a somewhat conventional character, implying at base that the productivity of resources employed in nonstandardized production shows the same changes as those in related standardized production, or the same productivity changes that producers believe they *could* have effectuated if products *were* standardized.

An even more pervasive problem is posed by the fact that the characteristics of many products change over time. Old models are abandoned and new models are introduced. In measuring production from the viewpoint of productivity analysis, the important question is whether the revised units of a product absorb a different volume of resources than the old units. If so, the real factor-cost weights of the new units should be adjusted by a ratio representing the proportion of factor cost required by the new model to that required by the old in an overlapping time period (or based on producer's estimates if there is no overlap). Fortunately, the Bureau of Labor Statistics, which computes most of the price indexes used in the deflation work underlying the real-product estimates, whenever feasible counts as "pure" price change only that change in market price which does not represent an alteration in the real cost of the materials and services consequent upon a model change.

There have been, of course, significant changes in the quality of many products apart from changes in real costs. This, however, is more of a problem for welfare than for productivity comparisons. There may be some effect on productivity as the proportion of resource inputs devoted to product development changes over time. In some industries, this proportion has tended to increase, a development that would impart some downward bias to the productivity ratio insofar as the associated quality improvements are not counted in output. A relative shift of production towards higher-quality goods within product families does increase real product; but productivity is not affected since the larger output is approximately offset by the larger volume of factor inputs required to produce the higher-valued product mix.

A somewhat different problem is introduced by new products. An advantage of a system of occasionally changing weights is that a new product can be weighted into the aggregate in the subperiod in which it appears in terms of its initial relative importance as measured by unit factor cost. If relative price and cost drop in succeeding subperiods, the relative weight of the product in the aggregate is reduced.

INPUTS

The basic inputs of the economy are the productive services of the factors of production. Input is the time-flow of services of the human and non-human factors available for use in the productive process; the result of the productive services is output, which is distributed as income to the factors. There are thus three dimensions to the various factor inputs: (1) the stocks of the primary factors available for use in production; (2) the time periods (usually hours) in which units of the factor-stocks are available for use in production, in terms of which the flow of services can be measured and their compensation or cost computed; and (3) the output or income resulting from their joint use, of which the shares accruing to each factor for its contribution to production can be used to weight the service-hours.

It would obviously defeat our purpose to measure inputs in terms of their result in the productive process alone, since we would then have a measure of output itself. But the changing efficiency of the inputs is revealed by comparing the available service-time of the real stocks of the factors, in "standard efficiency units" weighted by their unit shares of output (income) in a base period, with their actual output in a given period.[13] An ideal measure of input is thus *net* of any changes in quality over time, as it must be in order to have a basis for getting at efficiency changes through comparisons with output.

By weighting the available service-time of the factors by their base-period compensation, we obtain a measure of what the resources *would* have produced had technological and other conditions of efficiency remained the same as in the base period. By dividing this measure into the *actual* output in successive periods, we obtain a measure of the changes in the efficiency with which factor services are utilized in the processes of production, i.e., of their productivity, as discussed in Chapter 1.

We referred deliberately to the time periods in which the factors were *available* for use in production. This brings out the duality of the factors of production in a free-enterprise economy. Labor usually contracts to sell its services for specified time intervals, comprising a given number of hours per day or week or month. During the period of employment it is available for use in our sense, although it is not always fully utilized in production (as witness "stand-by" time in certain industries, not to mention the varying degrees of utilization of the latent potentials of employees depending on management or labor policies). But when not employed, labor is not available in an immediate sense to firms and is not a direct cost.

13 Cf. Kenneth E. Boulding, "Some Difficulties in the Concept of Economic Input," *Output, Input, and Productivity Measurement*, Studies in Income and Wealth, Volume 25, Princeton University Press (for NBER), 1961.

In the case of private capital, however, in principle it is wholly available during its lifetime, even if in periods of reduced activity some units are not utilized. It represents a cost which is quite apparent when the capital is leased, or has been financed by debt. Even when it represents equity there is a certain implicit average annual return that must be met if new capital is to be forthcoming. The fullness of utilization of the capital stock is one aspect of the efficiency of private management which is not relevant to the labor force outside employment. It is true that from a social viewpoint the total labor force is available for production and the degree of its utilization is an aspect of the efficiency of the economy; in Chapter 3 we construct one variant of the productivity measure from a social-cost standpoint. But otherwise our measures are constructed from the standpoint of the private-enterprise economy existing in this country, i.e., labor is counted as a cost only when employed, and thus available for use in production, while capital is counted as a cost when owned and thus available. This accords with the general treatment of cost in economic theory.

Another difference between the two major factor-stocks, as measured, is that the "man" provides a rough common denominator of the stock of labor, whereas in the case of capital the "constant dollar" must be used. Actually, the value of the capital represented by human beings differs from one group to another, and this is reflected in the varying rates of compensation. So instead of artificially estimating the real value of human capital in the various industries, adjusting for rates of utilization, and weighting by base-rates of compensation, we can skip a step by directly weighting manhours. In the case of capital, however, we must estimate the value of the stocks and weight by rates of return since there is no unit of capital even superficially uniform. Adjustment for rate of utilization is not necessary, since capital is available 8,760 hours a year, and the movement of "constant dollar capital-hours" would be the same as that of the index numbers of the real capital stock.

Labor Input

In the case of human resources, the "stock" of labor available for productive use is the labor force, of which a varying proportion over time is employed in the various occupations and industries. The majority of persons engaged in productive employment are paid by the hour; and manhours can also be estimated roughly for those not on an hourly rated basis, and their compensation translated to average hourly earnings for weighting purposes. Thus, we use manhours worked as the measure of the flow of available labor services. It is not a direct measure of input, but a measure derived from estimates of the employed stock of human resources and the average hours worked per person per year indicating the rate of utilization. Proprietors and unpaid family workers as well as employees are counted as

32

labor. When weighted by average hourly compensation in a base period, labor input indicates for a given period what the employed manhours would have contributed to output if productive efficiency had been the same as in the base period. The measure can also be interpreted in terms of the marginal disutility of work.

It is assumed that the inherent average physical and mental capacity of the persons employed in each occupation is constant over time. Insofar as the composition of persons employed in terms of basic aptitudes or capacities in relationship to their occupations changes over time, it cannot be said that the basic units are constant and that manhours would make the same contribution to output if technology and other dynamic factors were held constant between two periods. There are variations among individuals in the same occupations with respect to basic capacity; and there may be variations in the capacities of the same individual in different time periods as a result of aging[14] or of changing states of health. But taking large groups of individuals, the *average* output potential of the manhours worked, with given technical knowledge, should be relatively stable over time.

Perhaps the chief exception to this generalization is provided by the effect on potential labor services per manhour of reductions in the workweek from relatively high levels. In this situation, the energy input and potential output of a manhour may increase somewhat as hours of work are reduced with no change in technology. But as hours of work are progressively reduced, as they have been in this century, the effect on the potential services of a manhour probably becomes progressively smaller.[15] We choose to think of the manhour as the basic input unit, with changes in the length of the workweek or work-year as one of the factors influencing the output-input relationship. Furthermore, it can be maintained that reductions in the workweek have affected productivity less by increasing energy input per manhour than through putting pressure on management to improve its organization or equipment to offset the increase in hourly earnings which frequently accompanies a reduction in average hours.[16]

Since average hourly earnings differ among occupations, roughly reflecting different contributions to product and thus different "quantities" of labor service, manhours should be estimated and weighted separately

[14] A further discussion of changing average age is contained in Chapter 4, in the subsection, "Investment in persons."

[15] See Solomon Fabricant, *Employment in Manufacturing, 1899–1939: An Analysis of Its Relation to the Volume of Production*, New York (NBER), 1942, pp. 12–15. Fabricant cautions: "It is very difficult to determine from the cases described in these and other sources the extent to which changes in factors other than hours affected labor productivity" (*ibid.*, p. 13 n.).

[16] See Edward F. Denison, "Measurement of Labor Input, Some Questions of Definition and the Adequacy of Data," *Output, Input, and Productivity Measurement*, Studies in Income and Wealth, Volume 25.

for each occupation. But estimates of employment and hours are generally available over time only on an industry basis; so industry average hourly compensation estimates are used as weights. The aggregate of industry real labor input so computed will approximate the results obtained by weighting manhours worked by occupation so long as the occupational structures of the various industries are relatively stable.[17]

The labor input index thus holds the services per manhour constant in terms of the real income earned by manhours in each industry in the base period. This is the desired result, since the purpose of the productivity ratio is to compare the outputs actually produced in successive time periods with the outputs that *would* have been produced had the factor services not changed in efficiency. The efficiency changes reflect changes in the skill and degree of utilization of the basic capacities of workers in their jobs, as well as technological progress generally as reflected in improved organization and equipment.

This constancy of quality refers only to the same type of factor service, however. Relative shifts of resources to better-paying industries (in terms of base-period compensation) show up as an increase in labor input rather than as an increase in productivity. This result is also desirable, since from the viewpoint of technological efficiency we are interested in increases of output relative to input within the various industries. Shifts of resources among industries are interpreted as involving a changing quantity of resources, not changing technological efficiency. The proportionate increase in output attributable to a relative shift of resources can be estimated by dividing weighted inputs by undifferentiated inputs. However, this ratio would not reflect the effects of intra-industry shifts of resources, which may also be significant when industries are defined broadly.

Capital Input

The first step in measuring real capital services is to estimate the real net capital stock employed in the various industries; the next is to weight these figures by the base-period rates of return. It is assumed that within each industry relative prices of different types of real capital are proportionate to the present value of the anticipated future absolute returns, since rational management would increase the stock of each type of capital up to the point at which the final unit of each yielded the same rate of return. Different rates of return in the various industries presumably reflect

---

[17] "Presumably, there are qualitative differences in labor employed by different industries, since rather persistent interindustry wage differentials seem to exist" (Jacob Schmookler, "The Changing Efficiency of the American Economy; 1869–1938," *The Review of Economics and Statistics*, August 1952, p. 216). This accords with our own findings as reported in Chapter 7 and in Appendixes A and D.

different estimates of the degree of risk, different amounts of associated intangible capital resulting from industry investment in technical knowledge, or quasi-rents (positive or negative) resulting from superior (or inferior) adaptation of capital to market potentials. Roughly, we may say that the capital compensation in the several industries reflects the relative contributions to output (real income) of the capital stocks in each except to the extent that monopoly elements are present in differing degree.

Capital stocks (or capital formation data, from which the stock estimates are largely derived) are deflated to eliminate the effect of price changes in such wise that a new unit of a given type of plant or equipment is accorded the same base-period value, or weight, in all periods. Changes in the productive efficiency of new models as compared with the base-period model of a particular item of equipment are not reflected in the real value of the item (unless more resources are used). This is desirable from the viewpoint of productivity analysis, for the increased efficiency should show up in the output-input ratio. Since the units of various types of equipment are given the same weight over time, it is apparent that no allowance is made for changing productivity in the capital goods industries; we are interested in the relationship of outputs to the physical volume of inputs of base-period efficiency—not to the inputs required to replace other inputs in a given period. In the latter case, productivity gains would be double-counted.

Real stocks net of accumulated depreciation allowances are taken as a better measure of a basic capacity to contribute to production and revenue than gross stocks (i.e., the number of items in use, each weighted by base-period price regardless of age). Studies have shown that the gross output capacity of various types of machinery tends to fall with age, and the repair and maintenance charges rise so that the contribution to net revenue falls even more. More significantly, the marginal revenue products of older types of equipment are less than those of new, improved types because of technological advance and resulting obsolescence. This development occurs sporadically as far as a particular type of equipment is concerned, but may be assumed to occur gradually with respect to all the capital goods of an industry. The effect on the real marginal revenue product of groups of items over time is roughly approximated by the gradual decline in the depreciated real value of stock shown by the usual depreciation accounting procedures reflected in the national accounts.[18]

It may be objected that the use of depreciated real stocks seems to violate our basic principle of measuring stocks of resources employed in terms of units representing an equal capacity to contribute to output over

---

[18] See George Terborgh, *Realistic Depreciation Policy*, Chicago, Machinery and Allied Products Institute, 1954.

time, assuming base-period technical conditions throughout.[19] But in the base period itself, newly produced units of a given type presumably had a larger capacity to contribute to output and net revenue than older units—and the older the unit, the less the capacity. So, in effect, units are broken into age classes, and each is given a different value weight (roughly in proportion to the base-period net revenue produced by the items of varying age). It is assumed that the rate of technological advance and, thus, of obsolescence has been roughly the same throughout the entire period in that the life spans (reflecting both physical and economic factors) used to calculate depreciation are generally taken to be the same over time for given types of capital goods. If obsolescence speeded up, the net capital estimates as computed would have an upward bias, and productivity would be correspondingly understated.

In the case of land, of course, the depreciation problem is not involved since it is assumed that maintenance expenditures preserve the capacity of the various types of land to contribute to output at a constant level in a given technological framework. To the extent that land deteriorates, this would be reflected by a decline in the productivity ratios. The real stocks of land in each industry group are combined with other types of capital before being weighted by the rate of return to capital as a whole in each industry. In agriculture, the acreage of various types of land is estimated separately and combined by the average unit value of each type in order to get aggregate real stock prior to combination with other types of farm capital stocks (see Appendix B).

Inventory estimates represent average beginning- and end-of-year numbers of units of the various types of goods times the average price in the base period. For agriculture, real stocks of crops and livestock are estimated directly as described; in other areas, book value estimates are deflated by price indexes designed to convert to constant, base-year prices.

Sources of Basic Data and Reliability of Estimates

The sources of the basic data and the methods used for the estimates in this study are described in some detail in the appendixes. This material will be summarized here to give the general reader a quick picture of the statistical foundations of the study, and the technician an introduction to the appendixes.

An evaluation of the reliability of the productivity ratios rests primarily upon a qualitative appraisal of the accuracy and consistency of the data underlying the estimates of the outputs and the inputs in the economy

---

[19] Richard and Nancy Ruggles, "The Conceptual Basis for the Measurement of Real Capital Stock and Services," *Output, Input, and Productivity Measurement*, Studies in Income and Wealth, Volume 25.

and in the major industrial groupings. A considerable degree of interdependence between the output and the input data helps offset possible errors or bias in the sources since these tend to be offsetting in the ratios. We have compared economy estimates with weighted aggregates of industry estimates for output and the two input classes for all or parts of the period since 1889. Since the economy and industry estimates are based to varying degrees on different sources and methods, these comparisons will be summarized here because they will provide a partial test of accuracy. The comparisons also afford a check on the consistency of the two sets of numbers, which is important since in Part III we compare industry with economy trends.

OUTPUT

General Method

If complete basic data were at hand with respect to the physical quantities, prices, and values of all final transactions in the economy, it would be a matter of indifference whether the number of units of each type of commodity or service were weighted by the average final prices prevailing during the base period, or the current value of production were deflated by an index of the relevant prices with variable quantity weights. In terms of a formula, in which Q represents numbers of units of output; P, their average prices; and the subscripts $_0$ and $_1$, the base period and the given period, respectively:

$$\sum Q_1 P_0 = \sum Q_1 P_1 \div \frac{\sum P_1 Q_1}{\sum P_0 Q_1}$$

The same result could be obtained adding the real product (net output) originating in the various industrial divisions of the economy. If q stands for the quantities of goods produced by an industry and q' for the quantities purchased from other industries, while p and p' represent their respective average prices in the specified time periods, then

$$\sum Q_1 P_0 = \sum_{i=1}^{n} (q_1 p_0 - q'_1 p'_0)$$

The same result is obtained by deflating the value of output and of intermediate-product inputs for all industries by approximate variable-weighted price indexes and summing the differences.

Actually, although value estimates are generally available for the economy and its industrial divisions, neither quantity nor price data are complete. The choice of method for arriving at aggregate physical-volume estimates depends primarily on the representativeness of the sample of prices as compared with the adequacy of the sample of quantities and of the imputations involved in the coverage adjustments that are usually made to approximate total physical volume. The deflated-value approach has been used in obtaining the real products of the economy and of several industry divisions. Price-weighted quantity indexes have been used in the other industrial groupings. Both methods have advantages and short-comings, which will be noted in the following summary and appraisal. It should be mentioned here that only in the farm segment was true net output estimated by deducting real intermediate inputs from real gross output. In the other industry segments, either the component-industry physical output indexes were combined with value-added or national income weights as approximations to net output measures, or the current-value national product estimates were deflated directly. These two methods yield the same results as true net output measures only under special conditions.

Real National Product

The appraisal of the real-product estimates will be treated with respect first to the current-value estimates, and then to the deflators used to eliminate the effect of price changes. The current-dollar series from 1929 forward are based on the estimates of the Commerce Department; and for 1889–1929, on the revised estimates of Kuznets as adjusted. The sources and methods underlying both sets of data are basically the same and have been fully described by the authors;[20] we shall merely highlight some of the possible sources of error and attempt to appraise the general reliability of the over-all estimates.

The basic commodity flow data underlying the estimates for the important consumer and producer commodity segments are benchmarked on the periodic *Census of Manufactures*. They probably portray trends quite accurately, although annual changes interpolated from sample data are less reliable. Kuznets assumed constant distributive margins prior to 1919 because of a lack of readily available data. Later research by Harold Barger indicates a mild increase in margins between 1889 and 1919, so the early current-dollar estimates may have some downward bias, but this should not affect the constant-dollar series based on deflated producer values. Also prior to 1919, direct data are lacking for consumer expenditures for services. Kuznets used ratios of outlays for services to those for commodities, derived from occasional family budget studies. These estimates obviously have larger margins of error than the later estimates benchmarked on the *Census of Business* (first taken in 1929) and other direct information. Information on the "invisible" items of the net foreign balance is also scant before 1919.

Federal government purchase estimates are solidly based throughout. Data on state and local government purchases gradually improved over

[20] See references in Chap. 2, n. 2.

the period, but prior to the 1890 Census the noneducational outlay component is estimated indirectly. Practically no data are available on inventories prior to 1919, and Kuznets estimated net changes from extrapolation backwards of later relationships between stocks and commodity expenditures. Even after 1919, the annual net changes are subject to wide margins of error, although the cumulated net changes give a better indication of trends. The new-construction estimates, based as they are on a spreading of the value of construction permit or contract award data by assumed average monthly patterns of the value of construction put in place, are also less accurate as indicators of annual changes than of movements over longer periods.

Unfortunately, it is not possible to estimate the probable margins of error of the over-all national product estimates. As Milton Gilbert has put it: "The reason is that in the complex of factors that might lead to inaccuracy of the statistics, there are no measures of the errors arising out of most of them, and hence no way to assign them weights so as to arrive at a combined margin of error."[21] For some components, knowledge about the size and characteristics of the universe is lacking, while error due to faulty reporting, willful misstatements by respondents, or negligent enumeration is outside the scope of sampling error measurement. The Commerce Department experts have concluded: "A study of the statistical methodology underlying the national income estimates, supplemented by analysis of the statistical discrepancy and of the revisions, will remain the major avenue for obtaining an evaluation of their reliability."[22] Based on its own appraisal, the Commerce report concluded that "the foregoing survey may provide a sufficiently definitive basis for the general conclusion that the estimated annual totals of gross national product, national income, and personal income are subject to only a small percentage of error. . . ."[23]

Our brief review suggests that estimates for more recent years are probably better than those for earlier years owing to the existence of a somewhat larger body of census data since 1929, improved sample data for interpolations, and expanded administrative statistics. If Gilbert is correct in asserting that for the United States "the probability is all towards under-estimates . . . ,"[24] the improvement in the quality of the estimates might result in some upward bias over time. A review of sources does not suggest a major bias, and to the extent that it also affected the input estimates, it would not affect the productivity ratios. There can be no doubt that long-term changes in the national product estimates are

[21] Milton Gilbert, "Statistical Sources and Methods in National Accounts Estimates and the Problem of Reliability," *Income and Wealth, Series III,* p. 6.

[22] *National Income Supplement, 1954,* pp. 66–67.

[23] *Ibid.,* p. 66.

[24] Gilbert, *op. cit.,* p. 7.

subject to a smaller margin of error than are annual changes, which are based to a large extent on sample data. This conclusion is borne out by an examination of the effect of successive revisions on the estimates and by the movement of the statistical discrepancy between gross product and national income plus other charges against product.

The accuracy of the price deflators and the real national product estimates has not been evaluated by Kuznets or the Commerce Department, but the margins of error are almost certainly greater than those for the current values. In the first place, price indexes are not available to represent all products, even in the market area of the economy. The indexes are reasonably good for food, clothing, and many of the major categories of final product; but they are weak for certain types of consumer services (other than rents), particularly prior to 1935, and for many types of producer durable equipment before 1939, when the Bureau of Labor Statistics greatly expanded its price data collection program. At best, the price indexes used for deflation involve a considerable degree of imputation of price movements with respect to grades or "qualities" of a commodity, to various types of commodities in a given "family," and to commodity families within broader product classes. Sampling is also necessary with respect to types of distributive outlets, localities, and time periods. In recent years the Bureau of Labor Statistics, the chief source of price index numbers, has conducted periodic tests of the representativeness of its samples. It is not clear that price indexes from other sources are as representative of the product classes to which they are applied or that the imputations involved in the deflation procedure itself are reasonable. But in view of the large number of price series used, it is probable that the margins of error in the deflators for the standardized product groupings in the market area of the economy do not seriously distort trends in real product. Greater difficulties are encountered in the nonstandardized and in the nonmarket areas of the economy.

The price deflators for the value of output of nonstandard products such as ships and aircraft are unit cost indexes (weighted averages of materials prices and wage rates), and the construction cost deflators are partially of this character. The deflators for the estimated value (cost) of output of households (mainly domestic service) and of nonprofit institutions are of the same type (primarily average earnings series) as are the deflators for some types of professional services that are not standardized to any extent. The Commerce method of deflating the product of general government explicitly makes no allowance for possible changes in productivity, and Kuznets' estimates imply the same result.

Even assuming that productivity has not advanced as rapidly in these as in other areas of the economy, the relative magnitude of the value of output deflated by unit cost indexes suggests that the rate of growth of the resulting real private product estimates is subject to a downward bias approaching 10 per cent; while the bias in the growth rate of total product, including general government, is somewhat greater.

There is also some cyclical bias in the real-product estimates. The price indexes are usually based on quoted prices and do not take full account of changes in subsidiary terms of sale—special discounts, trade-in allowances, credit terms, prices of collateral equipment, and services or extras. "Net realized" prices tend to fluctuate more than quoted prices over the business cycle and thus the real-product estimates have a downward bias in depressed periods and an upward bias in recoveries. Comparisons of periods characterized by similar degrees of business activity should not be significantly affected.

Industry Output Measures

For our five basic segments and thirty-three industry groups, except for farming, output measures were obtained by weighting physical units and adjusting for incomplete coverage when necessary. In farming, although deflated value estimates are used, the results are virtually the same as those obtained by weighting quantities owing to the relative completeness and consistency of the value, price, and quantity data. For trade, we follow Barger in estimating the deflated value of goods passing through the various types of distributive outlets and weighting by the base-period distributive margins in each.[25] In the residual segments (construction, finance, and services), we have deflated the industry gross-product estimates since 1929 by the implicit deflators for the final products of those industries that enter the gross national product.

Data sources. With respect to the five basic segments, periodic industry censuses are available for agriculture, mining, manufacturing, water transportation, telephone and telegraph, and electric industries.[26] Inter-

[25] Harold Barger, *Distribution's Place in the American Economy since 1869*, Princeton University Press (for NBER), 1955, pp. 20ff.

[26] Census data are available as follows:

Agriculture: Decennial to 1920, quinquennial thereafter. Comprehensive annual data from sample surveys begin in 1910.

Mining: Decennial to 1939, except that a census was taken in 1902 instead of 1899; since 1939 censuses have been taken in 1954 and 1958. In addition, the Bureau of Mines publishes almost comprehensive annual production estimates by type of mineral in the *Minerals Yearbook*.

Manufacturing: Decennial to 1899; quinquennial, 1899–1919; biennial, 1919–39; and 1947, 1954, and 1958. Annual surveys of manufactures, conducted by the Census Bureau, are available beginning 1949 for noncensus years. Additional annual commodity data are contained in the Census *Facts for Industry* reports.

Water transportation: 1880, 1889, 1906, 1916, and 1926; estimates brought forward by relatively good data from the Maritime Commission and other agencies described in Appendix G.

Telephone and telegraph: 1880, 1890, and quinquennial, 1902–37.

Electric industries: 1882–1937 quinquennially, including electric railways.

state Commerce Commission annual statistics begin in 1890 for the railroads, 1936 for pipe lines, and 1939 for intercity buses and motor trucking.[27] Civil Aeronautics Authority (and predecessor agency) data are available for airlines beginning in 1929. American Transit Association reports contain annual data for electric railways (used to interpolate and extrapolate census data) and local bus lines. Annual data on production of manufactured and natural gas since 1929 come from the American Gas Association; before 1929, data on manufactured gas production are contained in the *Census of Manufactures*, and on natural gas production, in the *Minerals Yearbook*. When complete annual data are not available, we either show estimates for benchmark years only, or interpolate annually on the basis of sample surveys or fragmentary data. In the latter cases, the annual estimates are obviously less reliable than the benchmark estimates.

The commodity flow estimates involved in the trade output figures are based on the *Census of Manufactures* as processed by William Shaw for 1869–1929,[28] and by the Commerce Department thereafter. Distributive margins were first reported in censuses beginning in 1929; Barger used a variety of sources to estimate margins in earlier years. The gross product estimates for construction, finance, and services are based on the estimates of the Commerce Department that tie into census data first collected in 1929. The price deflators are those implicit in the real gross national product estimates, and are subject to the biases discussed earlier, particularly as regards construction and services orginating in households and nonprofit institutions. Our chief purpose in estimating real product and productivity in these segments was to make explicit the implications of the over-all estimates.

If the reliability of the benchmark census data is accepted, the accuracy of the derived estimates will depend largely on the nature of the output units and the adequacy of coverage adjustments or price imputations. It is to these matters that we now turn.

Nature of output units. In some instances, there is a choice as to the units in which production may be expressed, and judgment is required to determine the unit which would be most meaningful for productivity comparisons. For example, in the minerals industries, metallic content of ore was considered a preferable unit to the volume of ore; and in transportation of freight, ton-miles carried, rather than freight-car miles or tons of freight, was used.

A more serious problem arises because the available or preferable units are usually not entirely homogeneous, but comprise a number of qualities

[27] Harold Barger's estimates of pipe lines and intercity motor transport were pushed back roughly to 1919 on the basis of trade data as described in Appendix G.

[28] Simon Kuznets, *Commodity Flow and Capital Formation*, New York (NBER), 1938, Vol. 1; and William H. Shaw, *The Value of Commodity Output since 1869*, New York (NBER), 1947.

or types of goods that are lumped together for reporting purposes. For example, although numbers of pairs of leather shoes produced may be reported under the categories of men's, women's, and children's, there are many price lines within each of these classes. Shifts of demand and production among price lines would not affect production indexes based on gross units, but they would affect an ideal index based on a weighted aggregate of homogeneous units. Insofar as there has been a shift of demand towards higher qualities of goods over the long run or in cyclical expansions as real income advances, the gross-unit measures understate the increase in production. The reverse bias could affect the measures in contraction periods. In this regard, deflation of values by indexes of the prices of strictly specified representative goods is a preferable procedure, since shifts among qualities would show up as changes in the real values.

The probable downward bias in the physical-unit measures has decreased over time, however, since in manufacturing there has been a marked increase in the detail in which quantity data have been collected in the censuses (see Appendix D, subsection on "Physical units and weights"). A decreasing downward bias means that the estimates tend to increase relative to the true figures.

The problem of changes in quality of the same commodity, as distinguished from a change in quality-mix, was mentioned in the earlier conceptual discussion. Here, it should be noted that quality change will be greater in some industries than in others. Thus, manufactured goods are more susceptible to quality improvements than are farm products; and within manufacturing the quality of automobiles and machinery, for example, has probably improved more than that of lumber and lumber products. This should be kept in mind in interpreting relative changes in output and productivity by industry.

Coverage adjustments. A major problem in estimating the physical volume of production is posed by the fact that in many industry groups, particularly in the manufacturing segment, the physical-unit data do not relate to all of the production of the component industries, whereas the input data are comprehensive. Since it would be highly questionable to assume that uncovered output moved with the covered portion of output, F. C. Mills and Solomon Fabricant developed the technique of adjusting the partial quantity indexes to full coverage by an index of the ratio of the value of covered output to the total value of industry production. This involves the assumption that the average prices of the products for which quantity data are unavailable move with the average prices of the covered products. To obtain full coverage of industry groups or of the whole segment, the coverage adjustment was based on value-added ratios, a procedure which involves the assumption that unit values added in the covered and uncovered industries have parallel movements.

43

Since changes in relative price and unit value added reflect primarily relative changes in productivity over longer periods, the adequacy of the Mills-Fabricant coverage adjustment indirectly hinges on the assumption that productivity in the covered and uncovered areas moves similarly. In adjusting the manufacturing output indexes for 1947 relative to 1939, the Census Bureau and the Federal Reserve Board moved closer to this assumption by basing their adjustment factors on the ratios of employment in the covered area to total employment (see Appendix D). We have, likewise, used coverage adjustments based on employment ratios in the transportation and communications and public utility segments.

Tests using only part of the available data indicate that adjusted output indexes are better than unadjusted indexes. The degree of reliability depends on the validity of the underlying assumption and the relative size of the uncovered segment. As to the implicit assumption, it seems reasonable to suppose that productivity movements of parts of the same industry or industry group are more similar than productivity (or price) movements in less closely related areas. It has been suggested that the coverage adjustment leads to some downward bias since the uncovered area often includes relatively new products in the production of which prices tend to fall and productivity tends to rise in relation to the older products. This would be offset in some industries by the custom-built products for which unit data are not given since it might be expected that productivity increase would be less rapid in the case of these items. This same problem is, of course, present in the deflation of values. The imputation of price movements of covered to those of uncovered products has very similar limitations unless the imputations are periodically checked and adjusted.

With respect to the magnitude of the area uncovered by physical-volume or direct price information, a run-down by segment suggests that it comprises about one-fifth of the value of output in the private domestic economy in 1929. In farming and mining (except for nonmetallic mining and quarrying) coverage is virtually complete, whereas in manufacturing we estimate that about 53 per cent of the total value of production in the segment was not covered by quantity data in 1899, and 38 per cent in 1947—although these percentages were reduced somewhat by the use of deflated value estimates for some industries or groups.

In general, the uncovered area has declined over the decades as more quantity and price information has become available, so whatever bias is involved in coverage adjustments has tended to grow smaller. In addition, note that the real capital stock and input series also involve imputation of price deflators to uncovered items and have similar biases.

A different coverage problem is posed by the fact that certain types of output are included neither in the physical-unit nor the value measures, while the associated inputs enter the input measures. Force account construction activity, research and development, and in-plant training are included neither in the industry nor national output measures. Force account construction is significant in the extractive industries,[29] manufacturing, and the regulated industries, but its importance is declining. Research, development, and training are of increasing importance, and a significant factor in certain industry groups. Some downward bias is present in output and productivity indexes for these groups.

In some other cases, certain activities were not included in the physical-volume composites, nor did a basis for coverage adjustment exist—for example, in the transmission of television programs and in the rental of private wires by the telephone industry. Usually these outputs are minor relative to total output, but their omission impairs accuracy if their movement differs from that of covered output. It is likely that the bulk of uncovered activities are comparatively new and are growing relatively; so their omission results in an understatement of production and productivity increase.

Gross and net industry output. Only the farm real-product estimates are true net output measures, obtained by subtracting the deflated value of intermediate-product purchases from the real value of gross output. In the construction, finance, and service segments since 1929, we deflated gross product directly. This procedure yields true net output measures to the degree that output and intermediate input prices show parallel movements. This appears to have been the case in construction (see Appendix E). In finance and services the importance of intermediate products is relatively small, so the probable bias is slight. In the other segments, since we relate the gross output measures to factor inputs, we are assuming that the movement of gross measures approximates the movement of net measures. Based on scattered evidence for the United States, net output in nonfarm industries may have risen somewhat more than gross output as a result of materials savings and a shift towards more highly processed goods. Canadian estimates for recent decades, however, do not show much difference between the movements of nonfarm net and gross output measures, on balance.[30]

Comparison of Real Private Domestic Product and the Industry Output Aggregate

A comparison of aggregates of real final expenditures and of industry outputs in the private domestic economy since 1929 is contained in Table A-3. To some extent similar sources and methods were used; so the

[29] The crude petroleum production index was adjusted to include the construction of oil wells.

[30] V. R. Berlinguette and F. H. Leacy, "The Estimation of Real Domestic Product by Final Expenditure Categories and by Industry of Origin, Canada," *Output, Input, and Productivity Measurement*, Studies in Income and Wealth, Volume 25.

comparison is but a partial check on accuracy; it is more meaningful as a check on the consistency of the economy and the industry measures. Since consistent value estimates and the same deflators were used in the construction, finance, and service areas, both the economy and the segment estimates are subject to a downward bias on account of inadequate deflators. The implications of the real-product estimates with respect to the output of the trade segment are similar to those made explicit in the segment estimates. But in the other segments, the economy estimates are derived as deflated final expenditures while the industry estimates are generally weighted physical units with coverage adjustment.

It is, therefore, gratifying that relative to 1929, the two sets of estimates were only 2.2 per cent apart in 1953.[31] The higher level of the real-product estimate supports our surmise that weighted physical units, because of heterogeneity may have a secular downward bias relative to deflated values, or that net output estimates outside the extractive industries may tend to rise more than gross estimates due to reductions in intermediate materials consumption per unit of output, or that perhaps both explanations may apply. But the discrepancy is small enough to justify the comparison of industry and economy output and productivity estimates made in Part III.

The comparison prior to 1929 is less direct. Since output estimates for the finance and service segments are not available, an industry output aggregate for the other segments was used in conjunction with the real private domestic product estimates to derive output in the uncovered area as a residual. Between 1889 and 1929, the residual estimates of real product originating in the finance and service segments, when divided by the corresponding manhours, show virtually the same trend in output per manhour as do the estimates since 1929 (see Appendix A, end of section "Comparison of Real Product with an Aggregate of Industry Output"). This result is sufficiently plausible to suggest that the economy and the industry output estimates are reasonably consistent in the earlier period.[32]

LABOR INPUT

Estimates of labor input in the economy as a whole were built up from industry estimates and are, therefore, consistent. There are decennial external checks on the economy employment aggregates, and annual

---

[31] There was also close correspondence in a similar comparison for 1947–55, reported by Jack Alterman and Eva Jacobs, "Estimates of Real Product in the United States, 1947–55," *Output, Input, and Productivity Measurement*, Studies in Income and Wealth, Volume 25.

[32] Between 1869 and 1889, however, the estimates for finance and services show an absurdly large increase in output and productivity. This confirms the judgment that the 1869 estimate of national product is seriously understated, a judgment which led to the decision not to extend the economy analysis back of 1889.

checks on average hours and total manhours as well as on employment estimates since 1940. Further, there is throughout a close statistical interrelation between the output and employment estimates for the economy and some of the major industry segments.

The total-employment estimates appear to be quite good indicators of trends throughout the entire period, judging not only from the quality of the sources but also from their consistency with estimates of the labor force or the number of "gainful workers," adjusted for unemployment. The latter are largely independent of the employment estimates since 1929 and are partially so in earlier decades. Annual employment estimates are of a high degree of reliability only since 1939 when the Social Security reporting system began.

The estimates of average hours worked, which enter the manhour figures, are generally less reliable than the employment estimates. Correspondence between our industry-composite average hours estimates and those provided by the annual population surveys since 1940 is fairly good. The source data, while less abundant prior to the mid-1930's than after, provide broad benchmarks back to 1920. Before that date chief reliance had to be placed on available data relating to standard hours, which can be roughly adjusted to actual hours worked, and on estimates based on state data. Margins of error are probably high for the early decades. Despite its inadequacy, however, the statistical base is still broad enough to make unlikely any serious bias in the trend of the hours estimates, although estimates of annual changes prior to the mid-1930's may be subject to high margins of error. The industry labor compensation estimates used for weights are good and generally consistent with the employment data.

Employment

From 1929 forward, the Commerce Department estimates of numbers of employees and proprietors engaged in the various industries were used with only minor adjustment. From 1939 on, these are solidly based on comprehensive annual data provided by Social Security, Railroad Retirement, and federal civil service collections that cover over 95 per cent of employees, while collateral sources provide relatively good data for the remainder. Back to 1929, benchmarks are available from censuses covering almost all industries. The number of unpaid family workers was estimated back to 1940 on the basis of the Current Population Surveys, and prior to that date by applying the 1940 ratios to the number of proprietors in the several industry segments in earlier years. These estimates are weak, but the component is small. The Department of Agriculture estimates of farm employment were substituted for those of Commerce since the former include unpaid family workers.

Primary reliance on the Commerce estimates of persons engaged has the great advantage of providing a high degree of statistical inter-dependence with the real-product estimates. The estimates of employee compensation and proprietors' net income, derived from the same sources as the estimates of employees and proprietors, comprise almost three-fourths of the value of the national product. It is true that we use real-product estimates built up from expenditures rather than national income plus other charges; but over the period since 1929 there has been no notice-able trend in the statistical discrepancy between the two sets of estimates. For analysis of annual productivity changes, however, there would be some advantage in adjusting the real-product estimates by the statistical discrepancy. On the product side there is also interdependence, especially before 1939, when both output and employment estimates were drawn from the same censuses. This also applies to the industry output and employment estimates.

Prior to 1929, the employment estimates for manufacturing, mining, transportation, and public utilities were extrapolated by series, presented in National Bureau monographs, based on periodic industry censuses or agency reports. In some cases we pushed the monograph estimates back further by use of the same sources. For most of the remaining industry segments, for which censuses were not taken prior to 1929, it was necessary to rely on industrial distributions of gainful workers based on occupational data from the decennial population censuses, as prepared by Daniel Carson (see Appendix A) and roughly adjusted to an employment basis. Government employment estimates were based on Civil Service records and data from the Governments Division of the Census Bureau and from the Office of Education.

Annual estimates for many industry segments prior to 1929 could be interpolated between benchmarks on the basis of sample surveys or state data. For a few segments, interpolation was done on the basis of output series. For obvious reasons, such estimates are not presented in the industry productivity tables, but were merely used to build up the economy employment and manhour totals. Although the annual economy totals before 1929 are therefore not entirely independent of output series for intercensal years, they are dominated by independent data.

To combine the employment estimates with average hours estimates for a number of the segments, full- and part-time averages were appro-priate. For purposes of showing industrial distributions, as in Table A-VII, however, it is more meaningful to express employment in terms of full-time equivalents. On this basis, the industry aggregates are quite close to the population census totals for the labor force or for the number of gainful workers after adjustment to exclude the estimated number of persons unemployed. More significantly, the trends of the two aggregates between

1870 and 1950 are not far apart. The industry aggregate rose from 99 per cent of the adjusted labor force estimate in 1870 (or 100 per cent in 1890) to 103 per cent in 1950 (see Table A-VIII). Even though about half of estimated employment prior to 1929 was based on the labor force estimates, the correspondence between the totals is evidence that the economy trends are reasonable. The industry trends based on population census data are probably less accurate since allocation by industry of persons in occupations common to several industries cannot be precise. It is also evident that annual changes in the estimates up to 1939 are subject to wider margins of error than are the trends.

Edward Denison concluded a review of the employment estimates as follows:

> My judgment is that, for the period since 1939, the error introduced, by errors in the persons engaged series, into the year-to-year percentage change in gross national product per person engaged in production is not likely to exceed 0.2 percentage points. . . . The estimates from 1929 to 1938 are less reliable, but given the large productivity changes of that period, probably are good enough for meaningful year-to-year measurement, and should certainly be adequate for average changes over three or four years . . . at least back to 1880 their quality does not deteriorate much faster than is offset by the statistical advantage of a longer time period for computing an average rate of change in output per man for periods ending with the present.[33]

Average Hours and Manhours

From 1940 forward, estimates of average hours worked per week are available for all segments. The majority of the private-industry estimates are from the Bureau of Labor Statistics establishment surveys, although average hours worked in manufacturing groups since 1947 are taken from the Census annual surveys. For finance and services the chief source is the *Census of Population, 1940* and unpublished data from the Current Population Surveys. The weighted average of the industry estimates shows virtually the same trend and movements as the average hours estimates for the total civilian economy reported in the Census *Monthly Report on the Labor Force* (see Table A-XII). The manhours estimates based on the two sources also showed like trends, but year-to-year correspondence was less close, primarily because of divergences in annual changes in the employment estimates. Of the two sets of estimates, those based on establishment reports were chosen not only because they are statistically consistent with the output estimates, but also because the estimates based on Current

[33] Denison, *op. cit.*

Population Surveys rely on a small sample and are subject to wider margins of error.

In the conceptual discussion, it was noted that manhours worked, rather than manhours paid for, is the appropriate measure. The difference between the two concepts is not operationally significant prior to 1939,[34] but with the trend toward paid vacations, holidays, and sick leave during and after the war, the divergence has been increasing. Actually, our estimates are mixed, although comprising mainly hours worked. The BLS-based average hours are on a paid-for basis, while the census estimates (adjusted to exclude "0-hours") are hours worked. The farming and federal government manhour estimates are also on an hours worked basis.

The establishment-based estimates of average hours worked extend back to the mid- or early 1930's, and in the case of manufacturing to 1909. But estimates for most segments are available for 1920–22 from a survey by W. I. King for the National Bureau of Economic Research. For earlier years, standard weekly or daily hours estimates are available for manufacturing, mining, construction, railroads, and manufactured gas utilities. These are good trend indicators, although adjustments to an actual hours worked basis were made by correlations derived from estimates for periods when both types of estimates are available (see Appendixes A, C, D, E, and G).

For farming, Department of Agriculture estimates of manhours are available since 1910, based on technological studies of manhour requirements for various types of farm output. Prior to 1910, we accepted Barger's judgment that average hours in farming did not change significantly (see Appendix B). Estimates for most of the other private-industry segments are based on reports covering a number of states. Since the state data are fragmentary, the average hours estimates are weak for these segments. Civil Service Commission reports provide the basis for average hours worked per year by federal civilian employees. For the economy as a whole, the basis of the data for the average hours estimates is fairly broad, even in the latter part of the nineteenth century; but, unfortunately, there is no good method of subjecting the average hours and manhours estimates before 1940 to an external check.

Average hours data for some industries, notably manufacturing, relate to production workers. We imputed the same movements of average hours to nonproduction workers. Although nonproduction workers comprise a minor portion of total persons engaged, this assumption introduces additional possible sources of error, but more so in the annual fluctuations than in the trends. A similar imputation was made for average hours

[34] See Albert Rees, *New Measures of Wage-Earner Compensation in Manufacturing, 1914–57,* Occasional Paper 75, New York (NBR), 1960.

worked by proprietors and unpaid family workers, but an allowance was made for the higher level of average hours for this group relative to average hours for employees revealed by unpublished data from recent Current Population Surveys.

The labor compensation estimates used for weighting purposes are of the same order of reliability as the employment estimates and are generally consistent with them. That is, the Commerce Department estimates were used since 1929 and were extrapolated to 1919 by the Kuznets estimates after the latter were adjusted for consistency with our employment figures. The adjustment consisted of multiplying Kuznets' labor income estimates by the ratio of our employment estimates to his. In general, the 1919–29 weights were used for earlier subperiods. In any case, relative average hourly earnings in the various industries did not change very much over the decades (see Table A-5).

It should be noted that labor compensation includes supplements as well as wages and salaries. When this value is divided by manhours worked, the resultant average hourly earnings reflect the effect of changes in paid leave as well as in other supplements, which is consistent with our preferred treatment of manhours in the productivity ratios.

REAL CAPITAL STOCKS AND SERVICES

Since capital stock, unlike the labor force, is immediately available for use at all times, we have not adjusted for rate of utilization, counting this as an aspect of the efficiency with which the capital is used. Rather, weighting the real stock by its base-period rate of return, we measure the input of capital in constant dollars in successive years, assuming base-year efficiency in use of the instruments. Weighting is discussed in the next section; here we describe, in summary fashion, the real-stock estimates.[35]

For the major portion of the private nonfarm, nonresidential economy estimates, we used the reproducible real-wealth estimates prepared by Raymond Goldsmith for the period since 1896.[36] Goldsmith's basic method was to estimate annual gross outlays for plant and equipment by major types, deflate to 1929 prices, depreciate the real outlays by the straight-line method over average lengths of life as prescribed by *Bulletin "F"* of the Treasury Department,[37] and then cumulate the net additions to stock.

---

[35] A more detailed summary and discussion of the industry capital estimates is to be found in Daniel Creamer, "An Appraisal of Long-Term Capital Estimates: Some Reference Notes," *Output, Input, and Productivity Measurement*, Studies in Income and Wealth, Volume 25.

[36] *A Study of Saving in the United States*, Princeton, N.J., Princeton University Press, 1956, Volume III.

[37] *Income Tax Depreciation and Obsolescence, Estimated Useful Lives and Depreciation Rates*, Rev. Ed. (July 1942), Bureau of Internal Revenue (now Internal Revenue Service), 1942.

Site land was allowed for by applying the 1929 ratio of land value to value of structures to the constant-dollar value of the latter throughout. Inventories were estimated separately on a basis consistent with the national product component. To carry the reproducible stock estimates back of 1896, we successively deducted the corresponding annual net capital formation estimates contained in Kuznets' real national product estimates.

Goldsmith compared his "perpetual inventory" estimates with deflated census-type asset-value estimates, and found a good correspondence of trend.[38] Kuznets likewise compared cumulative totals of his net capital formation estimates with the deflated Census reproducible wealth estimates and found much the same net change over long periods, although there was considerable divergence over shorter periods.[39] It is his conclusion that the cumulative real net investment estimates provide a more reliable series than the deflated wealth estimates.

For this study, we made a somewhat different type of comparison. We subtracted the sum of the real fixed capital stock estimates for the private nonfarm industry segments that were available from the Goldsmith estimates (excluding residential real estate from both estimates), and compared the trends of the covered and residual sectors in relation to manhours worked in each. The estimates for the various groups in mining and manufacturing are based on deflated Census and Internal Revenue Service estimates of the value of assets (presumed to be at original cost), adjusted to exclude financial items.[40] Estimates for the groups included in the transportation, communications, and public utility segments were obtained chiefly by the method of cumulating real net investment, but this was done independently of the Goldsmith estimates.[41] It is these capital estimates that we use in the productivity estimates for the nonfarm industry groups.

The results of the comparison for key years beginning with 1899 are shown in Table A-6. The level of capital and particularly of capital per manhour in the uncovered sector is considerably lower than in the covered sector, but the trend of capital per manhour in the uncovered sector from 1909 on is moderately greater than in the covered sector. These results do not seem unreasonable (see Appendix A, section "Nonfarm Nonresidential Capital"), and confirmation of the 1939 level is provided

[38] Raymond W. Goldsmith, "A Perpetual Inventory of National Wealth," *Studies in Income and Wealth, Volume 14,* New York (NBER), 1952, pp. 46–57.

[39] Simon Kuznets, *National Product since 1869,* New York (NBER), 1946, pp. 193–199; see also *Capital in the American Economy: Its Formation and Financing,* in preparation.

[40] Israel Borenstein, *Capital and Output Trends in Mining Industries, 1870–1948,* Occasional Paper 45, New York (NBER), 1954; Daniel Creamer, *Capital and Output Trends in Manufacturing Industries, 1880–1948,* Occasional Paper 41, New York (NBER), 1954.

[41] Melville J. Ulmer, *Capital in Transportation, Communications, and Public Utilities: Its Formation and Financing,* Princeton University Press (for NBER), 1960.

by the results of the Harvard interindustry study group.[42] The increase of capital in the uncovered sector between 1899 and 1909 seems quite high, however, suggesting that the economy estimate for 1899 may be on the low side or that the covered-industry aggregate may be high. In general, the comparison does not indicate that the two sets of estimates are inconsistent. A similar comparison by Kuznets of the sum of his net investment estimates with the difference in the sum of industry capital stock between 1880 and 1922 showed only a 4 per cent discrepancy, although the correspondence in subperiods was not as close.[43]

Estimates of the stock of nonfarm residential structures in 1929 prices are those prepared by Leo Grebler, David M. Blank, and Louis Winnick.[44] The latter also cumulated real net additions to stock. Depreciation was computed by the declining balance method, using a rate of 2 per cent a year. A base in 1890 was provided by the product of the number of units in the stock and the deflated average value per unit given by the mortgage census of 1890.[45] The base agrees closely with the Kuznets independent estimate for this component of wealth. The estimates were carried back by subtracting Kuznets' estimates of real outlays for new nonfarm residential structures. The Grebler-Blank-Winnick estimates for 1950 relative to 1890 are about 5 per cent lower than independent census-type real-wealth estimates and about 10 per cent lower than Goldsmith's estimates. We used the Goldsmith method of applying a fixed percentage markup to obtain the real value of site land.

The estimates of farm capital other than machinery are those prepared by Alvin S. Tostlebe for census years 1870–1950,[46] interpolated annually and extrapolated forward by Goldsmith's estimates. Tostlebe used acres of farm land in the various states, by type, multiplied by the average value per acre in the base period. His weighted aggregate increases significantly less than a simple measure of acreage, reflecting the greater relative increase in unimproved compared to higher-value improved land. Tostlebe's estimates of inventories were obtained by multiplying numbers by average value per unit in the base period, by state. The changes in the real farm inventory values as estimated by Tostlebe accord closely with the corresponding gross national product (GNP) component.

Goldsmith's estimates were also used for the stock of net foreign assets,

[42] Research Project on the Structure of the American Economy, "The Capital Structure of the American Economy," *Studies in the Structure of the American Economy*, New York, Oxford University Press, 1953.

[43] Kuznets, *Capital in the American Economy*, Vol. II, Part D.

[44] *Capital Formation in Residential Real Estate: Trends and Prospects*, Princeton University Press (for NBER), 1956.

[45] *Census of the United States, 1890*, Vol. XII, *Report on Real Estate Mortgages*.

[46] *The Growth of Physical Capital in Agriculture, 1870–1950*, Occasional Paper 44, New York (NBER), 1954.

mentioned earlier, and as a basis for government-owned capital stock. In the latter category, we modified his land estimates somewhat; and for the sake of consistency with national product sectoring, we roughly estimated the capital stocks held by government enterprises to include them with the business sector rather than with general government.

It is not easy to appraise the accuracy of the real-stock estimates, given their conceptual basis.[47] The correspondence between long-run movements of the deflated book value estimates and the cumulated real net investment series is reassuring as to the basic value data, but these estimates are subject to common error on two scores. In the first place, the deflators for capital goods are not entirely satisfactory. This is true of construction throughout and of equipment particularly in the earlier decades. The probable downward bias in the plant physical-volume estimates is, of course, matched by a similar bias in the new-construction component of GNP. Secondly, the lengths of life of plant and equipment, according to which the gross capital outlays are depreciated by the perpetual inventory method, are also implicit in the book value estimates. Insofar as these are unrealistic, they affect the estimates of stock and associated capital services; or (more importantly), insofar as actual lengths of life have changed over the period, the estimates of real capital stock and associated capital inputs have somewhat distorted movements.

Comparisons of estimates based on the different approaches indicate that margins of error are probably greater in shorter-term movements than in the long-run trends. The statistical base of the capital outlay estimates is generally more solid for recent decades; so it is reasonable to suppose that the derived real capital stock estimates are more accurate in recent periods than in earlier years.

THE WEIGHTING SYSTEM

In many American industries, and in the economy, there tends to be a negative correlation between relative changes in outputs and in prices. This means that a late-period weight-base results in a smaller increase in the aggregate industry or economy output than an early-period weight-base. There is a similar, but less pronounced, tendency characterizing input aggregates, since capital per unit of labor input has increased, while unit capital compensation has declined, relative to wage rates. So, as we shall see, the weighting system makes less difference in the movement of total factor productivity than it does in the movement of real product. But the choice of a weighting system is still of consequence.

Ideally, in comparisons of an aggregate between two periods, one should use the relative weights of each period in order to bracket the difference

---

[47] See Creamer, "An Appraisal of Long-Term Capital Estimates: Some Reference Notes."

in change. This is hardly practical in presenting a long time series, and certainly not so for the many time series in this study. Accordingly, we have resorted to the weighting convention used in most of the other National Bureau studies of output. That is, in comparing movements between key years we have used arithmetic averages of the unit values in the two years to weight component units (the Marshall-Edgeworth formula), and then linked the resulting index numbers for the several sub-periods in order to form a continuous series, with 1929 as the reference base.

Although there is no unique solution to the index number problem, the chain index with occasionally changing weights seems to be a reasonable convention. The relative unit values for each time-segment of the index are consistent with the contemporaneous structure of production. Usually, structural changes are gradual enough to warrant only occasional changes in weights, but the changes cumulate so that over as long a period as we are studying frequent weight changes seem desirable. In comparing changes between the key years of the long period (1889–1957), it might be argued that cross-weights for these two years should be used. But differences in the nature of product are so great over as long a period as is considered here that this procedure would be impractical.

We have quantified the difference in movement of the output and input aggregates and of total factor productivity in the private domestic economy as a whole by using changing weights as compared with a fixed (1929) weight-base. With respect to real product, weighting by both systems was carried out in terms of about 200 product classes from 1929 on, and several dozen classes in the earlier years. Between 1889 and 1929, the chain index rose about 5 per cent more than the fixed-weight aggregate in line with the tendency for relative changes in prices and quantities to be inversely correlated. There is, however, very little difference between the two indexes between 1929 and 1953. One would have expected the fixed-weight (1929) aggregate to show a greater increase over this period, and its failure to do so seems to be connected with peculiarities of the post-World War II period (see Appendix A and Table A-XVIII). The input indexes were alternatively weighted in terms of 47 industrial groupings in the case of labor, and 25 in the case of capital, and the two broad input groups were also weighted together using both schemes. The fixed-weight aggregate rose about 2 per cent less than the chain index up to 1929 and then by about 1 per cent more between 1929 and 1953.

As a result of the relative movements described above, the productivity ratio showed less divergence of movement between 1889 and 1929 using the alternative weighting systems than was the case with real product, because the divergence of the input indexes was in the same direction as that of the output indexes up to 1929. Since 1929, however, the divergence was slightly greater, because whereas the fixed-weight input aggregate fell a bit relative to the chain index (in line with expectations), the divergence of the two real-product series was to a slight extent in the opposite direction (see Tables A-XVII and A-XVIII).

Some other comparisons of the effect of alternative weight-bases are made in the industry appendixes. In general, it appears that the effect of alternative weight-bases in groupings as broad as those used in this study is not great in relation to the large changes in the output and input aggregates and their ratios. But it is likewise clear that the changes vary somewhat depending on the particular weighting convention employed. The differences are minor, however, compared with differences in movement between weighted and unweighted input aggregates.

Finally, two deficiencies of the factor-cost estimates should be noted which affect their use for the analysis in Chapter 5 as well as for weighting purposes. They do not relate to the quality of the basic data, which is relatively good since 1919, but rather to methods of estimation. First, whereas the labor compensation estimates are based on plant data, in line with the principle of industry classification, the data on corporate profits relate to firms. Insofar as firms have establishments in several industries, there is some distortion since all profits are thrown into the industry in which the firm's major activities lie. We have transferred some of the profits reported for the petroleum refining industry (manufacturing) to the crude oil and natural gas producing industry (mining); but in several other cases distortions are probably significant enough to warrant adjustments, which, however, were not made because of lack of a firm statistical base. Second, whereas profits have been adjusted for the effect of inventory revaluation to current prices in the national accounts, a similar adjustment for depreciation revaluation has not been made. This is not so important in the relative weights assigned to the real capital stocks in the various sectors, but it is of somewhat greater importance in the relative weights accorded to labor and capital. In periods of rising prices, profits and the relative weight of capital tend to be overstated.

PART II

Productivity in the Total Economy

CHAPTER 3

Productivity Changes in the Economy

THIS chapter is devoted to a description of average changes in the private domestic economy since 1889. It provides the background for later analysis of the role of productivity in aggregate economic growth and a standard for comparison of productivity changes in the individual industries of the economy. The economy-wide estimates will also be useful for international comparison and analysis, but this use lies beyond the scope of the present volume.

Special interest attaches to over-all productivity indexes as the best available measures of net changes in the productive efficiency of the economy as a whole. In effect, the index of productivity in the private domestic economy is a weighted average of productivity indexes for the various industries. The component-industry measures show considerable dispersion and irregularity of movement. This is due partly to chance elements affecting invention, innovation, and the incidence of increasing returns, but it also reflects changing relative amounts of investment devoted to improvement of efficiency in the various industries. Only by study of the aggregate measure can we see the net effect of industry productivity changes and the degree of regularity of the forces promoting improved efficiency in the economy as a whole.

We shall examine both secular trends and shorter-period fluctuations in total factor productivity and the partial productivity ratios. The analysis is confined largely to the private domestic economy; the national product and productivity estimates are subject to some downward bias because of the method of estimating real product originating in the government and in the rest-of-the-world sectors. Since we later use the national productivity estimates for analysis of aggregate economic growth, however, we shall compare long-period productivity trends in the private domestic and total national economies. The differences are relatively minor, for the private domestic economy accounted for more than 90 per cent in all peacetime years.

Secular Trends

The long-term growth of total factor productivity and the partial productivity ratios will first be described in terms of average annual rates of change between 1889 and 1957. Inspection of the time series on an annual basis reveals a distinct change in trend about 1919; so rates of growth over the two segments of the long period will also be computed. More complicated methods of trend fitting are employed, but these give virtually the same average rates of change as are obtained by use of the simpler compound interest formula.

THE LONG PERIOD, 1889–1957

Total factor productivity—variant measures. Between the terminal years of the period 1889–1957, productivity increased at an average annual rate of approximately 1.7 per cent in the private domestic economy (see Table 1 and Chart 1). Since the real private domestic product grew at

TABLE 1

Private Domestic Economy:
Growth Rates in Real Product and Productivity Ratios, 1889–1957
(average annual percentage rates of change)

	Real Gross Product	*Real Gross Product per Unit of*			*Real Gross Product per Manhour* (unweighted)
		Total Factor Input	Labor Input	Capital Input	
1889–1957	3.5	1.7	2.0	1.0	2.4
1889–1919	3.9	1.3	1.6	0.5	2.0
1919–57	3.1	2.1	2.3	1.3	2.6

SOURCE: Table A-XXII.

an average annual rate of 3.5 per cent over the same sixty-eight year period, it is evident that about half of the growth in output was accounted for by additions to real labor and capital inputs, and half was contributed by increases in the efficiency with which the inputs were utilized, i.e., in productivity. The relative importance of productivity has been still greater in recent decades. But even the 1.7 per cent a year secular rate, when compounded, would result in a doubling of real private domestic product every forty years due to productivity growth alone; the 3.5 per cent annual rate of growth of real product as a whole results in a doubling every twenty years, on the average.

The rate of growth of productivity in the total national economy using the estimates of either the Commerce Department or Kuznets (national security version) is lower—1.6 per cent, as shown in Table 2. There is reason for thinking that these more comprehensive estimates understate actual productivity gains. The Commerce Department uses explicit conventions for estimating real product originating in the rest-of-the-world

CHART 1

Private Domestic Economy: Output, Inputs, and Productivity Ratios, Average Annual
Rates of Change, 1889–1957

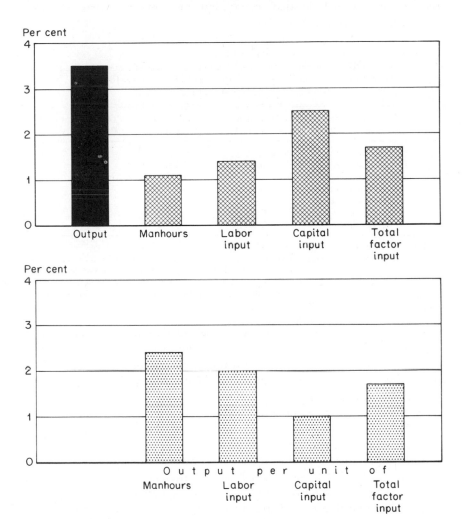

and general government that make no allowance for productivity change
in these sectors (which comprise the difference between the private domestic and total national economies).

Measurement of the physical volume of gross and net government output is not generally practicable; but it seems obvious a priori that the

61

productivity of public resources must have increased over the period since many of the same technological improvements have been introduced in government as in private industry.[1] This must also have been true of real net capital stocks located abroad, but the estimates of real net factor income from abroad do not reflect it.

TABLE 2

Alternative Economic Sectors and Variant Concepts of National Product:
Growth Rates in Real Product, Input, and Productivity, 1889–1957
(average annual percentage rates of change)

Economic Sector	Real Gross Product[a]	Total Real Factor Input	Total Factor Productivity
Private domestic	3.46	1.70	1.73
Private national	3.47	1.75	1.69
Total national:		1.92	
Commerce concept	3.50		1.55
Kuznets concepts:			
National security	3.50		1.55
Peacetime	3.39		1.44

SOURCE: Tables A-XIX through A-XXII.

[a] If real net product estimates are used, the growth rates are higher by 0.01 percentage point in the national security concept of the total economy; 0.02 percentage point higher in the private national economy; 0.03 percentage point higher in the Commerce national economy concept; and lower by 0.01 percentage point in the peacetime concept of the national economy.

Inclusion of the general-government and rest-of-the-world sectors raises real factor input proportionately more than real product in the total national economy as compared with the private domestic economy. The difference in average annual rates of change is 0.22 percentage point for input and 0.04 for real product.[2] Thus, the input of the two sectors rose even more than private domestic product. Reference to Table 2 indicates that the rest-of-the-world sector accounted for 0.04 percentage point of the difference between productivity growth in the private domestic and total national economies with the larger government sector accounting for the bulk of the total 0.18 percentage point difference. The proportionate difference between the two rates of growth differs somewhat by subperiod.

It is apparent that the differences shown are not major. Even if it were assumed that productivity in the total national economy rose at the 1.73

[1] See the experimental measures compiled by Henry Lytton, "Recent Productivity Trends in the Federal Government: An Exploratory Study," *The Review of Economic Statistics*, November 1959, p. 341.

[2] The greater relative discrepancy in the period since 1919 is traceable to our inclusion of the input of capital as well as of labor commanded by government, whereas the Commerce real government product estimates parallel the government labor input measure alone. Labor and capital inputs showed parallel movements between 1889 and 1919, but between 1919 and 1957 capital in this sector rose relative to labor input.

average annual percentage rate calculated for the private domestic economy instead of 1.55, then real national product would have risen at an average annual rate of 3.68 instead of at 3.50 as computed.

The Kuznets estimates (national security version) imply about the same rate of change in total factor productivity as the Commerce estimates, although there are several conceptual differences between the two series, as explained in Chapter 2. The chief difference is that Kuznets excludes estimated public services to business from final product while the Commerce Department includes all government purchases of goods and services. The amount involved is not large, and the conventions used by Kuznets to measure real government services to consumers and, by implication, real intermediate services to business result in a relatively stable ratio of the latter to real national product in the terminal years (see Appendix A, section on "Private purchases of goods and services"). Because the two sets of estimates yield much the same secular rate of productivity advance, it is plain that the Kuznets series also imply no advance in productivity of the factors employed in the public and foreign sectors. There is, however, some divergence in subperiod movements between the two series. Since the Kuznets conventions for excluding government real-cost services are quite arbitrary, the Commerce estimates are better suited to the study of productivity movements as such. Kuznets' estimates (national security version) will, nevertheless, be used for analysis of the interactions of productivity and economic growth because his national product estimates permit a complete breakdown by the broad purposes toward which economic activity is directed.

The rates of change in the Kuznets peacetime version of the national product are also shown in Table 2. In this version, Kuznets excludes national security outlays from final product on the grounds that they do not contribute directly to economic welfare but are merely a precondition for production and hence may be classed as intermediate. Since the proportion of total real gross national product devoted to national security purposes increased from 0.4 per cent in 1889 to 9.2 per cent in 1957, the average annual rate of growth of real product and productivity by the peacetime version was 0.11 percentage point lower over the sixty-eight-year period than by the national security version. Again, the differences vary by subperiod, depending on the changes in the distribution of the national product as between national security and civilian purposes.

We do not carry consideration of the peacetime version beyond this comparison and presentation of the basic estimates on which it is based (Tables A-I and A-II). It is only necessary to extend Kuznets' argument to read that national security is a goal equivalent to welfare in peacetime as well as in wartime to justify use of the more inclusive measures. In any case, from the standpoint of our interest in the productive capacity or productivity of resources, it is desirable to use measures that do not fluctuate with changes in the degree of international tension, since the resources devoted to national security can be shifted to the production of consumer or capital goods without substantially affecting total product inclusive of national security outlays. Subsequent analysis of national productivity movements is therefore based on national product measures, including the output of security items in all years.

A final comparison relates to product estimates gross and net of capital consumption allowances. In the next chapter, we use real net national product and productivity measures. These are theoretically preferable since the production of capital goods required to offset that part of the stock consumed in the production process does not add to welfare any more than does the output of any other intermediate goods and services. Actually, the estimation of real capital consumption presents serious conceptual and statistical problems that make the net measures less accurate than the gross. Further, since estimates of real capital consumption are not available for most industry groups, our analysis of real private product (used later for comparison with industry real-product estimates) is based on the gross estimates. The figures in the footnote to Table 2 indicate that the broad real gross and net product estimates are virtually interchangeable if Kuznets' estimates of real capital consumption are accepted. Ideal measures of net product, were they available, might show greater divergence of movement from the gross measures.

The partial productivity ratios. The index of total factor input is a weighted average of the indexes of the two major inputs, labor and capital, each of which may also be related to output. Since capital per unit of labor input increased by about 1 per cent a year on balance between 1889 and 1957, output per unit of capital input shows a significantly smaller average annual increase than output per unit of labor input—1 per cent as compared with 2 per cent (see Table 1).

For reasons adduced in Chapter 2, aggregate labor and capital inputs were computed by weighting manhours and real capital stocks in the various industry groups by the compensation per unit of labor and capital in each. Since both labor and capital inputs have shown a persistent tendency to increase more rapidly in the higher-paying industries, the weighted input indexes have increased more than the unweighted. This is a rough measure of the increasing quality of resources resulting from interindustry transfers of resources to the extent that relative unit compensations indicate the relative marginal productivities of the resources in the various uses.

When output is related to unweighted indexes of the two factor inputs, the productivity ratios rise faster than in the measures we have used. Output per manhour increases at an average rate of 2.4 per cent a year compared with the 2.0 per cent rise in output per unit of (weighted) labor input; and output per unit of capital (unweighted) increases by 1.1 per cent a year compared with 1.0 per cent for output per unit of (weighted) capital input. The ratio of output to a combination of both unweighted factor input indexes [3] increases at an average annual rate of 2.0 per cent compared with the 1.7 per cent shown by the preferred total factor productivity measure.

Our method of weighting inputs by industry has the distinct advantage that the productivity ratios are not affected merely by the relative shift of resources among industries[4]—the over-all productivity index is thus conceptually an internally weighted mean of the productivity indexes for the component industries. It can be compared with the industry indexes without the necessity of explaining that part of the change in the aggregate is due to interindustry shifts since these affect input rather than productivity by our procedure. The productivity indexes computed by using internal weights for the inputs are thus a purer measure of changes in technological efficiency as such. Another advantage is that they better indicate the extent to which rates of unit factor compensation in given employments can be raised consistent with stable average product prices. This is not true of productivity indexes using unweighted inputs since part of the "productivity" increase accrues to the factors as a result of upgrading.

THE BREAK IN TREND

Annual estimates of real private domestic product and associated factor inputs are plotted in Chart 2, and the derived estimates of total factor productivity, in Chart 3. Examination of the annual index numbers of total factor productivity reveals a distinctly higher trend since World War I than that which prevailed in the three prior decades. Rates of growth computed between the terminal years of the two periods are 1.3 per cent a year for 1889–1919 and 2.1 per cent for 1919–57. Actually, the change in trend could be interpreted as beginning in 1917, but it is more convenient for us to use the key year 1919 as the dividing point. The results are not substantially affected.

Trend lines fitted by the method of least squares to the two segments of the time series show the same rate of growth for the more recent period, but a somewhat lower rate for the early period—1.03 per cent. The difference arises because productivity in 1889 is below the trend line, whereas in 1919 it is above, as is apparent in Chart 3. Estimated productivity in both 1919 and 1953 is above the trend line; so the rate computed from terminal years is the same as that indicated by the method of least

---

[3] Manhours and unweighted capital input are combined by changing shares of national income in key years (see Table A-XXII).

[4] Effects of intra-industry shifts are not eliminated.

CHART 2

Private Domestic Economy: Real Gross Product and Factor Inputs, 1889–1957
(1929=100)

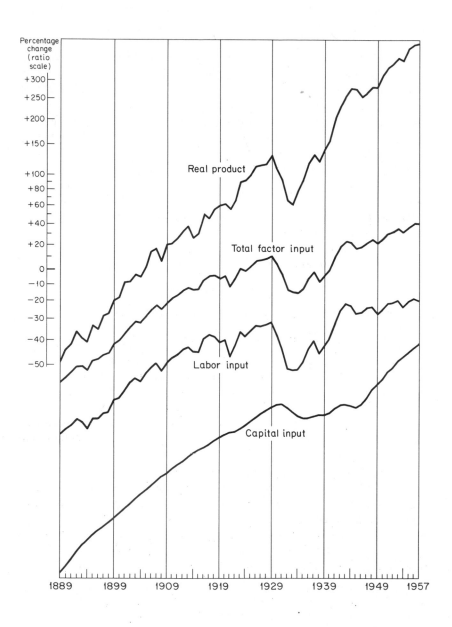

CHART 3

Private Domestic Economy: Trends in Total Factor Productivity, 1889–1957

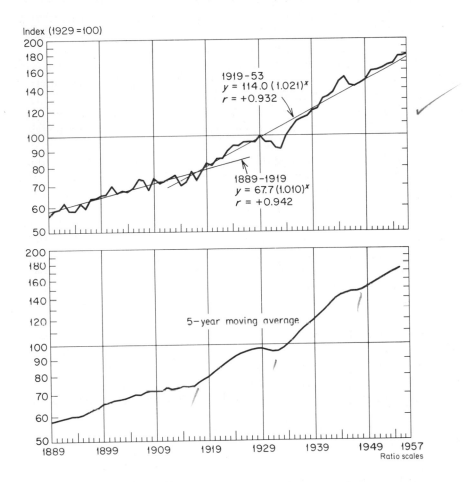

squares.[5] Subsequent estimates for 1953–57 continue to fall around the trend line, although 1957 is a bit lower relative to the trend than is 1953.

An alternative method of fitting a trend is illustrated, for 1919–53, by the dashed line in Chart 5. Here, the logarithms of total factor productivity are related to time and to the ratio of civilian employment to the civilian labor force. By holding the employment ratio constant at a relatively full employment level (0.965) the calculated net trend tends to pass through

[5] Glover's method, which minimizes the sum of the squares of arithmetic deviations, yields the same growth rate for the early period as the usual least squares method, but a higher average rate for the recent period (2.23 per cent versus 2.10 per cent).

the productivity estimates for years of high employment. The indicated trend rate of increase is 2.0 per cent a year. This type of net trend is useful for the projection of productivity to years in which full employment is assumed. The estimating equation indicates that for each 1.0 per cent decline in the employment ratio, productivity deviates from its calculated trend value by approximately 0.6 per cent.

Although it is preferable to calculate trend rates of growth by a method of least squares, we shall generally use the simpler compound interest formula applied to terminal years of subperiods or long periods. The differences between the two methods are not great since the terminal years are years of relatively high economic activity and, in any case, productivity indexes fluctuate less than most economic variables. The compound interest calculation is also used because annual estimates are not available for many of the industry productivity series with which the estimates for the private domestic economy are compared later.

Less confidence can be placed in estimates for decades prior to 1889, but it is of interest that the average rate of increase in total factor productivity between the decade averages for 1869–78 and 1889–98 is 1.2 per cent a year, which is in line with the 1.3 per cent for the subsequent quarter century. The rate would be somewhat less if correction were made for the downward bias of the estimates for the first decade, resulting from the undercount of the Census of 1870. This defect in the national product estimates results in the appearance of an extraordinarily high rate of increase in real product and productivity between 1869 and 1879, which is reduced by the use of the decennial averages. Because of doubts as to the accuracy of the early estimates, however, we confine the analysis of productivity changes to the period since 1889.

Between 1889 and 1919, the rates of growth of both of the major partial productivity ratios were significantly less than in the more recent period (see Chart 4). Acceleration after 1919 is much more marked in the output-capital ratio, with the average rate of change in this ratio rising from 0.5 per cent to 1.3 per cent a year. The average annual rates of increase in output per unit of labor were 1.6 per cent and 2.3 per cent in the two periods. In the early period, capital stocks, on balance, were being built up more rapidly relative to the labor force than they were after 1919. In some industries prior to World War I, capital was growing even faster than output; since then the reverse tendency has prevailed in almost all industries (see Chapter 6).

A similar picture emerges from an aggregate of independently estimated output series, accounting for more than half of the national income originating in the private domestic economy, in relation to independently derived capital series and to manhour series which are part of the broader aggregate. The pertinent growth rates are shown in Table 3. The acceler-

CHART 4

Private Domestic Economy: Partial Productivity Ratios, 1889–1957 (1929=100)

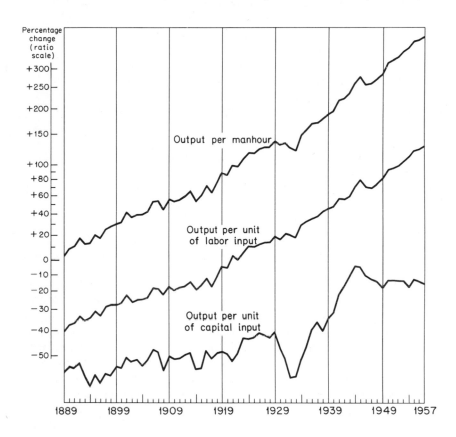

ation since 1919 is even more pronounced than it is in the sector as a whole, which confirms the notion of a distinct break in trend.

Although there is little evidence of further acceleration in total factor productivity over the years since World War I, the rate of increase in real private product per manhour since World War II has been higher than in the interwar period. This is discussed by Fabricant in his introduction, and in a report by the Bureau of Labor Statistics released as this volume was being prepared for press.[6] Using essentially the same series on real private product per manhour as is presented here, the BLS report notes that for 1909–58 a curvilinear trend fits the data better than a straight-line trend. When, however, the period 1919–58 is used, and when a

[6] *Trends in Output per Manhour in the Private Economy, 1909–1958*, BLS Bulletin 1249, December 1959.

variable is introduced to represent the rate of utilization of capacity, the degree of acceleration is sharply reduced. It is further reduced if the data back to 1889 are used. For the private nonfarm sector separately, no acceleration of real product per manhour is apparent after 1919.[7]

TABLE 3

Private Domestic Economy, Covered-Industry Sector[a]
Growth Rates in Output and Productivity Ratios, 1889–1953
(average annual percentage rates of change)

	Output	*Output per Unit of*		
		Total Factor Input	Labor Input	Capital Input
1889–1953	3.2	1.7	1.9	1.0
1889–1919	3.1	0.6	0.8	0.1
1919–53	3.2	2.6	2.8	1.9

Source: Table A-XXV.

[a] Aggregate of industry segments for which capital and labor input indexes as well as output indexes are available: farming, mining, manufacturing, transportation, and communications and public utilities; trade from 1929 forward.

Acceleration after 1947 in real product per manhour for the private economy can largely be explained in terms of a much higher rate of increase in real capital per manhour after World War II than in the interwar period. Acceleration is not significant in the total productivity measure since capital is included in the denominator of the ratio. Any projection of the postwar rate of increase in real private product per manhour would be predicated on a continuing high rate of increase in real capital stock per manhour, other things equal. But since this and the other causal forces are subject to change, any projection of a trend line beyond the historical period is hazardous.

It is not possible adequately to analyze the factors that may have been responsible for the change in productivity trend around the time of World War I, although it is a subject worthy of further investigation. A step in this direction can be taken by noting a few changes that occurred about the same time in associated variables. The scientific management movement, based on the ideas of Frederick W. Taylor, spread widely in the 1920's; college and graduate work in business administration expanded rapidly; and it was only after 1919 that organized research and development became a significant feature of the industrial landscape (see Chapter 4). It has also been suggested that the drastic change in national immigration policy promoted a more rapid increase in the average

[7] *Ibid.*, p. 27.

education of the labor force. That is, since the immigrants had less schooling, on the average, than the domestic labor force, the mass influx of workers from abroad prior to World War I had tended to retard the increase in average education.[8]

It is tempting to enumerate specific innovations that became important after 1919, such as mass or "flow" production techniques in manufacturing. Certainly, there was a remarkable acceleration in manufacturing productivity in the 1920's. But significant innovations were occurring throughout the whole period; short of a thorough study of their cost-reducing impact, it would not be possible to isolate those that contributed most to the speeding-up of productivity advance.

Temporal Variations in Growth Rates

SUBPERIOD CHANGES

In the private domestic economy as a whole, rates of growth over sub-periods of approximately a decade in length have been relatively close to the longer-term trend rates. They are notably more stable than the sub-period rates in most of the industry groups surveyed later because the variations of the industry rates tend to be offsetting. The offsetting nature of divergent industry rates may be in part a result of random factors and in part a result of interindustry shifts of the resources devoted to technological progress.

Over the period 1889–1957, the average deviation of the subperiod rates of change in total factor productivity from the average rate for the period as a whole is 0.4 per cent—less than one-quarter of the average annual rate of growth. The average deviations are less, of course, for each of the two major time-segments into which the trend was broken—0.2 and 0.3 per cent for 1889–1919 and 1919–57, respectively (see Table 4).

Taking the period as a whole again, for the sake of convenience, the average deviation of subperiod rates of change in output per unit of labor input is the same as that for total factor productivity—0.4 per cent. The deviation for output per unit of capital input is absolutely greater, and relatively much greater—0.7 per cent. Apparently, the forces that determine the growth of investment and capital stock in relation to output are comparatively irregular in their operation.

Irregularity in the subperiod rates of change in input proportions—or, to put it differently, in the rate of substitution of capital for labor—may be due to changes in relative factor prices, in the propensity to save, or in the nature of technological advance, all of which are interrelated. But the effect on changes in productive efficiency does not seem to be marked.

[8] The author is indebted to Milton Friedman for this suggestion.

There is, however, a mild tendency for subperiod rates of change in capital per unit of labor input to be positively correlated with subperiod rates of change in output per unit of labor input.[9] This tendency is consistent with the fact that the average deviation of subperiod rates of change in total factor productivity from the long-period rate is somewhat less than the weighted mean of the average deviations of subperiod changes in each of the partial productivity ratios from their secular rates of change.

TABLE 4

Private Domestic Economy:
Subperiod Rates of Change in Real Product and Productivity Ratios,
with Mean Deviations from Secular Rates, 1889–1957

| | *Real Product* | *Real Product Per Unit of* | | |
		Total Factor Input	Labor Input	Capital Input
AVERAGE ANNUAL PERCENTAGE RATES OF CHANGE				
1889–1899	4.5	1.6	2.0	0.4
1899–1909	4.2	1.2	1.3	0.8
1909–19	3.0	1.1	1.5	0.3
1919–29	3.7	2.0	2.2	1.4
1929–37	0.1	1.6	1.8	0.9
1937–48	4.5	2.3	2.2	2.7
1948–57	3.6	2.3	3.1	−0.2
MEAN SUBPERIOD DEVIATIONS FROM LONG-PERIOD RATES				
1889–1957	0.9	0.4	0.4	0.7
1889–1919	0.6	0.2	0.3	0.2
1919–57	1.3	0.3	0.4	0.9

SOURCE: Table A-XXII.

ANNUAL CHANGES

Charts 3 and 4 show that annual variations relative to trends are much greater than the relative subperiod variations. The average deviation of the yearly percentage changes in productivity from the 1.8 per cent average annual rate, 1889–1957, is 2.9; the average deviation of the change in output per unit of labor input is somewhat less, while that for the change in the output-capital ratio is much greater. The average annual deviations of percentage changes in total factor productivity and labor productivity are somewhat smaller when computed from the trend rates for 1919–57, but they are still large.

In a few cases, the variations in annual productivity changes appear to be erratic, traceable to random factors or, possibly, to erratic errors in the

[9] The coefficient of rank correlation is +.29 (which is, however, not significant at the 5 per cent level).

estimates. The sharp rises in 1901 and 1906, followed by partially offsetting drops, appear to be of this character. The lower-than-trend values in 1914, 1915, and 1917 may reflect the repercussions of World War I, although it should be noted that productivity was well above trend in 1944 and 1945.

Productivity and the business cycle. The major cause of annual fluctuations in productivity change appears to be short-term changes in the scale of production. Over those forty-seven years of the period 1889–1957 that are characterized as reference cycle expansions, the average percentage change in productivity was 2.8, compared with a 1.8 per cent average of annual changes over the entire period. Over the twenty-one years characterized as contractions, productivity fell by 0.5 per cent on the average (see Table 5). The average deviations of the percentage changes

TABLE 5

Private Domestic Economy:
Change in Real Product and Productivity Ratios,
Years of Expansion and of Contraction, 1889–1957
(average annual percentage change)

| | Years Covered (number) | Real Product | Real Product per Unit of | | |
			Total Factor Input	Labor Input	Capital Input
Years of expansion					
1889–1957	47	6.7	2.8	2.4	4.0
1889–1919	20	2.8	2.8	2.5	3.5
1919–57	27	6.7	2.9	2.3	4.4
Years of contraction					
1889–1957	21	−2.9	−0.5	1.3	−5.2
1889–1919	10	−1.5	−1.5	0.0	−4.9
1919–57	11	−4.1	0.3	2.5	−5.5

SOURCE: Table A-XXII.

during expansions are absolutely smaller and relatively much smaller than are the average deviations during contractions. Productivity fell during half of the contractions, and the fall was particularly marked during major contractions. But in the other reference contractions, productivity rose. Productivity rose by more than the trend rates of increase in the postwar readjustment, 1918–19, and in three subsequent recessions, two of which were very mild.

With respect to partial productivity, output per unit of labor input rose only one-half as much in contractions as in expansions. Presumably, certain types of "overhead" employees are kept on payrolls when output falls, but are not so fully utilized as when production is expanding. Also, when output falls below the point of the optimum combination of labor with fixed capital, it is to be expected that the productivity, or output per unit of each of the factors will decline. A partial offset might be provided by an increase in the efficiency of individual workers to the extent that less efficient workers are laid off first and those remaining exert more effort in view of growing unemployment. It is also probable that the pace of technological advance falls off a bit in recessions since investment in new plant and equipment tends to decline and research and development outlays to slacken despite the greater pressure towards cost reduction stemming from falling profit margins. On the other hand, some cost reductions can probably be achieved with little or no new capital and by concentrating production in more efficient plants.

Output per unit of capital input actually falls in contractions. This is, in part, a function of the technique of measuring capital input. We assume proportionality with real capital stocks, since from the standpoint of private ownership capital assets represent a real cost or charge regardless of the intensity with which they are employed. This is certainly the case when buildings or equipment are subject to long-term lease, or when they are financed by borrowed funds on which regular interest payments must be met. Even when equity capital is involved, presumably there must be some average rate of return over the lifetime of the underlying real assets, which is an implicit cost during recessions and must be incurred if capital is to remain in the industry.

Unlike labor, which can be laid off under conditions of declining activity (and subsequently does not represent a direct cost to private industry), capital stocks usually continue to increase in mild recessions— although the rate of increase declines as investment drops. Only in severe contractions does gross investment drop below capital consumption causing total capital stock to fall with output. Thus, when output falls, the output-capital ratio will drop even more, as a rule. This does not affect the subperiod or long-period changes since these are measured between years of high activity which give time for capital to be adjusted, more or less efficiently, to the volume of other inputs and to output.

Annual comparisons are, of course, a blunt instrument for cyclical analysis. Monthly estimates adjusted for seasonal variation permit a more refined analysis of changes in economic variables between turning points and during both expansion and contraction phases. This study has been confined to annual estimates, but a brief summary of the findings of Thor Hultgren with respect to movements of output per manhour over specific production cycles and the reference business cycle provides an illuminating supplement to our annual comparisons.[10]

[10] Thor Hultgren, *Changes in Labor Cost During Cycles in Production and Business*, Occasional Paper 74, New York (NBER), 1960.

Hultgren assembled monthly output per manhour estimates for 23 industries for one or more cycles between 1921 and 1956, giving him observations on 74 expansions and 83 contractions. In terms of the turning points identified in each industry output series (which mark production cycles), in 91 per cent of the expansions output per manhour increased, while in 72 per cent of the contractions output per manhour declined. There was, however, a declining proportion of increases in output per manhour during successive phases of expansion (from 88 to 68 per cent) and an increasing proportion of increases during successive phases of contraction (from 27 to 43 per cent).

At first glance, the positive relation between output and labor productivity movements seems to contradict our findings based on annual private domestic economy estimates, according to which output per manhour rises in contractions as well as in expansions, although in significantly lesser proportion. But it must be remembered that individual production cycles frequently do not coincide with the general reference cycle in timing. When they do not, the extent of the average industry expansion or contraction within the reference cycle dates is dampened. This influence is strong enough to reverse the picture of the relationship in contractions. In 76 per cent of Hultgren's 54 observations for reference expansions, output per manhour rose—a smaller percentage than prevailed during the production cycle expansions. But in 69 per cent of the 65 reference contractions, there was also a net increase in output per manhour as opposed to a majority of declines in production contractions. In other words, the adverse effect of declining volume is reduced, and the relative impact of technological advance is increased. The use of annual averages further accentuates the tendency towards rising output per manhour in contractions.

It is interesting to note also the relationships over the phases of the general business cycle. During expansions the percentage of observations in which output per manhour rose declined from 76 in the first phase to 63 in the last phase—a less pronounced decline than in individual production expansions. In the first phase of contraction, 48 per cent of the measures of industry output per manhour rose; in the last phase, 69 per cent were rising.

If monthly estimates of real capital stocks were available, it seems clear that the positive relation between output and the output-capital ratio would be more pronounced between turning points in the monthly reference cycle than between turning points on an annual basis. The positive relation would be still more pronounced over production cycles in which amplitudes of output fluctuation are greater than in the general business cycle.

Variant annual productivity measures. It would be possible crudely to adjust real capital stock estimates to make allowance for the hours of utilization

CHART 5

Private Domestic Economy: Trends in Alternative Productivity Measures, 1919–57

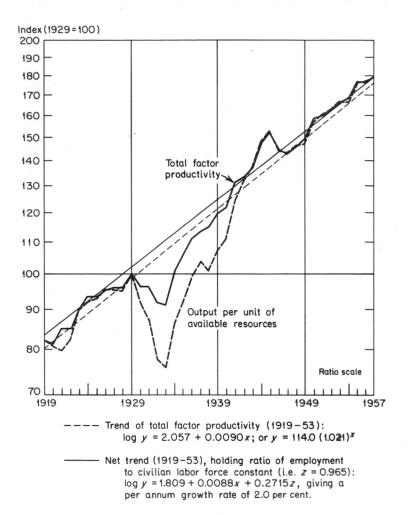

---- Trend of total factor productivity (1919–53):
$\log y = 2.057 + 0.0090x$; or $y = 114.0 \,(1.021)^x$

—— Net trend (1919–53), holding ratio of employment
to civilian labor force constant (i.e. $z = 0.965$):
$\log y = 1.809 + 0.0088x + 0.2715z$, giving a
per annum growth rate of 2.0 per cent.

and thus achieve a formal consistency with the treatment of labor input. If this were done, capital and total factor productivity would probably not decline in most contractions, although the rate of increase would be retarded, as in the case of labor productivity, since there would be departures from optimum factor combinations. But such an adjustment to capital would have a most tenuous statistical basis, and even theoretically would be purely formal, since in a real sense productive efficiency does decline when capacity is utilized at rates significantly below those for which it was created. In any case, the intermediate and long-term comparisons would not be affected because there is no clear-cut evidence of a marked trend in the degree of utilization of capital over time.[11]

A more interesting possible variant of the productivity series involves treating labor from the viewpoint of social cost, and counting unemployed members of the labor force over and above a normal "frictional" pool (say 3.5 per cent of the labor force) as part of labor cost. The further assumption is made that such persons—by definition willing and able to work—are desirous of working the same average hours as those put in by employed workers. This variant is shown for the period since 1919 in Chart 5. It is seen that productivity so calculated falls significantly more in years of marked depression than does our standard series—indicating that the efficiency with which society utilizes its potential resources drops more than does the productive efficiency of industry measured in terms of private-enterprise costs. The virtual identity in the movements of the alternative productivity series since World War II is a measure of the greater efficiency with which our social organization now provides for high levels of economic activity as compared with the 1930's and some earlier depressed periods.

[11] See Bert G. Hickman, "Capacity, Capacity Utilization, and the Acceleration Principle," *Problems of Capital Formation: Concepts, Measurement, and Controlling Factors,* Studies in Income and Wealth, Volume 19, Princeton University Press (for NBER), 1957, pp. 419–468.

CHAPTER 4

Productivity and Economic Growth

THERE are a number of measures of economic growth, each with its own meaning and uses. In this chapter, the relationship of productivity change to three aggregate growth measures is quantified. So also are certain characteristic trends in the composition of both output and input which seem to be related to the dynamics of economic growth in general and productivity advance in particular.

The most direct measure of economic growth is the real net national product. Increments to real product can be directly partitioned between increases in inputs and in productivity. The productivity increment is, of course, the gain in real income accruing to the factors of production, and the distribution of that gain will be analyzed in the next chapter.

From a broader viewpoint, only if real net product grows proportionately more than the population does is there economic progress. As a second measure, therefore, real net product per capita is used. We also look at changes in the ratio of consumption to total net product to see to what extent output growth has been used to raise potential economic welfare directly as compared with its use for investment goods or national security. Since the rise in real net product per capita results, in part, from an increase in input per capita, changes in the structure of factor input, and changes in certain types of nonfactor input as well, will be examined from the view-point of their relation to productivity advance.

The third type of measure is one that breaks down the real gross national product of each period between that part required to support the population and capital of the prior year, and a "margin over maintenance." Some of the margin must go for national security, but the rest may be used to support population increases, or to increase consumption and investment per capita as compared with the previous period. This approach reveals the anatomy of progress better than the conventional classification of the net national product and permits an appraisal of the relative importance of productivity gains in economic progress as defined. Certain significant types of investment are not included or identified as such in the national product measures, however, and this omission is repaired in a final section of the chapter.

National Output, Input, and Productivity

In this chapter, the national security version of the Kuznets estimates of real net national product is employed. It will be remembered that his measure comprises private and public consumer outlays and net investment, to which we have added national security expenditures. Although the statistical basis of Kuznets' segregation of government output between final and intermediate products (and thus the implied productivity of factors commanded by governments) is tenuous, use of his estimates makes possible a comprehensive analysis of national economic growth in terms of major social purposes. His estimates include real net income from abroad that contributes to American planes of living, even though the associated net capital stock is located abroad.

PARTITIONING OF CHANGES IN TOTAL REAL PRODUCT

Between 1889 and 1953, the real net national product grew from less than $20 billion to $187 billion (in 1929 prices). This nearly tenfold increase over the sixty-four years represents an average annual compound rate of growth of better than 3.5 per cent. As indicated in Table 6, the rate of growth was highest in the early part of the period and was subject to

TABLE 6

National Economy: Growth Rates in Real Product, Factor Input,
and Productivity, Subperiods, 1889–1957
(average annual percentage rates of change)

	Real Net National Product[a]	Total Factor Input	Total Factor Productivity
1889–1953	3.6	2.0	1.6
(1889–1957)	3.5	1.9	1.6
1889–1919	4.2	2.8	1.4
1919–53	3.1	1.3	1.7
1889–99	4.5	2.9	1.5
1899–1909	4.3	3.1	1.1
1909–19	3.8	2.3	1.5
1919–29	3.1	1.6	1.4
1929–37	0.2	−0.9	1.1
1937–48	4.4	2.2	2.2
1948–53	4.7	2.2	2.4
(1953–57)	2.2	0.7	1.5

SOURCE: Table A-XIX.
[a] Kuznets' concept, national security version.

progressive retardation right up through the prosperous 1920's. Following the stagnation of the 1930's, which saw little net gain in real output, the rate of growth picked up markedly and through 1953 was comparable with that of the pre-World War I decades (see Chart 6).

The rate of growth is slightly less when the long period is extended to 1957, as is shown in Table 6, for purposes of comparison with the data given in Chapter 3. This is due to the indicated retardation in the rate of growth between 1953 and 1957. At the time of writing, Kuznets' estimates were available only through 1953, and this terminal date is generally used in the rest of the chapter. For trend analysis, a few years more or less make little or no difference in the conclusions.

Over the period 1889–1953, national productivity increased at an average annual rate of 1.6 per cent a year, accounting for somewhat under half of the total growth of output. The rest of the expansion is attributable to the growth of input, which averaged 2.0 per cent a year. Up until 1919, however, productivity accounted for only one-third of the output increase, whereas since 1919 productivity has become, on balance, as important an element as input. This is partly the result of retardation in the rate of output growth and partly the result of an acceleration in the rate of increase in productivity. Based on the Kuznets estimates underlying this analysis, the productivity acceleration shows up after 1937; the growth rate averaged 1.3 per cent prior to 1937 and around 2.3 per cent thereafter. Judging from the real private domestic product estimates, however, the higher rate of growth began at about the end of the World War I.

Table 7 gives the results of a more elaborate attempt to partition the increments in real product between the factor input and productivity components. Since we are dealing with increments, averages were taken of annual changes over the several periods and subperiods. As first approximations to the input and productivity increments, the percentage changes in these variables were applied to the real net product of the previous year; the difference between the sum of these two increments and the total annual change in real net product (the "joint product" of the two components) was split equally between the variables in accordance with the procedure developed by Frederick C. Mills.[1] The general picture is similar to that obtained by comparing the relative rates of change in Table 6. Over the period as a whole, productivity is computed to have accounted for 48.5 per cent, as compared with 44.4 per cent, of the real-product increments. In a couple of the subperiods, however, the relative importance of the productivity increase is quite different when based on results obtained from the more painstaking method underlying Table 7.

[1] *Productivity and Economic Progress*, Occasional Paper 38, New York (NBER), 1952, p.31, n. 3. The equal division of the joint product has been criticized as being arbitrary.

CHART 6

National Economy: Real Net Product, Factor Input, and per Capita Measures, 1889–1957

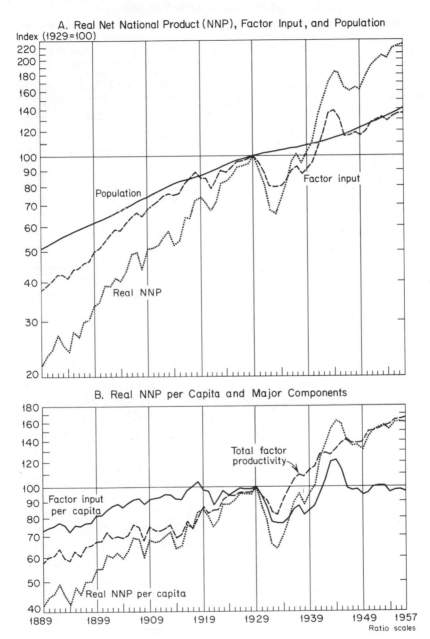

A. Real Net National Product (NNP), Factor Input, and Population

B. Real NNP per Capita and Major Components

TABLE 7

Partitioning of Increments in Real Net National Product between
Factor Input and Productivity, Subperiods, 1889–1953

PERIOD OF ANNUAL AVERAGE	REAL NNP[a] Millions of 1929 Dollars	INCREMENTS OF REAL NNP	ALLOCATION OF PRODUCT INCREMENTS[b]			
			Real Factor Input		Productivity	
			Millions of 1929 Dollars	Per Cent of Total	Millions of 1929 Dollars	Per Cent of Total
1889–1953	75,141	2,579	1,329	51.5	1,250	48.5
1889–1918	37,783	1,546	1,133	73.3	413	26.7
1919–53	107,163	3,464	1,497	43.2	1,967	56.8
1889–98	23,651	867	596	68.7	271	31.3
1899–1908	37,554	1,238	1,142	92.2	96	7.8
1909–18	52,142	2,534	1,661	65.5	873	34.5
1919–28	73,974	2,011	769	38.2	1,242	61.8
1929–36	74,390	150	−698	−465.3	848	565.3
1937–47	128,829	5,390	2,454	45.5	2,936	54.5
1948–53	166,454	6,774	3,874	57.2	2,900	42.8

[a] NNP = net national product. From Table A-XIX (Kuznets' concept, national security version); absolute figures estimated from 1929 value and weighted index of output.

[b] Estimated by procedure of F. C. Mills, *Productivity and Economic Progress*, Occasional Paper 38, New York (NBER), 1952, p. 31, n. 3.

PRODUCTIVITY AND CHANGES IN REAL PRODUCT

Between 1889 and 1953, while output was increasing between nine- and tenfold, the population of the nation grew from 62.5 million persons to over 160 million—roughly two and one-half times. Thus, output per capita grew by somewhat less than 300 per cent, which averages out at 2.1 per cent a year. On this basis, the gain of 1.6 per cent in the average annual rate of productivity accounts for about three-fourths of the increase in output per capita. The growth of input per capita accounts for the other fourth (see Chart 7, Panel A).[2]

Over the seven subperiods shown in Table 8, the rates of growth of real product per capita varied considerably; the weighted average deviation of the subperiod rates from the long-period rate of 2.1 per cent was 0.8 per cent. The larger part of the variation is traceable to variations in factor

[2] Solomon Fabricant has compared productivity changes in the private domestic economy with changes in real private domestic product per capita in *Basic Facts on Productivity Change*, Occasional Paper 63, New York (NBER), 1959, pp. 18–22. Since productivity rose more and real product less in the private domestic sector than in the total economy, the relative importance of productivity is greater by Fabricant's measure and differs somewhat over the subperiods in comparison with our measure.

CHART 7

Components of Real Net National Product per Capita, Average Annual Rates of Change,
1889–1953

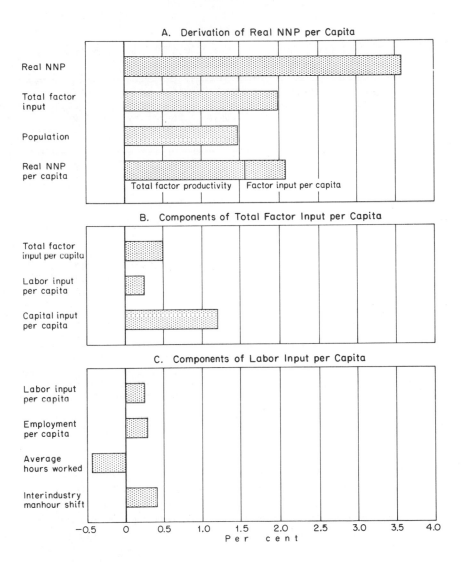

A. Derivation of Real NNP per Capita

Real NNP

Total factor input

Population

Real NNP per capita

Total factor productivity | Factor input per capita

B. Components of Total Factor Input per Capita

Total factor input per capita

Labor input per capita

Capital input per capita

C. Components of Labor Input per Capita

Labor input per capita

Employment per capita

Average hours worked

Interindustry manhour shift

−0.5 0 0.5 1.0 1.5 2.0 2.5 3.0 3.5 4.0
P e r   c e n t

input per capita. Productivity gains showed less variation; the average
subperiod deviation from the 1.6 per cent productivity growth rate over
the long period was 0.3 per cent. The several variables are plotted annually
in Chart 6. It will be noted from the chart and table that between 1919

and 1953 (or 1957) there has been virtually no net change in input per capita. Thus, productivity increase has accounted for the entire growth of real product per capita since 1919, on net balance.

TABLE 8

Productivity in Relation to Levels of Living, Subperiods, 1889–1957
(average annual percentage rates of change)

	Real NNP per Capita[a]	Ratio of Consumer Outlays to NNP	Real Consumer Outlays per Capita[a]	Total Factor Productivity	Factor Input per Capita	Addendum: Population
	(1)	(2)	(3)	(4)	(5)	(6)
1889–1953	2.1	−0.1	1.9	1.6	0.5	1.5
(1889–1957)	2.0	−0.1	1.8	1.6	0.4	1.5
1889–1919	2.4	−0.4	2.0	1.4	1.0	1.8
1919–53	1.8	0.1	1.7	1.7	0.1	1.2
1889–99	2.6	−0.4	2.2	1.5	1.1	1.8
1899–1909	2.3	0.1	2.4	1.1	1.2	1.9
1909–19	2.3	−1.0	1.3	1.5	0.8	1.5
1919–29	1.6	1.3	2.9	1.4	0.1	1.5
1929–37	−0.5	0.5	−0.1	1.1	−1.6	0.7
1937–48	3.2	−0.5	2.7	2.2	1.0	1.2
1948–53	3.0	−1.4	1.6	2.4	0.6	1.6
(1953–57)	0.4	0.1	0.5	1.5	−1.1	1.8

NNP = net national product.

Source: Real net national product and real consumer outlays: Kuznets' concepts, Table A-1, adjusted to conform with internal weighting method. Population: *Current Population Reports*, Dept. of Commerce, Series P-25, No. 114; population prior to 1900 extrapolated by Kuznets' estimates.

[a] When 100 is added to the average percentage rates, col. (1) = col. (4) × col. (5); and col. (3) = col. (1) × col. (2).

Real consumption expenditures per capita increased by slightly less than 2 per cent, since the ratio of consumer outlays to net national product was significantly lower in 1953 than in 1889 (see Table 8). This was a concomitant of the much higher proportion of resources devoted to national security purposes in the latter year. The somewhat erratic fluctuations in the consumption ratio were chiefly the result of changing requirements for national security. The main exception occurred during the 1929-37 period, when the proportion of resources devoted to investment declined substantially. As a result, real consumer outlays showed a negligible drop relative to population, although real net product per capita was 4.2 per cent lower in 1937 than in 1929.

PRODUCTIVITY AND ECONOMIC GROWTH

The Changing Structure of Inputs

Although the increase in productivity has been much larger than the growth of inputs relative to population, it is instructive to look at the structure of inputs per capita. Total factor input is a composite measure, and its growth relative to population is the net result of differential rates of change in the components. Examination of the changing composition of input not only fills in the arithmetic of economic growth, but also furnishes some clues as to the sources of productivity advance.

GROWTH OF CAPITAL RELATIVE TO LABOR INPUT

The average annual rates of change in labor and capital inputs per capita over the long period and the subperiods are shown in Table 9, together with their relative percentage weights. Total factor input is equal to the

TABLE 9

Labor and Capital Components of Input per Capita,
with Measures of Factor Substitution, Subperiods, 1889–1957
(average annual percentage rates of change and percentage weights)

	Total Factor Input per Capita[a] (1)	Labor Input Per Capita (2)	Weight (3)	Capital Input Per Capita (4)	Weight (5)	Capital per Labor Unit (6)	Total per Labor Unit[a] (7)
1889–1953	0.5	0.2	70	1.2	30	1.0	0.3
(1889–1957)	0.4	0.1	70	1.2	30	1.1	0.3
1889–1919	1.0	0.6	65	1.9	35	1.3	0.4
1919–53	0.1	−0.1	75	0.6	25	0.7	0.2
1889–99	1.1	0.6	64	2.4	36	1.7	0.5
1899–1909	1.2	0.9	64	1.7	36	0.8	0.3
1909–19	0.8	0.4	67	1.7	33	1.3	0.4
1919–29	0.1	−0.3	70	1.2	30	1.5	0.4
1929–37	−1.6	−1.7	75	−1.3	25	0.4	0.1
1937–48	1.0	1.2	77	0.5	23	−0.6	−0.1
1948–53	0.6	0.1	79	2.5	21	2.4	0.5
(1953–57)	−1.1	−1.8	79	1.4	21	3.3	0.8

SOURCE: Table A-XIX and population series from Table 8.
a When 100 is added to the average percentage rates col. (1) is approximately equal to cols. (2) plus (4) times their respective weights shown in cols. (3) and (5). Col. (7) equals col. (6) times col. (5), with allowance for the effects of rounding.

weighted sum of labor plus capital inputs. As between the two broad factor classes, the growth of capital has been much greater than the growth of labor input. Even after allowance for the smaller weight

85

accorded capital, it accounts for the larger part of the 0.54 per cent a year average increase in total input per capita (0.36 compared with 0.18).

Changes in inputs on a per capita basis have a somewhat different relative importance than straight changes. Thus, capital input increased at an average rate of 2.7 per cent a year, about 60 per cent more than the 1.7 per cent rate of increase in labor input. However, the 1.2 per cent rise in capital per head is four times the 0.3 per cent rise in labor input per head (see Chart 6, Panel B).

The relative importance of the factors in total input growth varied considerably over the subperiods. Whereas capital per unit of labor input increased by 1.0 per cent a year on the average over the period, the average deviation of subperiod rates was 0.7 per cent. The highest average rates of increase in capital per unit of labor input were in the first decade, 1889–99 (at 1.7 per cent a year), and the recent subperiod, 1948–57 (at 2.8 per cent). The postwar acceleration followed a low rate of advance between 1929 and 1937 and an actual decline in the 1937–48 period as a result of wartime restrictions on private investment and of early postwar capital shortages.

The last column of Table 9 shows the rates of substitution of capital for labor; the substitution rates are equivalent to average annual percentage changes in the index of capital per unit of labor input weighted by the relative shares of capital in the national income in the several subperiods. On the average, the share of capital was about 30 per cent, but it declined over the period, as indicated in column (5) (see Chapter 5 for a discussion of the relative prices of the factors).

TRENDS IN THE COMPONENTS OF LABOR INPUT

Our estimates of labor input (L) in relation to population (P) can be derived as the product of the ratio of the labor force (LF) to population, the ratio of employment (E) to the labor force, average hours worked per year (MH/E), and the ratio of labor input to manhours worked. In algebraic terms:

$$\frac{L}{P} = \frac{LF}{P} \times \frac{E}{LF} \times \frac{MH}{E} \times \frac{L}{MH}$$

To derive labor input as such, it is merely necessary to multiply both sides of the equation by population, which means substituting the labor force itself for the ratio of labor force to population on the right-hand side.

The various elements into which the labor input estimates may be divided are shown in Table 10 in terms of average annual percentage rates of change. In general, it is evident that the average increase of 0.2 per cent a year in labor input per capita is fully accounted for by the relative shift of workers and manhours into higher-paying industries (column 5). Unweighted manhours showed a slight downward tendency relative to population, as the increase in the ratios of labor force and employment to population was somewhat more than offset by the decline in average hours worked per year (see Chart 6, Panel C).

TABLE 10

Components of Labor Input per Capita, Subperiods, 1889–1957
(average annual percentage rates of change)

	Labor Input per Capita[a] (1)	Ratio of Labor Force to Population (2)	Ratio of Employment to Labor Force[b] (3)	Average Hours Worked per Year[c] (4)	Labor Input per Manhour[d] (5)
1889–1953	0.2	0.1	0.2	−0.4	0.4
(1889–1957)	0.1	0.1	0.1	−0.4	0.4
1889–1919	0.6	0.2	0.3	−0.3	0.4
1919–53	−0.1	0.0	0.1	−0.6	0.4
1889–99	0.6	0.4	0.0	0.0	0.3
1899–1909	0.9	0.4	0.3	−0.3	0.5
1909–19	0.4	0.0	0.5	−0.6	0.5
1919–29	−0.3	0.1	−0.4	−0.1	0.1
1929–37	−1.7	0.2	−0.8	−1.1	−0.1
1937–48	1.2	−0.1	0.9	−0.5	0.9
1948–53	0.1	−0.3	0.5	−0.7	0.6
(1953–57)	−1.8	−0.5	−0.8	−0.5	−0.1

[a] When 100 is added to the average annual percentage rates throughout, col. (1) = cols. (2) × (3) × (4) × (5).

[b] This ratio is influenced by the fact that our employment estimates were derived independently of the labor-force estimates. The rise in a ratio of consistent employment-to-labor-force figures is less (see Appendix A).

[c] The ratio of total manhours to the average annual employment estimates.

[d] The ratio of manhours weighted by average hourly earnings, by industry groups, to unweighted manhours.

Labor force and employment ratios. The increase in the proportion of the population participating in the labor force over the period was chiefly the result of a relative increase in the population of labor-force age. But even in relation to the population 14 years of age and over, there has been a slight increase in the labor-force ratio, as the rising participation ratios of women, especially in the 35–65 age bracket, have more than offset declines in some of the other brackets. The increasing labor-force participation of women may be traced in part to increasing productivity in household operation and to the shift of functions from the household to the business sector.

The ratio of employment to the labor force shows a small increase in our table due to the presumedly lower percentage of employment in 1889 than in 1953. It should not be inferred, however, that there has been an upward secular trend in the employment ratio. There is considerable variation from one key year to another. The most marked case is 1937 relative to 1929; the unemployment ratio was still relatively high in 1937, a year which saw a cycle peak, but not full recovery.

Average hours worked. Manhours worked have increased less than aggregate employment because of the secular trend toward a shorter workweek and work-year. From close to 54 hours in 1889 (60 in the nonfarm sector), the average annual workweek fell to 40 hours in 1953—an average annual decline of 0.4 per cent a year. The decline was by no means regular, however. Especially rapid reductions in average hours took place in the latter part of the 1909-19 decade, reflecting increased union strength in World War I and the effects of the Adamson Act, which established the eight-hour day for railroads; reductions took place again during the early 1930's, when shorter working hours were introduced over much of the economy as a means of sharing the work.[3]

It can be argued that reduction in the workweek helps promote productivity advance. There is some evidence to suggest that labor efficiency per hour increases as average weekly hours drop, but this force tends to wane with successive reductions in hours.[4] Of possibly greater importance is that insofar as shortening of standard hours comes at different times in different industries and establishments without corresponding reductions in the weekly wage, management is put under pressure to increase the degree of mechanization and the efficiency of operations generally.[5] The same reasoning would apply to increases in wage rates, hours remaining the same. The effect would vary depending upon such forces as the degree of price elasticity of demand for the products of the firms or industries affected.

The upgrading of labor. Since the effect of the declining length of the workweek on manhours offsets the increasing ratio of employment to population, the rise in labor input per capita may be ascribed to the impact on labor input of the relative shift of workers and manhours from lower- to higher-paying industries. It has been our contention that industry differentials in wage rates reflect, primarily, persistent differences

[3] Cf. Leo Wolman, *Hours of Work in American Industry*, Bulletin 71, New York (NBER), 1938.

[4] See Solomon Fabricant, *Employment in Manufacturing, 1899–1939: An Analysis of Its Relation to the Volume of Production*, New York (NBER), 1942, p. 13.

[5] This argument is developed by Edward F. Denison in "Measurement of Labor Input: Some Questions of Definition and the Adequacy of Data," *Output, Input, and Productivity Measurement*, Studies in Income and Wealth, Volume 25, Princeton University Press (for NBER), 1961.

in occupational structures and that wage rates in different occupations tend to reflect the differential contributions to product of different classes of workers. Thus, relative shifts of workers to higher-paying occupations and industries result in a greater "quantity" of labor input, reflecting the use of more valuable talents of individuals or a greater investment in training and development of innate skills. Interindustry shifts have gone on rather persistently throughout the whole period. The view that these movements have been associated with increased education per person is borne out by figures presented in Table 22. Table 11 makes clear that the

TABLE 11

Social-Economic Distribution of the Civilian Labor Force, 1890–1950
(per cent)

Group	1890	1910	1930	1950
Nonfarm	57.4	69.0	79.0	88.1
Proprietors, managers, etc.		6.6	7.5	8.8
Professional persons	3.7	4.4	6.1	8.6
Clerks and kindred workers	6.0	10.2	16.3	19.3
Skilled workers and foremen		11.7	12.9	14.2
Semiskilled workers		14.7	16.4	20.3
Unskilled workers		21.4	19.8	16.9
Farm	42.6	31.0	21.0	11.9
Proprietors, managers	23.1	16.5	12.4	7.5
Laborers	19.5	14.5	8.6	4.4

SOURCE: Estimates for 1910 and 1930 as compiled by Alba M. Edwards, *Census of Population, 1940, Comparative Occupation Statistics for the United States, 1870 to 1940,* Table XXVII, p. 187; estimates for 1890 based on occupational detail from the same source. Subgroups of nonfarm workers could not easily be identified except for professionals (*ibid.,* p. 111) and clerks (Edwards, "The White-Collar Workers," *Monthly Labor Review,* March 1934, p. 504). Estimates for 1950 from *Census of Population, 1950,* Vol. II, Part I.

shift toward higher-paying industries was indeed associated with relative shifts of the labor force towards more highly skilled or professional occupations, and from farms to generally more highly remunerated non-farm pursuits.[6]

Within the professional category of the labor force, there is one group that is of particular importance in germinating new ideas and incorporating them in improved technology—the scientists and engineers. Estimates are

[6] Another investigator, weighting the numbers of persons in the various socio-economic groupings by appropriate average earnings, found much the same difference between the movement of weighted and unweighted gainful workers from 1870 to 1950 that we found between manhours weighted and unweighted from 1889 to 1953 (see George Tolley, North Carolina State University, unpublished worksheets; see also his discussion of Denison's paper, *op. cit.*).

presented in Table 12 of the numbers of engineers and chemists, 1890–1950, and their ratio to the labor force. In 1950, chemists accounted for only about one-eighth of the total but were still a slightly larger group than the total of other natural scientists, such as physicists, mathematicians, biologists, and geologists (but excluding the medical professions), for whom data are not available prior to 1950. With around 90 per cent coverage, the estimates give a good general picture of the growth of the technological professions as a whole.[7]

TABLE 12

Distribution of Engineers and Chemists[a] in the Labor Force, Decennial, 1890–1950

	Number of Thousands	Per Cent of Labor Force
1890	33	0.14
1900	52	0.18
1910	105	0.28
1920	169	0.40
1930	273	0.56
1930	277	0.58
1940	338	0.63
1940	363	0.68
1950	636	1.08

SOURCE: David M. Blank and George J. Stigler, *The Demand and Supply of Scientific Personnel*, New York (NBER), 1957, Tables B-1 and B-2, pp. 144–47. The overlap in 1930 represents an adjustment of 1930 "gainful workers" to the labor force concept. The overlap in 1940 represents reconciliation of 1940 and 1950 Census counts of engineers. For full description and derivation see *ibid.*, notes to Table B-1 and Appendix E.

[a] Chemists include metallurgists, and engineers include surveyors. Surveyors cannot be segregated prior to 1930; they accounted for 0.024 per cent of the labor force in 1930, 0.031 per cent in 1940, and 0.044 per cent in 1950.

Over the sixty-year period, total numbers of engineers and chemists increased eighteenfold, after adjustment for discontinuities in the estimates for 1930 and 1940. As a percentage of the labor force, the increase was about sevenfold. This averages out as a 3.3 per cent a year relative increase, about double the rate of productivity advance. There is no retardation as yet apparent in the relative growth of the technological professions. The marked slowdown in the 1930's as a result of depressed economic conditions was virtually made good in the subsequent decade. It is obvious, however, that this relative growth rate cannot continue indefinitely.

[7] See David M. Blank and George J. Stigler, *The Demand and Supply of Scientific Personnel*, New York (NBER), 1957, p. 3.

Median age of labor force. The median age of labor-force participants increased by more than one-fifth between 1890 and 1955 (see Table 13). Some observers think that aging of the labor force results in decreased average personal efficiency, other things being equal, which would tend to restrain productivity advance. Certainly, people pass the peak of their physical strength and vigor at relatively early ages. This effect should tend to be mitigated, if not offset, however, by the shift in skill and occupational requirements that increases the average age at which individuals attain top proficiency. Peak earnings of professional people, for example, are not reached until the middle years or beyond. It would be

TABLE 13

Median Age of the Population and the Labor Force,
Selected Years, 1890–1955
(years)

	Total Population	Labor Force
1890	22.0	32.2
1920	25.3	34.3
1930	26.5	35.5
1940	29.0	36.0
1950	30.2	38.1
1955	30.0	39.1

SOURCE: *Economic Report of the President,* January 1957, Table C-4, p. 92.

hazardous to make any dogmatic statement about the relationship of average age to efficiency and to productivity advance in the face of technological changes that gradually alter the occupational composition of the labor force. In any case, the marked increase in the birth rate since 1940 has caused the median age of the population as a whole to decline in recent years, a development that will show up later as a drop in the median age of the labor force.

TRENDS IN THE COMPOSITION OF CAPITAL

Real capital stocks were weighted by rates of return in a number of sectors and industry groups to obtain an aggregate measure of real capital input. As was true of labor, although to a lesser degree, there was a relative shift of capital over the long period from industries with lower rates of return to those with higher rates of return on invested capital (see Table A-9). To the extent that higher rates of return are a result of greater intangible investment by the firms in an industry (for example the cumulation of technical knowledge from outlays on research and training), the weighted series reflects more fully the qualitative aspect of capital services.

91

Some of the major changes in the sectoral composition of capital stocks are shown in Table 14. The relative trends revealed clearly in this table seem to be typical concomitants of the process of economic development. Net investment abroad rose from negative figures prior to World War I to positive amounts in recent decades. The relative importance of the "social overhead" represented by publicly owned capital more than doubled between 1889 and 1953. Within the private domestic sector, the percentage of farm to total capital declined by almost two-thirds. Residential structures maintained a relatively constant ratio to total capital throughout, but showed a mild tendency to decline. Nonfarm, nonresidential plant, inventories, and equipment underwent a persistent and substantial relative increase.

TABLE 14

Distribution of Real Capital Stocks by Sector, Key Years, 1889–1953
(per cent)

	NATIONAL ECONOMY	REST-OF-THE-WORLD[a]	GOVERNMENT	PRIVATE DOMESTIC			
				Total	*Farm*	*Nonfarm*	
						Residential	Nonresidential
1889	100.0	−4.1	5.5	98.6	38.9	27.6	32.1
1899	100.0	−3.0	5.4	97.6	30.6	30.1	36.9
1909	100.0	−1.6	6.7	94.9	25.3	28.7	40.9
1919	100.0	1.4	7.6	91.0	22.2	26.3	42.5
1929	100.0	3.2	9.0	87.8	16.3	28.5	43.0
1937	100.0	1.4	13.2	85.4	15.9	28.3	41.2
1948	100.0	1.9	13.7	84.4	15.6	25.9	42.9
1953	100.0	1.8	13.1	85.1	14.4	25.5	45.2

SOURCE: Table A-XV.
[a] Net foreign assets.

An analysis (based on Table 15) of real capital stocks by major type is possible for the domestic economy. Structures and equipment, the two most important types of capital, each grew almost as much as real net product until 1929. There were some subperiod variations between the two output-capital ratios, but the trends were virtually parallel. The 1929-37 change was somewhat atypical, since real product and the stock of structures showed little change, while the stock of equipment fell relatively.

It is the trend since the late 1930's that diverges sharply from previous experience. Between 1937 and 1953 the stock of equipment showed a greater increase than real product. But the stock of structures showed little growth, and the output-structures ratio increased by almost 70 per cent. Various reasons can be adduced to explain this discrepant behavior;

for example, the greater relative increase in the cost of buildings than in the price of machinery and equipment, the development of space-saving innovations, and greater technological improvements in equipment than in structures. In some important industries, such as the utilities, fixed facilities are built up well ahead of demand, so beyond a point output increases faster than plant as the latter is utilized with increasing intensity.

TABLE 15

Domestic Economy: Major Types of Real Capital Stocks and
Relation to Real Net Product, Key Years, 1889–1953
(1929 = 100)

	Land, Farm and Forest	Structures	Equipment	Inventories
	REAL CAPITAL STOCK BY MAJOR TYPE			
1889	73	23	25	34
1899	86	40	33	42
1909	92	59	56	48
1919	98	72	80	73
1929	100	100	100	100
1937	101	101	89	101
1948	100	104	142	157
1953	104	120	203	188
	RATIOS OF REAL NET DOMESTIC PRODUCT TO REAL CAPITAL STOCK			
1889	32	103	95	68
1899	41	89	107	86
1909	58	91	95	110
1919	75	101	91	100
1929	100	100	100	100
1937	102	102	116	103
1948	165	158	116	105
1953	197	170	101	109

Source: Capital: Table A-XVI; real net domestic product (national security version): Table A-I, col. (7) minus Table A-III, col. (4).

To the extent that construction-cost deflators do not fully allow for productivity gains, the real-plant estimates obtained by deflation may have a downward bias. But the possible bias is unlikely to be so large as to account for a significant part of the divergent movement of the ratios of output to fixed capital by type.

The ratio of output to inventories has tended upward through most of the period. Between 1919 and 1953, the increase was about 10 per cent. The increase between 1889 and 1919 shown by our estimates was considerably greater—but it will be remembered that the private nonfarm portion of inventories prior to 1919 was not estimated independently of output. Yet it seems reasonable to suppose that there was a trend toward greater economy in the use of inventory stocks throughout the period as a result of steadily improving transportation and communication facilities and more efficient stock-control and merchandising methods generally.

The most striking increase was in the ratio of domestic output to land (farm and forest), which went up more than sixfold over the sixty-four years. Part of the rise is attributable to the less-than-proportionate increase in the demand for agricultural products as total real product rose. But gross farm output itself rose 30 per cent more than the acreage of farm land employed as crop yields per acre and production per animal unit were increased.

NONFACTOR INPUT TRENDS

Since the national product is measured net of intermediate products, a reduction in materials consumed per unit of output is reflected in a higher rate of increase in national product than would be shown if there were no economies in materials use. Transactions in semiprocessed goods or components are only of indirect significance in this connection, since changes in such transactions relative to the volume of final products reflect changes in raw materials use plus changes in the number of times materials change hands prior to final processing. Since the latter factor is largely a function of changes in the structure of business organization, we can see the basic phenomena better by looking directly at the consumption of raw materials relative to the national product rather than at the ratio of total intermediate-product purchases to product.

Productivity and raw material economies. Economies in consumption of materials per unit of output may result from fuller use of materials, a higher degree of processing, or a decline in the ratio of commodities to the national product.

Reliable estimates of domestic consumption of raw materials begin in 1900.[8] Over the half century 1900–52, total apparent consumption almost tripled, while real net national product increased close to sixfold. Thus, the ratio of output to raw materials input has more than doubled (Table 16), which means an average annual rate of increase of 1.4 per cent.

The foregoing comparison of real product with raw materials input, however, considerably overstates the contribution of materials economies to productivity gains since the value of raw materials obviously is much less than the value of final products. Approximations to the percentage-point increase in real national product and productivity attributable to the decrease in raw materials consumption per unit can be calculated in the following way: By adding the value of raw materials consumed to the net national product, both in 1929 dollars, we obtain a measure duplicative

[8] See *Raw Materials in the United States Economy, 1900–52*, Bureau of the Census Working Paper No. 1, 1954.

of raw materials input; if we then estimate a hypothetical real net national product by applying the 1929 ratio of the net measure to the measure gross of materials, we obtain estimates of what the net national product would have been had the requirements for raw materials remained constant at the 1929 proportion. The ratio of the actual to the hypothetical measure tells us by how much real product increased as a result of more economical

TABLE 16

Consumption of Raw Materials in Relation to Real Net
National Product, Key Years, 1900–52
(1929 = 100)

| | Real NNP[a] | Apparent Consumption of Raw Materials[b] | | | | Real NNP per Unit of Raw Materials Input |
		Total excl. Gold	Foods	Energy Materials	Physical-structure Materials	
1900	36.0	56.5	61.2	43.4	57.3	63.7
1909	52.8	72.2	76.5	56.6	75.9	73.1
1919	73.3	80.0	84.1	72.3	77.5	91.6
1929	100.0	100.0	100.0	100.0	100.0	100.0
1937	102.9	106.2	105.4	97.4	115.3	96.9
1948	163.7	140.3	131.0	141.7	159.4	116.7
1952	197.2	151.7	142.7	151.0	171.7	130.0

[a] NNP = net national product; Kuznets' concept, national security version (Table A-I).

[b] As estimated in *Raw Materials in the United States Economy, 1900–52*, Bureau of the Census Working Paper No. 1, 1954.

use of materials—assuming that resources are interchangeable between raw materials production and other uses without significant effect on over-all productivity. This computation is carried out in Table 17.

Over the period 1900–1952 as a whole, materials saving and greater processing accounted for a 0.25 per cent average annual increase in real net national product—or about one-sixth of the average percentage rate of increase in total factor productivity. The relative contribution from this source was more important in the early part of the period—from 1900 to 1919, the relative importance of materials economy was about one-third. Only in the period 1929–37 was there an increased use of materials per unit of output and a small negative influence on net product and productivity advance. Since 1948, the rate of saving in materials has been somewhat greater than the average over the half century.

Reductions in raw materials consumption per unit of output have also had an indirect influence on productivity change. If the hypothesis of a tendency towards diminishing returns in extractive industries is correct, then productivity advance in these industries and in the economy has been greater than would have been the case had raw materials production risen more nearly in proportion to national output. That is, a sixfold increase in raw materials production between 1900 and 1952, instead of the less than threefold increase that actually occurred, would have placed a greater strain on domestic natural resources and might possibly have resulted in lower rates of productivity advance than were realized.

TABLE 17

Estimated Effect of Raw Materials Savings on Growth of Real Net
National Product, Key Years, 1900–52

	Real NNP[a]	Consumption of Raw Materials[b]	Real Product Gross of Materials[c]	Hypothetical Real NNP at 1929 Materials Usage[d]	Effect of Materials Savings on Real NNP	
					Index[e] (1929 = 100)	Average Annual Rates of Change[f] (per cent)
		(millions of 1929 dollars)				
	(1)	(2)	(3)	(4)	(5)	(6)
1900	32.8	10.3	43.1	35.9	91.3	
1909	48.1	13.2	61.3	51.0	94.2	0.35
1919	66.7	14.6	81.3	67.7	98.5	0.45
1929	91.1	18.3	109.4	91.1	100.0	0.15
1937	93.7	19.4	113.1	94.2	99.5	−0.06
1948	149.2	25.6	174.8	145.6	102.4	0.26
1952	179.7	27.7	207.4	172.8	104.0	0.40

[a] NNP = net national product, Kuznets' concept, national security version (Table A-I).

[b] *Raw Materials in the United States Economy, 1900–52*, Bureau of the Census Working Paper No. 1, 1954.

[c] Col. (1) plus col. (2).

[d] Product of col. (3) and 1929 of col. (1) divided by 1929 of col. (3).

[e] Col. (1) divided by col. (4).

[f] Rates of change computed from col. (5) between terminal years of subperiods, ending with year shown in stub. The average annual percentage rate of change between 1900 and 1952 is 0.25.

Unit consumption by type of materials. The consumption of raw materials for food rose less in relation to real product than did the consumption of raw materials for other uses. This is due in part to a smaller increase in consumer outlays for food than in total real net product, especially prior to 1929. But there is also evidence that the real value of food production increased significantly in relation to raw materials input due primarily to greater processing but also to more complete use of the raw materials.

Economies in the use of physical-structure materials are partly a function of the increasing proportion of national product going into services rather than goods. Based on Kuznets' estimates, consumer services rose from 28 per cent of real net national product (national security variant) in 1900 to 37 per cent in 1929. The trend does not appear to have continued since 1929. Based on a careful study by the Commerce Department, the proportion of real gross national product accounted for by services, as distinguished from commodities and construction, increased only from 30 per cent in 1929 to 31 per cent in 1953.[9]

A more important factor in the declining raw materials proportion of the national product is the increase in the durable goods proportion—for the ratio of raw materials purchases to total value added is smaller in durable goods manufacture than in nondurable goods. The Commerce Department study indicates that durable goods increased from 18 per cent of the real GNP in 1929 to 22 per cent in 1953.[10] Based on the Kuznets estimates, consumer durables plus producer durable equipment increased from 13 per cent of real gross national product (national security version) in 1900 to 16 per cent in 1929. But in addition to the greater processing of goods resulting from technological advance and shifts in the composition of demand, there was also undoubtedly some saving of materials in the making of identical goods through reduction of waste, redesign, better quality controls, and so on.

It is apparent from Table 16 that real product went up considerably less in relation to energy materials than to physical-structure materials. A more illuminating picture is obtained by relating the consumption of energy materials to their direct output, and energy, in turn, to the factor inputs and real product.

Energy consumption, inputs, and output. While real product went up by less than two-thirds in relation to energy materials consumed between 1900 and 1952, the efficiency of conversion of the energy potential of inanimate energy resources into work output increased more than fourfold between 1900 and 1950.[11] In relating energy consumption to input and product, we employ a measure of energy used for work output that includes only operations which have been or could be performed by muscle power, and excludes energy used for space heating, lighting, or refrigeration. One such measure, in terms of horsepower-hours, is shown in Table 18.

In the 1870-80 decade, each manhour was provided with 0.55 horse-power-hours of animal or inanimate energy; by 1950, over 5 horsepower-hours were associated with each manhour—almost a tenfold increase over the seventy-five-year period. The average annual rate of increase in the ratio was 3.0 per cent, although after a period of accelerating advance the increase in horsepower-hours per manhour slowed to an average annual rate of 1.5 per cent in the 1930-50 period.

[9] "New Distribution of National Output by Goods, Services, and Construction, 1929–56," *Survey of Current Business,* June 1957, p. 9.
[10] *Ibid.,* p. 9.
[11] J. F. Dewhurst, *America's Needs and Resources, A New Survey,* New York, Twentieth Century Fund, 1955, Table I, p. 1,113.

TABLE 18

Energy Consumption for Work Performance in Relation to Output and Inputs, Decennial, 1870–1950

| | ENERGY CONSUMPTION FOR WORK PERFORMANCE Horsepower-Hours | | Horsepower-Hours per Manhour | | RATIO OF ENERGY CONSUMPTION TO | | | |
| | | | | | Real Capital | | Total Factor Input | Real Net National Product |
	Billions	Index	Hours	Index	Total	Equipment		
1870–80	22.0	5.1	0.55	14.3	34.5	41.5	21.1	35.7
1890	44.7	10.3	0.72	18.6	39.6	41.4	25.2	39.6
1900	74.3	17.1	0.98	25.5	43.4	50.3	31.8	44.5
1910	160.8	37.0	1.66	43.1	65.8	65.0	50.1	64.9
1920	283.3	65.1	2.64	68.4	85.0	81.7	72.8	82.6
1930	434.9	100.0	3.86	100.0	100.0	100.0	100.0	100.0
1940	491.9	113.1	4.35	112.7	119.3	124.4	113.2	92.0
1950	668.5	153.7	5.19	134.3	126.0	93.3	122.4	77.1

SOURCE: Energy consumption: J. F. Dewhurst, *America's Needs and Resources, A New Survey*, New York, Twentieth Century Fund, 1955, Table L, p. 1,116; manhours: Table A-X; equipment: Table A-XVI; net national product, total capital, and total factor input: Table A-XIX.

In relation to the real stock of capital, energy consumption more than tripled over the seventy-five years. Between 1930 and 1950, however, there was relatively little net increase. In relation to producer durable equipment the increase was less marked, with a net decline occurring between 1940 and 1950. Energy consumption per unit of real net product more than doubled over the entire period, but since 1930 the deceleration in its rate of increase relative to factor input was reflected in an actual decline relative to output.

There can be little doubt that the substantial increases in output per unit of input over the period were due in part to the striking increases in nonhuman energy relative to input. This trend was promoted by a decline in the relative price of energy as a result of marked increases in productivity in the energy-producing industries (see Chapter 6). Certainly, the increase in energy production was a necessary concomitant of the increase in equipment per worker and of faster and more powerful equipment. But the relation of energy to productivity is not a simple one, as evidenced by the deceleration in recent decades in the rate of increase in energy consumption per unit of input and a decline in relation to output at the same time that productivity advanced at a faster rate than it did in earlier decades.

The Changing Structure of Output

To complement the analysis of inputs as a means of gaining insight into the dynamics of productivity advance, one can also analyze the composition of output. Parts of output are devoted to increasing the quantity and quality of resources. Not all of these outlays are included or identified in the national product estimates.

MARGINS OVER MAINTENANCE OF PRODUCT

One helpful way of analyzing the composition of national product is in terms of the margin that remains after providing for the maintenance of the population of each previous year at the previous year's level of consumption and of net capital stock. This margin over maintenance, in turn, may be broken down into the portions required for national security, for growth of population, and a final "margin for economic progress" that may be invested in increasing the tangible or intangible capital per person. This margin gives us an alternative approach to the measurement of economic growth or progress. It was suggested, in somewhat different form, in an earlier National Bureau study by Mills.[12]

The real product necessary for maintenance of population is shown in Table 19 (column 2). It is computed annually as the real consumption of the previous year plus capital consumption allowances of the current year

[12] *Op. cit.*

TABLE 19

Margins over Maintenance of Real Gross National Product, Subperiods, 1889–1959

(annual averages)

PERIOD OF AVERAGE	REAL GROSS NATIONAL PRODUCT	MAINTENANCE OF POPULATION (CONSUMER AND CAPITAL GOODS)	MARGIN OVER MAINTENANCE OF POPULATION		MARGIN over Maintenance of Population and Security				
			Total	Maintenance of National Security	Total	Provision for Growth of Population (Consumption and Capital)	Margin for Economic Progress		
							Total	Consumption	Capital
	(1)	(2)	(3)	(4)	(5)	(6)	(7)	(8)	(9)
					MILLIONS OF 1929 DOLLARS				
1889–1953	84,291	70,641	13,650	6,488	7,162	3,817	3,345	1,215	2,130
1889–1918	42,610	35,857	6,753	813	5,940	2,745	3,195	580	2,615
1919–53	120,017	100,455	19,562	11,352	8,210	4,736	3,474	1,759	1,715
1889–98	26,781	22,264	4,517	143	4,374	1,785	2,589	314	2,275
1899–1908	42,111	35,180	6,931	334	6,597	2,906	3,691	648	3,043
1909–18	58,937	50,128	8,809	1,961	6,848	3,544	3,304	776	2,528
1919–28	83,181	71,058	12,123	1,380	10,743	4,284	6,459	1,690	4,769
1929–36	84,854	82,862	1,992	773	1,219	3,002	−1,783	71	−1,854
1937–47	142,417	109,583	32,834	24,944	7,890	4,388	3,502	3,077	425
1948–53	187,230	156,174	31,056	17,160	13,896	8,438	5,458	1,706	3,752
(1954–59)	226,324	190,389	35,935	21,914	14,021	9,732	4,289	2,745	1,544
					PERCENTAGE OF GROSS NATIONAL PRODUCT				
1889–1953	100.0	83.8	16.2	7.7	8.5	4.5	4.0	1.5	2.5
1889–1918	100.0	84.2	15.8	1.9	13.9	6.4	7.5	1.4	6.1
1919–53	100.0	83.7	16.3	9.5	6.8	3.9	2.9	1.5	1.4
1889–98	100.0	83.1	16.9	0.5	16.4	6.7	9.7	1.2	8.5
1899–1908	100.0	83.5	16.5	0.8	15.7	6.9	8.8	1.6	7.2
1909–18	100.0	85.1	14.9	3.3	11.6	6.0	5.6	1.3	4.3
1919–28	100.0	85.4	14.6	1.7	12.9	5.2	7.7	2.0	5.7
1929–36	100.0	97.7	2.3	0.9	1.4	3.5	−2.1	0.1	−2.2
1937–47	100.0	76.9	23.1	17.5	5.6	3.1	2.5	2.2	0.3
1948–53	100.0	83.4	16.6	9.2	7.4	4.5	2.9	0.9	2.0
(1954–59)	100.0	84.1	15.9	9.7	6.2	4.3	1.9	1.2	0.7

SOURCE: Gross national product, national security variant, Table A-XIX, allocated as described in text.

(averaged over the periods shown). The rest of the current-year real gross national product (column 3) is a margin over and above the requirements for maintenance of a given population with a constant level of capital and consumption goods per capita. This margin may be theoretically disposed of for purposes of growth—growth of population or of output per capita.

Some of the margin, however, is required for national security purposes —the amount depending on the interaction of international conditions and national foreign policy. Resources devoted to security purposes are *potentially* available to support economic growth (and a small portion of national security outlays does represent investment). But to calculate the *actual* margin available for economic growth (column 5), national security outlays must be deducted from the margin over maintenance of population.

The margin available for economic growth proper may be divided into two components—that necessary to support the growth of population, and that available for increased consumption or investment per capita. The former (column 6) is obtained by multiplying the net population increment of each year by the average per capita consumption and reproducible capital stock of the previous year. By subtracting the real consumption expenditures needed to support the population increment at the previous year's level from the total increment to consumption, that part of consumption outlay which serves to raise per capita consumption is obtained (column 8); an analagous procedure yields that portion of real investment which serves to increase capital stock per head (column 9). These last two components constitute what may be called a margin for economic progress, if the term is defined as the increase in real net economic output (excluding munitions) per capita.

Quite consistently for most of the subperiods, approximately 84 per cent of the real gross product has been required, on the average, to maintain the real personal consumption level of the previous year and to offset capital consumption. Of the remaining 16 per cent, national security required about 2 per cent of GNP, on the average, through 1929, and almost 14 per cent was available for population growth and economic progress. A little less than half of this margin over maintenance of population and security was needed to support the increase in population; the rest was devoted to raising real consumption and capital stocks per capita.

The 1930's were atypical in that there was little margin over maintenance of population and capital. Even with very low national security outlays, only 1.4 per cent of GNP was available for growth and progress between 1929 and 1937. More than this was required for consumption purposes by a growing population, and capital stocks per capita fell.

Since the 1930's, national security outlays have absorbed more than half the margin over maintenance. If we skip over the war years, and consider simply the period 1948–53, national security took 9 per cent of gross expenditures. Growth of population, while less than in the early decades, was up from the 1930's and required 4.5 per cent of GNP. Only 3 per cent of GNP has been available for economic progress—as compared with almost 8 per cent before 1929. It is interesting that provision for increased real consumption per capita has consistently absorbed between 1 and 2 per cent of GNP over the decades (except in the 1930's); therefore, the large increase in national security outlays since World War II compared with earlier periods has been mainly at the expense of the proportion of product devoted to increasing the capital stock per capita. In fact, there was no net increase in this component from 1929 until after World War II; since 1948, about 2 per cent of GNP has augmented capital per head.

This bears out the implications of the total and partial productivity ratios—rates of increase in capital per head or per manhour have little relation to rates of increase in total productivity. Productivity growth accelerated after World War I (after 1937, using the national measures) while capital per person showed smaller increases than before. A marked increase in the efficiency of given quantities of capital has been associated with the acceleration of productivity advance, and significant savings in capital as well as in labor per unit of output have been realized.

PRODUCTIVITY AND THE MARGIN FOR ECONOMIC PROGRESS

Over the sixty-four-year period, the productivity increment has been just slightly larger than necessary to provide for increases in real consumption per capita. As Table 20 indicates, prior to 1919 the productivity increment

TABLE 20

Productivity Increment
in Relation to Consumption Margin, 1889–1953
(annual averages)

Period of Average	Real GNP Millions of 1929 Dollars	Consumption Margin		Productivity Increment		
		Millions of 1929 Dollars	Per Cent of GNP	Millions of 1929 Dollars	Per Cent of GNP	Per Cent of Consumption Margin
1889–1953	84,291	1,215	1.5	1,250	1.5	103
1889–1919	42,610	580	1.4	413	1.0	71
1919–53	120,017	1,759	1.5	1,967	1.6	112
1948–53	187,230	1,706	0.9	2,900	1.5	170

SOURCE: Table 19.

was smaller, and after 1919 somewhat larger, than the margin for increased per capita consumption. The more ample relative dimensions of the productivity increment after 1919 are due to acceleration in its rate of growth, since the consumption margin averaged about 1.5 per cent of GNP in both periods. The much larger relative size of the 1948–53 productivity increment was due both to a greater-than-average rate of productivity growth and to a consumption margin that was squeezed to smaller-than-average proportions by high national security outlays and an expansion of net investment over that of the preceding two decades. During this period the productivity increment provided almost one-third of the capital margin in addition to the entire consumption margin.

On the surface, it might seem that there is some contradiction between Tables 8 and 20. That is, the preceding section indicated that the rate of productivity gain was less than the rate of increase in real consumption expenditures per capita—1.6 versus 1.9 per cent a year, on the average. But this is consistent with the analysis just presented, since the 1.6 per cent is reckoned on the net national product (NNP) base, which is about one-sixth higher than the consumption outlay base to which the 1.9 per cent applies.

If the increase in planes of living largely absorbed most of the productivity increment, the question may be asked as to the source of the rest of the margin over maintenance of population. First, it should be clear that the margin over maintenance, which averaged 16 per cent, is much larger than the average increment to the real national product, which has averaged 3.6 per cent. Productivity and input increments contribute less than one-quarter to the total margin; the remainder results from the spending-saving pattern of the community as influenced by the tax and expenditure policy of governments.

The most striking tendency revealed in Table 19 is the relatively small proportion of product since 1929 that has gone to increase the stock of capital per head. Even the 2.0 per cent contribution in 1948–53 is only one-third of the proportion in 1889–1919. The low ratio has been associated with a relatively high level of national security outlays (especially since 1939), as is shown in Table 19 and in Chart 8. The method of financing those outlays has obviously tended to reduce investment relatively more than consumption. During the war, capital goods were allocated directly; but since the war, the upward trend of the interest rate has been indicative of the tight capital supply situation.

It is true that even with the small increases in capital per worker since the 1920's, productivity gains have been greater than in the pre-1919 period, when the relative growth of capital was much greater. Widespread introduction of capital-saving technology has made this possible, but it cannot be said that productivity gains would not have been greater in recent years had capital been more abundant. There is the additional circumstance that the national accounts as now constructed do not identify, nor even include, all types of investment. It is to this matter that we now turn.

CHART 8

National Product, Margins over Maintenance of the Population at Levels of Previous Year, 1889–1918 and 1919–53

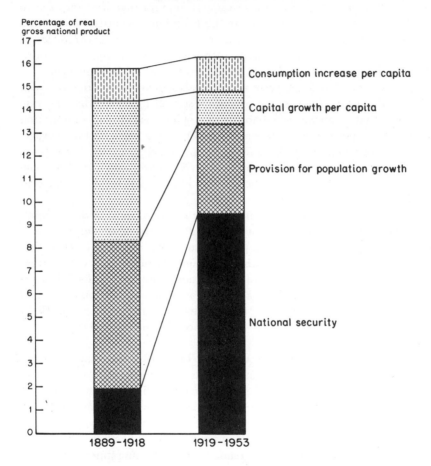

HIDDEN INVESTMENT

Investment may be defined as the application of resources and the incurrence of costs in the current period with the objective of increasing productive capacity and income in future periods. By this definition, it is apparent that some items included in consumption outlays are really "investment in self," in personal productive capacity.[13] Looked at broadly, most personal consumption outlays and standards of living generally have some connection with productive efficiency, from the aspects both of

[13] An intensive analysis of this form of investment is being undertaken by Gary Becker of the National Bureau staff.

capacity and of incentive. Also, some items charged to current expense in business accounting, such as exploratory and research outlays, are not included in national product, although they are really a form of investment. Government outlays for the same purpose are partially included in national security outlays; by the Commerce Department concept, total intangible and tangible public investment are included in government purchases but are not separately identified.

Investment in persons. The two chief types of personal consumption expenditures that fit the definition of investment are expenditures for education and for health services. The Commerce Department estimates of personal consumption expenditures plus public educational outlays can be extended back to 1909 by major category to furnish a general picture of total educational and private health expenditures (Table 21).

TABLE 21

Consumption Expenditures by Major Type, Key Years, 1909–53

	Total[a]	Food, Clothing, and Housing[b]	Personal Business[b]	Leisure Pursuits[b]	Medical Care	Education
		CURRENT DOLLARS (BILLIONS)				
1909	27.3	21.9	1.9	2.2	0.8	0.5
1919	60.3	46.6	6.5	4.2	1.9	1.1
1929	80.5	54.6	13.3	7.4	2.9	2.3
1937	69.0	47.6	10.7	5.7	2.7	2.3
1948	181.4	128.5	25.0	15.1	7.4	5.4
1953	236.6	159.6	38.8	19.6	10.1	8.5
		PERCENTAGE DISTRIBUTION OF CURRENT-DOLLAR OUTLAYS				
1909	100.0	80.4	7.0	8.0	2.8	1.8
1919	100.0	77.3	10.7	7.0	3.2	1.8
1929	100.0	67.8	16.5	9.2	3.7	2.8
1937	100.0	69.1	15.5	8.2	3.9	3.3
1948	100.0	70.8	13.8	8.3	4.1	3.0
1953	100.0	67.4	16.4	8.3	4.3	3.6
		REAL OUTLAYS PER CAPITA (1929 DOLLARS)				
1909	446	369	11	40	13	13
1919	508	374	57	41	19	17
1929	670	454	111	62	24	19
1937	654	452	106	54	23	19
1948	880	608	136	78	36	22
1953	958	641	161	91	40	25

[a] Estimates are those of the Department of Commerce for 1929 and later years, extrapolated to 1909 by the estimates contained in William H. Shaw, *Value of Commodity Output since 1869*, New York (NBER), 1947; and J. F. Dewhurst, *America's Needs and Resources* New York, Twentieth Century Fund, 1947. Estimates of public educational outlay (see Appendix K) were added to personal consumption expenditures.

[b] Housing includes household operations; personal business includes transportation; leisure pursuits include recreation, personal care, religious and welfare expenditures, and foreign travel.

Expenditures for education increased from 1.8 per cent of total consumption expenditures in 1909 to 3.6 per cent in 1953. Real educational outlays per capita went up by 98 per cent over the forty-four-year period, or at an average rate of 1.6 per cent a year. This probably represents an understatement—since the price deflator is the average pay of teachers, deflated expenditures are, in effect, labor input without allowance for productivity change. Understatement is also suggested by the fact that deflated educational outlays per capita went up less than total real consumption expenditures per capita, although the opposite relative movement is indicated by the current-dollar estimates.

The increasing personal and public investment in education is reflected in the data relating to school enrollments and degrees earned (Table 22).

TABLE 22

Enrollments and Graduates in Secondary Schools and Institutions
of Higher Education,[a] Decennial, 1890–1950
(per cent)

| | Secondary Schools | | Institutions of Higher Education | |
	Enrollment per 100 Persons 14–17 Years Old	Graduates per 100 Persons 17 Years Old	Resident enrollment per 100 Persons 18–21 Years Old	Earned Degrees per 100 Persons 21 Years Old
1890	6.7	3.5	3.0	1.2
1900	11.4	6.4	4.0	1.9
1910	15.4	8.8	4.8	2.1
1920	32.3	16.8	8.1	2.7
1930	51.4	29.0	12.2	5.5
1940	73.3	50.8	15.3	7.9
1950	76.5	59.0	19.3	18.8

SOURCE: *Higher Education for American Deomocracy*, President's Commission on Higher Education, 1947, Vol. VI; and the *Statistical Abstract of the United States, 1956*, Dept. of Commerce.

[a] Public and private.

Over the sixty-year period 1890–1950, enrollments in institutions of higher education as a percentage of the relevant age class increased more than sixfold, while secondary school enrollments per 100 in the 14–17 age class increased more than tenfold. Numbers of graduates showed much greater relative increases.

It seems inevitable that this striking advance in the educational attainments of the American people should have increased the skills, efficiency, and inventive potential of the labor force. It correlates with the picture, shown earlier, of the relative increase in the skilled and professional groups in the labor force, and with the relative shift of workers to higher-paying occupations and industries. To this extent, investment in self is reflected in our labor input measure. Within the same occupational groupings there must have been a trend towards higher educational attainment that should have increased the efficiency of labor within the various industries, but this part of the investment in persons does not affect labor input as measured.

Relative increases in private health outlays have also been striking (see Table 21). If public health expenditures were included, total levels, and possibly the increases as well, would be greater. The increasing outlays for health and related items were not without effect, if life expectancy may be taken as a criterion. As indicated in Table 23, the average life expectancy at birth in the United States increased from 47.3 years in 1900 to

TABLE 23

Average Length of Life and Survival Rates, by Sex and Color, Death-Registration States, Selected Years, 1900–55

	Total	White		Nonwhite	
		Male	Female	Male	Female
ESTIMATED AVERAGE LENGTH OF LIFE (YEARS)					
1900	47.3	46.6	48.7	32.5	33.5
1909	52.1	50.9	54.2	34.2	37.3
1919	54.7	54.5	57.4	44.5	44.4
1929	57.1	57.2	60.3	45.7	47.8
1937	60.0	59.3	63.8	48.3	52.5
1948	67.2	65.5	71.0	58.1	62.5
1953	68.8	66.8	72.9	59.7	64.4
1955	69.5	67.3	73.6	61.2	65.9
PROBABILITY OF SURVIVAL TO AGE 65 PER 100 PERSONS ATTAINING AGE 15					
1900–02		50.3	54.3	31.9	35.3
1919–21		58.5	61.2	41.3	37.0
1939–41		62.6	72.7	40.6	45.1
1953		66.9	80.9	50.0	59.6

SOURCE: *Abridged Life Tables: United States, 1954*, Vital Statistics—Special Reports: National Summaries, Vol. 44, No. 2, Department of Health, Education, and Welfare, May 15, 1956, Table 5 and derivation from Table 3.

69.5 years in 1955. The health and efficiency of labor-force members also probably improved over the period. More important, increasing survival rates mean that the investment in the birth, upbringing, and education of individuals yielded higher total returns.

There is a problem of distinguishing between gross and net investment in personal productive capacity. That part of investment-type outlays required to maintain the productivity of a given population at its previous level is akin to tangible investment designed to offset capital consumption.

The part of real outlays associated with increased population and increased outlays per person is a rough approximation of the net investment involved.

Although we have singled out two types of consumption expenditures for special comment, the rise in per capita consumption expenditures generally must have had a stimulating effect on personal efficiency and on productivity. Certainly, increasing per capita outlays for food, clothing, and shelter, for example, must have had some effect on health in addition to the effect of higher direct health outlays. More generally, the experience of rising planes of living, both for oneself and for those around one, must have raised standards and aspirations and so exerted a strong incentive effect on individuals to strive for further material progress.[14]

Intangible investment by business and government. There are several types of tangible and intangible investment that are charged by business firms to current expense. The Commerce Department attempts to estimate the volume of producers' durable equipment so charged and includes it in gross private domestic investment. Expenses of oil companies in drilling oil and gas wells are treated likewise. But several types of intangible investment, and certain mineral exploratory expenses, are not included in the national product or, in the case of public investment, are not segregated from other outlays.

Of the intangible investments, probably the most important types are expenditures for training and other ways of improving the efficiency of employees, and research and development outlays for the purpose of devising new equipment, processes, and procedures for increasing efficiency generally.

Unfortunately, data are not available to show the trend of training and educational costs incurred by industry. The total is undoubtedly large. In-plant training and various forms of apprenticeship have been practiced since time immemorial. If estimates were available for recent times, however, the general trend shown above by the estimates of public and private personal educational outlays would probably not be greatly modified by inclusion of business outlays for the same purpose.

Estimates are available for research and development outlays since 1920. The figures shown in Table 24 include publicly financed as well as business outlays. The estimates since 1941 are more reliable and more comprehensive than the earlier estimates. Although the two sets of estimates are not continuous, it is apparent that research and development expenditures

---

[14] This theme has been elaborated by Ruth Mack, "Trends in American Consumption and the Aspiration to Consume," *American Economic Review, Papers and Proceedings,* May 1956, pp. 55–68. She writes: "I hold that one cannot adequately explain . . . the growth in real consumption . . . without recognizing the unusual force of the drive to consume and its effect in activating productive effort" (p. 58).

have increased at a significantly higher rate than the net national product. The ratio of research and development outlays to national product has, however, not increased at an accelerating rate. The ratio more than doubled during the 1920's, doubled in the 1930's, and increased by one-half in the 1940's. On the basis of a McGraw-Hill survey of business

TABLE 24

Research and Development Expenditures in Relation to
Net National Product, Selected Years, 1920–55

| | | RESEARCH AND DEVELOPMENT OUTLAYS | | | |
| | | *Old Series*[b] | | *New Series*[c] | |
	NNP[a] Millions	Millions	Per cent of NNP	Millions	Per cent of NNP
1920	$78,100	$59	0.08		
1930	77,660	166	0.21		
1940	83,915	345	0.41		
1941	109,911			$ 900	0.82
1950	239,408			2,870	1.20
1955[p]	326,023			5,400	1.66

p = preliminary.
 a NNP = net national product, Kuznets' concept, national security version, in current dollars.
 b Estimated from figures shown in Vannevar Bush, *Science, the Endless Frontier,* A Report to the President, July 1945, p. 80.
 c *The Growth of Scientific Research and Development,* Dept. of Defense, 1953, p. 10, and preliminary reports of United States National Science Foundation. The estimates comprise expenditures by government, industry, and nonprofit institutions for basic and applied research in the sciences (including medicine) and engineering and for the design and development of prototypes and processes. Excluded are quality control, routine product testing, sales promotion or services, and research in the social sciences and psychology.

intentions to spend for research and development,[15] it appears that the ratio will again increase by more than one-half in the 1950's.

Before World War I, organized industrial research laboratories were much more the exception than the rule.[16] Invention and development had, of course, been going on in a more or less informal manner for a very long time. But it was the work of technically minded, and sometimes trained, individuals working chiefly as individuals—as proprietors or works managers in larger firms, as professional scientists, inventors, or both,

[15] McGraw-Hill Publishing Co., Dept. of Economics, *Business' Plans for New Plants and Equipment, 1958–1961, 11th Annual Survey,* New York, undated.
 [16] The first directory of industrial laboratories appeared in 1920 (*Research Laboratories in Industrial Establishments of the United States,* National Academy of Sciences).

or as production workers. In recent decades, invention and the development of innovations have become systematized and routinized, involving teams of scientists and engineers working in complex laboratories. The more informal type of innovation continues to be significant, but it is certainly of declining relative importance. Taking both informal and organized research and development together, its growth has extended over a much longer period of time and been more gradual than the growth of organized research and development alone—as witness the figures presented earlier on scientists and engineers in relation to the labor force. Even the latter comparisons probably overstate the growth of innovational activity, since untrained persons were relatively more important in earlier days.

Although we cannot measure it precisely, research and development activity is our best indication of the investment in scientific and technological advance that sooner or later results in productivity growth. We should not forget, however, that the volume and relative trend of this type of intangible investment depends on fundamental social values and institutions. The effect on productivity also depends partly on the rate at which cost-reducing innovations spread. This again is a function of social and institutional factors, such as the degree of competition, the availability and cost of financing, the availability of properly trained workers, and the state of long-run expectations.

CHAPTER 5
Productivity, Factor Prices, and Real Incomes

PRODUCTIVITY gains provide the increments to real product out of which the real incomes of the factors are increased. If productivity advances, wage rates and capital return necessarily rise in relation to the general product price level, since this is the means whereby the fruits of productivity gains are distributed to workers and investors by the market mechanism. The shares of the factors in the productivity increment depend on relative price movements. Changes in the factor shares in the national income as a whole depend on changes in the relative quantities of each used in the productive process as well as on changes in their relative prices.

In this chapter we shall quantify these relationships and attempt to say something about the forces underlying the divergent movements of the prices of the factors. We do not delve into the broader analysis of the dynamics of the price-cost-productivity relationship. The statement that the general price level always rises less than the average prices of the factors in proportion to the increase in total factor productivity is neutral with respect to the question of what causal forces produce price change. Nevertheless, effective price analysis requires estimates of the interrelated variables which this chapter seeks to provide. Our focus is on the increases in real income made possible by productivity advance and on the distribution of income and productivity increments between the factors.

The analysis is confined to the private domestic economy. Market price is the major means of allocating and compensating resources in this sector, and the estimates are more reliable than for the total economy including government. Most of the analysis relates to the period since 1919, for which the detailed Kuznets and Commerce estimates of income as well as product are available. It will be remembered that 1919 marked the beginning of a higher productivity trend, which has continued into the 1950's. Occasional reference will be made to changes in the variables between 1899 and 1919. These are based on current-dollar income estimates obtained by extrapolating the 1919 figures back by our estimates of gross national product and the reconciliation items and then splitting the resulting national income figures by ratios based on estimates by King and, more recently, by Budd.[1] The estimates for the earlier period are of

[1] See Willford I. King, *The National Income and Its Purchasing Power*, New York (NBER), 1930. The King estimates were used as a basis for extrapolating the factor proportions

111

poorer quality than those for the years since 1919, but the trends and relationships are similar to those in the later years.

Concepts and Measures

"Factor price" is used in this chapter as shorthand for the compensation (income) per unit of weighted factor input. Total factor price is obtained by dividing factor income by the sum of real labor and capital inputs, as shown in Table 25. Total factor price can be more specifically defined in terms of its components. The price of labor is the average compensation per manhour in the various industries, combined by changing manhour weights. This is a broader measure than wage rates, since it includes overtime and the cost of "fringe" benefits. Shifts of manhours among the forty or so industry groups for which manhours are estimated separately (see Appendix A) do not affect the over-all price index, but shifts among industries within these groups would.

The price, or average compensation per unit of capital input, is a compound variable, measuring, in effect, the product of the average price of capital goods and the average rate of return on the capital stock of the sector. This measure may also be interpreted as an index of the net rent earned per hour that the capital stock is available for use. As in the case of labor, the price of capital is not affected by relative shifts of capital among the twenty-five or so industry groups for which separate estimates were made, but it would be affected by intra-industry shifts.

Operationally, the average price of each of the two factor classes is obtained as the quotient of the total compensation of each and the corresponding real-input measure, as shown in Table 26. The derivation is not as simple as it may appear from the table. The national income estimates give employee compensation but do not break down the net income of proprietors between the returns on the labor and capital services furnished by proprietors. This we have done by imputing to proprietors of each industry segment the average hourly compensation of the employees of that industry. Other conventions, such as imputing the same rate of return to proprietors' capital as is earned by small corporations in the same industry, are possible, but differences stemming from alternative procedures are not crucial.[2]

---

from 1919 to 1909. Extrapolation from 1909 to 1899 was based on estimates from Edward C. Budd, "Factor Shares, 1850–1910," *Trends in the American Economy in the Nineteenth Century*, Studies in Income and Wealth, Volume 24, Princeton (for NBER), 1960.

[2] Kravis has experimented with four different methods of splitting the net income of proprietors. All methods give him the same general result, i.e., returns from property ownership have a declining share in the national income since 1900; but the degree of decline differs somewhat depending on the method (see Irving B. Kravis, "Relative Income Shares in Fact and Theory," *American Economic Review*, December 1959; for a discussion of the same problem for an earlier period, see Budd, *op. cit.*).

TABLE 25

Private Domestic Economy:
Factor Prices, Product Prices, and Productivity, Key Years and
Subperiods, 1899–1957

	Net Domestic Product at Factor Cost[a]		Factor Input	Factor Productivity[c]	Average Price	
	Current Dollars	1929 Dollars	1929 Dollars[b]		Factors[d]	Products[e]
	(1)	(2)	(3)	(4)	(5)	(6)
	MILLIONS OF DOLLARS			INDEX (1929 = 100)		
1899	13,767	28,438	44,054	64.6	31.3	48.4
1919	60,848	56,628	70,207	80.7	86.7	107.5
1929	82,669	82,669	82,669	100.0	100.0	100.0
1937	66,133	84,240	73,720	114.3	90.1	78.9
1948	203,191	135,991	92,827	146.5	218.9	149.4
1957	318,970	185,592	105,090	176.6	303.5	171.9
	LINK RELATIVES					
1899–1919	442.0	199.1	159.4	124.9	277.0	222.1
1919–57	524.1	327.7	149.7	218.8	350.1	159.9
1919–29	135.9	146.0	117.8	123.9	115.3	93.0
1929–37	80.4	101.9	89.2	114.3	90.1	78.9
1937–48	305.9	161.4	125.9	128.2	243.0	189.4
1948–57	157.0	136.5	113.2	120.5	138.6	115.1
	AVERAGE ANNUAL PERCENTAGE RATES OF CHANGE DERIVED FROM LINK RELATIVES					
1899–1919	7.7	3.5	2.4	1.1	5.2	4.1
1919–57	4.5	3.2	1.1	2.1	3.4	1.2
1919–29	3.1	3.9	1.7	2.2	1.4	−0.7
1929–37	−2.7	0.2	−1.4	1.7	−1.3	−2.9
1937–48	10.7	4.4	2.1	2.3	8.4	6.0
1948–57	5.1	3.5	1.4	2.1	3.7	1.6

NOTE: Table may not be internally consistent due to rounding.

a Differs from net domestic product at market prices chiefly by the amount of indirect business taxes. The estimate for 1929 is equal to the national income less income originating in the general-government and rest-of-the-world sectors.

b Factor input here is derived as the sum of labor and capital inputs in absolute terms (see Table 26). It differs slightly from the index given in the basic appendix tables, which represents a variable weighted average of indexes of labor and capital inputs.

c Col. (2) divided by col. (3).

d Col. (1) divided by col. (3).

e Col. (1) divided by col. (2) or col. (5) divided by col. (4).

Capital compensation is total income less employee compensation and the imputed labor compensation of proprietors. It represents the sum of net interest, rents, royalties, and profits (corporate and noncorporate). Since net profits are influenced by the method of depreciation accounting, it should be noted that the depreciation of nonfarm assets is based on original cost. Revaluation in terms of replacement cost would give somewhat different, but not substantially different, results. The Commerce Department did adjust book depreciation figures to eliminate the effect of the accelerated amortization allowed by the Internal Revenue Service beginning in 1950.

TABLE 26

Private Domestic Economy:
Input, Cost, and Average Price of Labor and of Capital,
Key Years, 1899–1957
(dollars in millions)

	Labor Cost		Average Price of Labor[a] (1929 = 100)	Capital Cost		Average Price of Capital[b] (1929 = 100)
	Current Dollars (1)	1929 Dollars (2)	(3)	Current Dollars (4)	1929 Dollars (5)	(6)
1899	9,623	33,878	28.4	4,144	10,176	40.7
1919	43,814	51,802	84.6	17,034	18,405	92.6
1929	59,749	59,749	100.0	22,920	22,920	100.0
1937	52,400	52,221	100.3	14,033	21,499	65.3
1948	154,769	66,859	231.5	48,422	25,968	186.5
1957	259,611	68,831	377.2	59,359	36,259	163.7

SOURCE: Current-dollar costs represent total labor compensation plus capital compensation derived as the difference between national income and labor compensation. Constant-dollar costs are computed from indexes of labor and capital input (Table A-XXII) multiplied by the 1929-dollar estimates.
[a] Col. (1) divided by col. (2).
[b] Col. (4) divided by col. (5).

Finally, since we deflate the compensation per unit of the factor inputs by an over-all price index to get real incomes, a few words should be said about the nature of the deflator used. To obtain an index of final-product prices consistent with the factor price index, it is necessary to compute the quotient of net private domestic product at factor cost in current prices and in constant prices. As a "net" measure, the implicit price deflator accords a smaller weight to the prices of capital goods than would a deflator of gross product, since the capital outlays required to offset capital consumption are excluded. By measuring the average prices of national product "at factor cost," the effect of indirect business taxes on market price is eliminated. In practice, the price index is obtained by dividing

114

income in the private domestic economy by the corresponding real net product at factor cost. The latter variable is computed by extrapolating base-period income by the index of real net product at market price, since the deflated net product at factor cost should show virtually the same movement as deflated net product at market price.[3]

Total Factor Price and Productivity

Between 1919 and 1957, total factor price more than tripled, which represents an average annual rate of advance of 3.4 per cent (see Chart 9). Average product prices went up by almost two-thirds over the same period, or at an average rate of 1.2 per cent a year. Therefore, the increase in real income per unit of total factor input amounted to 119 per cent—2.1 per cent a year on the average. By definition, the increase in real income per unit of total factor input is identical with the increase in total factor productivity, and both may be derived as the quotient of average total factor price and average product price (as defined above).[4]

Rough estimates for 1899–1919 imply an average annual rate of increase in total factor price of 5.2 per cent—more than in the succeeding thirty-eight years. But the average productivity advance of 1.1 per cent a year in the earlier period was significantly less than the later trend rate, and the average annual rise in the general-product price level was substantially greater—4.1 per cent compared with 1.2 per cent. Much of the increase occurred during the World War I period, but prices were already rising significantly by the turn of the century.

[3] See John W. Kendrick "The Estimation of Real National Product," *A Critique of the United States Income and Product Accounts*, Studies in Income and Wealth, Volume 22, Princeton University Press (for NBER), 1958. The implicit price deflators for the net product at factor cost and at market prices do not diverge substantially over the longer periods, as shown below. Nevertheless, for short-term analysis, I recommend the use of a market price index plus a reconciliation index to avoid possible misleading movements.

Implicit Price Deflators for Net Private Domestic Product,
Key Years, 1899–1957
(1929 = 100)

	At Market Prices	At Factor Cost	Ratio
1899	49.4	48.4	102.1
1919	108.4	107.5	100.8
1929	100.0	100.0	100.0
1937	82.1	78.9	104.1
1948	144.3	149.4	96.6
1957	172.5	171.9	100.3

[4] Let Y be total income, or product at factor cost, O the corresponding real product, and I the real factor input; then $O/I = Y/I \div Y/O$.

CHART 9

Private Domestic Economy: Factor Prices, Product Prices, and Productivity, Selected
Key Years, 1899–1957

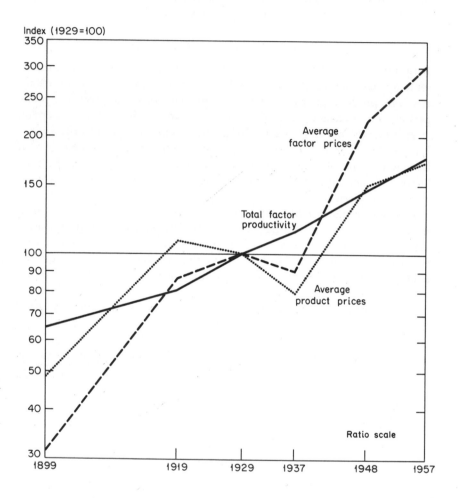

As shown in Table 25 and Chart 9, both price composites have risen
in the subperiods since 1937; in the subperiod 1929–37 both fell; from
1919 to 1929 factor price rose while product price fell. But whatever the
movement of average total factor price, it will exceed the average product
price movement in proportion to the productivity change, which is also
the measure of change in the real income per unit of total factor input.
Conversely, we may say that with any given increase in factor prices, the

movement of the general price level will be cushioned in proportion to the increase in productivity.

Although our estimates describe the relative movements of factor price, product price, and productivity, they do not permit us to explain the price movements. The latter is, of course, a very complex matter involving demand forces, monetary factors, supply elasticities, monopolistic pricing practices in product and factor markets, and other elements. Since many of the variables are interrelated in the sequence of price change, it would be very difficult to isolate the effect of individual elements, even if all the necessary detailed estimates were at hand.

Our estimates do permit us to analyze the movement of relative factor prices and, thus, relative changes in real income per unit of labor and capital input and in their shares of the national income and productivity increments. It is to these matters that the remainder of the chapter is devoted.

Relative Changes in Factor Prices and Income Shares

The index of total factor price is a composite. Each individual factor price may have changed by more or less than the weighted average of all. Average hourly labor compensation has changed in somewhat different proportions in the various occupational or industry groupings, and the price of capital has varied in different degree in the several industries. But the interindustry structures of wage rates and of capital compensation per unit have been relatively stable over time, in contrast to the marked difference in movement between the prices of the two major factor classes, labor and capital.

Between 1919 and 1957, average hourly labor compensation increased at an average annual rate of 4.0 per cent a year—more than double the 1.5 per cent average increase in the price of capital. The total increase over the thirty-eight years was 346 per cent in the case of labor rates compared with 77 per cent in the case of unit capital compensation. Reflecting the heavier weight of unit labor compensation, total factor compensation per unit rose by 250 per cent over the period, which reduces to an average annual gain of 3.4 per cent (see Table 27).

It will be noted that the 1.5 per cent average annual increase in the price of capital is somewhat higher than the rate of advance in average product prices generally. Since there was little trend in the rate of return on capital, the explanation lies primarily in a somewhat faster rise in the prices of capital goods as measured (especially plant) than in other final products. Insofar as the quality of capital goods increased more than the quality of other goods, the relative price rise is overstated.

In the earlier period, 1899–1919, the 5.2 per cent average gain in total factor price per year is a weighted average of 5.5 per cent for average hourly labor compensation and 4.2 per cent for capital compensation per unit. Since the relative increase in labor compensation per unit was less than in the subsequent period despite a faster growth of capital per man-hour, it may be inferred that innovation tended to be relatively more labor

TABLE 27

Private Domestic Economy:
Relative Factor Prices of Labor and of Capital, Key Years and
Subperiods, 1899–1957

| | Price per Unit of Factor Input | | | Reciprocal Ratios | |
| | Labor | Capital | Total | Labor to Capital [a] | Capital to Labor [b] |
	(1)	(2)	(3)	(4)	(5)
	INDEX (1929 = 100)				
1899	28.4	40.7	31.3	69.8	143.3
1919	84.6	92.6	86.7	91.4	109.5
1929	100.0	100.0	100.0	100.0	100.0
1937	100.3	65.3	90.1	153.6	65.1
1948	231.5	186.5	218.9	124.1	80.6
1957	377.2	163.7	303.5	230.4	43.4
	LINK RELATIVES				
1899–1919	297.9	227.5	277.0	130.9	76.4
1919–57	445.9	176.8	350.1	252.1	39.6
1919–29	118.2	108.0	115.3	109.4	91.3
1929–37	100.3	65.3	‿90.1	153.6	65.1
1937–48	230.8	285.6	243.0	80.8	123.8
1948–57	162.9	87.8	138.6	185.7	53.8
	AVERAGE ANNUAL PERCENTAGE RATES OF CHANGE				
1899–1919	5.5	4.2	5.2	1.3	−1.3
1919–57	4.0	1.5	3.4	2.5	−2.4
1919–29	1.7	0.8	1.4	0.9	−0.9
1929–37	0.0	−5.2	−1.3	5.5	−5.2
1937–48	7.9	10.0	8.4	−1.9	2.0
1948–57	5.6	−1.4	3.7	7.1	−6.7

SOURCE: Tables 25 and 26. Due to rounding, ratios may not exactly equal quotients of unit prices as shown.
[a] Col. (1) divided by col. (2).
[b] Col. (2) divided by col. (1).

saving in the earlier period. In this earlier period, the price of capital also showed a slightly greater increase than the general-product price level.

During the decade 1919–29, total factor price rose by 1.4 per cent a year—less than half its rate of increase over the whole period. The average increase in wage rates of 1.7 per cent was twice the average increase in the price of capital. Between 1929 and the submerged peak of 1937, wage rates barely held their own, while the price of capital, reflecting the incomplete recovery from the great depression, declined substantially. The next subperiod, 1937–48, was the only one in which the rate of increase in the price of capital exceeded that in the price of labor—10 per cent as compared with 8 per cent a year—a situation due both to the low 1937 base and to the postwar shortage of capital still prevailing at the high 1948 peak.

The relationship between factor prices reversed completely in the following period. Between 1948 and 1957, while the rate of increase in wage rates slowed somewhat, to a 5.6 per cent annual average, the price of capital declined absolutely as well as relatively. This reflected a decline in the rate of return on capital, since the prices of capital goods continued to rise.

Despite the decline in the actual average rate of return on capital in the postwar period, the expected marginal rate of return was still sufficient to induce a volume of new investment consistent with relatively full employment. In this connection, it should be noted that the early postwar rate of return on capital was abnormally high. But it is obvious that the rate of return could not continuously decline without dampening expectations and, thus, new-investment demand.

Assuming that the monetary authorities, with due regard for maintenance of high-level production, eventually pursue a policy permitting a stable or rising rate of return on capital, the partial offset to price inflation provided by a declining rate of return in the decade after 1948 would no longer operate. This would tend to promote a higher rate of advance in prices than in the 1948–57 period, unless productivity gains accelerate or the increase in wage rates relative to the price of capital slows as a result of changes in the variables we shall now examine.

THE INVERSE RELATION OF RELATIVE FACTOR PRICES AND QUANTITIES

Why has the relative price of capital fallen over most of the period under review? Two major influences stand out—one relating to the rate of return on capital and the other, to the prices of capital goods; the product of these two variables equals the price of capital as we define and measure it.

With respect to the first influence, the amount of net capital formation has been high enough secularly in this country to result in a significantly greater increase in real capital stocks and services than in the labor force and manhours worked. The law of diminishing marginal productivity states that under these circumstances, and in the absence of technological advance, the rate of return on capital will decline. Actually, technological advance has shifted the factor demand curves upwards; so there has been no pronounced trend in the rate of return to capital, while wage rates have risen more than the price level.

119

The second influence relates to the prices of capital goods. Increasing productivity in the capital goods industries, as in the economy generally, means that capital goods prices fall in relation to wage rates (or increase less), assuming relatively full employment and competitive conditions which tend to cause prices to approximate the cost of production per unit, and result in labor being paid in accordance with its (rising) marginal productivity. Since there has been no corresponding offset, i.e., no rising rate of return on capital over the long run, the decline in capital goods prices relative to wage rates is a built-in factor in dynamic economies that facilitates the substitution of capital for labor.

On the demand side, it is conceivable that inventions might be sufficiently capital-using (that is, require increasing quantities of capital relative to labor, given constant relative factor prices) to cause the demand for capital to increase more rapidly than the demand for labor. But if this has been the case (as distinguished from the substitution of capital for labor due to changing relative factor prices), the tendency has not been strong enough to offset the effect on relative price of the greater increases in the supply of capital than of labor—since the estimates show that wage rates have consistently risen relative to the price of capital in all periods when capital per unit of labor was rising.[5]

FACTOR SHARES IN NATIONAL INCOME

The national income accruing to each factor is the product of the quantity employed and its price (cost per unit). Aggregate national income is the sum of the compensations of all the factors. Thus, the share of each factor in total national income will vary in accordance with the net effect of changes in the quantity of the factor employed relative to total input, and in the price of the factor relative to average factor price.

It is apparent from Tables 26 and 29 that the input of capital rose substantially relative to labor input between 1899 and 1957 and in all subperiods except 1937–48. Between 1919 and 1957, the ratio of capital to labor input went up by 48 per cent. As a ratio to total factor input, the increase was only 32 per cent—since the marginal rate of substitution of capital for labor was more than three to one, based on the average weights accorded the two factors over the period. The ratios of the input of each factor to total factor input is shown in the first two columns of Table 28. From 1899 to 1919, the ratio of labor to total factor input had declined from 77 to 74 per cent; between 1919 and 1957 it fell further, to 66 per cent.

The decline in relative labor input was associated with a more than proportional increase in the price of labor services relative to total factor price. From 1899 to 1929, the ratio increased by 10 per cent; from 1929

---

[5] See Kravis, *op. cit.*, for further discussion of causal forces.

to 1957, the increase was 24 per cent (Table 28). Only in the subperiod 1937–48 did the relative price of labor decline. But in all subperiods, relative prices and relative inputs of the two factors moved inversely. Clearly, it was through relative price movements that the varying supplies of the two factors were absorbed by the productive system. That is,

TABLE 28

Private Domestic Economy:
Factor Shares of National Income, in Current and Constant Dollars,
Key Years, 1899–1957

	Distribution of Real Factor Cost in 1929 Prices		Relative Factor Prices[a]		Distribution of National Income in Current Prices	
	Labor	Capital	Labor	Capital	Labor[b]	Capital[c]
			(1929 = 100)			
	(1)	(2)	(3)	(4)	(5)	(6)
1899	76.9%	23.1%	90.7	130.0	69.9%	30.1%
1919	73.8	26.2	97.6	106.8	72.0	28.0
1929	72.3	27.7	100.0	100.0	72.3	27.7
1937	70.8	29.2	111.3	72.5	78.8	21.2
1948	72.0	28.0	105.8	85.2	76.2	23.8
1957	65.5	34.5	124.3	53.9	81.4	18.6

Source: Tables 26 and 27. Table may not be internally consistent due to rounding.
[a] Indexes of ratios of individual factor prices to total factor price (see Table 27).
[b] Col. (1) times col. (3).
[c] Col. (2) times col. (4).

producers achieved cost economies by substituting the factor that was becoming relatively cheaper for the one that was growing dearer as a result of changing relative supplies. Over the period since 1919, the ratio of the percentage change in relative factor inputs to the percentage change in relative factor prices was −0.2, as shown in Table 29. The elasticity of substitution varied considerably among the subperiods, however. Between 1899 and 1919, the coefficient was almost −0.5, whereas in the two decades since 1937, it has averaged about −0.3.

The last two columns of Table 28 show the net effect on income shares of the inverse movement of relative factor inputs and prices. There was little change in shares from 1899 to 1929. But after 1929, the decline in the relative input of labor was significantly smaller than the increase in relative labor price, and the share of labor increased from 72 per cent in 1929 to 81 per cent in 1957. The same percentages may be calculated directly from Table 26. Only in the subperiod 1937–48 did labor's share in the national income temporarily decline due to the peculiar circumstances described earlier. A picture of the movements of the several variables in key years since 1919 is given in Chart 10.

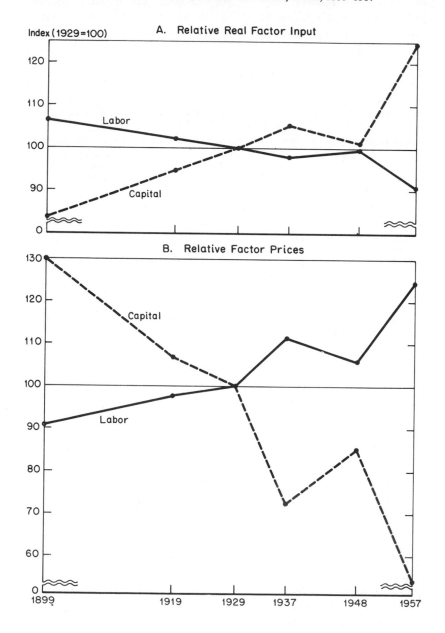

CHART 10

Private Domestic Economy: Relative Changes in Factor Inputs, Factor Prices, and Factor Shares of the National Income, Selected Key Years, 1899–1957

Relative inputs and prices are ratios of labor and capital inputs and prices to total factor input and price, respectively.

CHART 10, *continued*

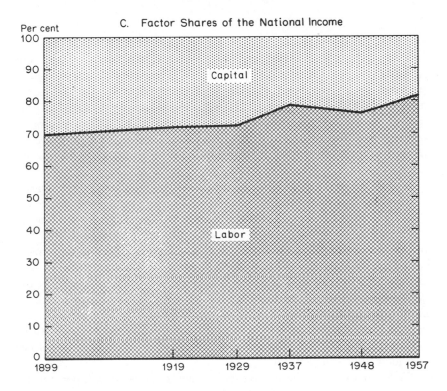

C. Factor Shares of the National Income

TABLE 29

Private Domestic Economy:
Relative Changes in Real Inputs and in Unit Compensations of the Factors,
Subperiods, 1899–1957
(link relatives)

	Real Factor Inputs			Unit Factor Compensations			Coefficient of
	Labor (1)	Capital (2)	Ratio (3)	Labor (4)	Capital (5)	Ratio (6)	Substitution[a] (7)
1899–1919	153	181	85	298	228	131	−0.48
1919–57	133	197	68	446	177	252	−0.21
1919–29	115	125	92	118	108	109	−0.89
1929–37	87	94	93	100	65	154	−0.13
1937–48	128	121	106	231	286	81	−0.32
1948–57	103	140	74	163	88	185	−0.31

SOURCE: Tables 26 and 27. Table may not be internally consistent due to rounding.
[a] [Col. (3) − 100] ÷ [Col. (6) − 100].

123

Relative Changes in Real Factor Compensation

REAL COMPENSATION PER UNIT

Once the prices of the factors have been calculated, it is easy to compute indexes of the real earnings per unit of each of the factor inputs. This involves dividing the factor prices (i.e., the current-dollar compensation per unit) by an index of the prices of products for which factor incomes are spent, directly or indirectly. For that index, we use the implicit price deflator for the net domestic product at factor cost. This index is composed of the prices of new capital goods and goods purchased by government, as well as consumer goods, although consumer goods have by far the largest weight.

It could be argued that labor income is distributed among these types of goods (i.e., among spending, saving, and taxes) somewhat differently than is the income accruing to the owners of capital; and, therefore, to measure the purchasing power of each type of compensation, different price indexes should be employed with weights based on the patterns of spending characteristic of each type of income. But both types of income are used for all the major types of final product, and it is statistically impossible to relate patterns of spending to type of factor income since most spending units do not receive a pure form of either. In any case, use of a different deflator would not substantially affect the results. Over the long period, 1919–57, the consumer price index increased by only 1 per cent more than our deflator.[6]

The results of deflating current-dollar factor compensation per unit by product price are shown in Table 30 in index number form. Since average hourly earnings increased substantially more than average compensation per unit of capital, it follows that the real increase in the former would also be greater. Between 1919 and 1957, real average earnings increased by 179 per cent, compared with an 11 per cent increase in real compensation per unit of capital. Between 1899 and 1919, the proportionate increase in real average hourly labor compensation was also much greater.

The gains in the real compensation of each factor can be compared with the gain in productivity, which may also be termed the gain in real income per composite unit of factor input (see Table 31 and Chart 11). The proportionate gain in the real average hourly earnings of labor was one-fourth greater than the percentage increase in productivity over the period since 1919, and between 1899 and 1919 the margin was even larger. The proportionate gain in real unit compensation of capital was

[6] Conceptually, a market price index would be preferable to our index at factor cost; but the differences between the two are minor and our index has the advantage of permitting precise definition of the relationships among productivity, prices, and unit factor costs.

CHART 11

Private Domestic Economy: Productivity and Real Income per Unit of Factor Input,
Selected Key Years, 1899–1957

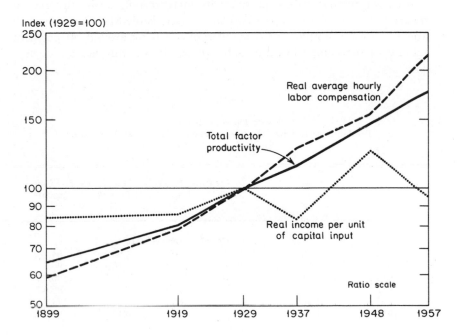

TABLE 30

Private Domestic Economy:
Derivation of Real Factor Income per Unit, Key Years, 1899–1957
(1929 = 100)

| | Current Income per Unit (Factor Price) | | Average Product | Real Income per Unit | |
| | Labor | Capital | Price | Labor[a] | Capital[b] |
	(1)	(2)	(3)	(4)	(5)
1899	28.4	40.7	48.4	58.7	84.1
1919	84.6	92.6	107.5	78.7	86.1
1929	100.0	100.0	100.0	100.0	100.0
1937	100.3	65.3	78.9	127.1	82.8
1948	231.5	186.5	149.4	155.0	124.8
1957	377.2	163.7	171.9	219.4	95.2

Source: Tables 25 and 27.
[a] Col. (1) divided by col. (3).
[b] Col. (2) divided by col. (3).

only about one-tenth of the productivity increase from 1919–57 and about the same in the earlier period.

The marked difference between the increases in real unit earnings of the two factors relative to the productivity increase reflects the differential movement in the prices of the two factors (see Table 31). Between 1919 and 1957, for example, the price of capital fell by around 50 per cent relative to the composite unit factor price. It was this relative decline

TABLE 31

Private Domestic Economy:
Productivity and Real Factor Income per Unit, Key Years and
Subperiods, 1899–1957

	Productivity[a] (1)	Relative Factor Prices Labor (2)	Capital (3)	Real Income per Unit Labor[b] (4)	Capital[c] (5)
	INDEX (1929 = 100)				
1899	64.6	90.7	130.0	58.7	84.1
1919	80.7	97.6	106.8	78.7	86.1
1929	100.0	100.0	100.0	100.0	100.0
1937	114.3	111.3	72.5	127.1	82.8
1948	146.5	105.8	85.2	155.0	124.8
1957	176.6	124.3	53.9	219.4	95.2
	LINK RELATIVES				
1899–1919	124.9	107.6	82.2	134.1	102.4
1919–57	218.8	127.4	50.5	278.8	110.6
1919–29	123.9	102.5	93.6	127.1	116.1
1929–37	114.3	111.3	72.5	127.1	82.8
1937–48	128.2	95.1	117.5	122.0	150.7
1948–57	120.5	117.5	63.3	141.5	76.3
	AVERAGE ANNUAL PERCENTAGE RATES OF CHANGE				
1899–1919	1.1	0.4	−1.0	1.5	0.1
1919–57	2.1	0.6	−1.8	2.7	0.3
1919–29	2.2	0.2	−0.7	2.4	1.5
1929–37	1.7	1.3	−3.9	3.0	−2.3
1937–48	2.3	−0.5	1.5	1.8	3.8
1948–57	2.1	1.8	−5.0	3.9	−3.0

SOURCE: Tables 25, 28, and 30. Table may not be internally consistent due to rounding.
 [a] Productivity index here differs slightly from that in the basic appendix tables because the input series was differently derived (see Table 25, note *b*).
 [b] Col. (1) times col. (2).
 [c] Col. (1) times col. (3).

that was associated with a smaller increase in real earnings per unit of capital than in productivity and made it possible for the real average earnings of labor to rise substantially more than the proportionate increase in productivity.[7]

Apparently, so long as capital services increase more rapidly than labor services and the price of capital rises less rapidly than wage rates, wage rates can rise somewhat faster than total factor productivity and still be consistent with a stable product price level. Beyond a point, however, increases in wage rates and the price of capital are associated with price inflation, as is indicated by this historical survey.

TOTAL REAL FACTOR INCOMES

Having estimated real income per factor unit by type, it is only necessary to multiply these estimates by the real input of each of the factors in order to obtain the total real incomes of each. The same result may be obtained by dividing the total current-dollar compensation of each of the factors by the product price deflator. But the more roundabout procedure of taking the product of the deflated unit compensations and inputs yields additional analytical material.

We already know that capital stocks and inputs rose in relation to labor input over the period under review. In absolute terms, between 1919 and 1957 labor input increased by one-third, while capital input almost doubled (Table 32). But we also know that relative changes in real income per factor unit were more pronounced and inverse to the relative input changes. Real capital compensation per unit rose by 11 per cent, while real unit labor compensation was up by 179 per cent over the thirty-eight-year period.

Putting the two variables together, we find that total real labor income rose by 270 per cent from 1919 to 1957, while real capital income rose by 118 per cent. Reduced to average annual rates of change, real labor income has grown by 3.5 per cent a year, or 1.4 percentage points more than the rate of growth of real capital income. The faster growth of real labor income prevailed in all subperiods except that of 1937–48.

The important fact is that the larger relative gains in real unit labor compensation more than offset the relative decline in labor input, leading to a greater rise in real labor income than in capital. The proportionate shares of the factors in real national income can be computed from Table 32, but these are the same as shown in Table 28 as computed from current-dollar national income, since the same price deflator was applied to both shares.

[7] For a fuller treatment of the real wage-productivity relation, see John W. Kendrick, "The Wage-Price-Productivity Issue," *California Management Review*, Spring 1960.

TABLE 32

Private Domestic Economy: Factor Inputs and Real Incomes 1899–1957

	LABOR			CAPITAL			TOTAL FACTORS		
	Input	Real Income Per Unit	Total^b	Input	Real Income Per Unit	Total^c	Input^a	Real Income Per Unit (Productivity)^a	Total (Product)^a
	(1)	(2)	(3)	(4)	(5)	(6)	(7)	(8)	(9)
	MILLIONS OF 1929 DOLLARS AND INDEX (1929 = 100)								
1899	$33,878	58.7	$19,882	$10,176	84.1	$8,556	$44,054	64.6	$28,438
1919	51,802	78.7	40,777	18,405	86.1	15,851	70,207	80.7	56,628
1929	59,749	100.0	59,749	22,920	100.0	22,920	82,669	100.0	82,669
1937	52,221	127.1	66,425	21,499	82.8	17,815	73,720	114.3	84,240
1948	66,859	155.0	103,594	25,968	124.8	32,397	92,827	146.5	135,991
1957	68,831	219.4	151,062	36,259	95.2	34,530	105,090	176.6	185,592
	LINK RELATIVES								
1899–1919	152.9	134.1	205.1	180.9	102.4	185.3	159.4	124.9	199.1
1919–57	132.9	278.8	370.5	197.0	110.6	217.8	149.7	218.8	327.7
1919–29	115.3	127.1	146.5	124.5	116.1	144.6	117.8	123.9	146.0
1929–37	87.4	127.1	111.2	93.8	82.8	77.7	89.2	114.3	101.9
1937–48	128.0	122.0	156.0	120.8	150.7	181.9	125.9	128.2	161.4
1948–57	102.9	141.5	145.8	139.6	76.3	106.6	113.2	120.5	136.5
	AVERAGE ANNUAL PERCENTAGE RATES OF CHANGE								
1899–1919	2.1	1.5	3.7	3.0	0.1	3.1	2.4	1.1	3.5
1919–57	0.8	2.7	3.5	1.8	0.3	2.1	1.1	2.1	3.2
1919–29	1.4	2.4	3.9	2.2	1.5	3.8	1.7	2.2	3.9
1929–37	-1.7	3.0	1.3	-0.8	-2.3	-3.1	-1.4	1.7	0.2
1937–48	2.3	1.8	4.1	1.7	3.8	5.6	2.1	2.3	4.4
1948–57	0.3	3.9	4.3	3.8	-3.0	0.7	1.4	2.1	3.5

SOURCE: Tables 25, 26, and 31. Table may not be internally consistent due to rounding.

^a Input and productivity series here differ slightly from those in the basic appendix tables because the input series was differently derived (see Table 25, notes a and b).

^b Col. (1) times col. (2).
^c Col. (4) times col. (5).
^a Col. (7) times col. (8).

Factor Shares of Productivity Gains

The fact that the labor share of national income rose in relation to the labor proportion of factor input implies that the labor share of productivity gains during the period was larger than its share of the national income at the beginning of the period. The estimates in Table 32 permit us to calculate the factor shares of the productivity increment, as shown in Table 33 for the period since 1919.

TABLE 33

Private Domestic Economy:
Factor Shares in Productivity Gains, Subperiods, 1919–57
(millions of 1929 dollars)

	1919–1957	1919–1929	1929–1937	1937–1948	1948–1957
Total					
1. Change in real income (product)	+128,964	+26,041	+1,571	+51,751	+49,601
2. Change in factor input	+34,883	+12,462	−8,949	+19,107	+12,263
3. Productivity gain (1 − 2)	+94,081	+13,579	+10,520	+32,644	+37,338
Labor					
4. Change in real income	+110,285	+18,972	+6,676	+37,169	+47,468
5. Change in input	+17,029	+7,947	−7,528	+14,638	+1,972
6. Labor gain (4 − 5)	+93,256	+11,025	+14,204	+22,531	+45,496
7. Labor share of total productivity gain (6 ÷ 3)	99.1%	81.2%	135.0%	69.0%	121.8%
Capital					
8. Change in real income	+18,679	+7,069	−5,105	+14,582	+2,133
9. Change in input	+17,854	+4,515	−1,421	+4,469	+10,291
10. Capital gain (8 − 9)	+825	+2,554	−3,684	+10,113	−8,158
11. Capital share of total productivity gain (10 ÷ 3)	0.9%	18.8%	−35.0%	31.0%	−21.8%

SOURCE: Changes in real income and input computed from estimates shown in Table 32.

For this purpose, we may estimate the real income resulting from productivity advance between two periods as the difference between the increment to real product and the increment to real factor input (cost).[8] Total factor input is an approximation to what real product would have been in the absence of productivity gain, since the volumes of inputs are weighted by the constant, base-period product (at factor cost) accruing

[8] This procedure is also suggested in the United Nations report, *A System of Price and Quantity Indexes for National Accounts*, Economic and Social Council, E/CN.3/C.46, New York, December 27, 1957 (mimeographed, limited distribution).

to each type of factor. Thus, to the extent that actual real product rises more than factor input, the difference represents that part of the increase in real product resulting from productivity advance.

Similarly, the increment to the real income of each of the factors is compared with its input increment. Real labor input, for example, indicates what the real income of labor would have been had there been no change in real compensation per manhour. The excess of increments to actual real labor income over increments of real labor input is one measure of labor's share in the total gain in real income due to productivity advance. The same reasoning holds for capital input.

Since the real incomes of each of the factors add up to total real product at factor cost, and since the inputs of each add to total factor input, the excess of real income of each factor over the real input adds up to the total productivity increment. Thus, the real income gain of each factor may be expressed as a proportion of the over-all productivity gain. It should be noted that one factor may appropriate more than the total productivity gain if the real unit income of the other factor actually declines in a given period.

Over the entire period, 1919–57, labor obtained 99 per cent of the productivity increment (Table 33). This is consistent with the increase in labor's share of the national income from 72 per cent in 1919 to 81 per cent in 1957, in contrast to its declining proportion of real factor input.

The only period in which labor's share of the productivity increment was less than its share of national income in the initial year was 1937–48. Between these years, labor commanded only 69 per cent of the productivity gain, and its share of national income declined from 79 to 76 per cent. In two of the periods, 1929–37 and 1948–57, labor obtained more than the total productivity increment. These were periods during which the rate of return on capital actually dropped—in the first, because of incomplete recovery from depression, and in the second, because of the readjustment from a condition of postwar capital shortage to a more normal situation. The estimates for the early period are not good enough for this sort of calculation, but the relative factor price movements indicate that the result would be similar to that obtained for the later period.

The mathematics of this approach indicates that labor would get the total productivity increment if the real compensation of capital per unit showed no change. Since the price of capital is the product of the average price of capital goods and the rate of return on capital, this would happen under two circumstances: first, if the average price of capital goods showed the same movement as average final product prices generally; and second, if the rate of return on capital remained constant. That capital obtained some of the productivity increment was due to a small relative increase in capital goods prices, not entirely offset by a slight decline in the rate of return on capital between 1919 and 1957.

PART III

Productivity Change by Industry

CHAPTER 6

Patterns of Productivity Change
by Industry Groupings

THE economy productivity measures are, in effect, weighted averages of productivity indexes for the component industries. Just as it was necessary to look at the aggregates for the macroeconomic analysis contained in Part II, so it is informative to disaggregate and look at the diverse productivity movements in the various industries. Not only do the industry productivity indexes reveal the sources of national productivity advance by industry of origin, but relative changes in productivity by industry can be related to relative changes in other variables in order to increase our understanding of causal factors and of the impact of productivity changes on the economic structure (treated in Chapter 7).

This chapter is primarily a summary description of productivity movements in the various industrial groupings of the private domestic economy between 1899 and 1953 and in the six component subperiods. Estimates of total factor productivity and the partial productivity ratios are available for five major segments of the economy and for thirty-three industrial groups within the five segments. Output per manhour measures are also available for three other major segments, for many Standard Industrial Classification 4-digit industries within the twenty manufacturing groups, for twelve groups within the farm segment, and for additional transportation industries.

As the analyst leaves the measures of productivity for the total economy and examines those for the industrial groupings, he is struck first by the considerable diversity of productivity movement. The industry rates of productivity change, while tending to cluster about their mean, show a considerable range of dispersion. The dispersion is markedly greater in the subperiods than it is over the long period, 1899–1953, and it is somewhat greater for the two partial productivity ratios than it is for total factor productivity. As would be expected, dispersion becomes greater the finer the industry detail that is subjected to analysis.

Consistent with these observations, variations in movements of the productivity ratios over the subperiods are greater for the industry groupings than for the economy as a whole; and variability tends to increase the more detailed the industrial classifications. The total factor productivity measures, however, tend to show less variability than the

133

partial productivity ratios. This indicates a positive correlation between relative changes in output per unit of labor input and in capital per unit of labor input.

Yet, despite the diversity of industry productivity movements, one is impressed by the strength and breadth of the underlying forces promoting productivity advance. Over the long period, no segment or group and very few individual industries experienced productivity declines. Even in the subperiods, productivity gains predominated heavily. Nevertheless, the difference in rates of productivity change is an intriguing topic for further investigation. Although we do not attempt a full-scale statistical explanation of industry differentials, in the concluding section of the chapter we speculate about some possible causal forces with reference to exploratory statistical studies.

Total Factor Productivity

SECULAR RATES OF CHANGE

Rates of change in total factor productivity are contained in Table 34. Over the long period, 1899–1953, the average annual rates of increase in the major segments range from 1.1 per cent in farming (on a net output basis) to 3.6 per cent in communications and public utilities. Mining and manufacturing each show about a 2 per cent yearly rate of advance, as does the covered sector as a whole, while transportation registers about 3 per cent (see Chart 12). Analysis of the interrelationships between relative changes in productivity and associated variables is deferred until the concluding section, but it may be helpful to mention here that there is a significant positive correlation between productivity and output changes. The ranking of the segments with respect to productivity change roughly corresponds to their ranking with respect to the growth of output.

Direct estimates of outputs and total factor inputs are available only for these five segments and their components; these accounted for 54 per cent of private domestic income in 1953. Since productivity estimates are available for the total private domestic economy, however, implicit estimates for the uncovered sector may be derived. Over the fifty-four-year period, total factor productivity grew at an average annual rate of 2.1 per cent in the covered sector compared with 1.7 per cent in the private domestic economy. This implies a 1.3 per cent rate of growth in the uncovered sector, which consists mainly of trade, finance, services, and construction. The estimate is necessarily crude, for reasons given in Appendix A; but the lower rate of growth in the residual area is consistent with direct estimates of real product per manhour for the component segments.

CHART 12

Private Domestic Economy: Total Factor Productivity, by Segment, Key Years, 1889–1953 (1929=100)

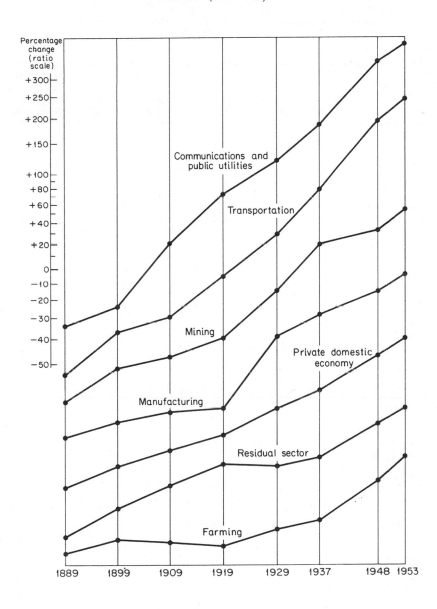

135

TABLE 34

Private Domestic Economy: Average Annual Rates of Change in Total Factor
Productivity, by Segment and by Group, with Measures of Dispersion,
Subperiods, 1899–1953
(per cent)

	Pre-1899	1899–1909	1909–1919	1919–1929	1929–1937	1937–1948	1948–1953	1899–1953	Mean Deviation of Subperiod Rates from Secular Rate
Farming	0.9	−0.2	−0.3	1.2	0.8	2.7	3.7	1.1	1.1
Mining	1.4	0.8	1.4	3.5	4.3	1.0	2.9	2.2	1.3
Metals		1.1	2.2	3.8	4.3	2.3	−2.6	2.2	1.3
Anthracite coal		−0.4	0.5	0.0	4.3	0.6	−0.3	0.7	1.0
Bituminous coal		1.2	1.8	2.4	1.0	0.3	3.9	1.6	0.8
Oil and gas		1.3	0.9	5.5	8.1	0.5	3.8	3.0	2.5
Nonmetals		1.6	0.4	5.9	0.7	4.4	1.2	2.6	2.0
Manufacturing	1.4	0.7	0.3	5.3	1.9	1.6	2.5	2.0	1.3
Foods		0.3	−0.4	5.3	1.5	1.5	2.2	1.7	1.5
Beverages		0.9	−5.6	−0.2	15.2	1.7	0.9	1.6	4.0
Tobacco		1.2	4.9	4.4	6.3	2.8	0.7	3.5	1.7
Textiles		1.1	0.9	2.9	4.6	2.5	2.6	2.4	1.0
Apparel		0.7	2.7	4.0	2.5	−0.7	1.3	1.7	1.4
Lumber products		−0.4	−1.2	2.5	0.4	2.2	3.8	1.0	1.5
Furniture		−0.8	−0.5	4.2	0.5	3.2	1.7	1.4	1.8
Paper		2.4	0.3	4.7	4.3	1.0	1.6	2.3	1.5
Printing, publishing		3.9	3.0	3.7	2.6	0.6	1.5	2.6	1.0
Chemicals		0.7	−0.7	7.4	3.0	3.7	4.1	2.9	2.2
Petroleum, coal products		0.7	−1.0	8.6	2.7	1.0	3.0	2.4	2.5
Rubber products		2.3	7.4	7.7	4.0	0.7	2.1	4.1	2.5
Leather products		0.1	0.5	2.9	3.6	0.4	0.0	1.2	1.3
Stone, clay, glass		2.2	0.7	5.7	2.3	2.0	2.4	2.6	1.2
Primary metals		2.7	−0.5	5.5	−1.3	3.2	0.5	1.9	2.1
Fabricated metals		2.3	1.8	4.6	1.0	1.6	5.1	2.6	1.2
Machinery, nonelectric		1.0	0.7	2.9	2.3	1.2	2.6	1.7	0.8
Electric machinery		0.6	0.3	3.5	3.2	2.1	5.0	2.2	1.3
Transportation equipment		1.1	7.0	8.4	−0.4	0.9	3.7	3.5	3.1
Miscellaneous		0.8	−0.6	4.6	2.9	2.0	3.0	2.0	1.4
Transportation	3.3	0.9	3.2	3.1	4.1	4.7	3.3	3.2	0.9
Railroads		1.8	3.4	1.9	1.7	3.6	2.7	2.6	0.8
Local transit		1.1	2.7	4.1	2.5	5.2	−4.3	2.5	1.8
Residual transport		−1.2	1.5	7.4	8.8	3.9	5.5	4.0	2.9

(continued)

TABLE 34 (concluded)

	Pre-1899	1899–1909	1909–1919	1919–1929	1929–1937	1937–1948	1948–1953	1899–1953	Mean Deviation of Subperiod Rates from Secular Rate
Communications and public utilities	1.2	4.6	3.7	2.5	3.3	4.3	2.7	3.6	0.7
Telephone		4.8	1.9	1.6	2.4	0.9	0.5	2.0	1.1
Telegraph		1.5	−1.2	4.3	2.1	2.1	2.4	1.8	1.2
Electric utilities		5.2	8.2	2.5	5.0	6.6	5.0	5.5	1.4
Manufactured gas		4.1	5.0	3.2	1.6	6.7	8.8	4.7	1.7
Natural gas		0.0	1.1	0.2	3.7	5.5	1.6	2.0	1.9
Residual sector	0.8	1.7	1.5	−0.1	0.8	2.2	2.3	1.3	0.7
Private domestic economy	1.2	1.2	1.1	2.0	1.6	2.3	2.7	1.7	0.5
Aggregate of 5 covered segments	1.6	0.7	0.8	3.7	2.3	2.4	2.9	2.1	1.0
Mean deviation from sector rates:									
5 segments	0.5	0.5	1.1	1.6	0.9	1.0	0.4	0.5	
33 groups		1.0	1.6	1.8	1.3	1.0	1.1	0.6	

Turning to the thirty-three industry groups for which total factor productivity estimates are available, we find a greater dispersion of trends. Over the long period, the average annual rates of productivity advance range from 0.7 per cent in anthracite coal mining to 5.5 per cent in electric utilities.

Within each of the four segments from which the group detail presented in Table 34 is drawn, the degree of dispersion is also pronounced (see Table 46 for statistical measures of dispersion). Within mining, average annual rates of advance range from less than 1 per cent for anthracite coal to 3 per cent for crude petroleum and natural gas. In manufacturing, the range is from 1 per cent for lumber products to 4 per cent for rubber products. Within transportation, both railroads and local-transit lines average a gain of about 2.5 per cent a year; but residual transportation, which includes motor transport, waterways, airlines, and pipe lines, averages 4 per cent a year. In the public utility segment, the range of the annual increase is from 1.8 per cent in the telegraph industry to 5.5 per cent for electric utilities.

A more graphic picture of the dispersion in the average annual rates of productivity change is given by the frequency distribution in Table 35

137

TABLE 35

Thirty-three Industry Groups: Frequency Distributions of Average Annual Rates of Change in Productivity Ratios, Subperiods, 1899–1953

Class Interval (per cent)	Total Factor Productivity							Output per Unit of Labor Input							Output per Unit of Capital Input						
	1899–1953	1899–1909	1909–1919	1919–1929	1929–1937	1937–1948	1948–1953	1899–1953	1899–1909	1909–1919	1919–1929	1929–1937	1937–1948	1948–1953	1899–1953	1899–1909	1909–1919	1919–1929	1929–1937	1937–1948	1948–1953
Under −5.0			1							1						1					4
−5.0 to −4.0							1										1				1
−4.0 to −3.0														1		1					1
−3.0 to −2.0			3		1		1			1						7	5	1	3		2
−2.0 to −1.0										1						7	7	2	1	1	5
−1.0 to 0		5	6	2	6	1	1		3	5	2	3	1	4		5	5	3	2	2	3
.0 to 1.0	1	8	9	1	3	10	5	1	4	8	3	6	9	5	4	5	4	2	1	4	3
1.0 to 2.0	12	11	4	3	9	4	6	10	15	4	8	2	7	8	5	2	4	2	4	8	6
2.0 to 3.0	14	5	3	6	4	9	7	14	5	5	5	9	7	6	17		1	6	5	6	3
3.0 to 4.0	3	1	2	5	5	4	7	4	5	3	1	3	4	2	4	2	3	6	6	1	1
4.0 to 5.0	2	2	1	7	1	1	1	2			6	5	1	3	1	2		5	3	2	2
5.0 to 6.0	1	1	1	5	1	2	3	1		1	2	1	2	2	2	1		4	4	3	1
6.0 to 7.0						2				2	2	2	2					1	2	4	2
7.0 to 8.0		2	2	2	1			1	1	1	3	1	1	1							
8.0 to 9.0		1	1	2	1		1				1						1	1		2	
9.0 and over					1			1	2			1							2		

CHART 13

Thirty-three Industry Groups: Divergence of Total Factor Productivity,
1953 Relative to 1899

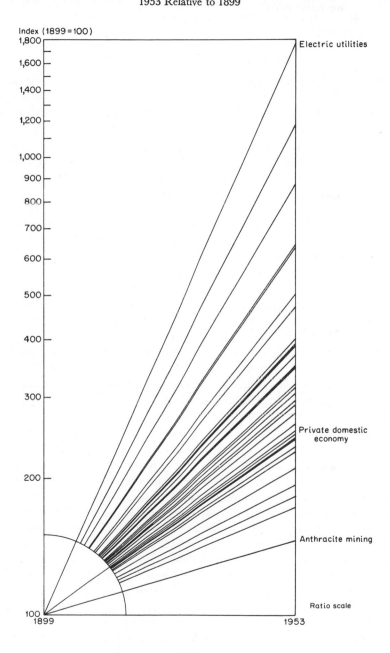

(first column) and Chart 13. The average annual rates are concentrated in the 1.0 to 3.0 per cent class intervals, but the distribution is somewhat skewed to the right. No group experienced secular declines in productivity, and six groups had gains that averaged more than 3 per cent a year over the long period.

PATTERNS OF PRODUCTIVITY MOVEMENT

Although we have been speaking of average annual rates of change, the course of productivity advance is not a smooth one. Between key years, rates of productivity change differ in each of the segments to a considerably greater extent than in the economy as a whole, and variability is even greater in the industry groups. Nevertheless, the major segment indexes show no actual declines in any of the subperiods except for a slight sag in farming prior to 1919. Among the groups, almost half show declines in one, or occasionally two, of the six subperiods.

As would be expected, annual changes in productivity exhibit still greater variability than average rates of change in the subperiods; and declines are more frequent on an annual basis, especially in periods of business recession. Due to the small number of total productivity series available on a yearly basis, annual fluctuations of all three productivity ratios are treated together in a later section of this chapter.

Each industry segment and group has had a unique pattern of productivity movement over the long period. The different group rates of change in the subperiods have tended to be offsetting in their effect on productivity change in the economy as a whole. The marked acceleration of productivity advance in the economy after 1919, for example, was not the result of acceleration in all groups at the same time, but rather a matter of "rolling acceleration" relative to pre-1919 rates of growth.

Thus, in terms of the segments shown in Chart 12, manufacturing and mining showed pronounced acceleration of productivity advance after 1919; but this lasted for only a decade in manufacturing and until 1937 in mining. Beginning around 1937, productivity advance accelerated in farming and in the residual service area, offsetting lower rates of advance elsewhere. Productivity gains in transportation were strong throughout the entire period after 1909, and especially so in the World War II subperiod. Persistently strong advance was already evident around 1899 in the communications and public utilities segment.

Productivity movements have not been graphed for the thirty-three groups, but to give a little more of the flavor of the industry patterns, we shall give a short summary of how they conform to or depart from the broader segment patterns. Variability in productivity changes over the subperiods was a little greater for the thirty-three industry groups, on the average, than for the five segments, as shown in Table 34. A few groups

140

showed even steadier rates of gain than the segments of which they are a part; examples include bituminous coal, nonelectric machinery, and the steam railroads. But, in general, group variability was somewhat higher and the greater stability in segment rates of advance was due to offsetting changes in rates of advance of the component groups.

In the mineral industries, the 1919–37 acceleration was widespread. Deceleration after 1937 was most marked in the metals group, which showed an absolute drop in total productivity in the 1948–53 subperiod. Only in bituminous coal was the rate of efficiency gain higher in the last subperiod than in any preceding. Yet it is too early to say that the tendency towards diminishing returns in the mineral industries is drawing ahead in the race with technological progress.

About half of the manufacturing groups followed the segment pattern of a slow rate of productivity advance between 1899 and 1919, marked acceleration in the 1920's, and a more moderate upward trend since 1929. In printing and publishing, however, a high rate of productivity advance was already evident in the first subperiod, 1899–1909; it continued through 1929, with some deceleration thereafter. Acceleration began in the 1909–19 subperiod for tobacco manufactures, apparel, rubber products, and transportation equipment. In the case of the latter two groups, this obviously reflected the dynamic early phase of the automobile era; productivity in both groups showed marked deceleration after 1929, although there was an improved rate of advance after 1948. The tobacco and apparel groups continued with higher-than-average productivity advance through 1937, but with deceleration thereafter. Some groups have shown their most rapid productivity growth since World War II, notably electric machinery, chemicals, and lumber products—influenced, no doubt, by high investment demand.

Within the transportation segment, which experienced a rather consistent upward trend, steam railroads showed accelerated average rates of productivity advance averaging around 3.5 per cent a year in each of the World War subperiods. Since 1948, the average annual rate of gain has been 2.7 per cent, close to the secular rate. The local transit group, consisting of electric railways and bus lines, showed almost as large a long-run rate of growth as steam railroads; but following acceleration during the World War II subperiod, there was an actual decline in both productivity and output after 1948. The residual transportation group has shown rapid productivity gains since World War I, as motor transportation, pipe lines, and finally airlines have become of increasing importance relative to waterways and the vanishing horse-drawn vehicle. Although rates of gain in this group are now below the 8 per cent annual average in the interwar period, the 5.5 per cent average rate between 1948 and 1953 keeps it one of the most technologically dynamic areas in the economy.

In the public utility segment, the smallest temporal variations in productivity advance relative to trend were in the electric utility group. Advances were consistently well above the economy average, although a very high rate of advance between 1909 and 1919 was succeeded by considerable deceleration in the following decade. Variations were also relatively small in the manufactured gas group, which showed advances in excess of the economy average in all subperiods after 1899. There was some deceleration in the 1929–37 subperiod, coincident with a drop in output. But in the 1948–53 subperiod, when output again declined, productivity showed its most rapid advance—averaging 8.8 per cent a year. The greatest relative variability in the segment was shown by the natural gas group. Production increased sharply after 1899, but productivity showed small gains prior to 1929. Large productivity increases between 1929 and 1948 were followed by more modest gains.

In the telephone industry, the largest productivity advances came in the early decades, and the smallest advances have been experienced since 1937—although this may be due partly to incomplete measurement of output (see Appendix H). Productivity advance in the telegraph industry has been steadily but moderately upwards since 1889, with the exception of a drop in the 1909–19 subperiod that was compensated for in the following decade.

MEASURES OF VARIABILITY AND DISPERSION

If one wishes to pin down the variability of subperiod rates of change in productivity, it is possible to measure the mean deviation of these rates from the long-term rate for each group or segment. These measures are shown in the last column of Table 34 and are summarized in Table 47. It can be seen that the mean deviation of subperiod rates so defined is 0.5 per cent for the private domestic economy as a whole and 1.0 for the five-segment aggregate, and averages 1.4 for the groups.

Variability in a few groups, as measured by the mean deviation of subperiod rates of change from the secular rate, was as high or higher than the secular rate itself. This was the case in anthracite coal mining, lumber products, products of petroleum and coal, primary metals, and beverages. In the case of beverages, however, variability was largely the result of the depressing effect of prohibition on productivity followed by the temporary stimulation of repeal. There is a tendency for the coefficients of variation to be inversely correlated with the secular mean rates of productivity change in the groups and segments.

That variability of productivity advance has not been uniform among the various groups, but has tended to be offsetting, suggests a larger dispersion of segment and group rates of change in the subperiods than over the period as a whole. In fact, as shown in Tables 34 and 46, the

142

mean deviation of segment and group productivity changes in the sub-periods from their average are approximately twice as great as the mean deviations from secular rates of change. Mean deviations of group rates of change relative to rates of change for the segment to which the groups belong are also approximately twice as great in the subperiods, on the average, as for the long period. The greater dispersion of subperiod rates of change is roughly what one would expect from the law of averages.

A graphic picture of dispersion in the subperiods compared with the period as a whole can be seen in the frequency distributions in the first panel of Table 35. It is apparent that there are more extreme rates of change in the subperiods than over the long period. Subperiod rates range from negative values to values exceeding 8 per cent a year. There is much less concentration of rates of change in the 1.0 to 3.0 per cent class intervals than is the case with the secular rates of change.

The question naturally arises as to whether the degree of dispersion of group rates of change from their mean has tended to lessen over the sub-periods. If so, this would be some indication of a more rapid rate of diffusion of innovations from one group to others, or of more similar rates of innovation arising within the several groups, or both. The answer seems clear-cut with respect to the mean deviations of the segments or groups as percentages of the rates of change in the covered sector, i.e., the coefficients of variation. For convenience, the coefficients of variation, based on the data underlying Table 34, are given in Table 36. By the last two subperiods, 1937–53, the coefficients had fallen sharply from their values for the first two subperiods, 1899–1919. The decline was relatively

TABLE 36

Trends in Relative Dispersion (Coefficient of Variation[a]) of Changes in
Total Factor Productivity, Subperiods, 1899–1953
(per cent)

	Covered Sector		Groups by Segment			
	Segments	Groups	Manu-facturing	Mining	Trans-portation	Communi-cations and Public Utilities
1899–1909	0.66	1.39	1.26	0.34	1.05	0.38
1909–19	1.31	2.02	6.07	0.45	0.21	0.51
1919–29	0.42	0.48	0.28	0.42	0.60	0.50
1929–37	0.41	0.59	0.76	0.60	0.56	0.16
1937–48	0.42	0.42	0.56	0.89	0.06	0.38
1948–53	0.15	0.39	0.42	0.69	0.46	0.63

[a] Coefficients show mean deviations of segment and group rates of productivity change from sector rates of change as ratios to the latter.

TABLE 37

Thirty-three Industry Groups: Deviations of Ranks of Rates of Change in Productivity Ratios in Six Subperiods from Mean Ranks, by Group, 1899–1953

	Total Factor Productivity			Output per Unit of Labor Input			Output per Unit of Capital Input		
	Mean Rank	Mean Deviation	Mean Deviation as Per Cent of Mean	Mean Rank	Mean Deviation	Mean Deviation as Per Cent of Mean	Mean Rank	Mean Deviation	Mean Deviation as Per Cent of Mean
Farming	11.8	7.8	66	13.7	10.2	74	11.2	4.6	41
Mining									
Metals	17.7	6.3	36	17.2	6.1	35	19.0	7.7	41
Anthracite coal	8.7	7.6	87	7.5	7.0	93	13.3	8.0	60
Bituminous coal	14.2	8.8	62	12.7	7.9	62	10.5	4.3	41
Oil and gas	21.2	6.8	32	20.5	6.3	31	18.0	11.0	61
Nonmetals	18.0	9.0	50	18.8	6.5	35	18.2	6.2	34
Manufacturing									
Foods	13.2	4.9	37	12.7	4.7	37	16.7	5.8	35
Beverages	11.8	8.5	72	12.7	7.7	61	15.3	9.7	63
Tobacco	22.0	6.0	27	24.0	8.3	35	12.5	8.5	68
Textiles	20.0	4.0	20	18.7	4.7	25	19.0	6.7	35
Apparel	13.7	6.3	46	12.3	6.8	55	13.0	8.3	64
Lumber products	10.7	8.6	80	11.2	8.5	76	10.7	8.0	75
Furniture	11.8	7.5	64	10.5	7.3	70	14.3	6.0	42
Paper	19.2	7.5	39	18.3	6.3	34	16.3	1.6	10
Printing, publishing	18.0	7.3	41	16.8	8.1	48	20.3	6.7	33

(continued)

TABLE 37 (concluded)

Manufacturing (continued)									
Chemicals	20.3	8.9	44	21.2	8.2	39	20.2	4.8	24
Petroleum, coal products	16.5	8.2	50	23.0	8.0	35	15.0	9.3	62
Rubber products	22.7	7.8	34	22.2	7.1	32	21.3	6.7	31
Leather products	10.3	6.0	58	10.2	5.9	58	13.7	9.2	67
Stone, clay, glass	19.3	4.8	25	18.7	5.7	30	16.5	5.2	32
Primary metals	16.0	11.3	71	16.2	10.2	63	13.5	8.2	61
Fabricated metals	20.8	6.6	32	19.3	5.9	31	18.8	4.5	24
Machinery, nonelectric	14.3	2.4	17	14.3	2.7	19	15.0	6.0	40
Electric machinery	17.3	6.3	36	17.7	4.7	27	17.2	8.5	49
Transportation equipment	19.0	10.3	54	17.5	10.2	58	23.2	8.2	35
Miscellaneous	16.7	5.1	31	14.8	6.2	42	17.8	6.1	34
Transportation.									
Railroads	19.3	7.2	37	19.0	6.7	35	16.8	11.2	45
Local transit	18.0	6.3	35	16.3	7.1	44	22.0	10.0	67
Communications and									
Public Utilities									
Telephone	14.8	8.8	59	14.5	9.0	62	15.8	11.2	71
Telegraph	15.2	5.4	36	14.8	4.3	29	22.0	7.3	33
Electric utilities	27.5	6.2	23	27.8	7.6	27	26.0	5.0	19
Manufactured gas	25.2	9.1	36	25.2	7.4	29	25.5	7.7	30
Natural gas	15.8	9.2	58	20.8	6.2	30	12.3	7.7	63
Average	17.0	7.2	42	17.0	7.0	41	17.0	7.3	43

small between the midperiod, 1919–37, and the last two subperiods. The tendency towards less dispersion has been marked in the manufacturing segment; but the reverse tendency has prevailed in mining, possibly due to a differential impact of the tendency towards diminishing returns. Perhaps improvement of data has had some influence.

The foregoing discussion implies that the relative positions, or ranks, of the various groups have fluctuated over the subperiods. Variations in rank were indeed marked, as shown in Table 37. The groups were first ranked with respect to rates of change in the subperiods, number 1 being the group with the smallest rate of advance, and number 33, with the largest. The averages of ranks in the subperiods are, of course, higher for the low industries and lower for the high industries than the ranks over the long period due to the fluctuations in rank. On the average, the mean deviations of the subperiod ranks from the average rank for the subperiods was 7.2, or about 42 per cent of the average rank for the subperiods.

Further analysis suggests that there has been a tendency for the groups with low average ranks to improve their position over the subperiods, while the high-ranking groups have tended to slip in the scale. Table 38

TABLE 38

Average Ranks of Quartiles and Halves of Thirty-three Industry Groups
Classified with Respect to Secular Rates of Change in Total Factor Productivity,
Subperiods, 1899–1953

Thirty-three Industry Groups	1899– 1953	1899– 1909	1909– 1919	1919– 1929	1929– 1937	1937– 1948	1948– 1953
First quartile	4.0	6.9	10.2	9.6	13.9	13.2	15.5
Second quartile	12.5	19.1	15.2	15.9	13.9	16.8	11.8
Third quartile	21.0	18.8	16.9	20.0	18.9	19.8	18.4
Fourth quartile	29.5	23.0	25.6	22.1	21.1	17.9	22.1
Lower half	8.5	13.0	12.8	12.8	13.9	15.0	13.6
Upper half	25.0	20.8	21.0	21.0	19.9	18.9	20.2

shows that the most striking trend was the improvement over the subperiods in the average rank of the first quartile, so designated with respect to average rank over all subperiods. The second quartile tended to drop in average rank, but not enough to prevent the groups in the lower half from rising in average rank. Both of the upper quartiles, and the higher half as a whole, showed some decline in average rank over the period. This tendency is to be expected between two periods, and has been called the "regression effect";[1] but when it persists it represents a real change. The

[1] Milton Friedman and Simon Kuznets, *Income from Independent Professional Practice*, New York (NBER), 1945, pp. 331–332n.

analysis of ranks was made of the groups excluding residual transportation. This group had one of the lowest ranks prior to 1919, but since then it has had one of the highest. If it had been included, the trends noted above would have been accentuated.

Changes in the Partial Productivity Ratios

STATISTICAL INTERRELATIONSHIPS AMONG THE PRODUCTIVITY RATIOS

Rates of change in output per unit of labor input have averaged around 13 per cent higher than the corresponding rates of change in total factor productivity in the industry groups of the private economy over the long period, and the ranks of the industry groups with respect to both ratios have been quite similar. These similarities are the outcome of two forces. In the first place, the relative weight accorded labor in the calculation of total factor input has averaged about three times the weight of capital over the period as a whole; so the movements of total productivity are much closer to the movements of output per unit of labor input than to the movements of the output-capital ratio in almost all industries. Secondly, capital has risen in relation to manhours in almost all industries; so output per manhour in most industry groups, and output per unit of labor input (weighted manhours) in all the segments and the private economy as a whole, have risen more than total factor productivity. The differences between the proportionate changes in the two ratios in the various industry groups and segments are largely a function of differences in proportionate changes in real capital input per unit of labor input in each. That is, the differences between the output-labor and total factor productivity ratios reflects the substitution of capital for labor, obtained directly as the quotient of total input and labor input, or as the proportionate change in capital per unit of labor input multiplied by the percentage weight of capital.

To illustrate the relationship, take the average annual percentage rates of change (plus 100.0) for the total private domestic economy, 1899–1953. The proportionate increase in output per unit of labor input (101.95) divided by that in total factor productivity (101.72) is 100.2. The 100.2 indicates the degree of substitution of capital for labor and is obviously the quotient of the proportionate increases in total factor input and labor input (101.57) and (101.34). Since total factor input is the weighted average of the two factor inputs, the substitution of capital for labor can also be obtained by weighting the proportionate rate of increase in capital per unit of labor input by the relative weight of capital (0.8 × 0.25 = 0.2).

Output per unit of capital input in the various industry groups has risen by less than output per unit of labor input to the degree that capital has risen in relation to labor input. This can be illustrated with reference to link relatives for the private domestic economy. The average proportionate increase in output per unit of capital input (101.16) is the quotient of the proportionate increases in output per unit of labor input (101.95) and in capital per unit of labor input (100.78). Since capital per unit of labor input is the strategic variable in explaining the relationships among the productivity ratios, we shall first review briefly the movement of this ratio for the covered segments and groups.

TABLE 39

Private Domestic Economy: Average Annual Rates of Change in Capital per Unit of Labor Input, by Segment and by Group, with Measures of Dispersion, Subperiods, 1899–1953
(per cent)

	Pre-1899	1899–1909	1909–1919	1919–1929	1929–1937	1937–1948	1948–1953	1899–1953	Mean Deviation of Subperiod Rates from Secular Rate
Farming	0.6	0.8	0.7	0.0	0.0	3.4	7.8	1.7	1.8
Mining	4.3	1.1	1.3	2.6	−2.3	0.6	5.1	1.2	1.3
Metals		1.5	0.4	2.6	−3.3	−0.6	8.7	1.0	2.2
Anthracite coal		−0.6	1.0	0.9	3.0	−3.8	8.9	0.7	2.4
Bituminous coal		3.6	3.7	−0.9	−1.2	−1.5	14.4	1.9	3.5
Oil and gas		4.1	4.3	1.6	−3.3	2.4	−4.3	1.4	2.4
Nonmetals		0.8	0.6	4.9	−1.0	−2.1	4.5	1.0	2.1
Manufacturing	3.5	2.8	2.8	1.3	−0.6	−0.7	2.2	1.2	1.3
Foods		1.5	2.6	0.3	−2.4	0.0	1.3	0.6	1.2
Beverages		0.9	−1.9	1.8	−1.8	−0.6	3.3	0.0	1.6
Tobacco		4.1	6.0	8.7	2.5	6.4	0.6	5.2	2.1
Textiles		1.8	4.3	−2.4	−0.9	−0.4	5.4	0.9	2.4
Apparel		2.5	6.2	0.0	−3.4	2.2	3.6	1.8	2.3
Lumber products		3.3	1.8	4.0	−4.0	0.9	3.1	1.5	1.9
Furniture		2.2	1.5	1.6	−2.2	−3.7	1.7	0.1	2.2
Paper		4.1	1.2	2.0	0.7	−1.0	2.7	1.5	1.4
Printing, publishing		0.7	1.5	0.1	0.3	−0.5	−0.6	0.3	0.6
Chemicals		2.2	1.5	2.1	0.0	0.5	4.8	1.6	1.0
Petroleum, coal products		4.8	4.5	0.5	4.4	−1.2	2.8	2.5	2.2
Rubber products		3.5	4.0	4.4	−2.8	0.3	1.0	1.9	2.2
Leather products		3.2	2.7	−2.1	−2.7	−0.5	3.0	0.5	2.3
Stone, clay, glass		5.2	2.1	3.1	−2.5	−2.7	4.2	1.3	2.8
Primary metals		6.0	0.6	1.0	1.5	−2.7	6.2	1.6	2.5
Fabricated metals		4.0	1.3	2.4	−2.0	−0.6	1.0	1.1	1.6
Machinery, nonelectric		3.6	−0.3	0.4	−1.3	0.6	1.6	0.8	1.2
Electric machinery		3.7	−1.5	2.3	−1.8	0.9	2.1	0.9	1.7
Transportation equipment		1.3	3.4	3.0	0.7	−1.5	−2.7	1.0	1.8
Miscellaneous		2.3	0.0	5.0	−2.9	0.1	0.4	1.0	2.0

(continued)

TABLE 39 (concluded)

	Pre-1899	1899–1909	1909–1919	1919–1929	1929–1937	1937–1948	1948–1953	1899–1953	Mean Deviation of Subperiod Rates from Secular Rate
Transportation	−1.4	−1.3	1.4	2.0	4.1	−2.5	3.9	0.8	2.1
Railroads		−3.1	0.9	2.9	5.2	−2.1	6.1	1.0	2.9
Local transit		0.7	−1.4	−1.9	1.5	−3.3	−0.3	−1.0	1.5
Residual transport		2.1	7.8	0.5	3.4	−2.2	4.1	2.3	2.7
Communications and public utilities	1.1	−1.0	−0.3	−0.2	4.5	−1.6	6.2	0.6	2.2
Telephone		−2.1	−4.0	0.9	6.8	−1.4	7.5	0.4	3.3
Telegraph		0.6	−4.0	−1.7	4.1	−4.0	2.2	−1.0	2.6
Electric utilities		4.0	0.3	−1.1	2.9	−0.3	5.1	1.4	2.1
Manfactured gas		−1.3	2.1	−1.0	2.8	−1.8	1.4	0.1	1.7
Natural gas		7.6	3.6	4.7	2.3	−2.3	3.9	3.1	2.5
Residual sector	−0.9	−0.3	0.5	0.0	1.9	−2.4	2.4	0.2	1.2
Private domestic economy	0.8	0.5	1.1	0.8	0.9	−0.5	3.3	0.8	0.6
Aggregate of 5 covered segments	2.2	1.3	1.7	1.4	0.5	0.6	4.1	1.3	0.6
Mean deviation from sector rates:									
5 segments	1.9	1.4	0.9	0.6	1.7	1.6	1.9	0.2	
33 groups		1.8	1.4	1.5	2.0	2.0	3.0	0.5	

CAPITAL PER UNIT OF LABOR INPUT

In the covered sector as a whole, capital per unit of labor input rose at an average rate of 1.3 per cent a year over the period 1899–1953. This rate compares with an average increase of 0.8 per cent a year in the total private domestic economy. The comparison implies that capital per unit of labor input in the uncovered sector rose at an annual rate of about 0.2 per cent—less than the increase in any of the covered segments.

Over the long period, there was relatively little dispersion of the segment rates of change from their weighted mean (see Table 39 and Chart 14). Mining and manufacturing each showed average increases of 1.2 per cent a year; the increase in farming was greater, while the increases in the transportation and the public utility segments were somewhat under 1 per cent a year.

The dispersion of group rates of change in capital per unit of labor input was considerably greater than the dispersion of segment rates, but was less than the dispersion of group rates of change in total factor productivity.

CHART 14

Private Domestic Economy: Capital per Unit of Labor Input, by Segment,
Key Years, 1889–1953 (1929=100)

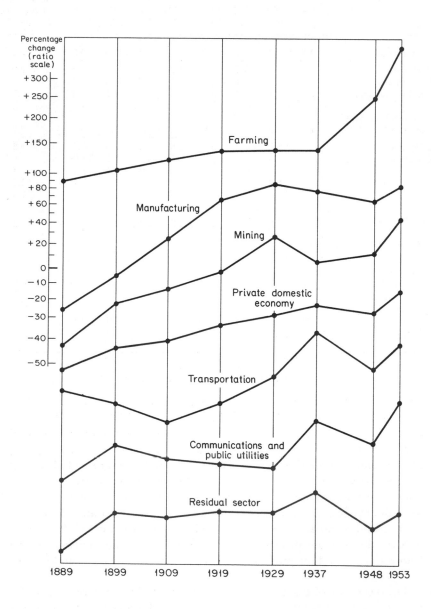

All but two of the thirty-three groups showed positive secular increases in capital per unit of labor input. Most of the group rates of increase clustered within the sector rate of increase of 1.3 per cent ± 0.6.

Significantly larger rates of increase in capital relative to labor input were shown by tobacco manufactures, natural gas utilities, and products of petroleum and coal. Very small rates of increase in the capital-labor ratio were evident in beverages, furniture, and manufactured gas utilities. The local transit and the telegraph groups each showed average declines of 1.0 per cent a year.

As would be expected, the subperiod rates of change in capital per unit of labor input fluctuated considerably in each of the groups. It will be recalled that in the private economy as a whole the rate of increase was fairly steady over the subperiods up to 1937; the subperiod 1937–48 was marked by a drop in the capital-labor ratio, while the years 1948 to 1953 saw an accelerated rate of advance. The pattern differs somewhat by industry groups. Declines in the capital-labor ratio characterized railway transportation from 1870 to 1909, and some of the communications and public utility groups in selected subperiods from 1899 to 1929, due to a prior build-up of plant and equipment beyond near-term requirements for output and labor input.

In the subperiod 1929–37, capital per unit of labor input dropped in the mining and manufacturing segments and in most of the component groups, although this was more than offset by increases in other segments. Apparently, the shorter life of equipment in these areas compared with transportation and public utilities made possible a quicker adjustment of capital stock to the decline in labor requirements experienced in this subperiod.

Between 1937 and 1948 declines in the capital-labor ratio were quite widespread as a result of wartime restrictions on civilian industry capital investment. A notable exception was farming, in which substitution of capital for labor was required to meet essential food and fiber needs because of the wartime farm labor shortage. A significant increase in capital per manhour in oil and gas production was also a major exception to the general tendency. In the 1948–53 subperiod, a substantial increase in capital per unit of labor input was quite general, only four groups showing declines.

Consistent with the large variability in subperiod movements, the dispersion of segment and group rates of change from the sector rate was much larger in the subperiods than over the period as a whole (see Table 46).

OUTPUT PER UNIT OF LABOR INPUT

Estimates of output per unit of labor input are available not only for the five covered segments and thirty-three groups, but also for three additional segments, a dozen groupings within farming, and eighty or more individual manufacturing industries. The behavior of labor productivity in the additional industries will be described, following a brief review of the covered area.

Covered segments and groups. There is no need to detail the movements of output per unit of labor input in the covered area, since they are quite similar to the patterns of change in total factor productivity, after allowing for the divergent movements of capital and labor inputs. Thus, with

TABLE 40

Private Domestic Economy: Average Annual Rates of Change in Output per Unit of Labor Input, by Segment and by Group, with Measures of Dispersion, Subperiods, 1899–1953
(per cent)

	Pre-1899	1899–1909	1909–1919	1919–1929	1929–1937	1937–1948	1948–1953	1899–1953	Mean Deviation of Subperiod Rates from Secular Rate
Farming	1.1	0.0	0.0	1.2	0.8	3.8	6.2	1.7	1.7
Mining	2.0	1.0	1.7	4.2	3.5	1.2	4.8	2.5	1.4
Metals		1.9	2.4	5.3	2.3	2.0	0.4	2.6	1.0
Anthracite coal		−0.4	0.5	0.0	4.3	0.1	0.5	0.7	1.1
Bituminous coal		1.2	2.0	2.4	0.9	0.0	5.7	1.7	1.1
Oil and gas		2.3	2.3	6.1	6.3	1.9	1.2	3.4	1.8
Nonmetals		1.9	0.6	7.8	0.4	3.5	2.9	2.9	2.0
Manufacturing	1.7	1.1	0.8	5.6	1.8	1.4	3.0	2.2	1.4
Foods		0.6	0.0	5.4	0.9	1.5	2.5	1.8	1.3
Beverages		1.3	−6.4	0.5	14.4	1.5	2.2	1.6	3.8
Tobacco		1.8	6.1	7.2	7.6	5.7	1.0	5.1	2.0
Textiles		1.4	1.7	2.4	4.4	2.3	3.9	2.5	0.8
Apparel		0.9	3.3	4.0	2.1	−0.5	1.7	1.9	1.4
Lumber products		−0.2	−1.0	3.0	−0.2	2.4	4.4	1.2	1.7
Furniture		−0.7	−0.4	4.3	0.3	2.6	1.9	1.3	1.7
Paper		3.0	0.5	5.1	4.5	0.7	2.5	2.6	1.6
Printing, publishing		4.0	3.3	3.7	2.7	0.5	1.4	2.7	1.1
Chemicals		1.3	−0.3	8.2	3.1	3.9	6.0	3.5	2.4
Petroleum, coal products		3.1	1.8	9.0	5.6	0.2	4.7	3.8	2.6
Rubber products		2.5	7.8	8.4	3.5	0.8	2.3	4.3	2.8
Leather products		0.5	0.9	2.5	3.2	0.3	0.5	1.3	1.0
Stone, clay, glass		2.8	1.0	6.3	1.7	1.3	3.3	2.7	1.5
Primary metals		3.8	−0.4	5.8	−0.9	2.5	2.1	2.3	2.0
Fabricated metals		2.9	2.0	5.1	0.5	1.6	5.2	2.7	1.4
Machinery, nonelectric		1.8	0.7	3.0	1.9	1.3	2.9	1.8	0.6
Electric machinery		1.3	0.0	4.0	2.9	2.3	5.5	2.4	1.3
Transportation equipment		1.3	7.7	9.1	−0.2	0.6	3.1	3.7	3.5
Miscellaneous		1.1	−0.6	5.5	2.2	2.0	3.1	2.1	1.4

(continued)

TABLE 40 (concluded)

	Pre-1899	1899-1909	1909-1919	1919-1929	1929-1937	1937-1948	1948-1953	1899-1953	Mean Deviation of Subperiod Rates from Secular Rate
Transportation	3.0	0.9	3.3	3.5	4.9	4.3	3.7	3.4	0.9
Railroads		1.1	3.6	2.6	2.9	3.2	3.7	2.8	0.7
Local transit		1.3	2.4	3.7	2.7	5.0	−4.4	2.4	1.7
Residual transport		−1.1	2.0	7.4	9.2	3.7	5.9	4.1	3.0
Communications and public utilities	1.7	4.1	3.5	2.4	5.5	3.7	4.6	3.8	0.7
Telephone		3.7	0.4	1.8	4.4	0.6	1.5	2.0	1.3
Telegraph		1.8	−2.4	3.9	2.8	1.9	2.5	1.6	1.5
Electric utilities		7.1	8.3	1.9	6.5	6.5	7.7	6.2	1.6
Manufactured gas		3.5	5.7	3.0	2.6	6.2	9.2	4.7	1.8
Natural gas		1.6	2.3	2.0	4.8	4.3	3.4	3.0	1.1
Residual sector	0.9	1.8	1.7	−0.1	1.1	1.8	2.7	1.4	0.8
Construction	1.5	4.3	−1.0	1.0	−0.5	0.5	3.6	1.1	1.6
Trade	0.6	1.5	0.4	1.1	1.6	2.2	1.8	1.4	0.5
Finance and services	1.8	2.0	1.6	−0.8	−0.9	3.0	2.6	1.2	1.4
Private domestic economy	1.4	1.3	1.5	2.2	1.8	2.2	3.4	2.0	0.5
Mean deviation of 8 segment rates from economy rate	0.5	0.7	0.8	2.2	1.3	1.0	1.0	0.6	
Aggregate of 5 covered segments	1.8	1.0	1.2	4.1	2.5	2.5	4.0	2.4	1.0
Mean deviation from sector rates:									
5 segments	0.4	0.4	0.9	1.5	1.3	1.3	1.2	0.5	
33 groups		1.0	1.8	1.8	1.4	1.2	1.6	0.6	

respect to the major segments, the differences between the long-period average rates of increase in total factor productivity and in output per unit of labor input were either 0.2 or 0.3 percentage points (compare Table 40 with Table 34, and Chart 15 with Chart 12). The larger difference, evident in farming, was not due to a higher rate of increase in capital per unit of labor input, but rather to a relatively larger weight accorded to capital because of the effect of net rents.

Among the thirty-three groups, differences between average annual rates of change in the output-labor ratio and total factor productivity were concentrated, for the most part, between 0.1 and 0.4 percentage points. In the local transit and the telegraph industries, output per unit of labor input rose slightly less than total factor productivity, since capital

CHART 15

Private Domestic Economy: Output per Unit of Labor Input, by Segment, Key Years, 1889–1953 (1929=100)

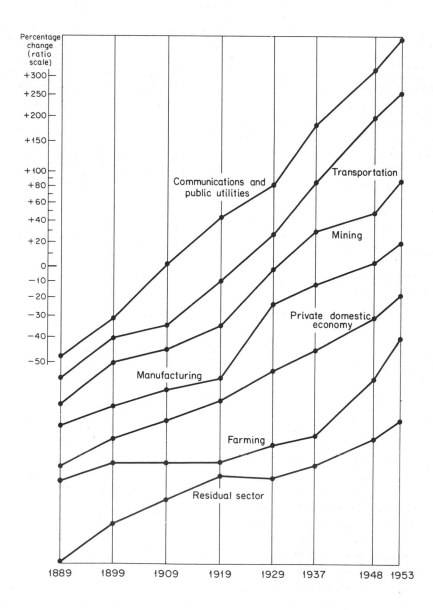

per manhour fell, as noted in the preceding section. In a few other groups, rates of change in both variables rounded out to the same amount due to small rates of increase in capital per manhour, or the small relative weight of capital, or both factors. On the other hand, several industries showed much larger average annual increases in output per unit of labor input than in total factor productivity. The largest percentage-point differences were 1.6 in tobacco manufactures, 1.4 in petroleum and coal products, and 1.0 in natural gas utilities. These are, of course, the groups in which capital per manhour rose most strongly.

Thus, the dispersion of group rates of change in output per unit of labor input was somewhat greater than that in total factor productivity, as measured in Table 46 and depicted in the frequency distributions of Table 35. The secular average annual rates of change in labor productivity ranged from 0.7 per cent for anthracite coal mining to 6.2 per cent for the electric utilities.

Despite different rates of change in the output-labor ratio and in total productivity, the ranking of the thirty-three groups was quite similar with respect to each. Several industries had significantly higher ranks with respect to labor productivity than with respect to total factor productivity because of relatively high rates of substitution of capital for labor. These include farming, natural gas utilities, petroleum and coal products, and tobacco manufactures. On the other hand, some groups stood lower with respect to output per unit of labor than to productivity, because of relatively low or negative rates of capital substitution; the telegraph and telephone, local transit, and printing and publishing groups are in this category. Electric utilities maintained top place in both rankings, although capital substitution was less than in some other groups. Anthracite coal mining stood at the bottom of both rankings, although capital substitution was positive.

Correlation of the ranks of the thirty-three groups with respect to both productivity ratios is highly positive (r = +.94, significant at the 1 per cent level). Thus, analyses of productivity change based on output-per-manhour measures should give results comparable to analyses based on total factor productivity. If available, measures of total productivity and the two partial productivity measures are, of course, preferable for analytical purposes, since they yield more information than output per manhour alone.

The movements of output per unit of labor input in the segments and groups are as described for total productivity, adjusted for movements in capital per unit of labor input appropriately weighted. The adjustment results in several major differences. In the first three subperiods, 1899–1929, labor productivity increased at rates that were generally higher than the rates of increase in total productivity, with the major exceptions found in transportation and in communications and public utilities, where the capital-labor ratio fell in one or more subperiods.

In the 1929–37 subperiod, labor productivity rose less than total productivity in most of the manufacturing and mining groups, because of a drop in the capital-labor ratio, and in the 1937–48 subperiod the smaller rise in labor productivity was widespread among all groups. In contrast, labor productivity rose substantially more than total productivity after 1948 in most groups because of large increases in the capital-labor ratio. With reference to the rates of advance recorded for total productivity after 1948 compared with the preceding period, acceleration, rather than deceleration, of gains in output per unit of labor occurred in the communications and public utility segment; deceleration was less marked in transportation; and acceleration was more marked in manufacturing, mining, farming, and the residual segments. In general, variability in the segment and group rates of change in output per unit of labor input over the subperiods was somewhat higher than that in total productivity. Subperiod dispersion was also greater, of course, as can be seen in the frequency distribution of Table 35, and in Table 46.

Residual segments. It will be recalled that total factor productivity of construction, trade, and finance and services as a whole could be estimated by a residual method. It is possible directly to estimate real product per manhour for each of the residual segments separately. The estimates, as shown in Table 40, indicate that real product per unit of labor input in each of the uncovered groups, as well as in the area as a whole, increased at a significantly lower rate than labor productivity in the private economy. According to our rough measures, the average annual rates of increase ranged from 1.1 per cent in construction to 1.4 per cent in trade.

In trade the rate of increase in output per unit of labor input over the subperiods was even steadier than in the covered segments. In contrast, variability was much greater in contract construction. Here, subperiod variations in rates of change in real product per manhour have been associated to some extent with the building cycle. There appears to have been little net gain in labor productivity in construction over much of the period, but the output estimates are undoubtedly subject to some downward bias (see Appendix E). Output per unit of labor input in the finance and services segment increased in all subperiods except those from 1919 to 1937.

It will be noted that there were larger-than-secular rates of advance in trade, finance, and services after 1937, and in construction after 1948. This acceleration of productivity advance in previously lagging segments of the economy is encouraging, if true. It must be stressed, however, that the real-product estimates for these segments are subject to a large margin of error, since they are derived from private real-product estimates, which are likewise somewhat unsatisfactory in this area due to inadequate price deflators.

Farm groups and regions. Although we have index numbers of total factor productivity only for the farm segment as a whole, index numbers of production per manhour have been prepared by the Department of Agriculture for the period from 1910 forward for twelve major groups of farm enterprises. These index numbers, based on gross production measures, show an average annual rate of increase per manhour between 1910 and 1953 of 2.3 per cent for the segment, contrasted with a 2.1 per cent rate of growth in our measures of net output per manhour.

Among the farm groups, the average annual rates of increase range from about 0.5 per cent for livestock and tobacco to 3.7 per cent for food grains and oil crops. In general, output per manhour has increased twice as fast for crops as for livestock and products (Table 41). The dispersion of the

TABLE 41

Farm Segment: Average Annual Rates of Change in Production per Manhour, by Groups of Enterprises, with Measures of Dispersion, Subperiods, 1910–53
(per cent)

	1910–1919	1919–1929	1929–1937	1937–1948	1948–1953	1910–1953	Mean Deviation of Subperiod Rates from Secular Rate
Livestock and products	0.3	0.5	−0.3	2.6	3.0	1.1	1.2
Meat animals	0.3	0.7	−0.4	1.2	1.2	0.6	0.5
Milk cows	0.5	1.1	−0.5	2.9	2.9	1.4	1.2
Poultry	0.0	0.7	0.7	2.1	5.4	1.4	1.2
Crops	0.7	0.8	2.0	4.9	3.2	2.3	1.5
Feed grains	0.6	0.9	1.8	7.0	7.1	3.3	2.8
Hay and forage	−0.2	0.7	1.3	4.3	4.4	2.0	1.8
Food grains	0.8	3.9	1.1	7.2	5.1	3.7	2.1
Vegetables	0.0	1.5	0.7	2.5	1.5	1.3	0.7
Fruits and nuts	2.8	1.5	2.3	0.8	2.4	1.8	0.7
Sugar crops	−1.0	2.2	1.1	2.6	7.7	2.1	1.7
Cotton	0.2	0.8	4.4	3.1	5.3	2.5	1.7
Tobacco	−0.5	−0.3	0.6	2.1	−0.2	0.4	0.9
Oil crops	−1.1	2.4	2.1	7.7	9.3	3.7	3.3
Total farm production per manhour	0.5	1.2	2.1	4.5	3.4	2.3	1.4
Mean deviation from total farm sector	0.7	0.8	0.9	2.0	2.3	0.9	

SOURCE: *Changes in Farm Production and Efficiency: A Summary Report*, Dept. of Agriculture, Statistical Bulletin No. 233, August 1958, Table 15. A revised edition was published in September 1959, too late to incorporate the revisions into this volume. Presented here, for comparison, are the revised rates of change for total farm production per manhour: 1910–19, 0.5; 1919–29, 1.5; 1929–37, 1.7; 1937–48, 4.8; 1948–53, 4.7; and for the long period (1910–53), 2.5.

group rates of change over the long period from their weighted average in farming is not much greater than in the nonfarm economy; the average deviation of group rates of change from their mean (2.3 per cent) is 0.9 per cent.

It will be seen in Table 41 that there was a definite acceleration in rates of advance over the subperiods from 1910 to 1948 in all groups except fruits and nuts. Tobacco was the only group in which there were declines in production per manhour in more than one of the subperiods. Whereas production per manhour in several major groups and the total showed a somewhat smaller advance in the 1948–53 subperiod than in the preceding subperiod, further acceleration was marked in poultry raising, sugar crops, cotton, oil crops, and fruits and nuts.

Variability of productivity changes in the farm segment was not significantly greater than in the other segments. The mean deviation of subperiod average annual rates of change from the secular rates was 1.4 per cent for the segment and 1.5 per cent, on the average, for the groups— almost precisely the same figures that apply in manufacturing. Apparently the weather and other relatively uncontrollable factors do not cause wider variations of productivity advance in farming than in other segments over intervals as long as the subperiods used in this study.

Farming is the only segment for which regional productivity indexes are readily available (Table 42). The dispersion of rates of change in production

TABLE 42

Farm Segment: Average Annual Rates of Change in Production per Manhour, by Geographical Division, with Measures of Dispersion, Subperiods, 1919–53
(per cent)

	1919–1929	1929–1937	1937–1948	1948–1953	1919–1953	Mean Deviation of Subperiod Rates from Secular Rate
New England	1.9	1.0	4.2	3.0	2.6	1.2
Middle Atlantic	1.3	2.2	3.7	3.7	2.6	1.0
East North Central	1.2	2.4	4.7	4.1	2.8	1.4
West North Central	1.9	0.7	6.2	2.3	3.0	2.1
South Atlantic	1.6	1.9	3.2	3.3	2.4	0.8
East South Central	1.2	2.6	3.1	2.5	2.3	0.6
West South Central	0.0	3.8	4.3	4.3	2.9	1.7
Mountain	3.1	1.1	5.3	4.0	3.5	1.3
Pacific	1.6	1.8	3.5	3.5	2.5	0.9
United States	1.2	2.1	4.5	3.4	2.8	1.3
Mean Deviation from Total Farm Sector	0.5	0.7	0.8	0.6	0.3	

CHART 16

Farm Segment: Divergence of Gross Production per Manhour

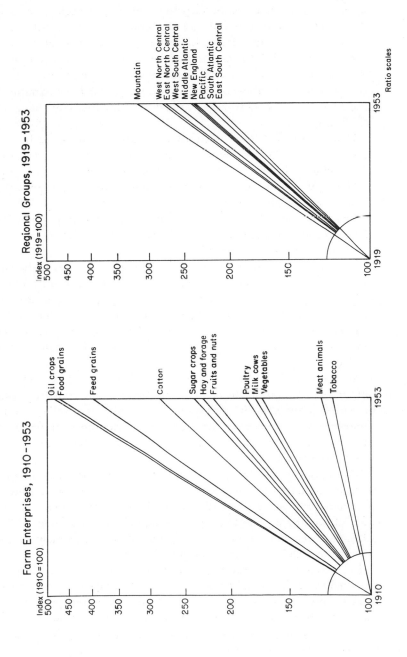

Farm Enterprises, 1910–1953

Regional Groups, 1919–1953

per manhour between 1919 and 1953 among the nine regions shown is only about one-third as great as the dispersion of group rates of change (see Chart 16). This is not surprising since most regions participate to some extent in most types of farming, although in different proportions.

Variability of productivity changes in the nine regional groupings was no greater than that for farming in the country as a whole from 1919 to 1953 (Table 42). The several divisions of the Central Region were the only ones to show above-average variability, which is undoubtedly associated with the above-average variability of productivity changes in food and feed grains.

Manufacturing industries. Output per manhour measures beginning in 1899 are available for eighty manufacturing industries, as defined by SIC 4-digit classifications or combinations thereof[2] (see Appendix Tables D-V and D-VI). The simple mean of the average annual rates of change in the eighty industries between 1899 and 1954 is 2.2 per cent, the same increase as in the manufacturing segment as a whole. The changes range from a few small negatives to a high of 5.8 per cent a year for cigars and cigarettes (see Table 43).

A frequency distribution of the average annual rates is shown in the first column of Table 44. It is similar to the frequency distribution of the group rates of change (see Table 35). About 70 per cent of the industries had rates of change between 1.0 and 3.0 per cent a year. The distribution is also somewhat skewed to the right, reflecting the greater tendency for industries to have high rates of productivity advance than to experience declines.

As measured by mean deviations, the dispersion of rates of change in output per manhour in the eighty industries is 50 per cent greater than the dispersion of the manufacturing-group rates of change. This confirms the impression that the greater the degree of industry detail in terms of which the productivity ratios are constructed, the greater the degree of dispersion —and also of variability.

The majority of the eighty manufacturing industries followed the segment pattern of movement. There was, generally, a slow rate of productivity advance from 1899 to 1919, and even some declines. This was followed by a period of relatively rapid advance in the 1920's. After 1929, however, most industries saw a rate of advance which was less than that of the 1920's but above the pre-1919 rate.

In a few industries, the higher rate of advance achieved in the 1920's persisted thereafter, as in fertilizers, paints, and cigars and cigarettes. In at least a dozen industries, the rate of advance in output per manhour was fairly steadily upward from 1899 on—as in canning of fruits and vegetables,

[2] In several instances, the measures of output per manhour for groups are used if no component-industry measure is available.

TABLE 43

Output per Manhour in Manufacturing Industries:
Average Deviations of Subperiod Rates of Growth and Ranks from
Subperiod Averages, 1899–1954

Industry	EIGHTY MANUFACTURING INDUSTRIES			
	Average Annual Rate of Change, 1899–1954	Average Deviation of Subperiod Rates	Subperiod Ranks	
			Average	Average Deviation
Cigars and cigarettes	5.8%	2.4%	63.0	18.3
Motor vehicles and equipment	5.0	5.8	41.0	26.0
Silk and rayon goods	4.6	2.2	61.3	17.6
Rubber products group	4.4	2.7	55.5	15.5
Chemicals, n.e.c., rayon, gases	4.3	2.1	62.2	12.4
Beet sugar	4.1	3.5	50.8	20.8
Canning, fruits and vegetables	4.1	0.8	63.5	8.7
Glass products	3.6	1.6	56.2	14.1
Blast furnace products	3.5	3.7	43.0	26.0
Knitting mills	3.5	0.9	54.7	17.0
Petroleum refining	3.5	3.4	49.8	26.9
Coke oven products	3.4	2.7	48.7	22.4
Fertilizers	3.3	1.8	54.2	16.8
Primary nonferrous metals	3.3	2.4	53.7	18.1
Chewing and smoking tobacco	3.2	1.6	52.7	20.3
Cement, lime, concrete	3.1	1.9	49.5	15.8
Heating and cooking apparatus	3.0	0.9	51.0	17.7
Converted paper products	2.9	1.2	47.8	13.8
Raw cane sugar	2.8	3.7	48.8	26.9
Dairy products	2.8	1.0	48.2	10.5
Tanning and dyeing materials	2.8	2.8	46.7	20.7
Printing and publishing group	2.7	1.1	44.8	18.8
Bolts, nuts, screw machine products	2.7	2.6	44.8	23.5
Sheet metal work	2.6	2.1	44.5	22.2
Pianos	2.6	1.3	45.5	22.7
Carbon black	2.6	3.0	43.0	26.7
Manufactured ice	2.5	1.3	43.8	14.9
Nonferrous metal products, n.e.c.	2.5	1.4	46.0	17.0
Paper and pulp mills	2.4	2.0	42.8	17.6
Electric machinery group	2.4	1.4	43.2	11.8
Wirework, n.e.c.	2.3	3.0	36.7	25.2
Cotton goods	2.3	0.9	44.2	15.1
Rice cleaning	2.2	2.5	40.0	18.7
Steel mill products	2.2	1.9	39.7	20.0
Hats, wool felt	2.1	3.3	42.2	25.4
Glue and gelatin	2.1	1.5	39.7	12.1
Misc. mfg. incl. instruments	2.1	1.7	39.7	12.1
Salt	2.1	1.2	39.7	10.0
Soap and glycerine	2.1	1.9	39.5	14.5
Carpets and rugs, wool	2.0	0.5	40.7	17.3
Agricultural machinery	2.0	1.2	40.3	12.3
Jute and linen goods	2.0	0.8	41.2	11.8

n.e.c. = not elsewhere classified.

(continued)

TABLE 43 (concluded)

Industry	Average Annual Rate of Change, 1899–1954	Average Deviation of Subperiod Rates	Subperiod Ranks Average	Average Deviation
	EIGHTY MANUFACTURING INDUSTRIES			
Cottonseed oil mills	2.0	3.2	41.0	23.7
Woolen and worsted goods	2.0	0.9	41.5	11.8
Leather tanning and finishing	2.0	1.1	37.3	15.7
Explosives	1.9	4.0	39.8	27.8
Apparel group	1.9	1.3	33.5	15.8
Paints and allied products	1.9	1.2	36.2	16.2
Linseed oil mills	1.9	3.8	39.2	30.5
Corn products	1.8	1.6	35.2	18.2
Office and store machines	1.8	2.2	37.0	17.7
Foundry and machine shop products	1.8	0.6	37.2	7.2
Wood distillation	1.8	1.7	38.8	10.6
Cane-sugar refining	1.8	2.7	38.2	19.8
Structural steel products	1.8	2.1	35.0	19.3
Leather gloves and mittens	1.8	1.1	37.2	17.5
Grease and tallow	1.7	3.6	38.2	23.2
Cutlery and edge tools	1.7	2.2	38.8	19.2
Beverages group	1.7	3.7	32.3	20.3
Carriages, wagons, sleighs	1.6	1.5	34.0	21.0
Bakery products	1.6	0.9	34.5	19.2
Furniture group	1.6	1.9	37.0	15.3
Cordage and twine	1.6	1.4	32.3	12.3
Clay and pottery products	1.5	0.9	33.0	10.0
Vinegar and cider	1.5	1.4	33.7	12.8
Hand tools	1.5	1.8	30.0	15.3
Nails and spikes	1.5	1.3	31.7	13.3
Canning, fish	1.4	1.6	33.2	20.9
Flour and meal	1.4	1.9	34.3	14.0
Hats, fur felt	1.4	1.1	33.8	19.8
Footwear, leather	1.3	1.1	30.3	18.4
Leather belting	1.2	1.8	32.0	13.3
Liquors, distilled	1.1	12.1	21.2	24.9
Lumber mills	1.1	1.9	32.0	17.3
Gum naval stores	0.7	1.6	29.2	25.2
Meat packing	0.5	1.5	18.7	8.3
Ships and boats	0.3	1.4	22.7	15.9
Saddlery, harness	−0.2	2.3	21.2	17.6
Locomotives and parts	−0.5	3.1	26.0	23.7
Railroad and street cars	−0.7	1.9	19.0	22.0
Average of 80 covered industries	2.2	2.1[a]	40.5	17.9

[a] 2.1 is the unweighted average of the industry subperiod deviations. The average deviation of subperiod rates taken about the average change for the average of all covered industries is 1.0.

knitting mills, glass, converted paper products, industrial chemicals, and nonferrous metal products. In others, there was a straight-line trend, but with some subperiod irregularity, as in foundry and machine shop products, agricultural machinery, and clay and pottery products. These industries were usually the technologically older ones, in which acceleration in productivity advance had occurred prior to 1899.

Some industries advanced rapidly in the early decades and then experienced retardation or decline—for example, cement, lime, and concrete, the sugar industries, and leather gloves and mittens. On the other hand, some industries showed renewed acceleration of productivity advance after World War II, particularly in the stone, clay, and glass and the machinery groups.

TABLE 44

Manufacturing Industries:[a] Frequency Distributions of Average Annual Rates of Change in Output per Manhour, Subperiods, 1899–1954

Class Interval (per cent)	1899–1954 A	1899–1909 A	B	1909–19 A	B	1919–29 A	B	1929–37 A	B	1937–47 A	B	1947–54 A	B
Under −2.0		4	4	9	11	2	2	7	11	2	6	2	6
−2.0 to −1.0		6	7	4	5	1	1	4	10	1	11		4
−1.0 to −0.0	3	5	6	15	18	2	3	13	20	11	21	5	12
0.0 to 1.0	3	7	7	18	17	3	5	11	28	16	31	7	29
1.0 to 2.0	29	22	21	10	18	7	10	6	17	20	31	9	43
2.0 to 3.0	28	12	14	9	10	7	11	12	16	17	31	17	50
3.0 to 4.0	10	13	15	10	13	10	16	14	22	6	15	14	38
4.0 to 5.0	6	5	5	2	3	13	18	5	13	4	12	5	29
5.0 to 6.0	1	2	2		1	15	18	1	6	1	3	12	28
6.0 to 7.0		2	5			5	9	2	6	2	3	4	22
7.0 to 8.0		1	1	2	2	4	7	1	3		1	3	10
8.0 to 9.0		1	1			7	9	1				0	11
9.0 to 10.0						1	3	1	1		1	2	13
10.0 and over				1	1	3	4	2	5				12
Total number of industries	80	80	88	80	99	80	116	80	158	80	166	80	307

[a] The "A" distributions refer to a constant sample of eighty industries; the "B" distributions refer to a varying number of industries, the progressive increase in number of industries in successive subperiods stemming from finer breakdowns of the preceding industry classification and from the introduction of estimates for additional industries.

Finally, a few industries have been stagnant or have actually experienced irregularly declining output per manhour in this century: meat packing, saddlery and harness, ships and boats, and railroad equipment. In the latter two industries, however, the apparent decline in output per manhour may be due to the use of broad quantity measures that do not reflect shifts in production to higher value-added types of the product groupings; output per manhour indexes based on deflated value-of-product measures show slight increases.

Just as there was generally greater variability in productivity changes between key years in the twenty manufacturing groups than in the segment, so there is still greater average variability in industry movements. The mean deviations of subperiod rates of change in output per manhour from the secular rate in the eighty industries average 2.1 per cent compared with 1.6 per cent for the groups and 1.4 per cent for the manufacturing segment as a whole. It is clear that variations in productivity changes in components tend to be offsetting; hence productivity movements of aggregates are less variable than those of the components. Also, as in the groups, there were large fluctuations in the rank of the manufacturing industries with respect to changes in output per manhour. The coefficient of variation of ranks in the subperiods from average rank was more than 40 per cent (see Table 43).

Dispersion of the rates of change in the eighty manufacturing industries in the subperiods is pictured in the frequency distributions of Table 44. The greater range of change and the lesser degree of central tendency in the subperiods than in the long period and for the individual industries compared with the manufacturing and other groups (see Table 35) stand out clearly. There is even greater dispersion when a larger, variable sample of manufacturing industries is used, comprising up to 307 industries in the last subperiod (the "B" columns of Table 44).

Other industries. Estimates of output per manhour are available for five of the industries that constitute the residual transportation group. As shown in Table 40, the average annual rate of increase for the residual was 4.1 per cent between 1899 and 1953 compared with 3.4 per cent for transportation as a whole. Within the residual, output per manhour for waterways, which showed the smallest increase (approximately 3 per cent a year), was still above the economy average. Much larger rates of increase were shown by the newer forms of transportation. Between 1919 and 1953, output per manhour for pipe lines increased at an average annual rate of 7.5 per cent. This was also approximately the average rate of advance for intercity motor transport; trucking advanced somewhat more and passenger buses somewhat less. Between 1929 and 1953, the airlines experienced a better-than-9-per-cent average annual gain in output per manhour.

A few scattered series are available for other industries. Rough estimates for fisheries (see Appendix B) show an average annual rate of advance of 0.9 per cent a year in output per worker between 1899 and 1953. In the government-enterprise segment, estimates are available for the postal service. Here, output per manhour rose at an average rate of 1.8 per cent a year over the long period (see Appendix J), which compares favorably with private-industry experience.

OUTPUT PER UNIT OF CAPITAL INPUT

Despite the substitution of capital for labor over most of the period under review, substantial savings in capital per unit of output[3] were realized in

---

[3] The "capital coefficient," which is the reciprocal of "capital productivity" (i.e., output per unit of capital input), fell over the period.

the economy and its major segments between 1899 and 1953. Output per unit of capital input increased at an average annual rate of 1.2 per cent in the private domestic economy, and 1.0 per cent in the covered sector, implying an average rate of increase of 1.3 per cent a year in the uncovered sector.

Among the segments, the average annual rates of advance in the output-capital ratio range from practically no change in farming to 2.5 and 3.2 per cent in transportation and communications, respectively, with near-average changes in mining and manufacturing (see Table 45 and Chart 17). The differences in rates of advance are associated not only with the technological characteristics of the several industries, but also with the dates, which differed considerably, at which relatively full mechanization was achieved.

Although the segment rates of change in output per unit of capital input over the long period run lower than those in total factor productivity, the dispersion is virtually the same in absolute terms (see Table 46). This is also true of average rates of change in the group output-capital ratios, which range from a small negative in lumber products to 4.7 per cent a year in electric utilities. A frequency distribution of changes in output per unit of capital input in the groups (Table 35, last panel) shows that the modal class is between 1 and 2 per cent a year, instead of between 2 and 3 per cent, as in the case of changes in total productivity and the output-labor ratio. The peaking of the distribution is sharper, and the distribution has a more normal shape.

The time sequence differs, but there is a typical pattern of movement of output per unit of capital input in the various segments and groups. The first phase is characterized by a rapid build-up of capital as mechanized processes are substituted for hand processes or as plant is constructed in anticipation of gradually increasing demand and rates of utilization. During this phase, output per unit of capital input generally declines. Then, once production processes have been made as capital-using as current technology and relative factor prices warrant, resources are devoted primarily to refining equipment and production processes. Capital-saving innovations are more numerous in this phase since possibilities of cutting costs along these lines are greater because of the larger relative quantity of capital, and output per unit of capital input begins to rise.

The timing of the early shift in output per unit of capital input from a downward to an upward direction varied widely among the segments. The low points of the ratio (in terms of our key years) were 1919 in manufacturing, 1909 in mining, and 1879 in communications and public utilities. In the last case, there was little net change in the ratio between 1869 and 1899, as increases in the older groups tended to be offset by declines in the burgeoning groups. The period of "capital deepening" in transportation, dominated by the railroads, had apparently ended before the beginning of our estimates in 1870. This was also true in farming, but the farm output-capital ratio showed a renewed decline during the build-up of the second technological revolution in the early twentieth century.

Within each segment, the pattern varied somewhat by group. In mining, the low point of output per unit of capital input for anthracite coal came

TABLE 45

Private Domestic Economy: Average Annual Rates of Change in Output per Unit of Capital Input, by Segment and by Group, with Measures of Dispersion, Subperiods, 1899–1953
(per cent)

	Pre-1899	1899–1909	1909–1919	1919–1929	1929–1937	1937–1948	1948–1953	1899–1953	Mean Deviation of Subperiod Rates from Secular Rate
Farming	0.5	−0.7	−0.7	1.2	0.8	0.4	−1.5	0.0	0.8
Mining	−2.2	−0.1	0.4	1.5	6.0	0.6	−0.3	1.3	1.5
Metals		0.3	2.0	2.7	5.9	2.6	−7.6	1.6	2.2
Anthracite coal		0.2	−0.4	−0.9	1.3	4.1	−7.7	0.0	2.0
Bituminous coal		−2.3	−1.7	3.3	2.2	1.6	−7.5	−0.2	2.7
Oil and gas		−1.8	−1.9	4.5	9.9	−0.5	5.8	2.0	3.9
Nonmetals		1.1	0.0	2.7	1.4	5.8	−1.5	1.9	1.8
Manufacturing	−1.8	−1.6	−1.9	4.3	2.4	2.1	0.8	1.0	2.1
Foods		−0.9	−2.5	5.1	3.4	1.5	1.2	1.2	2.2
Beverages		0.4	−4.6	−1.2	16.6	2.0	−1.1	1.6	4.4
Tobacco		−2.2	0.0	−1.3	4.9	−0.7	0.0	0.0	1.6
Textiles		−0.3	−2.5	4.9	5.4	2.8	−1.4	1.6	2.8
Apparel		−1.6	−2.6	4.0	5.7	−2.6	−1.9	0.0	3.1
Lumber products		−3.4	−2.8	−1.0	3.9	1.5	1.2	−0.4	2.3
Furniture		−2.9	−1.9	2.7	2.5	6.6	0.2	1.3	3.0
Paper		−1.0	−0.7	2.9	3.8	1.7	−0.2	1.1	1.7
Printing, publishing		3.2	1.8	3.7	2.4	1.0	2.0	2.3	0.8
Chemicals		−0.9	−1.7	6.0	3.0	3.4	1.2	1.8	2.5
Petroleum, coal products		−1.6	−2.6	8.4	1.2	1.4	1.8	1.3	2.7
Rubber products		−0.9	3.7	3.8	6.4	0.5	1.3	2.4	2.2
Leather products		−2.6	−1.8	4.7	6.1	0.9	−2.4	0.9	2.9
Stone, clay, glass		−2.3	−1.0	3.1	4.4	4.2	−0.8	1.4	2.6
Primary metals		−2.1	−0.9	4.8	−2.4	5.4	−3.9	0.6	3.4
Fabricated metals		−1.1	0.7	2.6	2.6	2.2	4.2	1.6	1.3
Machinery, nonelectric		−1.8	1.0	2.5	3.3	0.7	1.3	1.1	1.2
Electric machinery		−2.3	1.5	1.6	4.8	1.4	3.3	1.4	1.4
Transportation equipment	0.0	4.1	5.9	−0.9	2.2	5.9	2.7	2.3	
Miscellaneous		−1.2	−0.7	0.4	5.3	2.0	2.7	1.1	1.8

(continued)

166

TABLE 45 (concluded)

	Pre-1899	1899–1909	1909–1919	1919–1929	1929–1937	1937–1948	1948–1953	1899–1953	Mean Deviation of Subperiod Rates from Secular Rate
Transportation	4.5	2.2	1.8	1.5	0.8	6.9	−0.1	2.5	1.8
Railroads		4.3	2.7	−0.3	−2.1	5.4	−2.2	1.8	2.7
Local transit		0.5	3.8	5.7	1.2	8.7	−4.1	3.4	3.1
Residual transport		−3.2	−5.4	6.9	5.6	6.0	1.8	1.8	4.6
Communications and public utilities	0.5	5.1	3.8	2.7	1.0	5.3	−1.5	3.2	1.8
Telephone		5.9	4.6	0.9	−2.2	2.0	−5.5	1.6	2.8
Telegraph		1.2	1.6	5.7	−1.2	6.1	0.4	2.6	2.5
Electric utilities		3.0	8.1	3.1	3.5	6.8	2.4	4.7	2.0
Manufactured gas		4.9	3.5	3.9	−0.2	8.1	7.6	4.6	2.1
Natural gas		−5.7	−1.2	−2.6	2.4	6.8	−0.5	−0.1	3.5
Residual sector	1.8	2.1	1.2	−0.1	−0.8	4.3	0.3	1.3	1.4
Private domestic economy	0.6	0.8	0.3	1.4	0.9	2.7	0.1	1.2	0.7
Aggregate of 5 covered segments	−0.3	0.3	−0.5	2.7	2.0	1.9	0.0	1.0	1.3
Mean deviations from sector rates:									
5 segments	1.5	1.4	1.3	1.4	1.1	1.1	0.9	0.6	
33 groups		1.5	1.7	1.9	2.4	1.5	2.6	0.8	

in 1879, although the ratio showed little trend in subsequent decades. In metal and nonmetal mining and quarrying, the low point was reached in 1889. In bituminous coal and in crude petroleum and natural gas production, the output-capital ratios did not reach bottom until 1919.

In manufacturing, the majority of groups followed the segment pattern of declines up to 1919, followed by increases (at a decreasing rate) in the succeeding subperiods. All groups but printing and publishing and beverages showed declines in output per unit of capital input in the 1899–1909 subperiod. Between 1909 and 1919, six of the twenty groups registered increases in advance of the segment as a whole. Although there were relatively few drops in output per unit of capital input in the three subperiods between 1919 and 1948, seven groups registered declines in the last subperiod reviewed here, 1948–53. It will be interesting to see if this increasing dispersion foreshadows a reversal of movement, as was the case in the 1909–19 subperiod.

CHART 17

Private Domestic Economy: Output per Unit of Capital Input, by Segment,
Key Years, 1889–1953 (1929=100)

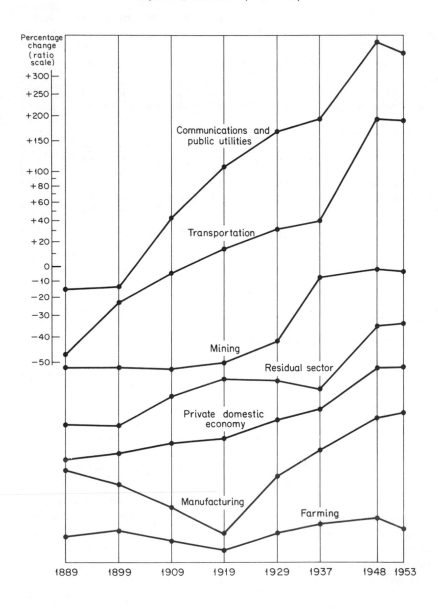

In the transportation segment, output per unit of capital input for the railroads was already advancing sharply in the first decade for which we have estimates, 1869–79. The big build-up of roadbed and, to a lesser degree, equipment had already occurred. The turning point in the output-capital ratio for local transit came in 1899. In the residual transportation segment, the turn appears to have come nearest the key year 1919, influenced by the early phase of capital-building in pipe lines and in motor transport.

In the utilities segment, low points in the output-capital ratios were reached in 1889 in the telephone industry, 1899 in electric utilities and manufactured gas, and not until 1929 in natural gas. In the telegraph industry, the early phase of plant expansion relative to output apparently took place prior to the first decade for which data are available (1879–89).

Once begun, the rise in output per unit of capital input continued in most areas, but with major irregularities in the last two subperiods as a result of World War II. Due to wartime restrictions and early-postwar capital shortages, the growth of capital stocks was retarded and the rise in the output-capital ratio was accelerated in the economy. Conversely, between 1948 and 1953 capital was expanded about as rapidly as was output in the covered sector and in the economy. In all segments, output per unit of capital input either fell or showed only small increase. Taking 1937–53 as a whole, the rate of increase was in line with past experience. Whether the pattern since 1948 has merely been a "catching-up" with the trend, to be followed by further substantial increases in the output-capital ratio, or whether part of it represents a new period of deepening of capital, is not clear. It seems reasonable to assume that output per unit of capital input will resume some advance in the economy as a whole. Despite the fact that a catching-up was undoubtedly involved in the capital expansion from 1948 to 1953, the ratio remained fairly stable. On the other hand, some of the major postwar technological developments suggest that the intermediate-term trend in output per unit of capital may be less steep than the 1899–1953 trend, particularly so long as high-level employment, income, and investment are maintained.

As this review suggests, variability in rates of change of output per unit of capital input in the segments and groups between key years was considerably greater, on the average, than was variability in rates of change in output per unit of labor input (see Table 47). Among the segments, variability in rates of change of the output-capital ratio relative to the output-labor ratio was particularly large in transportation and in communications and public utilities. This would seem to indicate even less flexibility in these segments than in manufacturing in adjusting capital to changes in output over subperiods as compared with adjusting labor to output. Variability in rates of change in the output-capital ratio was considerably higher in the groups than in the segments of which they are components; so the group variations must have been partially offsetting.

Dispersion of rates of change in output per unit of capital input in the segments was about twice as great in the subperiods as for the period as a whole, and greater still with respect to the thirty-three group measures. If anything, the degree of dispersion has tended to increase with time.

COMPARISON OF DISPERSION AND VARIABILITY IN THE PRODUCTIVITY AND INPUT RATIOS

Dispersion. If there were no systematic relationship between changes in the two partial productivity ratios, we could expect that the mean deviation of the segment or group rates of change in total factor productivity from their mean would approximate a weighted average of the mean deviations of rates of change in the two partial productivity measures from their means. But the measures of dispersion of rates of change in total factor productivity generally fall below the average dispersion of rates of change in the two partial productivity ratios, whether measured over the long period or subperiods (see Table 46).

This indicates that the deviations of segment and group rates of change in the two partial productivity ratios from their means must be inversely correlated. Looked at differently, segment and group rates of change in capital per unit of labor input and output per unit of labor input must be positively correlated. Rank correlation of the latter two variables for the thirty-three groups over the long period yields a coefficient of $+.40$, significant at the 5 per cent level. Actually, total input per unit of labor input, which gives capital its appropriate weight, is more closely correlated with output per unit of labor input; the Spearman coefficient of rank correlation between these variables for the thirty-three groups is $+.60$, significant at the 1 per cent level.

Inspection of Table 46 makes it clear that, on the average, the dispersion of rates of change in total productivity is more decisively below the average dispersion in rates of change in the two partial productivity ratios in the subperiods than over the long period. The lesser dispersion is also more pronounced with reference to changes in the thirty-three group rates than in those of the five segments. Dispersion differs somewhat within each segment, as shown in the table.

The fact that there is less difference between group rates of change in total factor productivity than in labor productivity suggests that the same result may obtain in international comparisons. That is, difference in rates of change, and in levels, of productivity among nations might well be less if capital as well as labor input were used in the denominators of productivity ratios. Sufficient information with respect to capital input

TABLE 46

Private Domestic Economy: Comparison of Dispersion in Rates of Change in Productivity Ratios, by Segment, 1899–1953

(per cent)

	MEAN DEVIATIONS OF COMPONENT RATES OF CHANGE FROM RATES OF CHANGE IN THE AGGREGATE							
	Long Period, 1899–1953				Subperiod Averages			
	Total Factor Productivity	Output per Unit of Labor Input	Output per Unit of Capital Input	Capital per Unit of Labor Input	Total Factor Productivity	Output per Unit of Labor Input	Output per Unit of Capital Input	Capital per Unit of Labor Input
Covered sector								
5 segments	0.5	0.5	0.6	0.2	1.0	1.1	1.2	1.3
33 groups	0.6	0.6	0.8	0.5	1.3	1.4	1.8	1.8
Segments								
Mining								
5 groups	0.7	0.8	0.4	0.4	1.2	1.3	1.9	1.9
Manufacturing								
20 groups	0.5	0.6	0.5	0.5	1.3	1.3	1.6	1.4
Transportation								
3 groups	0.6	0.6	0.2	0.6	1.2	1.1	1.4	1.5
Communications and public utilities								
5 groups	0.8	1.2	0.8	0.7	1.4	1.5	2.2	1.7

in other countries has not been compiled to make possible a test of this hypothesis.

It can also be seen in Table 46 that dispersion in group rates of change over the long period in capital per unit of labor input is somewhat less than in capital or labor in relation to output. In other words, trends in requirements by industry group for either input provide a better guide to trends in requirements for the other input than do secular changes in output.

Subperiod variability. Variability in rates of change in total factor productivity over the subperiods is generally distinctly less than average variability in subperiod rates of change in the two partial productivity ratios. In fact, variability in subperiod rates of change in total productivity is below the corresponding measure of variability in output per unit of labor input in the segment and group measures, on the average, and in some of the groups as combined by segment (Table 47). The reason behind the greater stability of rates of change in total productivity compared with the partial productivity ratios must be that there is, generally, an inverse correlation between the deviations of the subperiod rates of change in the two partial ratios from their secular rates of change. Or, subperiod rates of change in output per unit of labor input and capital (or total input) per unit of labor input must be positively correlated.[4] To put it differently, in those subperiods in which capital per unit of labor input shows greater-than-average increases, output per unit of labor input often rises by more than the average, while output per unit of capital input tends to show less-than-average increases.

It will also be noted that over the subperiods, movements of capital are generally more closely related to movements of labor input than to movements of output. This is indicated by the lesser variability in subperiod rates of change in capital per unit of labor input than in output per unit of capital input. The greater stability of rates of change in the capital-labor ratio is particularly pronounced in the measure for the covered sector of the economy, but is also significant in the group measures, on the average, and in the manufacturing groups in particular.

The reader who is interested in intermediate- or long-range economic projections will note certain relevant implications of the comparisons of our variability measures. For example, the lesser variability of total factor productivity than of output per unit of labor input suggests that the composite measure would be a better vehicle for projection. Likewise, the capital-labor ratio is a better means of projection than the capital-output ratio, since it shows less than half as much variability in the private

[4] As we noted above, the coefficient of rank correlation is +.40 when changes in the output-labor and the capital-labor ratios are used, and +.60 when changes in the output-labor and total input-labor ratios are used.

TABLE 47

Private Domestic Economy: Comparison of Variability in Subperiod Rates of Change in Productivity Ratios, by Segment, 1899–1953
(per cent)

	MEAN DEVIATIONS OF SUBPERIOD RATES OF CHANGE FROM SECULAR RATE							
	Aggregate Measures				*Component Averages*			
	Total Factor Productivity	Output per Unit of Labor Input	Output per Unit of Capital Input	Capital per Unit of Labor Input	Total Factor Productivity	Output per Unit of Labor Input	Output per Unit of Capital Input	Capital per Unit of Labor Input
Covered sector 5 segments 33 groups	1.0	1.0	1.3	0.6	1.2 1.4	1.3 1.0	1.7 2.1	1.6 2.0
Segments Mining 5 groups	1.3	1.4	1.5	1.3	1.6	1.3	3.2	2.8
Manufacturing 20 groups	1.3	1.4	2.1	1.3	1.6	1.6	2.3	1.8
Transportation 3 groups	0.9	0.9	1.8	2.1	1.4	1.5	3.0	2.7
Communications and public utilities 5 groups	0.7	0.7	1.8	2.2	1.3	1.5	2.8	2.7

domestic economy as a whole. Also, the lesser variability of all measures for the economy than for the segments or groups means that a projection of an aggregate as a whole is likely to be more accurate than an average of projections of the constituent elements, although the latter would be necessary to forecasts of economic structure.

Annual variability. In the several segments or groups for which annual estimates are available, the mean deviations of annual percentage changes in the productivity ratios from the secular rates are much larger than the subperiod mean deviations. They are generally well above the secular rates of advance themselves. This is also true of the mean deviations of the annual percentage changes in the productivity ratios for the private domestic economy as a whole, but weighted averages of the group mean annual deviations are somewhat larger than those in the aggregate measure (Table 48).

TABLE 48

Private Domestic Economy: Mean Deviations of Annual Rates of Change in the Productivity Ratios from Average Annual Secular Rates of Change, 1899–1953
(per cent)

| | Total Factor Productivity | Output per Unit of | |
		Labor Input	Capital Input
Private domestic economy			
Secular rate of change	1.8	2.0	1.4
Mean deviation of:			
Subperiod rates	0.5	0.5	0.7
Annual rates	3.0	2.9	5.3
Covered groups[a]			
Secular rate of change	1.8	2.3 (2.4)[b]	0.9
Mean deviation of:			
Subperiod rates	1.1	1.4 (1.4)[b]	1.4
Annual rates	4.6	4.1 (4.3)[b]	5.9

[a] Weighted measures for farming, railroads, local transit, electric utilities, telephone communications, and natural gas utilities.

[b] The figures in parentheses include, in addition, mining, manufacturing, and manufactured gas utilities, for which annual estimates of output per unit of labor input alone are available.

It is possibly somewhat surprising that the mean annual percentage deviations of the group and economy total productivity measures lie below the average mean annual percentage deviations of the corresponding partial productivity ratios. As was true in the subperiods, this indicates that annual changes in capital per unit of labor input are positively

TABLE 49

Private Domestic Economy: Average Annual Percentage Changes in
Productivity, Expansions versus Contractions, by Major Segment
and by Selected Groups, 1899–1953

	Total Factor Productivity	Output per Unit of	
		Labor Input	Capital Input
Private domestic economy			
Expansions	2.7	2.2	4.1
Contractions	−0.3	1.6	−5.2
Farming			
Expansions	1.3	1.5	0.4
Contractions	1.4	3.0	−0.2
Private domestic nonfarm economy			
Expansions	3.0	2.5	4.6
Contractions	−0.5	1.5	−6.2
Mining			
Expansions		2.7	
Contractions		2.2	
Manufacturing			
Expansions		3.4	
Contractions		−0.1	
Railroads			
Expansions	5.1	4.4	7.9
Contractions	−2.8	−0.6	−10.2
Local transit			
Expansions	3.3	3.0	5.4
Contractions	1.0	1.2	−0.3
Electric utilities			
Expansions	7.6	7.9	7.2
Contractions	1.1	3.0	−0.4
Telephone communications			
Expansions	2.8	2.3	3.3
Contractions	0.7	1.6	−1.5
Manufactured gas utilities			
Expansions		5.0	
Contractions		4.6	
Natural gas utilities			
Expansions	3.1	3.3	2.4
Contractions	−0.2	2.8	−5.2

CHART 18

Private Domestic Economy: Output per Unit of Labor Input, by Selected Industry Group,
1889–1953 (1929=100)

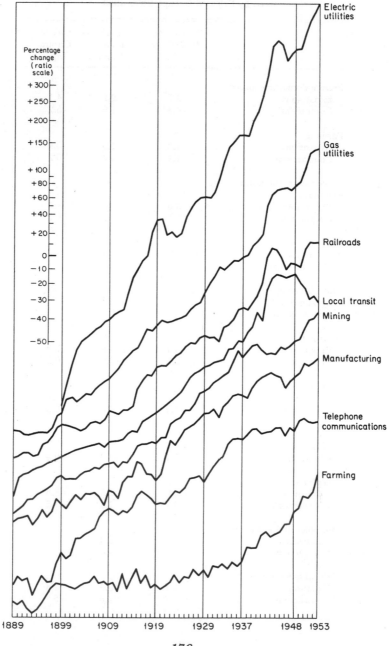

correlated with annual changes in output per unit of labor input. Apparently, the tendency for these variables to vary together is strong enough to overcome the tendency in years of recession for capital per unit of labor input to rise (since capital stocks are relatively inflexible), while output per unit of labor input shows less-than-average increases or actual declines.

The importance of the cycle in explaining differences in annual changes in the group or segment productivity ratios is brought out in Table 49 and Chart 18 (see the discussion with respect to the influence of the cycle on economy annual changes in Chapter 3). The tendency for productivity to rise more in expansions than in contractions prevails in all groups for which we have annual measures except farming.

The smaller productivity increases, or actual declines, in nonfarm industries are due principally to a drop in capital productivity as measured; but even output per unit of labor input rises only half as much in contractions as in expansions. In the farm economy, to the contrary, total factor productivity has actually risen somewhat more in general business contractions than in expansions—1.4 per cent compared with 1.3 per cent, on the average. Although farm output is influenced primarily by weather, political controls, and other factors outside the general business cycle, it appears that the squeeze on net farm income that results from the sensitivity of farm prices to the business cycle tends to spur efficiency gains. This may also be true in nonfarm industries, but the adverse effect of falling rates of utilization of capacity more than offsets the tightening up of operations induced by falling profit margins.

Some Forces Underlying Industry Changes

The forces underlying the pervasive productivity advance by industry are highly complex. They comprise the cultural values that affect the motivations of individuals and direct their energies; the socio-economic organization or "institutional" framework that enables or promotes the pursuit of efficiency; and, more directly, the changes in technology that affect the organization, processes, and instruments of production in the individual enterprises of the economy. A discussion of these matters must, of necessity, be somewhat speculative, although reference will be made to some quantitative analyses by ourselves and by another investigator, who used our measures of total factor productivity for the manufacturing industry groups.[5]

Although the quantitative analysis is fragmentary and at best could not be conclusive in the face of the complex interrelationships involved, it is

[5] See Nestor E. Terleckyj, "Factors Underlying Productivity: Some Empirical Observations," *Journal of the American Statistical Association*, June 1958, p. 593; also, his unpublished doctoral dissertation for Columbia University, *Sources of Productivity Change. A Pilot Study Based on the Experience of American Manufacturing Industries, 1899–1953*, 1959.

important to try to explain the causal forces. In order to project changes in relative prices and other structural aspects of the economy, it is necessary to project productivity by industry, a task that requires knowledge of the underlying forces. More important, if we wish to take action to affect productivity advance, we must have knowledge of its causes. This section is but an introduction to the subject, and it is hoped that our productivity indexes will be useful to others who wish to carry the analysis further.

PERVASIVE FORCES

During our review of industry productivity trends, we remarked that despite differences in rates of change, all industry groups advanced over the long period, and practically all smaller component industries did likewise. Indeed, average rates of increase were heavily concentrated at between 1.0 and 3.0 per cent a year. This indicates that there are certain broad, pervasive forces that promote productive efficiency throughout the economy. Before taking up reasons for differences among industries, we shall consider some factors that have a fairly even incidence on all industries.

The social factors alluded to above are usually taken for granted by the inhabitants of a nation and often overlooked in explaining economic developments. Yet the values of a people and the institutions through which they work are fundamental, although the actions taken to alter the productive mechanism are more apparent and immediately related to productivity change. The prevalence of similar values and institutions throughout our society is a major reason for the breadth of productivity advance. We shall discuss several of the more important social factors briefly; they are not generally susceptible to quantification.

A prerequisite for productivity increase is the *desire* for material advance on the part of the people of a society—not for fixed goals, the attainment of which removes incentive for further advance, but for standards of living that continually stay ahead of attained levels. A rising standard of living has been characteristic of the United States, and it has been strengthened by the crafts of advertising. The desire for material advance has not been directed solely toward rising consumption levels, however; it has embraced the goals of providing increased capital for future generations and a broader material base for national security.

Another basic social value, which is in line with our liberal heritage, is the belief in maintaining maximum economic as well as political freedom consistent with the general welfare. Our concepts of the proper role for government activity have changed as the economy has evolved; but in general, public opinion has favored retention of the maximum possible role for individual initiative. This has helped foster a creative and dynamic economy.

When coupled with the institutions of private property, the profit motive, and competition, economic freedom has been a powerful means of promoting the material welfare of the community as well as of the individual. This tenet of economic liberalism is based on the premise that each person, seeking to maximize his income, will employ his labor and capital in their most productive uses. Further, in order to increase their profits, entrepreneurs develop and introduce new products or cost-reducing methods of producing existing products. Under the spur of competition, other firms of an industry must imitate the management of firms that have pioneered the innovations, or else their profit margins disappear, and they go into bankruptcy. Thus, prospective profit is the carrot and competition the stick that motivate progress. Other systems of rewards and penalties are possible, but it has yet to be demonstrated that they are as effective in achieving productivity advance; and, certainly, they do not allow as much scope for individual freedom, which many people value even more than material progress.

The reports of many European productivity teams that have visited the United States stress the importance of a relatively high degree of competition in spurring technological progress. Some writers, to the contrary, have maintained that a degree of market control is conducive to progress, since the greater financial strength and stability of sheltered firms make possible the large-scale research and development work necessary for continuous innovation.

In an attempt to test these hypotheses, Nestor Terleckyj correlated rates of total productivity advance in manufacturing industry groups with each of two measures of phenomena related to the extent of competition in the several industries. One is a measure of rates of entry, based on the number of births of new firms relative to the size of the industry groups as measured by value added. The other is a measure of concentration, representing weighted averages of the proportions of sales accounted for by the four largest firms in the 4-digit industries constituting the manufacturing-industry groups (see Table 50).

There is no significant correlation between productivity changes and levels of these two measures. It would seem either that there is a sufficient degree of competition throughout American industry to provide a fairly uniform stimulus to productivity advance and, therefore, interindustry differentials are due to other factors, or that the negative aspects of competition, if any, approximately offset the positive effects on productivity change. This conclusion is tentative, since the two measures used are not ideal indexes of the extent of competition.

Besides institutional factors, there are forces that directly affect technology across a broad industrial front. Most industries benefit from the growth of the whole economy: As markets become more concentrated,

TABLE 50

Entry of New Firms, Entry Rates, and Concentration Ratios, by
Industry Group, 1947 and 1948

	New Firms, 1948	Firms in Operation at Beginning of 1948	Entry Rate, 1948[a]	Concentration Index 1947[b]
	(number in thousands)			
All industries	393.3	3872.9	102	
Manufacturing	34.6	315.4	110	
Foods incl. beverages	3.5	39.0	90	35.9[c]
Textile mills	0.7	9.2	76	21.9
Apparel	4.1	39.7	103	11.1
Lumber, basic products	10.9	49.7	219	20.6
Furniture	1.4	12.3	114	20.3
Paper and products	0.3	3.7	81	22.0
Printing, publishing	2.3	39.8	58	19.7
Chemicals	0.9	11.5	78	45.8
Petroleum, coal products	0.1	0.9	111	39.6
Rubber products	0.1	1.0	100	77.2
Leather and products	0.5	6.9	72	26.2
Stone, clay, glass products	1.3	13.8	94	44.3
Primary metals	0.4	5.7	70	42.1
Fabricated metals	2.2	20.7	106	28.4
Machinery, nonelectric	2.2	22.8	96	37.5
Electric machinery	0.5	4.8	104	62.2
Transportation equipment	0.5	5.3	94	86.3
Miscellaneous incl. tobacco	2.7	28.6	94	31.6[d]
Mining and quarrying	5.3	36.3	146	
Contract construction	65.0	310.3	209	
Trade	275.6	1984.7	139	
Transportation, communications and public utilities	23.9	175.9	136	
Finance, insurance, real estate	16.0	322.4	50	
Services	72.9	728.0	100	

SOURCE: Betty C. Churchill, "Recent Business Population Movements," *Survey of Current Business*, Dept. of Commerce, January 1954, pp. 15 and 16; and Nestor E. Terleckyj, *Sources of Productivity Change. A Pilot Study Based on the Experience of American Manufacturing Industries, 1899–1953*, unpublished doctoral dissertation, New York, Columbia University, 1959, based on *Report of the Federal Trade Commission on Changes in Concentration in Manufacturing, 1935 to 1937 and 1954*, 1954. The entry rate shown here is not the same as the one used by Terleckyj.

[a] Number of new entries per 1,000 firms in operation.

[b] Weighted averages of the proportions of sales accounted for by the four largest firms in the Standard Industrial Classification 4-digit industries constituting the manufacturing industry groups.

[c] Excluding beverages, for which the index is 33.5.

[d] Excluding tobacco, for which the index is 76.4.

greater specialization is made possible, and the average education and training of the labor force is increased. Progress in certain strategic industries benefits all. For example, as transportation and communication facilities have improved, it has been possible for industry to reduce inventory-sales ratios and thus increase total productivity. Certain types of new products developed by the machinery and other producer industries have broad applications across industry lines. Examples include office equipment, furnishings, and supplies; materials handling equipment; and heating, lighting, and power equipment. Innovations made in more specialized industries may also have applications across industry lines. Such "linked" innovations probably spread with some lag, as is suggested by the variability of industry ranks over the subperiods that we noted earlier in the chapter. But linked innovations are a cause of widespread productivity advance over longer periods.

So far, the factors discussed are ones believed to affect most, if not all, industries. Even these pervasive forces may have a somewhat different impact by industry. But the main forces explaining relative industry changes in productivity are the ones that directly affect the technology of the individual industries.

FORCES WITH DIFFERENTIAL IMPACT

Terleckyj has done a rather elaborate quantitative study of the relationship between changes in our estimates of total productivity and ten explanatory variables for twenty 2-digit and up to twenty-five 3-digit manufacturing industry groups for one or more of our subperiods or combinations of subperiods between 1899 and 1953. On the basis of simple rank correlations, multiple regressions, and graphic techniques, he concluded that three of the explanatory variables were significantly related to relative industry rates of change in productivity: rates of change in output, amplitudes of cyclical fluctuations, and ratios of research and development outlays to sales or of research and development personnel to total manhours worked. The reader who wants the technical details of the Terleckyj study may refer to the sources noted. We observe here only that neither the simple nor the multiple correlation coefficients were very high; they varied considerably from one period to another, as between subperiods and longer periods, and also as between the analysis based on the 2-digit and that based on the 3-digit industry groups. Yet, the findings are suggestive.

In the light of our a priori discussion of causal forces in Chapters 1 and 4, it is not surprising that the three variables named above turned out to be significant in explaining relative changes in productivity. On the other hand, in view of the deficiencies of the measures and the complexity of the underlying forces, it is also not surprising that the unexplained variance in both the simple and multiple correlations remained relatively large. We turn briefly to a discussion of the reasons why each of the three explanatory variables may be significant, and of the limitations of these measures.

Research and development activity. Since technological change is a chief cause of productivity advance, measures of innovational activity in the various industries should be significantly correlated with relative productivity changes. But even if we could catalogue all the innovations made by the firms of each industry in successive periods, further difficulties would be met in trying to weight each in accordance with its relative importance. At best, only indirect measures of innovational activity, such as the number of patents issued, are possible. ·

Perhaps the best indirect measure is research and development outlays in relation to sales, of which estimates are available for recent periods (see Table 51). Estimates by industry of research and development

TABLE 51

Research and Development Outlays, Dollar Volume and Ratios to Sales, by Manufacturing Industry Group, 1953

	Research and Development Expenditures	Estimated Sales	Research and Development Expenditures Relative to Sales
	(millions of dollars)		(per cent)
All manufacturing	3,467.8	293,871	1.180
Foods	46.7	40,160	0.116
Beverages	7.5	7,874	0.095
Tobacco	4.0	4,248	0.094
Textiles	25.1	12,927	0.194
Apparel	2.9	11,848	0.024
Lumber products	27.6	7,328	0.377
Furniture	24.7	3,835	0.644
Paper	27.9	8,442	0.330
Printing, publishing	22.4	9,127	0.245
Chemicals	361.1	18,997	1.901
Petroleum, coal products	145.9	25,492	0.572
Rubber products	53.6	5,000	1.072
Leather products	17.8	3,512	0.507
Stone, clay, glass	38.0	6,906	0.550
Primary metals	59.8	23,264	0.257
Fabricated metals	103.3	15,885	0.650
Machinery, nonelectric	318.9	24,170	1.319
Electric machinery	743.3	17,429	4.265
Transportation equipment	1,111.0	36,387	3.053
Miscellaneous	326.3	11,040	2.956

SOURCE: Nester E. Terleckyj, *Sources of Productivity Change.* The research and development expenditures are based on *Science and Engineering in American Industry, Final Report on a 1953–1954 Survey*, National Science Foundation, NSF 56-16, Washington, 1956; sales estimated from *Statistics of Income, 1953*, Internal Revenue Service; and *Census of Manufactures, 1947.*

personnel in relation to total employment or manhours, which Terleckyj also used, have the advantage of being available for prewar years. These measures indicate the relative intensity of investment in activities designed to produce commercially applicable inventions and, thus, eventual innovation.

Despite a relatively good correlation with productivity changes (see Chart 19), the measures of research and development intensity are not

CHART 19

Twenty Manufacturing Groups: Relation between Rates of Change in Total Factor Productivity, 1948–53, and Ratios of Research and Development Outlays to Sales, 1953

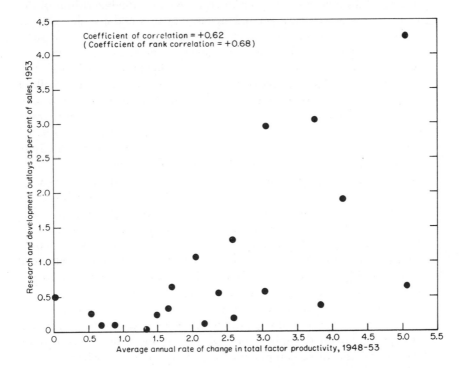

ideal indicators of the relative flows of innovation. Some innovation results from unorganized activities, such as changes conceived of by works managers or by production workers and other nonresearch employees (or by proprietors, in the case of noncorporate enterprise). Some of the most important developments affecting the productivity of an industry may originate with equipment manufacturers or suppliers in other industries. Government research is important for certain industries, such as agriculture. Basic scientific research carried on in universities and in government and nonprofit organizations, as well as in business firms, may have widespread application across industry lines. Further, the volume of commercially applicable inventions resulting from research and development outlays will vary from time to time and from industry to industry, due to chance. There will also be different time-lags between the development of an innovation and its commercial application, although changes in research ratios are probably gradual enough so that use of lagged relationships would not significantly change the relationships of subperiod averages.

It is interesting that Terleckyj's net regression coefficients indicate that rates of productivity advance differ by approximately 0.5 per cent for each tenfold difference in research intensity.[6] Since the logarithms of the research-intensity ratio are related linearly to productivity change, the effect of a given absolute increase in the research and development ratio on productivity advance becomes less the larger the ratio.

A related measure used by Terleckyj is the ratio of numbers of engineers and chemists per 10,000 employees in the several industries. The bulk of the engineers are not engaged primarily in organized research and development work, and the proportion has undoubtedly changed over time. Although the engineer and scientist ratios were significantly related to the research and development ratios, they are not related to productivity changes except in the simple correlations for the last subperiod.

Another indirect approach to the volume of innovational activity is by measures of financial strength in the various industries. Presumably, firms with relatively high rates of return on capital would be more disposed to spend money on research and development (which, in turn, should contribute to earnings) and would be in a better position to borrow funds than firms with less satisfactory earnings. Further, firms with a good financial position would be better able to make the necessary investment to improve efficiency, both from retained earnings and loans—which would be easier to arrange and probably cost less than if profit margins were lower.

As a by-product of our input estimates, we were able to compute rates of return on invested capital for the thirty-three industry groups for 1929–53 and the three component subperiods. The coefficients of rank correlation between the rates of return and the rates of change in total factor productivity turned out to be not significant.

Relative changes in industry output. As shown in the next chapter, there is a significant degree of correlation between relative changes in output and in total productivity for the thirty-three industry groups over the long period and in most subperiods. Terleckyj found the same result with respect to the twenty manufacturing groups. His net regression coefficient

---

[6] See Terleckyj's dissertation, p. 64.

indicates that for every 3 per cent difference in growth rates among industries, productivity advance differed by about 1 per cent, on the average.[7] This relationship cannot be interpreted as reflecting primarily the effect of relative changes in scale. Index numbers of output provide, at best, a crude measure of the effects of scale. Furthermore, interpretation is complicated because a two-way relationship is involved.

We have already noted that an increase in industry output makes possible increased specialization of production among the plants and firms of an industry and the emergence of new industries providing specialized services, materials, or equipment which further reduce real unit costs. Growth also provides a favorable environment for innovation, whether output is expanded by an increase in the number of firms or by an increase in size of firms as optimum size itself is increased by technological progress. In either case, the planning of new facilities spurs rethinking of production technology. It is also clear that a larger proportion of plant and equipment is of the newest, most efficient type in an expanding industry than in one in which new-equipment purchases are chiefly for replacement.

There are several drawbacks, however, to using relative changes in output as an indicator of the relative impact of economies of scale. Such economies do not occur automatically, and it is unlikely that they bear a linear, or any other regular, relationship to output. External economies may be greater in one phase of industry expansion than in another; by the same token, similar rates of expansion in different industries probably result in different degrees of induced advance in efficiency, with possible lags of differing length.

In the second place, other factors favorable to productivity advance are intercorrelated with rates of growth. Terleckyj's correlations indicate that rapidly growing industries tend to employ more engineers and do more research, are composed of somewhat larger firms and plants, are more concentrated, have slightly greater barriers to entry, and are subject to less frequent business fluctuations. Thus, rates of growth stand for a complex of interconnected factors and cannot indicate external economies alone.

Possibly the most important objection to the growth measure as an explanatory variable is that it is intercorrelated with productivity itself. That is, autonomous innovations may reduce the relative cost and price of the products of an industry; the relative quantity sold will expand as a consequence if demand is price elastic and other demand influences are equal. In this case, the relative expansion of output is a result of the relative rise in productivity. Yet, the increased output, in turn, may be expected to result in economies of scale that will reinforce the productivity

[7] *Ibid.*, p. 62.

advance. Growth of productivity and output not only induces economies of scale, but may also create conditions more favorable to autonomous innovation—such as by strengthening the financial position of the firms involved so that more resources may be devoted to research and development.

In any case, it is clear that the output-productivity relation does not provide an unambiguous measure of scale effects. The picture is complicated further by the possibility that part of the positive association may be spurious (see Chapter 7). Recognizing the mutual influence of relative changes in output and productivity, Terleckyj tried relating productivity changes to the measures of research intensity and cyclical amplitude alone. These two variables jointly explained about 55 per cent of the variability in rates of productivity change for 1919–53, but were less successful for shorter periods.[8]

Cyclical and structural factors. Terleckyj's simple rank correlations reveal a significant degree of correlation between amplitude of cyclical fluctuation and productivity change in 3-digit manufacturing industries in the 1929–37 subperiod. There was a significant but lower coefficient of correlation between frequency of cyclical fluctuation and productivity change in the 2-digit groups in the 1948–53 subperiod. But only the amplitude measure showed up as significant in the multiple regressions. In part, this may occur because frequency of cyclical fluctuation shows a higher and more consistent negative correlation with growth than does the measure of cycle amplitude.

It seems plausible that wide cyclical fluctuations should adversely affect the average productivity of an industry. Some degree of organizational stability is prerequisite to steady improvements in productive efficiency. Frequent or large changes in the size of staff of firms, or cyclical fluctuations in the number of firms in business, would not seem to be conducive to innovation. This factor has often been mentioned as a reason for technological backwardness in the construction industry, for example. The associated lack of financial stability would hardly promote a policy of expenditures for research and development and would have an adverse effect on access to financial markets for investment funds. On the other hand, it could be argued that mild fluctuations provide a spur to efficiency. In Terleckyj's regressions, differences in cyclical amplitude were much less important than differences in research intensity in explaining relative productivity changes.

It might be argued that certain industries, because of various structural features, are more susceptible to innovation than others. Terleckyj introduced several variables of this sort into his correlations: ratios of

[8] *Ibid.*, p. 96.

capital stock to manhours worked; and average sizes of plants and firms in the various industries (as measured by average numbers of employees and average total dollar assets, respectively). None was significantly associated with productivity change in any of the statistical approaches. It is interesting that the average sizes of plants and firms were highly correlated with the measures of concentration and entry that were not correlated with productivity advance, as noted above. We also tried a measure of the ratio of purchased materials to the value of output and found this, too, to be unrelated to relative productivity changes.

CONCLUDING OBSERVATIONS

Although the explanatory variables included in the multiple correlations with relative rates of productivity change by industry reflect what are probably the major factors influencing productivity—innovation, scale, and business cycles—it is not surprising that about half the variance remains unexplained.

In the first place, there are undoubtedly errors in the estimates of the variables. For example, the productivity indexes (except for agriculture) are based on the assumption that gross and net industry output show the same movements, whereas true net output series may have somewhat different movements from gross series.

Secondly, it should be emphasized again that research and development outlays are only an indirect indication of the volume of innovation. Not only are variable lags involved, but identical outlays probably result in different amounts of eventual cost reduction. Results cannot be predicted accurately when the outlay is authorized, and the chance element must be substantial. This is supported by the presence of greater fluctuations in industry ranks with respect to productivity change than with respect to research and development outlays.

Further, research and development expenditures are not the only source of innovations. Although we did not succeed in identifying differences of industry structure that have a bearing on relative productivity change, it does seem reasonable to suppose that some industries are more amenable to cost reduction than others, and more so at one period than another. Also, the rates at which initial innovations spread over the firms of an industry undoubtedly differ from one period to another and from one industry to another. It is likewise probable that the effects on industry organization of proportionate changes in scale, if the scale factor could be isolated, would be found to vary between time periods and industries.

Finally, there are other factors that affect productivity besides changes in industry output and the intensity of investment designed to produce innovation. We have mentioned that the pervasive forces affecting the economy as a whole may have a somewhat different industry impact.

For example, the growth of management consulting services, as the economy has grown, is of greater advantage to the firms of some industries than of others. The rate of innovation may also be affected by additional specific factors, such as availability of financing, average entrepreneurial ability, and so forth, that we could not quantify.

At least, empirical analysis lends modest support to our deductive reasoning as to the forces that are important in explaining productivity advance. It is also significant in appearing to eliminate certain hypotheses, such as those that associate different degrees of competition in various industries with different rates of productivity change.

CHAPTER 7

Relative Changes in Productivity, Prices, and Resource Allocation

THUS far in Part III we have reviewed productivity movements in the various industries and industry groupings and have suggested some of the chief factors that may explain the different rates of change. It remains to explore the impact on economic structure of industry productivity changes.

Briefly, in this chapter it will be demonstrated that there is little connection between relative changes in productivity and factor prices in the several industries; there is, consequently, a significant negative correlation between relative changes in productivity and product prices. Through its effect on price, productivity is one of several factors affecting relative changes in quantities produced. On the average, the industry groupings of firms that increase their productive efficiency relative to the economy average are able to reduce the prices of their products relative to the general price level and thereby gain an increasing share of the market. Given relative changes in output, relative changes in productivity and factor substitutions provide a statistical explanation of relative changes in resource employment in the several industries. Firms in the technologically more progressive industries have tended to increase their employment of labor and use of capital somewhat more than industry as a whole—a fact which contradicts the notion of "technological unemployment" in any long-run sense.

Relative Changes in Productivity and in Prices

The interrelationship among productivity, product price, and factor price at the economy level was developed in Chapter 5. The interrelationships at the industry level are analogous, but more complex. Certain more or less realistic assumptions can be made, however, in order to simplify the relationship.

COMPONENTS OF INDUSTRY PRICE CHANGE

At the industry level, the basic identity of national product originating (at factor cost) with the quotient of factor price (product per unit of real input) and factor productivity holds, as at the economy level. To repeat the identity, but using VA (value added) as the symbol for national product originating in an industry:

$$VA/O = (VA/I) \div (O/I)$$

But this formulation does not tell us what we want to know about price. For the economy, the sum of the value added in each industry is equal to the value of all final products, to which a general price index for the economy applies. But in a component industry, value added is only a part of the value of production. The value of purchased intermediate products (materials and services) is the other part, to which value is added by processing within the given industry, i.e., by applying the services of labor and capital commanded by the given industry to the products purchased from other industries. So value added per unit of industry output is not the whole story of what happens to price, which also reflects prices of intermediate products. The value of production per unit of output (VP/O) is the relevant variable. Unit value of production would have the same movement as a variable-weighted price index if units of all types of output were separately weighted by base-period prices. In practice, there is generally some difference in movement between the unit value and the price of the output of an industry because, first, outputs are often measured in terms of somewhat heterogeneous units, so shifts in composition of output as well as changes in the price of identical units over time affect unit value; and, second, price and output indexes generally involve differing degrees of imputation, and weighting systems may not be fully consistent.

In the empirical investigation that follows, unit value indexes will be generally employed as price indicators since they are statistically consistent with the other variables of the system. Unit value indexes have another advantage over price indexes: They reflect changes in net realized price, which is desired, whereas price indexes are usually based on quoted prices, with more or less inadequate allowance for changes in discounts and other terms of sale. One drawback to their use is that errors in the output indexes and therefore in the productivity indexes affect the unit value indexes to the same degree in the opposite direction. Therefore, coefficients of correlation between relative changes in unit value and in productivity may contain a spurious element of uncertain magnitude. As a check on correlations involving unit value, therefore, we shall occasionally substitute price indexes since their derivation is wholly independent of the productivity variable.

Now, if we substitute unit value for unit value added in the left-hand side of the previous equation, we shall have to add the variables that explain changes in materials cost per unit of output (VM/O) to the right-hand side. Unit materials cost is the product of the price of materials and unit materials requirements. The price of materials may be expressed as

VM/M, where M is the physical volume of purchased materials (and services), obtained in practice by deflating the value of materials by the prices of the various intermediate products purchased by the given industry. Unit materials requirements (M/O) is the inverse of the "partial intermediate-product productivity ratio," if we wish to maintain parallelism with the partial factor productivity terminology. If consistent index numbers are used as the variables, the two terms on the right-hand side will have to be weighted by the base-period proportions of the value of product accounted for by value added and by value of purchased materials and services, designated by the subscripts wa and wm, respectively. Thus:

$$\frac{VP}{O} = \left(\frac{VA}{I} \div \frac{O}{I}\right)_{wa} + \left(\frac{VM}{M} \div \frac{O}{M}\right)_{wm}$$

An identity of this sort obviously does not explain the causal factors behind price change generally—the factors that cause changes in money demand to deviate from changes in the supply of goods. But the variables in the identity do enable us to analyze the components of a given relative price change. Also, given the rate of productivity advance in an industry and its unit materials cost, we can specify the change in factor price that is consistent with stable product prices.

PRODUCTIVITY-PRICE RELATIONS IN ILLUSTRATIVE INDUSTRY GROUPS

To indicate the type of price analysis that is possible when the several productivity and price variables identified in the equation above are known, we shall present the relevant index numbers for two important groups in the economy, farming and manufactured foods. These groups were chosen primarily because relatively good estimates could be prepared for all the variables. They are also suitable for illustrative purposes because of their different behavior.

The figures for the farm sector are shown in Table 52. Percentage changes in the variables over the entire period can be seen in the last line of the table. Between 1899 and 1953, composite factor price (wage rates and the unit compensation of capital), computed as the quotient of value added (national income) per unit of real factor input, rose over eightfold (column 3). But productivity (physical volume of gross output per unit of real factor input) more than doubled (column 4); so value added per unit of output increased by 233 per cent (column 2). The price of purchased materials and services consumed in the production process more than tripled over the period. This was far less of an increase than that in factor price; but materials consumption per unit of output, instead of declining, as did factor use per unit of output (the inverse of factor productivity), rose about two-and-one-half times (column 7). Thus,

TABLE 52

Farm Segment: Productivity and Prices of Outputs and Inputs, Key Years and Subperiods, 1899–1953

	Unit Value of Output^a (price) (1)	Value Added Per Unit of Output^b (2)	Value Added Per Unit of Input (3)	Productivity (4)	Cost of Materials Per Unit of Output^c (5)	Cost of Materials Per Unit of Materials Input (6)	Unit Materials Requirements (7)	Relative Weight of Materials (per cent) (8)
				INDEX (1929 = 100)				
1899	41.5	44.6	37.7	84.6	30.3	47.2	64.3	
1909	64.7	69.9	58.7	84.0	45.1	64.0	70.4	
1919	143.6	150.6	128.9	85.6	117.6	133.7	88.0	
1929	100.0	100.0	100.0	100.0	100.0	100.0	100.0	21.4
1937	81.2	79.5	85.1	107.1	87.8	86.1	102.0	
1948	187.5	171.6	283.8	165.4	246.2	162.0	152.0	
1953	170.8	148.5	307.2	206.8	252.9	154.6	163.6	
				LINK RELATIVES				
1899–1909	155.9	156.7	155.7	99.3	148.8	135.6	109.5	15.6
1909–19	221.9	215.5	219.6	101.9	260.8	208.9	125.0	14.8
1919–29	69.6	66.4	77.6	116.8	85.0	74.8	113.6	17.4
1929–37	81.2	79.5	85.1	107.1	87.8	86.1	102.0	21.4
1937–48	230.9	215.8	333.5	154.4	280.4	188.2	149.0	23.0
1948–53	91.1	86.5	108.2	125.0	102.7	95.4	107.6	28.0
1899–1953	411.6	333.0	814.9	244.4	834.7	327.5	254.4	15.6

^a Price is gross value of product divided by gross output. It may also be derived as the weighted average of value added per unit of output (col. 2) and cost of materials per unit of output (col. 5); weights for materials are given in col. 8; for value added, 100 − col. (8).
^b Col. (3) divided by col. (4).
^c Col. (6) times col. (7).

CHART 20

Farm Segment: Components of Price Movements, Key Years, 1899–1953

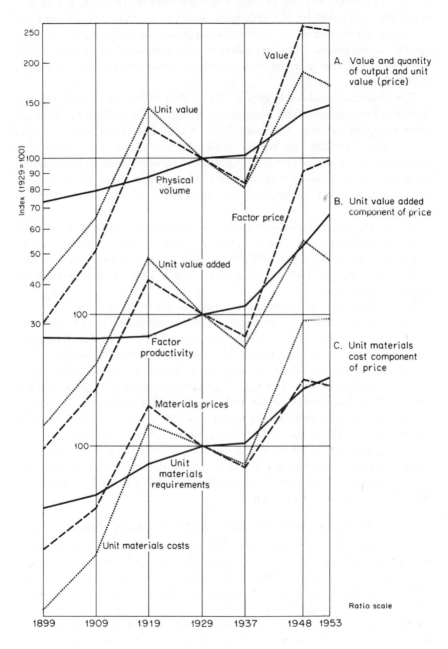

materials cost per unit of output (column 5) went up more than eightfold, compared with the tripling of factor cost per unit of output. But the effect of the very large increase in unit materials cost on final price was substantially mitigated by the relatively low proportion—16 per cent—of total cost accounted for by materials purchases in 1899, the base period for this comparison. The net effect of the several changes was a little more than fourfold increase in the average price (unit value) of output (Chart 20).

The manufactured-foods group (Table 53) differs in several respects from the farm sector. The average price (unit value) of output approximately tripled between 1899 and 1953. Value added per unit of output quadrupled, but the cost of materials per unit of output rose to only 263 per cent of the base value. In contrast to farming, materials accounted for a large proportion of total cost in the base period, and the change in unit materials cost dominated the movement of manufactured-foods prices.

The fourfold increase in unit value added was the resultant of a tenfold increase in factor price (value added per unit of input) reduced in its impact on value added per unit of output by an almost two-and-one-half-fold increase in total factor productivity, which amounts to a 60 per cent decline in real factor cost per unit of output.

Materials prices averaged better than a threefold increase over the fifty-four-year period, but the effect of this rise on materials costs per unit of output was cushioned by a reduction of one-fourth in materials requirements per unit of output. As a result, both unit materials costs and final prices of manufactured foods increased less than threefold over the period.

The reduction in unit materials requirements was largely the result of a shift in the product-mix of the industry toward more highly processed foods, but there was some saving of materials in the individual component industries. It will be noted that the reduction of materials requirements was accomplished in the 1899–1937 period; since 1937, unit materials requirements have increased somewhat. It is also striking that the very large productivity advance of the 1920's has not been closely approached either before or since that decade.

RELATIVE CHANGES IN PRODUCTIVITY, COSTS, AND PRICES

If one had consistent estimates for all industries of the four variables into which price changes can be decomposed, then relative price changes could be subject to full statistical description. It is interesting and useful, however, to see to what extent relative productivity changes alone can explain relative changes in prices or in unit values of output. An annex has been included at the end of this chapter, presenting most of the variables with which productivity has been correlated in the subsequent sections.

TABLE 53

Manufactured-Foods Industry:a Productivity and Prices of Outputs and Inputs, Key Years and Subperiods, 1899–1953

	Unit Value of Output^b (price) (1)	Value Added Per Unit of Output^c (2)	Value Added Per Unit of Input (3)	Productivity (4)	Cost of Materials Per Unit of Output^d (5)	Cost of Materials Per Unit of Materials Input (6)	Unit Materials Requirements (7)	Relative Weight of Materials (per cent) (8)
			INDEX (1929 = 100)					
1899	63.9	44.9	27.2	60.6	71.1	55.8	127.5	
1909	74.8	53.2	34.5	64.9	83.1	67.9	122.4	
1919	151.4	104.4	69.0	66.1	169.5	155.9	108.7	
1929	100.0	100.0	100.0	100.0	100.0	100.0	100.0	72.1
1937	85.1	83.1	93.5	112.5	85.9	89.7	95.8	
1948	186.2	170.4	225.3	132.2	192.4	204.0	94.3	
1953	185.2	180.8	266.4	147.3	186.9	187.3	99.8	
			LINK RELATIVES					
1899–1909	117.1	118.5	126.8	107.1	116.9	121.7	96.0	80.4
1909–19	202.4	196.2	200.0	101.8	204.0	229.6	88.8	80.1
1919–29	66.1	95.8	144.9	151.3	59.0	64.1	92.0	80.7
1929–37	85.1	83.1	93.5	112.5	85.9	89.7	95.8	72.1
1937–48	218.8	205.1	241.0	117.5	224.0	227.4	98.4	72.7
1948–53	99.5	106.1	118.2	111.4	97.1	91.8	105.8	74.4
1899–1953	289.8	402.7	979.4	243.1	262.9	335.7	78.3	80.4

a This table represents a special study of the foods group. The output index is based on complete coverage of food industries, using deflated value when no quantity data are available; in other tables the output index is based on quantity data, by industry, with an adequacy adjustment to estimate full coverage for the group. The index of materials prices is based on a Marshall-Edgeworth weighted average of deflated materials costs (computed for each industry in the foods group); in the other tables the materials price index was imputed from the ratio of the sum of materials costs in current and constant dollars. In other tables for other groups, the materials price index was computed for the group as a whole on the basis of weights obtained from the BLS Interindustry Relations Study, 1947, Division of Interindustry Economics, October 1952.

b Price is computed from value of product in index form divided by the output index. It may also be derived as the weighted average of value added per unit of output, col. (2), and cost of materials per unit of output, col. (5); weights are given for materials in col. (8), for value added, 100 − col. (8).

c Col. (3) divided by col. (4).

d Col. (6) times col. (7).

Before correlating these variables, it will be helpful to investigate the relationship between productivity changes and changes in each of the other three price-related variables. If, for example, there were highly positive correlations between changes in productivity and changes in factor prices, or in unit materials costs, or both, then relative changes in real factor costs per unit of output (the inverse of productivity) would be offset by relative changes in the opposite direction in the other cost elements, and the degree of correlation between relative changes in prices and in productivity would be low. That is, productivity gains in varying amounts would accrue to the factors or to suppliers of materials, and relative prices would not change.

Actually, we know that there are substantial relative changes in prices. Economic theory suggests that factor prices, rather than product prices, in the various industries tend to show the same proportionate changes under competitive conditions, given time for labor and capital to flow into the industries in which factor prices have risen relatively and out of those in which their unit compensation is temporarily depressed. Under these conditions, there should be little relationship between relative changes in productivity and factor prices, but a high degree of correlation between relative changes in productivity and in unit value added. It is more difficult to argue a priori with respect to the relative movements of productivity and unit materials costs. But if relative industry efficiency in the use of factors carried over to the use of materials, then there should be a negative rather than a positive relationship between relative changes in productivity and in unit materials cost.

Relative changes in factor prices. Analysis of the data bearing on the subject can be carried out by relating relative productivity changes to changes in average hourly earnings and in the price of capital separately, and then to total factor compensation per unit of input.

That changes in the average hourly earnings of labor are not closely related to productivity changes is indicated by our estimates of the former for the key years. The interindustry structure of average hourly earnings has not changed very much over the various subperiods of the fifty-four-year period, as shown by relative rankings of the thirty-three industry groups in this respect in Table 54. For percentage changes in average hourly earnings in the various groups relative to the mean change, the coefficient of variation is +.14 for the long period and averages +.09 for the six subperiods; this is considerably less than the coefficient of variation of percentage changes in productivity (cf. Table 36). Serial correlation of the group ranks with respect to average hourly earnings in each subperiod with ranks in the previous subperiod yields coefficients above +.9 in all subperiods except between the first two.

TABLE 54

Ranking of Average Hourly Earnings in Thirty-three Industry Groups,
Subperiods, 1899–1953

	1899– 1953[a]	1899– 1909	1909– 1919	1919– 1929	1929– 1937	1937– 1948	1948– 1953
Farming	1	1	1	1	1	1	1
Mining							
Metals	16	31	31	15	13	15	15
Anthracite coal	31	24	27	32	30	31	30
Bituminous coal	32	29	33	30	23	32	31
Oil and gas	24	14	29	25	20	21	21
Nonmetals	7	32	13	6	5	4	7
Manufacturing							
Foods	11	15	14	12	9	10	12
Beverages	27	33	32	31	28	18	18
Tobacco	2	7	2	2	2	3	3
Textiles	4	2	5	3	4	6	5
Apparel	12	9	19	20	14	11	8
Lumber products	3	3	3	4	3	2	2
Furniture	5	6	7	8	6	5	6
Paper	13	5	9	9	12	16	16
Printing, publishing	29	28	23	28	32	29	27
Chemicals	22	22	21	22	21	20	25
Petroleum, coal products	33	16	24	27	33	33	33
Rubber products	23	17	22	23	25	23	22
Leather products	8	8	12	11	8	7	4
Stone, clay, glass	15	18	16	17	16	14	14
Primary metals	28	26	30	29	27	27	28
Fabricated metals	18	20	18	21	18	17	17
Machinery, nonelectric	25	27	25	24	24	22	23
Electric machinery	19	25	20	19	22	19	19
Transportation equipment	30	10	28	33	31	30	29
Miscellaneous	14	19	15	18	17	13	13
Transportation							
Railroads	10	4	10	13	15	9	10
Local transit	9	12	8	10	10	12	9
Communications and public utilities							
Telephone	21	21	11	16	26	26	20
Telegraph	6	11	4	5	7	8	11
Electric utilities	26	30	26	26	29	28	26
Manufactured gas	17	13	6	7	11	25	32
Natural gas	20	23	17	14	19	24	24

[a] Rank of average of absolute hourly earnings in subperiods weighted by length of each subperiod. Hourly earnings for each subperiod represent an average of hourly earnings in the terminal years of the subperiod.

So it is not surprising that the coefficient of rank correlation between proportionate changes in productivity and in average hourly labor compensation, while positive, is barely significant, either over the long period or the subperiods, for the thirty-three groups or the eighty manufacturing industries (see Table 55). It will be noted that the highest coefficients are

TABLE 55

Coefficients of Rank Correlation[a] of Relative Changes in Productivity
and in Factor Prices, Subperiods, 1899–1953

	1899– 1953	1899– 1909	1909– 1919	1919– 1929	1929– 1937	1937– 1948	1948– 1953
33 industry groups							
Total productivity versus							
Average hourly labor							
compensation	0.24	−0.33	0.24	0.0	0.41	0.14	0.11
Capital compensation per unit	0.22[b]				0.20	−0.35	0.04
Factor compensation per unit	0.05	−0.22	0.03	0.19	0.62	−0.22	−0.01
Capital compensation per unit versus average hourly labor							
compensation	0.11[b]				0.13	0.19	0.19
80 manufacturing industries[c]							
Output per manhour versus average hourly labor							
compensation	0.26	0.39	0.27	0.21	0.44	0.42	0.20

[a] For $N = 33$, the value of the coefficient of rank correlation which is significant at the 0.05 level is 0.31; at the 0.01 level, 0.43. For $N = 80$, the comparable figures are 0.22 and 0.28.

[b] 1929–53.

[c] For the eighty manufacturing industries, the long period refers to 1899–1954, and the last two subperiods are 1937–47 and 1947–54.

for 1929–37. Apparently, relative changes in productivity are a more important determinant of changes in industry wage rates in a period of subnormal aggregate demand than at other times. Note that in the eighty manufacturing industries, in which average hourly earnings are probably less influenced by changing occupational structure, percentage changes in average hourly earnings are often more closely correlated with percentage changes in output per manhour in the subperiods than over the long period. It seems logical that the longer the period for adjustments, the more nearly alike will be the movements of wage rates. Over time, competition will tend to equalize changes in rates of compensation in the various industries—except insofar as these are a result of changing occupational structure or changes in basic supply and demand forces that alter the relation of wage rates among occupations.

Estimates of compensation per unit of real capital services are of poorer quality than the labor compensation estimates, particularly before 1929. But essentially the same result emerges from a correlation between proportionate changes in capital compensation per unit and in productivity. While the coefficient is positive in two out of three subperiods, it is not significantly high. The relatively high negative coefficient of rank correlation in the 1937–48 subperiod is interesting. With a high aggregate demand in the latter year, profitability was more affected by demand factors (such as war-born backlogs of requirements in certain areas) than by unit costs, although the firms of some industries set their own price ceilings.

Changes in total compensation per unit of composite factor input show a coefficient of rank correlation with productivity changes of less than +.1 for the long period; in three of the subperiods the coefficient was negative; and in all except that of 1929–37 it was low (see Table 55). This being so, one would expect a high negative correlation between relative industry changes in value added per unit of output and in productivity. The coefficient shown in Table 57 is —.74; while significant, it is not as high as might be expected, because the census value-added estimates used in getting most of the unit value-added figures for the correlation include certain intermediate services as well as factor compensation proper. Also, our capital compensation estimates are not necessarily consistent with the value-added figures.

But we are more interested in total unit values or prices of industry outputs than in unit values added since the former are the prices that influence sales. The extent to which relative industry price changes may be explained by relative productivity changes depends not only on factor prices but also on the patterns of change in the unit value of purchased materials and services, to which we now turn.

Relative changes in unit materials costs. The cost of purchased materials per unit of output is the product of the quantity of materials consumed per unit and the prices of the materials. Correlating the ranks of the percentage changes in each of these variables with percentage changes in productivity over the long period, we obtain a coefficient of almost —.4 in each case (see Table 56).

It is of interest that those industries with higher-than-average increases in factor productivity also tend to have larger-than-average savings in materials. This suggests that management efficiency in use of the factors carries over with respect to the use of intermediate products, and/or that the industries with relative increases in productivity tend also to be industries in which there are relative increases in the degree of processing of purchased materials. Perhaps an increasing degree of processing generally or a shift in the composition of output to types of products requiring greater processing offers improved opportunities for productivity advance. It is not as easy to suggest reasons why the prices of purchased materials should fall relatively in the industries experiencing relative productivity increases.

TABLE 56

Coefficients of Rank Correlation[a] of Relative Changes in Productivity and in Unit Cost of Materials, Thirty-three Industry Groups, Subperiods, 1899–1953

	1899– 1953	1899– 1909	1909– 1919	1919– 1929	1929– 1937	1937– 1948	1948– 1953
Total factor productivity versus							
Materials cost per unit of output	−0.59	−0.55	−0.50	−0.58	−0.55	−0.36	−0.52
Real materials cost per unit	−0.39	−0.36	−0.38	−0.25	−0.22	−0.15	−0.10
Value (price) of materials per unit	−0.38	−0.37	−0.01	−0.51	−0.50	−0.28	−0.52
Real materials cost per unit versus materials price	−0.22	−0.16	−0.21	−0.22	−0.05	−0.04	−0.13

[a] For $N = 33$, the value of the coefficient of rank correlation which is significant at the 0.05 level is 0.31; at the 0.01 level, 0.43.

When relative productivity changes are correlated with the costs of purchased materials per unit of output, the coefficient (−.59) is substantially higher than is obtained using changes in either of the cost components. The result reflects a slight negative correlation between relative changes in unit consumption and prices of purchased materials (see Table 56). Apparently, industries facing relative increases in materials prices make more strenuous attempts to economize on materials or to substitute other inputs, but such possibilties are limited.

Relative changes in unit values of output. To the extent that there have been variations in the relative movements of factor prices and of materials costs per unit of output associated with relative changes in productivity, the degree of correlation between relative changes in productivity and prices will be reduced. Relative changes in factor prices have not been great, and neither has their degree of correlation with relative productivity changes. Relative changes in unit materials costs have been much greater than those in factor prices, and their degree of correlation with relative productivity changes has been substantially greater, although still not high. Therefore, it is not surprising that the coefficients of correlation between changes in productivity and in unit value or price are significant at the 1 per cent level (see Table 57 and Chart 21).

Although productivity is but one of four variables into which relative price change can be decomposed, the coefficient of rank correlation of −.72 between relative changes in productivity and in unit value means that approximately one-half of the variance in changes of unit values is explained by productivity changes. The coefficients of correlation are almost as high in relationships between relative changes in output per manhour and in unit values of output for the eighty manufacturing industries and the twelve farm groups.

TABLE 57

Coefficients of Rank Correlation[a] of Relative Changes in Unit Values or Prices and in Productivity or Related Variables, Subperiods, 1899–1953

	1899–1953	1899–1909	1909–1919	1919–1929	1929–1937	1937–1948	1948–1953
33 industry groups							
Total factor productivity versus							
Unit value added	−0.74	−0.79	−0.65	−0.46	−0.29	−0.64	−0.68
Unit value of output	−0.72	−0.74	−0.59	−0.61	−0.44	−0.60	−0.66
Price	−0.55	−0.62	−0.49	−0.60	−0.23	−0.41	−0.49
Unit labor cost versus							
Unit value of output	0.62	0.63	0.64	0.78	0.75	0.80	0.64
Price	0.55	0.47	0.50	0.69	0.41	0.68	0.64
80 manufacturing industries[b]							
Output per manhour versus							
unit value of output	−0.57	−0.76	−0.41	−0.54	−0.73	−0.33	−0.49
Unit labor cost versus							
unit value of output	0.69	0.76	0.61	0.70	0.74	0.72	0.49
12 farm groups[c]							
Output per manhour versus							
price	−0.55		−0.32	−0.43	0.03	0.31	−0.27

[a] Significance of rank correlation coefficients:

N	0.05 Level	0.01 Level
12	0.51	0.71
33	0.31	0.43
80	0.22	0.28

[b] For the eighty manufacturing industries, the long period refers to 1899–1954, and the last two subperiods are 1937–47 and 1947–54.

[c] For the twelve farm groups, the long period covers 1910–53, and the first available subperiod covers 1910–19.

It will be noted in Table 57 that the coefficient of correlation is not as high when changes in composite price indexes are used in the relationship instead of changes in unit values. As mentioned earlier, the unit value measures rest on the same output indexes that are used in the productivity calculations. Therefore, to the extent that there are errors in the output measures, the degree of correlation between changes in unit values and changes in productivity is overstated.

CHART 21

Thirty-three Industry Groups: Relation between Total Factor Productivity and Unit
Value of Output, 1953 Relative to 1899

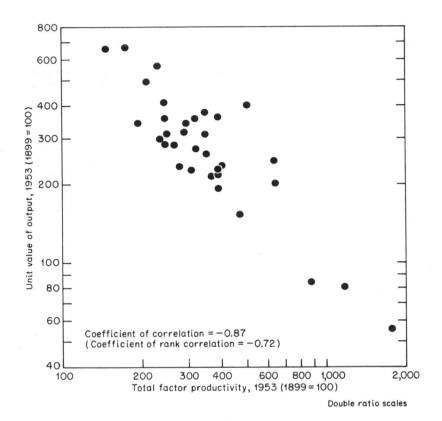

Double ratio scales

In the thirty-three groups, the degree of association between changes in productivity and changes in both unit values and prices has generally been lower in the subperiods since 1929 than earlier.

In Table 57, we have also shown coefficients of rank correlation between relative changes in prices and in unit labor costs (labor cost per unit of output). Although unit labor cost indexes are the quotient of average hourly earnings and output per manhour and thus measure but partially two of the four component variables of price change, the coefficients are almost as high as those obtained from relationships between productivity and prices (disregarding sign). This reflects the heavy weight of labor in both the productivity and the factor price measures.

A comparison of total factor productivity and prices reveals that relative changes in prices are less than proportionate to relative changes in productivity. A regression equation fitted to the percentage changes in the two sets of estimates for the thirty-three groups indicates that a 10 per cent change in productivity is associated with an 8 per cent change in price, on the average.[1] It is consistent with this relation that the dispersion of relative price changes is less than the dispersion of relative productivity changes: the coefficient of variation for proportionate changes in productivity in the thirty-three groups, 1899–1953, is +.46, whereas for unit value it is +.34. This is consistent with the fact that high-productivity industries tend also to reduce their unit materials cost more than average.

Relative Changes in Output, Productivity, and the Employment of Resources by Industry

Relative changes in output of the various industries of the economy are the result of three major sets of forces: (1) the income elasticities of demand for the various groups of products by which the industries are distinguished; (2) the price elasticities of demand for the various groups of products; and (3) shifts in demand as tastes of consumers change and new or modified products are introduced.

It is not our purpose here to present a full statistical explanation of changes in relative demand; instead, we shall focus on the relative changes in the distribution of resources among industries that result from relative changes in productivity. The main question to be answered is whether or not the interaction of relative changes in output and in productivity, acting through relative price changes and the other demand variables, has operated to produce a positive association with relative changes in productivity and in resource employment. If not, then the industries with greater-than-average productivity gains would be characterized by a declining proportion of the resources employed in the economy. Our analysis will show that the reverse tendency has prevailed over the longer periods.

RELATIVE CHANGES IN OUTPUT, PRICES, AND PRODUCTIVITY

Output and prices. There is a significant negative correlation between relative changes in productivity and prices; if there is likewise a negative association between relative changes in prices and in output, as would be expected, then it follows that productivity and output will be positively associated. Table 58, showing average annual percentage changes in

---

[1] The regression equation fitted to the logarithms of index numbers of unit values (y) and logs of index numbers of productivity (x) for 1953 (1899 = 100) is:
$$y = 4.7267 - 0.9013x$$
$$r = -.87$$

output by segment and by group for the long period, 1899–1953, and the subperiods, is provided for reference purposes. It will be noted that the dispersion of relative output changes is considerably greater than the dispersion of relative changes in productivity—more so for the long period

TABLE 58

Private Domestic Economy: Average Annual Rates of Change in Physical Volume of Output, by Segment and by Group, with Measures of Dispersion, Subperiods, 1899–1953
(per cent)

	Pre-1899	1899–1909	1909–1919	1919–1929	1929–1937	1937–1948	1948–1953	1899–1953	Mean Deviation of Subperiod Rates from Secular Rate
Farming	2.6	0.7	0.6	1.0	0.2	1.4	0.4	0.8	0.4
Mining	5.9	5.9	2.2	3.8	−0.5	3.1	0.7	2.8	1.6
Metals		5.5	0.9	3.2	−0.2	0.1	1.8	1.9	1.8
Anthracite coal		3.0	0.8	−1.8	−4.3	0.9	−11.6	−1.2	3.1
Bituminous coal		7.0	2.1	1.4	−2.3	2.7	−5.3	1.6	2.6
Oil and gas		7.3	7.3	9.1	2.6	4.2	4.8	6.1	2.0
Nonmetals		7.9	−0.5	7.5	−4.4	5.4	5.2	3.6	3.9
Manufacturing	4.8	4.7	3.5	5.1	0.4	5.4	5.7	4.1	1.4
Foods		4.0	3.8	4.4	0.5	3.6	2.0	3.3	1.0
Beverages		3.9	−9.6	−4.5	27.2	6.3	0.7	2.9	8.3
Tobacco		3.8	5.0	3.7	2.0	4.3	1.8	3.6	0.8
Textiles		4.1	1.6	3.5	1.0	3.7	0.8	2.7	1.2
Apparel		5.3	2.4	4.5	0.5	3.6	2.1	3.3	1.4
Lumber products		2.5	−2.7	1.3	−3.6	3.0	2.0	0.4	2.4
Furniture		2.9	0.3	7.0	−3.3	6.9	2.8	3.0	3.0
Paper		7.2	3.7	6.6	2.5	4.5	4.8	5.0	1.4
Printing, publishing		7.6	4.3	6.4	0.2	3.4	2.8	4.3	1.9
Chemicals		5.4	5.1	6.9	2.7	8.7	8.7	6.2	1.7
Petroleum, coal products		6.4	9.3	9.9	1.6	5.3	4.8	6.5	2.3
Rubber products		6.0	21.4	6.4	−1.2	5.9	4.6	7.5	5.1
Leather products		2.6	0.8	1.0	1.0	0.9	−0.1	1.1	0.5
Stone, clay, glass		6.5	−0.1	6.0	−0.1	5.4	3.9	3.7	2.5
Primary metals		7.2	3.6	4.9	−1.4	5.5	3.8	4.1	1.9
Fabricated metals		7.2	3.8	5.2	−0.8	6.2	11.5	5.2	2.3
Machinery, nonelectric		4.7	5.2	3.1	0.1	7.3	5.6	4.4	1.8
Electric machinery		9.2	9.4	8.0	−0.8	9.4	12.7	7.9	2.6
Transportation equipment		3.9	19.0	5.1	−1.2	5.5	13.7	7.2	5.5
Miscellaneous		6.4	2.4	3.7	0.8	7.1	5.9	4.4	2.1
Transportation	7.4	4.6	3.9	2.0	0.4	6.8	1.6	3.5	1.9
Railroads		6.1	4.4	0.8	−2.6	5.2	−1.5	2.6	3.0
Local transit		7.4	3.9	2.6	−2.5	3.6	−8.7	2.0	3.4
Residual transport		−0.7	1.8	6.7	7.5	7.5	8.0	4.7	3.2

(continued)

TABLE 58 (concluded)

Private Domestic Economy: Average Annual Rates of Change in Physical Volume of
Output, by Segment and by Group, with Measures of Dispersion, Subperiods, 1899–1953
(per cent)

	Pre-1899	1899–1909	1909–1919	1919–1929	1929–1937	1937–1948	1948–1953	1899–1953	Mean Deviation of Subperiod Rates from Secular Rate
Communications and public utilities	6.8	12.9	7.3	8.1	1.8	7.3	6.1	7.5	2.2
Telephone		18.2	4.9	7.5	−0.9	7.2	2.6	7.1	4.1
Telegraph		3.7	2.6	8.0	−2.0	0.2	−2.4	2.1	2.9
Electric utilities		17.1	14.0	10.8	4.1	7.8	9.3	10.7	3.5
Manufactured gas		9.3	6.5	3.5	−1.3	4.5	−2.0	4.0	3.0
Natural gas		8.4	4.8	5.1	3.5	8.4	11.9	6.7	2.3
Residual sector	4.1	4.2	3.0	3.7	−0.2	4.3	5.3	3.3	1.2
Construction	4.3	5.7	−2.9	5.9	−5.9	7.2	5.6	2.6	4.7
Trade	4.6	3.9	2.2	4.2	0.5	4.4	2.6	3.1	1.2
Finance and services	5.4	5.2	2.5	3.4	−1.4	3.6	4.3	3.0	1.5
Private domestic economy	4.5	4.2	3.0	3.7	0.1	4.5	4.4	3.3	1.1
Mean deviation of 8 segment rates from economy rate	0.8	1.2	1.2	1.3	1.2	1.3	1.8	0.8	
Aggregate of 5 covered segments	4.8	4.1	3.0	3.7	0.4	4.6	3.7	3.3	1.0
Mean deviation from sector rates:									
5 segments	1.1	1.7	1.3	1.8	0.2	1.7	2.4	1.3	
33 groups		2.6	2.8	2.1	1.4	2.0	3.4	1.9	

than for the subperiods. Since there is greater dispersion in group rates
of change in productivity than in prices, it is clear that relative changes in
output are much more widely dispersed than relative changes in prices
by industry group. Variability in group rates of output change over the
subperiods is likewise considerably greater than that of productivity
changes in the groups, although there is little difference in the variability
of the two measures at the segment and economy levels.

The coefficient of correlation between relative changes in output and
in price (unit value) for the thirty-three groups is —.48 for the long period.
It averages somewhat less in the subperiods, as is shown in Table 59.
This means that about one-fourth of the variance in relative output changes
may be explained by relative changes in the prices (unit values) of the
products of the thirty-three groups over the long period. We have noted

that about one-half of the variance in relative price changes may be explained by relative changes in productivity. Yet the degree of association between relative changes in output and in productivity is greater than might be inferred from these correlations.

TABLE 59

Coefficients of Rank Correlation[a] of Relative Changes in Unit Values or Prices and in Output, Subperiods, 1899–1953

	1899–1953	1899–1909	1909–1919	1919–1929	1929–1937	1937–1948	1948–1953
33 industry groups							
Price versus output	−0.34	−0.54	−0.50	−0.26	−0.18	−0.49	0.07
Unit value versus output	−0.48	−0.64	−0.56	−0.16	−0.35	−0.57	−0.11
Manufacturing							
20 groups							
Price versus output	−0.45	−0.66	−0.78	−0.18	−0.39	−0.50	0.33
Unit value versus output	−0.54	−0.69	−0.69	−0.22	−0.65	−0.64	0.02
80 industries[b]							
Unit value versus output	−0.52	−0.51	−0.29	−0.19	−0.64	−0.42	−0.13
12 farm groups[c]							
Price versus output	0.22		0.07	0.47	−0.20	0.09	0.33

[a] Significance of rank correlation coefficients:

N	0.05 Level	0.01 Level
12	0.51	0.71
20	0.38	0.53
33	0.31	0.43
80	0.22	0.28

[b] For the eighty manufacturing industries, the long period refers to 1899–1954, and the last two subperiods are 1937–47 and 1947–54.

[c] For the twelve farm groups, the long period covers 1910–53, and the first available subperiod covers 1910–19.

Output and productivity. The coefficients obtained from correlating relative rates of change in productivity and output are shown in Table 60. The correlations were carried out separately for the thirty-three industry groups and the twenty manufacturing groups, using both total factor productivity and output per unit of labor input as the dependent variables. For the eighty manufacturing industries and the twelve farm groups, output per unit of labor input (manhours) alone could be used. The results are shown graphically by the scatter diagrams in Charts 22 and 23.

The degree of correlation is significantly positive in all cases except that of farming. The coefficient using the twenty manufacturing groups (+.66) is somewhat higher than that (+.64) obtained using all groups.

It makes little difference in the correlation whether rates of change in total factor productivity or in output per manhour are used for the twenty groups. In the case of the eighty manufacturing industries, the coefficient of rank correlation between rates of change in output and in output per manhour is +.67, almost as high as for the groups. In all cases, the degree of correlation is somewhat higher over the long period than in the subperiods, on the average.

TABLE 60

Coefficients of Rank Correlation[a] of Relative Changes in Productivity
and in Output, Subperiods, 1899–1953

	1899–1953	1899–1909	1909–1919	1919–1929	1929–1937	1937–1948	1948–1953
33 industry groups							
O/I versus O	0.64	0.64	0.48	0.56	0.67	0.29	0.37
O/L versus O	0.68	0.69	0.53	0.49	0.61	0.25	0.30
Manufacturing							
20 groups							
O/I versus O	0.66	0.61	0.44	0.63	0.73	0.41	0.69
O/L versus O	0.69	0.72	0.55	0.55	0.79	0.36	0.60
80 industries[b]							
O/L versus O	0.67	0.57	0.22	0.49	0.69	0.31	0.67
12 farm groups[c]							
O/L versus O	−0.10		−0.17	−0.07	0.52	0.25	−0.02

NOTE: O = output; I = total input; L = labor input.

[a] Significance of rank correlation coefficients:

N	*0.05 Level*	*0.01 Level*
12	0.51	0.71
20	0.38	0.53
33	0.31	0.43
80	0.22	0.28

[b] For the eighty manufacturing industries, the long period refers to 1899–1954, and the last two subperiods are 1937–47 and 1947–54.

[c] For the twelve farm groups, the long period covers 1910–53, and the first available subperiod covers 1910–19.

Again, the possibility of a spurious element in the correlations due to errors in the output indexes should be kept in mind. For the twelve farm groups, relative changes in output and in output per manhour are not closely correlated; the coefficient is −.10 for the long period, which is not significant at the 5 per cent level. The result for farming is not surprising in view of the generally low price elasticity of demand for farm products. Also, the reciprocal influence of scale on productivity could hardly be expected to operate in extractive industry.

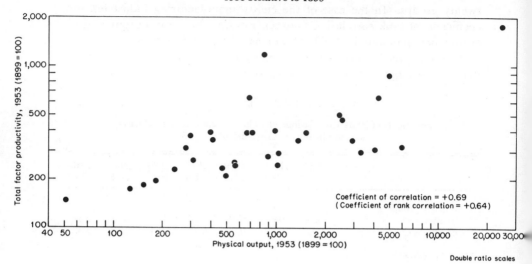

CHART 22
Thirty-three Industry Groups: Relation between Output and Total Factor Productivity,
1953 Relative to 1899

Total factor productivity, 1953 (1899 = 100)

Coefficient of correlation = +0.69
(Coefficient of rank correlation = +0.64)

Physical output, 1953 (1899 = 100)

Double ratio scales

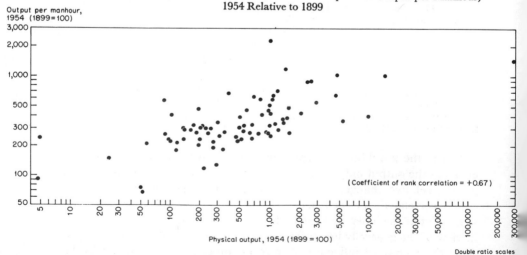

CHART 23
Eighty Manufacturing Industries: Relation between Output and Output per Manhour,
1954 Relative to 1899

Output per manhour,
1954 (1899 = 100)

(Coefficient of rank correlation = +0.67)

Physical output, 1954 (1899 = 100)

Double ratio scales

The significant association between relative changes in productivity and in output is not due just to the influence of productivity on price and therefore on sales. As it has already been emphasized, increases in output make possible economies of scale that augment autonomous innovation in producing productivity advance. In fact, our analysis suggests that the influence of relative changes in scale on relative productivity changes may be more important than the reverse influence working through relative price changes. The problem is complicated by the possibility that other demand forces may tend to reinforce the productivity-price effect on output. For example, shifts in demand due to changing consumer preferences and increases in income probably favor new products, and productivity in industries producing new items generally rises faster than in industries producing older products.[2]

We cannot attempt a full analysis of relative output changes; this in itself would be a major research undertaking. From here on, we take the relative changes in output by industry as given and analyze the effect of relative productivity changes on the employment of labor and of capital in the various industries. The question is whether relative increases in output have been large enough to more than offset relative decreases in unit factor requirements and to result in rising resource employment in the technologically progressive industries.

VARIABLES EXPLAINING RELATIVE CHANGES IN THE EMPLOYMENT OF LABOR

In Table 61, index numbers of total factor productivity and other variables required to reconcile relatives of output and of employment (total persons engaged) are shown for major segments for 1953 on an 1899 base. By dividing output (O) by total factor productivity (O/I), total input (I) is obtained, and the quotient of total input and total input per unit of labor input (a measure of the substitution of capital for labor) is labor input (L). But labor input is manhours in component groups weighted by average hourly compensation, whereas our major interest is in employment of persons (E). The latter can be obtained as the quotient of labor input and labor input per person, which reflects the net effect of changes in average hours worked and interindustry shifts of manhours among groups with varying hourly compensation. To summarize:

$$E = O \div \frac{O}{I} \div \frac{I}{L} \div \frac{L}{E}$$

To illustrate by the manufacturing segment, output increased almost ninefold over the fifty-four years, while productivity and total factor input both approximately tripled. Since capital input increased somewhat more

[2] Solomon Fabricant, *Employment in Manufacturing, 1899–1939: An Analysis of Its Relation to the Volume of Production*, New York (NBER), 1942, p. 64.

than labor input, labor input increased to 270 per cent of the base. Labor input per person employed declined over the period, as the reduction in the workweek more than offset the upward influence of shifts of manhours from lower- to higher-paying groups; so employment rose to 325 per cent of the base figure. It is clear that productivity change is the chief variable relating output to employment changes, but other adjustments are also necessary to get a precise reconciliation.

TABLE 61

Private Domestic Economy: Output, Productivity, Persons Engaged, and Related Variables, by Major Segment, 1953 Relative to 1899

	Output (1)	Total Factor Productivity (2)	Factor Substitution[a] (3)	Labor Input (4)	Labor Input per Person (6)	Persons Engaged (6)
Private domestic economy	586	254	112	207	94	221
Farming	153	184	135	62	88	70
Mining	442	316	120	117	88	133
Manufacturing	885	291	113	270	83	325
Transportation	641	545	109	108	69	156
Communications and public utilities	5,015	680	113	655	78	839
Construction	400	184[b]		217	77	282
Trade	525	213[b]		246	58	424
Finance and services	484	193[b]		251	85	296

[a] Substitution of capital for labor as measured by the ratio of total factor input to labor input.

[b] Rough estimates of output per manhour for construction and trade, and of output per unit of labor input for finance and services.

To explain *relative* changes in employment by industry group—that is, changes in the proportions of total employment absorbed by each group—it is necessary to express the index numbers for each variable as percentages of the corresponding index numbers for the private domestic economy as a whole. This is done in Table 62. To illustrate again by the manufacturing segment, the ninefold increase in output was 150 per cent greater than the sixfold increase in real private domestic product. Total factor productivity went up 14 per cent more in manufacturing than in the economy, but factor substitution was about the same. Consequently, manufacturing labor input increased by about 30 per cent more than total labor input; but since labor input per person declined more in manufacturing than in the economy, the relative increase in persons employed was almost 50 per cent. This reconciles precisely with the increase in the manufacturing proportion of total persons employed in the private domestic economy, from 21 per cent in 1899 to 31 per cent in 1953.

How typical is the manufacturing segment in exhibiting relative increases in *both* productivity and employment? Of the twenty-four groups showing greater-than-average productivity gains over the period, fourteen showed relative increases in employment and one showed no change. One of the most amazing cases is the electric light and power industry, in which the productivity advance was seven times greater than the economy average; and yet relative employment increased sixfold as a result of a forty-twofold relative output gain! The nine groups experiencing relative productivity increases but declines in relative employment comprised two manufacturing groups (tobacco products and textile mill products), the metal and nonmetal mining groups, all three transportation groups, and the telegraph and manufactured gas utilities.

In the aggregate, employment in the twenty-four industries with relative productivity gains rose from 20 per cent of total employment in private domestic industries in 1899 to 28 per cent in 1953. This 40 per cent gain in relative employment is convincing evidence that relative productivity increase in the long run is not associated with relative declines in employment.

It will be observed, however, that of the thirteen industry groups or segments experiencing relative declines in productivity or in output per manhour, only five likewise showed drops in relative employment. But the large relative decline in farm employment was more than enough to offset relative employment increases in other technologically less progressive areas, of which trade and services were the largest. In these areas, whereas relative output fell somewhat, the productivity decline was relatively greater and was associated with substantial gains in the proportion of total employment absorbed by the trade and service industries.

RELATIVE CHANGES IN PRODUCTIVITY AND IN FACTOR INPUTS

Another way to measure the association between relative changes in productivity and in factor input is through correlation analysis. The coefficients of correlation obtained by using ranks of proportionate changes in productivity and in each of the factor inputs and the total are summarized in Table 63. Here, errors in the input estimates would tend to bias the correlations negatively.

All the correlations show a mildly positive association between relative changes in productivity and relative input changes over the long period. The association is somewhat stronger in the case of capital input than in the case of either manhours or persons employed, and the coefficient of rank correlation using total factor input lies between the coefficients obtained using the capital and labor variables. In the eighty manufacturing industries, the association between relative changes in output per

TABLE 62

Private Domestic Economy, by Segment and by Group: Factors Influencing Relative Changes in Employment, 1953 Relative to 1899;[a] and Distribution of Persons Engaged, 1899 and 1953 (per cent)

	Output	Total Factor Productivity	Factor Substitution[b]	Labor Input[c]	Labor Input per Person	Persons Engaged[a]	Distribution of Persons Engaged 1899	Distribution of Persons Engaged 1953
	(1)	(2)	(3)	(4)	(5)	(6)	(7)	(8)
Farming	26	72	121	30	94	32	37.8	12.0
Mining	75	124	107	57	94	60	2.5	1.5
Metal	48	125	110	35	99	35	0.5	0.2
Anthracite coal	9	58	90	17	94	18	0.5	0.1
Bituminous coal	40	91	97	46	89	52	1.0	0.5
Oil and gas	415	197	109	194	62	312	0.2	0.5
Nonmetals	114	153	108	69	115	60	0.3	0.2
Manufacturing	151	114	101	131	89	147	20.8	30.5
Foods	96	96	94	107	78	137	1.6	2.2
Beverages	80	93	91	95	80	118	0.3	0.3
Tobacco	116	252	208	22	83	27	0.6	0.2
Textiles	71	138	98	53	75	70	3.0	2.1
Apparel	96	99	98	99	73	135	1.6	2.2
Lumber products	21	68	97	32	80	41	2.8	1.1
Furniture	84	83	87	116	81	143	0.4	0.6
Paper	233	137	102	166	79	210	0.4	0.9
Printing, publishing	168	158	92	115	80	144	1.1	1.6
Chemicals	432	185	120	194	80	243	0.6	1.4

(continued)

TABLE 62 (concluded)

	(1)	(2)	(3)	(4)	(5)	(6)	(7)	(8)
Petroleum, coal products	498	138	187	193	65	288	0.1	0.4
Rubber products	844	345	245	100	83	295	0.2	0.5
Leather products	31	77	44	93	72	61	1.1	0.7
Stone, clay, glass	123	154	83	96	83	100	1.1	1.1
Primary metals	152	109	129	108	79	164	1.3	2.2
Fabricated metals	259	153	173	98	82	211	1.3	2.7
Machinery, nonelectric	175	96	186	98	84	221	1.7	3.9
Electric machinery	1,014	126	820	98	78	1,053	0.2	2.1
Transportation equipment	726	251	297	97	81	365	0.9	3.3
Miscellaneous	176	114	161	96	84	192	0.5	1.0
Transportation	109	214	52	98	74	71	7.4	5.2
Railroads	68	153	44	101	71	62	3.9	2.4
Local transit	50	146	41	85	82	51	0.5	0.2
Residual transport	209	323	67	97	78	85	3.0	2.6
Communications and public utilities	855	267	317	101	83	380	0.7	2.5
Telephone	690	121	673	85	76	881	0.1	1.2
Telegraph	53	103	63	82	75	84	0.1	0.1
Electric utilities	4,186	693	464	130	78	597	0.1	0.6
Manufactured gas	144	462	34	93	72	47	0.2	0.1
Natural gas	565	116	326	149	73	446	0.1	0.3
Construction	68	65[e]	105		82	128	5.0	6.5
Trade	90	75[e]	119		62	192	11.2	21.5
Finance and services	83	68[e]	121		90	134	13.6	18.3

[a] Index numbers, for 1953 on an 1899 base, for the several segments and groups, are expressed as percentages of corresponding index numbers for the private domestic economy as a whole.

[b] Capital for labor.

[c] Col. (1) divided by col. (2) divided by col. (3).

[d] Col. (4) divided by col. (5) or col. (8) divided by col. (7).

[e] Output per manhour (for construction and trade) or per unit of labor input (for finance and services) relative to labor productivity in the private domestic economy as a whole.

CHART 24

Thirty-three Industry Groups: Relation between Total Factor Productivity and Persons
Engaged, 1953 Relative to 1899

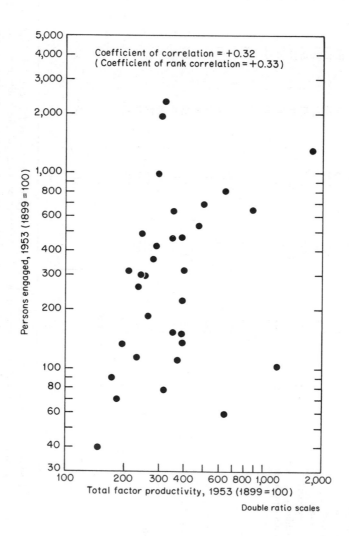

Double ratio scales

CHART 25

Thirty-three Industry Groups: Relation between Total Factor Productivity and Capital
Input, 1953 Relative to 1899

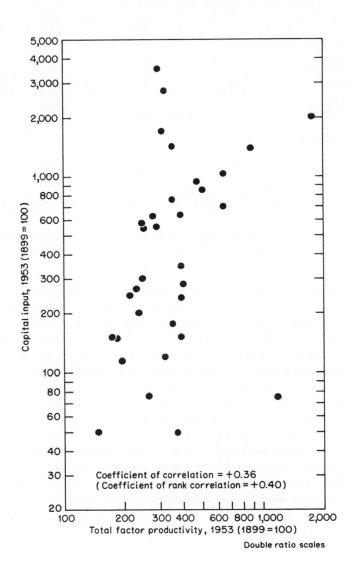

Coefficient of correlation = +0.36
(Coefficient of rank correlation = +0.40)

Capital input, 1953 (1899 = 100)

Total factor productivity, 1953 (1899 = 100)

Double ratio scales

TABLE 63

Coefficients of Rank Correlation[a] of Relative Changes in Productivity and in
Factor Inputs, Subperiods, 1899–1953

	1899–1953	1899–1909	1909–1919	1919–1929	1929–1937	1937–1948	1948–1953
33 industry groups							
Total factor productivity versus							
Persons engaged	0.33	0.35	0.11	−0.04	0.05	−0.19	0.19
Manhours	0.33	0.31	0.05	−0.08	−0.10	−0.34	0.15
Capital input	0.40	0.24	0.20	0.15	0.00	−0.40	0.03
Total factor input	0.35	0.29	0.06	0.03	−0.10	−0.37	0.10
80 manufacturing industries[b]							
Output per manhour versus							
Persons engaged	0.33	−0.01	−0.28	−0.05	0.09	−0.19	−0.12

[a] For $N = 33$, the value of the coefficient of rank correlation which is significant at the 0.05 level is 0.31; at the 0.01 level, 0.43. For $N = 80$, the comparable figures are 0.22 and 0.28.

[b] For the eighty manufacturing industries, the long period refers to 1899–1954, and the last two subperiods are 1937–47 and 1947–54.

manhour and in persons employed is somewhat lower than that obtained for the thirty-three groups. The results are pictured in Charts 24 and 25.

Table 63 indicates clearly that the correlations between relative changes in productivity and factor inputs are generally lower in the subperiods than over the long period. This is particularly marked in the eighty manufacturing industries. The associations are all negative in the 1937–48 subperiod, and occasionally so in other periods. The phenomenon of higher correlations over the long period than in the subperiods is consistent with the like results obtained in correlations between relative changes in productivity, prices, and output. Apparently, the theoretical propositions that prices tend to equal unit costs and that industries with declining relative unit costs tend to enjoy increases in relative demand and output describe the operations of the real economy more aptly if a rather long period is allowed for the adjustments to take place.

Annex: Variables Used in the Industry Analysis

For the convenience of other analysts, we present here tables showing for the thirty-three groups in key years the variables with which the productivity indexes were correlated. As described in the following notes, the index numbers of values per unit of output for mining and manufacturing should be relatively good, based as they are on consistent census data, but they are rougher for some of the other segments. Data on average hourly labor earnings are based on consistent earnings and employment estimates, but would be influenced by possible errors in our estimates of average hours worked per year. The estimates of capital compensation per unit of real capital are subject to a wider margin of error than the other series. Our industry price indexes have not been included because of their incomplete coverage for certain industries. However, the description and sources of price indexes used for the manufacturing industries are given in the Technical Note to Appendix D.

	1929=100					
	1899	1909	1919	1937	1948	1953
FARMING						
Unit value of product	41.5	64.7	143.6	81.2	187.5	170.8
Unit value added	44.6	69.9	150.6	79.5	171.6	148.6
Unit materials cost	30.3	45.1	117.6	87.8	246.2	252.9
Average hourly earnings	34.9	50.8	110.2	71.1	238.0	276.5
Capital compensation per unit of real capital	30.3	66.0	160.2	92.7	196.8	116.3
MINING: METALS						
Unit value of product	83.6	76.6	126.5	101.0	222.0	298.3
Unit value added	85.7	72.8	120.1	102.2	223.1	298.6
Unit materials cost	75.2	91.7	152.0	96.0	217.5	296.7
Average hourly earnings	46.6	56.0	107.4	122.6	251.1	357.3
Capital compensation per unit of real capital			119.6	151.2	230.8	96.9
MINING: ANTHRACITE COAL						
Unit value of product	28.0	35.2	79.3	73.1	156.3	185.0
Unit value added	27.3	33.9	74.6	69.5	132.3	147.0
Unit materials cost	31.5	42.4	105.5	93.3	291.9	399.0
Average hourly earnings	25.6	31.1	76.8	104.8	217.2	297.7
Capital compensation per unit of real capital			89.5	−31.6	573.7	115.8
MINING: BITUMINOUS COAL						
Unit value of product	48.8	59.9	139.8	108.9	280.2	276.2
Unit value added	52.4	62.8	138.6	107.2	264.9	255.7
Unit materials cost	28.5	43.7	147.3	117.5	364.9	390.0
Average hourly earnings	30.0	47.4	111.5	125.7	278.7	364.2
Capital compensation per unit of real capital			103.8	115.4	2023.1	253.3
MINING: OIL AND GAS						
Unit value of product	49.5	48.3	142.4	96.3	208.4	199.3
Unit value added	45.1	43.5	129.0	105.3	232.0	223.8
Unit materials cost	76.5	72.9	212.9	48.9	84.6	70.9
Average hourly earnings	25.5	35.5	103.3	125.3	252.6	334.8
Capital compensation per unit of real capital			95.2	256.5	514.7	661.3
MINING: NONMETALS						
Unit value of product	63.6	62.0	127.2	91.1	125.4	145.6
Unit value added	68.2	64.6	119.1	91.1	120.9	137.7
Unit materials cost	45.6	52.8	157.6	91.1	142.5	175.2
Average hourly earnings	67.6	59.4	91.3	107.2	250.0	342.1
Capital compensation per unit of real capital			104.1	82.4	312.2	275.7
MANUFACTURING: FOODS						
Unit value of product	64.4	78.0	167.9	85.1	186.9	188.2
Unit value added	45.2	55.5	115.8	83.1	171.1	183.8
Unit materials cost	71.6	86.6	188.0	85.9	193.1	189.9
Average hourly earnings	29.0	38.0	82.9	101.4	213.3	286.6
Capital compensation per unit of real capital				126.6	301.8	277.7

(continued)

	1899	1909	1919	1937	1948	1953
				1929=100		

	1899	1909	1919	1937	1948	1953
MANUFACTURING: BEVERAGES						
Unit value of product	36.8	44.2	107.5	59.0	96.7	108.6
Unit value added	50.4	58.2	123.3	65.4	93.7	101.9
Unit materials cost	20.1	27.1	88.0	50.9	100.5	116.7
Average hourly earnings	37.9	49.6	86.2	114.1	194.2	272.2
Capital compensation per unit of real capital				233.3	550.0	447.2
MANUFACTURING: TOBACCO PRODUCTS						
Unit value of product	70.5	76.3	115.9	87.1	131.8	147.4
Unit value added	69.5	66.6	92.1	92.7	131.3	175.1
Unit materials cost	71.8	94.5	161.2	76.5	132.6	91.2
Average hourly earnings	38.3	47.0	91.3	108.7	250.6	339.3
Capital compensation per unit of real capital				106.3	119.8	189.2
MANUFACTURING: TEXTILES						
Unit value of product	47.1	57.2	151.6	72.2	148.0	158.9
Unit value added	47.5	53.9	140.2	74.0	169.4	156.3
Unit materials cost	46.6	59.5	160.2	70.7	132.0	160.8
Average hourly earnings	27.5	34.9	94.4	116.0	276.9	333.5
Capital compensation per unit of real capital				126.5	577.4	195.1
MANUFACTURING: APPAREL						
Unit value of product	51.0	62.6	138.3	70.4	153.1	162.7
Unit value added	51.6	62.2	129.4	72.2	173.4	188.4
Unit materials cost	50.7	63.0	144.7	69.0	138.6	144.4
Average hourly earnings	24.4	33.4	91.0	96.3	207.5	245.0
Capital compensation per unit of real capital				70.3	183.7	104.1
MANUFACTURING: LUMBER PRODUCTS						
Unit value of product	37.6	45.5	109.8	88.6	233.6	246.3
Unit value added	33.8	44.2	109.7	83.5	224.9	244.6
Unit materials cost	42.4	47.1	110.0	95.0	244.4	248.2
Average hourly earnings	27.1	35.8	83.4	88.6	214.2	290.8
Capital compensation per unit of real capital				149.1	785.3	376.9
MANUFACTURING: FURNITURE						
Unit value of product	37.3	51.5	120.6	90.5	138.0	186.9
Unit value added	38.4	50.7	118.6	87.6	137.2	175.0
Unit materials cost	36.2	52.4	122.9	93.9	139.0	205.6
Average hourly earnings	27.6	36.3	77.4	95.2	217.5	288.6
Capital compensation per unit of real capital				120.0	770.0	690.3
MANUFACTURING: PAPER						
Unit value of product	56.8	59.4	125.6	87.2	183.4	208.0
Unit value added	60.7	58.0	125.6	84.8	176.0	200.7
Unit materials cost	54.1	60.8	125.6	88.9	188.9	213.4
Average hourly earnings	26.9	36.0	83.8	119.3	259.7	349.8
Capital compensation per unit of real capital				76.8	497.6	492.0

(continued)

	1899	1909	1919	1937	1948	1953
MANUFACTURING: PRINTING AND PUBLISHING						
Unit value of product	74.3	67.0	101.3	80.5	140.9	161.9
Unit value added	73.1	64.5	88.7	79.2	132.6	147.3
Unit materials cost	80.1	75.5	139.4	80.8	144.3	180.1
Average hourly earnings	26.3	35.8	67.1	105.9	209.0	271.5
Capital compensation per unit of real capital				55.3	171.8	174.1
MANUFACTURING: CHEMICALS						
Unit value of product	73.1	86.6	171.1	81.3	129.2	121.3
Unit value added	60.8	70.4	130.9	82.4	117.7	126.8
Unit materials cost	84.4	101.9	208.3	80.3	139.9	116.3
Average hourly earnings	27.3	37.0	79.1	107.6	232.4	331.0
Capital compensation per unit of real capital				104.7	233.3	224.1
MANUFACTURING: PETROLEUM AND COAL PRODUCTS						
Unit value of product	64.8	71.4	170.3	83.6	189.8	174.1
Unit value added	66.2	63.4	169.1	67.8	158.5	134.1
Unit materials cost	64.3	73.9	170.6	88.8	200.0	187.1
Average hourly earnings	24.6	33.7	85.8	145.8	310.2	456.3
Capital compensation per unit of real capital				40.1	215.1	148.4
MANUFACTURING: RUBBER PRODUCTS						
Unit value of product	209.3	229.9	189.9	87.2	138.7	177.3
Unit value added	172.1	180.5	187.9	75.7	140.7	176.4
Unit materials cost	241.9	275.3	191.6	98.0	136.7	178.2
Average hourly earnings	27.3	34.3	88.2	124.2	237.4	325.4
Capital compensation per unit of real capital				123.6	315.3	530.6
MANUFACTURING: LEATHER AND PRODUCTS						
Unit value of product	47.7	62.8	151.7	72.1	172.0	161.2
Unit value added	37.3	50.2	128.4	71.1	180.8	191.0
Unit materials cost	54.5	71.4	167.4	72.9	166.2	141.1
Average hourly earnings	28.2	36.8	90.8	102.2	224.0	277.3
Capital compensation per unit of real capital				49.5	323.8	234.3
MANUFACTURING: STONE, CLAY, AND GLASS PRODUCTS						
Unit value of product	54.2	56.5	125.2	90.9	159.7	186.7
Unit value added	56.9	56.0	115.7	86.2	148.7	170.4
Unit materials cost	49.5	57.4	142.0	98.8	180.6	215.6
Average hourly earnings	26.4	34.6	73.1	95.8	202.3	283.1
Capital compensation per unit of real capital				124.1	385.2	423.5
MANUFACTURING: PRIMARY METAL PRODUCTS						
Unit value of product	84.9	74.3	128.8	101.1	150.6	194.7
Unit value added	78.0	55.2	124.8	107.7	161.1	215.4
Unit materials cost	88.1	83.9	130.8	97.9	145.3	184.3
Average hourly earnings	27.7	34.2	85.0	113.8	224.7	326.0
Capital compensation per unit of real capital				53.2	230.5	258.2

(continued)

	1899	1909	1919	1937	1948	1953
					1929=100	
MANUFACTURING: FABRICATED METAL PRODUCTS						
Unit value of product	70.9	69.7	122.6	95.7	159.4	207.2
Unit value added	64.6	63.4	111.1	87.9	151.4	196.8
Unit materials cost	80.1	78.0	138.1	106.1	170.1	221.0
Average hourly earnings	27.2	35.4	76.4	100.1	220.9	303.4
Capital compensation per unit of real capital				80.6	190.7	154.4
MANUFACTURING: MACHINERY, NONELECTRIC						
Unit value of product	52.3	53.7	108.4	94.1	163.7	182.9
Unit value added	45.9	49.0	101.4	88.7	142.4	162.4
Unit materials cost	64.1	61.6	120.8	103.6	200.6	218.2
Average hourly earnings	29.8	38.4	83.7	113.9	232.3	318.8
Capital compensation per unit of real capital				98.9	191.3	222.1
MANUFACTURING: ELECTRIC MACHINERY						
Unit value of product	50.6	52.4	104.1	85.2	136.6	132.6
Unit value added	41.2	47.0	104.1	85.7	125.7	123.7
Unit materials cost	64.4	60.0	103.9	84.8	151.5	144.6
Average hourly earnings	30.0	39.8	81.8	121.4	238.2	319.6
Capital compensation per unit of real capital				118.6	253.7	331.6
MANUFACTURING: TRANSPORTATION EQUIPMENT						
Unit value of product	81.9	98.1	152.3	109.5	178.7	211.7
Unit value added	94.5	116.8	167.4	77.7	162.5	195.3
Unit materials cost	74.0	86.9	142.4	122.8	189.1	222.3
Average hourly earnings	24.0	24.2	88.0	111.7	219.5	306.6
Capital compensation per unit of real capital				77.0	229.2	356.2
MANUFACTURING: MISCELLANEOUS						
Unit value of product	51.2	62.5	122.2	77.5	142.7	160.9
Unit value added	44.7	53.7	109.1	73.6	138.7	156.3
Unit materials cost	60.4	75.9	141.9	83.3	148.6	167.6
Average hourly earnings	27.1	34.4	73.0	95.4	201.3	275.1
Capital compensation per unit of real capital				106.6	122.8	155.5
TRANSPORTATION: RAILROADS						
Unit value of product	66.3	68.9	88.8	82.0	108.3	128.6
Unit value added	69.6	67.6	75.9	81.0	107.3	130.1
Unit materials cost	54.5	73.3	133.3	85.5	111.6	123.5
Average hourly earnings	25.6	30.5	85.1	106.3	200.1	289.2
Capital compensation per unit of real capital			57.3	34.6	109.2	98.3
TRANSPORTATION: LOCAL TRANSIT (ELECTRIC RAILWAYS AND BUSES)						
Unit value of product	87.2	97.5	116.0	85.4	117.3	188.1
Unit value added	87.6	97.5	116.1	85.4	117.5	188.4
Unit materials cost	86.8	97.7	115.7	85.3	117.3	188.1
Average hourly earnings	30.4	36.3	80.9	114.4	225.5	289.5
Capital compensation per unit of real capital			80.2	27.9	41.4	157.7

(continued)

	1899	1909	1919	1937	1948	1953
			1929=100			
COMMUNICATIONS: TELEGRAPH						
Unit value of product	54.0	69.3	105.4	81.9	125.7	154.1
Unit value added	44.6	65.2	99.1	77.4	135.5	170.5
Unit materials cost	107.8	95.1	145.3	109.3	63.5	50.9
Average hourly earnings	33.2	37.7	72.5	106.7	242.5	326.4
Capital compensation per unit of real capital				26.6	25.9	148.0
COMMUNICATIONS: TELEPHONE						
Unit value of product	77.5	58.5	72.7	105.4	120.8	176.4
Unit value added	79.3	54.2	60.5	101.4	132.8	179.2
Unit materials cost	72.5	70.9	108.3	116.9	86.2	168.2
Average hourly earnings	32.7	33.9	73.6	139.2	233.5	323.3
Capital compensation per unit of real capital				67.6	57.6	116.8
PUBLIC UTILITIES: ELECTRIC UTILITIES						
Unit value of product	112.0	117.5	123.3	76.9	64.0	62.6
Unit value added	106.5	112.4	110.3	75.9	50.4	51.2
Unit materials cost	161.5	160.8	238.6	86.0	184.6	164.0
Average hourly earnings	34.4	37.7	81.5	126.6	228.7	319.5
Capital compensation per unit of real capital	24.6	25.3	38.4	89.5	112.3	164.0
PUBLIC UTILITIES: MANUFACTURED GAS						
Unit value of product	101.3	83.9	86.0	96.4	91.7	81.6
Unit value added	116.0	90.5	70.8	111.2	84.2	65.7
Unit materials cost	76.3	72.4	112.4	71.0	104.6	109.0
Average hourly earnings	34.0	37.0	80.5	126.8	323.4	470.2
Capital compensation per unit of real capital	23.3	66.7	24.2	142.9	111.1	312.0
PUBLIC UTILITIES: NATURAL GAS						
Unit value of product	34.2	48.0	69.1	94.0	90.7	117.1
Unit value added	30.6	43.8	58.4	103.0	100.8	131.4
Unit materials cost	51.2	71.7	95.7	46.9	36.8	41.3
Average hourly earnings	33.9	37.2	80.6	126.6	254.9	362.2
Capital compensation per unit of real capital	43.0	46.1	113.8	132.1	300.8	391.3

SOURCES

Farming: For the output index see Appendix B, section on "Gross Farm Output." Gross value of farm production and value of materials and other intermediate products are estimates of Department of Commerce, the former extrapolated by Strauss and Bean (see Appendix B, Note 2). Value added is the difference between value of product and cost of materials. Average hourly earnings of labor is the Department of Agriculture series, farm wages without room and board. Capital compensation per unit of real capital is described in Appendix B, section on "Factor Weights in Farming."

Mining: For output measures see Appendix C, section on "Output." Value of production is taken from *Minerals Yearbook*, Bureau of Mines. Value of materials is estimated from the ratio of value of materials to value of product (Israel Borenstein, *Capital and Output Trends in Mining Industries, 1870–1948*, Occasional Paper 45, New York (NBER), 1954, Table 5). Value added is computed as the difference between value of product and cost of materials. Hourly earnings in mining are obtained from Leo Wolman's unpublished data. Capital compensation per unit is described in Appendix C, end of section on "Capital."

Manufacturing: For output indexes see Appendix D, section on "Output Estimates." Value of product, value added, and cost of materials are based on data from *Census of Manufactures* adjusted for census-to-census consistency. Hourly earnings are computed from wages and salaries of production workers and salaried employees divided by hours worked per week; these are from the *Census of Manufactures*, 1899–1929, and from the Office of Business Economics, Department of Commerce, 1929–53; Census data on hours were supplemented by BLS studies. Capital compensation per unit is described in Appendix D, section on "Capital Stocks and Input."

Transportation, Railroads: For output index see Appendix G, section on "Output." Value of product is represented by passenger and freight revenues (*Statistics of Railways in the United States*, Interstate Commerce Commission, annual). Cost of materials for Class I steam railroads (fuels, stationery and printing, advertising, and other miscellaneous materials and supplies) is available in *Statistics of Railways*. The ratio of cost of materials to operating revenues of Class I roads was applied to revenues of all roads to obtain cost of materials for all roads. Value added is computed as the difference between value of product and cost of materials. An index of hourly earnings was built up by linking monthly earnings in Class I steam railroads as estimated by the Bureau of Labor Statistics, 1929–53; unpublished series of Leo Troy, 1918–29; Paul Douglas's series, 1899–1919 (in his *Real Wages in the United States*, Boston, Houghton Mifflin, 1930). Capital compensation per unit is derived as the quotient of nonlabor compensation (the difference between Commerce's income originating in railroads and total labor compensation) and the index of real capital input.

Local Transit: For output index see Appendix G, sections on "Electric Railroads" and on "The Local-Transit Group." Value of product is the sum of operating revenue of electric railways (*Census of Electrical Industries*) and trolley, coach, and motor-bus operating revenues (*Transit Fact Book*, American Transit Association, New York). Value added is assumed to be a constant 75 per cent of value of product, the average ratio of income originating in railways (Department of Commerce) and operating revenues in 1929 and 1937. Cost of materials is therefore assumed to be 25 per cent of value of product. The hourly earnings index is a link of Bureau of Labor Statistics data (1932–53) and Douglas's average yearly wage adjusted by an hours series (1899–1932). Capital compensation per unit is derived as the quotient of nonlabor compensation (Commerce income originating in local transit less total labor compensation) and the index of real capital input.

Communications and Public Utilities: For output indexes see relevant sections of Appendix H. Values of product are represented by revenue: for the communications groups, from Census and Federal Communications Commission data; for electric utilities, from Census and Edison Electric Institute data; for the gas utilities from Census and American Gas Association data and from Jacob M. Gould, *Output and Productivity in the Electric and Gas Utilities, 1899–1942*, New York (NBER), 1946. For the communications groups, value added is national income, and material costs, the difference between value of product and value added. For electric utilities, the value of fuel consumption in bituminous coal equivalents (Gould and Edison Electric Institute) represents materials costs; and value added, the difference between value of product and materials cost. For manufactured gas, value added and cost of materials are given in *Census of Manufactures*. For natural gas, cost of materials is estimated by applying to value of product the ratios of materials cost to value of product for the oil and gas mining industry. Value added is the difference between value of product and estimated materials cost. Average hourly earnings of labor are computed from indexes of labor compensation and manhours. Estimates in absolute terms are derived by dividing 1929 labor compensation by the product of 1929 employment and average hours per man-year and applying to these 1929 estimates the indexes of hourly earnings. Capital compensation per unit is described, under the subsection "Total Input" in Appendix H, in the relevant section for each industry.

223

DIRECTOR'S COMMENT

by Stanley H. Ruttenberg

John Kendrick's text and monumental array of data, and Solomon Fabricant's Introduction as well, represent a considerable effort that will be useful to economists who specialize in the field of productivity. Much of this work is of a provisional nature, however, and its conclusions, in my opinion, are frequently less than definite or firm.

While Kendrick has performed a worthy pioneering task, the essential value of this work is experimental. Unfortunately, its exploratory nature is often covered by overstated conclusions that are based on provisional and inadequate analysis.

A new measure of productivity is introduced, for example, but its conceptual framework and proper use or uses are not clearly developed. The absence of a conceptual framework may add to existing difficulties in the application of productivity measures as tools for economic analysis and policy development. It has already added some confusion in the area of the greatest practical application of productivity—the area of collective bargaining and labor-management relationships.

There are many unanswered, basic questions concerning total factor productivity, as the new measure is called. Furthermore, this exploratory volume raises many additional problems, which are dismissed or only inadequately examined. Among these various issues are the following:

1. Should a productivity measure be called total factor productivity, when it excludes measurement of many intangible factors other than labor and capital?

The new productivity measure is an attempt to measure output per combined labor and capital inputs. It does not measure numerous other inputs, such as education, science, technology, social organization, cultural heritage, and the quality of human skills and ingenuity which are essential to rising productivity.

I am not advocating a combined measure of all the various tangible and intangible inputs. It seems to me, however, that the all-encompassing terms "total factor productivity" and "total productivity" are misleading when they are applied to a limited measure of two inputs.

2. What is the conceptual basis for the new productivity measure, which is output per unit of combined actual manhours and available capital?

This question is unanswered, except for the brief implication that the new productivity measure is a measure of efficiency, which is never defined. Does total factor productivity purport to measure efficiency, in terms of dollar costs to business, alone? Or does total factor productivity attempt to measure efficiency in terms of costs to the economy and society as a whole?

As developed in this volume, it would seem that total factor productivity attempts to measure the dollar costs to business of entrepreneurial decisions concerning investment, capital stock, and employment, including the costs of the entire capital stock, whether or not it is utilized, and the actual manhours that are worked. There are additional costs, however, which are not measured—such as the unemployment compensation and public assistance costs of underutilization of the potential labor force, the social waste of unused or underutilized manpower and labor skills, the social cost of business investment decisions which may involve the elimination of some existing departments or plants and investment in new locations.

It would appear that it is a limited type of efficiency that total factor productivity attempts to measure. The brief implication of a conceptual basis for the newly introduced measure, therefore, is most inadequate.

3. Although total factor productivity is a new measure, and it is referred to as a superior measure, its proper uses and applications are not developed.

In the absence of an adequate conceptual framework and a clear statement of purposes, uses, and appropriate applications, it is difficult to comprehend Kendrick's and Fabricant's views of the newly introduced productivity measure.

Total factor productivity is described as better than other measures, but why and how it is superior are not adequately explained. Since each productivity measure is good in itself for its own specific and limited purposes, if it is conceptually and mathematically valid, it is conceivable that the new measure may be superior to other measures for some purposes, inferior for other purposes, and inappropriate for still other purposes. The uses and appropriate applications of total factor productivity, however, are not developed and the supposed superiority of this measure is declared, but not explained.

4. Is there any relevance to be drawn from direct or implied comparisons of changes in real average hourly employee compensation and total factor productivity over periods of time? Kendrick and Fabricant assure me that they do not mean that total factor productivity is the appropriate yardstick for wage and salary policy decisions, but some readers may be misled.

This issue is important since it deals with the distribution of income and, in effect, with part of the basic structure of our economy and society.

Since total factor productivity rises at a slower rate than output per manhour, is it meant that real average hourly employee compensation should properly rise at a rate that is equal to the rate of total factor productivity and less than the rate of output per manhour? A practical application of this policy would result in a decline of the wage and salary share of national income and a rise in the national income share that goes to the return to capital.

If, in the view of Kendrick and Fabricant, real average hourly employee compensation should properly rise somewhat faster than total factor productivity, then the question is, how much faster—more rapidly than total factor productivity and less than output per manhour, proportionate to the rise of output per manhour, or more rapidly than output per manhour?

These questions are raised by the comparisons that are made. The relevance of the comparisons and answers to these questions, however, is not presented.

In other publications, Kendrick has indicated the impropriety of using total factor productivity as a yardstick for wage-productivity comparisons. Since the new productivity measure is admittedly not an appropriate yardstick, why are the comparisons made at all? Furthermore, what is the basis for apparently abandoning the usual comparison of real average hourly employee compensation with output per manhour?

These questions concern the use of productivity measures in collective bargaining, which is, at present, the area of its greatest application. There is, however, no direct discussion of this subject. The effect, therefore, is to add confusion in a difficult area of social and economic policy that involves the distribution of income.

5. Is total factor productivity a valid productivity measure, since it combines two conceptually different measures—output per unit of *actual* manhours and output per unit of *available* capital?

Output per manhour is a measure that is based on actual manhours, excluding the unemployed, the underemployed, and those who are out of the labor force because appropriate work is not available. This measure, therefore, is one of output per unit of *actual* inputs.

Output per unit of capital, on the other hand, is a measure that is based on available capital, including the total capital stock after depreciation, regardless of whether or not it is utilized. This measure, therefore, is one of output per unit of *available* inputs.

Is it appropriate to combine two such different measures into one new productivity measure? If there is some conceptual basis for combining these two differing measures, is the resultant factor productivity a measure of efficiency, as claimed? Would it not be more appropriate to leave these conceptually different measures as two distinctly separate measures of output per units of differing qualities and quantities of inputs? If any combination is presented as a measure of total factor productivity, it should be only one of the "variants" that Kendrick includes in his third chapter. In that combination, total labor supply—whether employed or unemployed—is counted as an input, just as is total capital—whether employed or unemployed.

These basic issues concerning the newly introduced productivity measure are not examined in any clear manner.

In addition, there are a number of difficult problems concerning capital productivity that are not adequately discussed. In measuring the available capital stock, there are problems of actual depreciation as contrasted with book depreciation and serious difficulties of price deflation. Any discussion of output per unit of capital should include a careful exposition of these difficulties, which are considerably greater than measuring employee manhours, with which there are many years of experience.

6. Is there validity to Kendrick's claim that the wage and salary share of national income has risen sharply?

The evidence of experts who have studied national income shares for many years casts serious doubt on Kendrick's claim of a sharp increase of the labor share of national income. Most students have concluded that the wage and salary share of national income has increased slowly over the past several decades or has remained relatively stable. They point, for example, to the necessity of accounting for the effects of labor force shifts before reaching any conclusions about the trend of the wage and salary share of national income. Kendrick mentions the effect of labor force shifts in one part of his book, but fails to give the matter the emphasis it deserves.

Although Kendrick declares that the wage and salary share of national income has risen sharply, the considerable body of literature of a contrary nature is not discussed adequately or refuted.

These comments indicate, in my opinion, the need for a considerable amount of continuing work in the area of productivity measurement and analysis. Kendrick's massive effort is just a beginning. It permits one to draw very tentative conclusions, but certainly no firm conclusions. His work does raise many issues, however, for much further research.

AUTHOR'S NOTE

Since most of the issues raised by Mr. Ruttenberg are discussed in some detail in the text, an additional "reply" is unnecessary. The reader may judge for himself the validity of Mr. Ruttenberg's comments. I should, however, like to reaffirm my conviction concerning the analytical usefulness of having measures of input, price, and productivity of tangible capital separately and in combination with labor, in addition to the labor measures alone. In Chapter 5, for example, far from "adding confusion," the full set of estimates makes possible a more complete statistical analysis of relative changes in factor incomes in the United States than any previously attempted.

JOHN W. KENDRICK.

PART IV

Appendixes A–K

APPENDIX A
The National Economy

THIS appendix contains a description of the sources and methods used in estimating the real-output and -input components of the productivity estimates for the national economy and major sectors. Conceptual problems are alluded to where pertinent; they are treated more fully in Part I of the text. The estimates of the chief components and the summary index numbers of the output-input ratios are presented in the tables at the end of this appendix. To some extent, the general methodological description in this appendix is applicable to the industry estimates of productivity as well as to the national estimates and will not be repeated in the subsquent appendixes.

The estimates of aggregate national output and of aggregate capital stocks have been made independently of the corresponding estimates for the several industrial divisions of the economy described in succeeding appendixes because industry estimates are lacking in certain areas. We do, however, compare the aggregate output and capital estimates with the sum of the available industry estimates in order to obtain some idea of their consistency by making explicit the implications for the residual, uncovered area.

In the case of manhours worked, the national estimates were obtained by aggregating the estimates for all the various industry groups of the economy. Here, the question of consistency does not arise. Aggregate manhours do not show the same movement as total "labor input" in the nation, however, since manhours worked in the several industry groups were weighted in accordance with average hourly compensation. A system of occasionally changing weights was consistently applied to both labor and capital inputs and to the real national product estimates before computation of productivity ratios.

Output

Estimates of the national product, adjusted to eliminate the effect of price changes, provide the broadest available measure of the real final output of the national economy. It is this measure, in several variant forms, that we employ as the numerator of the ratios of productivity in the total economy. A weighted average of output index numbers for the several industrial divisions of the economy, as described in succeeding appendixes, is used for comparison; but it cannot suitably serve as the primary measure Reliable direct estimates for the broad area of finance and services, as well as for several lesser industries, are not available. Moreover, the industry output estimates are generally gross of products purchased from other industries, and therefore do not add up to the national product, except on certain assumptions. Hence, we must rely on the sum-of-final-products approach to the estimation of aggregate national product.

The conceptual differences among the several available sets of product estimates, as prepared by Kuznets and by the Department of Commerce,[1] were discussed in Chapter 2.[2] These differences will be reviewed briefly in subsequent sections as they bear on the methodology of estimation. It may be noted here that we use a recent "statistical variant" of the Kuznets estimates identical with the Commerce estimates for the common components. Thus, the differences among the several versions of the two sets of estimates are wholly due to the somewhat different concepts or the sectoring underlying each.

Before summarizing the methods used to estimate the several versions of national product, the system of weights will be described. The same weighting system has been used for all versions in computing the productivity ratios.

WEIGHTING SYSTEM

Deflation of the national product, by type of expenditure, by index numbers of the market prices of the various final goods and services is, in effect, the same as weighting physical units of the products by base-period market prices. Theoretically, we should prefer factor-cost weights for reasons developed in Chapter 2, but it is unlikely that real product at factor cost would move very differently from real product at market price in the United States economy.[3] In combining industry output indexes, as noted later, we have used the more appropriate value-added or gross factor-cost weights.

Although the comparison base of our constant-dollar estimates and output index numbers is 1929, we have used changing weight bases, as

---

[1] The Department of Commerce series are described in *National Income Supplement, 1954, Survey of Current Business*; and the recent estimates by Simon Kuznets are described, and references to his earlier works provided, in *Capital in the American Economy: Its Formation and Financing*, in press.

[2] For further literature on concepts, see the references in Chapter 2, note 1.

[3] This judgment is supported by the opinion of two national income specialists, who write: "Although this measure is perhaps conceptually superior as a gauge of the productivity of resources, we believe the practical difficulties associated with a strict application of the factor cost method are so serious that a market price measure is a better 'all purpose' valuation scheme" [Everett E. Hagen and Edward C. Budd, "The Product Side: Some Theoretical Aspects," *A Critique of the United States Income and Product Accounts*, Studies in Income and Wealth, Volume 22, Princeton University Press (for NBER), 1958, p. 243, n. 24].

indicated in Chapters 1 and 2. The price index numbers for the terminal years of each subperiod were averaged and set equal to 100 before deflating values for all years in the subperiods; then the deflated values were chained to the 1929 values to form a continuous series.

It was on this principle that most of the National Bureau estimates of physical volumes of output by industry were prepared (see succeeding appendixes), and the principle is also used in the Federal Reserve index of industrial production. To provide significant comparisons for trend analysis, key years were selected from periods of relatively high business activity. In the case of manufacturing, the years selected by Fabricant were 1899, 1909, 1919, 1929, and 1937; to these we added the business cycle peaks 1948, 1953, and 1957. The index numbers for successive pairs of these key years were cross-weighted by the average unit value added in successive pairs of years, and these were chained to form a continuous series on a 1929 comparison base. Index numbers for intervening census years were weighted by the average unit value of the given year and the succeeding key year. The output indexes for other industries were prepared in similar fashion, although the key years vary slightly depending on the dates of the pertinent industrial censuses.

Since we use the estimates of real private product on the Commerce basis for comparisons with the industry output estimates, and over the subperiods as defined above, we first reweighted the product detail of this series by the average prices in the terminal years of the various subperiods from 1889 to 1953. Since product detail is slender prior to 1889, we have used average prices for 1889 and 1899. For the years since 1953, we have used the 1954 weight-base incorporated in the most recent Commerce estimates.[4]

The reweighting from 1929 forward was carried out on the basis of worksheet detail provided by the National Income Division of the Department of Commerce, which covers several hundred product-classes together with the corresponding price deflators. Prior to 1929, we used the commodity detail given by William H. Shaw,[5] to derive the adjustments necessary to convert the deflators for these segments to a 1929 base,

---

[4] *U.S. Income and Output, 1958 Supplement, Survey of Current Business.*
Our real-product estimates for 1929–53 are based on the Commerce series published in the *National Income Supplement, 1954*, as revised in subsequent July numbers of the *Survey* through 1957. *U.S. Income and Output, 1958 Supplement* contained further revisions of the national product numbers and associated estimates of persons engaged from 1946 forward, but it was not feasible for us to incorporate the revisions into our basic series through 1953. Fortunately, the revisions were less than 1 per cent in the upward direction for both product and persons engaged; so the derived productivity estimates would not be significantly affected. Our estimates for 1953–57, however, are based on the estimates contained in *U.S. Income and Output, 1958 Supplement.*
[5] *Value of Commodity Output since 1869*, New York (NBER), 1947.

plus a direct conversion of the real-product estimates in the other categories, in order to arrive at aggregate real product on the desired basis of changing weights.

Table A-1 shows changes in the Commerce national product estimates

TABLE A-1

Effect of Alternative Weighting Systems on Subperiod Movements of
Real Gross National Product, Commerce Concept, 1889–1953
(per cent)

	Change in Real GNP Weighted by			
	1929 Prices	Changing Prices	1947 Prices	1954 Prices
1889–99	52.4	54.8		
1899–1909	50.4	50.9		
1909–19	32.7	38.2		
1919–29	40.8	40.3		
1929–37	4.5	3.3	2.8	0.9
1937–48	58.6	60.8	58.9	59.7
1948–53	23.7	25.5	25.2	25.9

converted to constant dollars by the single (1929)-base and changing-base weighting schemes just discussed, as well as in 1947 and 1954 dollars as estimated by Commerce for the recent period. Presumably, much the same differences would characterize the Kuznets estimates if they were reweighted correspondingly; and for consistency, we have applied the same reweighting factors to index numbers of the Kuznets estimates in 1929 dollars.

NATIONAL PRODUCT AS ESTIMATED BY KUZNETS

We are fortunate in having the revised estimates of national product by Kuznets on an annual basis back to 1869.[6] These are largely the result of previous work in the field at the National Bureau of Economic Research, summarized by Kuznets in an earlier volume.[7] The new series also draws heavily on the estimates of national product by the Commerce Department for the period since 1929, although the degree of reliability differs in the three statistical variants presented by Kuznets.

The peacetime version: statistical variants. Variant I represents the original estimates presented by Kuznets[8] as later revised to incorporate more recently available data and estimates. These estimates are based on the

---

[6] *Capital in the American Economy.*
[7] *National Product since 1869*, New York (NBER), 1946.
[8] *National Income and Its Composition, 1919–1938*, New York (NBER), 1941.

income payments approach, with consumer expenditures for services derived as a residual. The various components of product were extrapolated from the late 1930's by Commerce estimates of the corresponding components. The estimates under Variant II are the same as those under Variant I, except that direct estimates of service expenditures are substituted for those obtained as a residual, thus introducing a "statistical discrepancy" between the Kuznets income and product estimates (which are equal in the first variant). In Variant III, Kuznets uses the Department's estimates, adapted to his conceptual framework, for the years since 1929, and extrapolates back the various components by the corresponding components of Variant I, except for services, which are extrapolated by the direct estimates used in Variant II.

It should be emphasized that the three recent variants prepared by Kuznets are purely *statistical* variants and that they all embody the same basic concept of national product. In each, national product is taken as the flow of goods to consumers and into capital formation; government purchases are included only to the extent that they are interpreted as falling into one or the other of these categories of final product. In this study, we make use of Kuznets' Variant III only (see Table A-I). Statistically, this variant is practically identical with the common components of the Commerce series. We can thus focus attention on the conceptual basis of different trends in output and productivity using the two basic alternative series. Kuznets has stated that "there are no compelling reasons for preferring any one of the three variants in the study of long-term trends: they yield almost identical results."[9] In view of this fact, there is no reason to complicate the picture by dealing with more than one of the Kuznets sets of national product estimates, although we do present several *conceptual* variants of both the Kuznets and the Commerce product series.

The national security version. In his book, *National Product in Wartime*,[10] Kuznets developed supplementary estimates of the national product for the years of the two world wars, based on the assumption of two end purposes of a nation's economic life. In addition to the peacetime goal of satisfaction of the wants of individual consumers, he maintained that in wartime the preservation of the nation also becomes a prime purpose of economic activity, ". . . and war output is properly treated as a final product." In *National Product since 1869*, he presented revised annual estimates of national product from 1919 through 1943 on the basis of both the "peacetime" and "wartime" concepts. His most recent estimates, however, are presented only in terms of the peacetime concept, which he has consistently maintained is appropriate for long-term comparisons.

[9] *Capital in the American Economy*, Vol. II, p. B-18.
[10] New York (NBER), 1945.

As an alternative basis for productivity comparisons, in Table A-I we reintroduce estimates that are basically adjustments of the recent Kuznets product estimates to the wartime concept. In this, we follow Frederick C. Mills.[11] As developed earlier, the rationale for this procedure lies in the argument that in a world of national states, national security is *at all times* a prime social objective. On these grounds, we have shifted from the term "wartime" to the more general term "national security," which accords with the designation by Commerce of the relevant government outlays.

In order to estimate the national security version, one must first deduct outlays for durable war goods from the Kuznets peacetime estimates and then add total national security outlays, which include durable war equipment and new construction. Estimates of government purchases of durable war goods—munitions and new construction—consistent with the revised aggregates are contained in Kuznets' *Capital in the American Economy*.[12]

Kuznets also presents a supplemental series showing "gross war output," 1914–53.[13] In assembling this series, he uses the Commerce estimates of national security purchases for the years available—1939 forward. The estimates for earlier years are derived as described in *National Product since 1869*, Table I-9. We have likewise used the Commerce estimates of national security purchases from 1939 on. We have made several adjustments, based on his worksheet detail, to the Kuznets estimates in order to achieve more precise comparability with the Commerce estimates of total federal government purchases and the national security component for later years. Specifically, we have deducted foreign loans and added back payments of principal and interest on such loans. These adjustments are of some importance from 1917 to 1933. We have also added back sales of war supplies, since the Commerce procedure is to deduct total government sales of goods from total purchases rather than to allocate this item by type of purchase. We thus have a series that may be related to the government-purchases component of the Commerce national product estimates as well as used to build up the national security variant of the Kuznets product estimates. For the years before 1914, we have based our estimates of federal military (War and Navy Departments) expenditures on those presented by M. Slade Kendrick.[14] These estimates have been converted from fiscal years to calendar years by use of the factors described below in the explanation of the total federal-purchases estimates.

[11] *Productivity and Economic Progress*, Occasional Paper 38, New York (NBER), 1952, Note 1.
[12] Vol. II, Table 7.
[13] *Ibid.*, Table 6.
[14] *A Century and a Half of Federal Expenditures*, Occasional Paper 48, New York (NBER), 1955, Table B-1.

Deflation of national security purchases was accomplished with a view to maintaining consistency with the relevant constant-price estimates of both Kuznets and Commerce. The current-dollar estimates were first broken down into four components: government purchases of durable war goods, as estimated by Kuznets; pay of the armed forces (including value of subsistence and clothing provision), estimated as described in Appendix K; pay of civilian employees of the Defense Department (formerly War and Navy Departments), estimated as the product of the number employed[15] and the average annual compensation of federal civilian general-government employees, as described in Appendix K; and an "all other" residual, which includes nondurable munitions. The fact that the "all other" estimates are low and relatively stable in peacetime years gives some support to the validity of the total security estimates and their breakdown, although the detail is used primarily for deflation purposes.

The constant-dollar estimates for the first three components were derived as described in the sources cited for the current value series. Thus, we use the Kuznets figures for munitions and war construction in real terms; and the base-period pay of the armed forces and of civilian employees of the Defense Department is extrapolated by employment, consistent with the Commerce estimates of real government purchases. The deflator for all other purchases is the same general price index used for total "all other" federal-government purchases, as described below, through 1940. From 1941 to date, however, with a much more substantial volume of other purchases due to the increased amount of nondurable munitions procurement, we have combined the "all other" price deflator with the price deflator used by the Commerce Department for munitions. Kuznets also used the Commerce munitions deflator for durable munitions outlays since 1939. But since the deflator is composed of price series for both durable and nondurable munitions, by weighting it into the deflator for residual purchases including nondurable munitions we obtain constant-dollar totals for the broader category of munitions plus other war purchases that are similar to those contained in the Commerce figures.

Capital consumption and net product. The recent estimates by Kuznets of capital consumption and net national product in 1929 dollars, adjusted to eliminate his allowance for real depreciation on munitions, are shown in Table A-I. The adjustment was made for the sake of consistency with our input estimates since we do not include durable munitions as part of the stock and input of productive capital.

Kuznets' capital consumption figures were generally derived from his estimates of fixed capital formation in constant dollars, depreciated in

---

15 Solomon Fabricant, *The Trend of Government Activity in the United States since 1900*, New York (NBER), 1952, Tables B-6 and B-7.

accordance with estimated life spans of major classes of producer goods. Possible errors of estimate can arise as a result of errors in the capital formation estimates, the lengths of economic life employed, the assumption of a constant length of life, and the time-shape of the depreciation charge. It is Kuznets' judgment, however, that the deduction of capital consumption as estimated from gross national product for the purpose of trend analysis "yields a smaller error than no adjustment."[16] Between the years 1880 and 1922, Kuznets finds considerable agreement between the sum of his real net capital formation estimates and the change in real wealth, estimated independently.[17]

It is important to understand that the real capital consumption estimates do not purport to measure the volume of capital goods production necessary to maintain intact the productive capacity of the economy. Rather, they should be interpreted as measuring the resources required to maintain the income-producing ability of the capital stock in terms of base-period prices. A given amount of capital goods in constant prices, whether for expansion or for replacement, would be expected to have a greater output capacity in one period than in another as a result of technological advance. It is this concept of capital that accords with the requirements of productivity analysis.

NATIONAL PRODUCT ON THE COMMERCE BASIS

The Commerce Department has published estimates of the gross national product in constant dollars as well as at current market prices for the years since 1929. We converted these estimates through 1953 to a 1929 base (accepting the Kuznets estimates in 1929 dollars that were based on the Commerce estimates and shifting the deflator for the remaining components) before reweighting as described earlier. In order to obtain estimates on the Commerce conceptual basis prior to 1929, the Kuznets Variant III estimates of the components that were consistent with the Commerce framework were used, independent estimates being made of the components that had to be added to the adjusted Kuznets figures to arrive at totals on the Commerce basis.

Specifically, this means that implicit government services to consumers had to be estimated and subtracted from Kuznets' flow of goods to consumers, and "services furnished without payment by financial intermediaries other than life insurance companies" added; public capital formation and the net change in stocks of monetary metals had to be subtracted from Kuznets' total capital formation; and, most important, total government purchases of goods and services had to be estimated and added to the estimates of private purchases of goods and services.

[16] *National Product in Wartime*, p. 20.
[17] See *Capital in the American Economy*.

The following sections describe the methods used to estimate the reconciliation items in current and 1929 dollars prior to 1929. Table A-IIa contains estimates in 1929 dollars for the entire period through 1957, since the Commerce estimates on a 1929 price base are not published elsewhere. In presenting these figures we accept the conversion by Kuznets of the Commerce estimates from a 1947 to a 1929 price base, although it should be noted that the conversion was done on the basis of broad product groupings rather than in the full product detail in which the Commerce current value estimates were made. Table A-IIb contains annual estimates in current values for 1929 and earlier years only, as the estimates for later years are readily available from Department of Commerce publications— although estimates for selected key years of more recent periods are provided as a further guide to those who wish to make their own reconciliation between the Kuznets and Commerce series.

Private purchases of goods and services. Two adjustments are necessary to go from Kuznets' "flow of goods to consumers" to the Commerce "consumption expenditures" estimates. The first is the deduction of government direct services to consumers, which Kuznets roughly approximated in current values by the use of estimates of personal tax and nontax payments for the years through 1940; for 1941 and subsequent years, because of the effect of war and national security requirements on personal taxes, he applied the 1929–40 ratio (0.036) of personal taxes to consumption expenditures (excluding unpaid financial services) to these expenditures in the later years. The price index applied is the implicit deflator for total consumer expenditures for services.

For 1929 to 1890, we have estimated personal tax and nontax payments independently since they are not shown explicitly in Kuznets' series. Federal income tax liabilities of individuals for the calendar years 1913–29 were estimated from the *Annual Report of the Commissioner of Internal Revenue.* Fiscal-year totals for the estate and gift taxes were taken from the *Annual Report of the Secretary of the Treasury* and were averaged to obtain calendar-year receipts. The sum of these two series was used to extrapolate back the 1929 Commerce estimate of federal personal tax payments. The relatively small amount of nontax payments was extrapolated by civilian population figures.

State personal tax receipts back to 1915 were estimated annually on the basis of data collected by the Governments Division of the Bureau of the Census. Certain categories were split between personal taxes and indirect business taxes on the same basis as that used by the National Income Division. Census figures were also available for 1890, 1902, and 1913. Estimates for intervening years were obtained by straight-line interpolation, and the entire series was adjusted to the Commerce level in 1929. Personal tax receipts of local government units were extrapolated by property tax revenues for 1927, 1922, 1913, 1902, and 1890, as reported in the Census Bureau special studies of state and local government finances (see note 25.) Annual interpolations to 1902 were made on the basis of property tax revenues in cities of over 30,000 population; from 1902 to 1890 the interpolation was on a straight-line basis. The special-assessment portion of nontax payments was also estimated on the basis of reports on this item by cities of over 30,000 population. The residual nontax payments were handled in the same manner as federal nontax payments.

Because of the lack prior to 1890 of aggregate data on state and local tax receipts, which loomed much larger than federal at that time, we have resorted to the device used by Kuznets after 1940. For 1889 and earlier years, the value of imputed direct services by governments to consumers was held at a constant ratio to the value of the flow of other consumer goods. The ratio used was 0.015, slightly below the 1890 ratio of personal tax and nontax payments to consumer outlays. This ratio was used in preference to a ratio based on several years of experience, since there was some upward drift after 1890.

Our estimates of personal tax and nontax payments are the same as those included in the Kuznets aggregate estimates from 1929 forward, since both are based on the Commerce series. From 1919 to 1929, our estimates differ slightly from those shown by Kuznets,[18] but our figures are consistent with both the later and the earlier estimates. It should be noted that the consistency of our series with the Kuznets estimates of the flow of goods to consumers cannot be precisely determined. They are consistent to the extent that the ratios of services to commodities, by which Kuznets built up his totals, take account of the trend in tax receipts revealed by direct estimate.[19]

Kuznets is aware that his method of imputing a value to the direct services to individuals by governments is a rough convention, tolerable only because the magnitudes involved have been small until recent years. His preferred method, given sufficient resources, would be to make a functional classification of all government outlays and segregate the magnitudes representing final services, such as health, education, recreation, and the like. Judging from the occasional attempts at a specific approach, with due allowance for interpretation of the dividing line between direct and cost services, Kuznets does not consider the results of his convention to be unreasonable for the 1929–38 decade. Furthermore, as Table A-2 shows, the portion of government purchases (excluding war output and new construction) assumed to represent final purchases has fluctuated between the 0.3 and 0.5 ratios indicated for 1939 and 1929, respectively. The ratio of final government services to national product

[18] *National Product since 1869*, Table 1 4B.
[19] Cf. *ibid.*, Part III.

has tended to rise over the long run, but this is a reflection of the expanding role of government in the economy rather than the result of an assumption that government has devoted an increasing share of its services to the ultimate consumer.

The other item necessary to reconcile the Kuznets and Commerce consumption expenditure estimates is "services furnished without payment by financial intermediaries except insurance companies." This item, not included by Kuznets, represents the imputed value of banking services furnished to individuals without charge. The current values are approximated by the operating expense of banks, which is equivalent to their property income less interest payments to customers by type. In translating this item into real terms, we have used the Commerce procedure and assumed that the flow of real services is proportionate to the dollar volume of deposits of individuals, adjusted for changes in the purchasing power of the dollar by the consumer price index.

TABLE A-2

Government Services to Consumers in Relation to
Net National Product and Total Government Outlays, Key Years, 1870–1953

	NET NATIONAL PRODUCT, KUZNETS	GOVERNMENT OUTLAYS[a]	IMPUTED DIRECT GOVERNMENT SERVICES		
			Value	Proportion of	
				Net National Product	Government Outlays
	(billions of dollars)			(per cent)	
1870	5.49	0.23	0.07	1.3	30
1890	11.45	0.48	0.15	1.3	31
1910	28.97	1.3	0.44	1.5	34
1929	90.3	5.2	2.6	2.9	50
1939	73.8	8.4	2.4	3.3	29
1948	192.8	15.9	6.3	3.3	40
1953	258.8	23.1	8.2	3.2	35

[a] Exclusive of outlays for national security and new construction.

We have also used the Commerce approach in extending the estimates to earlier years. The current value estimate in 1929 was extrapolated by the estimated gross earnings of all banks in the United States. This was obtained by blowing up the gross earnings of national banks by the ratio of total deposits in all banks to those in national banks.[20] The constant-dollar estimates were extrapolated by the total deposits of all banks, which were deflated by the consumer price index of the Bureau of Labor Statistics (shifted to a 1929 base and extrapolated for years prior to 1913

[20] *Historical Statistics of the United States, 1789–1945*, Dept. of Commerce, 1949, Series N 61, N 26, and N 34.

by the index prepared by the Federal Reserve Bank of New York).[21] It should be noted that this procedure involves the assumption that the portion of bank deposits held by individuals as consumers did not change significantly prior to 1929.

Despite the roughness of the estimating procedure, the results seem reasonable. The imputed services of financial intermediaries rise from about 0.5 per cent of consumption expenditures in 1870 to 1.5 per cent in 1929. Because the value of these services is consistently below the imputed value of direct government services, the Kuznets estimates of consumer goods are slightly higher than those on the Commerce basis. Since the absolute increases (but not the percentage increases) in government services exceed those in financial services, the Kuznets estimates of consumer goods show a slightly higher rate of growth over the period as a whole than those based on the Commerce concept.

In the field of fixed investments, the necessary adjustments are simple. As we later add total government purchases, here we deduct public purchases of durable equipment (including munitions) and new public construction from the Kuznets estimates. Because of his estimating procedure, Kuznets' estimates of the flow of durable equipment include not only government purchases, but also a small statistical discrepancy as compared with the Commerce estimates. Since we extrapolate the latter estimates back of 1929 by the Kuznets estimates exclusive of munitions, we are in effect holding the small amount of nonwar equipment purchased by the government plus whatever statistical discrepancy remains at its 1929 ratio to the total Kuznets estimates of nonwar equipment purchases.

The only difference between the Kuznets and Commerce estimates of the change in business inventories is that the former include the net change in inventories of monetary metals. The figures shown in Table A-II are the Kuznets estimates exclusive of his explicit estimates of the value of the change in monetary metal stocks from 1919 forward. The latter series is not shown here, but can be obtained as the difference between these figures and those published by Kuznets. The monetary metal item is generally quite small. Prior to 1919, Kuznets did not explicitly estimate this item; indeed, his estimates of the change in business inventories were based on an extrapolation of the regression of total inventories on commodity flow since 1919. We have taken his estimates of inventory change prior to 1919 without adjustment as being essentially comparable with the later Commerce figures. Because of the large margins of error attaching to the inventory change estimates in the early period, a minor adjustment would be meaningless.

Kuznets' estimates of "net changes in claims against foreign countries" in current values are identical with the Commerce estimates of "net

[21] *Ibid.*, Series L 36.

foreign investment" since 1929 and are conceptually comparable with the latter in the earlier years. A difference exists, however, between the two sets of estimates in constant dollars. Commerce deflated exports and imports of goods and services (receipts and payments) separately by the price indexes applicable to each. Kuznets, on the other hand, deflated the *net* balance by a general price index (the implicit deflator for the rest of national product). The Commerce method can be justified from a production standpoint, while the Kuznets method conforms to a welfare approach, since changes in the terms of trade between the United States and the rest of the world affect the real income of the nation.[22] The results of the two methodologies can be significantly different, particularly from year to year, as a result of divergent movements between export and import prices and shifts in the composition of trade.

In view of the generally small magnitude of the balance and the deterioration of the quantity and quality of data necessary to implement the Commerce approach in the earlier period, we have used the Kuznets constant-dollar estimates for the years prior to 1929.

Federal government purchases. Having derived estimates of private purchases of final goods and services on the Commerce basis, the remaining task was to estimate total government purchases of goods and services. This was a major endeavor, and we will describe the sources and methods separately for federal and for state and local government purchases.

It was possible to estimate total federal purchases annually from 1869 to 1929 by essentially the same methods as those used by the Commerce Department for more recent years. The basic source was the *Annual Report of the Secretary of the Treasury*, supplemented for 1921–29 by Budget documents. The point of departure was the series on total ordinary administrative budget expenditures. These data were adjusted to a "purchases" basis by deduction or addition of the various items described generally in the *National Income Supplement, 1954*, pp. 146–47. The resulting estimates, which relate to fiscal years, were than converted to a calendar-year basis.

The expenditures data, as transcribed, were already net of debt retirement and premiums. The major nonpurchase items deducted were, in the earlier years, pensions and interest on the public debt. Of much smaller magnitude were District of Columbia expenditures, grants-in-aid, tax refunds, budgetary expenditures relating to government enterprises, and purchases of existing assets. Grants-in-aid to state and local governments were not a significant deduction until World War I. The government-enterprise item was confined to the Post Office in the nineteenth century;

---

[22] A discussion of this point is contained in a paper by Solomon Fabricant, "Capital Consumption and Net Capital Formation," *A Critique of the United States Income and Product Accounts*, Studies in Income and Wealth, Volume 22, p. 440.

but various other enterprises growing out of the war and its aftermath required substantial adjustments from 1917 on—as did loans and purchases of foreign obligations, and capital formation of government enterprises. The deduction for government sales, necessary to arrive at net purchases, was of some consequence throughout the period.

Adjustment of the estimates from a fiscal- to a calendar-year basis was somewhat rough because only gross-expenditure data were available by months in the *Annual Report of the Secretary of the Treasury*. The proportions of fiscal-year expenditures falling in each half-year period were computed, and these proportions applied to the fiscal-year purchases estimates. Somewhat more than half the expenditures tended to fall in the first six months of the fiscal year. The half-year purchases figures were recombined to yield calendar-year totals.

For purposes of deflating the current value estimates, federal government purchases were split into three broad categories: labor compensation, new construction, and other purchases of goods and services. The method of estimating compensation of general-government employees is described in Appendix K. Since the compensation in constant dollars was extrapolated by the employment estimates, the implicit deflator was the average annual compensation per employee.

The estimates of federal government new construction from 1929 to 1915 are those published by the Department of Commerce.[23] The deflator was derived from the same source by allocating the constant-dollar estimates for the various types of public construction between federal and state and local governments by the same proportions as those applied to the current values, and then dividing the constant into the current values. The current-dollar values, by major types, were extrapolated back to 1869 on the basis of the estimates reproduced in *Historical Statistics*, Series H 27–32. The deflator was extrapolated from 1915 back by that used by Kuznets for total new public construction.

Other federal government purchases in current dollars were derived as a residual. The deflator for this component, used by the Commerce Department since 1929, consists broadly of components of the Bureau of Labor Statistics wholesale price index, reweighted in accordance with the relative importance of the various types of purchases in 1938 as revealed by detailed estimates assembled by the Temporary National Economic Committee. Since federal agencies purchase such a wide variety of goods, the implicit deflator so derived moves closely with the composite wholesale price index excluding agricultural products, and with the food component reduced in weight to 2 per cent of the total, in line with its relatively small importance in federal agency procurement. This somewhat modified

[23] *Construction Volume and Costs, 1915–52*, May 1953 Statistical Supplement, *Construction and Building Materials*.

composite wholesale price index was used to extend the Commerce deflator from 1929 back. Prior to 1890, the BLS wholesale price composite was extrapolated to 1869 by a weighted average of wholesale prices for the various product groups contained in the Aldrich Report, including farm products.[24] The weights were those underlying the BLS index for 1909, except for the smaller weight assigned the food group.

State and local government purchases. The estimates of purchases of state and local governments are not quite so reliable as those of the federal government, particularly with regard to annual changes; but the indicated trends should be relatively accurate at least as far back as 1890. Estimates of state and local government expenditures have been prepared by the Governments Division of the Bureau of the Census for 1890, 1902, 1913, 1922, 1927, 1932, and thereafter biennially.[25]

The census estimates represent direct general expenditures on a consolidated basis net of most intergovernmental transactions. To convert these to a purchases basis, it was necessary to deduct interest on general debt and purchases of existing assets, and to add capital outlays of state and local government enterprises (utilities and liquor stores). The interest item is shown in the cited studies. Purchases of land and existing assets were estimated to be one-third of the estimate shown for these items plus new equipment, the proportion being based on that in later years when separate estimates were available for existing and new assets. Enterprise capital outlays were estimated by applying to total capital outlays the ratios of enterprise expenditures to total expenditures.

The Census Bureau estimates relate to fiscal years ending in the calendar years indicated, except for 1913 when all data were adjusted to a fiscal year ending June 30. Apparently, in the years with which we are concerned, most local governments (nonschool) and many state governments operated on a calendar-year basis. Accordingly, in the years other than 1913 we have adjusted only the estimates of school expenditures by adding one-half the difference between expenditures for the school year ending in the given calendar year and those in the succeeding school year to the former. In 1913, the same type of adjustment was made to total state and local expenditures. Even in 1913, the adjustment amounted to only about 3 per cent of the fiscal-year purchases.

Annual interpolations of state and local government purchases were made between the benchmark years from 1902 to 1927, and between the

[24] *Wholesale Prices, Wages, and Transportation,* Committee on Finance, Senate Report No. 1394, 52d Cong., 2d sess., 1893.

[25] *Historical Review of State and Local Government Finances,* Special Studies No. 25, 1948; and *Historical Statistics on State and Local Government Finances, 1902–1953,* Special Studies No. 38, 1955. The estimates for 1922 and 1927 were based on less-than-complete coverage of all government units, but the available data were blown up to approximately full coverage by the Census Bureau.

adjusted Census estimate for 1927 and the Commerce estimate for 1929 on the basis of partial annual data collected by the Census Bureau. From 1915 to 1929, the data relate to expenditures of state governments and of cities of over 30,000 population. Prior to 1915, only municipal government data were available for annual interpolations. For a few scattered years, data were not collected; these cases were handled by straight-line interpolation in constant dollars, with reflation of the interpolated estimates. The derivation of annual estimates prior to 1902 will be described following a summary description of the deflation procedures.

Deflation was carried out in terms of three major components. Estimates of the compensation of state and local school and nonschool employees, the first component, were available in current and constant dollars annually back to 1869, based on methods described in Appendix K. Estimates of new construction, the second component, were obtained by subtracting federal government new construction (see preceding section) from the estimates of total new public construction prepared by Kuznets, in both current and constant dollars. The residual "other" purchases by state and local governments in current dollars for 1890, 1902, and subsequent years were than deflated. The deflator was the Commerce series extrapolated by the wholesale price index excluding food and farm products (described in the preceding section), weighted 0.82, and the index of wholesale food prices, weighted 0.18. The relative weights are those employed in the Commerce deflator.

Annual estimates of other purchases prior to 1902 were prepared in the following way. A straight-line interpolation between the 1890 and 1902 constant-dollar residual purchases was made; the resulting annual estimates were then reflated by the price deflator in order to obtain current-dollar figures. The estimates for residual purchases, in current and constant dollars, were then added to the corresponding estimates of employee compensation and new construction in order to obtain total state and local purchases for the intervening years. Estimates of other purchases for the years prior to 1890 were obtained first in constant dollars by extrapolating the 1890–1953 trend in this item on a per capita basis, and applying the extrapolated figures to population estimates for the earlier years. The constant-dollar estimates so derived were then reflated by the price index to obtain current-dollar figures. Total state and local purchases were then obtained as the sum of the three components, in current and in constant dollars.

Since one of the components was derived by extrapolation prior to the 1890 benchmark, the earlier estimates are clearly less reliable than those for 1890 and subsequent years. Other purchases, in real terms per capita, have shown a remarkably steady growth since 1890, however; and it does not seem unreasonable to assume a similar trend in earlier decades, since forces such as urbanization were at play throughout the entire period.

VARIANT FORMS OF THE COMMERCE ESTIMATES

Table A-III contains several variant forms of real product on the Commerce basis. Only one of these, the gross "domestic product," represents a competing aggregate concept, covering as it does the product of factors located in the national geographical area as contrasted with the "national product" of factor services provided by residents of the area. The net national product estimates are designed to portray final product after allowance for capital consumption as defined by Commerce. The estimates of gross private domestic product represent a different level of aggregation with respect to industry coverage—the product of government factors is excluded in order to give a better basis for productivity comparisons in view of the Commerce method of estimating real government product. This variant is shown on a domestic basis, gross of capital consumption, for greater comparability with the output of the various private-industry groups.

Net national product. The Commerce estimates of capital consumption have a somewhat narrower coverage than those of Kuznets described earlier. They do not include depletion "since the value of the corresponding discoveries of natural resources is not an element of capital formation or profits."[26] Neither do they include depreciation on publicly owned capital goods, presumably because this procedure is not followed in public accounting.

In order to obtain estimates of capital consumption in constant dollars on the Commerce basis, we have subtracted the depletion and public depreciation components from the Kuznets totals in 1929 dollars. This was done for the years after 1929 as well as for prior years, since Commerce has not yet published estimates of capital consumption in constant dollars. The resulting aggregates comprise depreciation on private stocks of fixed capital (including owner-occupied residences), capital outlays charged to current expense, and accidental damage to fixed capital. While having the same coverage as the Commerce estimates, the constant-dollar aggregates do not necessarily embody the same accounting conventions pertaining to lengths of life and methods of charging depreciation as those underlying the Commerce estimates unadjusted for price changes. The nonfarm depreciation portions of the latter estimates are in terms of original cost, as contrasted with the Kuznets estimates in current, replacement values. This does not concern us in general, since our focus is on physical-volume series; it does explain, however, why the estimate of capital consumption for 1929 in Table A-III deviates somewhat from the one published by Commerce.

---

[26] *National Income Supplement, 1954,* p. 42.

As a rough check on the comparability of the capital consumption estimates on the Commerce basis derived from Kuznets, and the Commerce estimates since 1929, we have deflated the latter by appropriate price indexes drawn largely from the work of Raymond Goldsmith. Although the movements of the two series are quite close, we have used the adjusted Kuznets estimates of capital consumption in deriving net national product on the Commerce basis. This not only provides consistency throughout the long period, but also conforms to our objective of minimizing the purely statistical differences between the Kuznets and Commerce series.

Domestic product. Both Commerce and Kuznets define national product in terms of the output attributable to the factors of production supplied by residents of the continental United States. Thus, the income from capital invested in foreign countries by United States residents is added to income and product, while the income accruing to residents of foreign countries from their capital investment here is deducted. Kuznets deflates the current-dollar "net payments of factor income from abroad"[27] by the general national product deflator, and an analogous general price index is used by Commerce.

If the net payments are deducted from national product, or not included to begin with, the corresponding aggregate is called the "domestic product." By this concept, the criterion for inclusion in income or product becomes the physical location of the factors themselves. Thus, the return to capital owned abroad but located in this country is included, while the income from capital located abroad but owned by United States residents is not added. From a strict welfare viewpoint, the national concept seems appropriate, since we are concerned with the real income that the residents of a nation derive from productive activity. Real national income or product differs from the output of goods and services within the country (deducting purchases from abroad) to the extent of net factor payments from abroad.

As indicated in Table A-III, net factor income from abroad is a small item, fluctuating between −0.5 per cent of national product in the late nineteenth century and +0.5 per cent in recent years. Yet, for purposes of productivity comparisons, except when these are related to real-income comparisons with welfare connotations, as in Chapter 4, there are advantages in using the domestic product concept. Estimates of net investments abroad, which must be included in input on a nationality basis, are subject to greater margins of error than domestic capital stock estimates. Furthermore, the flow of real income from foreign-owned capital bears an erratic

[27] The estimates from 1929 forward are given in *National Income Supplement, 1954,* Table 11, p. 174; those for earlier years are described in Kuznets, *Capital in the American Economy,* Vol. II, pp. A-41 and B-30 to B-32.

relationship to the output of the industries concerned and to the capital stock itself; this association tends to distort the capital and total factor output-input ratios. Finally, if aggregate productivity is to be compared with productivity in various industries, the aggregate should be on a domestic basis, since the industry input estimates are available only on this basis.

Private domestic product. Because of the difficulties of measuring real government product, it is desirable to exclude the government sector and study productivity movements in the private domestic sector. National income and product originating in general government is defined by Commerce as the compensation of the productive factors employed by government units. In practice, Commerce counts only the compensation of general-government employees, although it can be argued that an imputed return to publicly owned capital stocks should also be included (see Appendix K). But in either case, the product of the private domestic economy (which includes government enterprise) is obtained by deducting government product from total domestic product. In Table A-III, estimates of private product are shown gross of capital consumption, since we later compare them with industry output estimates that are on a gross basis; but net private product can easily be computed from the information provided.

COMPARISON OF REAL PRODUCT WITH AN AGGREGATE OF INDUSTRY OUTPUT

The comparisons in this section are intended primarily to give some indication of the consistency, since 1889, between total real gross product originating and the output measures for the several industrial divisions of the private domestic economy. The comparison is also a rough external check on the reliability of the real-product estimates, subject to qualifications noted below.

There is actually no objective way of assessing the margins of error in the real-product estimates. On the basis of a critical examination of source materials, the Commerce Department technicians tentatively concluded "that the estimated annual totals of gross national product, national income, and personal income are subject to only a small percentage of error."[28] This statement applies only to the estimates since 1929, and it is generally accepted that the quality deteriorates as the estimates are extended backward. The product estimates for 1869–79 are notably weak because of deficiencies in the Census of 1870, a fact that is confirmed by the analysis of this section. It is for this reason that we begin our annual real-product estimates with 1889 and have recourse to annual averages for the two earlier decades.

[28] *National Income Supplement, 1954,* p. 66.

The process of price deflation was carried out in terms of more than 200 product classes after 1929, using the wide variety of sources available. For the earlier period, fewer price series were available, and the deflation was done on a more aggregate basis. Thus, the real-product as well as the current value estimates are presumably less accurate in the early period, although the "physical-volume" figures are subject to various qualifications throughout, as noted in Chapter 2. Nevertheless, the fact that the productivity estimates from 1889 on show a comparatively regular movement over the subperiods and appear generally plausible is some indication of the broad reliability or at least the consistency of both the real-product and the input estimates.

It is only for the period since 1929 that an appraisal of the real-product estimates could be made on the basis of an aggregate of output measures for all industry segments. Even for this period, the industry aggregate is not perfectly adapted for our purposes. Only in the farm, construction, and finance and services areas are the measures true net output or "real product originating" measures. The other industry estimates are gross of intermediate products consumed in the production process and therefore are fully comparable conceptually with aggregate real product only on the assumption that the real gross and net output measures have moved proportionately. In a number of segments, it was necessary to apply "coverage adjustments" to the extent that the value of the physical units underlying the industry composite fell short of the total value of production.[29] The coverage adjustments are not generally large; but, insofar as the underlying assumption that either unit value or productivity in the uncovered areas moved with the like variable in the covered industries is not valid, some distortion may be introduced. Further, in the construction and the finance and services areas, current-dollar gross national product originating was deflated directly by product price indexes. This procedure introduces possible distortions in the results, apart from shortcomings in the deflators (see Appendixes E and J). It is implicitly assumed that average prices of intermediate products move with average prices of gross output. Since the intermediate-product ratio is not large in the finance and service areas, distortions from this source should be minor.

To obtain the aggregate industry output index, gross national income originating in the various segments in 1929 was extrapolated by the output indexes shown in Table A-IV. Correspondingly, the real gross product index was based on the fixed-weight 1929-dollar estimates of Table A-III. From the comparison of aggregate industry output with real product (Table A-IV) for the years since 1929, it is apparent that real product rose somewhat more over the period as a whole, and in two of the three subperiods. The evidence is summarized in Table A-3.

[29] See Appendix D for discussion of coverage adjustments.

The divergence between the two measures over the whole period is not unreasonable in view of differences in their construction. In the first place, the ratio of net to gross output has probably increased over the period under review, except in the extractive industries. A larger increase in real product than in gross output results from savings in materials and greater processing per unit. This was true in manufacturing since 1939,[30] and in the earlier decade it was probably also the case in electric and gas utilities with respect to the major intermediate input, coal.[31]

TABLE A-3

Private Domestic Economy: Comparison of Movements in Real Gross Product
and Aggregate Industry Output, Subperiods, 1929–53
(link relatives)

	Aggregate Industry Output	Real Gross Product	Ratio: Gross Product to Industry Output
1929–37	97.8	102.5	104.8
1937–48	164.7	159.8	97.0
1948–53	121.8	122.5	100.6
1929–53	196.3	200.7	102.2

Secondly, insofar as there is a trend towards higher-priced grades of products as real income grows secularly, physical-volume indexes tend to have a downward bias. That is, if the basic units used for composite physical-volume measures are heterogeneous, the indexes do not show shifts among grades as changes in volume. Deflated value estimates do, of course, reflect such shifts. Finally, the coverage adjustments may not adequately reflect the growing output of new products whose prices are falling relative to average prices.

Thus, it seems reasonable that the gross output aggregate should rise less than real product. The reversal of this tendency in the 1937–48 subperiod may well be associated with the effects of postwar reconversion, which were still in evidence in 1948. The results of this comparison are, of course, no proof of the accuracy of the real-product estimates. Possibly the divergence between the two aggegates should be greater. And since the series in question are based on many of the same sources, they may have either errors in common or errors peculiar to each that work in the

[30] See *Trends in Output per Man-hour and Man-hours per Unit of Output—Manufacturing, 1939–53*, BLS Report No. 100, 1955.

[31] See Jacob M. Gould, *Output and Productivity in the Electric and Gas Utilities, 1899–1942*, New York (NBER), 1946, pp. 172–83.

same direction. But, at least, the two series appear to be relatively consistent, when account is taken of the conceptual and methodological differences between them.

The appraisal of the real-product estimates prior to 1929 must be made on a different basis. Estimates of national income or product originating in finance and services are not available for the earlier period; neither are estimates of physical output. Real gross income originating in the finance and services segment can be derived as a residual, however, by the subtraction of covered real gross income from total real gross income of the private domestic economy. The relevant indexes are shown in Table A-IV. The same qualifications apply to this comparison as were mentioned in connection with the post-1929 comparisons. For example, insofar as the ratio of nonfarm net to gross output has increased, the growth of real product in the finance and services segment would tend to be overstated in the residual measure.

The implied growth of output in the finance and services areas prior to 1929 was much greater than that shown by the direct measure after that date. But when compared with labor input, the average annual rate of increase in the partial productivity ratio was 1.5 per cent for 1889–1929 compared with 1.6 per cent for 1929–53. Although somewhat irregular over the subperiods, the indicated trends in finance and services output per unit of labor input do not appear to be prima facie evidence of distortion in the trend of the total real-output measure.

Prior to 1889, the movement of output per unit of labor input for finance and services throws considerable doubt on the validity of the aggregate measure. A large increase between 1869 and 1879 is followed by a decline between 1879 and 1889. These gyrations certainly confirm Kuznets' opinion that real product in 1869 is understated, possibly by 10 per cent or so, partly because of the well-known undercoverage of the Census of 1870. The 1879 aggregate, on the other hand, may possibly be overstated. It was partly because of the behavior of the residual real-product estimates that we decided not to show annual estimates for the aggregates prior to 1889. The decade averages do, however, yield productivity results that are more in line with later experience.

Labor Input

Based on the concepts developed in Chapter 2, labor input has been estimated by weighting manhours worked in the various industrial divisions of the economy by average hourly compensation in each. All classes of workers are included in the estimates of persons engaged, manhours, and labor input: proprietors and the self-employed, unpaid family workers, and employees of all categories including nonproduction as well as production workers. The labor variables were estimated by industrial segment and then aggregated to obtain economy totals. Thus, the problem of consistency between the aggregates and the industry components does not arise as it does in the cases of output and capital. We shall, however, compare our aggregates with estimates based on other sources.

The sources and methods used in deriving the labor series for the various industry segments are described fully in succeeding appendixes; only a summary description is given in this section. Weighting procedures, however, are fully explained. Annual estimates of employment and manhours are presented for broad sectors. The distribution by industry is shown only for key years; but the reader can compute the numbers in greater detail for all years from the industry appendix tables. Annual index numbers of labor input are shown in the productivity summary tables for the national economy and the private domestic sector at the end of this Appendix.

EMPLOYMENT

Our chief interest in employment is as a means of obtaining estimates of manhours and labor input for the productivity ratios. Where direct manhour data are available, employment figures are used to derive estimates of average hours worked. They are also of interest as a measure of resource allocation as analyzed in Chapter 7. Consequently, estimates of employment as well as of manhours and labor input are presented in the appendix tables.

Employment concepts. The employment estimates used in this study are based on establishment reports, or they represent extrapolations of establishment-based employment estimates. Establishment reports are collected in connection with industrial censuses or Census surveys, social security and similar administrative programs, and Labor Department and trade-association reporting programs. In this type of report, all workers employed in a given time period are counted, including part-time workers whose primary employment is in another establishment in the same or a different industry, and workers who have shifted jobs during the period. In contrast, in reports prepared by the Census Bureau from decennial population censuses or current population surveys of the labor force, each worker is counted only once, in the industry in which he is primarily employed. This is the major difference between the two estimates. However, the Census estimates also tend to be lower, since a minimum age limit is invoked (fourteen years since 1930; ten years before then). Even today, particularly in agriculture, many children under fourteen and even under ten years of age are employed (usually as unpaid family workers) for parts of the year.

A substantial portion of the difference between establishment and labor-force reporting disappears when numbers of employees are converted to a "full-time equivalent" basis. The distribution of employment among industries differs, however, to the extent that part-time work performed elsewhere by primary workers of a given industry is not precisely offset by part-time work performed in the given industry by outside workers. The employment estimates shown in this report are generally approximations to full-time equivalents, since this provides a better basis for analyzing the industrial distribution of manpower by giving a more comparable content to the average job in each industry. Manhours actually worked is, of course, an even better basis for such an investigation.

As will be seen from the comparison in Table A-VIII, estimates of employment on a labor-force basis and of persons engaged on an establishment basis (which comprise full-time equivalent employees plus proprietors and unpaid family workers) do not precisely coincide as to level and and movement. This is largely because proprietors and unpaid family workers have not been reduced to a full-time equivalent basis. About 5 per cent of this class of worker are multiple job-holders. To the extent that they are employees in a secondary activity, they serve to swell the establishment employee count but not the labor force enumeration. However, the estimates of establishment employment even on a full-time equivalent basis are swollen relative to Census employment estimates to the extent that outside employment lifts a person's workweek above the prevailing average.

The labor force estimates suffer from the disadvantage that population censuses are taken less frequently than industrial censuses and surveys. Also, prior to the 1950 Census, the labor force estimates were not broken down by industrial attachment. Although industry estimates have been built up from occupational detail, a considerable margin of error is involved because of the problem of allocating "repeater" occupations. Further, derivation of employment estimates from the labor force figures by deducting unemployment estimates is somewhat hazardous, particularly on an industry basis. Since 1940, we have had monthly Census population surveys of both the labor force and employment; but since these are based on a small sample they are subject to considerable sampling variability, particularly with respect to the unpublished industry detail.

For the purpose of combining employment with average hours estimates in order to obtain manhours, full- and part-time employment estimates are frequently appropriate. Much of the material on hours relates to averages based on both full-time and part-time employees of establishments; therefore, our worksheets contain industrial employment estimates on both bases. Estimates of full- and part-time employment for the aggregate are shown in Table A-V.

Finally, something should be said as to the temporal dimensions of employment averages. Employment is usually reported as the total number of persons on the payroll during a specified period of time—frequently, one week in each month. Annual averages are thus averages of temporal samples. To the extent that these samples are not representative of the whole period under review, the annual average is not entirely "true." The same observation holds for average hours estimates. Some of the estimates of persons engaged, particularly proprietors, relate to even fewer periods in the year, or possibly to only one date. In such cases, it is evident that seasonal and cyclical fluctuations affect the adequacy of the estimates as annual averages. This is more serious with respect to annual changes than to trends.

Ideally, we should like to have a daily count of all persons at work in establishments or self-employed for days in which operations are conducted. Then the tally could be averaged for all operational days per year to arrive at average annual employment. If daily hours actually worked by the persons engaged were also tabulated, then average hours worked per day, or per year, could be computed. Even such an "ideal" setup would have its problems. Days when operations were significantly below normal would pull down the averages, which would then not reflect average employment under full operating conditions. Similarly, average annual hours would not reflect the average work-year of fully employed workers to the extent that layoffs occur. Total manhours worked would, however, be obtained; and this is the prime desideratum for productivity estimates. Averages of employment and hours are inevitably subject to problems of interpretation of the sort indicated. Manhours, which refer to totals rather than averages, are less ambiguous, although the problem of errors resulting from temporal sampling remains. The statistical problem of measuring manhours worked as distinct from manhours paid for will be treated later.

Sources and methods. The estimates of persons engaged used in this study are drawn for the most part from secondary sources. For 1929 and subsequent years we have used, with a few exceptions, the estimates of the National Income Division of the Department of Commerce, which have been carefully prepared and are consistent with the estimates of national income and product.[32] The Commerce estimates for agriculture, mining, manufacturing, much of transportation, communications and public utilities, and government, have been extrapolated back by estimates based on establishment reports in census years, and by other government surveys or trade-association data. Many of these estimates are contained in previous National Bureau studies of output and employment, extended for the present study by the use of parallel sources and methods. Employment

---

[32] *National Income Supplement, 1954,* and *Technical Notes, Sources and Methods Used in the Derivation of National Income Statistics,* National Income Divsion, Office of Business Economics, mimeo, 1948. See Chapter 2 for discussion of the importance of consistency with national product.

in the other areas of the economy was extrapolated back of 1929 largely by Daniel Carson's estimates [33] of gainful workers in the various industry divisions, based on *Census of Population* occupational data; Carson's figures were adjusted for changes in the ratio of employment to the labor force as estimated for the total economy by Clarence D. Long. [34] In a few service segments, employment estimates made by Stanley Lebergott for the years back to 1900 were used, since his series appeared to be the most carefully prepared of those that were available.[35] Lebergott also made heavy use of the census data on gainful workers by occupation.

The estimates for 1929 and subsequent years, and particularly those since 1939, are considerably more reliable than the earlier figures. This statement is more applicable to the industry distribution than to the aggregate, and to year-to-year changes than to trends.

Since 1939, the Commerce employment estimates have been based on Social Security and Railroad Retirement data, which cover almost four-fifths of all workers. Another 15 per cent or so of the workers are government employees, for whom relatively reliable estimates are made, based on data gathered by the Civil Service Commission and the State and Local Government Division of the Census Bureau. Since complete coverage is thus obtained for almost 95 per cent of employees, and estimates for many of the uncovered industries derive from relatively reliable sources, the quality of the employment estimates is very good. The quality of the estimates for persons engaged, which include proprietors and the self-employed, is not so good, because before and after 1950 interpolations and extrapolations for nonfarm proprietors were based largely on estimates of numbers of firms derived from sample surveys. Also, we added the estimates of unpaid nonfarm family workers, based on the Census Bureau's current population survey, back to 1941. These are subject to considerable sampling variability at the half-million level involved in this category in 1941.

From 1929 to 1939, the estimates are also quite firmly based. Occasional censuses were taken, beginning in 1929, of most major industrial divisions. Annual movements, frequently based on the BLS employment estimates derived from establishment surveys, are less reliable than the indicated longer-term trends.

Prior to 1929, industrial censuses were not taken for trade, services, and construction. In these areas, chief reliance has been placed on the decennial occupation data. In order to obtain annual estimates for the

[33] "Changes in the Industrial Composition of Manpower since the Civil War," *Studies in Income and Wealth, Volume 11,* New York (NBER), 1949.

[34] *The Labor Force under Changing Income and Employment,* Princeton University Press (for NBER), 1958.

[35] *Estimates of the Labor Force, Employment, and Unemployment, 1900–1950,* Office of Statistical Standards Bureau of the Budget.

economy, employment in a few industrial divisions has been interpolated between census years on the basis of the relationship to output. Clearly, annual productivity comparisons are meaningless for an industry for which the estimates are thus derived. In such cases, comparisons have been confined to decennial years or averages.

Even in the areas in which industrial censuses were taken periodically, annual interpolations were generally based on samples or partial state data; so the year-to-year movements are less significant than changes between census years.

Characteristics of the estimates. Since the estimates for earlier years have been used to extrapolate the worker estimates of the Commerce Department, they are thereby adjusted to establishment-count levels, even when the extrapolator is an adjusted population-count series. The Commerce Department publishes two different sets of employee estimates: full-time equivalents and full- and part-time employment. The full-time equivalent employee is not defined in terms of a set number of hours per week, but rather in the approximate terms of the prevailing workweek. In practice, Commerce has made the conversion by dividing payrolls of part-time employees by the average pay of full-time employees on the basis of segregated payroll data that were available from some of the industry censuses and from Social Security data. Therefore, short-period changes in the relationship between the two series prior to 1940 are not significant since the ratio of one to another was determined by the benchmark information for selected years. Even with constant industry ratios, however, the ratio of full- and part-time employees to full-time equivalents in the economy as a whole is affected by interindustry shifts of employment. Part-time employment is significantly large only in certain industrial segments, such as trade and services. In other segments, such as manufacturing, it is so small a portion of the total that actual employment is used to approximate full-time equivalent employment.

In estimating employment prior to 1929, we have extended both full-time equivalent and full- and part-time employment by the same series in each of the industries. This implies that the proportion between the two in each of the segments remained constant at the 1929 ratio. Thus, changes in the ratios at the national level prior to 1929 reflect only inter-industry employment shifts. Table A-V shows the two series for selected years throughout the period.

Numbers of proprietors (including self-employed) have generally been estimated directly, as indicated in the succeeding appendixes. Estimates of nonfarm unpaid family workers, however, were available only for 1941 and subsequent years. These estimates, based on the Current Population Surveys, cover the nonfarm economy as a whole and were distributed by industry in proportion to the number of proprietors. Prior to 1941, unpaid family workers were extrapolated back by the numbers of proprietors, using the 1941 proportion. This is obviously a crude expedient, but as of 1941 only 0.5 million persons were involved, and total employment including even these rough estimates should be better than estimates not allowing for the unpaid. Numbers of unpaid family workers are greater in agriculture than in the rest of the economy; and the farm employment estimates of the Department of Agriculture include this class of worker, although they are not separated from proprietors.

Table A-V also shows the numbers of proprietors and unpaid family workers and their importance relative to total persons engaged. The total from 1929 forward differs from the Commerce Department estimates in two respects: (1) the Department of Agriculture series on farm employment has been substituted for that used by the Commerce Department (the former includes unpaid family workers and is estimated somewhat differently); (2) we have added estimates of unpaid nonfarm family workers not covered by Commerce.

Annual estimates of employment in the national economy by major sector are given in Table A-VI. The industrial distribution of the estimates of total persons engaged is shown for key years in Table A-VII. As indicated earlier, employees are on a full-time equivalent basis, family workers are not. Proprietors are included if they work more than half-time in their establishments, and unpaid family workers, if they work fifteen hours or more. Since 5 per cent of family workers on farms and almost 4 per cent of nonfarm family workers have secondary jobs (in 1950),[36] there obviously could be some distortion in the industrial distribution presented.

Comparison with the Census estimates. In Table A-VIII, our estimates of total persons engaged are compared with estimates based on population census data, prepared by Long[37] for census years 1890–1950, extrapolated to 1870. Although estimates based on establishment reports can be expected to differ from those based on the population censuses for reasons cited earlier, it would be disturbing if the movements of the two series were widely different. The labor-force estimates are tied into relatively reliable population figures, and the levels and movements of labor-force participation ratios by age-sex classes have been relatively persistent. Considerable confidence can therefore be placed in the trends revealed by the labor-force estimates, despite the need for assorted adjustments at various dates, as described in some detail by Long. The adjustment necessary to derive an employment figure is subject to a considerable margin of error, but the unemployment ratio is generally so small that

---

[36] "Multiple Employment and Pay Status of Persons with Job but not at Work, July 1950," *Current Population Reports*, Series P-50, No. 30., Dept. of Commerce, 1951.
[37] *Op. cit.*, Table C-1.

inaccuracy here should not seriously affect the indicated employment trends.

The comparison indicates that the broad movements of the two sets of estimates are reasonably consonant. The series used in this study, however, is largely independent of the labor-force estimates only since 1929. In earlier years, estimates for industries accounting for more than half the total number of persons engaged have been tied into the Census figures. Despite this fact, the ratios of our estimates to those of Long show a small upward drift, amounting to about 4 per cent over the eighty-year span.

This could be due to the fact that prior to 1929 we assumed that full-time equivalent employment moved with full- and part-time employment within the industrial segments for which independent data were available. Part-time work may well have increased over the period as a result of the declining length of the workweek, which permitted more secondary (part-time) job-holding, and the increasing labor-force participation of women, to some degree on a part-time basis. The rise in the ratio of the industry employment aggregate to the census-based estimate in 1940 may be due to an inadequate adjustment of full- and part-time employment to a full-time equivalent basis, but between 1930 and 1950 the two series show almost precisely the same changes.

The long-term difference between the two series is not large enough to warrant adjustment of the industry aggregate, even if the census-based employment series could be taken as perfectly accurate. Apart from the adjustments required in the labor-force data, there are possibilities of error in the employment ratios.

AVERAGE HOURS AND MANHOURS WORKED

In general, estimates of manhours worked in the economy were obtained by multiplying employment by average hours worked per year in the various industrial groupings.[38] Various sources of data and types of average hours series were used for the several industries. These are described in some detail in the succeeding industry appendixes. Here we shall summarize briefly the chief sources used and the major qualifications attaching to the aggregate average hours and manhour estimates.

It has only been since 1940 that comprehensive average hours estimates for the economy have been collected in the current population surveys of the Census Bureau (*Monthly Report on the Labor Force*), and these have been based on a relatively small sample of households.[39] Because we were

[38] In steam railroads back to 1916 and farming back to 1910, direct estimates of manhours were available. In these cases, average hours worked were obtained as the quotient of manhours and employment.

[39] For 1940, an industrial distribution of employment by average hours classes for the week of March 24–30 is available in the *Census of Population, 1940*.

interested in average hours and manhours by industry group consistent with total economy estimates, as well as in continuity, we continued to build up economy manhours estimates by industry despite the availability of a comprehensive series after 1940. Census Bureau average hours estimates (provided from unpublished tabulations) were useful, however, in filling gaps in the finance and services areas.

Sources and methods. For federal government classified and "blue collar" civilian employees, information concerning the standard workday, workweek, and holiday and leave provisions was contained in records of the Civil Service Commission. Special studies gave some indication of leave actually taken so average hours worked per year could be estimated. No similar information was available for the armed services; indeed, the meaningfulness of an hours measure of input is questionable for this category. But to maintain consistency in the measure of labor input throughout the economy, average hours worked by federal civilian employees were imputed to members of the armed services. At the state and local level, information concerning the average workday of persons engaged in public education was obtained and multiplied by the average number of days worked per year; the latter is available annually from the Office of Education. There is no central source of information on average hours worked by nonschool employees, but the occupations included in this category are so diverse that average hours worked in the rest of the nonfarm economy were used. This was the broadest imputation required in the manhour estimates.

For the private farm economy, direct estimates of average hours worked are available from the *Monthly Report on the Labor Force*, and these were used beginning with 1950. The Department of Agriculture has made annual estimates of farm manhour requirements back to 1910, based on periodic technical studies. With minor adjustments, these seemed appropriate to our purposes. When divided by the farm employment estimates, the implicit average hours worked per year showed little trend. This relative stability can be rationalized (see Appendix B), and we assumed a constant average in years prior to 1910.

It is in the private nonfarm sector that the widest variety of sources was used. The broadest coverage of average hours is provided by the BLS, which has published estimates over a varying number of years for manufacturing, mining, contract construction, trade, communications and public utilities, and a few service industries. The manufacturing series begins in 1909, but most of the others begin in the 1930's.

The BLS bases its average hours estimates on data, collected from a sample of establishments in each industry, relating to average full- and part-time employment and the corresponding manhours paid for. The manhours estimates cannot be used as such since they are based on a sample;

but the average hours estimates derived therefrom may be multiplied by full- and part-time employment estimates for the several industries as a whole in order to obtain total manhours. The use of sample information implies that both the level and the movement of the average hours series is subject to some error. Because the BLS employs a "cutoff" sample and not a probability design, the sampling variability of the estimates cannot be calculated. The samples used are relatively large, however, particularly for manufacturing, and have been broadened on several occasions. The BLS schedules cover production and related workers in the manufacturing and mining segments, and nonsupervisory workers in the other industries. Hours paid for but not worked are carried at the level prevailing for employees actually at work in the reporting establishments.

The average hours estimates based on BLS or other establishment reports,[40] and extrapolations of these series, have been multiplied by the average number of full- and part-time employees in the several industries, and then by 52 to obtain manhours per year. To the extent that average hours of salaried or supervisory employees were not covered, it was assumed that they were the same as the average hours of the covered workers—an assumption which is probably more valid with regard to trends than to short-term fluctuations. In those industries in which proprietors and unpaid family workers were an insignificant proportion of persons engaged, the same imputation was made.

The most serious limitation of the BLS estimates in recent years, from the standpoint of our concept, is that they relate to average hours paid for rather than worked. This limitation is probably not important prior to World War II,[41] although the derived level of manhours may be a little higher than one representing hours actually worked. But during and since the war, labor has obtained a gradual increase in paid leave. Thus, over the last decade, our average hours and manhour estimates have some upward bias as a measure of time actually worked. This bias has been mitigated, however, because beginning in 1947 average hours worked in manufacturing were derived from the Census Bureau's *Annual Survey of Manufactures*, in which manhours relate to time actually worked. Also, in the general-government and the finance and services segments, the estimates are for hours actually worked.

For finance and services, we employed unpublished estimates based on tabulations made by the Bureau of the Census from the Current Population Survey data beginning with 1944. These estimates are based on averages

[40] Some of the hours series formerly compiled by the National Industrial Conference Board have also been employed.

[41] See, for example, "Holiday Provisions in Union Agreements in 1952–53," *Monthly Labor Review*, Bureau of Labor Statistics, February 1954: "Prior to World War II, paid holidays for wage earners in manufacturing, construction, and mining industries were found in few agreements" (p. 128).

that exclude the influence of zero-hour workers and thus represent hours actually worked. Since by the labor-force concept the average hours estimates refer to workers whose main job is in the primary industry, we assumed that the hours of part-time primary workers were offset by hours worked in other industries by other primary employees. The Census average hours estimates were therefore multiplied by full-time equivalent employees in order to arrive at manhours. An average hours figure for this segment for 1940 was computed from the *Census of Population*. Estimates were available for 1920–22 from the National Bureau study by Willford I. King,[42] which was also used for some other industries. Prior to 1920, it was necessary to do what Harold Barger[43] did in trade—to estimate average hours worked from state data. The data were fragmentary and, therefore, not too reliable, but the indicated trends appear to be reasonable.

In manufacturing, construction, steam railroads, and gas utilities, the average hours estimates were pushed back to earlier decades by means of available estimates of the standard, or full-time, workweek. The latter were adjusted to represent average hours actually worked by means of a regression between the ratios of actual to full-time average hours and the ratios of employment to the labor force in the industry, calculated from estimates for years in which actual average hours estimates were available.[44] Although the coefficients of correlation are high, it is clear that the average hours series are better indicators of trend than of annual movement, in the earlier decades.[45]

In the several nonagricultural industries in which proprietors and unpaid family workers were a significant portion of the total working force, an adjustment in the level of average hours was made. Estimates made by the Census Bureau in connection with the *Monthly Report on the Labor Force* reveal that since 1944, when separate data became available, this class of worker has persistently worked substantially longer hours per week than employees. The Census Bureau prepared, on request, a tabulation showing average hours worked by proprietors and unpaid family workers in 1954 for all the industry segments in which they were a factor: contract construction, trade, finance, and services. These industry estimates were extrapolated back to 1946 by the average hours worked by all proprietors and family workers, and to years before 1946, by the average hours worked

[42] *Employment, Hours and Earnings in Prosperity and Depression, United States, 1920–1922*, 2nd ed., New York (NBER), 1923.

[43] *Distribution's Place in the American Economy since 1869*, Princeton University Press (for NBER), 1955.

[44] See Leo Wolman, *Hours of Work in American Industry*, Bulletin 71, New York (NBER), 1938: "In the long run, actual hours will, in all probability, have the same general trend as full-time hours, but deviations of one from the other will occasionally be more or less sharp, depending on the state of business and employment" (p. 5).

[45] As Wolman points out: "Comparing similar periods of business activity, percentages of time lost appear remarkably steady" (*ibid.*, p. 18).

by employees. A somewhat different procedure was used by Barger, whose figures on average hours worked by all persons engaged in trade were used prior to 1919 (see Appendix F).

For key years, a summary of the industry and sector average hours worked per week is shown in Table A-IX. In interpreting this table, it must be remembered that the weekly averages represent the quotient of average annual hours per person and 52. Thus, slack time in the farm sector pulls down the average weekly hours per year as compared with hours worked during full-time weeks. Average hours worked by government employees are low due to generous leave provisions for federal employees throughout the period and to the summer holidays of public school teachers. In the latter case, an increasing number of school days per year increased the average hours worked per year up to 1909 and thus the average hours per week as we compute it, although the length of the weeks actually worked presumably did not change significantly. Total manhours worked in major sectors of the economy are shown annually in Table A-X. A distribution of manhours by industrial segments is shown for key years in Table A-XI.

Comparison with the Census survey estimates. For the period since 1940, it is possible to compare our estimates of average hours, manhours, and persons engaged in civilian industry with like estimates contained in the Census Bureau's *Monthly Report on the Labor Force* (MRLF); we do so in Table A-XII. The MRLF average hours estimates are based on a weighted distribution of persons engaged classified by single hours-of-work classes exclusive of zero hours. To obtain manhours, the average hours so computed (adjusted to eliminate the effect of holidays falling in the survey week) were multiplied by the average number of all workers, excluding persons with a job but not at work.

The derivation of the total manhours estimates used in this study was as outlined above and described in more detail in the following appendixes. Average annual hours estimates are the quotient of manhours and persons engaged (which includes employees in terms of full-time equivalents as estimated by the Department of Commerce). It should be remembered, however, that except in the farm sector, no attempt was made to reduce proprietors and unpaid family workers to full-time equivalents. Average annual hours were divided by 52 to convert them to a weekly basis.

With respect to the average hours comparison, it will first be noted that the MRLF series averages about 2.5 per cent higher than our series. This is partly because our employment estimates for some industries (other than general government, farming, manufacturing since 1947, and finance and services) include persons who are on paid leave. Based on a special Census survey which revealed that 67 per cent of the persons with a job but not at work in the week of July 2–8, 1950 were on paid leave, we have estimated that this factor accounts for almost half the discrepancy in 1950. It could, however, be more important in helping explain why the MRLF series shows a somewhat greater decline in the postwar period than the industry composite. The MRLF figures in Table A-4 show that an increasing proportion of persons with a job are not at work, a development which is undoubtedly due primarily to the increasing trend towards paid leave.

TABLE A-4

Civilian Economy: Persons with a Job but Not at Work in Relation to Total with a Job, 1940–57

	Total with Job (000)	*With Job but Not at Work*	
		Number (000)	Per Cent of Total
1940	47,520	1,190	2.5
1941	50,350	980	1.9
1942	53,750	1,100	2.0
1943	54,470	1,220	2.2
1944	53,960	1,760	3.3
1945	52,820	2,010	3.8
1946	55,250	2,260	4.1
1947	58,027	2,474	4.3
1948	59,378	2,751	4.6
1949	58,710	2,530	4.3
1950	59,957	2,648	4.4
1951	61,005	2,680	4.4
1952	61,293	2,814	4.6
1953	62,213	2,798	4.5
1954	61,238	3,036	5.0
1955	63,193	2,932	4.6
1956	64,979	3,160	4.9
1957	65,011	3,017	4.6

Another important reason for the difference in level is that the MRLF shows a higher workweek in agriculture than that implied by our figures. This is due in part to the inclusion in our series of children under fourteen years of age, seasonal immigrants, and certain part-time workers not covered by the Census Bureau (see Appendix B).

A noticeable feature of the average hours comparison is the somewhat greater increase in average hours shown by MRLF than by the industry composite during World War II, especially in 1943. This may be explained by the nature of the Commerce Department's full-time equivalent employment estimates. Standard factors were developed to convert full- and part-time employment to a full-time equivalent basis. During World

War II, the volume of part-time employment increased. A correct year-to-year adjustment to a full-time basis would have yielded a smaller increase in persons engaged and a larger increase in average hours worked during these years. But this bias is partially compensated for in the manhour estimates by the difference in the employment estimates.

The composite-industry employment estimates average 4.3 per cent higher than the MRLF estimates because of the lower age cutoff in the latter, the fact that proprietors and unpaid family workers have generally not been reduced to full-time equivalents in the former, and other factors mentioned earlier. The discrepancy more than offsets the opposite differential in average hours; so the aggregate of industry manhours is larger than the MRLF total. This is to be expected in view of the different concepts underlying the two measures.

A more important consideration is the relative movements of the two manhours series. Over the period 1940–53 as a whole, the MRLF total increased by 21.6 per cent compared with an 18.0 per cent increase in the industry aggregate. Hence, our broad conclusions as to trends in productivity would not be significantly affected by the use of one series rather than the other. Year-to-year changes show considerably less correspondence; this underscores the frequent warning not to place too much stress on the precise magnitude of annual changes. In general, because of the small sample on which the MRLF is based and the greater possibility of household respondent errors, the industry composite should be the more reliable series. Certainly, the industry employment estimates, based largely on Social Security and other comprehensive government reporting systems, are more accurate. The average hours series are less reliable on both bases, but the industry-composite average hours series shows closer agreement with the MRLF averages than do the employment estimates.

LABOR INPUT (WEIGHTED MANHOURS)

In accordance with our basic concepts, manhours worked in the various industry groups or segments were weighted by average hourly earnings in order to obtain aggregate measures of labor input. These indexes, shown in the productivity summary tables, are used in direct comparisons with output and in comparisons in which they are combined with capital input to form measures of total factor input. Since interest also attaches to employment and manhours (unweighted) in relation to output, these ratios are also generally shown in the summaries.

Sources and methods. As described in later appendixes, manhours were weighted by average hourly employee compensation by industry groupings within the segments of mining, manufacturing, transportation, and communications and public utilities. In order to get a measure of real labor input in the economy as a whole, indexes of manhours or of real labor input in the several industrial divisions were weighted as follows: Average hourly labor compensation was computed from the Commerce estimates of labor compensation and our employee manhours estimates (based on the Commerce employment estimates that are consistent with the compensation figures) for 1929, 1937, 1948, and 1953; similar estimates were made for 1929 and 1919 using the Kuznets compensation and employment series in conjunction with our average hours estimates; these were linked to the Commerce estimates in order to form a continuous series.

In effect, the annual manhours estimates (or base-period 1929 manhours extrapolated by real labor input in the four segments noted above) were weighted in each of the subperiods by the mean of average hourly compensation of the first and last year of each subperiod. In practice, we extrapolated the base-period 1929 compensation (blown up to include compensation for the labor of proprietors and unpaid family workers) by the indexes of average hourly compensation in each segment, the latter being obtained for the four segments by dividing current-dollar compensation by real labor input. From the resulting figures we computed the industry proportions of the aggregate in each key year, and averaged these ratios for the two bounding years of each subperiod to use as weights for the annual indexes of manhours or of real labor input. This gives the same result as weighting manhours directly. The 1919–29 average weights were applied to prior years, since average earnings estimates before 1919 could not readily be made for some of the segments. The relative industry weights for the several subperiods are shown in Table A-5.

Effect of weighting. The weights for most of the industry divisions are so stable over the subperiods that there is little difference between aggregates obtained by using changing weights based on the Marshall-Edgeworth formula and those obtained by using fixed (1929) weights. This comparison is not shown for the economy, but a similar comparison for the manufacturing segment points up the minor effect of alternative weighting schemes (see Table D-11). The persistence of interindustry wage-rate differentials is the result of similar percentage changes in wage rates in the various industry groups over intermediate periods.

However, weighting manhours by industry compensation rates yields a labor input aggregate that moves very differently from an unweighted manhour aggregate. As shown in Table A-XIII, weighted labor input in the economy rose almost 40 per cent more between 1869 and 1953 than manhours worked. This is the result of interindustry differentials in average hourly earnings and of the relative shift of persons and manhours towards the higher-paying industries.

The effect on labor input of the growing relative importance of general government is noticeable, but not very great since the low pay of the armed forces tends to pull average hourly earnings of government employees down to the level of average pay in the private economy. Almost half of the greater proportionate rise in aggregate labor input than in manhours is due to the relative shift of manhours from the farm sector to the private nonfarm sector (Table A-XIII, column 11). The balance is largely attributable to the relative shift of manhours worked within the private nonfarm sector toward the better-paying industries. If manhours could have been weighted in greater industry detail than the forty-seven groups used for that purpose, labor input might well have risen even more than indicated by our calculations.

Although Table A-XIII shows only key years, annual indexes of manhours and of labor input are shown in Tables A-XIX and A-XXII for the national economy and the private domestic sector. From these tables, the annual effect of interindustry manhour shifts on labor input can be computed.

TABLE A-5

National Economy: Relative Weights of Labor Input,
by Sector and by Industrial Division, Subperiods, 1919–53
(per cent)

	1919–29	1929–37	1937–48	1948–53
Total economy	100.0	100.0	100.0	100.0
General government	6.2	6.8	5.7	5.1
Private economy	93.8	93.2	94.3	94.9
Farm	9.9	7.5	11.4	11.9
Nonfarm	83.9	85.7	82.9	83.0
Agricultural services, forestry, fisheries	0.3	0.4	0.4	0.4
Mining	2.8	2.7	2.8	2.9
Construction	6.8	6.5	6.0	6.1
Manufacturing	25.2	25.9	25.0	25.1
Trade	21.0	20.4	20.3	20.0
Finance, insurance, real estate	5.1	5.0	4.1	3.7
Transportation	7.8	8.3	8.3	8.6
Communications and public utilities	2.3	2.7	2.8	2.7
Services, domestic	2.4	2.6	3.4	3.9
Services, other than domestic	9.1	9.9	8.6	8.5
Government enterprise	1.1	1.3	1.2	1.1

Industry distributions. Much of the statistical work relating to labor is summarized for selected years in Table A-XIV. The percentage distributions of employment, manhours, and labor inputs are based on the preceding analyses. The distributions reveal the relative shifts of labor among the major sectors and industries of the economy. They also show the different relative importance of the various industries depending on which labor measure is used.

The distribution of manhours depends not only on the number of persons engaged in the various industries, but also on the average number of hours worked per person. Thus, the relative importance of government is less on a manhours basis than on an employment basis because of the lower average number of hours worked per year by federal employees and public school teachers; the relative importance of the service industries is higher because of the greater-than-average number of hours worked per year. The relative importance of industries by the criterion of real labor input is again different as a result of industrial differences in average hourly earnings. Thus, farming and the service industries have a much lower share of labor input than of manhours because of relatively low earnings, while the converse is true, for example, of construction and manufacturing. The several percentage distributions have also shown somewhat different relative changes over time as a result of differing relative changes in the workweek and in wage rates among industries.

Real Capital Stocks and Services

In Chapter 2, the rationale was developed for the proposition that real capital input tends to parallel the movement of real capital stocks, net of depreciation in the case of reproducible fixed capital assets. Here we describe the sources and methods used in estimating capital stocks in constant dollars and rates of capital compensation by sector. The latter are used to translate the stock figures into real capital services, or input, thus making it possible to combine capital services in the several sectors with each other and with the estimates of labor input.

The real capital stock estimates have been built up by major sectors corresponding to those used for the national product estimates. However, no breakdown by industry segment within the private nonfarm sector was attempted. The wealth estimates of Raymond Goldsmith[46] were used for net foreign assets and, with some modification, for the general-government and private nonfarm nonresidential sectors. The capital stock estimates by Alvin Tostlcbe,[47] supplemented by Goldsmith's estimates, were used for the farm sector; and those by Leo Grebler, David M. Blank, and Louis Winnick[48] were used for nonfarm residential property. A summary of annual constant-dollar stock figures by sector is shown in Table A-XV.

The capital estimates for the domestic economy were recombined by major types of tangible assets in order to permit the calculation of ratios

[46] *A Study of Saving in the United States*, Princeton University Press, 1956, Vol. III, Table W-3, p. 20. These data are carried forward in the *Postwar Capital Market Study* (unpublished).

[47] *Capital in Agriculture: Its Formation and Financing since 1870*, Princeton University Press (for NBER), 1957, Table 9, p. 66.

[48] *Capital Formation in Residential Real Estate: Trends and Prospects*, Princeton University Press (for NBER), 1956, Table D-1, p. 360.

of output to capital by type. This could be done for structures, equipment, and inventories. Estimates of agricultural land also seemed sufficiently reliable for this purpose. In the case of nonfarm site land, the Goldsmith convention of assuming proportionality to the real value of structures was followed; so estimates for this class of land could not be meaningfully related to output. The estimates of capital stock by type are presented in Table A-XVI.

NET FOREIGN ASSETS

Since the national income is defined in terms of the income accruing to the labor or capital supplied by the permanent residents of the nation, it is necessary to include in the national capital the value of assets owned by United States residents and located abroad less the value of foreign-owned assets located in the United States. When the role of productivity in increasing real income per capita is being considered, it is necessary to relate real income to population and to input on a national basis, since the real income produced by net asset holdings in foreign countries may be a significant factor in the plane of living of the nation's residents. However, for reasons developed earlier, it is desirable for some purposes to exclude net income from abroad from national income estimates and, correspondingly, to exclude net foreign assets from capital estimates. The income and capital tables have therefore been set up in such a way that productivity comparisons can be made on a domestic as well as on a national basis.

The capital items involved in the computation of net holdings of foreign assets comprise not only direct investments in real productive facilities, but also financial claims. This is in contrast to our treatment of domestic capital, whereby we include only real items, and not the claims thereto, in order to avoid double counting. Underlying financial holdings abroad, however, are real income-producing assets that are not otherwise counted, whereas financial resources of foreigners in this country are offsets against the value of real capital domestically located, since part of the income must go to the foreign holders. For this reason, it was not feasible to break down net foreign assets by type of real capital, as is done in Table A-XVI for domestic capital.

The estimates used are those prepared by Goldsmith as published through 1945, and as revised and extended from 1946, benchmarked on the Treasury Department *Census of Foreign-Owned Assets in the United States* (1945) and *Census of American-Owned Assets in Foreign Countries* (1947). Goldsmith's current value figures from 1929 forward are based on unpublished estimates prepared by Robert Sammons and extrapolated by published and unpublished estimates of the Department of Commerce going back to the 1920's and by capital movement statistics collected regularly by the Treasury Department. Estimates for earlier years were based on a variety of sources, described in the notes to the relevant tables.

A rough check on the movement of the current value net foreign asset estimates is provided by the net foreign investment component of the national product. Theoretically, this item measures net sales (purchases) to (from) foreigners on capital account. A positive foreign balance, for example, may be associated with a net increase in American capital holdings abroad or a net decrease in foreign investments in the United States. If the basic data underlying the foreign accounts were perfect, the change in net foreign assets should equal net foreign investment.

Goldsmith calculated that over the period 1897–1949 net holdings of assets abroad increased by about $50 billion, as a result of an increase in foreign assets held by Americans of $59 billion offset by total net foreign investments in the United States over the same period of about $9 billion. Net foreign investment, estimated by the balance-of-payments current account approach, shows cumulated net capital exports (for net acquisition of foreign assets) of about $44 billion. "The difference of nearly $6 billion, or about 12 per cent, for the period as a whole appears moderate in view of the nature of the data from which both estimates were derived."[49] It should be noted, however, that the difference was generally in the opposite direction until the mid-1930's.

Deflation of net foreign assets poses difficult conceptual as well as statistical problems. Even for each of the two capital categories—domestic and foreign—there are no specified underlying assets that can be priced, and the difference between the two value aggregates is even further removed from tangible assets. Goldsmith used a generalized purchasing power index for deflation. This is consistent with the deflation procedure for net factor income from abroad. Yet it could be argued that the deflator for domestic investment is more appropriate in the sense that it would roughly indicate what the net foreign capital would purchase, if liquidated, in terms of tangible domestic assets.

GOVERNMENT CAPITAL

The estimates of reproducible civilian capital stocks owned by federal, state, and local governments are those of Raymond Goldsmith. We narrowed somewhat his estimate of public land holdings and extrapolated the base-period value by different methods. For the sake of consistency with national product sectoring, we estimated roughly the capital stocks held by government enterprises for inclusion in the business sector. Similarly, we subtracted these estimates from the adjusted Goldsmith figures to obtain public capital held by civilian general government.

[49] Goldsmith, *op. cit.*, Vol. II, p. 601; cf. Table B-91, p. 602.

For structures, the chief component of general-government capital, we used the 1929-dollar estimates of Goldsmith.[50] These were derived by cumulating net investment in 1929 prices, starting with the estimated value in 1896. The latter was obtained by cumulating gross outlays less depreciation for the number of years preceding 1896 corresponding to the assumed length of life of the category of asset involved. The sources of the outlay estimates, the lengths of life assumed, and the deflators employed are referred to in Goldsmith's Table W-7. We pushed the Goldsmith real-stock estimates back of 1896 by cumulatively subtracting Kuznets' net public nonwar construction expenditure estimates in 1929 prices.[51]

Federal government equipment expenditures were taken from Budget Bureau compilations of obligations by object of expenditure and from other fiscal statements for earlier years.[52] Local government equipment expenditures were estimated roughly as a fixed percentage of total capital outlays less street and highway construction, based on capital expenditure estimates of the Governments Division of the Census Bureau (see notes to Goldsmith's Table G-6). An average life of twelve years was assumed in calculating depreciation—approximately the same average used in business accounting. Deflation was accomplished by the over-all implicit price deflator for nonfarm producer durable equipment.

Goldsmith's estimates of the stock of equipment held by governments seem to be seriously understated. The current value estimates for 1939 are substantially below Reeve's.[53] The depreciated value of all state and local capital assets, excluding roads and streets, is also substantially below the estimate by Fabricant.[54] As Goldsmith points out, the lack of distinction between current and capital outlays in the Treasury accounts raises the danger of missing certain expenditures that would be capitalized by business. This is particularly true of equipment, since independent estimates of government construction outlays are available. Not only are the basic data for state and local governments incomplete, but the segregation of equipment outlays is largely conventional. At any event, no allowance is made in Goldsmith's estimates for equipment expenditures of state governments. Since the estimate by Reeve for 1939 seems more realistic as to level, we raised the Goldsmith estimates of the real stock of public equipment (exclusive of Reconstruction Finance Corporation stocks) throughout by the ratio of his estimate for 1939 to the Reeve calculation.

[50] *Ibid.*, Vol. III, Table W-3 (col. 10).
[51] *Capital in the American Economy.*
[52] See Goldsmith, *op. cit.*, Vol. I, notes to Tables F-2 and F-16.
[53] J. E. Reeve *et al.*, "Government Component in the National Wealth," *Studies in Income and Wealth, Volume 12*, New York (NBER), 1950, Table 5, p. 487.
[54] Goldsmith, *op. cit.*, Vol. II, pp. 578–79.

The Goldsmith estimates of inventories, which we use, cover federal government corporations and credit agencies and state and local governments, based on the sources already described. The price deflator was the wholesale price index, except for federal corporations from 1935 on, for which the index for wholesale prices of farm products was used because of the predominance of Commodity Credit Corporation inventories. Goldsmith did not include federal general-government inventories. These are presumably quite small, since the much larger state and local government inventories were valued at only $60 million in 1929.

The final step in the estimation procedure was to deduct estimates of reproducible assets (by type) held by government enterprises from the Goldsmith totals, as adjusted. This was simple in the case of assets of federal corporations and other enterprises (except the Post Office), since separate estimates are presented by Goldsmith. The case of other enterprise assets was handled by a fixed percentage deduction of one-seventh from assets net of those just mentioned. This percentage was based on a 1939 estimate for state and local enterprises derived from Fabricant[55] plus an estimate for the value of Post Office assets of around half a billion dollars. An examination of functional classifications by Fabricant of state and local capital assets[56] does not indicate any decided trend in the proportion of the total accounted for by enterprises. Similarly, the ratio of public buildings outside the District of Columbia (a substantial part of which is Post Office property) to total federal nondefense assets excluding corporations and credit agencies has been relatively stable in this century. It is clear that a flat deduction to remove government-enterprise assets from the totals for structures and equipment is somewhat arbitrary. However, errors from this source should have little effect on the movement of either general-government reproducible capital or private nonfarm reproducible assets. At the same time, the relative magnitudes of capital assets in the two sectors should be more accurately reflected in the adjusted figures.

The Goldsmith estimates of public lands are tied into the Reeve estimates for 1939 and 1946, with an allowance for the value of land beneath streets and highways. We have accepted the base values, with two exceptions. First, in line with procedure in the private economy, we did not include the value of subsoil assets, primarily because of the conceptual and statistical measurement problems and the relatively small magnitude of the associated net royalty. Second, we excluded the value of land in the public domain not withdrawn for specific use. Although this has been a relatively small item since 1939, it was much larger in earlier times. As there is little connection between this domain and current production, it did not seem appropriate to include it for purposes of productivity comparisons.

[55] *The Trend of Government Activity*, Table C3, p. 209.
[56] *Ibid.*, Tables C5 and C7, pp. 211, 213.

In extrapolating the base-period land values, Goldsmith used the value of tax-exempt land, deflated by the wholesale price index. Since tax-exempt land includes more than public land, and since the unit values of such land may deviate widely from wholesale prices in movement, we used a different procedure. Site land, which comprises the bulk of the value of public land, was extrapolated by the real value of public structures and other improvements, in line with procedure in the private nonfarm economy. The other public land included consists of forest land, and the much less important park areas. Estimates of the constant-dollar value of public forest land are those prepared by Reuss.[57] They have been extrapolated forward, and back to 1920, by estimates of the acreage of public forest and woodland supplemented by estimates of forest acreage under the Forest Service Administration.[58] Allowance was made for the downward trend in lumber stands and thus in real value per acre, which is apparent in the 1929–46 estimates. Prior to 1910, the real value was extrapolated by available estimates of total forest acreage.[59]

Estimates of the acreage of public park lands were made by Reuss for 1929, 1939, and 1944.[60] These estimates were interpolated and extrapolated forward, and back to 1916, by acreage under the National Park Service, which accounts for the bulk of the total.[61] Park areas have grown even faster than urban population since 1916, but we used the latter series to extrapolate earlier years. Since the 1929 dollar value of park areas was only about $25 million in 1916, errors in the extrapolation procedure are unimportant. The base-period value of $52 million was computed as an extrapolation of a 1939 estimate by Reeve.[62]

FARM CAPITAL

The derivation of estimates in this sector is described in Appendix B. Briefly, our series are based on the estimates by Tostlebe, interpolated and supplemented by the estimates of Goldsmith.

NONFARM RESIDENTIAL REAL ESTATE

The estimates of the stock of nonfarm residential structures in 1929 dollars, prepared by Grebler, Blank, and Winnick,[63] are the basis of the capital series for this sector. The Grebler estimates represent a cumulation of

---

[57] Lawrence A. Reuss, "Land Utilization Data as Background Information for the National Balance Sheet and Approximations of the Value of Forest Lands," *Studies in Income and Wealth, Volume 12*, p. 231.

[58] *Historical Statistics*, Series F 45 and F 70.

[59] *Ibid.*, Series F 35.

[60] *Op. cit.*, Table 3, p. 228.

[61] *Historical Statistics*, Series F 17.

[62] *Op. cit.*, p. 518.

[63] *Op. cit.*, Table D-1, pp. 360–61.

annual net additions in 1929 dollars to the permanent nonfarm housing stock.

The underlying estimates of gross expenditures for new units, additions, and alterations were those of the Commerce Department back to 1921, extended to 1889 by estimates prepared by David M. Blank.[64] The deflator was the construction cost index compiled by E. H. Boeckh and Associates (Cincinnati, Ohio, and Washington, D.C.) extrapolated to 1889 by a weighted average of wage rates and materials prices. Comparison indicates a high degree of conformity over the long period between the Boeckh index and indexes of market prices of standard nonfarm residential structures.[65] The expenditure estimates were tied into an initial wealth estimate based on the number of units in 1890 and the average value per unit derived from the Census *Report on Real Estate Mortgages, 1890*. Although independently derived, the 1890 wealth estimate agrees quite closely with Kuznets' estimate for the same date.[66] In going from 1890 to 1869, we have subtracted Kuznets' annual estimates of net nonfarm residential outlays in 1929 dollars from the Grebler end-of-year stock estimate for 1889.

Depreciation was computed by the declining balance method, a rate of 2 per cent being applied to the cumulated value of structures as of the end of each preceding year, and a half-year's depreciation charged against current-year construction. A relatively small additional allowance for demolition was added to depreciation to obtain total capital consumption. This method differs from Goldsmith's method, which involved straight-line depreciation over sixty years for one- to four-family structures, fifty years for multifamily structures, and thirty years for additions and alterations. The Grebler approach [67] implies a somewhat longer average length of life and produces higher depreciation charges during the first two decades or so, and smaller charges thereafter. Further, some value remains indefinitely in the stock, although it eventually becomes negligible. On the basis of an appraisal by the Federal Housing Administration of a sample of houses during 1939, and other evidence, the Grebler method seems somewhat more realistic than the Goldsmith technique.

In practice, the results obtained in the two investigations do not differ greatly. Starting from approximately the same level at the end of 1896, the Goldsmith estimates of the real stock of structures rise somewhat less rapidly than the Grebler estimates until 1909 but catch up with the latter by 1919. The rates of increase during the twenties are such that the

[64] *The Volume of Residential Construction in 1889–1950*, Technical Paper 9, New York (NBER), 1954.

[65] Grebler, Blank, and Winnick, *op. cit.*, Appendix C.

[66] *Ibid.*, p. 365.

[67] Cf. *ibid.*, p. 379.

Goldsmith estimate is over 10 per cent higher than the Grebler estimate by the end of 1929. Approximately the same differential prevails at the end of 1949. The difference in behavior is presumably due to the different methods of calculating capital consumption, since both investigators used the Commerce Department gross expenditure estimates.

The authors of the estimates used here have compared their stock and net capital formation estimates with several independent sets of wealth estimates for various years from 1890 to 1950. There are, of course, difficulties in such comparisons as a result of certain differences in coverage, valuation, and the treatment of the land factor relative to the stock of structures. In general, over relatively long periods of time, the correspondence between the two types of estimates is fairly close. In terms of net capital formation, between 1890 and 1930 the two sets of estimates differ by less than 1 per cent, since subperiod discrepancies are virtually canceling. From 1930 to 1940, however, cumulated net investment is only slightly negative, compared with a considerably larger decrement indicated by the wealth estimates. Conversely, from 1940 to 1950 the housing censuses indicate a much larger volume of net capital formation than is shown by the estimated capital formation series. The net shortage by 1950 is almost 5 per cent of the stock estimate; which suggests that the postwar stock of nonfarm residential capital may be understated in the estimates used here.

With the Grebler-Blank-Winnick estimates of the real stock of structures accepted, there remained the problem of estimating the real value of the underlying land. On the basis of FHA appraisal and tax assessment data beginning in the 1930's, a benchmark estimate in the 1920's, and an estimate for 1907, the authors conclude that the proportion of land to total nonfarm residential real estate, in current values, fell linearly from 40 per cent in 1890 to about 17 per cent in 1953. The principal force adduced to explain this trend is suburbanization.

The statistical basis for the trend seems quite slender, particularly prior to the 1930's. Goldsmith chose to use a constant land-structure ratio for the period since 1896, although it appears that the basis for this technique is more tenuous than that underlying the Grebler procedure. Even if certain land-structure ratios based on current values are accepted, there is no warrant for applying these to constant value structure estimates (and Grebler explicitly refrains from doing so), since the implication would be that land and building prices move proportionately. This seems unlikely, although data on land prices are sadly lacking.

In view of our ignorance in this area, we chose to assume a constant ratio between real land and structure values over time. It is true that the relationship in real values may deviate from the physical-volume relationship as the average quality of structures changes or as relative shifts occur in the types of land utilized with respect to price classes.[68] But the proportionality assumption is clear and unambiguous, and makes it possible to interpret the ratios of the real capital involved to the output measures as essentially structure-output ratios. However, a base-period markup of the structures to cover land values is necessary in order to portray more accurately the relative size of capital stocks in the various industries or sectors and to obtain more accurately weighted aggregate capital inputs.

The Grebler ratio of the value of land to structures for 1929 has been chosen in preference to the somewhat lower Goldsmith ratio, since the information used by Goldsmith relates entirely to 1930 or later years, whereas Grebler and his associates had more relevant data, some of it relating to the 1920's.

NONFARM NONRESIDENTIAL CAPITAL

This is the largest portion of the capital estimates, comprising all private industries except farming and residential real estate. The total was estimated by summing Goldsmith's series for the several types of capital goods in constant dollars for the sector, with a few adjustments to his figures such as the inclusion of government-enterprise capital. For weighting, the total was split between manufacturing (derived as indicated in Appendix D) and an "all other" residual. Although we did not attempt a finer breakdown by industry, a comparison was made, in selected years, with the sum of the available industry estimates used in the industry productivity comparisons.

The stock of structures was estimated as the sum of nonfarm nonresidential, underground mining, and institutional structures,[69] plus government-enterprise structures estimated as described above. The sum of these categories was carried back from 1896 to 1869 by cumulatively deducting Kuznets' estimates of net private nonresidential construction in 1929 dollars, less the net change in the real value of farm structures estimated as described in Appendix B. The sources of Goldsmith's gross outlay estimates, deflators, and depreciation rates are described in his Table W-7.[70]

The real value of site land was obtained by applying a constant ratio (0.39) to the estimates of the real value of structures. The ratio was obtained from the 1929 estimates for structures in relation to those for land, as built up by Goldsmith from land-structures ratios for several types of property, but excluding his estimate of the value of vacant lots.[71] To the

---

[68] The shift of population to the suburbs has increased the proportion of relatively less valuable lands; this has tended to be offset by a concomitant increase in the average size of lots.

[69] Goldsmith, *op. cit.*, Vol. III, Table W-3 (cols. 6, 7, and 9).

[70] *Ibid.*, pp. 32–33.

[71] *Ibid.*, Vol. I, Table B-51; Vol. III, note to Table W-1, p. 12.

estimates for site land were added the Goldsmith estimates for private nonfarm forest land,[72] extrapolated prior to 1900 by the same over-all series used for public forest land.

For the stock of producers durable equipment, we started with the Goldsmith estimates,[73] less his estimates of the real stock of farm equipment.[74] In general, Goldsmith used the gross outlay figures of the Commerce Department, extrapolated by the estimates of William H. Shaw, with lengths of life used for depreciation drawn from those allowed for tax purposes by the Internal Revenue Service as shown in *Bulletin "F"*.[75] Goldsmith's estimates include only 10 per cent of the real value of passenger cars, compared with a 30 per cent allowance for business use in the investment component of the gross national product. For the sake of consistency with national output, we adjusted the Goldsmith business passenger-car stocks upwards accordingly, after taking account of the fact that 10 per cent or so of the stock is already included in the farm-equipment stock estimates. We have also eliminated that part of the equipment stock estimates which represents equipment owned by general government. The end-of-year real-stock estimate for 1896 served as a base from which estimates by Kuznets of annual net expenditures for producers durable equipment in 1929 prices (after deduction of net changes in equipment stocks of farmers and general government) were successively subtracted back to 1869.[76]

Goldsmith's estimates of private nonfarm inventories in 1929 dollars are given in his Volume III, Table W-3 (column 17). The 1896 figure was carried back to 1869 by cumulatively deducting Kuznets' estimates of the real net change in business inventories[77] less our estimates of the net change in farm inventories described in Appendix B. It should be noted that prior to 1919 the inventory estimates are largely based on a relationship to the national product since no adequate benchmarks are available in the early period. To obtain a total for the sector, we have added inventories held by the government corporations, described above, to the estimates by Goldsmith.

Total real capital stocks in the private nonfarm nonresidential sector are the sum of the estimates for structures, land, equipment, and inventories. Since the stock estimates are on a year-end basis, two-year moving averages were taken in order roughly to convert them to a calendar-year basis.

---

[72] *Ibid.*, Vol. III, Table W-3 (col. 24).
[73] *Ibid.*, Vol. III, Table W-3 (col. 12).
[74] *Ibid.*, Table W-7, p. 35.
[75] *Income Tax Depreciation and Obsolescence, Estimated Useful Lives and Depreciation Rates*, rev. ed., 1942; Goldsmith's lengths of life, *op. cit.*, Table W-7; Shaw's estimates, *Value of Commodity Output since 1869*, New York (NBER), 1947.
[76] *Capital in the American Economy.*
[77] *Ibid.*

Having been built up independently, the capital stock estimates for the sector are not necessarily consistent with those for the several industry segments described in later appendixes: manufacturing, mining, transportation, and communications and public utilities. It is possible, however, to subtract the sum of fixed capital (excluding land) in the covered segments from the private nonfarm, nonresidential aggregate in order to obtain a residual, which may be assessed for reasonableness. This has been done in Table A-6 for the key years of the period, 1899–1953, for which Goldsmith's estimates were used to obtain the aggregate. The stock estimates have been related to manhours in both the covered and uncovered segments.

The level of capital per manhour in the uncovered area is less than half that in the covered segment. This does not seem unreasonable inasmuch as the uncovered area consists chiefly of trade, finance (excluding residential real estate and property rented to the covered segments), and services. Also, the comparison excludes inventories, which account for about half of trade capital, and land, which is the chief factor in the uncovered forestry industry. The movement of capital per manhour in the two areas is broadly similar. The rise between 1899 and 1909 of capital relative to manhours in the uncovered segment appears steep compared with other decade changes in either area—suggesting that the 1899 estimate for total capital may be low or that the aggregate of the covered segments may be high. In general, however, the greater rise of capital stocks in the uncovered sector than in the covered seems plausible.

The aggregate estimates and the estimates for the covered segments were independently prepared. The estimates for manufacturing and mining are deflated Census and Internal Revenue Service asset data, rather than a cumulation of deflated net investment as are Goldsmith's estimates. The estimates by Melville J. Ulmer[78] of capital in the regulated industries were obtained by the same method as that used by Goldsmith but were based on independent capital outlay estimates. Also, Ulmer based his initial 1870 stock estimate on a Census figure, whereas Goldsmith obtained his initial stock estimate by cumulating net investment of previous years. So the levels of the two series are not necessarily consistent.

Goldsmith has compared his wealth estimates based on the "perpetual inventory" approach with Census-type estimates, and found the general correspondence to be good—better for the long trend than for shorter movements. This was also true of a comparison involving the largest component, nonfarm land and structures, except in the census year 1912, when the Goldsmith estimate is significantly lower.[79] In an earlier

[78] *Capital in Transportation, Communications, and Public Utilities: Its Formation and Financing*, Princeton University Press (for NBER), 1960.

[79] Raymond W. Goldsmith, "A Perpetual Inventory of National Wealth," *Studies in Income and Wealth, Volume 14*, New York (NBER), 1952, pp. 46–57.

TABLE A-6

Private Nonfarm, Nonresidential Economy: Fixed Reproducible Capital in Relation to Manhours, Covered Industries, Residual Uncovered Sector, and Total, Key Years, 1899–1953

	Capital			Manhours			Capital per Manhour		
	Total	Covered Sector	Residual	Total	Covered Sector	Residual	Total	Covered Sector	Residual
	(billions of 1929 dollars)			(billions)			(1929 dollars)		
1899	37.0	30.1	6.9	49.5	23.0	26.5	0.75	1.31	0.26
1909	60.5	46.4	14.1	66.6	32.5	34.1	0.91	1.43	0.41
1919	79.9	60.9	19.0	75.4	38.6	36.8	1.06	1.58	0.52
1929	104.6	78.7	25.9	89.5	37.1	52.4	1.17	2.12	0.49
1937	97.9	70.1	27.8	77.6	30.8	46.8	1.26	2.28	0.59
1948	114.6	84.7	29.9	101.3	44.5	56.8	1.13	1.90	0.53
1953	145.5	101.8	43.7	108.0	47.5	60.5	1.35	2.14	0.72

NOTE: Covered sector comprises manufacturing, mining, transportation, and communications and public utilities; uncovered sector comprises construction, trade, finance, services, agricultural services, forestry, fisheries, and government enterprises.

comparison, Kuznets also found a fair correspondence between his real net capital formation estimates and changes in real wealth estimates based on Census information, a chief exception being the decade 1912–22, when the sum of net capital outlays substantially exceeded the wealth increase.[80]

More pertinent for our purposes is a recent analysis by Kuznets of the difference between his net capital formation estimates and the changes in the aggregate of the industry capital estimates, used in this study, plus Kuznets' own Census-type estimates of stocks in the uncovered segments. Between 1880 and 1900 (for most of these years we pushed back the capital stock estimates by cumulating the Kuznets net capital formation estimates), the sum of Kuznets' net investment almost exactly equals the change in the sum of industry capital stocks, both expressed in 1929 dollars.[81] This correspondence is the result of offsetting discrepancies. During 1880–90, the change in industry stocks exceeded the net investment estimates by about $5 billion, and during 1890–1900 it fell short by about the same amount. During 1900–22, the stock change continued to fall somewhat below the sum of net investment. But for the entire period, 1880–1922, the discrepancy is only about $6 billion out of a total change, based on cumulated net investment, of about $147 billion. It is Kuznets' opinion that the cumulation of net investment yields better real-stock estimates, particularly for purposes of comparing changes over intermediate periods. It is with this in mind that we have used the cumulation method in going back of the Goldsmith estimates, rather than the Census estimates for 1880 and 1890.

CAPITAL WEIGHTING SYSTEM

Index numbers of real capital stocks were weighted in terms of the major sectors or industry groups shown in Table A-7. The sector stocks are unweighted, with the exception of manufacturing, in which the index numbers are a weighted average of index numbers of capital in the twenty component groups (see Appendix D). Current-dollar compensation of capital was obtained by subtracting labor compensation, including an imputed compensation for proprietors as described above, from national income originating in the several sectors in the key years beginning with 1919. Capital compensation was then divided by the index numbers of real capital stocks to get "capital compensation per unit"; these estimates were totaled for successive pairs of key years in order to obtain relative weights in the subperiods for the components of the several sectors.

This procedure parallels that used in weighting the index numbers of labor input described above. It yields the same result as that obtained by applying average rates of return of the beginning and end years of each

[80] Kuznets, *National Product since 1869*, pp. 193–99.
[81] *Capital in the American Economy*, Vol. II, Part D.

TABLE A-7

National Economy: Relative Weight of Real Capital Input, by Major Sector, Subperiods, 1919-53

(per cent)

	1919-29 Weight in		1929-37 Weight in		1937-48 Weight in		1948-53 Weight in	
	Sector	Total	Sector	Total	Sector	Total	Sector	Total
Manufacturing	28.2	20.0	32.0	23.8	39.4	30.1	38.3	30.8
Nonmanufacturing, non-residential	54.7	38.6	52.1	38.8	49.8	38.1	49.0	39.3
Residential	17.1	12.1	15.9	11.9	10.8	8.3	12.7	10.2
Private nonfarm	100.0		100.0		100.0		100.0	
Private nonfarm	80.0	70.7	82.9	74.5	83.1	76.5	87.2	80.3
Farm	20.0	17.7	17.1	15.4	16.9	15.6	12.8	11.8
Private domestic	100.0		100.0		100.0		100.0	
Private domestic	93.4	88.4	93.2	89.9	95.5	92.1	95.9	92.1
General government	6.6	6.3	6.8	6.6	4.5	4.3	4.1	3.9
Total domestic	100.0		100.0		100.0		100.0	
Domestic economy	94.7	94.7	96.5	96.5	96.4	96.4	96.0	96.0
Rest-of-world	5.3	5.3	3.5	3.5	3.6	3.6	4.0	4.0
National Economy	100.0	100.0	100.0	100.0	100.0	100.0	100.0	100.0

subperiod to the real-stock estimates themselves and then linking from 1929. Consistent with the labor weighting procedure, the 1919–29 weights were used in earlier years. The use of fixed weights, as compared with changing weights, makes a somewhat greater difference with respect to aggregate capital input measures than it does with respect to aggregate labor input, since relative rates of return on capital have varied more over time than has the wage structure. This can be seen in the Table A-7 summary of weights. The compensation per unit of nonfarm residential capital, total farm capital, and since 1929, of government capital decline relatively, while the compensation of capital in manufacturing rises relatively over the entire period.

The capital compensation estimates from 1929 forward were derived from the national income estimates of the Department of Commerce. The derivation for 1929 is illustrated in Table A-8. All of the underlying estimates are contained in the *National Income Supplement, 1954*, with two exceptions. Net rents of nonfarm residential dwellings were obtained from a special article in the June 1953 *Survey of Current Business*. The return to

TABLE A-8

National Economy: Derivation of Capital Compensation Estimates,
by Major Sector, 1929

Line No.		Millions of Dollars
1	National income	87,814
2	Rest-of-world (net capital income)	810
3	Domestic income (1–2)	87,004
4	General government[a]	(5,880)
5	Labor compensation	4,335
6	Capital compensation[a]	(1,545)
7	Private domestic income (3–5)	82,669
8	Farm income[b]	8,569
9	Labor compensation[c]	5,206
10	Capital compensation[b] (8–9)	3,363
11	Private nonfarm domestic income (7–8)	74,100
12	Manufacturing	21,888
13	Labor compensation[c]	16,464
14	Capital compensation (12–13)	5,424
15	Residential (capital compensation)	3,650
16	Nonmanufacturing, nonresidential (11–12–15)	48,562
17	Labor compensation[c]	38,079
18	Capital compensation (16–17)	10,483

[a] Compensation of general-government capital is not included in the Commerce Department national income total shown in line 1.

[b] Includes net rents paid to nonfarm landlords.

[c] Includes an imputed compensation for manhours worked by proprietors and unpaid family workers.

general-government capital, not included in the national accounts, was obtained by applying the average rate of interest paid on the public debt to our estimates of the current-dollar value of the stock of public capital. The average rate was obtained by dividing monetary interest paid by governments (*National Income Supplement, 1954*, Table 37) by the gross interest-bearing debt of federal, state, and local governments (*Survey of Current Business*, September 1953 and May 1956). The labor compensation estimates are higher than the published "employee compensation" estimates by the amount of imputed compensation for the labor of proprietors and their families.

The Commerce estimates for the private nonfarm domestic economy were extrapolated back from 1929 to 1919 by the estimates of Kuznets contained in *National Income and Its Composition, 1919–1938*. Kuznets' wage-salary estimates were adjusted for comparability with our estimates of employment by multiplying them by the ratio of our employment estimates to his. They were further adjusted to include estimated compensation of proprietors and unpaid family workers and then used to extrapolate the 1929 labor compensation estimates. National income in 1919 was obtained by extrapolating the 1929 ratio to labor compensation by similar ratios obtained from the Kuznets estimates for 1919 and 1929. Manufacturing was treated similarly. The return to residential capital was computed by applying the 1929 rate of return to the current-dollar value of residential real estate in 1919. The estimate for the nonmanufacturing, nonresidential sector was obtained as a residual, in line with the procedure for 1929 and subsequent years.

Total national income was built up by adding estimates for the other sectors, derived as follows: Farm national income was estimated from recent Agricultural Department publications (see Appendix B); compensation of general-government employees was estimated as described in Appendix K; government capital compensation, by applying the 1929 rate of return to the current-dollar value of assets in 1919; net property income from abroad in 1919 was available from the Commerce Department.

The real capital input estimates obtained by sector weighting of the capital stocks show a greater increase between 1869 and 1957 than do the unweighted aggregate real-stock figures. Table A-9 indicates that the weighted series rises by almost 10 per cent more than the unweighted over the period as a whole. The result is in the same direction as that shown by weighted labor input in relation to unweighted manhours, but to a lesser degree. This may be due in part to the fact that the labor inputs were weighted in somewhat greater detail than the capital inputs—forty-seven groups compared with twenty-five.

It will be noted from Table A-9 that weighted capital declined relative to unweighted capital between 1869 and 1889. This is due primarily to a large relative increase in residential real estate, which has the lowest relative rate of return of the various sectors or groups.

TABLE A-9

National Economy: Comparison of Weighted and Unweighted
Real Capital Input, Key Years, 1869–1957
(1929 = 100)

| | Capital Input | | Ratio of |
	Weighted by Sector[a]	Unweighted	Weighted to Unweighted
1869	11.6	11.8	0.983
1879	17.4	18.0	0.967
1889	25.5	27.4	0.931
1899	38.7	41.6	0.930
1909	55.7	57.9	0.962
1919	76.7	74.8	1.025
1929	100.0	100.0	1.000
1937	95.3	97.9	0.973
1948	115.6	112.3	1.029
1953	141.6	133.6	1.060
1957	160.4	151.0	1.062

[a] Marshall-Edgeworth weights, as described in text.

Total Factor Input

Two approaches to the measurement of total input are possible. First, total capital input may be combined with total labor input. In this case the relative weights are obtained from the quotients of total capital compensation and the index of weighted capital stocks, and of total labor compensation and the index of weighted manhours; estimation of factor compensation has already been described. The results of this method are shown in Table A-10.

Alternatively, total inputs in the various sectors may be combined. In this case relative weights are obtained by dividing total factor compensation in each sector by the index of weighted input. That these two methods result in the same total input indexes is illustrated in Table A-11 for the two subperiods that link automatically on a 1929 basis.

As when combining the various types of each of the inputs, changing weights based on the Marshall-Edgeworth formula were used to combine the input classes for each of the subperiods, and the subperiod relatives were linked forward and backward from the 1929 base. The system of changing weights results in a somewhat larger increase in input for the national economy prior to 1929 than does the use of fixed 1929 weights (see Table A-XVII). This is the result of the inverse relation between relative factor weights and relative factor inputs. The use of 1929 weights should give a larger increase in total input since 1929 than the use of changing weights; but the tendency is not marked, as the table shows. Between 1937 and 1948 capital input did not grow as rapidly as labor input, while capital compensation per unit temporarily reversed its downward trend in relation to average hourly labor compensation. But after 1948, relative capital inputs increased, and the relative price of capital declined; so recent weights yield a lesser increase in total real input than is obtained using 1929 weights.

TABLE A-10

National Economy: Relative Weights of Labor and Capital Inputs, by Major Sectors, Subperiods, 1899–1953
(per cent)

| | NATIONAL ECONOMY | | PRIVATE DOMESTIC ECONOMY | | | | | |
| | *Labor* | *Capital* | *Total* | | *Nonfarm* | | *Farm* | |
			Labor	Capital	Labor	Capital	Labor	Capital
1899–1909	64	36	65	35	63	37	63	37
1909–19	67	33	68	32	71	29	56	44
1919–29	70	30	71	29	74	26	57	43
1929–37	75	25	76	24	78	22	60	40
1937–48	77	23	78	22	78	22	71	29
1948–53	79	21	79	21	79	21	79	21

One cannot speak strictly of an "unweighted input" index, since manhours and capital are not additive without the use of a common denominator. But, the combination of unweighted real capital stocks and unweighted manhours by their relative unit compensation in 1929 represents the minimum weighting possible. This total input measure increases far less than either of the indexes using internal weights for each of the factor classes (see Table A-XVII, columns 3 and 5). The ratios of weighted to unweighted indexes reflect the relative shift of inputs to higher-paying uses, which was pointed out in connection with labor and capital inputs separately.

The indexes of factor input are shown for the national and private domestic economies annually, and in other sectors for key years, in the productivity summary tables, A-XIX through A-XXIII.

The Productivity Ratios

Having described the nature and derivation of the real-product and factor input measures, little remains to be said about the productivity index numbers shown in the tables at the end of this appendix. The indexes

TABLE A-11

National Economy: Alternative Methods of Weighting Inputs, by Major Sector,
Key Years and Subperiods, 1919–37

| | Total Input | Input by Type | | Input by Sector | | | |
		Labor	Capital	Private Nonfarm	Farm	Government	Rest-of-world
				WEIGHTS (PER CENT)			
1919–29		70	30	80	12	6	2
1929–37		75	25	83	9	7	1
				INDEX (1929 = 100)			
1919	85.1	88.7	76.7	82.3	102.0	103.8	32.3
1929	100.0	100.0	100.0	100.0	100.0	100.0	100.0
1937	92.8	92.0	95.3	88.2	95.6	151.5	42.3

were computed from ratios of real product to the corresponding partial and total factor input measures in each of the several broad sectors of the economy distinguished in this study.

CONSISTENCY OF OUTPUT AND INPUT WEIGHTING SCHEMES

The real-product series in index form (Tables A-XIX to A-XXII) do not show the same movement as the real-product series expressed in constant-dollar aggregates (Tables A-I to A-III). This results from different systems of weights. The various types of goods and services comprising the constant-dollar product estimates are weighted by 1929 prices. The indexes, on the other hand, are based on a reweighting of the goods and services produced in the private domestic sector for each of the subperiods by average prices in the terminal years in accordance with the Marshall-Edgeworth formula (see Table A-XVIII for the reweighting effects in key years).

The index numbers of manhours are wholly unweighted, whereas those of labor input represent manhours in the various industry groups and segments weighted by the mean of average hourly earnings in the bounding years of each subperiod beginning with 1919; manhours in the earlier years are weighted by the average of 1919–29 average hourly earnings. The same time-pattern of weights is used in obtaining capital input. That is, average unit capital compensation weights were calculated for subperiods beginning with 1919 and applied to the index numbers of real capital stock in the various industry groups and sectors.

A superficial inconsistency in the weighting procedure for product and the two input classes will be noted. The Marshall-Edgeworth weights for product were changed each subperiod (and the real-product estimates linked) back to 1889–99, whereas reliable weights for the two input classes could not be obtained prior to 1919–29. This is probably not important, however, since the use of changing weights as compared with fixed weights makes little difference in the movement of capital input and even less in that of labor. In combining labor and capital inputs, weights have been changed in subperiods back to 1899–1909; this is more consistent with the product weighting procedure.

The use of changing, as compared with fixed, weights makes somewhat less difference in the movement of the productivity indexes than it does in the movement of real product. That is, the movement of the ratio of the input aggregate using changing weights to that using fixed weights is in the same direction as the comparable ratio of the two real-product aggregates, but to a lesser extent (see Table A-XVIII). This is true not only of the long period, 1869 or 1899 to 1953, but also of all the subperiods with the exception of 1948–53. In general, the effect of alternative weighting systems on productivity movements is not marked in relation to the total movement of the series over the long period and each subperiod. One exception is the decade 1909–19, in which contemporary weights yield about a 4 per cent greater increase in real product and productivity than 1929 weights. But that larger increase merely serves to put the rate of productivity change in 1909–19 in line with the growth rate in the two earlier decades.

RELIABILITY OF THE PRODUCTIVITY RATIOS

In appraising the reliability of the productivity ratios, one must keep in mind the various limitations attaching to both the output and input measures. It is not true, however, that the productivity ratios are no better than their component parts. If errors in the numerator and the denominator are in an opposite direction, the effect on the ratios is magnified. However, it is likely that errors in output and input measures are in the same direction and therefore offsetting. Many of the output and input estimates for the economy and its industrial divisions are based on the same basic source materials. Thus, varying degrees of coverage, and response, and certain other reporting errors would tend to affect both outputs and inputs similarly. The very fact that the productivity series, whether based on real-product or on industry aggregates, tend to exhibit rather regular secular movements and to yield significant analytical results, is a pragmatic indication of the broad reliability of the estimates. There is, however, no direct means of measuring the probable margins of error of the estimates (see Chapter 2).

THE PRODUCTIVITY SUMMARY TABLES

Tables A-XIX through A-XXV, following this section, give index numbers of the partial and total factor productivity ratios and the underlying variables for the national economy, using the three chief concepts of national product discussed earlier; the private domestic economy; the private domestic nonfarm economy; the sector for which output can be derived as a weighted aggregate of industry output indexes; and the somewhat smaller sector in which industry capital as well as output and labor input indexes are available.

Of the three national economy tables (A-XIX, XX, and XXI), only the one based on the national security version of the Kuznets estimates is given annually, since this is the preferred concept and underlies the analysis of Chapter 4. The other two tables are for key years; and the input index numbers are not repeated since these are the same throughout— the only variation among the three tables is in the concept of national product. National product is shown net of capital consumption allowances (without allowance for depreciation of munitions, however), since this is appropriate for the purposes for which the national economy series are used—temporal comparisons of material well-being. Factors permitting adjustment of net product and derived productivity indexes to a basis gross of capital consumption are provided for those who are interested in this form of data. Likewise, in Table XXI, factors are provided that permit conversion of the national economy measures to a domestic basis.

Table XXII, giving estimates for the private domestic economy, Commerce concept, is also on an annual basis since this is the series used for detailed examination of temporal productivity changes because of its presumed greater accuracy. The product estimates in this sector are gross of capital consumption, partly because annual changes in gross measures are more meaningful than annual changes in net measures, and partly because they are used for comparison with the industry estimates, which are likewise gross. The farm and nonfarm components of the private domestic economy may be found in Tables B-I and A-XXIII.

The two industry aggregate summaries (Tables A-XXIV and A-XXV) are for key years only, since they are used chiefly as broad confirmations of the general movements revealed by the aggregate private domestic economy measures.

One further note, which will refer to all index numbers in this volume, is necessary. Due to the use of changing weights for different periods in a time series and the method of linking the several segments into a continuous series, indexes for totals may not be averages of the linked component indexes. For example, the index number for total gas utilities output in 1909 relative to 1929 is 37.5, which lies outside the range of the index numbers of 38.0 and 38.1 for manufactured and natural gas outputs, respectively. For another example, the index number of total factor productivity in the metal mining group in 1953 is higher than the index numbers of the two partial productivity ratios (see Table C-III).

TABLE A-I

Gross and Net National Product, Adjusted Kuznets Concepts,
Peacetime and National Security Versions, 1869–1957
(millions of 1929 dollars)

| | Gross National Product (1) | Capital Consumption^a (2) | Net National Product (1) − (2) (3) | Gross War Construction and Munitions (4) | National Security Outlays (5) | National Product: National Security Version | | Addendum: National Security Outlays (current dollars) (8) |
						Gross (1) − (4) + (5) (6)	Net (6) − (2) (7)	
1869–78^b	10,755	995	9,760		73	10,828	9,833	59
1879–88^b	20,149	1,926	18,223		81	20,230	18,304	47
1889	23,284	2,651	20,633		97	23,381	20,730	54
1890	25,042	2,817	22,225		101	25,143	22,326	56
1891	26,200	2,983	23,217		104	26,304	23,321	58
1892	28,783	3,135	25,648		112	28,895	25,760	62
1893	27,306	3,274	24,032		118	27,424	24,150	64
1894	26,351	3,378	22,973		119	26,470	23,092	62
1895	29,744	3,475	26,269		110	29,854	26,379	58
1896	29,104	3,593	25,511		121	29,225	25,632	63
1897	31,855	3,727	28,128		179	32,034	28,307	91
1898	32,255	3,859	28,396		440	32,695	28,836	217
1899	35,443	3,999	31,444		413	35,856	31,857	216
1900	36,574	4,140	32,434		338	36,912	32,772	174
1901	40,931	4,288	36,643		324	41,255	36,967	166
1902	41,337	4,447	36,890		317	41,654	37,207	168
1903	43,391	4,628	38,763		328	43,719	39,091	179
1904	42,836	4,803	38,033		368	43,204	38,401	205
1905	45,947	4,983	40,964		360	46,307	41,324	205
1906	51,544	5,214	46,330		333	51,877	46,663	190
1907	52,201	5,486	46,715		328	52,529	47,043	194
1908	47,203	5,726	41,477		391	47,594	41,868	232
1909	53,615	5,920	47,695		393	54,008	48,088	241

(continued)

TABLE A-I (continued)

Year								
1910	54,263	6,158	48,105		385	54,648	48,490	239
1911	55,341	6,402	48,939		403	55,744	49,342	242
1912	58,171	6,637	51,534		393	58,564	51,927	240
1913	60,828	6,886	53,942		405	61,233	54,347	252
1914	55,755	7,109	48,646	205	558	56,108	48,999	322
1915	57,434	7,285	50,149	182	542	57,794	50,509	319
1916	66,356	7,489	58,867	277	716	66,795	59,306	460
1917	64,692	7,754	56,938	1,882	3,287	66,097	58,343	2,530
1918	63,640	8,019	55,621	3,854	12,610	72,396	64,377	12,730
1919	70,271	8,650	61,621	2,215	7,337	75,393	66,743	8,283
1920	71,383	8,603	62,780	430	1,739	72,692	64,089	2,241
1921	68,355	8,183	60,172	334	1,377	69,398	61,215	1,481
1922	73,150	8,663	64,487	145	829	73,834	65,171	818
1923	82,994	8,905	74,089	89	741	83,646	74,741	735
1924	85,222	9,043	76,179	103	732	85,851	76,808	697
1925	87,359	9,407	77,952	111	703	87,951	78,544	690
1926	93,438	10,086	83,352	104	683	94,017	83,931	688
1927	94,161	10,163	83,998	112	701	94,750	84,587	697
1928	95,715	10,592	85,123	174	796	96,337	85,745	789
1929	101,444	10,994	90,450	190	843	102,097	91,103	843
1930	91,513	10,902	80,611	203	903	92,213	81,311	869
1931	84,300	10,662	73,638	324	958	84,934	74,272	908
1932	70,682	10,246	60,436	349	910	71,243	60,997	826
1933	68,337	9,960	58,377	287	840	68,890	58,930	708
1934	74,609	9,995	64,614	407	974	75,176	65,181	862
1935	85,806	10,188	75,618	457	1,046	86,395	76,207	951
1936	95,798	10,563	85,235	614	1,299	96,483	85,920	1,205
1937	103,917	10,884	93,033	550	1,263	104,630	93,746	1,189
1938	96,670	10,923	85,747	607	1,414	97,477	86,554	1,328
1939	103,736	11,086	92,650	400	1,173	104,509	93,423	1,258

(continued)

TABLE A-I (concluded)

Gross and Net National Product, Adjusted Kuznets Concepts,
Peacetime and National Security Versions, 1869–1957
(millions of 1929 dollars)

	Gross National Product (1)	Capital Consumption[a] (2)	Net National Product (1) − (2) (3)	Gross War Construction and Munitions (4)	National Security Outlays (5)	National Product: National Security Version Gross (1) − (4) + (5) (6)	Net (6) − (2) (7)	Addendum: National Security Outlays (current dollars) (8)
1940	112,961	11,401	101,560	626	2,311	114,646	103,245	2,223
1941	126,237	12,457	113,780	2,822	11,131	134,546	122,089	13,794
1942	122,571	13,934	108,637	10,537	39,992	152,026	138,092	49,567
1943	121,918	14,785	107,133	16,316	62,208	167,810	153,025	80,384
1944	126,633	15,907	110,726	17,684	71,206	180,155	164,248	88,615
1945	130,218	16,217	114,001	12,098	60,917	179,037	162,820	75,923
1946	151,895	14,658	137,237	2,311	14,207	163,791	149,133	21,188
1947	153,515	16,558	136,957	1,341	8,124	160,298	143,740	13,349
1948	158,828	18,012	140,816	1,478	9,828	167,178	149,166	15,984
1949	153,970	19,014	134,956	1,585	11,579	163,964	144,950	19,288
1950	172,756	19,849	152,907	1,565	10,247	181,438	161,589	18,511
1951	178,565	21,201	157,364	3,821	19,059	193,803	172,602	37,260
1952	180,234	20,696	159,538	5,795	25,956	200,395	179,699	48,823
1953	184,993	21,776	163,217	6,287	28,455	207,161	185,385	51,475
1957p	210,574	25,593	184,981	3,794	21,006	227,786	202,193	46,473

p = preliminary.
a This is the series presented by Simon Kuznets in *Capital in the American Economy: Its Formation and Financing*, New York (NBER), in press, except that no allowance has been made for depreciation of durable munitions.
b Annual average for decade.

TABLE A-IIa

Gross National Product, Commerce Concept, Derivation from Kuznets Estimates[a], 1869–1957
(millions of 1929 dollars)

| | CONSUMPTION EXPENDITURES | | | | GROSS PRIVATE DOMESTIC INVESTMENT | | | | NET | GOVERNMENT | GROSS |
| | Total, Kuznets Estimates | Personal Tax and Nontax Payments | Unpaid Services of Financial Intermediaries | Total, Commerce Basis $(1)-(2)+(3)$ | New Construction and Equipment Kuznets Estimates | Public Investment | Commerce Basis $(5)-(6)$ | Change in Business Inventories | FOREIGN INVESTMENT[b] | PURCHASES OF GOODS AND SERVICES | NATIONAL PRODUCT, COMMERCE CONCEPT $(4)+(7)+(8)+(9)+(10)$ |
	(1)	(2)	(3)	(4)	(5)	(6)	(7)	(8)	(9)	(10)	(11)
1869–78[c]	8,284	136	66	8,214	2,147	222	1,925	445	−122	1,001	11,463
1879–88[c]	15,662	236	143	15,569	4,019	408	3,611	544	−76	1,400	21,048
1889	18,063	270	211	18,004	5,009	523	4,486	383	−171	1,689	24,391
1890	18,012	281	224	17,955	6,776	545	6,231	479	−225	1,756	26,196
1891	19,319	307	235	19,247	6,495	588	5,907	438	−52	1,825	27,365
1892	20,215	321	263	20,157	8,112	624	7,488	566	−110	1,909	30,010
1893	20,334	336	258	20,256	6,854	635	6,219	201	−83	1,976	28,569
1894	19,697	314	276	19,659	6,470	583	5,887	180	4	2,026	27,756
1895	22,184	355	290	22,119	7,050	646	6,404	788	−278	2,049	31,082
1896	22,122	350	284	22,056	6,433	699	5,734	354	195	2,105	30,444
1897	23,887	388	295	23,794	6,856	659	6,197	799	313	2,224	33,327
1898	24,268	410	335	24,193	6,538	691	5,847	558	891	2,579	34,068
1899	27,130	469	392	27,053	6,635	776	5,859	1,117	561	2,582	37,172
1900	27,384	494	406	27,296	7,636	868	6,768	723	831	2,579	38,197
1901	30,744	554	461	30,651	8,373	903	7,470	1,135	679	2,652	42,587
1902	31,005	578	484	30,911	9,399	989	8,410	632	301	2,750	43,004
1903	32,883	608	486	32,761	9,379	1,149	8,230	689	440	3,003	45,123
1904	33,282	615	521	33,188	8,943	1,182	7,761	318	293	2,999	44,559

(continued)

Gross National Product, Commerce Concept, Derivation from Kuznets Estimates[a], 1869–1957
(millions of 1929 dollars)

	CONSUMPTION EXPENDITURES				GROSS PRIVATE DOMESTIC INVESTMENT				NET FOREIGN INVEST-MENT[b]	GOVERNMENT PURCHASES OF GOODS AND SERVICES	GROSS NATIONAL PRODUCT, COMMERCE CONCEPT (4) + (7) + (8) + (9) + (10)
	Total, Kuznets Estimates	Personal Tax and Nontax Payments	Unpaid Services of Financial Intermediaries	Total, Commerce Basis (1) − (2) + (3)	New Construction and Equipment Kuznets Estimates	Public Investment	Commerce Basis (5) − (6)	Change in Business Inventories			
	(1)	(2)	(3)	(4)	(5)	(6)	(7)	(8)	(9)	(10)	(11)
1905	35,138	633	585	35,090	9,682	1,252	8,430	817	310	3,223	47,870
1906	38,995	633	603	38,965	10,992	1,376	9,616	1,283	274	3,282	53,420
1907	39,742	659	619	39,702	11,586	1,524	10,062	663	210	3,640	54,277
1908	37,243	681	635	37,197	9,943	1,452	8,491	−400	417	4,085	49,790
1909	41,267	698	700	41,269	11,229	1,481	9,748	1,395	−276	3,757	55,893
1910	42,057	723	700	42,034	11,595	1,639	9,956	875	−264	3,898	56,499
1911	44,051	727	740	44,064	10,500	1,628	8,872	706	84	4,586	58,312
1912	45,198	727	740	45,211	11,741	1,714	10,027	1,159	73	4,588	61,058
1913	46,717	787	771	46,701	12,684	1,813	10,871	1,158	269	4,476	63,475
1914	46,124	804	804	46,124	9,786	1,968	7,818	27	−182	4,849	58,636
1915	45,333	833	822	45,322	9,406	2,014	7,392	229	2,466	5,015	60,424
1916	49,447	956	917	49,408	11,226	2,180	9,046	1,667	4,016	4,733	68,870
1917	49,177	1,733	898	48,342	11,428	3,572	7,856	486	3,601	6,979	67,264
1918	49,595	2,294	820	48,121	11,465	5,314	6,151	529	2,051	16,509	73,361
1919	52,205	2,783	823	50,245	11,749	3,880	7,869	2,865	3,502	9,677	74,158
1920	54,160	2,234	787	52,713	10,726	2,279	8,447	4,313	2,284	5,556	73,313
1921	56,970	1,706	818	56,082	9,891	2,330	7,561	−122	1,536	6,526	71,583
1922	59,240	2,020	929	58,149	12,944	2,571	10,373	253	653	6,360	75,788
1923	64,265	1,820	982	63,427	15,435	2,632	12,803	2,775	469	6,345	85,819
1924	68,979	1,908	1,056	68,127	16,193	2,857	13,336	−984	984	6,898	88,361
1925	67,064	2,047	1,120	66,137	18,022	3,253	14,769	1,602	671	7,350	90,529
1926	72,514	2,121	1,155	71,548	19,312	3,406	15,906	1,157	435	7,359	96,405
1927	74,240	2,320	1,237	73,157	18,785	3,591	15,194	378	718	7,890	97,337
1928	76,321	2,796	1,288	74,813	18,763	3,867	14,896	−417	1,008	8,203	98,503
1929	80,317	2,643	1,278	78,952	18,678	4,121	14,557	1,674	771	8,482	104,436

(continued)

TABLE A-IIa (concluded)

Year										
1930	75,897	2,620	1,388	74,665	15,428	4,417	11,011	−558	9,435	95,130
1931	73,168	2,076	1,425	72,517	11,579	4,110	7,469	−717	9,965	89,454
1932	66,371	1,766	1,420	66,025	7,318	3,210	4,108	−3,268	9,483	76,403
1933	65,008	1,931	1,489	64,566	6,370	2,678	3,692	−3,348	9,415	74,178
1934	68,590	2,113	1,493	67,970	8,096	3,521	4,575	−2,790	10,924	80,781
1935	73,108	2,491	1,670	72,287	9,881	3,651	6,230	2,551	10,972	91,435
1936	80,750	2,925	1,827	79,652	14,123	5,544	8,579	717	12,689	100,907
1937	84,429	3,656	1,851	82,624	14,717	4,675	10,042	4,544	12,349	109,112
1938	83,022	3,542	1,851	81,331	12,963	5,164	7,799	−957	13,999	103,232
1939	87,006	3,020	1,896	85,882	14,788	5,480	9,308	638	14,369	110,994
1940	91,662	3,203	2,012	90,471	16,201	5,073	11,128	3,109	15,062	121,008
1941	97,865	3,468	2,021	96,418	21,007	7,945	13,062	5,819	23,002	138,698
1942	96,165	3,609	2,106	94,662	24,157	16,719	7,438	2,391	51,221	154,656
1943	98,755	3,842	2,386	97,299	26,006	20,363	5,643	−957	71,391	170,206
1944	102,155	4,015	3,086	101,226	27,113	20,105	7,008	−1,036	79,506	183,584
1945	109,052	4,337	3,886	108,601	23,531	13,932	9,599	−1,275	66,448	180,939
1946	122,298	4,980	3,623	120,941	19,705	4,425	15,280	6,218	20,093	165,605
1947	124,925	5,212	2,858	122,571	23,118	4,065	19,053	−797	17,548	164,134
1948	127,542	5,299	2,882	125,125	25,879	4,967	20,912	4,065	21,852	173,021
1949	130,700	5,235	3,004	128,469	25,667	6,218	19,449	−2,790	25,350	170,637
1950	138,723	5,499	3,075	136,299	29,825	6,540	23,285	5,580	23,433	187,411
1951	139,780	5,665	3,060	137,175	32,369	9,458	22,911	6,218	32,036	199,419
1952	143,967	5,739	3,130	141,358	34,557	11,834	22,723	1,754	39,167	205,800
1953	149,989	5,803	3,359	147,545	36,335	12,576	23,759	−239	43,040	213,964
1957p	171,926	6,505	4,524	169,945	36,728	10,461	26,267	677	38,180	236,002

p = preliminary.

a Using Kuznets, statistical variant III, *Capital in the American Economy: Its Formation and Financing*, New York (NBER), in press.

b For 1929 and prior years, the estimates are those prepared by Kuznets, although his method of deflation differs from that of the Commerce Department (see text). After 1929, the estimates are those of the Department.

c Annual average for decade.

TABLE A-IIb

Gross National Product, Commerce Concept, Derivation from Kuznets Estimates, 1869–1929; and Reconciliation with Kuznets Estimates, 1937, 1948, and 1953

(millions of current dollars)

	CONSUMPTION EXPENDITURES				GROSS PRIVATE DOMESTIC INVESTMENT				NET FOREIGN INVEST-MENT	GOVERNMENT PURCHASES OF GOODS AND SERVICES	GROSS NATIONAL PRODUCT, COMMERCE CONCEPT (4) + (7) + (8) + (9) + (10)
	Total, Kuznets Estimates	Personal Tax and Nontax Payments	Unpaid Services of Financial Intermediaries	Total, Commerce Basis (1) − (2) + (3)	New Construction and Equipment Kuznets Estimates	Public Investment	Commerce Basis (5) − (6)	Change in Business Inventories			
	(1)	(2)	(3)	(4)	(5)	(6)	(7)	(8)	(9)	(10)	(11)
1869–78a	5,777	86	38	5,729	1,163	133	1,030	361	−94	383	7,409
1879–88a	8,780	132	77	8,725	1,887	202	1,685	349	−40	492	11,211
1889	9,737	146	103	9,694	2,272	245	2,027	231	−90	623	12,485
1890	9,549	150	113	9,512	3,042	254	2,788	283	−115	661	13,129
1891	10,108	162	122	10,068	2,795	258	2,537	257	−26	694	13,530
1892	10,218	167	115	10,166	3,396	268	3,128	310	−53	722	14,273
1893	10,487	174	134	10,447	2,843	269	2,574	113	−41	756	13,849
1894	9,465	160	112	9,417	2,596	240	2,356	91	2	753	12,619
1895	10,439	180	111	10,370	2,764	256	2,508	403	−126	773	13,928
1896	10,080	176	124	10,028	2,475	266	2,209	173	86	799	13,295
1897	10,933	195	113	10,851	2,656	264	2,392	391	139	844	14,617
1898	11,407	206	114	11,315	2,641	294	2,347	284	408	1,034	15,388
1899	12,917	238	118	12,797	2,943	360	2,583	612	266	1,098	17,356
1900	13,731	256	155	13,630	3,506	414	3,092	426	412	1,124	18,684
1901	15,334	291	148	15,191	3,762	425	3,337	658	334	1,148	20,668
1902	16,043	309	179	15,913	4,337	477	3,860	391	153	1,237	21,554
1903	17,109	330	194	16,973	4,371	549	3,822	431	225	1,413	22,864
1904	17,651	339	207	17,519	4,177	563	3,614	199	152	1,366	22,850
1905	18,980	354	208	18,834	4,689	615	4,074	516	165	1,527	25,116
1906	21,279	358	236	21,157	5,670	707	4,963	831	149	1,620	28,720
1907	22,667	380	265	22,552	6,206	817	5,389	453	119	1,891	30,404
1908	21,354	397	270	21,227	5,141	748	4,393	−264	235	2,108	27,699
1909	24,372	416	281	24,237	5,965	788	5,177	989	−161	1,924	32,166

(continued)

TABLE A-IIb (concluded)

1910	25,564	442	331	25,453	6,267	890	5,377	647	−158	2,041	33,360
1911	26,498	453	351	26,396	5,781	904	4,877	481	50	2,464	34,268
1912	28,398	465	373	28,306	6,553	962	5,591	840	45	2,529	37,311
1913	29,466	513	418	29,371	7,241	1,042	6,199	848	167	2,482	39,067
1914	29,542	542	436	29,436	5,519	1,114	4,405	19	−114	2,678	36,424
1915	29,977	588	447	29,836	5,527	1,198	4,329	167	1,598	2,808	38,738
1916	36,715	715	483	36,483	7,414	1,492	5,922	1,495	2,952	2,916	49,768
1917	45,116	1,395	538	44,259	9,392	2,961	6,431	599	3,295	5,361	59,945
1918	52,027	1,966	640	50,701	11,714	5,354	6,360	729	2,190	16,196	76,176
1919	54,659	2,193	794	53,260	12,590	4,277	8,313	4,054	3,824	9,456	78,907
1920	63,671	2,044	997	62,624	13,029	2,906	10,123	7,361	2,844	5,904	88,856
1921	58,931	1,692	969	58,208	10,384	2,631	7,753	63	1,613	6,301	73,938
1922	58,425	2,000	891	57,316	12,155	2,608	9,547	530	645	5,952	73,990
1923	64,645	1,824	946	63,767	15,537	2,844	12,693	2,992	477	6,186	86,115
1924	68,620	1,942	964	67,642	16,233	3,066	13,167	−936	987	6,701	87,561
1925	68,279	2,098	1,026	67,207	17,815	3,406	14,409	1,752	684	7,256	91,308
1926	74,044	2,172	1,076	72,948	18,979	3,498	15,481	1,523	445	7,297	97,694
1927	73,883	2,362	1,081	72,602	18,363	3,673	14,690	407	716	7,864	96,279
1928	76,528	2,818	1,181	74,891	18,336	3,880	14,456	−379	1,012	8,184	98,164
1929	80,317	2,643	1,278	78,952	18,678	4,121	14,557	1,674	771	8,482	104,436
1937	69,304	2,921	876	67,259	14,110	4,612	9,498	2,249	62	11,712	90,780
1948	182,231	6,332	1,710	177,609	45,675	8,661	37,014	4,162	1,956	36,584	257,325
1953	235,943	8,199	2,798	230,542	74,281	24,210	50,071	254	−2,017	84,368	363,218
1953r				232,649			49,893	447	−2,017	84,413	365,385
1957p				284,442			64,339	953	3,462	87,132	440,328

a Annual average for decade.

p = preliminary.

r = revised (U.S. Income and Output, 1958 Supplement, Survey of Current Business, Dept. of Commerce).

TABLE A-III

National Product, Commerce Concept, by Sector, 1869–1957
(millions of 1929 dollars)

	Gross National Product (1)	Capital Consumption Allowances (2)	Net National Product (1) − (2) (3)	Net Factor Income from Abroad (4)	Gross Domestic Product (1) − (4) (5)	Government Product (6)	Gross Private Domestic Product (5) − (6) (7)	Addendum: Farm Gross Product[a] (8)
1869–78[b]	11,463	877	10,586	−113	11,576	695	10,881	4,289
1879–88[b]	21,048	1,724	19,324	−143	21,191	954	20,237	6,002
1889	24,391	2,388	22,003	−190	24,581	1,124	23,457	6,824
1890	26,196	2,540	23,656	−203	26,399	1,148	25,251	6,715
1891	27,365	2,691	24,674	−198	27,563	1,171	26,392	6,987
1892	30,010	2,829	27,181	−198	30,208	1,203	29,005	6,635
1893	28,569	2,954	25,615	−189	28,758	1,235	27,523	6,464
1894	27,756	3,046	24,710	−193	27,949	1,272	26,677	6,689
1895	31,082	3,131	27,951	−198	31,280	1,301	29,979	7,112
1896	30,444	3,236	27,208	−213	30,657	1,322	29,335	7,627
1897	33,327	3,355	29,972	−252	33,579	1,347	32,232	8,198
1898	34,068	3,472	30,596	−236	34,304	1,549	32,755	8,561
1899	37,172	3,595	33,577	−217	37,389	1,526	35,863	8,557
1900	38,197	3,719	34,478	−200	38,397	1,575	36,822	8,637
1901	42,587	3,848	38,739	−179	42,766	1,632	41,134	8,583
1902	43,004	3,989	39,015	−157	43,161	1,662	41,499	8,514
1903	45,123	4,146	40,977	−141	45,264	1,697	43,567	8,772
1904	44,559	4,298	40,261	−137	44,696	1,753	42,943	9,001
1905	47,870	4,453	43,417	−130	48,000	1,822	46,178	9,107
1906	53,420	4,657	48,763	−114	53,534	1,899	51,635	9,594
1907	54,277	4,897	49,380	−116	54,393	1,986	52,407	9,162
1908	49,790	5,104	44,686	−126	49,916	2,088	47,828	9,342
1909	55,893	5,268	50,625	−110	56,003	2,187	53,816	9,152

(continued)

TABLE A-III (continued)

1910	56,499	5,473	51,026	−107	56,606	2,285	54,321	9,411
1911	58,312	5,681	52,631	−128	58,440	2,365	56,075	8,880
1912	61,058	5,879	55,179	−120	61,178	2,454	58,724	10,498
1913	63,475	6,092	57,383	−118	63,593	2,523	61,070	9,133
1914	58,636	6,276	52,360	−88	58,724	2,642	56,082	10,196
1915	60,424	6,413	54,011	99	60,325	2,737	57,588	10,912
1916	68,870	6,577	62,293	180	68,690	2,802	65,888	9,595
1917	67,264	6,786	60,478	273	66,991	3,710	63,281	10,586
1918	73,361	6,958	66,403	328	73,033	7,056	65,977	9,612
1919	74,158	7,463	65,695	539	73,619	4,960	68,659	9,674
1920	73,313	7,380	65,933	382	72,931	3,655	69,276	9,542
1921	71,583	6,950	64,633	324	71,259	3,580	67,679	8,981
1922	75,788	7,365	63,423	572	75,216	3,537	71,679	9,595
1923	85,819	7,565	73,254	699	85,120	3,589	81,531	10,246
1924	88,361	7,661	80,700	620	87,741	3,739	84,002	9,718
1925	90,529	7,959	82,570	727	89,802	3,888	85,914	10,433
1926	96,405	8,546	87,859	735	95,670	3,976	91,694	10,328
1927	97,337	8,569	88,768	743	96,594	4,114	92,480	10,647
1928	98,503	8,912	89,591	802	97,701	4,198	93,503	10,406
1929	104,436	9,232	95,204	810	103,626	4,335	99,291	10,729

(continued)

TABLE A-III (continued)

	Gross National Product (1)	Capital Consumption Allowances (2)	Net National Product (1) − (2) (3)	Net Factor Income from Abroad (4)	Gross Domestic Product (1) − (4) (5)	Government Product (6)	Gross Private Domestic Product (5) − (6) (7)	Addendum: Farm Gross Product[a] (8)
1930	95,130	9,060	86,070	768	94,362	4,554	89,808	9,991
1931	89,454	8,742	80,712	627	88,827	4,630	84,197	11,176
1932	76,403	8,281	68,122	506	75,897	4,536	71,361	10,696
1933	74,178	7,961	66,217	420	73,758	4,988	68,770	10,998
1934	80,781	7,951	72,830	368	80,413	5,900	74,513	9,472
1935	91,435	8,084	83,351	455	90,980	6,315	84,665	10,444
1936	100,907	8,377	92,530	359	100,548	7,517	93,031	9,753
1937	109,112	8,623	100,489	335	108,777	6,966	101,811	10,927
1938	103,232	8,638	94,594	457	102,775	7,611	95,164	11,421
1939	110,994	8,774	102,220	373	110,621	7,639	102,982	11,452
1940	121,008	9,010	111,998	420	120,588	7,909	112,679	11,366
1941	138,698	9,883	128,815	398	138,300	9,574	128,726	12,311
1942	154,656	11,038	143,618	353	154,303	13,671	140,632	13,198
1943	170,206	11,628	158,578	326	169,880	21,015	148,865	12,591
1944	183,584	12,583	171,001	364	183,220	24,032	159,188	12,718

(continued)

TABLE A-III (concluded)

1945	180,939	12,829	163,110	309	180,630	23,420	157,210	12,158
1946	165,605	11,373	154,232	449	165,156	12,452	152,704	12,416
1947	164,134	13,114	151,020	601	163,533	9,602	153,931	11,909
1948	173,021	14,436	158,585	702	172,319	9,639	162,680	12,785
1949	170,637	15,316	155,321	696	169,941	10,097	159,844	12,722
1950	187,411	16,053	171,358	812	186,599	10,449	176,150	12,890
1951	199,419	17,253	182,166	921	198,498	12,951	185,547	12,149
1952	205,800	16,709	189,091	858	204,942	13,866	191,076	12,212
1953	213,964	17,635	196,329	856	213,108	13,787	199,321	13,057
1957ᵖ	236,002	20,774	215,228	1,338	234,664	13,952	220,712	13,939

ᵖ = preliminary.

ᵃ Farm gross product is equivalent to net farm output of Appendix B, which is net of intermediary products but gross of capital consumption.

ᵇ Annual average for decade.

TABLE
Private Domestic Economy: Comparison of Industry Output
(1929

	Farm[a]	Fisheries	Mining	Construc-tion	Manufac-turing	Trade[b]
1869	32.4	44.9	5.1	11.8	7.1	7.2
1879	50.3	54.5	9.8	18.4	10.2	14.3
1889	63.1	54.8	18.7	33.4	18.3	21.5
1899	79.2	59.8	31.3	43.5	27.5	32.6
1909	84.8	66.1	55.3	75.7	43.4	48.5
1919	89.9	76.9	68.7	56.3	61.0	64.6
1929	100.0	100.0	100.0	100.0	100.0	100.0
1937	102.3	120.6	95.7	61.4	103.3	104.2
1948	120.2	137.5	133.3	132.3	184.2	167.3
1953	123.8	143.0	138.4	174.1	243.4	190.2

[a] Adjusted to cover agricultural services.
[b] Adjusted to cover garages prior to 1929.
[c] Adjusted for full coverage.

A-IV
Aggregate with Real Gross Product, Key Years, 1869–1953
=100)

Transpor-tation[c]	Communi-cations and Public Utilities[c]	Post Office	Industry Aggregate Excluding Finance and Services[d]	Finance and Services[e]	Industry Aggregate	Real Gross Product[f]
4.0	0.9	2.4	10.3	2.9		8.2
7.9	1.7	5.8	16.7	14.9		16.2
20.2	3.2	11.3	25.9	17.9		23.6
35.7	6.7	19.8	37.1	33.6		36.1
55.8	22.6	42.3	53.5	56.0		54.2
82.2	45.8	71.8	68.1	71.7		69.1
100.0	100.0	100.0	100.0	100.0	100.0	100.0
103.1	115.5	92.0	101.2	89.2	97.8	102.5
211.8	249.5	148.8	172.7	132.0	161.1	163.8
228.9	336.0	174.4	209.7	162.6	196.3	200.7

[d] Adjusted to cover forestry and government enterprises other than Post Office.
[e] Derived as a residual, 1869–1929; and by deflation of national product originating in sectors, 1929–53.
[f] Index of real gross product, employing 1929 constant price weights.

TABLE A-V

Private Economy: Persons Engaged, by Class of Worker, Key Years, 1869–1957

		Employees				Addendum:
	Proprietors and Unpaid Family Workers[a]	Full-Time Equivalent	Full- and Part-Time	Persons Engaged (1) + (2)	Proprietors and Family Workers as Proportion of Persons Engaged	Full- and Part-Time Employees as Proportion of Full-Time Equivalents
	(1)	(2)	(3)	(4)	(5)	(6)
	(n u m b e r i n t h o u s a n d s)				(per cent)	
1869	4,657	6,874	7,755	11,531	40.4	112.8
1879	6,490	8,608	9,626	15,098	43.0	111.8
1889	8,753	12,142	13,349	20,895	41.9	109.9
1899	10,101	15,767	17,244	25,868	39.0	109.4
1909	11,465	21,924	23,606	33,389	34.3	107.7
1919	11,752	27,238	29,029	38,990	30.1	106.6
1929	12,445	32,391	34,598	44,836	27.8	106.8
1937	12,253	30,924	33,027	43,177	28.4	106.8
1948	12,357	41,786	44,112	54,143	22.8	105.6
1953	11,374	45,706	48,191	57,080	19.9	105.4
1953r	11,824	45,718	48,439	57,542	20.5	106.0
1957p	11,571	47,106	50,143	58,677	19.7	106.4

p = preliminary.
r = revised (*U. S. Income and Output, 1958 Supplement, Survey of Current Business,* Dept. of Commerce).

[a] For the farm sector, proprietors and family workers are adjusted to full-time equivalents.

TABLE A-VI

National Economy: Persons Engaged, by Major Sector, 1869–1957

(thousands)

	Total		General Government[a]			Private		
	Incl. Military	Civilian	Total	Military	Civilian	Total	Farm	Non-farm[b]
1869–78[c]	13,412	13,371	458	41	417	12,954	6,490	6,464
1879–88[c]	18,435	18,398	618	37	581	17,817	8,200	9,617
1889	21,620	21,581	725	39	686	20,895	8,886	12,009
1890	22,327	22,290	739	37	702	21,588	9,009	12,579
1891	22,890	22,854	754	36	718	22,136	9,094	13,042
1892	23,573	23,536	774	37	737	22,799	9,178	13,621
1893	23,498	23,460	795	38	757	22,703	9,263	13,440
1894	23,031	22,990	819	41	778	22,212	9,348	12,864
1895	24,209	24,168	837	41	796	23,372	9,432	13,940
1896	24,332	24,292	849	40	809	23,483	9,517	13,966
1897	25,040	24,999	866	41	825	24,174	9,602	14,572
1898	25,400	25,217	1,028	183	845	24,372	9,687	14,685
1899	26,861	26,741	993	120	873	25,868	9,771	16,097
1900	27,295	27,172	1,023	123	900	26,272	9,856	16,416
1901	28,425	28,309	1,055	116	939	27,370	9,914	17,456
1902	29,647	29,544	1,071	103	968	28,576	9,972	18,604
1903	30,525	30,422	1,096	103	993	29,429	10,030	19,399
1904	30,419	30,312	1,130	107	1,023	29,289	10,089	19,200
1905	31,814	31,709	1,167	105	1,062	30,647	10,146	20,501
1906	33,071	32,962	1,213	109	1,104	31,858	10,205	21,653
1907	33,848	33,742	1,265	106	1,159	32,583	10,263	22,320
1908	33,086	32,961	1,333	125	1,208	31,753	10,321	21,432
1909	34,785	34,647	1,396	138	1,258	33,389	10,379	23,010

(continued)

TABLE A-VI (continued)

National Economy: Persons Engaged, by Major Sector, 1869–1957

(thousands)

	Total		General Government[a]			Private		
	Incl. Military	Civilian	Total	Military	Civilian	Total	Farm	Non-farm[b]
1910	35,708	35,573	1,453	135	1,318	34,255	10,437	23,818
1911	36,274	36,133	1,506	141	1,365	34,768	10,425	24,343
1912	37,341	37,192	1,565	149	1,416	35,776	10,440	25,336
1913	37,896	37,745	1,611	151	1,460	36,285	10,450	25,835
1914	37,475	37,314	1,688	161	1,527	35,787	10,456	25,331
1915	37,669	37,500	1,753	169	1,584	35,916	10,466	25,450
1916	40,126	39,952	1,794	174	1,620	38,332	10,497	27,835
1917	41,531	40,696	2,527	835	1,692	39,004	10,447	28,557
1918	43,998	41,030	5,060	2,968	2,092	38,938	10,311	28,627
1919	42,313	41,047	3,323	1,266	2,057	38,990	10,197	28,793
1920	41,497	41,144	2,314	353	1,961	39,183	10,343	28,840
1921	39,361	39,006	2,302	355	1,947	37,059	10,316	26,743
1922	41,383	41,117	2,264	266	1,998	39,119	10,269	28,850
1923	43,938	43,693	2,297	245	2,052	41,641	10,135	31,506
1924	43,315	43,054	2,399	261	2,138	40,916	10,034	30,882
1925	44,512	44,257	2,492	255	2,237	42,020	10,038	31,982
1926	45,795	45,544	2,553	251	2,302	43,242	9,992	33,250
1927	45,900	45,646	2,642	254	2,388	43,258	9,734	33,524
1928	46,382	46,126	2,695	256	2,439	43,687	9,772	33,915
1929	47,611	47,350	2,775	261	2,514	44,836	9,828	35,008

(continued)

TABLE A-VI (concluded)

1930	45,465	45,204	2,902	261	2,641	42,563	9,623	32,940
1931	42,607	42,350	2,984	257	2,727	39,623	9,814	29,809
1932	39,274	39,023	2,960	251	2,709	36,314	9,868	26,446
1933	39,615	39,366	3,473	249	3,224	36,142	9,809	26,333
1934	42,739	42,489	4,303	250	4,053	38,436	9,723	28,713
1935	44,224	43,961	4,585	263	4,322	39,639	9,804	29,835
1936	47,078	46,788	5,686	290	5,396	41,392	9,495	31,897
1937	48,233	47,920	5,056	313	4,743	43,177	9,223	33,954
1938	46,379	46,053	5,661	326	5,335	40,718	8,949	31,769
1939	47,769	47,427	5,630	342	5,288	42,139	8,730	33,409
1940	49,606	49,057	5,732	549	5,183	43,874	8,454	35,420
1941	54,097	52,421	6,748	1,676	5,072	47,349	8,215	39,134
1942	59,056	54,902	9,171	4,154	5,017	49,885	8,088	41,797
1943	64,864	55,835	14,208	9,029	5,179	50,656	8,043	42,613
1944	66,020	54,655	16,507	11,365	5,142	49,513	7,869	41,644
1945	64,363	53,061	16,369	11,302	5,067	47,994	7,700	40,294
1946	58,917	55,483	8,104	3,434	4,670	50,813	7,927	42,886
1947	59,264	57,665	6,068	1,599	4,469	53,196	7,994	45,202
1948	60,216	58,748	6,073	1,468	4,605	54,143	7,980	46,163
1949	58,702	57,098	6,389	1,604	4,785	52,313	7,672	44,641
1950	60,491	58,797	6,614	1,694	4,920	53,877	7,643	46,234
1951	64,191	61,067	8,475	3,124	5,351	55,716	7,350	48,366
1952	65,264	61,626	9,182	3,638	5,544	56,082	7,045	49,037
1953r	66,219	62,674	9,139	3,545	5,594	57,080	6,825	50,255
1953r	66,693	63,148	9,151	3,545	5,606	57,542	6,825	50,717
1957p	67,728	64,943	9,051	2,785	6,266	58,677	5,834	52,843

p = preliminary.
r = revised (*U.S. Income and Output, 1958 Supplement, Survey of Current Business*, Dept. of Commerce).
a For detail, see Appendix K.
b Segment detail for key years is given in Table A-VII. Additional data and, in some cases, annual indexes for segments and groups are given in Appendixes C–J.
c Annual average for decade.

307

TABLE A-VII

National Economy: Persons Engaged, by Sector and by Industrial Division, Key Years, 1869–1957
(thousands)

	1869	1879	1889	1899	1909	1919	1929	1937	1948	1953	1953r	1957p
National economy[a]	11,910	15,639	21,620	26,861	34,785	42,313	47,611	48,233	60,216	66,219	66,693	67,728
Civilian economy	11,859	15,602	21,581	26,741	34,647	41,047	47,350	47,920	58,748	62,674	63,148	64,943
General government	328	504	686	873	1,258	2,057	2,514	4,743	4,605	5,594	5,606	6,266
Private economy	11,531	15,098	20,895	25,868	33,389	38,990	44,836	43,177	54,143	57,080	57,542	58,677
Farm	5,721	7,577	8,886	9,771	10,379	10,197	9,828	9,223	7,980	6,825	6,825	5,834
Nonfarm	5,810	7,521	12,009	16,097	23,010	28,793	35,008	33,954	46,163	50,255	50,717	52,843
Agricultural services, forestry, fisheries	37	63	110	141	183	221	247	261	273	300	300	327
Mining	151	281	507	659	1,079	1,145	1,057	963	1,005	873	877	839
Construction	580	645	964	1,315	1,744	1,516	2,392	1,807	3,326	3,716	3,878	4,259
Manufacturing	2,100	2,810	4,049	5,365	7,679	10,600	10,570	10,696	15,481	17,428	17,476	17,065
Trade	926	1,232	2,104	2,892	4,089	5,603	8,028	8,384	11,474	12,266	12,447	13,187
Finance, insurance, real estate	48	65	172	325	559	904	1,592	1,538	1,942	2,235	2,339	2,749
Transportation	569	766	1,435	1,908	2,691	3,357	3,051	2,351	3,013	2,974	3,010	2,867
Communications and public utilities	35	50	96	167	368	629	1,034	901	1,282	1,401	1,404	1,516
Services	1,323	1,547	2,481	3,204	4,360	4,514	6,628	6,579	7,647	8,220	8,144	9,160
Government enterprises	41	62	91	121	258	304	409	474	720	842	842	874

p = preliminary.
r = revised (U.S. Income and Output, 1958 Supplement, Survey of Current Business, Dept. of Commerce).

[a] With respect to labor, the national and domestic economies are practically identical.

TABLE A-VIII

National Economy: Persons Engaged, Comparison of Industry Aggregate
and Census-based Series, Decennial, 1870–1950

	Based on *Census of Population* Data (millions)	Industry Aggregate	Ratio: Industry Aggregate to Census
1870	12.1	12.0	0.99
1880	16.5	16.6	1.01
1890	22.4	22.3	1.00
1900	27.1	27.3	1.01
1910	35.5	35.7	1.01
1920	40.8	41.5	1.02
1930	44.0	45.5	1.03
1940	46.4	49.6	1.07
1950	58.5	60.4	1.03

SOURCE: For 1890–1950, see Clarence D. Long, *The Labor Force under Changing Income and Employment*, Princeton University Press (for NBER) 1958, Table C-1; 1870 and 1880 are based on estimates of gainful workers by Daniel Carson, "Changes in the Industrial Composition of Manpower since the Civil War," *Studies in Income and Wealth*, Vol. 11, New York (NBER) 1949, p. 47, adjusted for unemployment.

TABLE A-IX

National Economy: Average Hours Worked per Week, by Sector and by Industrial Division, Key Years, 1869–1957
(number)

	1869	1879	1889	1899	1909	1919	1929	1937	1948	1953	1957p
National economy[a]	53.7	52.8	53.5	53.4	52.0	49.1	48.6	44.4	41.8	40.3	39.6
Civilian economy	53.8	52.8	53.5	53.4	52.0	49.4	48.7	44.5	42.0	40.6	39.8
General government	34.6	35.1	36.3	37.4	39.0	37.1	37.4	36.5	34.6	34.3	33.8
Private economy	54.3	53.4	54.1	54.0	52.5	50.0	49.3	45.4	42.7	41.3	40.5
Farm	45.9	45.5	45.5	45.5	45.7	49.0	49.8	50.7	45.4	40.1	41.0
Nonfarm	62.7	61.3	60.4	59.1	55.6	50.4	49.2	43.9	42.2	41.4	40.4
Agricultural services, forestry, fisheries	52.5	51.9	51.2	51.3	50.9	48.7	47.7	44.1	44.9	44.3	43.5
Mining	46.6	48.2	45.4	42.6	41.8	40.5	42.1	33.8	39.3	37.6	38.3
Construction	55.6	55.1	51.8	51.2	44.1	41.8	42.6	36.0	39.8	39.4	38.7
Manufacturing	55.9	54.5	53.5	52.7	51.0	46.3	44.2	38.6	40.1	39.8	38.8
Trade	70.2	70.2	70.2	69.1	62.6	58.3	56.4	49.6	45.8	44.9	43.9
Finance, insurance, real estate	54.1	52.7	51.5	50.7	49.1	44.5	45.5	43.9	40.7	40.6	39.3
Transportation	61.9	62.2	64.3	63.5	62.0	52.4	50.1	46.8	47.8	43.5	43.1
Communications and public utilities	64.8	65.8	64.5	58.0	55.2	46.0	46.8	40.3	40.6	40.1	40.0
Services	74.3	72.1	68.8	66.5	63.0	56.2	52.8	49.1	41.3	40.9	39.2
Government enterprises	48.8	49.0	47.8	46.6	45.8	44.3	44.9	37.1	37.4	37.3	37.2

p = preliminary.

[a] With respect to labor, the national and domestic economies are practically identical.

Source: Manhours estimates (Table A-XI) divided by corresponding estimates of persons engaged (Table A-VII) and 52 (weeks in the year). The average hours estimates for 1953 are virtually the same using either the unrevised or revised manhour and persons engaged series, although in a few instances there were differences of more than 0.2, due chiefly to changes in the Commerce estimates of full-time equivalents relative to full- and part-time employment.

TABLE A-X

National Economy: Manhours, by Major Sector, 1869–1957
(millions)

	Total		General Government[a]			Private		
	Incl. Military	Civilian	Total	Military	Civilian	Total	Farm	Non-farm[b]
1869–78[c]	37,046	36,954	848	92	756	36,198	15,381	20,817
1879–88[c]	51,192	51,110	1,162	82	1,080	50,030	19,422	30,608
1889	60,133	60,049	1,378	84	1,294	58,755	21,045	37,710
1890	62,280	62,200	1,411	80	1,331	60,869	21,337	39,532
1891	63,896	63,819	1,443	77	1,366	62,453	21,538	40,915
1892	66,002	65,923	1,491	79	1,412	64,511	21,738	42,773
1893	65,309	65,228	1,525	81	1,444	63,784	21,939	41,845
1894	63,096	63,009	1,571	87	1,484	61,525	22,139	39,386
1895	66,921	66,834	1,613	87	1,526	65,308	22,340	42,968
1896	66,917	66,834	1,633	83	1,550	65,284	22,541	42,743
1897	68,990	68,906	1,670	84	1,586	67,320	22,741	44,579
1898	69,718	69,343	2,005	375	1,630	67,713	22,942	44,771
1899	74,558	74,312	1,945	246	1,699	72,613	23,142	49,471
1900	75,486	75,235	2,007	251	1,756	73,479	23,343	50,136
1901	78,764	78,528	2,080	236	1,844	76,684	23,489	53,195
1902	82,109	81,899	2,117	210	1,907	79,992	23,635	56,357
1903	84,524	84,314	2,183	210	1,973	82,341	23,781	58,560
1904	83,351	83,130	2,250	221	2,029	81,101	23,927	57,174
1905	87,459	87,242	2,352	217	2,135	85,107	24,072	61,035
1906	90,904	90,679	2,450	225	2,225	88,454	24,218	64,236
1907	92,980	92,761	2,570	219	2,351	90,410	24,364	66,046
1908	89,188	88,931	2,693	257	2,436	86,495	24,510	61,985
1909	94,054	93,771	2,835	283	2,552	91,219	24,656	66,563

(continued)

Table A-X (continued)

National Economy: Manhours, by Major Sector, 1869–1957

(millions)

	Total		General Government[a]			Private		
	Incl. Military	Civilian	Total	Military	Civilian	Total	Farm	Non-farm[b]
1910	96,605	96,329	2,972	276	2,696	93,633	24,802	68,831
1911	98,500	98,211	3,079	289	2,790	95,421	25,319	70,102
1912	101,647	101,342	3,210	305	2,905	98,437	25,651	72,786
1913	102,466	102,158	3,302	308	2,994	99,164	25,325	73,839
1914	100,745	100,416	3,435	329	3,106	97,310	26,100	71,210
1915	99,982	99,638	3,555	344	3,211	96,427	25,568	70,859
1916	107,072	106,718	3,647	354	3,293	103,425	25,418	78,007
1917	110,690	108,993	5,105	1,697	3,408	105,585	26,126	79,459
1918	114,876	108,913	10,113	5,963	4,150	104,763	26,480	78,283
1919	107,930	105,387	6,516	2,543	3,973	101,414	25,992	75,422
1920	107,226	106,519	4,496	707	3,789	102,730	26,394	76,336
1921	96,877	96,175	4,362	702	3,660	92,515	24,348	68,167
1922	103,770	103,244	4,311	526	3,785	99,459	25,190	74,269
1923	111,793	111,308	4,432	485	3,947	107,361	25,367	81,994
1924	109,475	108,959	4,623	516	4,107	104,852	25,655	79,197
1925	113,442	112,938	4,833	504	4,329	108,609	26,180	82,429
1926	117,354	116,858	4,961	496	4,465	112,393	26,266	86,127
1927	116,906	116,406	5,155	500	4,655	111,751	25,243	86,508
1928	118,028	117,524	5,253	504	4,749	112,775	25,692	87,083
1929	120,338	119,825	5,397	513	4,884	114,941	25,474	89,467

(continued)

Table A-X (concluded)

1930	112,632	112,119	5,565	513	5,052	107,067	25,213	81,854
1931	103,769	103,284	5,613	485	5,128	98,156	25,770	72,386
1932	92,383	91,908	5,448	475	4,973	86,935	24,866	62,069
1933	92,552	92,079	6,495	473	6,022	86,057	24,809	61,248
1934	92,619	92,155	7,998	464	7,534	84,621	22,255	62,366
1935	97,756	97,277	8,576	479	8,097	89,180	23,157	66,023
1936	106,835	106,320	10,925	515	10,410	95,910	22,484	73,426
1937	111,443	110,887	9,568	556	9,012	101,875	24,307	77,568
1938	103,788	103,211	10,693	577	10,116	93,095	22,635	70,460
1939	108,532	107,927	10,653	605	10,048	97,879	22,748	75,131
1940	112,978	112,007	10,797	971	9,826	102,181	22,847	79,694
1941	124,204	121,006	12,874	3,198	9,676	111,330	22,054	89,276
1942	138,323	129,762	18,333	8,561	9,772	119,990	22,934	97,056
1943	156,325	135,269	31,942	21,056	10,886	124,383	22,750	101,633
1944	160,012	133,509	37,358	26,503	10,855	122,654	22,530	100,124
1945	150,012	126,029	34,073	23,983	10,090	115,939	21,019	94,920
1946	131,474	125,375	14,538	6,099	8,439	116,936	20,265	96,671
1947	130,317	127,477	10,893	2,840	8,053	119,424	19,352	100,072
1948	131,019	128,412	10,887	2,607	8,280	120,132	18,828	101,304
1949	126,402	123,553	11,399	2,849	8,550	115,003	18,219	96,784
1950	128,914	125,905	11,812	3,009	8,803	117,102	16,750	100,352
1951	135,876	130,328	15,096	5,548	9,548	120,780	15,979	104,801
1952	137,927	131,379	16,475	6,548	9,927	121,452	15,284	106,168
1953	138,567	132,186	16,361	6,381	9,980	122,206	14,231	107,975
1953r	139,819	133,438	16,393	6,381	10,012	123,426	14,231	109,195
1957p	139,577	134,564	16,028	5,013	11,015	123,549	12,445	111,104

p = preliminary.

r = revised (based on estimates of persons engaged as revised in U. S. Income and Output, 1958 Supplement, Survey of Current Business, Dept. of Commerce).

a For detail, see Appendix K.

b Segment detail for key years is given in Table A-XI. Additional group detail and, in some cases, annual indexes of segments and groups are given in Appendixes C through J.

c Annual average for decade.

TABLE A-XI

National Economy: Manhours, by Sector and by Industrial Division,
Key Years, 1869–1957
(millions)

	1869	1879	1889	1899	1909	1919	1929	1937	1948	1953	1953r	1957p
National economy[a]	33,280	42,916	60,133	74,558	94,054	107,930	120,338	111,443	131,019	138,567	139,819	139,577
Civilian economy	33,166	42,833	60,049	74,312	93,771	105,387	119,825	110,887	128,412	132,186	133,438	134,564
General government	591	921	1,294	1,699	2,552	3,973	4,884	9,012	8,280	9,980	10,012	11,015
Private economy	32,575	41,912	58,755	72,613	91,219	101,414	114,941	101,875	120,132	122,206	123,426	123,549
Farm	13,642	17,945	21,045	23,142	24,656	25,992	25,474	24,307	18,828	14,231	14,231	12,445
Nonfarm	18,933	23,967	37,710	49,471	66,563	75,422	89,467	77,568	101,304	107,975	109,195	111,104
Agricultural services, forestry, fisheries	101	170	293	376	484	560	613	599	637	693	691	739
Mining	366	704	1,198	1,459	2,342	2,412	2,313	1,690	2,056	1,716	1,716	1,672
Construction	1,676	1,848	2,596	3,498	4,001	3,292	5,304	3,380	6,890	7,595	7,947	8,575
Manufacturing	6,105	7,964	11,264	14,700	20,365	25,525	24,290	21,467	32,278	36,076	36,175	34,438
Trade	3,381	4,496	7,677	10,394	13,310	16,979	23,555	21,616	27,334	28,489	29,048	30,106
Finance, insurance, real estate	135	178	461	857	1,427	2,092	3,767	3,511	4,109	4,718	4,937	5,619
Transportation	1,833	2,477	4,801	6,303	8,681	9,154	7,949	5,725	7,485	6,810	6,811	6,432
Communications and public utilities	118	171	322	504	1,056	1,506	2,517	1,886	2,709	2,906	2,925	3,154
Services	5,114	5,801	8,872	11,087	14,283	13,201	18,204	16,780	16,406	17,347	17,311	18,679
Government enterprises	104	158	226	293	614	701	955	914	1,400	1,625	1,634	1,690

p = preliminary.
r = revised (based on estimates of persons engaged as revised in U.S. Income and Output, 1958 Supplement, Survey of Current Business, Dept. of Commerce).

[a] With respect to labor, the national and domestic economies are practically identical.

TABLE A-XII

Civilian Economy: Employment, Average Hours, and Manhours, Comparison of Industry Composite with Census Survey Estimates, 1940–57

	Employment			Average Hours Worked per Week			Manhours		
	MRLF[a] (thousands)	Industry Composite[b]	Ratio (2) ÷ (1)	MRLF[c]	Industry Composite (8) ÷ (2) ÷ 52	Ratio (5) ÷ (4)	MRLF (1) × (4) × 52 (millions)	Industry Composite (millions)	Ratio (8) ÷ (7)
	(1)	(2)	(3)	(4)	(5)	(6)	(7)	(8)	(9)
1940	46,330	49,057	1.059	44.5	43.9	0.987	107,208	112,007	1.045
1941	49,370	52,421	1.062	45.6	44.4	0.974	117,066	121,006	1.034
1942	52,650	54,902	1.043	46.6	45.5	0.976	127,581	129,762	1.017
1943	53,250	55,835	1.049	48.6	46.6	0.959	134,573	135,269	1.005
1944	52,200	54,655	1.047	48.0	47.0	0.979	130,291	133,509	1.025
1945	50,810	53,061	1.044	46.3	45.7	0.987	122,330	126,029	1.030
1946	52,990	55,483	1.047	44.2	43.5	0.984	121,792	125,375	1.029
1947	55,554	57,665	1.038	43.5	42.5	0.977	125,663	127,477	1.014
1948	56,626	58,748	1.037	43.2	42.0	0.972	127,205	128,412	1.009
1949	56,180	57,098	1.016	42.6	41.6	0.977	124,450	123,553	0.993
1950	57,309	58,797	1.026	42.4	41.2	0.972	126,355	125,905	0.996
1951	58,325	61,067	1.047	42.5	41.0	0.965	128,898	130,328	1.011
1952	58,479	61,626	1.054	42.4	41.0	0.967	128,934	131,379	1.019
1953	59,415	62,674	1.055	42.2	40.6	0.962	130,380	132,186	1.014
1953r	59,415	63,148	1.063	42.2	40.6	0.962	130,380	133,438	1.023
1957p	61,994	64,943	1.048	41.1	39.8	0.968	132,494	134,564	1.016

p = preliminary.
r = revised (*U.S. Income and Output, 1958 Supplement, Survey of Current Business*, Dept. of Commerce).

[a] MRLF = *Monthly Reports on the Labor Force*, Series P–57, Bureau of the Census. Excluding persons with job but not at work.
[b] Including employees as full-time equivalents.
[c] Adjusted for holiday weeks.

TABLE
National Economy: Real Labor Input and Manhours, Effect of
1929

	National Economy			Private Economy		
	Labor Input (1)	Man-hours (2)	Ratio (1) ÷ (2) (3)	Labor Input (4)	Man-hours (5)	Ratio (4) ÷ (5) (6)
1869	22.4	27.7	0.809	23.0	28.3	0.813
1879	29.1	35.7	0.815	29.8	36.5	0.816
1889	43.4	50.0	0.868	44.6	51.1	0.873
1899	55.4	62.0	0.894	56.7	63.2	0.897
1909	73.5	78.2	0.940	74.9	79.4	0.943
1919	88.7	89.7	0.989	88.6	88.2	0.983
1929	100.0	100.0	1.000	100.0	100.0	1.000
1937	92.0	92.6	0.994	87.4	88.6	0.986
1948	119.3	108.9	1.096	111.9	104.5	1.071
1953	129.9	115.1	1.129	117.2	106.3	1.103
1957^p	129.4	114.9	1.126	116.9	106.4	1.099

p = preliminary.

A-XIII
Interindustry Manhour Shifts, by Major Sector, Key Years, 1869–1957
= 100

Private Nonfarm Economy			Effect of Government-Private Shifts	Effect of Farm-Nonfarm Shifts
Labor Input (7)	Man-hours (8)	Ratio (7) ÷ (8) (9)	(3) ÷ (6) (10)	(6) ÷ (9) (11)
19.4	21.2	0.915	0.995	0.889
25.0	26.8	0.933	0.999	0.875
39.6	42.1	0.941	0.994	0.928
52.7	55.3	0.953	0.997	0.941
72.3	74.4	0.972	0.997	0.970
84.9	84.3	1.007	1.006	0.976
100.0	100.0	1.000	1.000	1.000
86.7	8.86	1.000	1.008	0.986
117.6	113.2	1.039	1.023	1.031
126.3	120.7	1.046	1.024	1.054
126.9	122.8	1.033	1.025	1.064

Distribution of Labor Input, Manhours, and Persons Engaged, by
(per

	1869			1899
	Persons Engaged	Man-hours	Labor Input^a	Persons Engaged
National economy	100.0	100.0	100.0	100.0
Military	0.4	0.3	0.5	0.4
Civilian	99.6	99.7	99.5	99.6
General government	2.8	1.8	3.5	3.3
Private economy	96.8	97.9	96.0	96.3
Farm	48.0	41.0	20.0	36.4
Nonfarm	48.8	56.9	76.0	59.9
Agricultural services, forestry, fisheries	0.3	0.3	0.3	0.5
Mining	1.3	1.1	1.9	2.5
Construction	4.9	5.0	9.8	4.9
Manufacturing	17.6	18.3	28.2	20.0
Trade	7.8	10.2	13.6	10.8
Transportation	4.8	5.5	7.8	7.1
Communications and public utilities	0.3	0.4	0.5	0.6
Finance, insurance, and real estate	0.4	0.4	0.9	1.2
Services	11.1	15.4	12.4	11.9
Government enterprises	0.3	0.3	0.6	0.4

^{a} Absolute figures on which these percentages are based were derived by multiplying 1929 labor compensation by labor input indexes for industries and summing to sector totals.

A-XIV
Sector and by Industrial Division, 1869, 1899, 1929, and 1957
cent)

	1899		1929			1957[p]		
	Man-hours	Labor Input[a]	Persons Engaged	Man-hours	Labor Input[a]	Persons Engaged	Man-hours	Labor Input[a]
	100.0	100.0	100.0	100.0	100.0	100.0	100.0	100.0
	0.3	0.4	0.5	0.4	0.5	4.1	3.6	3.5
	99.7	99.6	99.5	99.6	99.5	95.9	96.4	96.5
	2.3	4.0	5.3	4.1	6.3	9.3	7.9	12.2
	97.4	95.6	94.2	95.5	93.2	86.6	88.5	84.3
	31.0	13.5	20.7	21.2	8.1	8.6	8.9	3.0
	66.4	82.1	73.5	74.3	85.1	78.0	79.6	81.3
	0.5	0.4	0.5	0.5	0.4	0.5	0.5	0.3
	2.0	3.0	2.2	1.9	2.6	1.2	1.2	1.3
	4.7	8.2	5.0	4.4	6.7	6.3	6.1	7.8
	19.7	27.1	22.2	20.2	25.7	25.2	24.7	28.6
	13.9	16.6	16.9	19.6	20.6	19.5	21.6	19.3
	8.5	10.9	6.4	6.6	7.9	4.2	4.6	4.2
	0.7	0.8	2.2	2.1	2.4	2.2	2.3	2.3
	1.1	2.2	3.3	3.1	5.2	4.1	4.0	5.6
	14.9	12.2	13.9	15.1	12.4	13.5	13.4	10.3
	0.4	0.7	0.9	0.8	1.2	1.3	1.2	1.6

p = preliminary.

TABLE A-XV

National Economy: Real Capital Stocks, by Major Sector, 1869–1957

(millions of 1929 dollars)

	NATIONAL ECONOMY	NET FOREIGN ASSETS	DOMESTIC ECONOMY	GENERAL GOVERNMENT	PRIVATE DOMESTIC ECONOMY			
					Total	Farm	*Private Nonfarm*	
							Residential	Nonresidential
1869–78[a]	54,098	−3,175	57,273	3,335	53,938	27,447	9,677	16,814
1879–88[a]	83,327	−3,425	86,752	4,717	82,035	36,276	18,465	27,294
1889	103,190	−4,250	107,440	5,722	101,718	40,132	28,448	33,138
1890	108,189	−4,448	112,637	5,920	106,717	40,848	30,845	35,024
1891	114,155	−4,586	118,741	6,106	112,635	41,683	32,888	38,064
1892	120,846	−4,667	125,513	6,268	119,245	42,401	34,926	41,918
1893	126,929	−4,764	131,693	6,430	125,263	42,872	36,903	45,488
1894	131,263	−4,803	136,066	6,610	129,456	43,472	38,576	47,408
1895	136,407	−4,940	141,347	6,811	134,536	44,193	40,456	49,887
1896	141,477	−4,982	146,459	7,048	139,411	44,989	42,326	52,096
1897	146,191	−4,908	151,099	7,440	143,659	45,992	44,104	53,563
1898	151,476	−4,938	156,414	7,959	148,455	47,073	45,748	55,634
1899	156,795	−4,750	161,545	8,448	153,097	48,004	47,138	57,955
1900	162,309	−4,638	166,947	8,920	158,027	48,799	48,122	61,106
1901	167,394	−4,573	171,967	9,425	162,542	49,298	49,042	64,202
1902	173,289	−4,288	177,577	9,901	167,676	50,234	50,156	67,286
1903	179,821	−4,082	183,903	10,448	173,455	51,231	51,182	71,042
1904	184,890	−3,968	188,858	11,110	177,748	51,876	52,384	73,488
1905	190,778	−3,876	194,654	11,770	182,884	52,701	54,381	75,802
1906	198,451	−3,804	202,255	12,359	189,896	53,562	56,844	79,490
1907	206,344	−3,580	209,924	12,974	196,950	54,096	58,858	83,996
1908	212,942	−3,410	216,352	13,758	202,594	54,524	60,628	87,442
1909	218,302	−3,507	221,809	14,554	207,255	55,295	62,665	89,295

(continued)

TABLE A-XV (continued)

Year								
1910	224,805	−3,554	228,359	15,320	213,039	56,229	64,538	92,272
1911	231,628	−3,508	235,136	16,177	218,959	57,627	65,974	95,358
1912	237,020	−3,367	240,387	17,053	223,334	58,178	67,462	97,694
1913	243,881	−3,244	247,125	17,871	229,254	58,602	69,070	101,582
1914	250,563	−3,094	253,657	18,662	234,995	59,079	70,644	105,272
1915	258,025	−1,702	259,727	19,688	240,039	60,627	72,246	107,166
1916	266,294	1,834	264,460	20,787	243,673	60,729	73,900	109,044
1917	273,796	4,017	269,779	21,525	248,254	61,353	74,780	112,121
1918	278,079	3,742	274,337	21,767	252,570	62,082	74,442	116,046
1919	281,995	3,874	278,121	21,594	256,527	62,600	74,243	119,684
1920	287,157	4,617	282,540	21,380	261,160	62,563	74,320	124,277
1921	292,222	5,942	286,280	21,800	264,480	61,766	74,763	127,951
1922	297,948	7,512	290,436	22,867	267,569	61,089	76,912	129,568
1923	306,702	8,176	298,526	24,069	274,457	60,420	80,458	133,579
1924	317,047	8,500	308,547	25,617	282,930	59,950	84,834	138,146
1925	328,372	9,146	319,226	27,318	291,908	60,003	89,860	142,045
1926	341,716	9,652	332,064	28,794	303,270	60,493	95,043	147,734
1927	354,297	10,164	344,133	30,388	313,745	60,605	99,904	153,236
1928	365,829	11,020	354,809	32,140	322,669	61,181	104,224	157,264
1929	377,073	11,984	365,089	34,024	331,065	61,463	107,336	162,266
1930	385,841	12,744	373,097	36,463	336,634	61,120	108,572	166,942
1931	389,232	12,934	376,298	39,032	337,266	61,542	108,680	167,044
1932	385,653	12,478	373,175	41,160	332,015	61,838	108,022	162,155
1933	376,913	11,486	365,427	42,360	323,067	60,950	106,649	155,468
1934	368,941	10,516	358,425	43,257	315,168	59,017	105,254	150,897
1935	365,700	8,892	356,808	44,988	311,820	58,788	104,304	148,728
1936	365,202	6,662	358,540	46,884	311,656	58,396	104,100	149,160
1937	369,145	5,067	364,078	48,682	315,396	58,877	104,382	152,137
1938	372,153	4,096	368,057	50,643	317,414	59,438	104,791	153,185
1939	373,890	2,960	370,930	53,228	317,702	59,629	105,675	152,398

(continued)

TABLE A-XV (concluded)

National Economy: Real Capital Stocks, by Major Sector, 1869–1957

(millions of 1929 dollars)

	NATIONAL ECONOMY	NET FOREIGN ASSETS	DOMESTIC ECONOMY	GENERAL GOVERNMENT	PRIVATE DOMESTIC ECONOMY			
					Total	Farm	Private Nonfarm	
							Residential	Nonresidential
1940	380,676	1,514	379,162	56,972	322,190	60,952	107,102	154,136
1941	391,178	1,434	389,744	59,659	330,085	62,559	108,804	158,722
1942	398,536	1,920	396,616	60,278	336,338	64,399	109,532	162,407
1943	397,961	1,766	396,195	59,968	336,227	65,216	108,646	162,365
1944	393,473	1,476	391,997	58,662	333,335	65,307	107,220	160,808
1945	386,955	−274	387,229	57,204	330,025	64,765	105,847	159,413
1946	390,364	97	390,267	56,382	333,885	64,691	105,754	163,440
1947	405,751	4,760	400,991	56,700	344,291	64,478	107,355	172,458
1948	423,472	7,980	415,492	58,022	357,470	65,884	109,923	181,663
1949	439,184	8,760	430,424	59,546	370,878	68,262	112,880	189,736
1950	454,555	8,691	445,864	60,738	385,126	70,431	116,962	197,733
1951	472,716	8,507	464,209	62,010	402,199	72,023	121,420	208,756
1952	489,322	8,674	480,648	64,074	416,574	72,748	124,998	218,828
1953	503,932	9,029	494,903	65,988	428,915	72,521	128,604	227,790
1957p	569,370	10,110	559,260	74,160	485,100	73,331	n.a.	n.a.

p = preliminary.

a Annual average for decade.

n.a. = not available.

TABLE A-XVI

Domestic Economy and Private Sectors:[a] Real Capital Stocks, by Major Type, 1869–1953
(millions of 1929 dollars)

	DOMESTIC ECONOMY					PRIVATE DOMESTIC ECONOMY				
	Farm, Forest, and Park Land	Structures (Including Site Land)	Equipment	Inventories	Monetary Gold and Silver	Farm and Forest Land	Structures[b] Total	Nonresidential	Equipment	Inventories
1869–78[c]	21,320	24,205	5,029	6,543	176	19,447	23,025	13,348	4,929	6,537
1879–88[c]	26,204	40,714	8,216	10,993	625	24,442	38,566	20,101	8,044	10,983
1889	28,264	55,010	10,503	12,772	891	26,581	52,099	23,651	10,279	12,759
1890	28,634	58,787	10,921	13,377	918	26,965	55,700	24,855	10,689	13,363
1891	29,137	63,349	11,389	13,942	924	27,483	60,077	27,189	11,147	13,928
1892	29,641	68,513	11,879	14,590	890	28,001	65,042	30,116	11,627	14,575
1893	30,142	73,771	12,337	14,601	842	28,516	70,087	33,184	12,075	14,585
1894	30,644	78,037	12,554	14,022	809	29,034	74,130	35,554	12,288	14,004
1895	31,148	82,362	12,707	14,336	794	29,552	78,227	37,771	12,439	14,318
1896	31,648	86,181	13,095	14,723	812	30,068	81,820	39,494	12,819	14,704
1897	32,186	89,958	13,494	14,566	895	30,620	85,298	41,194	13,194	14,547
1898	32,769	93,938	13,805	14,874	1,028	31,218	88,908	43,160	13,474	14,855
1899	33,174	97,401	14,252	15,572	1,146	31,637	92,009	44,871	13,896	15,555
1900	33,614	100,825	14,935	16,331	1,242	32,092	95,063	46,941	14,557	16,315
1901	33,885	104,849	15,716	16,188	1,329	32,375	98,683	49,641	15,312	16,172
1902	34,012	109,293	16,631	16,250	1,391	32,511	102,722	52,566	16,209	16,234
1903	34,240	113,460	17,774	16,977	1,452	32,748	106,420	55,238	17,326	16,961
1904	34,516	117,257	18,755	16,804	1,526	33,034	109,649	57,265	18,277	16,788
1905	34,751	121,718	19,665	16,913	1,607	33,279	113,545	59,164	19,163	16,897
1906	34,990	126,968	20,923	17,677	1,697	33,527	118,291	61,447	20,417	17,661
1907	35,251	132,399	22,469	18,030	1,775	33,798	123,190	64,332	21,947	18,015
1908	35,537	137,511	23,552	17,925	1,827	34,093	127,627	66,999	22,964	17,910
1909	35,668	142,488	24,158	17,646	1,849	34,233	131,884	69,219	23,508	17,630

(continued)

TABLE A-XVI (continued)

Domestic Economy and Private Sectors:ª Real Capital Stocks, by Major Type, 1869–1953

(millions of 1929 dollars)

| | DOMESTIC ECONOMY | | | | | PRIVATE DOMESTIC ECONOMY | | | | |
	Farm, Forest, and Park Land	Structures (including Site Land)	Equipment	Inventories	Monetary Gold and Silver	Farm and Forest Land	Structures^b Total	Nonresidential	Equipment	Inventories
1910	35,922	147,338	25,017	18,199	1,883	34,497	136,047	71,509	24,315	18,180
1911	37,253	151,246	25,826	18,852	1,959	35,837	139,230	73,256	25,064	18,828
1912	37,534	155,300	26,712	18,790	2,051	36,127	142,549	75,087	25,894	18,764
1913	37,453	160,040	27,985	19,535	2,112	36,055	146,569	77,499	27,123	19,507
1914	37,723	164,547	28,940	20,373	2,074	36,335	150,281	79,637	28,038	20,341
1915	38,526	168,236	29,334	21,366	2,265	37,147	153,139	80,893	28,421	21,332
1916	37,920	171,926	30,134	21,677	2,803	36,550	156,212	82,312	29,264	21,647
1917	37,564	174,823	31,757	22,335	3,300	36,204	158,772	83,992	30,967	22,311
1918	37,618	175,743	33,402	24,110	3,464	36,268	159,513	85,071	32,700	24,089
1919	37,806	176,456	34,378	26,158	3,323	36,464	160,156	85,913	33,774	26,133
1920	37,790	177,477	35,030	29,098	3,145	36,456	161,118	86,798	34,524	29,062
1921	38,121	178,995	35,031	30,725	3,408	36,791	162,404	87,641	34,607	30,678
1922	38,159	182,867	34,711	30,805	3,894	36,827	165,665	88,753	34,314	30,763
1923	37,298	189,124	35,454	32,443	4,207	35,964	171,083	90,625	35,008	32,402
1924	37,126	196,899	36,642	33,380	4,500	35,789	177,746	92,912	36,065	33,330
1925	37,257	206,021	37,815	33,555	4,578	35,918	185,433	95,573	37,056	33,501
1926	37,774	215,764	39,210	34,763	4,553	36,434	193,820	98,777	38,309	34,707
1927	37,947	225,721	40,398	35,564	4,503	36,603	202,305	102,401	39,330	35,507
1928	38,408	235,141	41,385	35,567	4,308	37,061	209,995	105,771	40,104	35,509
1929	38,720	243,320	42,806	36,001	4,242	37,370	216,418	109,082	41,332	35,945

(continued)

TABLE A-XVI (concluded)

Year										
1930	38,850	249,494	43,932	36,416	4,405	37,500	220,530	111,958	42,248	36,356
1931	39,452	253,203	43,528	35,696	4,419	38,106	221,892	113,212	41,642	35,626
1932	39,792	253,806	41,562	33,678	4,337	38,450	220,400	112,378	39,565	33,600
1933	39,460	251,705	38,983	31,011	4,268	38,122	217,019	110,370	36,991	30,935
1934	38,968	248,544	37,030	29,225	4,658	37,636	213,271	108,017	35,108	29,153
1935	39,269	246,180	36,201	29,375	5,783	37,937	210,284	105,980	34,296	29,303
1936	38,918	245,398	36,695	30,792	6,737	37,585	208,638	104,538	34,710	30,723
1937	39,165	246,288	38,096	33,034	7,495	37,833	208,577	104,195	36,020	32,966
1938	39,137	247,272	38,736	34,425	8,487	37,803	208,626	103,835	36,632	34,353
1939	39,053	248,352	38,835	34,733	9,957	37,718	208,642	102,967	36,682	34,660
1940	39,906	250,397	39,948	36,747	12,164	38,574	209,299	102,197	37,648	36,669
1941	40,224	253,333	42,178	40,337	13,672	38,896	211,164	102,360	39,781	40,244
1942	40,437	254,397	43,704	44,136	13,942	39,115	211,954	102,422	41,248	44,021
1943	40,472	252,531	43,785	45,624	13,783	39,155	210,314	101,668	41,275	45,483
1944	40,587	248,938	43,850	45,404	13,218	39,276	207,402	100,182	41,421	45,236
1945	40,038	245,234	44,780	44,385	12,792	38,734	204,566	98,719	42,498	44,227
1946	39,542	245,063	47,676	45,111	12,875	38,244	205,289	99,535	45,341	45,011
1947	38,754	248,183	53,443	46,940	13,671	37,457	209,131	101,776	50,827	46,876
1948	38,559	252,863	60,864	48,435	14,771	37,261	213,975	104,052	57,859	48,375
1949	39,302	258,830	67,106	49,910	15,276	38,003	219,283	106,403	63,744	49,848
1950	40,805	266,694	72,395	51,128	14,842	39,503	225,717	108,755	68,838	51,068
1951	41,084	275,621	77,921	55,233	14,350	39,780	233,049	111,629	74,193	55,177
1952	40,648	283,870	82,749	58,874	14,507	39,344	239,664	114,666	78,749	58,817
1953	40,227	292,235	86,978	61,134	14,329	38,922	246,261	117,657	82,652	61,080

[a] Totals shown in Table A-XV are not repeated here. General-government capital by type may be derived as the difference between the sector totals by type. The farm component by type is shown in Table B-III (for key years), so that private domestic nonfarm capital could also be derived as a residual.

[b] The residential (nonfarm) component is shown separately in Table A-XV.

[c] Annual average for decade.

TABLE A-XVII

National Economy: Total Factor Input,
Effect of Alternative Weighting Systems, Key Years, 1869–1957

	Changing Weights	Fixed (1929) Weights	Unweighted Components[a]	Relative Movements: Ratio of Changing Weights to	
				Fixed Weights	Un- weighted
	(1 9 2 9	=	1 0 0)		
1869	18.7	19.3	23.2	0.969	0.806
1879	25.1	25.8	30.7	0.973	0.818
1889	37.4	38.3	43.6	0.977	0.858
1899	50.0	50.7	56.2	0.986	0.890
1909	67.9	68.5	72.5	0.991	0.937
1919	85.1	85.3	85.5	0.998	0.995
1929	100.0	100.0	100.0	1.000	1.000
1937	92.8	92.9	94.1	0.999	0.986
1948	118.4	118.3	109.9	1.001	1.077
1953	132.3	133.2	120.3	0.993	1.100
1957[p]	135.9	138.2	125.1	0.983	1.086

[p] = Preliminary.
[a] Indexes of unweighted manhours and unweighted real capital stock combined by relative shares in national income in 1929.

TABLE A-XVIII

Private Domestic Economy: Total Factor Productivity,
Effect of Alternative Product and Input Weights, Key Years, 1869–1957
(1929 = 100)

	Real Product			Real Input			Total Factor Productivity		
	Changing Weights (1)	Fixed Weights (2)	Ratio (1) ÷ (2) (3)	Changing Weights (4)	Fixed Weights (5)	Ratio (4) ÷ (5) (6)	Changing Weights (7)	Fixed Weights (8)	Ratio (7) ÷ (8) (9)
1869	7.7	8.2	0.939	19.9	20.4	0.975	38.7	40.2	0.963
1879	15.6	16.2	0.965	26.9	27.2	0.989	58.0	59.6	0.973
1889	22.3	23.6	0.946	39.8	40.5	0.983	56.0	58.3	0.961
1899	34.6	36.1	0.959	52.9	53.3	0.992	65.4	67.7	0.966
1909	52.1	54.2	0.961	71.0	71.3	0.996	73.4	76.0	0.966
1919	69.7	69.1	1.008	84.9	84.9	1.000	82.1	81.4	1.009
1929	100.0	100.0	1.000	100.0	100.0	1.000	100.0	100.0	1.000
1937	101.0	102.5	0.985	88.9	89.2	0.997	113.6	114.9	0.989
1948	163.8	163.8	1.000	112.3	112.3	1.000	145.9	145.9	1.000
1953	202.9	200.7	1.011	121.9	123.4	0.988	166.4	162.6	1.023
1957ᵖ	225.2	222.3	1.013	125.5	128.3	0.978	179.4	173.3	1.035

p = preliminary.

TABLE A-XIX

National Economy: Real Net Product, Inputs, and Productivity Ratios, Kuznets Concept, National Security Version, 1869–1957
(1929 = 100)

	Output (Real Net Product)	Persons Engaged	Output per Person Engaged	Man-hours	Output per Manhour	Labor Input	Output per Unit of Labor Input	Capital Input	Output per Unit of Capital Input	Total Factor Input	Total Factor Productivity	Addendum: Output (Real Gross Product)
1869–78[a]	10.3	28.2	36.5	30.8	33.4	24.9	41.4	13.9	74.1	21.2	48.6	10.1
1879–88[a]	19.2	38.7	49.6	42.5	45.2	35.9	53.5	21.3	90.1	31.0	61.9	18.9
1889	21.5	45.4	47.4	50.0	43.0	43.4	49.5	25.5	84.3	37.4	57.5	21.7
1890	23.3	46.9	49.7	51.8	45.0	45.0	51.8	26.6	87.6	38.8	60.1	23.4
1891	24.4	48.1	50.7	53.1	46.0	46.3	52.7	28.1	86.8	40.2	60.7	24.6
1892	26.8	49.5	54.1	54.8	48.9	48.2	55.6	29.9	89.6	42.1	63.7	26.9
1893	25.1	49.4	50.8	54.3	46.2	47.4	53.0	31.4	79.9	42.2	59.5	25.5
1894	24.0	48.4	49.6	52.4	45.8	45.1	53.2	32.4	74.1	41.0	58.5	24.6
1895	27.6	50.8	54.3	55.6	49.6	48.6	56.8	33.7	81.9	43.8	63.0	27.9
1896	26.8	51.1	52.4	55.6	48.2	48.6	55.1	35.0	76.6	44.2	60.6	27.2
1897	29.7	52.6	56.5	57.3	51.8	50.4	58.9	36.1	82.3	45.8	64.8	30.0
1898	30.3	53.3	56.8	57.9	52.3	50.9	59.5	37.4	81.0	46.6	65.0	30.7
1899	33.5	56.4	59.4	62.0	54.0	55.4	60.5	38.7	86.6	50.0	67.0	33.7
1900	34.4	57.3	60.0	62.7	54.9	56.2	61.2	40.4	85.1	51.1	67.3	34.6
1901	38.8	59.7	65.0	65.5	59.2	59.3	65.4	41.8	92.8	53.6	72.4	38.7
1902	38.9	62.3	62.4	68.2	57.0	62.7	62.0	43.6	89.2	56.4	69.0	38.9
1903	41.0	64.1	64.0	70.2	58.4	64.9	63.2	45.4	90.3	58.6	70.0	40.9
1904	40.2	63.9	62.9	69.3	58.0	63.4	63.4	47.0	85.5	58.2	69.1	40.3
1905	43.2	66.8	64.7	72.7	59.4	67.4	64.1	48.4	89.?	61.3	70.5	43.2
1906	48.8	69.5	70.2	75.5	64.6	70.7	69.0	50.4	96.8	64.2	76.0	48.4
1907	49.4	71.1	69.5	77.3	63.9	72.6	68.0	52.6	93.9	66.2	74.6	49.2
1908	43.9	69.5	63.2	74.1	59.2	68.8	63.8	54.5	80.6	64.5	68.1	44.6
1909	50.8	73.1	69.5	78.2	65.0	73.5	69.1	55.7	91.2	67.9	74.8	50.9

(continued)

TABLE A-XIX (continued)

1910	51.1	75.0	68.1	80.3	63.6	76.0	67.2	57.6	88.7	70.2	72.8	51.4
1911	52.3	76.2	68.6	81.9	63.9	77.6	67.4	59.5	87.9	71.9	72.7	52.7
1912	55.2	78.4	70.4	84.5	65.3	80.7	68.4	61.2	90.2	74.6	74.0	55.6
1913	57.9	79.6	72.7	85.1	68.0	81.8	70.8	63.2	91.6	76.0	76.2	58.2
1914	52.2	78.7	66.3	83.7	62.4	79.6	65.6	65.3	79.9	75.3	69.3	53.3
1915	54.0	79.1	68.3	83.1	65.0	79.4	68.0	67.6	79.9	75.9	71.1	55.1
1916	63.9	84.3	75.8	89.0	71.8	86.9	73.5	70.4	90.8	81.8	78.1	64.2
1917	63.3	87.2	72.6	92.0	68.8	90.7	69.8	73.2	86.5	85.3	74.2	64.0
1918	71.7	92.4	77.6	95.5	75.1	95.3	75.2	75.0	95.6	89.0	80.6	72.0
1919	73.8	88.9	83.0	89.7	82.3	88.7	83.2	76.7	96.2	85.1	86.7	74.4
1920	70.6	87.2	81.0	89.1	79.2	87.7	80.5	78.5	89.9	85.0	83.1	71.4
1921	66.6	82.7	80.5	80.5	82.7	78.0	85.4	80.2	83.0	78.7	84.6	67.4
1922	71.1	86.9	81.8	86.2	82.5	84.3	84.3	81.6	87.1	83.5	85.1	71.9
1923	81.9	92.3	88.7	92.9	88.2	92.3	88.7	83.6	98.0	89.7	91.3	81.8
1924	83.3	91.0	91.5	91.0	91.5	89.7	92.9	86.1	96.7	88.6	94.0	83.1
1925	86.3	93.5	92.3	94.3	91.5	93.3	92.5	88.5	97.5	91.9	93.9	86.2
1926	91.8	96.2	95.4	97.5	94.2	97.1	94.5	91.6	100.2	95.5	96.1	91.8
1927	92.7	96.4	96.2	97.1	95.5	97.2	95.4	94.5	98.1	96.4	96.2	92.7
1928	93.8	97.4	96.3	98.1	95.6	97.8	95.9	97.2	96.5	97.6	96.1	94.1
1929	100.0	100.0	100.0	100.0	100.0	100.0	100.0	100.0	100.0	100.0	100.0	100.0
1930	89.6	95.5	93.8	93.6	95.7	92.7	96.7	102.5	87.4	95.1	94.2	90.6
1931	80.7	89.5	90.2	86.2	93.6	83.7	96.4	103.2	78.2	88.5	91.2	82.4
1932	66.9	82.5	81.1	76.8	87.1	73.3	91.3	101.4	66.0	80.2	83.4	69.8
1933	65.3	83.2	78.5	76.9	84.9	73.5	88.8	98.4	66.4	79.7	81.9	68.2
1934	73.3	89.8	81.6	77.0	95.2	75.2	97.5	95.8	76.5	80.3	91.3	75.5
1935	82.2	92.9	88.5	81.2	101.2	79.8	103.0	94.5	87.0	83.4	98.6	83.2
1936	95.1	98.9	96.2	88.8	107.1	88.5	107.5	94.2	101.0	89.9	105.8	95.3
1937	101.4	101.3	100.1	92.6	109.5	92.0	110.2	95.3	106.4	92.8	109.3	100.9
1938	94.6	97.4	97.1	86.2	109.7	84.9	111.4	95.9	98.6	87.4	108.2	95.0
1939	102.9	100.3	102.6	90.2	114.1	89.7	114.7	95.8	107.4	91.1	113.0	102.7

(continued)

TABLE A-XIX (concluded)

National Economy: Real Net Product, Inputs, and Productivity Ratios, Kuznets Concept, National Security Version, 1869–1957
(1929 = 100)

	Output (Real Net Product)	Persons Engaged	Output per Person Engaged	Man-hours	Output per Manhour	Labor Input	Output per Unit of Labor Input	Capital Input	Output per Unit of Capital Input	Total Factor Input	Total Factor Productivity	Addendum: Output (Real Gross Product)
1940	110.1	104.2	105.7	93.9	117.3	94.4	116.6	97.2	113.3	95.0	115.9	109.1
1941	134.8	113.6	118.7	103.2	130.6	107.6	125.3	100.5	134.1	106.0	127.2	132.6
1942	152.6	124.0	123.1	114.9	132.8	123.7	123.4	103.2	147.9	119.0	128.2	149.9
1943	171.5	136.2	125.9	129.9	132.0	145.2	118.1	103.3	166.0	135.6	126.5	167.8
1944	183.1	138.7	132.0	133.0	137.7	149.6	122.4	102.1	179.3	138.8	131.9	179.2
1945	181.0	135.2	133.9	124.7	145.1	139.6	129.7	100.5	180.1	130.7	138.5	177.6
1946	163.3	123.7	132.0	109.3	149.4	119.2	137.0	102.6	159.2	115.4	141.5	160.1
1947	160.2	124.5	128.7	108.3	147.9	118.2	135.5	108.9	147.1	116.1	138.0	159.4
1948	163.6	126.5	129.3	108.9	150.2	119.3	137.1	115.6	141.5	118.4	138.2	163.7
1949	161.0	123.3	130.6	105.0	153.3	114.8	140.2	120.5	133.6	115.9	138.9	162.5
1950	178.6	127.1	140.5	107.1	166.8	118.1	151.2	125.0	142.9	119.4	149.6	179.0
1951	191.1	134.8	141.8	112.9	169.3	126.0	151.7	131.0	145.9	126.9	150.6	191.5
1952	198.9	137.1	145.1	114.6	173.6	128.7	154.5	135.3	147.0	130.0	153.0	197.9
1953	205.7	139.1	147.9	115.1	178.7	129.9	158.4	141.6	145.3	132.3	155.5	205.1
1954p	202.3	135.1	149.7	110.7	182.7	124.4	162.6	145.5	139.0	128.7	157.2	203.0
1955p	216.9	138.2	156.9	114.4	189.6	128.5	168.8	149.8	144.8	132.9	163.2	217.0
1956p	221.8	140.8	157.5	116.1	191.0	130.6	169.8	155.1	143.0	135.6	163.6	222.4
1957p	224.3	141.3	158.7	114.9	195.2	129.4	173.3	160.4	139.8	135.9	165.0	225.5

p = preliminary.
a Annual average for decade.

TABLE A-XX

National Economy: Real Net Product and Productivity Ratios,
Kuznets Concept, Peacetime Version, Key Years, 1869–1957
(1929 = 100)

	Output (Real Net Product)[a]	Output per Unit of Labor Input	Output per Unit of Capital Input	Total Factor Productivity	Addendum: Output (Real Gross Product)[a]
1869	7.7	34.2	66.0	41.0	7.5
1879	15.5	53.3	89.1	61.8	15.2
1889	21.6	49.8	84.7	57.8	21.7
1899	33.3	60.1	86.0	66.6	33.5
1909	50.7	69.0	91.0	74.7	50.8
1919	68.7	77.5	89.6	80.7	69.8
1929	100.0	100.0	100.0	100.0	100.0
1937	101.3	110.1	106.3	109.2	100.9
1948	155.6	130.4	134.6	131.4	156.5
1953	182.4	140.4	128.8	137.9	184.3
1957[p]	206.7	159.7	128.9	152.1	209.8

p = preliminary.

[a] This is the series presented by Simon Kuznets, except that no allowance has been made for depreciation of munitions; and an adjustment has been applied to make output indexes comparable with the weighting scheme used in computing input indexes.

TABLE A-XXI

National Economy: Real Net Product and Productivity Ratios, Commerce Concept, Key Years, 1869–1957

(1929 = 100)

	OUTPUT, REAL NET PRODUCT	OUTPUT PER UNIT OF LABOR INPUT	OUTPUT PER UNIT OF CAPITAL INPUT	FACTOR PRODUCTIVITY	Ratio of Gross to Net Product	ADDENDUM Ratios of Domestic to National Economy Indexes			
						Net Product	Capital Input	Total Input	Factor Productivity (Net Product)
1869	7.8	35.0	67.7	42.0	98.1	102.3	114.7	103.7	98.6
1879	15.7	54.0	90.2	62.5	98.1	101.3	114.4	104.0	97.4
1889	21.8	50.2	85.5	58.3	101.4	101.8	113.3	103.5	98.5
1899	33.9	61.2	87.6	67.8	100.9	101.5	111.4	103.0	98.5
1909	51.3	69.8	92.1	75.6	100.6	101.0	108.6	102.5	98.4
1919	70.3	79.3	91.7	82.6	101.4	100.0	103.3	101.1	98.9
1929	100.0	100.0	100.0	100.0	100.0	100.0	100.0	100.0	100.0
1937	104.4	113.5	109.5	112.5	98.9	100.6	102.0	100.4	100.2
1948	167.0	140.0	144.5	141.0	99.5	100.4	101.5	100.4	100.0
1953	209.9	161.6	148.2	158.7	99.3	100.4	101.6	100.4	100.0
1957ᴾ	230.1	177.8	143.5	169.3	99.9	100.3	101.7	100.3	100.0

ᴾ = preliminary.

TABLE A-XXII

Private Domestic Economy: Real Gross Product, Inputs, and Productivity Ratios, Commerce Concept, 1869–1957
(1929 = 100)

	Output (Real Gross Product)	Persons Engaged	Output per Person Engaged	Man-hours	Output per Manhour	Labor Input	Output per Unit of Labor Input	Capital Input	Output per Unit of Capital Input	Total Input	Total Factor Productivity	Addendum: Output (Real Net Product)
1869–78[a]	10.4	28.9	36.0	31.5	33.0	25.6	40.6	16.6	62.7	22.6	46.0	10.6
1879–88[a]	19.5	39.7	49.1	43.5	44.8	36.8	53.0	24.8	78.6	33.0	59.1	19.7
1889	22.3	46.6	47.9	51.1	43.6	44.6	50.0	29.8	74.8	39.8	56.0	22.1
1890	24.2	48.1	50.3	53.0	45.7	46.2	52.4	31.1	77.8	41.3	58.6	24.0
1891	25.3	49.4	51.3	54.3	46.6	47.6	53.2	32.8	77.1	42.8	59.1	25.1
1892	27.7	50.8	54.5	56.1	49.4	49.5	56.0	34.8	79.6	44.8	61.8	27.6
1893	26.3	50.6	52.0	55.5	47.4	48.6	54.1	36.6	71.9	44.8	58.7	25.8
1894	25.5	49.5	51.5	53.5	47.7	46.1	55.3	37.7	67.6	43.6	58.5	24.9
1895	28.8	52.1	55.3	56.8	50.7	49.9	57.7	39.2	73.5	46.7	61.7	28.5
1896	28.1	52.4	53.6	56.8	49.5	49.9	56.3	40.6	69.2	47.2	59.5	27.6
1897	31.0	53.9	57.5	58.6	52.9	51.7	60.0	41.7	74.3	48.7	63.7	30.6
1898	31.6	54.4	58.1	58.9	53.7	51.9	60.9	43.1	73.3	49.3	64.1	31.2
1899	34.6	57.7	60.0	63.2	54.7	56.7	61.0	44.4	77.9	52.9	65.4	34.4
1900	35.5	58.6	60.6	63.9	55.6	57.5	61.7	46.1	77.0	54.0	65.7	35.2
1901	39.6	61.0	64.9	66.7	59.4	60.7	65.2	47.6	83.2	56.7	69.8	39.6
1902	39.8	63.7	62.5	69.6	57.2	64.3	61.9	49.3	80.7	59.7	66.7	39.7
1903	41.9	65.6	63.9	71.6	58.5	66.6	62.9	51.3	81.7	61.9	67.7	41.8
1904	41.2	65.3	63.1	70.6	58.4	64.9	63.5	52.8	78.0	61.3	67.2	40.9
1905	44.3	68.4	64.8	74.0	59.9	69.0	64.2	54.2	81.7	64.4	68.8	44.2
1906	49.6	71.1	69.8	77.0	64.4	72.4	68.5	56.3	88.1	67.5	73.5	49.7
1907	50.5	72.7	69.5	78.7	64.2	74.3	68.0	58.6	86.2	69.5	72.7	50.5
1908	46.0	70.8	65.0	75.3	61.1	70.1	65.6	60.4	76.2	67.4	68.2	45.3
1909	52.1	74.5	69.9	79.4	65.6	74.9	69.6	61.8	84.3	71.0	73.4	51.8

(continued)

TABLE A-XXII (continued)

Private Domestic Economy: Real Gross Product, Inputs, and Productivity Ratios, Commerce Concept, 1869–1957
(1929 = 100)

	Output (Real Gross Product)	Persons Engaged	Output per Person Engaged	Man-hours	Output per Manhour	Labor Input	Output per Unit of Labor Input	Capital Input	Output per Unit of Capital Input	Total Input	Total Factor Productivity	Addendum: Output (Real Net Product)
1910	52.5	76.4	68.7	81.5	64.4	77.5	67.7	63.7	82.4	73.3	71.6	52.1
1911	54.5	77.5	70.3	83.0	65.7	79.0	69.0	65.7	83.0	75.0	72.7	54.0
1912	57.3	79.8	71.8	85.6	66.9	82.2	69.7	67.3	85.1	77.7	73.7	56.9
1913	59.7	80.9	73.8	86.3	69.2	83.2	71.8	69.4	86.0	79.0	75.6	59.2
1914	54.8	79.8	68.7	84.7	64.7	80.7	67.9	71.5	76.6	78.0	70.3	53.7
1915	56.4	80.1	70.4	83.9	67.2	80.4	70.2	73.2	77.0	78.3	72.0	55.3
1916	65.1	85.5	76.1	90.0	72.3	88.3	73.7	74.4	87.5	84.1	77.4	64.7
1917	63.0	87.0	72.4	91.9	68.6	90.7	69.5	76.3	82.6	86.3	73.0	62.0
1918	67.5	86.8	77.8	91.1	74.1	90.0	75.0	78.4	86.1	86.5	78.0	66.5
1919	69.7	87.0	80.1	88.2	79.0	86.7	80.4	80.3	86.8	84.9	82.1	68.5
1920	70.0	87.4	80.1	89.4	78.3	87.9	79.6	82.0	85.4	86.2	81.2	69.0
1921	67.5	82.7	81.6	80.5	83.8	77.8	86.8	83.2	81.1	79.3	85.1	66.8
1922	71.8	87.2	82.3	86.5	83.0	84.6	84.9	83.8	85.7	84.4	85.1	71.0
1923	82.0	92.9	88.3	93.4	87.8	93.0	88.2	85.5	95.9	90.9	90.2	82.0
1924	83.6	91.3	91.6	91.2	91.7	90.0	92.9	87.7	95.3	89.3	93.6	83.7
1925	86.6	93.7	92.4	94.5	91.6	93.6	92.5	89.8	96.4	92.5	93.6	86.6
1926	92.0	96.4	95.4	97.8	94.1	97.5	94.4	92.7	99.2	96.1	95.7	92.0
1927	93.0	96.5	96.4	97.2	95.7	97.3	95.6	95.4	97.5	96.8	96.1	93.0
1928	93.9	97.4	96.4	98.1	95.7	97.9	95.9	97.7	96.1	97.8	96.0	93.6
1929	100.0	100.0	100.0	100.0	100.0	100.0	100.0	100.0	100.0	100.0	100.0	100.0

(continued)

TABLE A-XXII (concluded)

Year												
1930	90.8	94.9	95.7	93.1	97.5	91.9	98.8	102.0	89.0	94.3	96.3	90.0
1931	84.0	88.4	95.0	85.4	98.4	82.3	102.1	102.1	82.3	87.1	96.4	83.0
1932	71.8	81.0	88.6	75.6	95.0	71.2	100.8	99.9	71.9	78.1	91.9	70.0
1933	70.0	80.6	86.8	74.9	93.5	70.5	99.3	96.5	72.5	76.7	91.3	68.2
1934	76.9	85.7	89.7	73.6	104.5	70.8	108.6	93.8	82.0	76.3	100.8	75.8
1935	83.8	88.4	94.8	77.6	108.0	74.9	111.9	92.5	90.6	79.1	105.9	83.6
1936	94.5	92.3	102.4	83.4	113.3	82.6	114.4	92.5	102.2	85.0	111.2	94.8
1937	101.0	96.3	104.9	88.6	114.0	87.4	115.6	93.8	107.7	88.9	113.6	101.9
1938	95.4	90.8	105.1	81.0	117.8	79.3	120.3	94.6	100.8	82.8	115.2	95.6
1939	104.1	94.0	110.7	85.2	122.2	84.2	123.6	94.3	110.4	86.6	120.2	105.0
1940	110.2	97.9	112.6	88.9	124.0	88.6	124.4	95.9	114.9	90.3	122.0	111.8
1941	130.4	105.6	123.5	96.9	134.6	99.3	131.3	99.0	131.7	99.3	131.3	132.7
1942	142.6	111.3	128.1	104.4	136.6	108.6	131.3	101.7	140.2	107.1	133.1	144.9
1943	153.1	113.0	135.5	108.2	141.5	114.2	134.1	101.8	150.4	111.5	137.3	155.6
1944	162.8	110.4	147.5	106.7	152.6	112.7	144.5	100.9	161.3	110.1	147.9	165.3
1945	160.4	107.0	149.9	100.9	159.0	106.3	150.9	99.8	160.7	104.9	152.9	162.4
1946	153.5	113.3	135.5	101.7	150.9	107.3	143.1	102.1	150.3	106.2	144.5	156.6
1947	157.4	118.6	132.7	103.9	151.5	110.6	142.3	107.3	146.7	110.0	143.1	158.8
1948	163.8	120.8	135.6	104.5	156.7	111.9	146.4	113.3	144.6	112.3	145.9	164.5
1949	162.9	116.7	139.6	100.1	162.7	106.6	152.8	118.1	137.9	109.1	149.3	162.4
1950	178.7	120.2	148.7	101.9	175.4	109.8	162.8	122.8	145.5	112.6	158.7	179.0
1951	188.5	124.3	151.6	105.1	179.4	114.4	164.8	129.1	146.0	117.5	160.4	188.5
1952	194.0	125.1	155.1	105.7	183.5	115.7	167.7	133.2	145.6	119.4	162.5	195.2
1953	202.9	127.3	159.4	106.3	190.9	117.2	173.1	139.6	145.3	121.9	166.4	203.9
1954p	199.5	123.6	161.4	102.1	195.4	111.8	178.4	143.6	138.9	118.5	168.4	199.3
1955p	217.3	127.0	171.1	106.1	204.8	116.3	186.8	148.0	146.8	122.9	176.8	217.5
1956p	222.6	129.5	171.9	107.8	206.5	118.4	188.0	153.4	145.1	125.7	177.1	222.4
1957p	225.2	129.8	173.5	106.4	211.7	116.9	192.6	158.2	142.4	125.5	179.4	224.4

a Annual average for decade.

p = preliminary.

TABLE A-XXII: Supplement

Private Domestic Economy: Productivity Ratios Based on Unweighted Inputs, 1869–1957

(1929 = 100)

	Unweighted Capital Input (measured in 1929 prices)	Output per Unit of Unweighted Capital Input	Total Input (weighted average of manhours and un-weighted capital)	Output per Unit of Total Input (weighted average of manhours and un-weighted capital)
1869–78[a]	16.3	63.8	26.5	39.2
1879–88[a]	24.8	78.6	37.4	52.1
1889	30.7	72.6	44.5	50.1
1890	32.2	75.2	46.3	52.3
1891	34.0	74.4	47.8	52.9
1892	36.0	76.9	49.6	55.8
1893	37.8	69.6	49.9	52.7
1894	39.1	65.2	49.0	52.0
1895	40.6	70.9	51.8	55.6
1896	42.1	66.7	52.3	53.7
1897	43.4	71.4	53.9	57.5
1898	44.8	70.5	54.6	57.9
1899	46.2	74.9	57.9	59.8
1900	47.7	74.4	58.9	60.3
1901	49.1	80.7	61.3	64.6
1902	50.6	78.7	63.7	62.5
1903	52.4	80.0	65.6	63.9
1904	53.7	76.7	65.4	63.0
1905	55.2	80.3	68.2	65.0
1906	57.4	86.4	71.0	69.9
1907	59.5	84.9	72.8	69.4
1908	61.2	75.2	71.2	64.6
1909	62.6	83.2	74.4	70.0
1910	64.4	81.5	76.4	68.7
1911	66.1	82.5	77.9	70.0
1912	67.5	84.9	80.2	71.4
1913	69.2	86.3	81.2	73.5
1914	71.0	77.2	80.7	67.9
1915	72.5	77.8	80.6	70.0
1916	73.6	88.5	85.1	76.5
1917	75.0	84.0	86.8	72.6
1918	76.3	88.5	86.7	77.9
1919	77.5	89.9	85.1	81.9
1920	78.9	88.7	86.4	81.0
1921	79.8	84.6	80.3	84.1
1922	80.8	88.9	84.9	84.6
1923	82.9	98.9	90.4	90.7
1924	85.5	97.8	89.6	93.3

(continued)

Table A-XXII: Supplement (concluded)

	Unweighted Capital Input (measured in 1929 Prices)	Output per Unit of Unweighted Capital Input	Total Input (weighted average of manhours and unweighted capital)	Output per Unit Total of Input (weighted average of manhours and unweighted capital)
1925	88.2	98.2	92.7	93.4
1926	91.6	100.4	96.0	95.8
1927	94.6	98.3	96.5	96.4
1928	97.5	96.3	97.9	95.9
1929	100.0	100.0	100.0	100.0
1930	101.7	89.3	95.2	95.4
1931	101.9	82.4	89.4	94.0
1932	100.3	71.6	81.5	88.1
1933	97.6	71.7	80.3	87.2
1934	95.2	80.8	78.8	97.6
1935	94.2	89.0	81.6	102.7
1936	94.1	100.4	86.0	109.9
1937	95.3	106.0	90.2	112.0
1938	95.9	99.5	84.4	113.0
1939	96.0	108.4	87.7	118.7
1940	97.3	113.3	90.9	121.2
1941	99.7	130.8	97.6	133.6
1942	101.6	140.4	103.9	137.2
1943	101.6	150.7	106.8	143.4
1944	100.7	161.7	105.5	154.3
1945	99.7	160.9	100.7	159.3
1946	100.9	152.1	101.6	151.1
1947	104.0	151.3	104.0	151.3
1948	108.0	151.7	105.4	155.4
1949	112.2	145.2	102.8	158.5
1950	116.3	153.7	105.0	170.2
1951	121.5	155.1	108.6	173.6
1952	125.8	154.2	110.0	176.4
1953	129.6	156.6	111.3	182.3
1954p	133.0	150.0	108.6	183.7
1955p	137.1	158.5	112.6	193.0
1956p	142.1	156.7	115.0	193.6
1957p	146.5	153.7	114.8	196.2

a Annual average for decade.

p = preliminary.

TABLE A-XXIII

Private Domestic Nonfarm Economy: Real Gross Product, Inputs, and Productivity Ratios, Commerce Concept, 1869–1957
(1929 = 100)

	Output (Real Gross Product)	Persons Engaged	Output per Person	Manhours	Output per Manhour	Labor Input	Output per Unit of Labor Input	Capital Input	Output per Unit of Capital Input	Total Factor Input	Total Factor Productivity
1869–78[a]	6.8	18.5	36.8	23.3	29.2	21.5	31.6	9.6	70.8	17.5	38.9
1879–88[a]	15.1	27.5	54.9	34.2	44.2	32.2	46.9	16.2	93.2	26.9	56.1
1889	17.3	34.3	50.4	42.1	41.1	39.6	43.7	20.9	82.8	33.5	51.6
1890	19.5	35.9	54.3	44.2	44.1	41.8	46.7	22.2	87.8	35.3	55.2
1891	20.5	37.3	55.0	45.7	44.9	43.2	47.5	24.0	85.4	37.0	55.4
1892	23.6	38.9	60.7	47.8	49.4	45.3	52.1	26.2	90.1	39.1	60.4
1893	22.1	38.4	57.6	46.8	47.2	44.2	50.0	28.3	78.1	39.2	56.4
1894	21.0	36.7	57.2	44.0	47.7	41.3	50.8	29.5	71.2	37.8	55.6
1895	24.3	39.8	61.1	48.0	50.6	45.4	53.5	31.0	78.4	41.0	59.3
1896	22.9	39.9	57.4	47.8	47.9	45.3	50.6	32.4	70.7	41.5	55.2
1897	25.5	41.6	61.3	49.8	51.2	47.3	53.9	33.4	76.3	43.1	59.2
1898	25.8	41.9	61.6	50.0	51.6	47.4	54.4	34.7	74.4	43.7	59.0
1899	29.2	46.0	63.5	55.3	52.8	52.7	55.4	36.0	81.1	47.6	61.3
1900	30.0	46.9	64.0	56.0	53.6	53.5	56.1	37.8	79.4	48.8	61.5
1901	34.8	49.9	69.7	59.5	58.5	57.0	61.1	39.5	88.1	51.7	67.3
1902	35.1	53.1	66.1	63.0	55.7	60.9	57.6	41.2	85.2	54.8	64.1
1903	37.1	55.4	67.0	65.5	56.6	63.4	58.5	43.3	85.7	57.2	64.9
1904	36.1	54.8	65.9	63.9	56.5	61.5	58.7	44.9	80.4	56.6	63.8
1905	39.4	58.6	67.2	68.2	57.8	66.0	59.7	46.3	85.1	60.0	65.7
1906	44.7	61.9	72.2	71.8	62.3	69.7	64.1	48.6	92.0	63.3	70.6
1907	46.3	63.8	72.6	73.8	62.7	71.8	64.5	51.3	90.3	65.7	70.5
1908	41.1	61.2	67.2	69.3	59.3	67.0	61.3	53.3	77.1	63.3	64.9

(continued)

Year											
1909	48.1	65.7	73.2	74.4	64.7	72.3	66.5	54.7	87.9	67.3	71.5
1910	48.2	68.0	70.9	76.9	62.7	75.1	64.2	56.7	85.0	70.0	68.9
1911	51.1	69.5	73.5	78.4	65.2	76.6	66.7	58.7	87.1	71.6	71.4
1912	52.4	72.4	72.4	81.4	64.4	80.0	65.5	60.5	86.6	74.6	70.2
1913	56.6	73.8	76.7	82.5	68.6	81.3	69.6	62.9	90.0	76.2	74.3
1914	49.9	72.4	68.9	79.6	62.7	78.1	63.9	65.3	76.4	74.6	66.9
1915	51.0	72.7	70.2	79.2	64.4	78.0	65.4	66.8	76.3	75.0	68.0
1916	62.2	79.5	78.2	87.2	71.3	86.9	71.6	68.3	91.1	81.7	76.1
1917	58.6	81.6	71.8	88.8	66.0	89.3	65.6	70.4	83.2	84.0	69.8
1918	64.8	81.8	79.2	87.5	74.1	88.4	73.3	72.7	89.1	84.1	77.1
1919	67.2	82.2	81.8	84.3	79.7	84.9	79.2	74.9	89.7	82.3	81.7
1920	67.7	82.4	82.2	85.3	79.4	86.0	78.7	77.1	87.8	83.7	80.9
1921	65.6	76.4	85.9	76.2	86.1	75.7	86.7	78.9	83.1	76.5	85.8
1922	69.7	82.4	84.6	83.0	84.0	82.9	84.1	79.9	87.2	82.1	84.9
1923	80.4	90.0	89.3	91.6	87.8	92.2	87.2	82.3	97.7	89.6	89.7
1924	82.7	88.2	93.8	88.5	93.4	88.7	93.2	85.2	97.1	87.8	94.2
1925	85.3	91.4	93.3	92.1	92.6	92.5	92.2	87.8	97.2	91.3	93.4
1926	91.5	95.0	96.3	96.3	95.0	96.8	94.5	91.3	100.2	95.4	95.9
1927	92.2	95.8	96.2	96.7	95.3	97.1	95.0	94.6	97.5	96.4	95.6
1928	93.5	96.9	96.5	97.3	96.1	97.5	95.9	97.2	96.2	97.4	96.0
1929	100.0	100.0	100.0	100.0	100.0	100.0	100.0	100.0	100.0	100.0	100.0
1930	90.5	94.1	96.2	91.5	98.9	91.3	99.1	102.5	88.3	93.8	96.5
1931	81.5	85.1	95.8	80.9	100.7	80.6	101.1	102.5	79.5	85.5	95.3
1932	68.5	75.5	90.7	69.4	98.7	68.9	99.4	99.7	68.7	75.7	90.5
1933	66.0	75.2	87.8	68.5	96.4	68.2	96.8	96.0	68.8	74.4	88.7
1934	75.6	82.0	92.2	69.7	108.5	69.4	108.9	93.3	81.0	74.7	101.2
1935	82.2	85.2	96.5	73.8	111.4	73.5	111.8	91.9	89.4	77.6	105.9
1936	94.9	91.1	104.2	82.1	115.6	82.1	115.6	92.0	103.2	84.3	112.6
1937	100.9	97.0	104.0	86.7	116.4	86.7	116.4	93.4	108.0	88.2	114.4
1938	94.1	90.7	103.7	78.8	119.4	78.3	120.2	94.2	99.9	81.8	115.0

(continued)

TABLE A-XXIII (concluded)

Private Domestic Nonfarm Economy: Real Gross Product, Inputs, and Productivity Ratios, Commerce Concept, 1869–1957

(1929 = 100)

	Output (Real Gross Product)	Persons Engaged	Output per Person	Manhours	Output per Manhour	Labor Input	Output per Unit of Labor Input	Capital Input	Output per Unit of Capital Input	Total Factor Input	Total Factor Productivity
1939	103.8	95.4	108.8	84.0	123.6	83.9	123.7	93.8	110.7	86.9	119.4
1940	110.8	101.2	109.5	89.1	124.4	89.1	124.4	95.2	116.4	90.5	122.4
1941	132.3	111.8	118.3	99.8	132.6	101.5	130.3	98.4	134.5	100.2	132.0
1942	145.0	119.4	121.4	108.5	133.6	111.6	129.9	101.1	143.4	109.4	132.5
1943	157.4	121.7	129.3	113.6	138.6	118.2	133.2	100.9	156.0	104.6	150.5
1944	168.2	119.0	141.3	111.9	150.3	116.6	144.3	99.8	168.5	113.1	148.7
1945	166.1	115.1	144.3	106.1	156.6	110.0	151.0	98.7	168.3	107.7	154.2
1946	158.0	122.5	129.0	108.1	146.2	111.6	141.6	101.4	155.8	109.5	144.3
1947	163.0	129.1	126.3	111.9	145.7	115.9	140.6	107.8	151.2	114.3	142.6
1948	169.2	131.9	128.3	113.2	149.5	117.6	143.9	114.6	147.6	117.1	144.5
1949	168.3	127.5	132.0	108.2	155.5	111.9	150.4	119.6	140.7	113.6	148.2
1950	185.8	132.1	140.7	112.2	165.6	116.3	159.8	124.6	149.1	118.1	157.3
1951	197.6	138.2	143.0	117.1	168.7	122.1	161.8	131.4	150.4	124.4	158.8
1952	203.8	140.1	145.5	118.7	171.7	124.0	164.4	135.9	150.0	126.6	161.0
1953	212.8	143.6	148.2	120.7	176.3	126.3	168.5	143.3	148.5	129.9	163.8
1954p	208.3	139.3	149.5	115.8	179.9	120.3	173.2	147.9	140.8	126.2	165.1
1955p	227.0	144.3	157.3	120.6	188.2	125.3	181.2	153.0	148.4	131.1	173.2
1956p	232.8	148.7	156.6	123.4	188.7	128.0	181.9	159.6	145.9	134.6	173.0
1957p	236.2	149.6	157.9	122.8	192.3	126.9	186.1	165.5	142.7	135.0	175.0

a Annual average for decade.

p = preliminary.

TABLE A-XXIV

Private Domestic Economy, Aggregate of Industry Segments Covered by Output Data:
Output, Inputs, and Productivity Ratios, Key Years, 1869–1953
(1929 = 100)

	Output	Persons Engaged	Output per Person	Manhours	Output per Manhour	Labor Input	Output per Unit of Labor Input
1869	10.9	27.7	39.4	29.4	37.1	24.5	44.5
1879	17.5	36.8	47.6	38.6	45.3	32.2	54.3
1889	26.7	49.8	53.6	53.2	50.2	47.3	56.4
1899	38.1	61.0	62.5	65.3	58.3	59.4	64.1
1909	54.1	77.8	69.5	81.2	66.6	77.9	69.4
1919	68.6	91.7	74.8	92.6	74.1	91.1	75.3
1929	100.0	100.0	100.0	100.0	100.0	100.0	100.0
1937	101.0	95.7	105.5	87.8	115.0	85.4	118.3
1948	169.8	121.7	139.5	107.1	158.5	113.5	149.6
1953	204.0	126.7	161.0	110.3	185.0	119.6	170.6

NOTE: Aggregate indexes are exclusive of finance and services throughout.

TABLE A-XXV

Private Domestic Economy, Aggregate of Industry Segments Covered by Capital Data: Output, Inputs, and Productivity Ratios, Key Years, 1869–1953

(1929 = 100)

	Output	Persons Engaged	Output per Person	Manhours	Output per Manhour	Labor Input	Output per Unit of Labor Input	Capital Input	Output per Unit of Capital Input	Total Factor Input	Total Factor Productivity
1869	12.1	33.6	36.0	35.3	34.3	28.4	42.6	18.2	66.5	25.4	47.6
1879	18.7	45.0	41.6	46.8	40.0	37.9	49.3	27.2	68.8	34.8	53.7
1889	28.2	58.6	48.1	61.8	45.6	53.1	53.1	38.0	74.1	48.7	57.9
1899	39.8	70.0	56.9	73.7	54.0	65.8	60.5	50.0	79.6	61.2	65.0
1909	54.6	86.9	62.8	91.3	59.8	87.9	62.1	69.5	78.6	82.5	66.2
1919	70.7	101.5	69.7	103.3	68.4	103.9	68.0	93.2	75.9	100.8	70.1
1929	100.0	100.0	100.0	100.0	100.0	100.0	100.0	100.0	100.0	100.0	100.0
1937	103.6	96.9	106.9	89.1	116.3	87.1	118.9	88.9	116.5	87.5	118.4
1948	171.9	119.9	143.4	105.3	163.2	111.7	153.9	117.4	146.4	113.0	152.1
1953	204.9	123.8	165.5	107.6	190.4	116.9	175.3	143.2	143.1	122.3	167.5

NOTE: Aggregate indexes are exclusive of trade prior to 1929 and of construction, finance and services, agricultural services, forestry, fisheries, and government enterprises throughout.

APPENDIX B

Agriculture, Forestry, and Fisheries

IT IS convenient to treat this segment in terms of two major groupings: farming and all other groups combined. Farming is by far the most important of these. It accounted for 98 per cent of national income originating in the segment in 1929 (more in earlier years), and 94 per cent in 1957. Farming occupies such a distinctive position in the economy—both because of its processes and products and because of the rural location of the resources engaged—that it is often treated as a "sector" in the national accounts. Unusually complete historical data are available, particularly for the period since 1910, making possible estimates of capital as well as of labor inputs, and of net as well as of gross output.

The remaining three groups (agricultural services, forestry, and fisheries) are combined, primarily for the purpose of presenting estimates of employment and manhours worked. Capital estimates are not available. Adequate output measures are lacking, although it is possible to construct a crude series of fisheries output (shown in the final section of this appendix). In the case of agricultural services it can be argued that the product is included in gross farm output.

Farm Output

There is a greater choice of indexes of the physical volume of output in farming than in other segments of the economy. In this study we use basically two measures: one relating to gross output and the other to net output (real value added). These are both parts of the Commerce Department constant-dollar national product estimates;[1] as such they are based primarily on information supplied by the Department of Agriculture. These estimates are available only for the period since 1910, but it has been possible to extend them to 1869 on the basis of estimates by Strauss and Bean.[2] The gross output index is comparable in concept and in movement with the Agriculture Department index of farm output, and we use the latter for output per manhour comparisons by major types of

[1] See *Survey of Current Business*, Dept. of Commerce: "Gross National Farm Product in Constant Dollars, 1910–50," September 1951; "Farm Income and Gross Farm Product," August 1954; "Note on Gross Farm Product," October 1958.

[2] Frederick Strauss and Louis H. Bean, *Gross Farm Income and Indices of Farm Production and Prices in the United States, 1869–1937*, Dept. of Agriculture, Technical Bulletin No. 703, 1940.

livestock and crop production. Other farm output indexes have been described and compared by Tostlebe;[3] we shall allude to them in the course of describing the indexes used here.

The Commerce measure of gross farm output is obtained by summing the deflated values of the following items: cash receipts from farm marketings and Commodity Credit Corporation loans, net change in farm inventories, farm products consumed directly in farm households, and the gross rental value of farm homes. It is necessary to add inventory change to sales (marketings) in order to approximate production. Since a significant (although declining) portion of farm output is consumed on farms where produced, this must be added to production for the market or to inventory in order to arrive at total output. In the national accounts, the rental value of farm residences is also included as part of the income and product of the farm sector. It is perhaps somewhat artificial to regard farming as an "enclave" within the economy and treat farm residences apart from nonfarm residences whose rental value is included in the real estate industry. However, estimates of the real stock of farm buildings cover both residential and nonresidential structures, and a separation would be arbitrary. Also, farm houses are used to some extent for productive purposes as well as for dwellings.

The Department of Commerce estimates have embodied several different weight-bases: 1939, 1947–49, and 1954. The several implicit deflators for total output do not differ substantially in movement; in line with our general procedure of using changing weights, however, and for comparability with the farm output index of the Agriculture Department, we used the 1939-base deflators through 1940, the 1947–49-base deflators from 1940 to 1953, and the 1954 base thereafter. Also, the four major components were recombined, using average prices in the several successive pairs of key years described in Appendix A. The constant-dollar estimates so obtained were linked forward and backward in time from the 1929 current values, since 1929 is the comparison base used for the tables.

This gross output measure differs from that used by Tostlebe in estimating farm capital coefficients in two respects. Tostlebe excluded the rental value of farm residences from gross farm income, and he deflated the current values by the over-all index (1929 = 100) of prices received by farmers. The movement of the two series is nevertheless quite close. Inclusion of the real rental value of farm homes makes less than 1 per cent difference in the increase of gross output between 1910 and 1953, and the simpler deflation procedure used by Tostlebe likewise has little effect.

[3] Alvin S. Tostlebe, *Capital in Agriculture: Its Formation and Financing since 1870*, Princeton University Press (for NBER), 1957, Appendix H.

In comparison with our gross output measure, the Department of Agriculture index of farm output shows slightly less increase over the period 1910–53. The Agriculture index is designed to show the annual volume of farm production available for eventual human use through marketings or home consumption. Thus, the production of seeds is excluded; and in combining livestock and crop production to form total farm output, the value of feed consumed (other than pasture) is excluded from the weight given livestock because it is already included in crop production. To the extent that feed and seed are produced and consumed in the production process on the same farm, they are not included in our measure; to the extent that they enter into marketings, they are included, and our measure is more gross than that of Agriculture. The practical difference, however, is small. Department of Agriculture economists used 1947–49 price weights for the period since 1940, and a 1935–39 base for earlier years.

Harold Barger and Hans H. Landsberg[4] likewise attempted to measure farm output net of intermediate products produced and consumed within the farm sector. Their measure is somewhat more net than the Department's in that it excludes milk fed to calves, eggs used for hatching, and the like; but the trend of their index is very similar to that of the farm output index, showing only a slightly smaller increase between 1910–14 and 1935–39. Since the Agriculture Department measure was available on a current basis, it seemed preferable to use this index rather than to attempt to carry forward the closely similar Barger and Landsberg index.

Also comparable with our measure of gross farm output is the index of farm production since 1869, prepared by Strauss and Bean for the Department of Agriculture and the National Bureau of Economic Research.[5] Strauss and Bean attempted to measure the output sold by farm producers to the nonfarm economy and that consumed in the producers' households. The output of feed and seed was generally excluded, although interstate sales of grain crops could not be eliminated. Livestock production for sale was adjusted for inventory change; data were not at hand regarding the value of changes in crop inventories; but the production trend should not be affected seriously by this omission since crop inventories are only about one-fourth the value of all inventories. A geometric mean of farm prices in 1910–14 and in the current year was used for weighting physical units.

Despite the several conceptual differences, the Strauss and Bean index exhibits virtually the same trend as ours over the period 1910–37. Therefore, we have extrapolated our estimates of real gross output, exclusive of

[4] *American Agriculture, 1899–1937: A Study of Output, Employment and Productivity*, New York (NBER), 1942.

[5] Strauss and Bean, *op. cit.*, p. 126.

the rental value of farm homes, by the Strauss and Bean calendar-year index back to 1869, splicing the two series by the 1910 overlap. The real gross rental value of farm homes was extrapolated by Tostlebe's estimates of the real stock of farm buildings. Estimates by Goldsmith indicated that residences comprised a virtually constant proportion of the total between 1900 and 1929[6] (although a rising proportion after 1929), and our extrapolation procedure implies that the proportion was constant prior to 1900.

NET FARM OUTPUT

Net farm output is gross farm output, as defined above, less farmers' purchases of intermediate products consumed in the production process.[7] These include feed, seed, fertilizer, motor fuel, irrigation aids, insecticides, veterinary services, and other items charged to current expense. Some items represent market purchases by farmers from each other, but most of them represent purchases from the nonfarm economy. Their deduction yields an output figure which is net in the sense that it represents the value added by farming to the national product. Estimation of net output is particularly important in the farm sector because, due to a large relative increase in purchases from other industries, net output has risen significantly less than gross output (see Table B-1).

As defined, net farm output is equivalent to the national product originating in farming as estimated by the Department of Commerce, with one qualification. The Department deducts gross rents paid to nonfarm landlords, as well as intermediate products, in order to arrive at the farm gross national product (gross only of capital consumption allowances). By Commerce definition, farm product is confined to the net output produced by factors located within the sector. In our measure, however, we include the portion of farm output that represents the return to capital used in farming, irrespective of the location of the owner. Accordingly, our estimates of capital, including land, comprise total real capital employed in farming. A breakdown of capital by ownership would tend to be arbitrary and possibly distort the productivity relationship. Actually, the trend of net output practically parallels that of the real national product originating, since real gross rents paid to nonfarm landlords increased proportionately with real farm product between 1910 and 1953.

Although the Commerce Department deflated intermediate products by detailed product classes, only the implicit deflators for the aggregate were published—on the 1939, 1947–49, and 1954 bases. The implicit

---

[6] Raymond W. Goldsmith, *A Study of Saving in the United States*, Princeton University Press, 1956, Vol. III, Table W-27, p. 75.

[7] Gross output is already net of intermediate products that were produced and utilized on the same farm or that did not pass through organized markets.

TABLE B-1

Gross and Net Farm Output, Key Years, 1869–1957

	Gross Farm Output[a]	Intermediate Products Consumed[b]	Net Farm Output[c]	Ratio of Net to Gross (per cent)
		(millions of 1929 dollars)		
1869	3,950	440	3,510	88.9
1879	6,180	730	5,450	88.2
1889	7,820	1,000	6,820	87.2
1899	9,920	1,360	8,560	86.3
(1909)	10,770	1,620	9,150[d]	
1910	11,080	1,660	9,420	85.0
1919	11,930	2,250	9,680	81.1
1929	13,670	2,940	10,730	78.5
1937	13,990	3,060	10,930	78.1
1948	18,880	6,100	12,780	67.7
1953	20,100	7,040	13,060	65.0
1957[p]	21,920	7,980	13,940	63.6

[p] = preliminary (based on estimates in Dept. of Commerce, *Survey of Current Business*, October 1958).

NOTE ON WEIGHTING: For the four components of gross output and for intermediate products as a whole, Commerce deflators on a 1939 base, converted to a 1929 base, were used to 1940, linked to deflators on a 1947–49 base for the period 1940–53 and to deflators on a 1954 base for the subsequent years. Then the components were reweighted by average prices in the terminal years of each subperiod according to the Marshall-Edgeworth formula, and linked to the 1929 values before aggregation of the output components and subtraction of the intermediate-product total.

[a] Equals "total value of farm output," as given in the *Survey of Current Business*, August 1954, Table 1, line 1, p. 22, deflated and extrapolated to 1869 as described in the text and in note above.

[b] *Ibid.*, line 7 minus line 9 to 1910; 1869–1909 based on extrapolation of the ratios of intermediate products to gross farm output by ratios based on the constant-dollar estimates, 1860–1900, by Marvin T. Towne and Wayne D. Rasmussen (see Appendix B, note 8), interpolated linearly and extrapolated to 1909 by the 1890–1900 rate of change in the ratio.

[c] This is equivalent to the Commerce Department's "farm gross national product" (*op. cit.*, line 10) *inclusive* of rents paid to nonfarm landlords (*op. cit.*, line 8), but with deflation procedures altered as described in note above.

[d] Estimated by applying the 1910 ratio of net to gross to the 1909 estimate of real gross farm output.

deflators rise substantially more over the 1910–57 period when a relatively recent base is employed than when a 1939 base is used, and the physical volume of intermediate products rises correspondingly less. We have used 1939 weights for the years prior to 1940, 1947–49 weights for 1940–53, and 1954 weights since 1953. Ideally, we should like to have used averages of key-year weights throughout, but published detail did not permit this refinement.

The important feature of our real net output calculation is that a chain of estimates for the subperiods, using the Marshall-Edgeworth weighting system, was employed for gross output and aggregate intermediate products separately before the difference was calculated. As shown in Table B-1, the physical volume of intermediate products increased significantly more than gross output, and thus net output increased less. Since the ratio of prices received to prices paid by farmers was higher in 1947–49 and lower in 1939 than the average of the key-year ratios, the use of changing weights results in a smaller increase in net output over the whole period than is obtained by use of 1947–49 weights, and a larger increase than is obtained by use of 1939 weights. The difference between results based on changing weights and those based on 1954 weights is less marked.

The Department of Commerce farm real-product estimates are available back to 1910. Estimates for the censal years 1870–1900 have recently been prepared by Towne and Rasmussen as part of a larger study,[8] and their estimates of the ratios of intermediate-product purchases to total output in 1910–14 dollars have been used to extrapolate the Commerce ratios. Although the Towne and Rasmussen estimates purport to be largely consistent with those of the Commerce Department, it was apparent that they did not include all intermediate-products purchases. Accordingly, we have extrapolated the ratio to 1910 by the 1890–1900 rate of increase and linked it to the ratio based on Commerce estimates.

Farm Labor Input

EMPLOYMENT

Full- and part-time employment of family and hired workers on farms has been estimated for the years since 1909 by the Agricultural Marketing Service (formerly the Bureau of Agricultural Economics) of the Department of Agriculture.[9] Since 1925, the annual estimates have been averages of persons engaged in the last complete calendar week of each month based on responses by 15,000–20,000 farmers to mail questionnaires. The sample estimates have been tied into benchmarks provided by the *Census of Agriculture*, supplemented by the *Census of Population* occupational data. Prior to 1925, the annual estimates represented interpolations between census benchmarks on the basis of production and other indirect information; hence, they are not so accurate an indication of annual changes. Prior to 1910, estimates have been made by Agriculture for only the

---

[8] Marvin W. Towne and Wayne D. Rasmussen, "Farm Gross Product and Gross Investment during the Nineteenth Century," *Trends in the American Economy in the Twentieth Century, Studies in Income and Wealth*, Volume 24, Princeton University Press (for NBER), 1960.

[9] See the periodic *Farm Labor* report.

decennial years in which census data are available.[10] We have interpolated linearly between census years before 1910 in order to obtain farm
employment estimates as a component of national totals. Although this
procedure lends stability to the farm component of the annual employment estimates, it is well known that farm employment is not sensitive
to general cyclical swings.

The Agriculture employment totals are broken down by class of worker
beginning in 1910. Farm operators (owners or tenants) are counted as
employed if they spend one hour or more on farm work during the survey
week. Unpaid members of the operator's household are counted if they
work fifteen hours or more. These two groups are classed together as
"family workers." All persons, including members of the operator's
family, doing one or more hours of farm work for pay during the survey
week are counted as employees, or "hired workers."

For the purposes of this study, it was necessary to break down farm
employment between family workers and hired workers prior to 1910.
This was done on the basis of information provided by *Census of Population*
occupational data as reworked by Alba M. Edwards.[11] It was noted that
the ratios of each class of worker to total employment indicated by the
Agriculture Department estimates for 1910 were the same as those indicated by the Census, if 797,000 workers were deducted from the latter
because of an overcount of unpaid family workers, as suggested by Edwards.
The 1910 proportions were also found to hold for 1900 if the 670,000
workers added by Edwards were put in the hired worker category.
Earlier censuses do not provide a breakdown of laborers between hired
and family workers, but the latter category was extrapolated by the
estimates for owners and tenants, while the figures for hired workers were
obtained by subtracting unpaid family workers so derived from total
laborers. The 1890 ratios are close to those for 1900 and subsequent years;
but the proportion of hired workers to the total fell significantly between
1870 and 1890, reflecting the increasing extent of farm ownership in those
decades.

It should be noted that the Agriculture Department total farm employment estimates prior to 1910 are closely tied into the Edwards estimates of
gainful workers in agriculture. These latter estimates show much the
same decennial movements from 1880 to 1910 as the estimates subsequently prepared by Carson.[12] But the Carson estimate for 1870 is 6.5 per

[10] *Changes in Farm Production and Efficiency, 1955 Summary*, Agricultural Research Service,
June 1956, pp. 41–43.

[11] *Census of Population, 1940, Comparative Occupation Statistics for the United States, 1870 to
1940*, p. 104.

[12] See Daniel Carson, "Changes in the Industrial Composition of Manpower since the
Civil War," *Studies in Income and Wealth, Volume 11*, New York (NBER), 1949, especially
pp. 128–32.

cent under the Edwards estimate and, thus, indicative of a much larger employment increase between 1870 and 1880. Essentially, Edwards interpolated the number of farm workers between benchmarks by rural population. Carson, on the other hand, interpolated by the acreage of improved farm land. His method would seem to be subject to less margin of error, and his estimates definitely yield a more reasonable productivity movement than the estimates based on Edwards. We have, accordingly, adjusted the Agriculture estimate for 1870 down to 7.5 million.

An attempt was made to convert the employment estimates to a full-time equivalent basis. This conversion has no relevance to the farm productivity ratios, since the manhour estimates are independent of the employment series, and since the conversion factor applied to the Agriculture Department employment series is a constant. It was made for the purpose of comparing persons engaged in the various industrial segments of the economy (see Table A-VII). Because of the importance of proprietors and unpaid family workers in farming, we have converted total persons engaged to a full-time basis, in contrast to the Commerce Department's practice of converting only employees.

In order to arrive at a conversion factor, estimates of full-time equivalent persons engaged in farming were made from the Census Bureau Current Population Surveys (CPS) for 1940 and subsequent years. The *Monthly Report on the Labor Force* (MRLF) shows agricultural employment by broad average hours categories. We followed the Census Bureau in classing persons working less than 35 hours a week as part-time workers. To obtain full-time equivalents, the average number of persons working 1 to 14 hours a week was divided by 7, and the number working 15 to 34 hours, divided by 2, on grounds that the "standard" full-time workweek in agriculture is in the neighborhood of 50 hours. The sum of the converted figures and the average number working 35 hours a week and more represents full-time equivalents of persons covered by the CPS.

The Agriculture Department estimates cover more persons and jobs than the population survey estimates, however, and have run substantially higher than the latter estimates. The sources of difference between the two series in a recent year may be analyzed as follows, based on a special survey conducted by the Census Bureau in August 1951, surveys of multiple job-holding on other dates, and contemporary discussion in the *Farm Labor* report.

The total difference between the two series amounted to 2.1 million in 1951, after excluding zero-hour workers from the CPS estimates. Of this number, approximately half may be attributed to multiple job-holdings. Something more than 0.3 million represent secondary jobs held by persons engaged in farming. The total hours worked by such persons are already included in the Census Bureau figures, and no further adjustment is necessary. Around 0.7 million represent secondary jobs of persons primarily engaged in nonfarm industries. But such jobs are largely offset by nonfarm jobs held by persons who are classed in farming, and little adjustment to the Census totals would be required on this score. The remaining million or so workers included by Agriculture but not by Census consist of children between the ages of six and thirteen; unpaid family workers who work close to fifteen hours a week; and the excess of imported foreign workers and migratory workers, not living in private households, included by Agriculture but not by Census, over agricultural service workers, included by Census but not by Agriculture. Of the total difference, it is our judgment that 0.6 million represents the full-time equivalent number that should be added to the Census adjusted average for consistency with the Department of Agriculture series. This represents about 6.7 per cent of the Agriculture total.

For the other years from 1940 on, we have converted the Census estimates to a full-time equivalent basis as described and added 6.7 per cent of the Agriculture estimates in order to obtain full-time equivalents on the Agriculture basis. The series thus derived fluctuates in a fairly narrow range of 71 to 75 per cent of full- and part-time employment in the postwar period, 1946–55, although the ratio is higher during the war years. It is possible that the ratio was affected by the change in the design of the population survey in mid-1945. In any case, year-to-year changes would not be significant in view of the sampling errors that affect both the MRLF and Agriculture series. We have, therefore, computed the ratio of estimated full-time equivalent to full- and part-time employment, 1940–55 (77 per cent) and converted the latter by this constant. The resultant certainly furnishes a better basis for broad comparisons with the volume of labor input in other industries and with labor-force estimates.

MANHOURS AND AVERAGE HOURS

Estimates of farm manhours for years since 1910 have been made by the Production Economics Research Branch of the Agricultural Research Service, Department of Agriculture.[13] The Agriculture estimates are in terms of "man-equivalent" hours. Since certain farm workers accomplish less than average adult males, total actual hours of farm work exceed total man-equivalent hours, and we have made a level adjustment for the sake of greater comparability with nonfarm manhours.

Agriculture estimates are based on studies, for selected years, of labor used per acre of crops and per head or unit of livestock production. Data for individual enterprises are averaged and applied to official estimates of acres and numbers made by the Crop Reporting Board. State estimates

---

[13] See *Changes in Farm Production and Efficiency, 1955 Summary.*

are converted to a regional basis and then combined into national aggregates. Benchmarks for 1910, 1919, and 1929 were developed from data collected in extensive field surveys and published in the Works Progress Administration National Research Project reports. Surveys for 1939, 1944, and 1950 were based on secondary data reported in state experiment station bulletins and on special studies of farm practices.

Annual estimates, by type of production, were interpolated between benchmarks, on the basis of data relating to such factors as unit yields and quantity and quality of capital goods employed. Manhours spent in farm maintenance or general overhead work (including construction by farm workers) were calculated separately and added to the direct hours for crops and livestock.

We have used the Agriculture Department manhour estimates for 1910–50 but raised them by 10 per cent in order to come closer to an actual hours-worked concept. This factor was based on an informal opinion by some of the Department's technicians that actual hours would run 5 to 10 per cent above man-equivalent hours. We have taken the higher figure, since actual manhours computed from the Census Bureau Current Population Surveys for recent years (1950–55) averaged almost 10 per cent higher than the man-equivalent hours figures; and, as we noted above, the agricultural category of the MRLF does not include all persons engaged in farm work. The movement of the adjusted series is still that of the man-equivalent hours series; this is desirable for productivity purposes since no scheme is used to weight hours internally in accordance with the differential productivity of various categories of workers. Man-equivalence is a step in this direction.

It is obvious that the manhour estimates are only as good as the basic technical studies. It is also clear that the manhour and derived productivity estimates are better as indications of trend than of year-to-year movements. As of 1958, the last benchmark used by the Department of Agriculture for its manhour estimates was 1950. The series since 1950 has shown significantly less decline than the product of the Census Bureau estimates of employment and average hours worked in agriculture. We have linked in 1950 to the latter series, as it appears that the Department will revise its series downward on the basis of data from a 1954 benchmark study. The estimates based on the Census Bureau figures are those adjusted by the Bureau of Labor Statistics Division of Productivity to allow for the effect of the 1953 increase in the sample underlying the Current Population Surveys.

Because farm manhours and employment estimates differ in concept and sources, their quotient cannot be considered a precise measure of average hours worked on farms. It can, however, be used as a basis for assessing the reasonableness and consistency of the two sets of estimates in the light of some general information concerning average hours of work on farms. Disregarding annual fluctuations, which are generally not large, implicit average hours increase by around 3 per cent from the decade 1910–19 to 1920–29, then fall slightly in the 1930–39 period to the average for the first twenty years. After 1939, average hours rise 10 per cent to a peak in 1944, but by 1947–50 they are down to a lower level than that of the interwar period. The Census Bureau estimates of average hours worked in agriculture show a persistent decline in the period 1950–57.

Over the entire period, 1910–57, only a mild reduction in average hours worked was recorded, and this came after World War II. This may seem surprising in view of the undeniable downtrend in nonfarm average hours, which might be expected to affect the farm sector and particularly hired labor. But there are several reasons for believing that the implications of the farm manhours and employment estimates are broadly reasonable.

In the first place, average hours in the farm sector as a whole are affected by relative shifts in persons engaged among the several types of farming in which levels of average hours differ. Even though the nominal workweek in individual branches of agriculture may have fallen, downward pressure from this source has tended to be offset by relative shifts of workers to more demanding farm occupations. Specifically, there have been distinct relative increases of employment in the several types of livestock farming. Average hours worked per year are typically higher in livestock products than in the more seasonal staple crops.[14]

While mechanization has reduced unit labor requirements, it has not necessarily reduced average hours worked per year. Farmers' earnings are closely related to the amount of work done in critical seasons. Whereas the hours that can be worked per day with animals are limited, use of the tractor lifts these limitations. Hopkins has written: "In most areas, it is found that the farmers and their hired men put in 0.2 to 0.3 hours more per field day on farms with a tractor than on farms using only horses. . . . This effect is most pronounced in the small-grain area, in which the greatest pressure to seed or harvest crops within limited seasons is found."[15]

More generally, a farmer's income from both his labor and capital is closely related to the hours he and available members of his family work. This being so, there is a more direct incentive than in nonfarm work to maintain hours, especially since proprietors are a more important part of the work force in farming than elsewhere. Hired farm labor would be more influenced by the trend towards shorter hours elsewhere, but this tendency has probably been mitigated by the frequently close work association between operator and hired hand and by the absence of extensive

[14] See John A. Hopkins, *Changing Technology and Employment in Farming*, Dept. of Agriculture, 1941, pp. 22–25.
[15] *Ibid.*, p. 25.

unionization in agriculture. There is some evidence that average hours of farm labor have decreased;[16] but since employees account for only one-fourth of the total, the effect on average hours of all persons engaged is lessened proportionately.

In sum, we do not have much direct information about average hours worked on farms, but the considerations listed suggest that the small changes indicated by the manhours and employment estimates are not unreasonable. It is Barger's conclusion that average hours in agriculture have been virtually constant over the whole period 1870–1950.[17] In view of the lack of trend exhibited by our estimates for the period since 1910, we have extrapolated the manhours estimates by employment from 1870 to 1910, thus accepting Barger's judgment that average hours were relatively constant before as well as for several decades after 1910.

Farm Capital

With the exception of the farm machinery component, the estimates of farm capital are those prepared by Alvin Tostlebe for census years 1870–1950,[18] interpolated annually by major category between 1900 and 1950 and extrapolated after 1950 by the estimates of Goldsmith.[19] Goldsmith's estimates of the real stock of farm machinery were used for the period since 1900, in preference to the Tostlebe estimates, for reasons given below. The stock of land was estimated separately, and reproducible capital was subdivided into buildings, equipment, and inventories of crops and live-stock (including and excluding workstock).

FARM REAL ESTATE

Tostlebe estimated the real value of farm real estate in considerable detail. For the thirty-seven humid states, he calculated the base-period value per acre of "improved" and "unimproved" land in each state and applied these estimates to the number of acres of each type of land as reported by states in censuses. The constant-dollar depreciated value of farm buildings in these states was calculated from the Agriculture Department estimates

16 Willford I. King, *Employment, Hours, and Earnings in Prosperity and Depression, United States, 1920–1922*, New York (NBER), 1923, p. 82. King estimated that average weekly hours of farm employees from 1920 to 1922 were almost fifty-two. In 1953, the Current Population Survey implied they were about six hours lower. Much of this may have occurred in the postwar years.

17 Harold Barger, *Distribution's Place in the American Economy since 1869*, Princeton University Press (for NBER), 1955, pp. 10–12. See also Barger and Landsberg, *op. cit.*, pp. 268–72.

18 Tostlebe, *op. cit.* An earlier description of his sources and methods is contained in his *The Growth of Physical Capital in Agriculture, 1870–1950*, Occasional Paper 44, New York (NBER), 1954.

19 Goldsmith, *op. cit.* Revised and extended estimates for 1945–55 have been supplied by the author, and linked to his published estimates as of 1945.

for the country as a whole. For the eleven western states, acreages of irrigated, dry farming, and grazing land, as reported in the censuses, were weighted by the estimated value per acre of each in the base period. Although Tostlebe estimated the real value of land and buildings together in the second instance, he made available a breakdown so that these items could be treated separately.

The procedure followed by Tostlebe has merit in that shifts in the quality composition of land are reflected in the real-stock estimates. Thus, since 1925 the total acreage of farm land has risen by 12 per cent more than the real-value estimates, reflecting the greater relative increase in unimproved land than in higher-value improved land. Goldsmith used a simpler estimating procedure. His real-value estimates closely parallel Tostlebe's but increase by 4 per cent more between 1900 and 1950. Goldsmith's annual figures, based on Agriculture Department information, were used for interpolation from 1910 on; prior to 1910, we followed Goldsmith's procedure of interpolating linearly between census dates.

Goldsmith's estimates of the real value of buildings were used to interpolate Tostlebe's census-year estimates back to 1900; before this date interpolations were linear. The stock-of-buildings figures of Goldsmith also show a somewhat greater increase than those of Tostlebe over the first half of the century.

MACHINERY AND EQUIPMENT

Goldsmith's estimates of the real net stock of farm equipment plus estimates of the real stock of passenger cars for farm business were used for this category. The Goldsmith estimates represent cumulated net expenditures for machinery and equipment (exclusive of passenger cars).[20] His gross expenditure figures are somewhat higher than those of the Agriculture Department, partly because he includes subsidiary durable items not counted by Agriculture, partly because he uses different depreciation periods. The Goldsmith real-stock figures are considerably higher than those of Tostlebe, and move differently. Tostlebe's basic procedure was to deflate the Census value data by a current price index. Yet there is much uncertainty about the method of valuation used by farmers in reporting and the consistency among farmers in the valuations over time. As Tostlebe warns, his method is in error to the extent that Census values deviate from depreciated values at current prices. Since Goldsmith's estimates are based on a clear and consistent method of derivation and valuation, they have been used. Also, Goldsmith's procedure of deflating by components is preferable to Tostlebe's procedure of deflating by one composite index based on fixed quantity weights.

[20] *Ibid.*, Vol. I, pp. 773–79, and Vol. II, pp. 443–68.

The real value of farm automobiles for business use was likewise estimated by cumulating real net additions. Current-dollar estimates of gross outlays and depreciation since 1910 were available from the Agriculture Department. The Department assumed that 40 per cent of the use of farm automobiles was for business purposes (50 per cent from 1942 to 1945). The corresponding percentage of a cumulation of Goldsmith's real net saving through farm passenger cars, 1900–10, was used for the first decade, and his deflator as extended was applied to Agriculture's current value net outlay figures. The Goldsmith price index from 1910 on is based on the Department of Agriculture estimates of prices paid by farmers for new automobiles, extrapolated to 1900 by wholesale prices of new cars.

The Goldsmith estimates, adjusted to include farm automobiles for business use, show a smaller increase than the Tostlebe estimates between 1910 and 1950. This is partly because Tostlebe included the deflated value of all farm automobiles and partly because of the different methods of establishing current values. Since Tostlebe's price deflator rises more than Goldsmith's over the period, the difference in deflation procedure would have worked in the opposite direction.

INVENTORIES

For livestock, Department of Agriculture estimates of number of head on January 1 of each year are available for the entire period, with the exception of chickens prior to 1925.[21] Numbers, by type of state, were multiplied by average value per unit on or near January 1, 1929. Estimates by Agriculture of the physical volume of crops stored on farms are far less comprehensive, except for recent years. Coverage becomes progressively thinner in going back to 1910. The general procedure followed by Tostlebe was to average the ratio of inventories to production by state for the earliest five-year period for which both series were available and apply these ratios to state crop-production data as reported by censuses back to 1870.[22] The continuous quantity estimates were then weighted by base-period average prices by states.

The Tostlebe constant-price inventory totals show almost exactly the same net change between 1910 and 1920 and over subsequent quinquennial periods as the "net change in all farm inventories" component of the Commerce gross farm output estimates converted to a 1929 price base. The totals also move quite similarly to Goldsmith's estimates of crop and livestock inventories in 1929 prices, and these latter estimates were used for annual interpolations back to 1900.[23] Prior to 1900, we estimated

---

[21] Number of chickens 1870–1920 were estimated by Tostlebe as described in *The Growth of Physical Capital in Agriculture, 1870–1950*, Occasional Paper 44, Appendix D.
[22] *Ibid.*, Appendix E.
[23] Goldsmith, *op. cit.*, Vol. I, Table A-31, p. 795.

livestock inventories annually by the sources and methods described by Tostlebe, and adjusted to his benchmarks where necessary. Annual interpolations between his decennial crop inventory figures from 1900 back were made on the basis of the crop production estimates of Strauss and Bean.

Work stock was segregated from other inventories for analytical purposes. The numbers of horses and mules and their average values in the base period were taken from the same Agriculture Department data used by the other estimators.

Factor Weights in Farming

As a basis for obtaining weights to apply to indexes of farm labor and capital, estimates of national income originating in farming were compiled for key years. Department of Commerce estimates, based on Agriculture Department series, are available back to 1910.[24] These were extended to 1899 by estimates prepared by Raymond Goldsmith.[25] Since capital provided by nonfarm landlords was included in our farm capital estimates, net rents paid to nonfarm landlords were added to the farm national income estimates. Nonfarm rents were available from the Department of Agriculture back to 1910;[26] this series was extrapolated to 1899 by farm national income adjusted for the estimated change in the proportion of farms owned by nonfarm landlords.[27]

The compensation of employees, including the value of pay in kind, is available from the Commerce Department from 1929 forward. This series was extended to 1910 by the Agriculture Department estimates for the same category.[28] Extrapolation to 1899 was by means of the product of our employee manhour estimates and an index of the composite wage rate in agriculture.[29] Average earnings of employees were imputed to proprietors and unpaid family workers by multiplying the employee compensation estimates by the ratio of total manhours worked to employee manhours. Capital compensation was derived as the difference between national income, as adjusted, and labor compensation.

Labor and capital compensation were divided by the indexes of real labor and capital input, respectively, in order to obtain unit compensation figures. These were totaled for successive key years to arrive at the percentage weights to apply to the input indexes for the years within each of the subperiods bounded by the key years. The procedure is shown in some

[24] *Survey of Current Business*, August 1954, pp. 22–23.

[25] *Op. cit.*, Vol. I, Table A-4, p. 757.

[26] *Farm Income Situation*, No. 159, 1956, Table 15, p. 32.

[27] Goldsmith, *op. cit.*, Vol. I, Table A-14, p. 770.

[28] *Farm Income Situation*, No. 159, Table 16, p. 33.

[29] *Historical Statistics of the United States, 1789–1945*, Dept. of Commerce, 1949, Series D 176.

detail in Table B-2, both for its intrinsic interest and to provide an illustration of the general weighting scheme (used in other industries but not usually shown in such detail). Also in line with our general procedure, the 1899–1909 weights were applied to the input indexes for earlier years.

TABLE B-2

Farm Segment: Derivation of Factor Weights, Annual Averages in Successive Pairs of Key Years, 1899–1953

Line No.	1899– 1909	1909 –19	1929 –29	1929 –37	1937 –48	1948 –53
1. Farm national income,[a] millions of $	4,012	8,602	10,297	7,962	14,464	19,766
2. Employee compensation, millions of $	614	1,121	1,398	1,142	2,016	2,922
3. Employee manhours as per cent of total manhours	23.47	23.07	23.81	23.85	21.39	21.00
4. Total labor compensation, millions of $ (2) ÷ (3)	2,616	4,860	5,872	4,788	9,423	13,912
5. Index of manhours (1929 = 100)	94.41	100.25	101.10	97.85	77.99	69.46
6. Unit labor compensation millions of $ (4) ÷ (5)	2,771	4,848	5,808	4,893	12,083	20,028
7. Capital compensation, millions of $ (1) − (4)	1,396	3,742	4,425	3,174	5,041	5,854
8. Index of real capital (1929 = 100)	86.17	98.37	101.16	97.96	103.55	111.21
9. Unit capital compensation, millions of $ (7) ÷ (8)	1,620	3,804	4,374	3,240	4,868	5,264
Relative weights (per cent)						
10. Labor (6) ÷ (6 + 9)	63.1	56.0	57.0	60.2	71.3	79.2
11. Capital (9) ÷ (6 + 9)	36.9	44.0	43.0	39.8	28.7	20.8

[a] Adjusted to include net rents to nonfarm landlords.

Agricultural Services, Forestry, and Fisheries

These residual groups of the segment are small compared with farming, and we combined them into one major grouping. The groups are residual in the sense that adequate output measures were not available for them,[30] although rough estimates for fisheries could be put together as described in the following section.

Agricultural services (Standard Industrial Classification, Major Group 07) includes such diverse activities as cotton ginning, grist milling, corn shelling, hay baling, threshing services, animal husbandry services, horticultural services, etc., usually on a contract basis. Hunting, trapping, and game propagation are also included. Forestry (Major Group 08) includes the growing of trees, gathering of tree products, forestry services, but not logging. Fisheries (Major Group 09) involves the catching (or taking) of fish or other marine products and fishery services, such as the operation of fish hatcheries or fishing preserves.

EMPLOYMENT AND MANHOURS

From 1929 forward, the Commerce Department estimates of persons engaged were used. In the pre-Social Security period, *Census of Manufactures* estimates of employment in the gum turpentine and rosin industry were the chief source for the forestry group. Employment in fisheries was based on the 1930 and 1940 *Census of Population* occupational data, with selected intervening years based on Bureau of Fisheries estimates (which are more than twice as high as the Census figures, presumably because of part-time workers). For agricultural services, use was made of the 1935 and 1939 *Census of Service Establishments* and of the relation of employment in this group to that in agricultural production.

In going back of 1929 for forestry and fisheries, Carson's labor force estimates, adjusted to an employment basis (see Appendix A), were used for census years. The same method was used to obtain the information for fisheries alone, except that before 1910 it was necessary to use the Edwards estimates for fisheries, which are roughly comparable with the Carson totals. Annual interpolations were made for the two groups together from 1929 back to 1900 by the published estimates of the National Industrial Conference Board.[31] The Board's estimates were based on data from the Bureau of Fisheries and the Forestry Service.

The pre-1929 estimates of persons engaged in agricultural services are the only component of the economy aggregate not tied into selected benchmarks. Instead, use was made of the relationship from 1929 to 1953 between numbers of persons engaged in farming and those in agricultural services. The ratio of agricultural service employment to farm employment rose steadily after 1929, reflecting the increasing use by

---

[30] Resources for the Future has made estimates of timber output, but these imply a decline in output per worker, and they have not been used here. See N. Potter and F. T. Christy, Jr., "Employment and Output in the Natural Resource Industries, 1870–1955," *Output, Input, and Productivity Measurement*, Studies in Income and Wealth, Volume 25, Princeton University Press (for NBER), 1961.

[31] *Historical Statistics*, Series D 67.

farmers of certain intermediate services and the growing tendency to obtain certain services on a contract basis. It seemed reasonable to suppose that this was a secular tendency because we knew, for example, that the ratio of all intermediate products to farm output had exhibited a generally rising trend from 1910 on. Accordingly, we extrapolated the rate of change in the ratio since 1929 back to the beginning of the period and applied the extrapolated ratios to the estimates of farm employment in order to derive estimates of employment in agricultural services.

As for average hours worked, since agricultural services include certain processing activities, we have assumed that the workweek has behaved more like that in manufacturing than that in farming. Consequently, numbers of full-time equivalent employees were multiplied by average hours worked in all manufacturing. Numbers of proprietors and unpaid family workers were multiplied by the same series raised by 10 per cent to take account of the longer hours worked by this class of worker in the economy generally.

In the case of forestry and fisheries, however, we assumed that because of the necessity of accommodating work time to seasonal and weather conditions, average hours did not change significantly over the period under review. Accordingly, we held average hours per week for employees constant at the 46.8 figure indicated by the 1940 *Census of Population* and used 110 per cent of this figure for proprietors and unpaid family workers.

Our information regarding average hours worked in agricultural services, forestry, and fisheries is scantier than in any other grouping in the economy. However, this group is so small that possible errors here would have a negligible effect on total manhours in the private economy.

FISHERIES OUTPUT

Estimates of the United States catch of fish have been made by the Fish and Wild Life Service and its predecessor agency, the Bureau of Fisheries, over a relatively long period of time. Estimates of the number of pounds caught in the United States annually since 1929 can be derived from data shown in *Historical Statistics* (Series F 155, for the United States and Alaska, less Series F 189, for Alaska); and Arthur F. Burns[32] provides estimates for 1880–1929 consistent with the later series. The estimates are based on "intermittent statistical canvasses," with interpolations made by the official agencies, and are more accurate in indicating trends than annual movements. Furthermore, the series is an unweighted quantity aggregate; ideally, the catch of each type of fish should be weighted by base-period unit values; but this time-consuming refinement was not undertaken.

[32] *Production Trends in the United States since 1870*, New York (NBER), 1934.

Index numbers of the output of the fisheries, as measured by total poundage caught, are shown in Table B-3. The corresponding estimates of persons engaged are also shown for comparison. The relative movement of the two series does not seem unreasonable, in that output rose

TABLE B-3

Fisheries: Output and Persons Engaged, Key Years, 1889–1953
(1929 = 100)

	Output	Persons Engaged
1889	55	70
1899	60	80
1909	66	89
1919	77	79
1929	100	100
1937	121	92
1948	137	111
1953	143	118

more rapidly than employment between 1889 and 1953. In both world war periods, however, employment rose relative to output. The two series are too rough, however, to permit confident use of their ratio as a productivity indicator.

TABLE B-I

Farm Segment: Net Output, Inputs, and Productivity Ratios, 1869–1957
(1929 = 100)

	Net Output[a]	Persons Engaged[b]	Net Output per Person	Manhours[b]	Net Output per Manhour	Capital Input	Net Output per Unit of Capital Input	Total Factor Input	Total Factor Productivity
1869	32.7	58.2	56.2	53.6	61.0	37.7	86.7	47.5	68.8
1879	50.8	77.1	65.9	70.4	72.2	53.6	94.8	63.9	79.5
1889	63.6	90.4	70.4	82.6	77.0	65.3	97.4	75.8	83.9
1890	62.6	91.7	68.3	83.8	74.7	66.5	94.1	77.0	81.3
1891	65.1	92.5	70.4	84.5	77.0	67.8	96.0	77.9	83.6
1892	61.8	93.4	66.2	85.3	72.5	69.0	89.6	78.9	78.3
1893	60.2	94.3	63.8	86.1	69.9	69.8	86.2	79.7	75.5
1894	62.3	95.1	65.5	86.9	71.7	70.7	88.1	80.5	77.3
1895	66.3	96.0	69.1	87.7	75.6	71.9	92.2	81.5	81.4
1896	71.1	96.8	73.5	88.5	80.3	73.2	97.1	82.4	86.3
1897	76.4	97.7	78.2	89.3	85.6	74.8	102.1	83.5	91.5
1898	79.8	98.6	80.9	90.1	88.6	76.6	104.2	84.7	94.2
1899	79.8	99.4	80.3	90.8	87.9	78.1	102.2	85.7	93.1
1900	80.5	100.3	80.3	91.6	87.9	79.4	101.4	86.7	92.3
1901	80.0	100.9	79.3	92.2	86.8	80.2	99.8	87.3	91.0
1902	79.4	101.5	78.2	92.8	85.6	81.7	97.2	88.2	90.6
1903	81.8	102.1	80.1	93.4	87.6	83.4	98.1	89.3	91.6
1904	83.9	102.7	81.7	93.9	89.4	84.4	99.4	89.9	93.8
1905	84.9	103.2	82.3	94.5	89.8	85.7	99.1	90.8	93.5
1906	89.4	103.8	86.1	95.1	94.0	87.1	102.6	91.7	97.5
1907	85.4	104.4	81.8	95.6	89.3	88.0	97.0	92.3	92.5
1908	87.1	105.0	83.0	96.2	90.5	88.7	98.2	93.0	93.7
1909	85.3	105.6	80.8	96.8	88.1	90.0	94.8	93.8	90.9

(continued)

1910	87.7	106.2	82.6	97.4	90.0	91.5	95.8	94.8	92.5
1911	82.8	106.1	78.0	99.4	83.3	93.8	88.3	96.9	85.4
1912	97.9	106.2	92.2	100.7	97.2	94.7	103.4	98.1	99.8
1913	85.1	106.3	80.1	99.4	85.6	95.3	89.3	97.6	87.2
1914	95.0	106.4	89.3	102.5	92.7	96.1	98.9	99.7	95.3
1915	101.7	106.5	95.5	100.4	101.3	98.6	103.1	99.6	102.1
1916	89.4	106.8	83.7	99.8	89.6	98.8	90.5	99.4	89.9
1917	98.7	106.3	92.9	102.6	96.2	99.8	98.9	101.4	97.3
1918	89.6	104.9	85.4	103.9	86.2	101.0	88.7	102.6	87.3
1919	90.2	103.8	86.9	102.0	88.4	101.9	88.5	102.0	88.4
1920	88.9	105.2	84.5	103.6	85.8	101.8	87.3	102.8	86.5
1921	83.7	105.0	79.7	95.6	87.6	100.5	83.3	97.7	85.7
1922	89.4	104.5	85.6	98.9	90.4	99.4	89.9	99.1	90.2
1923	95.5	103.1	92.6	99.6	95.9	98.3	97.2	99.0	96.5
1924	90.6	102.1	88.7	100.7	90.0	97.5	92.9	99.3	91.2
1925	97.2	102.1	95.2	102.8	94.6	97.6	99.6	100.6	96.6
1926	96.3	101.7	94.7	103.1	93.4	98.4	97.9	101.1	95.3
1927	99.2	99.0	100.2	99.1	100.1	98.6	100.6	98.9	100.3
1928	97.0	99.4	97.6	100.9	96.1	99.5	97.5	100.3	96.7
1929	100.0	100.0	100.0	100.0	100.0	100.0	100.0	100.0	100.0
1930	93.1	97.9	95.1	99.0	94.0	99.4	93.7	99.2	93.9
1931	104.2	99.9	104.3	101.2	103.0	100.1	104.1	100.8	103.4
1932	99.7	100.4	99.3	97.6	102.2	100.6	99.1	98.8	100.9
1933	102.5	99.8	102.7	97.4	105.2	99.2	103.3	98.1	104.5
1934	88.3	98.9	89.3	87.4	101.0	96.0	92.0	90.8	97.2
1935	97.3	99.8	97.5	90.9	107.0	95.6	101.8	92.8	104.8
1936	90.9	96.6	94.1	88.3	102.9	95.0	95.7	91.0	99.9
1937	101.9	93.8	108.6	95.4	106.8	95.8	106.4	95.6	106.6
1938	106.5	91.1	116.9	88.9	119.8	96.7	110.1	91.2	116.8
1939	106.7	88.8	120.2	89.3	119.5	97.0	110.0	91.6	116.5

(continued)

TABLE B-I (concluded)

Farm Segment: Net Output, Inputs, and Productivity Ratios, 1869–1957
(1929 = 100)

	Net Output[a]	Persons Engaged[b]	Net Output per Person	Manhours[b]	Net Output per Manhour	Capital Input	Net Output per Unit of Capital Input	Total Factor Input	Total Factor Productivity
1940	105.9	86.0	123.1	88.3	119.9	99.2	106.8	91.5	115.7
1941	114.8	83.6	137.3	86.6	132.6	101.8	112.8	91.0	126.2
1942	123.0	82.3	149.5	90.0	136.7	104.8	117.4	94.3	130.4
1943	117.4	81.8	143.5	89.3	131.5	106.1	110.7	94.2	124.6
1944	118.5	80.1	147.9	88.4	134.0	106.2	111.6	93.6	126.6
1945	113.3	78.3	144.7	82.5	137.3	105.4	107.5	89.1	127.2
1946	115.7	80.7	143.4	79.6	145.4	105.3	109.9	87.0	133.0
1947	111.0	81.3	136.5	76.0	146.1	104.9	105.8	84.3	131.7
1948	119.2	81.2	146.8	73.9	161.3	107.2	111.2	83.5	142.8
1949	118.6	78.1	151.9	71.5	165.9	111.1	106.8	82.4	143.9
1950	120.1	77.8	154.4	65.8	182.5	114.6	104.8	78.5	153.0
1951	113.2	74.8	151.3	62.8	180.3	117.2	96.6	76.6	147.8
1952	113.8	71.7	158.7	60.0	189.7	118.4	96.1	74.5	152.8
1953	121.7	69.5	175.1	55.9	217.7	118.0	103.1	71.1	171.2
1954	126.6	67.7	187.0	54.4	232.7	118.0	107.3	69.9	181.1
1955	133.1	65.5	203.2	55.4	240.3	118.9	111.9	70.9	187.7
1956	134.1	61.3	218.8	53.1	252.5	119.3	112.4	69.1	194.1
1957[p]	129.9	59.4	218.7	48.9	265.6	119.3	108.9	65.6	198.0

p = preliminary.
a Net of intermediate products but gross of capital consumption.
b Absolute numbers of persons engaged and manhours are given in Tables A-VI and A-X.

TABLE B-II

Farm Segment: Gross Output and Productivity Ratios,[a] 1869–1957
(1929 = 100)

	Gross Output	Gross Output per Person	Gross Output per Manhour	Gross Output per Unit of Capital Input	Total Factor Productivity
1869	28.9	49.7	53.9	76.7	60.8
1879	45.2	58.6	64.2	84.3	70.7
1889	57.2	63.3	69.2	87.6	75.5
1890	56.3	61.4	67.2	84.7	73.1
1891	58.7	63.5	69.5	86.6	75.4
1892	55.8	59.7	65.4	80.9	70.7
1893	54.4	57.7	63.2	77.9	68.3
1894	56.4	59.3	64.9	79.8	70.1
1895	60.0	62.5	68.4	83.4	73.6
1896	64.4	66.5	72.8	88.0	78.2
1897	69.3	70.9	77.6	92.6	83.0
1898	72.5	73.5	80.5	94.6	85.6
1899	72.5	72.9	79.8	92.8	84.6
1900	73.3	73.1	80.0	92.3	84.5
1901	73.0	72.3	79.2	91.0	83.6
1902	72.5	71.4	78.1	88.7	82.2
1903	74.8	73.3	80.1	89.7	83.8
1904	76.9	74.9	81.9	91.1	85.5
1905	77.9	75.5	82.4	90.9	85.8
1906	82.2	79.2	86.4	94.4	89.6
1907	78.6	75.3	82.2	89.3	85.2
1908	80.3	76.5	83.5	90.5	86.3
1909	78.8	74.6	81.4	87.6	84.0
1910	81.0	76.3	83.2	88.5	85.4
1911	77.1	72.7	77.6	82.2	79.6
1912	89.4	84.2	88.8	94.4	91.1
1913	79.7	75.0	80.2	83.6	81.7
1914	87.5	82.2	85.4	91.1	87.8
1915	92.0	86.4	91.6	93.3	92.4
1916	83.4	78.1	83.6	84.4	83.9
1917	91.1	85.7	88.8	91.3	89.8
1918	87.2	83.1	83.9	86.3	85.0
1919	87.3	84.1	85.6	85.7	85.6

(continued)

TABLE B-II (concluded)

Farm Segment: Gross Output and Productivity Ratios,[a] 1869–1957
(1929 = 100)

	Gross Output	Gross Output per Person	Gross Output per Manhour	Gross Output per Unit of Capital Input	Total Factor Productivity
1920	87.0	82.7	84.0	85.5	84.6
1921	82.5	78.6	86.3	82.1	84.4
1922	87.6	83.8	88.6	88.1	88.4
1923	92.6	89.8	93.0	94.2	93.5
1924	91.0	89.1	90.4	93.3	91.6
1925	96.2	94.2	93.6	98.6	95.6
1926	96.2	94.6	93.3	97.8	95.2
1927	98.8	99.8	99.7	100.2	99.9
1928	98.1	98.7	97.2	98.6	97.8
1929	100.0	100.0	100.0	100.0	100.0
1930	94.5	96.5	95.5	95.1	95.3
1931	102.3	102.4	101.1	102.2	101.5
1932	98.1	97.7	100.5	97.5	99.3
1933	100.2	100.4	102.9	101.0	102.1
1934	88.1	89.1	100.8	91.8	97.0
1935	95.2	95.4	104.7	99.6	102.6
1936	92.6	95.9	104.9	97.5	101.8
1937	102.4	109.2	107.3	106.9	107.1
1938	106.7	117.1	120.0	110.3	117.0
1939	109.8	123.6	123.0	113.2	119.9
1940	112.2	130.5	127.1	113.1	122.6
1941	120.4	144.0	139.0	118.3	132.3
1942	131.8	160.1	146.4	125.8	139.8
1943	129.3	158.1	144.8	121.9	137.3
1944	131.1	163.7	148.3	123.4	140.1
1945	130.4	166.5	158.1	123.7	146.4
1946	134.0	166.0	168.3	127.3	154.0
1947	131.9	162.2	173.6	125.7	156.5
1948	138.1	170.1	186.9	128.8	165.4
1949	137.6	176.2	192.4	123.9	167.0
1950	141.9	182.4	215.7	123.8	180.8
1951	139.4	186.4	222.0	118.9	182.0
1952	143.2	199.7	238.7	120.9	192.2
1953	147.0	211.5	263.0	124.6	206.8
1954	152.3	225.0	280.0	129.1	217.9
1955	158.7	242.3	286.5	133.5	223.8
1956	162.1	264.4	305.3	135.9	234.6
1957[p]	160.3	269.9	327.8	134.4	244.4

[p] = preliminary.
[a] Index numbers of the inputs are the same as those shown in Table B-I.

TABLE B-III

Farm Segment: Real Capital Stock, by Type, Key Years, 1869–1953
(millions of 1929 dollars)

	Total Farm Capital	*Land*	*Structures*	*Machinery and Equipment*	*Work Stock*	*Inventories* Livestock Excluding Work Animals	*Crops*
1869	23,145	13,836	4,578	564	623	2,697	847
1879	32,941	19,643	6,367	828	906	3,643	1,554
1889	40,132	23,863	7,006	1,217	1,274	4,698	2,074
1899	48,004	29,107	8,057	1,900	1,504	4,770	2,666
1909	55,295	31,735	11,255	3,012	1,739	4,960	2,594
1919	62,600	34,254	13,671	3,984	1,906	5,745	3,040
1929	61,463	34,365	13,409	4,132	1,436	5,183	2,938
1937	58,877	34,686	11,663	3,651	1,147	5,300	2,430
1948	65,884	34,218	13,110	8,012	659	5,945	3,940
1953	72,521	36,032	14,781	10,753	379	6,768	3,808

APPENDIX C
Mining

THE indexes of output, employment, and manhours in the mining segment and the five major groups of mining industries are built upon those published by Harold Barger and Sam Schurr.[1] Their methods have had to be modified at a number of points so as to achieve consistency with other industry measures contained in this volume. Also, the Barger and Schurr estimates have had to be extended back of 1899 and forward from 1939. So far as the early period is concerned, the task of extension was made easier by several previous studies, in particular those conducted by the Works Progress Administration National Research Project (NRP).[2] It was, however, necessary to amend somewhat the estimates published in these studies; in the case of stone quarrying, it seemed preferable for our purposes to devise new methods for estimating output.

The indexes of real net capital assets are those of Israel Borenstein,[3] adjusted for consistency with our output and employment indexes and extended to 1953 by Borenstein.

The emphasis in this appendix will be placed on the modifications and extensions of the works of Barger and Schurr and Borenstein since their volumes contain full descriptions of the sources and methods that they have used. High priority was given to an effort to make our measures of output and input complete and consistent both over time and with each other. The reconciliation of the two requirements was not always easy because of the nature of the basic data.

For the purposes of this study, every form of mineral extraction carried on underground and at the surface is called mining. Thus, the segment includes quarrying of stone and production of crude petroleum and natural gas, in addition to mining proper. To avoid duplication of items included in the manufacturing segment, Barger and Schurr arranged data so that, ". . . within practical limits, a uniform definition might apply in measuring output and employment, and [so] that this definition might include all processes up to, but not beyond, the point where operations of a kind covered by the Census of Manufactures begin."[4]

[1] *The Mining Industries, 1899–1939: A Study of Output, Employment and Productivity*, New York (NBER), 1944.

[2] Especially, Vivian E. Spencer, *Production, Employment, and Productivity in the Mineral Extractive Industries, 1880–1938*, Report S-2, Philadelphia, June 1940.

[3] *Capital and Output Trends in Mining Industries, 1870–1948*, Occasional Paper 45, New York (NBER), 1945.

[4] Barger and Schurr, *op. cit.*, pp.7–8.

The classification of mining into groups of mineral industries was handled in more or less identical fashion in all our primary sources.[5] Consequently, mining industries are classified in this report as follows: metal mining, Pennsylvania anthracite coal, bituminous coal, petroleum and natural gas, nonmetallic mining and quarrying.[6]

More detailed industry classifications within the metals group raise difficulties. In this group, complex ores and concentrates are produced by single plants, and the primary sources differ as to whether data should be presented on an industry or on a product basis (a fuller discussion is presented in the section on metal mining). With this exception, definitions of industries within the mining segment introduce no intricate problems of the kind met in the manufacturing segment since the industries and products generally coincide. In this study, however, we confine ourselves to the five major groups.

The estimates in the Appendix C tables are presented for the same key years used for other groups. The selection of the key years was based mainly on two considerations: availability of data and approximate elimination of the effects of cyclical movements. Since a census of mineral industries was taken in 1902 instead of 1900, the 1899 estimates generally had to be interpolated.

At the end of the appendix will be found the summary tables showing output, the two inputs, and the output-input ratios, all in the form of index numbers for each group of mineral industries separately and for the mining segment as a whole. Text tables with footnotes contribute to the description of sources and methods.

Output

By way of introduction to the sections on individual groups of mining industries, a few points common to all will be discussed. Weighting methods closely approximate those used in the other segments. The output indexes for each group of mining industries were constructed using changing weights computed on the basis of the Marshall-Edgeworth formula.[7] The weighting factor was price, or unit mine values, whenever

[5] And in most secondary sources, the exceptions being the Paley Commission report and, to some extent, the study of Y. S. Leong, "Index of the Physical Volume of Production of Minerals, 1880–1948," *Journal of the American Statistical Association*, March 1950, pp. 15–29.

[6] It is to be noted that the fifth group, nonmetallic mining and quarrying, is recognized as such only in the SIC; the components are not combined by either the Bureau of the Census or the Bureau of Mines.

[7] The same formula was applied by Barger and Schurr, *op. cit.*, pp. 271–72, as in other National Bureau studies. Their method consists of two steps: first, comparisons were made between 1899 and 1909, 1909 and 1919, 1919 and 1929, and 1929 and 1937; second, a chain index was computed for the entire period, 1899–1939, and this annual series was fitted into the framework provided by the four comparisons mentioned.

available. We combined output indexes of the five groups into a composite index of output for the mining segment using national income per unit of output as the weighting factor (see Table C-1). The latter was obtained

TABLE C-1

Mining: Relative Unit National Income Weights for Output Indexes,
by Group, Subperiods, 1919–53
(per cent)

	1919–1929	1929–1937	1937–1948	1948–1953
Bituminous coal	28.0	29.9	37.9	39.0
Pennsylvania anthracite	9.0	10.5	9.3	10.0
Metals	21.6	20.2	16.2	14.4
Oil and gas wells	33.0	30.3	27.9	28.0
Nonmetallic mining and quarrying	8.4	9.1	8.7	8.6

by dividing the national income originating in each group of mining industries by the appropriate output index in successive key years beginning with 1919. In this, as in all the aggregate index numbers in the mining segment, average 1919–29 weights were applied in earlier years.

Only in the nonmetallic mining and quarrying group was the deficiency of output coverage serious enough to justify adjustments. The nature of the coverage adjustments will be discussed in the appropriate section below. Whenever there was a compelling need to adjust either output or input figures in order to make them consistent with each other, statistical expediency required that the former should give way to the latter.[8]

A final topic of general character with respect to mining output concerns the estimates for 1869. No specific figures for quantities produced and prices are listed in the following sections because, given the paucity of information, the index numbers for that year were derived by extrapolating the 1880 index number by estimates from the Borenstein work. The latter were based on Census data supplemented by the Bureau of Mines figures.

COAL MINING

The output indexes for bituminous coal and Pennsylvania anthracite were based directly on homogeneous quantity data. Table C-2 tells the whole story. The figures on coal are probably the most complete in terms of coverage among our five groups of mining industries. There are two minor shortcomings: first, Alaskan production could not be separated

[8] Barger and Schurr, *op. cit.*, Chapter 3 and Appendix A.

and excluded until 1916; second, information was not collected on the output of mines producing less than 1,000 tons a year. However, both of these defects in coverage may be considered negligible.[9]

TABLE C-2

Coal Production, Key Years, 1880–1953
(millions of short tons)

	Bituminous	Pennsylvania Anthracite
1880	42[a]	29
1889	96	46
1899	193	60
1909	380	81
1919	466	88
1929	535	74
1937	445	52
1948	600	57
1953	457	31

SOURCE: Bureau of Mines.

[a] Including coal mines west of longitude 100 degrees West, as given in *Report on the Mining Industries of the United States, 1880*, Bureau of the Census.

METAL MINING

Table C-3 shows the quantities produced and the prices used in the derivation of output index numbers for those key years that are not covered in the Barger and Schurr study. The year 1899 has been included in order to give an overlap with the estimates presented in that study.

With respect to coverage, the metal mining group, following Barger and Schurr, contains some nonmetals (fluorspar of Illinois and Kentucky and pyrites) while a metal (placer gold) is excluded. This adjustment in classification was necessitated by peculiarities in data on labor input[10] and had to be used to preserve consistency between output and employment figures. The adjustment itself presented no difficulty for the two late key years, but for 1880 and 1889 it was virtually impossible to separate placer from lode gold. The point is of some importance, although it does appear on first sight that placering might have been negligible at the time.[11] A more thorough look into the matter reveals that hydraulic placering

[9] W. E. Hotchkiss, *et al.*, *Mechanization, Employment, and Output per Man in Bituminous-Coal Mining*, WPA-NRP Report E-9, Philadelphia, 1939, pp. 357–358; Barger and Schurr, *op. cit.*, p. 298.

[10] See Barger and Schurr, *op. cit.*, p. 315.

[11] Much the greater part of placer gold is produced by dredging operations, and these had their commercial beginnings in 1896 (*Mineral Resources, 1921*, Bureau of Mines, Part I, p. 453).

TABLE C-3

Metal Mining: Production and Unit Values, by Type of Ore,
Selected Key Years, 1880–1953

		1880	1889	1899	1948	1953
Iron ore[a]	(mill. l.t.)	7.1	14.5	26.4	126.2	117.4
	($ per l.t.)	3.25	2.30	1.41	3.91	6.76
Manganese ore	(thous. l.t.)	5.8	24.2	9.9	117.0	140.7[b]
	($ per l.t.)	15.00	9.92	8.28	37.50	88.50
Manganiferous ore[a]	(thous. l.t.)		65	109	1,198	1,107[b]
	($ per l.t.)		3.50	3.25	4.62	6.28
Lode gold, early period[c]	(mill. f. oz.)	1.74	1.54	3.34		
	($ per f. oz.)	20.67	20.67	20.67		
Silver, early period[c]	(mill. f. oz.)	30.3	51.4	56.5		
	($ per f. oz.)	1.15	.94	.60		
Gold, late period From copper ore Outside Mississippi	(thous. f. oz.)				450	617
Valley	(thous. f. oz.)				1,170	
	($ per f. oz.)				35.00	35.00
Silver, late period From copper ore Outside Mississippi	(mill. f. oz.)				7.91	9.16
Valley	(mill. f. oz.)				30.1	
	($ per f. oz.)				0.905	
Copper	(thous. s.t.)	30	113	284	834	926
	($ per s.t.)	428	270	342	434	574
Lead, early period[c]	(thous. s.t.)	96	152	202		
	($ per s.t.)	100	78	90		
Zinc, early period[c]	(thous. s.t.)	23	59	129		
	($ per s.t.)	110	100	116		
Lead, late period Outside Mississippi Valley	(thous. s.t.)				260	
Mississippi Valley	(thous. s.t.)				130	
	($ per s.t.				358	
Zinc, late period Outside Mississippi Valley	(thous. s.t.)				522	
Mississippi Valley	(thous. s.t.)				108	
	($ per s.t.)				266	

(continued)

TABLE C-3 (concluded)

		1880	1889	1899	1948	1953
Fluorspar[d], Ill. and Ky.	(thous. s.t.)	4	11	16	257	
	($ per s.t.)	4.00	4.70	5.49	35.00	
Bauxites	(thous. l.t.)		.73[e]	32.9	1,376	
	($ per. l.t.)		3.25	3.56	6.69	
Mercury	(thous. flks.)[f]	60.3	26.7	30.7	14.4	
	($ per flask)	30.8	44.7	47.4	76.5	
Molybdenum	(mill. lb.)				26.7	
	($ per lb.)				.688	
Tungsten	(thous. s.t.)				4.21	9.74[g]
	($ per s.t.)				1,576	3,748

SOURCE: For 1880, 1889, and 1899: Vivian E. Spencer, *Production, Employment, and Productivity in the Mineral Extractive Industries, 1880–1938*, WPA–NRP Report S-2, Philadelphia, 1940; Nicholas Yaworski *et al.*, *Technology, Employment, and Output per Man in Iron Mining*, WPA–NRP Report E-13, Philadelphia, 1940; *Report on Mining Industries, 1880* and *Report on Mineral Industries in the United States at the Eleventh Census, 1890*, Bureau of the Census; *Mineral Resources*, 1899–1925; and Harold Barger and Sam H. Schurr, *The Mining Industries, 1899–1939: A Study of Output, Employment and Productivity*, New York (NBER), 1944, Table A-1.

For 1940 and 1953: *Minerals Yearbook*, Bureau of Mines, annual issues and preprints. for 1953; data for 1953 are incomplete and are subject to revision.

[a] Ores containing less than 5 per cent of manganese are included in iron ore. Our primary sources also include, in early years, manganiferous ore (5 to 25–40 per cent manganese) with iron ore (see Spencer, *op. cit.*, Table B-6, note k). These quantities are shown separately in our table and have been deducted from iron ore. Manganiferous ore was negligible in 1880.

[b] The 1953 data for manganese and manganiferous ores are slightly defective because the *Minerals Yearbook* preprints make the distinction with reference to battery ores only between the ores containing less than 25 per cent and 25 per cent or more manganese. For all other varieties 35 per cent of manganese is the dividing point. However, the error involved is not very serious as the total of battery ore represents 1.3 per cent of the sum of manganese and manganiferous ores in 1953.

[c] Production of gold in Alaska is excluded throughout. Prior to 1906, gold, silver, copper, lead, and zinc are expressed in terms of product, rather than by industry breakdown (see discussion in text). Moreover, the early figures represent metal recovered, rather than recoverable metallic content, a distinction also discussed in the text.

[d] The fluorspar series begins in Barger and Schurr, *op. cit.*, in 1909. However, data are available for earlier years in *Minerals Yearbook, 1925*, Part II, p. 13; and they are included, since employment in fluorspar, reported on an industry basis, is part of lead and zinc employment.

[e] The 1889 data are from *Mineral Resources, 1918*, Part I, p. 516, the only issue where corrected figures were published.

[f] The flask as defined in early issues of *Mineral Resources* equals 76.5 pounds and was converted into 76-pound flasks, the basis for later data.

[g] Estimated on the basis of 1952 relationship of 60 per cent tungsten oxide short ton and 1,000 pound tungsten content.

was booming in the 1880's in California until restrictive legislation put a stop to it. The problem was solved here by including placer gold prior to 1899 and by linking in 1899 to the series excluding it.

The problem of consistency between output and employment figures arises in the nonferrous metal industries. The Bureau of Mines publishes its output data in *Minerals Yearbook* on a commodity basis, while its employment data, found in the accident bulletins, are presented on an industry basis. The difficulty looms large in the Barger and Schurr work; their solution is by way of adjusting the output data to make them correspond to the employment data.[12] However, it was possible to follow that procedure only beginning with 1906. Prior to that date, the data do not permit allocation of nonferrous metals to the several industries producing them and the data had to be used on a product basis for the output index of the total metal group. The link between the two sets of figures is easily obtained at the group level, and the problem of inconsistency with employment figures does not enter on this level. This obviates the need for elaborate adjustments of the kind to be found in Barger and Schurr in this volume, which is confined to the broader groupings of mineral industries. The Barger and Schurr procedure was, however, applied in 1948 and 1953 (see Table C-3).

A broader problem arises because metals can be measured in terms of quantities of ore or as the recovered or recoverable content of that ore. These measures would not yield the same picture of the movement of output, particularly in the nonferrous metal industries, because the qualities of ores change. Conceptually, the metallic content of ore is a more meaningful measure of output than the ore itself, since the derived productivity measure is influenced by the quality as well as the quantity of ore mined. The distinction between recoverable and recovered metallic content is of lesser significance; Barger and Schurr prefer the former because of the lag in time necessary for recoverable to become recovered metallic content and, also, because of considerations related to the separation of mining from manufacturing industries.[13] Our early figures are integrated with the Barger and Schurr pre-1906 data, and our later figures, with their post-1906 data. The link between the two is provided in their work.

As a final point of interest with reference to the output of metals, the index computed for the years prior to 1899 on the basis of data described above may be compared with some other published indexes. The comparison with the index implicit in Borenstein's output table[14] turns out

---

[12] For details see Barger and Schurr, *op. cit.*, notes to Table A–1 and Appendix B.

[13] Barger and Schurr, *op. cit.*, Appendixes B and D.

[14] *Op. cit.*, Table A–2. It may be noted that this index is derived by weighting output data throughout by 1929 prices.

TABLE C-4

Crude Petroleum and Natural Gas: Production and Unit Values, Key Years, 1880–1953

	Crude Petroleum		Natural Gas		Natural Gasoline		Well Drilling	
	(mil. bbl.)	($ per bbl.)	(bil. cu. ft.)	($ per th. cu. ft.)	(mil. gal.)	($ per gal.)	(mil. ft.)	($ per ft.)
1880	26	0.94	0	0	0	0	0	0
1889	35	0.77	250	0.0800	0	0	6.7	2.60
1899	57	1.13	223	0.0900	0	0	17.8	2.53
1909	183	0.70	481	0.1300	0	0	28.4	2.55
1919	378	2.01	746	0.2160[a] 0.0826[a]	352	0.1830	68.6	4.47
1929	1,007	1.27	1,918	0.0822	2,234	0.0709	88.1	4.76
1937	1,279	1.18	2,408	0.0513	2,065	0.0470	105.1	
1948	2,020	2.60	5,148	0.0647	6,162	0.0740	136.7	7.69
1953	2,360	2.68	8,397	0.0920	10,020	0.0600	198.4	8.36

SOURCE: For petroleum, natural gas, and natural gasoline, the data for 1880 and 1889 are from O. E. Kiessling et al., *Technology, Employment, and Output per Man in the Petroleum and Natural-Gas Industries*, WPA–NRP Report E-10, Philadelphia, 1939, pp. 321 and 322 (value per unit of natural gas production in 1889 was derived from value data in *Mineral Resources, 1912*, p. 302); for 1899–1937 from Barger and Schurr, *The Mining Industries*, p. 285; for 1948 and 1953 from *Minerals Yearbook, 1948*, and 1953 preprints. For well drilling, the series since 1929 is based on Department of Commerce data, extended to earlier years by using numbers of wells drilled as an extrapolator.

[a] In 1919, first figure, comparable with earlier years, refers to value at point of consumption; second figure, comparable with later years, refers to value at well.

favorably in the sense that the differences do not exceed one index point, and they are consistently in the same direction. The movement of our index in the early years is also almost perfectly parallel with that of the Leong index, despite somewhat different coverage and methods of weighting.[15] Finally, if an index for metal mining had been presented in the Spencer study, strong parallelism could have been expected because many of the underlying data and estimates are identical.

CRUDE PETROLEUM AND NATURAL GAS

The derivation of the quantities and the unit values used as weights in the output index for the oil and gas producing industry group can be seen in Table C-4. One point in the table deserves specific comment. The inclusion of well drilling in the composite output index of oil and gas wells is an innovation. The idea itself is not new; Barger and Schurr recognized that the peculiar importance of development activity in the oil and gas portion of the mining sector posed a conceptual problem with regard to the index of productivity, inasmuch as the labor input estimates include manhours spent in drilling. The inclusion of well drilling in the output index is justified as a means of improving consistency between the output and employment figures.[16] Table C-5 shows the extent to which inclusion of well drilling modifies the output index of the oil and gas group. The productivity indexes show a more regular movement when based on the output measure inclusive of drilling.

TABLE C-5

Crude Petroleum and Natural Gas: Alternative Indexes of Output, Key Years, 1880-1953
(1929 = 100)

	1880	1889	1899	1909	1919	1929	1937	1948	1953
Excluding drilling	2.8	6.1	8.1	18.3	34.7	100.0	123.8	207.2	254.6
Including drilling	2.2	6.2	10.2	20.7	41.7	100.0	122.8	196.6	248.3

NONMETALLIC MINING AND QUARRYING

In extending the Barger and Schurr indexes for the three components of this group—stone, gypsum, and phosphate rock—from 1909 back to 1880, the latter two minerals presented no special difficulties. Extrapolation

[15] Our modifications in classification have been already discussed. Moreover Leong's coverage is broader since he did not have to deal with employment data as well. Also, he weighted quantity data by the average 1935–39 unit values.

[16] For more detailed discussion, see Barger and Schurr, *op. cit.*, pp. 190 ff. It should also be noted that the figures of the Office of Business Economics, which we have used after 1929, take into account cost differences due to varying depths of wells. Numbers of wells, the unit used prior to 1929, is a less precise real-cost measure.

was by means of the Spencer indexes, which are based on physical units. In the case of stone, however, a major problem was encountered.

In the 1909 and subsequent censuses, production of the various types of stone was reported in terms of short tons, whereas in the 1890 Census different units were employed, varying with the categories of stone and the uses to which they were put. Spencer and Leong avoided the problem of converting units by deflating estimates of the value of stone production by the wholesale price index of building materials. This procedure is unsatisfactory, since the index is based on prices of materials other than stone. The more difficult alternative involved converting the units of measurement employed in the 1890 Census to short tons and thus obtaining quantity figures more or less consistent with the later data. Experimentation with this procedure, and computation of comparable unit values for the various categories, suggested that average unit values had increased significantly less than the wholesale price index for building materials and that the deflated value estimate for 1889 had an upward bias relative to 1909. When completed, our index number of output (1929 = 100) for the stone industry in 1889 was 31.0 compared with Spencer's 55.7 and Leong's 44.6 (for the construction group).

Interpolation between 1889 and 1909 and extrapolation to 1880 were done on the basis of deflated value,[17] but the establishment of a quite different 1889 benchmark from those previously available changes the trend of the series significantly. Some explanation of the 1889 estimate is therefore in order.

For about two-thirds of the categories of stone production, as indicated by the asterisks in Table C-6, relatively reliable conversion factors were available. These factors were derived from output figures for later years reported by the Bureau of Mines both in short tons and in the other physical units involved—cubic feet, square feet, linear feet, number of paving blocks, etc. We computed the conversion factors for each variety and use of stone given in the published figures for some six individual years covering a span of over twenty years. The conversion factors were found to be almost constant through time, a circumstance expected because the use of stone within each variety is determined by its qualities, among which the degree of porosity and specific gravity are important ones.

For the remaining items, other than limestone used for lime and cement, conversion factors were obtained by consulting the technical literature.[18]

---

[17] The 1880 value of output was deflated by an extension of the 1889 average unit value by the Warren and Pearson index of the prices of building materials, instead of the BLS index. G. F. Warren and F. A. Pearson, *Wholesale Prices for 213 Years, 1720 to 1932*, Ithaca, Cornell University Agricultural Experiment Station, Memoir 142, 1932.

[18] In particular, Oliver Bowles, *The Stone Industries*, New York, McGraw-Hill, 1939.

The factors ranged from 11 to 12 cubic feet per short ton for quality stone (used for construction, monuments, and decoration) to over 21 cubic feet per short ton for crushed stone (which was relatively unimportant in 1889). While the conversion factors were not wholly stable in some instances, they seemed to be firmly enough based to be used.

TABLE C-6

Varieties of Stone: Distribution of Value of Production by Use, 1889
(per cent)

	Type of Stone				Total
	Granite	Marble	Limestone	Sandstone	
Building	13.7[a]		12.0[a]	15.8[a]	41.5
Monumental and decorative	5.3[a]	7.8[a]			13.1
Paving	6.6[a]		{5.1 0.7[a]		12.4
Other streetwork, bridges, dams, railways	6.1		8.2	2.3	16.6
Lime[b]			3.7		3.7
Cement[b]			4.5		4.5
Flux			3.5[a]		3.5
Abrasive				1.3	1.3
Miscellaneous	0.5		0.3[c]	2.6	3.4
Total	32.2	7.8	32.2	27.8	100.0
Items with reliable conversion factors[a]	25.6	7.8	15.5	16.5	65.4

Source: The percentages are based on value figures given in *Report on Mineral Industries, 1890*.

[a] Conversion factors were derived from production data in alternative units, given in *Mineral Resources* and the *Minerals Yearbook* for a number of years and considered to be reliable. The estimate for monumental and decorative marble is based on statements of a general nature in *Report on Mineral Industries, 1890*, p. 618. The proportion in terms of value for all other uses does not exceed 2.3 per cent in later years.

[b] Derivation is discussed in the text.

[c] The figure consists of two parts: 0.1 per cent is the miscellaneous category gven by *Report on Mineral Industries, 1890*; 0.2 per cent is due to discrepancies in estimates made for the limestone used for making lime.

With respect to limestone used for making lime, Bowles estimated that 100 pounds of stone are required to produce 56 pounds of lime.[19] By means of this ratio, the quantity data on lime production in the 1890 Census were converted to quantities of limestone. The conversion was more difficult in the case of limestone used for making cement. A conversion factor could be found only for the relationship between limestone and Portland cement. By applying this factor to the output of Portland cement in 1909, the limestone used to produce natural cement could be derived as a residual. The 1909 ratio between estimated limestone consumption and natural cement production was used to derive the 1889 limestone output (see Table C-7).

TABLE C-7

Estimated Limestone Used in Cement Production, 1889 and 1909

	1889		1909	
	Output of Cement[a] (thousands of barrels)	Limestone Used (millions of short tons)	Output of Cement[a] (thousands of barrels)	Limestone Used (millions of short tons)
Natural cement	6,532	9.34[b]	1,538	2.2[c]
Portland cement	300	0.07[d]	64,991	14.6[d]
Total		9.41		16.8[e]

[a] Statistical Appendix to *Minerals Yearbook, 1935*, p. 178. Apart from natural and Portland cement, there is a third kind, pozzuolan, but only the first two are made of limestone.

[b] Estimated by applying the 1909 ratio of limestone used for natural cement to output of natural cement.

[c] By deduction of stone used for Portland cement from stone used for total cement.

[d] Estimated by using the relationship quoted in E. C. Eckel, *Cements, Limes and Plasters*, 2nd. ed., New York, Wiley, 1922, p. 275, of 225 tons of limestone per 1,000 barrels of Portland cement.

[e] Barger and Schurr, *The Mining Industries*, p. 289.

The result of the conversion of the various types of stone output to short tons in 1889, together with other nonmetallic mining output, is summarized in Table C-8. A final word should be said about slate, which is treated separately from stone in the censuses. The 1890 Census reported roofing slate in numbers of squares. The squares were converted to short tons by use of a three-to-one ratio.[20] The output of other slate was

[19] *Ibid.* pp. 387–88.
[20] Based on *Mineral Resources, 1925*, Part II, p. 66.

reported only in value terms. Here, the estimated 1909 price per short ton[21] was extrapolated to 1889 by means of the price index for building materials, and the physical volume was obtained by deflation of value. Use of the unsatisfactory deflation procedure in this minor instance could hardly affect the level of the 1889 index.

TABLE C-8

Nonmetallic Mining and Quarrying: Production and Unit Values,
by Type of Stone, 1889

	Quantity (thousands of short tons)	Unit Value (dollars per short ton)
Granite	4,320	3.35
Marble	284	12.29
Limestone	28,713	0.50
Sandstone	6,227	2.01
Slate	295	11.80
Gypsum	268	1.13
Phosphate Rock	607	5.98

Extension to recent years. The 1948 and 1953 quantities and prices represent a simple continuation of the Barger and Schurr series for stone, gypsum, and phosphate rock, based on data from the *Minerals Yearbook.* The detail is presented in Table C-9.

Coverage adjustment. Once the Barger and Schurr figures were extended to 1880–1953, the question of serious undercoverage of the nonmetallic mining and quarrying industries called for a solution. To this end, an adjustment ratio was applied in each key year to the group output index derived on the basis of estimates described in the preceding pages.

The adjustment ratios for each key year were obtained from the value of product for Barger and Schurr coverage (i.e., stone, including slate, gypsum, and phosphate rock) and from the total value of product for full coverage. In addition to stone, gypsum, and phosphate, the latter includes asbestos, asphalt and bitumens, barite, borates, bromine, clay (including Fuller's earth), emery (including corundum), feldspar, gems and precious stones, graphite, magnesite, magnesium chloride and sulfate, marl, mica, millstones (and buhrstones), monazite and zircon, peat, potash, sand and gravel, silica and silicates, calcium chloride, sodium carbonates and sulfates, sulfur, and talc (and soapstone). Tests indicated that the difference between the true total and our "full coverage" was within 1 per cent.

---

[21] After conversion of the reported square feet to short tons using the ratio of 300:1 based on *Mineral Resources, 1925,* Part II, p. 66.

TABLE C-9

Nonmetallic Mining and Quarrying: Production and Unit Values, by Type of Stone,
1948 and 1953

	1948		1953	
	Quantity (thousands of short tons)	Unit Value (dollars per short ton)	Quantity (thousands of short tons)	Unit Value (dollars per short ton)
Dimension stone				
Granite	639	34.92	604	40.49
Marble	83	110.10	76	110.56
Nondimension marble	193	6.81	377	9.96
Limestone	607	17.43	799	19.40
Sandstone	204	20.41	354	24.43
Slate	141	48.90	153	43.72
Nondimension slate	659	9.13	546	10.91
Miscellaneous dimension stone	80	22.07	65	42.23
Nondimension stone				
Nondimension basalt	20,600	1.45	30,000	1.54
Dimension basalt	58	1.33	59	3.65
Granite	13,050	1.26	22,890	1.37
Limestone	180,700	1.23	243,260	1.35
Limestone used for cement	56,500	0.61	66,300	0.75
Sandstone	7,090	1.96	8,300	2.37
Miscellaneous nondimension	16,810	0.87	18,980	1.08
Gypsum	7,250	2.63	8,290	2.79
Phosphate rock	9,390	5.83	12,500	6.13

Table C-10 shows both the corrected and uncorrected indexes for nonmetallic mining and quarrying. The validity of the adjustment rests on the reasonableness of the underlying assumption that unit values of the covered and uncovered products showed parallel movement (see Appendix D for a general discussion of coverage adjustments).

TABLE C-10

Nonmetallic Mining and Quarrying: Output Indexes,
Unadjusted and Adjusted for Coverage, Key Years, 1880–1953

	Unadjusted Index (1929 = 100)	Coverage Adjustment		Adjusted Index (1929 = 100)
		Per Cent	Index	
1880	12.0	0.9452	165.6	7.2
1889	28.1	0.9452	165.6	17.0
1899	36.9	0.8803	154.2	23.9
1909	66.6	0.7429	130.2	51.1
1919	50.6	0.5945	104.2	48.6
1929	100.0	0.5708	100.0	100.0
1937	68.3	0.5580	97.7	69.9
1948	117.5	0.5402	94.6	124.2
1953	151.6	0.5400	94.6	160.3

ANNUAL DATA

The annual indexes of output have been taken from primary sources wherever readily available; in other cases, they have been estimated by interpolation between the key years. Indexes of output for groups of mining industries, constructed by Leong and by the Board of Governors of the Federal Reserve System for the later period, and an index that we constructed on an annual basis using all available quantity data served as interpolators.

Labor Input

The backbone of the estimates of employment and manhours in the mining groups is the work of Barger and Schurr for 1899–1939. Their data required certain adjustments and supplementation to achieve full coverage of class of worker and industry for the key years used in this study. They were extrapolated back to 1880 largely by data in the censuses of 1880 and 1889, and forward to 1957 by the employment estimates of the Department of Commerce and the average hour estimates of the Department of Labor.

First, we shall describe briefly the sources and methods used by Barger and Schurr and point up some of the general conceptual and statistical problems. Then we shall describe, by industry, the sources and methods used to supplement and extrapolate the Barger and Schurr estimates. The sources used for the recent estimates can be described in a single section, since they are uniform for all segments. Finally, the method of estimating proprietors throughout the entire period will be explained, and the weighting system by which total manhours in the various groups are combined into labor input for the segment as a whole will be described.

SOME GENERAL PROBLEMS

The estimates by Barger and Schurr of employment and mandays worked in the mining groups other than oil and gas were derived for the most part from the accident reports of the Bureau of Mines and the 1902 Census. Except for 1902, then, the output and employment estimates are based on two separate canvasses by the Bureau of Mines, but Barger and Schurr maintain that with a few exceptions, the industry coverage of the two sets of estimates is comparable. In the few cases of patent undercoverage of certain parts of the industry groups, they have made adjustments. The industry coverage in the quarrying and nonmetallic minerals groups, while the same for labor as for output, is admittedly partial for both, and we have applied coverage adjustments to manhours as well as to output.

The employment data of the Bureau of Mines relate to "active-period averages," that is, averages of monthly counts for only those months in which the reporting establishments were active; in some cases in the latter years of the period, the estimates represent the actual number of mandays worked, as tabulated for payroll purposes, divided by the number of days per year that the mines were operated. The active-period average employment series are not well suited for comparison with output since they do not reflect changes in the extent of mine operation from year to year and are closer to a labor force concept. Accordingly, Barger and Schurr compared output with mandays and manhours worked. The manday estimates usually represent the active-period average number of employees multiplied by the average number of days the mine was active (computed separately for each enterprise by the Bureau of Mines), but they may also represent actual payroll records of mandays worked. The manhours estimates represent mandays multiplied by nominal hours worked per day. For consistency with the other segments, our emphasis is on the manhour estimates, and we computed ratios of output to manhours rather than to mandays.

Although the relationship of average employment to output is less meaningful in mining than in other segments, we needed employment estimates to arrive at economy aggregates. For consistency of treatment with that of other segments, the Commerce employment estimates from 1929 forward were used and were extrapolated back by the Barger series as extended to 1870 by data from the censuses. The Commerce estimates represent full-period averages and, thus, the extrapolation by active-period averages[22] represents a break in continuity. Active-period average employment shows less volatility over the cycle and, conversely, the implicit series on average hours worked per year are more volatile. However, the levels of the two types of employment estimates tend to be close together in years of sustained activity, and the employment trend in the spliced series should evidence continuity. In the petroleum and natural gas group, the estimates for the early period are on a full-period average basis consistent with the later estimates. Differences between estimates on the alternative bases in this group would be negligible anyway, since operations are generally continuous.

A further problem is introduced by the fact that the accident bulletins of the Bureau of Mines report only employees "in and about mines." Thus, proprietors and certain categories of salaried workers such as general officers and clerks are not covered. On the basis of detailed information presented in the censuses of 1889, 1902, and 1939, the percentages of total employment accounted for by these categories could be estimated. The proportions involved are small and have not changed drastically; but to approximate our ideal of full coverage of persons engaged, we applied the coverage adjustments in Table C-11 to the

TABLE C-11

Coal and Metal Mining: Adjustment Ratios for Coverage of Number Employed and Manhours, 1889, 1902, and 1939

	1889	1902	1939
Bituminous	0.980	0.980	0.971
Pennsylvania anthracite	0.980	0.980	0.962
Metals	0.980	0.952	0.952

Barger and Schurr estimates for three groups of mining industries, interpolating linearly between benchmarks. The adjustment for quarrying and nonmetallic mining was included in our over-all industry coverage adjustment, described later. The available employment estimates for the oil and gas group cover wage earners only; so total salaried employment was estimated as described in the section on that group.

[22] The 1902 Census employment estimates were on a 300-day basis, but were converted to active-period averages by the method used by Barger and Schurr in metal mining (*op. cit.*, p. 300). The 1889 Census definitely reverts to active-period averages, and whereas the 1880 Census is not explicit on this point, the indications are that the employment estimates are consistent with those for 1889.

Under this heading we present, by group, the basic data and estimates for key years for which no figures are available in the Barger and Schurr volume.

Coal. The figures in Table C-12 are consistent with the Barger and Schurr estimates. The estimates for 1899 were obtained by multiplying their estimates of mandays by estimated average hours worked per day.

TABLE C-12

Coal: Employment and Manhours, 1880, 1889, and 1902

	Number Employed		Manhours	
	Bituminous	Pennsylvania Anthracite	Bituminous	Pennsylvania Anthracite
	(t h o u s a n d s)		(m i l l i o n s)	
1880	100.0	70.7	215.7	145.0
1889	175.2	124.3	376.2	236.2
1902	370.1	148.1	749.0	163.2

SOURCE: 1880: Spencer, *Mineral Extractive Industries*, pp. 153–54; and W. E. Hotchkiss *et al.*, *Mechanization, Employment, and Output per Man in Bituminous-Coal Mining*, WPA–NRP Report E-9, Philadelphia, 1939, p. 358, adjusted to include salaried employees "in and about mines" on the basis of data in *Report on Mining, 1880* for the "administrative force."

1889: Employment data are from *Report on Mineral Industries, 1890*, p. 347; manhours was estimated by using data in *Mineral Resources, 1925*, Part II, p. 410, on average number of days per year and estimates by Spencer, *Mineral Extractive Industries*, on average number of hours per day.

1902: Barger and Schurr, *The Mining Industries*, Table A-3, p. 312.

Metals. The figures for employment and manhours in the metal mining industries have been derived for 1880 and 1889 by components (see Table C-13).

In metal mining, the key years of 1899 and 1909 were not covered by Barger and Schurr. We have made estimates separately for iron ore, copper, and the group of other nonferrous metals by making a linear interpolation of the ratio of output to mandays between 1889 and 1902 and between 1902 and 1911,[23] and then applying the interpolated ratio to the output index numbers for 1899 and 1909. Adjustments for the average number of active days per year and the average number of hours worked per day[24] yielded numbers employed and manhours, respectively. The results are presented in Table C-14.

[23] Data for 1902 and 1911 are to be found in the Barger and Schurr volume. However, for the 1899 interpolation, the 1902 figures had to be adjusted to include placer gold.

[24] Both have been estimated separately for iron ore, copper, and the group of other nonferrous metals.

TABLE C-13

Metal Mining: Employment and Manhours, by Type of Ore, 1880 and 1889

	1880		1889	
	Number Employed (thousands)	Manhours (millions)	Number Employed (thousands)	Manhours (millions)
Iron ore	31.67	72.4	38.23	93.5
Copper	6.26	16.8	9.82	26.4
Manganese	0.23	0.7	0.60	1.6
Gold and silver	30.00	91.2	56.92	117.4
Lead	7.48	20.2	9.00	15.6
Mercury	2.20	6.5	1.00	2.7
Total[a]	78	208	115	257

SOURCE: *Report on Mining, 1880; Report on Mineral Industries, 1890; Census of Mineral Industries, 1939;* Spencer, *Mineral Extractive Industries;* Y. S. Leong *et al., Technology, Employment, and Output per Man in Copper Mining,* WPA–NRP Report E-12, Philadelphia, 1940; Yaworski *et al., Iron Mining.* The figures include placer gold. Correction was made to make the employment data consistent with that for output with respect to manganiferous ore. On both points, see discussion in the text in section on output. Employment in bauxite mining was negligible.

[a] The totals are adjusted with respect to fluorspar in Illinois and Kentucky and to pyrites (see section in text on output).

Oil and gas wells. In terms of available information with respect to employment and manhours, this is the most difficult group of mining industries. Barger and Schurr put it this way:

Prior to the Census of Mineral Industries for 1939 there was no comprehensive survey of employment in the petroleum and natural gas industry. Bureau of Mines statistics similar to those we have used for most other important mineral industries are not available except for a few recent years. For years prior to 1939, information from the decennial Censuses is either lacking altogether, or deficient. In 1929, for instance, no attempt whatever was made to cover the industry. In the reports on the industry in 1909 and 1919 a very important part of total operations—that conducted by contractors—remain untouched. Only in the Census of 1902 was information collected in anything approaching as comprehensive a fashion as that of the Census of 1939.[25]

For the period between 1902 and 1939 Barger and Schurr published estimates only for 1929 and 1935–38. However, the NRP offers estimates

[25] *Op. cit.,* p. 325.

TABLE C-14

Metal Mining: Employment and Manhours, by Type of Ore, 1899 and 1909

| | Iron Ore | | Copper | | Other Nonferrous Metals | | Total | |
	Number Employed (thousands)	Manhours (millions)	Number Employed (thousands)	Manhours (millions)	Number Employed (thousands)	Manhours (millions)	Number Employed (thousands)	Manhours (millions)
1899	36.6	93.1	24.2	62.4	73.3	141.7	134.1	297.2
1909	62.9	156.7	62.1	140.6	77.6	155.2	202.6	452.5

TABLE C-15

Oil and Gas Group: Wage Earner Employment and Manhours,
Key Years, 1880–1937

	Number Employed (thousands)	Manhours (millions)
1880	11.48	41.3
1889	18.50	67.3
1899	45.80	167.3
1909	46.75	140.9
1919	111.20	275.3
1929	179.00	413.3
1937	159.80	315.9

SOURCE: Kiessling *et al.*, *Natural-Gas Industries*, p. 327. The 1899 estimates were derived by interpolation between 1889 and 1902, following the same principle as in the case of metal mining.

TABLE C-16

Oil and Gas Group: Estimates of Salaried Employees, Key Years, 1889–1939

	Number Employed			Estimated Annual Number of Hours per Employee[a]	Total Manhours of Salaried Employees (thousands)
	Producing Operations[b]	Contractors[c]	Total		
1889	2,305	336	2,641	3,579	9,452
1902	4,596	645	5,241	3,558	18,647
1909	6,128	590	6,718	3,034	20,382
1919	24,400	1,289	25,689	2,470	63,452
1929	33,115	3,082	36,197	2,310	83,615
1937	25,888	2,406	28,294	1,977	55,937
1939	32,327	5,153	37,480	1,779	66,677

[a] Kiessling *et al.*, *Natural-Gas Industries*. The figures refer to wage earners, and the assumption is made that they apply also to salaried employees.

[b] The figures here refer to total salaried employees, not to salaried employees in and about mines. Sources of data are: 1889: *Report on Mineral Industries, 1890*; 1900, 1902, 1909, 1919, and 1939: *Census of Mineral Industries, 1939*; 1929 and 1937: estimated by interpolation of ratio of wage earners to salaried employees.

[c] Estimates are based on the assumption that the ratio of salaried employees to wage earners for contractors and for regular producers showed the same movement. Thus, two kinds of movements are taken into account: that of the ratio of wage earners to salaried employees in the oil industry, as represented by regular producers, and of employment in contracting services, as represented by number of wage earners. 1939 figure is from *Census of Mineral Industries, 1939*.

for many of the other key years within the 1880–1937 period. These estimates, in the words of Barger and Schurr, ". . . represent the abstract of an enormous amount of research . . ." and are the best available. Since the difference between full-period and active-period averages is of no practical significance for the group of oil and gas wells, it was easier for us to rely heavily on the NRP study. Moreover, this study takes into account workers employed by contractors. The series in Table C-15 represent only the wage earners, including those employed by contractors. Estimates of all salaried employees in the industry are contained in Table C-16; our sources and methods of derivation are explained in the footnotes.

Nonmetallic mining and quarrying. As in the case of output, the data on employment and manhours for this group of mining industries are poor. In consequence, our estimates are not entirely satisfactory, but they are sufficiently consistent with the output figures; so the productivity trends for the group, and especially for the mining segment, should not be distorted. Our basic estimates cover stone, gypsum, and phosphate rock. The estimates for this part of the group for the key years not covered in the Barger and Schurr study are given in Table C-17; the footnote describes the sources and methods used.

TABLE C-17

Nonmetallic Mining and Quarrying: Employment and Manhours, Key Years, 1880–1919

	Number Employed (thousands)	Manhours (millions)
1880	39.6	89.4
1889	80.8	182.5
1899	94.2	166.7
1909	127.2	259.2
1919	78.4	185.8

SOURCE: 1880: Number employed was estimated by using the figure on manhours and some evidence found in *Census of Mines and Quarries, 1902,* concerning average hours worked in 1880. Manhours was extrapolated by the Spencer estimates (*Mineral Extractive Industries*) on manhours.

1889: Data of *Report on Mineral Industries, 1890* on employment adjusted to exclude lime (see discussion in the section on output). Manhour figures were obtained with the help of census data on average number of days worked per year and an estimate of the average number of hours per day.

1899 and 1909: Estimated by interpolation between 1889 and 1902 and between 1902 and 1911 (figures for 1902 converted from 300-day workers to active-period averages). The method of interpolation was similar to that described in the section on metal mining above.

1919: Sum of Barger and Schurr figures (*The Mining Industries*) on gypsum and phosphate rock plus our estimate for stone. The latter was derived by applying to the Barger and Schurr estimate of mandays the figures from *Quarry Accidents,* Bureau of Mines, on average number of mandays per year and average number of hours per day.

Since a significant and increasing portion of the segment was not covered by the continuous industry estimates, adjustments for full coverage were worked out from census data for 1889, 1902, and 1939 (Table C-18). The adjustment ratios for employment and manhours were interpolated for key years between 1902 and 1939 by means of the adjustment ratios for output, described in a preceding section and presented in Table C-10.

TABLE C-18

Nonmetallic Mining and Quarrying: Adjustment Ratios for Full Coverage of Employment, Manhours, and Output, Key Years, 1889–1939

	Number Employed	Manhours	Output
1889	0.9346	0.9320	0.9452
1902	0.9050	0.8993	0.8881
1909	0.7536	0.7435	0.7429
1919	0.5988	0.5851	0.5945
1929	0.5708	0.5519	0.5708
1939	0.5476	0.5238	0.5513

RECENT-PERIOD ESTIMATES

Although the Commerce estimates of employment in the mining groups were generally used beginning 1929, for the petroleum and natural gas group the Commerce estimates have been used only since 1939. Careful examination of this series and the NRP series has convinced us that the latter is a more accurate representation of employment movements between 1929 and 1939. The Barger and Schurr estimates, as supplemented and extended, were linked to the Commerce estimates in the year indicated.

Estimates of average hours worked per week prepared by BLS are available since the mid-1930's for mineral industries. These are consistent with the OBE full-period employment estimates, and the two series have been used jointly to obtain estimates of manhours worked for 1939 and later years. The absolute levels of manhours so derived are quite close to the manhours estimates of Barger and Schurr after adjustment in the several instances already noted. This serves to confirm our impression that the two sets of estimates are reasonably consistent in industry and class-of-worker coverage. Unfortunately, it has not been possible to compare the current movement of the OBE-BLS-based manhour estimates with manhours prepared by the Barger method, since the Bureau of Mines has discontinued publishing some of the information needed.

PROPRIETORS

Proprietors represent a category that has been considered part of labor input throughout this volume. Therefore, although information is scanty, an effort has been made to include them in the mining sector as well.

Our procedure of estimating the number of proprietors in each group of mineral industries is based on the 1939 figures of the *Census of Mineral Industries*,[26] extrapolated forward, and back to 1929, by the OBE series. For 1909 and 1919 the figures given in the mining censuses for those years were adopted. The 1902 estimates were derived by extrapolation of the 1909 figures by data on the number of unincorporated firms. Finally, for all years previous to 1902, the estimates of total persons engaged were linked to the employee estimates, a procedure which is equivalent to extrapolation of 1902 proprietors by the sum of wage earners and salaried employees.

The oil and gas wells group again introduced special problems. In the first place, data on the contractors' portion of the industry were lacking, and our estimates had to be based on the same principles as those applied to salaried employees. Secondly, the 1902 estimates obtained in the fashion just described seemed improbably high; this forced another exception to the procedure followed elsewhere, and the link of 1902 was in this case moved to 1909.

Hours worked by proprietors have been derived by applying to the estimated number of proprietors either BLS average weekly hours for those years in which they are available or the average hours implicit in the Barger and Schurr study for the earlier period, multiplied by the estimated number of weeks worked per year and days worked per year respectively. In the case of oil and gas wells, since Barger and Schurr offer only a few figures on labor input, our estimates for the rest of the key years were based on NRP Report E-10.[27] The estimates of number of proprietors and manhours are given in Table C-19.

With the help of Borenstein's 1870 estimates of the number of wage earners and of the average number of hours worked per year,[28] the manhour figures for 1870 can be derived by extrapolation for each of the five components of the mining segment. When compared with the output estimates, however, the computed productivity ratios seemed high relative to 1880; consequently, we do not publish the 1870 figures but use the manhour estimates in deriving economy totals.

WEIGHTING SYSTEM

In accordance with the basic procedures in this study, manhours in each of the five mineral groups were weighted by average hourly compensation in order to obtain labor input in the segment as a whole. The average

[26] This represents a modification of the methods applied in other sectors of the economy, where the OBE figures were used as given; but the 1939 Census data seemed, on several grounds, more reliable for our purposes and yielded more reasonable results when extrapolated backwards.

[27] O. E. Kiessling *et. al.*, *Technology, Employment, and Output per Man in the Petroleum and Natural-Gas Industries*, WPA–NRP Report E-10, Philadelphia, 1939.

[28] *Op. cit.*, Table 3.

TABLE C-19

Mining: Estimates of Proprietors, by Group, Key Years, 1902–53

	Number (Thousands)				Manhours (Millions)			
	Bituminous Coal	Metals	Oil and Gas Wells	Nonmetallic Mining and Quarrying[a]	Bituminous Coal	Metals	Oil and Gas Wells	Nonmetallic Mining and Quarrying[a]
1902	6.3	5.3	n.a.	6.3	8	13.9	n.a.	18.0
1909	3.7	4.2	26.7	3.5	8	11.1	80.9	10.0
1919	4.2	1.4	20.0	1.8	7	3.4	49.4	4.9
1929	3.0	0.4	7.0	1.6	10	0.9	16.2	4.3
1937	4.6	0.8	7.8	2.1	9	1.5	15.4	4.1
1939	4.6	0.8	7.8	2.1	16	1.5	14.2	3.9
1948	5.8	0.4	10.9	2.1	10	0.8	20.7	4.4
1953	5.2	0.2	10.9	2.5	8	0.4	20.5	5.3

NOTE: In the Pennsylvania anthracite coal industry numbers of proprietors and manhours worked were negligible.

n.a. = not available.
[a] After adjustment for coverage.

compensation estimates were based on the total compensation series of the Department of Commerce for 1929 and subsequent years, extrapolated to 1919 by Kuznets' estimates. The relative weights used to combine the five manhour indexes in each of the subperiods are shown in Table C-20.

TABLE C-20

Mining: Relative Weight of Manhours, by Group, Subperiods, 1919–53
(per cent)

	1919–29	1929–37	1937–48	1948–53
Bituminous	42.2	38.3	40.6	42.4
Pennsylvania anthracite	14.2	15.3	13.7	13.3
Metals	12.2	12.8	13.5	13.9
Oil and gas wells	24.9	26.0	25.7	24.5
Nonmetallic mining and quarrying	6.5	7.6	6.5	5.9

Capital

Our measures of capital are built upon those of Israel Borenstein.[29] Capital is defined by Borenstein as follows: "The depreciated net value of structures and equipment is designated as 'plant,' and the sum of inventories, cash, and receivables as 'working capital.' The net value of surface land and mineral resources owned by the mining establishment, excluding leased land, we designate 'land.' The sum of plant and working capital we call 'capital,' and the sum of capital and land, 'total capital.' "[30]

For our purposes, capital is defined as plant plus inventories. The cash and receivables are eliminated from working capital. Land is not included owing to the difficulties of deflating the book values into meaningful real terms, a fact that has been noted by Borenstein.[31] Consequently, our capital figures in Table C-21 are taken from the worksheets underlying Tables A-3 and A-4 in Borenstein's study. Generally speaking, Borenstein's figures up to 1919 are based on the censuses of mineral industries and on the data of the Internal Revenue Service, adjusted to Census coverage, for the years beginning with 1929. The value of reproducible capital was converted to constant 1929 prices.

In terms of the consistency in coverage with output and labor input, the capital figures are satisfactory for the study of trends. As a matter of fact, for a considerable number of the key years, Borenstein's coverage is identical to ours. The two exceptions, oil and gas wells and nonmetallic mining and quarrying, are noted in Table C-21.

[29] *Op. cit.* ,Tables A–3 and A–4.
[30] *Ibid.*, p. 16.
[31] *Ibid.*, pp. 42–43 and Appendix D.

TABLE C-21

Mining: Plant and Inventories, by Group, Key Years, 1870–1953
(millions of 1929 dollars)

	Bituminous		Pennsylvania Anthracite		Metals		Oil and Gas Wells	Nonmetallic Mining and Quarrying[b]		Total
	Plant	Inventories	Plant	Inventories	Plant	Inventories	Plant and Inventories[a]	Plant	Inventories	
1870	23.3	1.4	32.7	0.7	33.8	2.3	17.7	6.5	0.6	119.0
1880	40.2	2.2	80.8	1.6	160.0	7.6	92.8	15.8	2.1	403.1
1889	100.6	2.7	106.1	1.4	309.5	25.9	325.0	63.2	7.8	942.2
1909	605.9	16.7	180.2	4.1	802.6	158.3	1,505.0	154.7	15.6	3,443.1
1919	882.8	23.9	205.0	4.7	693.2	169.4	3,675.0	{ 146.7	14.8	5,815.5
								218.4	22.0	5,894.4
1929	700.0	51.0	173.7	19.2	704.0	208.2	5,698.8	298.1	80.7	7,933.7
1937	483.3	43.0	111.9	10.5	434.1	133.8	3,289.1	181.9	54.3	4,741.9
1948	521.8	73.0	75.0	11.4	352.6	80.9	5,571.5	190.4	35.7	6,912.3
1953	596.2	74.3	52.5	17.3	561.6	145.5	5,309.2	262.4	52.6	7,071.6

SOURCE: Israel Borenstein, *Capital and Output Trends in Mining Industries, 1870–1948*, Occasional Paper 45, New York (NBER) 1954, worksheets underlying Tables A-3 and A-4.

[a] The sum of plants and inventories was adjusted to cover contracting operations (which are mostly in drilling; see section on oil and gas wells output). The ratio of the total number of employed in the oil industry to the number employed by regular producers served as the adjustment factor.

[b] The figures refer to what we have called "full coverage" (see discussion of this group in output and labor input sections). In 1919 the first figure is comparable with the earlier years, the second with the later years.

Table C-21 contains no data for 1899 because they were not available. The estimates of capital input we have used for that year were derived by interpolation. The variable we interpolated between 1889 and 1902 was the ratio of output to capital, from which the estimated value of capital was then derived from the available output estimates.

The composite index of capital input for the mining sector was obtained by combining the indexes for the five groups of mining industries. The weighting factors—unit capital compensation—are based on OBE data on national income originating, extrapolated by the Kuznets national income estimates, less labor compensation. The relative weights are shown in Table C-22. This method contains one imperfection, which, however,

TABLE C-22

Mining: Relative Weight of Capital Input, by Group, Subperiods, 1919–53
(per cent)

	1919–29	1929–37	1937–48	1948–53
Bituminous	3.8	3.0	13.2	10.7
Pennsylvania anthracite	2.6	0.7	2.5	2.4
Metals	41.1	34.4	23.6	15.7
Oil and gas wells	41.6	54.8	53.7	63.2
Nonmetallic mining and quarrying	10.9	7.1	7.0	8.0

does not substantially affect the results: Royalties, the compensation for land, could not be entirely eliminated from the capital compensation estimates underlying the computation of weights. The trend rate of growth of the unweighted composite capital index is, on the whole, somewhat greater than that of the weighted index.

Total Factor Input

The index of total input was constructed by weighting the indexes of labor and of capital inputs by the unit compensation of each in the mining segment as a whole, as shown in Table C-23. This procedure yields the

TABLE C-23

Mining: Relative Weights of Labor and Capital Inputs, Subperiods, 1919–53
(per cent)

	Labor	Capital
1919–29	70.0	30.0
1929–37	65.4	34.6
1937–48	58.1	41.9
1948–53	63.3	36.7

same result as that obtained by weighting the total factor input of each group by the corresponding unit factor compensation.

TABLE C-I

Mining: Output, Inputs, and Productivity Ratios, Key Years, 1879–1953

(1929 = 100)

	Output	Persons Engaged	Output per Person	Manhours	Output per Manhour	Labor Input	Output Per Unit of Labor Input	Capital Input	Output per Unit of Capital Input	Total Factor Input	Total Factor Productivity
1879	9.8	26.6	36.8	30.4	32.2	31.1	31.5	10.3	95.1	24.9	39.4
1889	18.7	48.0	39.0	51.8	36.1	50.2	37.3	22.5	83.1	41.9	44.6
1899	31.3	62.3	50.2	63.1	49.6	62.0	50.5	37.8	82.8	54.7	57.2
1909	55.3	102.1	54.2	101.3	54.6	99.0	55.9	67.2	82.3	89.5	61.8
1919	68.7	108.3	63.4	104.3	65.9	103.8	66.2	80.0	85.9	96.7	71.0
1929	100.0	100.0	100.0	100.0	100.0	100.0	100.0	100.0	100.0	100.0	100.0
1937	95.7	91.1	105.0	73.1	130.9	72.5	132.0	60.0	159.5	68.2	140.3
1948	133.3	95.1	140.2	88.9	149.9	88.5	150.6	78.3	170.2	85.3	156.3
1953	138.4	82.6	167.6	74.2	186.5	72.6	190.6	82.5	167.8	76.6	180.7

TABLE C-II

Mining: Output, Labor Inputs, and Productivity Ratios, 1879–1957
(1929 = 100)

	Output	Persons Engaged	Output per Person	Manhours	Output per Manhour	Labor Input	Output per Unit of Labor Input
1879	9.8	26.6	36.8	30.4	32.2	31.1	31.5
1889	18.7	48.0	39.0	51.8	36.1	50.2	37.3
1890	20.5	50.7	40.4	55.0	37.3	53.3	38.5
1891	21.7	51.9	41.8	56.2	38.6	54.7	39.7
1892	22.9	53.4	42.9	56.7	40.4	55.1	41.6
1893	22.4	53.1	42.2	54.2	41.3	53.4	41.9
1894	21.6	53.2	40.6	50.6	42.7	49.8	43.4
1895	24.3	55.1	44.1	55.1	44.1	54.6	44.5
1896	25.0	57.2	43.7	55.6	45.0	55.1	45.4
1897	24.9	56.8	43.8	53.9	46.2	53.2	46.8
1898	27.6	59.1	46.7	56.3	49.0	55.4	49.8
1899	31.3	62.3	50.2	63.1	49.6	62.0	50.5
1900	33.1	67.4	49.1	68.0	48.7	67.1	49.3
1901	35.9	73.0	49.2	73.7	48.7	72.5	49.5
1902	36.2	78.6	46.1	75.5	47.9	73.3	49.4
1903	41.9	82.7	50.7	83.4	50.2	82.2	51.0
1904	42.6	86.3	49.4	82.7	51.5	80.9	52.6
1905	47.0	91.1	51.6	90.4	52.0	88.8	52.9
1906	48.4	92.9	52.1	91.1	53.1	89.1	54.3
1907	53.4	96.3	55.5	100.7	53.0	99.4	53.7
1908	49.3	95.0	51.9	90.3	54.6	88.8	55.5
1909	55.3	102.1	54.2	101.3	54.6	99.0	55.9
1910	58.9	103.5	56.9	106.4	55.4	104.4	56.4
1911	58.4	102.2	57.1	109.6	53.3	107.0	54.6
1912	62.4	103.9	60.1	113.1	55.2	109.9	56.8
1913	66.2	107.8	61.4	119.6	55.4	117.1	56.5
1914	61.7	104.9	58.8	104.8	58.9	103.6	59.6
1915	66.5	102.6	64.8	104.5	63.6	102.8	64.7
1916	75.3	107.0	70.4	116.6	64.6	114.9	65.5
1917	80.2	111.4	72.0	123.0	65.2	121.9	65.8
1918	80.5	109.0	73.9	120.5	66.8	120.7	66.7
1919	68.7	108.3	63.4	104.3	65.9	103.8	66.2
1920	77.8	110.2	70.6	114.0	68.2	112.7	69.0
1921	61.5	107.6	57.2	88.5	69.5	89.0	69.1
1922	65.9	112.1	58.8	86.8	75.9	85.4	77.2
1923	90.2	121.4	74.3	114.4	78.8	113.1	79.8
1924	84.4	113.3	74.5	106.3	79.4	104.4	80.8
1925	86.7	109.1	79.5	102.1	84.9	100.6	86.2
1926	93.8	109.0	86.1	109.2	85.9	108.9	86.1
1927	93.5	109.6	85.3	102.8	91.0	102.6	91.1
1928	92.7	98.9	93.7	94.6	98.0	94.0	98.6
1929	100.0	100.0	100.0	100.0	100.0	100.0	100.0

(continued)

TABLE C-II (concluded)

	Output	Persons Engaged	Output per Person	Manhours	Output per Manhour	Labor Input	Output per Unit of Labor Input
1930	87.3	92.5	94.4	84.8	102.9	84.8	102.9
1931	72.2	82.0	88.0	66.3	108.9	66.9	107.9
1932	57.8	68.1	84.9	51.2	112.9	52.0	111.1
1933	63.1	69.2	91.2	54.4	116.0	55.2	114.3
1934	68.3	77.4	88.2	57.4	119.0	58.2	117.4
1935	73.9	79.6	92.8	57.9	127.6	58.1	127.2
1936	95.2	85.2	111.7	68.7	138.6	68.5	139.0
1937	95.7	91.1	105.0	73.1	130.9	72.5	132.0
1938	80.5	81.3	99.0	58.0	138.8	57.9	139.0
1939	89.4	80.2	111.5	61.7	144.9	61.6	145.1
1940	100.5	89.2	112.7	69.0	145.6	68.5	146.7
1941	106.5	93.9	113.4	77.0	138.3	76.0	140.1
1942	109.8	94.9	115.7	82.4	133.2	80.8	135.9
1943	113.0	88.5	127.7	83.5	135.3	82.4	137.1
1944	120.1	84.6	142.0	88.2	136.2	88.3	136.0
1945	117.9	79.8	147.7	81.8	144.1	82.1	143.6
1946	115.9	84.0	138.0	82.2	141.0	81.7	141.8
1947	126.6	90.5	139.9	87.8	144.2	87.2	145.2
1948	133.3	95.1	140.2	88.9	149.9	88.5	150.6
1949	114.7	88.2	130.0	75.5	151.9	74.7	153.5
1950	129.6	88.4	146.6	79.0	164.0	78.2	165.7
1951	141.1	88.9	158.7	80.4	175.5	79.2	178.1
1952	137.2	86.4	158.8	77.6	176.8	76.1	180.3
1953	138.4	82.6	167.6	74.2	186.5	72.6	190.6
1954	130.6	75.3	173.4	66.3	197.0	64.5	202.5
1955	145.0	75.8	191.3	70.3	206.3	68.4	212.0
1956	153.1	79.6	192.3	74.3	206.1	72.2	212.0
1957	152.2	79.0	192.7	72.3	210.5	70.3	216.5

TABLE G-III

Mining: Output, Inputs, and Productivity Ratios, by Group, Key Years, 1879–1953
(1929 = 100)

	Output	Persons Engaged	Output per Person	Manhours	Output per Manhour	Capital Input	Output per Unit of Capital Input	Total Factor Input	Total Factor Productivity
METAL MINING									
1879	12.9	65.3	19.8	69.7	18.5	18.4	70.1	39.4	32.7
1889	21.7	96.0	22.6	86.6	25.1	36.8	59.0	57.2	37.9
1899	39.1	111.3	35.1	100.3	39.0	64.0	61.1	78.8	49.6
1909	66.6	150.0	44.4	141.7	47.0	105.3	63.2	120.2	55.4
1919	72.7	124.2	58.5	121.7	59.7	94.6	76.8	105.7	68.8
1929	100.0	100.0	100.0	100.0	100.0	100.0	100.0	100.0	100.0
1937	98.2	96.8	101.4	81.8	120.0	62.3	157.6	70.3	139.7
1948	99.6	81.5	122.2	66.6	149.5	47.5	209.7	55.4	179.8
1953	109.2	86.3	126.5	71.7	152.3	77.5	140.9	69.4	157.3
PENNSYLVANIA ANTHRACITE MINING									
1879	38.8	45.7	84.9	52.5	73.9	42.7	90.9	51.8	74.9
1889	61.7	80.8	76.4	85.5	72.2	55.7	110.8	83.3	74.1
1899	81.8	90.7	90.2	83.0	98.6	72.5	112.8	82.2	99.5
1909	109.8	113.2	97.0	116.3	94.4	95.6	114.9	114.8	95.6
1919	119.3	101.0	118.1	120.0	99.4	108.7	109.8	119.2	100.1
1929	100.0	100.0	100.0	100.0	100.0	100.0	100.0	100.0	100.0
1937	70.2	64.9	108.2	50.0	140.4	63.5	110.6	50.3	139.6
1948	77.4	53.6	144.4	54.3	142.5	44.8	172.8	52.0	148.8
1953	41.9	35.8	117.0	28.7	146.0	36.2	115.7	28.6	146.5

(continued)

TABLE C-III (continued)

Mining: Output, Inputs, and Productivity Ratios, by Group, Key Years, 1879–1953

(1929 = 100)

	Output	Persons Engaged	Output per Person	Manhours	Output per Manhour	Capital Input	Output per Unit of Capital Input	Total Factor Input	Total Factor Productivity
BITUMINOUS MINING									
1879	7.9	20.0	39.5	24.2	32.6	5.6	141.1	23.5	33.6
1889	17.9	35.0	51.1	42.4	42.2	13.8	129.7	41.3	43.3
1899	36.1	54.0	66.9	62.8	57.5	33.5	107.8	61.7	58.5
1909	71.0	107.6	66.0	109.1	65.1	82.9	85.6	108.1	65.7
1919	87.1	123.6	70.5	110.1	79.1	120.7	72.2	110.5	78.8
1929	100.0	100.0	100.0	100.0	100.0	100.0	100.0	100.0	100.0
1937	83.3	100.2	83.1	77.4	107.6	70.1	118.8	77.1	108.0
1948	112.1	96.6	116.0	103.8	108.0	79.2	141.5	100.5	111.5
1953	85.4	61.6	138.6	59.8	142.8	89.3	95.6	63.4	134.7
CRUDE PETROLEUM AND NATURAL GAS									
1879	2.2	7.8	28.2	11.3	19.5	1.6	137.5	7.2	30.6
1889	6.2	14.7	42.2	21.2	29.2	5.7	108.8	14.7	42.2
1899	10.2	20.6	49.5	29.2	34.9	10.9	93.6	21.6	47.2
1909	20.7	36.2	57.2	47.2	43.9	26.4	78.4	38.5	53.8
1919	41.7	70.6	59.1	75.6	55.2	64.5	64.7	71.0	58.7
1929	100.0	100.0	100.0	100.0	100.0	100.0	100.0	100.0	100.0
1937	122.8	88.1	139.4	75.4	162.9	57.7	212.8	66.1	185.8
1948	196.6	122.0	161.1	98.4	199.8	97.8	201.0	100.0	196.6
1953	248.3	142.2	174.6	117.2	211.9	93.2	266.4	104.9	236.7

(continued)

TABLE C-III (concluded)

Mining: Output, Inputs, and Productivity Ratios, by Group, Key Years, 1879–1953

(1929 = 100)

	Output	Persons Engaged	Output per Person	Manhours	Output per Manhour	Capital Input	Output per Unit of Capital Input	Total Factor Input	Total Factor Productivity
				NONMETALLIC MINING AND QUARRYING					
1879	7.2	36.7	19.6	32.3	22.2	7.0	102.9	21.7	33.2
1889	17.0	75.6	22.5	65.9	25.8	27.9	60.9	50.1	33.9
1899	23.9	92.2	25.9	64.2	37.2	34.8	68.7	51.9	46.1
1909	51.1	141.1	36.2	114.0	44.8	66.9	76.4	94.4	54.1
1919	48.6	108.9	44.6	102.5	47.4	63.5	76.5	86.2	56.4
1929	100.0	100.0	100.0	100.0	100.0	100.0	100.0	100.0	100.0
1937	69.9	86.7	80.6	67.7	103.2	62.4	112.0	66.0	105.9
1948	124.2	110.0	112.9	82.1	151.3	59.7	208.0	73.1	169.9
1953	160.3	122.2	131.2	91.8	174.6	83.2	192.7	89.1	179.9

TABLE C-IV

Mining: Persons Engaged and Manhours, by Group, 1929

	Persons Engaged (thousands)	Manhours (millions)
Metals	124	314
Pennsylvania anthracite	151	282
Bituminous	474	925
Crude petroleum and natural gas	218	513
Nonmetallic mining and quarrying	90	279
Total	1,057	2,313

APPENDIX D

Manufacturing

THE indexes of output and employment in the manufacturing segment, groups, and industries are built primarily upon those constructed by Solomon Fabricant[1] and extended by the Census Bureau.[2] The indexes of real net capital assets for manufacturing groups and selected subgroups of industries are based on those prepared by Daniel Creamer,[3] adjusted for consistency of coverage with the Fabricant indexes.

We went somewhat further afield than previous National Bureau investigators in exploiting average hours data from the Census and other sources to combine with the employment series. This was necessary to achieve the goal of using weighted manhours throughout as a measure of real labor input for combination with capital input in constant dollars. We have also occasionally supplemented the Fabricant output indexes, which are based exclusively on physical quantity data, by deflated value estimates in those cases in which price information was available. For manufactured foods, we supplemented estimates of gross output in constant dollars by estimates of the deflated value of intermediate products consumed in order to arrive at estimates of real net output.

Since earlier National Bureau volumes contain full descriptions of the sources and methods underlying the basic estimates, these will be summarized only briefly here. In these notes, we will be more concerned with areas in which we have extended, supplemented, or adjusted the original indexes. Similarly, the major appendix tables are largely confined to indexes, since most of the basic data are readily accessible in the previous Bureau volumes, and the data underlying the estimates used for extension and supplementation may be found in the sources cited. Total and partial productivity ratios are presented for all the manufacturing groups and selected subgroups, and output per manhour estimates are presented for a wide range of SIC 4-digit industries or combinations thereof.

[1] *The Output of Manufacturing Industries in the United States, 1899–1937*, New York (NBER), 1940; and *Employment in Manufacturing, 1899–1939: An Analysis of Its Relation to the Volume of Production*, New York (NBER), 1942.

[2] *Census of Manufactures, 1947, Indexes of Production*; and *Census of Manufactures, 1954*, Vol. IV, *Indexes of Production*.

[3] Daniel Creamer, Sergei Dobrovolsky, and Israel Borenstein, *Capital in Manufacturing and Mining: Its Formation and Financing*, Princeton University Press (for NBER), 1960.

Classification

MANUFACTURING SEGMENT

The basic source of data relating to manufacturing activities is the *Census of Manufactures*. The classification and definition of industries and industry groupings used in the 1947 and 1954 Censuses is almost identical with that outlined in the Budget Bureau's *Standard Industrial Classification Manual*, Volume I, of November 1945. The Census quotes the *Manual* definition of manufacturing as follows: "the mechanical or chemical transformation of inorganic or organic substances into new products. These activities are usually carried on in plants, factories, or mills, which characteristically use power-driven machines and materials-handling equipment. Manufacturing production is usually carried on for the wholesale market, for interplant transfer, or to order of industrial users rather than for direct sale to the household consumer."[4]

Over the years the scope of the activities classed as manufacturing by the Census has changed somewhat. The tendency has been to drop industries whose inclusion in manufacturing seemed doubtful. A major change occurred in 1904, when neighborhood industries and hand trades were excluded, and figures for 1899 were reclassified accordingly. Some other important industries subsequently dropped are motion picture production, manufactured gas, automobile repairing, and railroad repair shop products. Fabricant adjusted the Census data for earlier years to conform to the 1937 definition of manufacturing.[5] Since the differences in scope of the 1947 and 1954 Censuses compared with the 1937 Census were quite minor,[6] the Fabricant segmental output and employment indexes for 1939 were extrapolated forward by the Census indexes for 1939, 1947, and 1954 without further adjustment.

[4] *Census of Manufactures, 1947*, Bureau of the Census, Vol. I, p. 3. The further discussion clarifies the definition as it relates to borderline areas, departures from common usage, and the several instances in which the Census departs from the SIC (see also *ibid.*, Appendixes C and E). The SIC was amended to some extent prior to the 1954 Census, but the changes were not basic.

[5] See Fabricant, *The Output of Manufacturing Industries* Appendix C, pp. 637–639. A very informative general discussion of the *Census of Manufactures* is contained in a book that appeared as the present study was being prepared for press: Frank A. Hanna, *The Compilation of Manufacturing Statistics*, Bureau of the Census, 1959.

[6] In 1947, two activities—coffee and spice roasting and grinding and tobacco stemming and redrying—accounting for $147 million of value added, were newly included; eight activities were dropped, of which bakery products produced in retail bakeries, logging camps and contractors, and certain repair activities were the most important, accounting for $96 million of value added (*Census of Manufactures, 1947*, Vol. I, pp. 6–7). In 1954, establishments engaged primarily in processing milk and in packaging seafood were added. The 1947–54 comparisons were adjusted accordingly (see *Census of Manufactures, 1954*, Vol. I, Appendix A; see also *Historical Comparability of Census of Manufactures Industries, 1929–1958*, Bureau of the Census Working Paper No. 9, 1959).

Within the manufacturing segment as defined, the Census Bureau has collected data from virtually the entire universe of establishments, with the exception of the very small. The degree of coverage probably did not vary significantly over the years until 1954. In the 1939 and earlier biennial censuses, the cutoff point for establishments to be included was at a value of product of $5,000. In 1947, the criterion was changed to exclude establishments with no employees—a procedure which made possible use of the Social Security Administration files. "This change in procedure has not, however, appreciably affected the comparability of the figures for 1947 with those for earlier years except for the figures on number of establishments."[7] The Census officials, on the basis of a carefully conducted sample survey, estimated that in 1947 the Census tables included 98.2 per cent of all manufacturing employment and 98.7 per cent of total wages and salaries. In addition to omission of the small establishments, there was some undercoverage of establishments whose classification in manufacturing was questionable and of establishments that operated during only part of the census year. Coverage in 1954 was believed to be complete, however. Consequently, for purposes of comparison, the Census Bureau adjusted upwards its estimates of output in all manufacturing and the major groups for 1947 by the estimated percentages of undercoverage.

MANUFACTURING INDUSTRIES

The basic grouping of establishments for which we compute productivity ratios is the "industry," identified by SIC 4-digit code numbers. In order to interpret productivity measures in terms of the real activities they describe, it is necessary to understand the Census definition of an industry and the principles by which the definition is implemented statistically. The classification is designed to "conform to the existing structure of American industry."[8] The industry is defined as an economically significant group of establishments engaged primarily in the same or similar lines of productive activity generally characterized by the products made or manufacturing processes employed. The establishment is generally identified in terms of a single physical location where a distinctive and reportable activity takes place.

It would be convenient if industries and products were coterminous— performance measures would be simpler to understand and less complicated to construct. But most establishments produce a number of products, and whereas output data can be collected on a product basis, cost data can not be so allocated except on a grossly arbitrary basis. Consequently, an industry is usually defined in terms of a group of products which are

[7] *Census of Manufactures, 1947*, Vol. I, p. 6.
[8] *Ibid.*, p. 7.

"primary" to it. Descriptions of the various industries and groups by principal primary products, together with code numbers and titles, are given in the censuses.[9]

The Census classification scheme places primary emphasis on aspects of supply—homogeneity of production or of technology—rather than on economic demand characteristics, such as close substitutability and high "cross-elasticity." The two criteria may frequently coincide. On the other hand, similar types of products may not be substitutable, or substitute commodities may be placed in different industries (e.g., tin cans and glass containers).

The Census Bureau attempts to apply the classification principles so as to maximize the homogeneity or similarity of activity of the establishments in an industry. That is, the industry is defined in terms of a range of products typically produced in large proportion by a number of establishments; and an establishment is assigned to a given industry if the plurality of its products (processes or operations)—usually as measured by value of products shipped—comes within the industry definition. The classification scheme is affected by the extent to which most of the establishments within an industry tend to produce the full range of primary products. If a significant number of the establishments concentrated on but a portion of the activities defining the industry, this would constitute a basis for further subdivision.

Homogeneity and overlapping. The average "industry homogeneity" for all manufacturing establishments in 1947 was 90 per cent (the proportion of value of output comprising primary products). Only twenty-five industries, accounting for less than 6 per cent of total value added in manufacturing, were completely homogeneous in the sense that their shipments comprised primary products exclusively. It should be kept in mind, however, that homogeneity is relative to the definition of the industry, and the products which are primary to an industry may exhibit considerable variety.

Table D-1 shows the distribution of industries in the 1947 Census according to degree of homogeneity. Since our classifications involve quite a few combinations of the 1947 industries, the homogeneity of the combined industries is even higher. That is, the more broadly an industry is defined, the greater the homogeneity of a given group of establishments. This partially explains why the data given by Fabricant for 1929 on the basis of 285 industries show greater homogeneity, or "degree of specialization" as it is called there, than the data for the 453 industries distinguished in 1947.[10] If the industries that appear to be defined identically in 1929

---

[9] See *Census of Manufactures, 1947*, Vol. I, Appendix C; and *Census of Manufactures 1954*, Vol. I, Appendix A.

[10] Fabricant, *The Output of Manufacturing Industries*, Table A-2, p. 336.

and 1947 were analyzed, the average homogeneity measure would provide some indication of the changing degree of diversification of establishment output.

TABLE D-1

Frequency Distribution of Manufacturing Industries, by Degree of Homogeneity and Extent of Overlapping of Products, 1947

	Degree of Homogeneity[a]		*Extent of Overlapping*[b]	
Percentage Class	Number of Industries	Value Added (millions)	Number of Industries	Value Added (millions)
Less than 50	...	$ ...	19	$ 1,737
50–59	1	18	9	479
60–69	6	439	19	1,231
70–79	37	2,772	50	4,226
80–89	129	19,238	110	16,458
90–99	255	47,820	207	38,212
100	25	4,139	35	11,909
No data	...	...	4	174
Total	453	74,426	453	74,426

Source: *Census of Manufactures, 1947*, Vol. II, Table 5, for each industry. Summary adapted from Maxwell R. Conklin and Howe T. Goldstein, "Census Principles of Industry and Product Classification, Manufacturing Industries," *Business Concentration and Price Policy*, Special Conference Series, Vol. 5, Princeton Unversity Press (for NBER), 1955, Tables A-4 and A-5, pp. 33–34.

For a similar tabulation for 1954, see *Census of Manufactures, 1954*, Vol. I, Appendix A, Table 1, p. A-1; a comparison of substantially identical industries for 1947 and 1954 is shown in Table 2, p. A-2.

[a] Value of primary products as percentage of total value of industry output.

[b] Value of primary products as percentage of value of total output of these products.

The corollary of the fact that establishments in most industries produce secondary products is that the establishments of many industries do not account for all of the output of the primary products which define those industries. The second part of Table D-1 shows the distribution of establishments according to the "extent of overlapping" (percentage coverage of primary activity). The average amount of overlapping in 1947 was also about 10 per cent. Changes in both ratios were relatively minor between 1947 and 1954. Whereas more industries accounted for all of their primary activity than the number that produced only primary products, there were more industries with 30 per cent or more overlapping than was the case with the homogeneity measure. It is the degree of homogeneity, however, that is significant as regards the validity of "coverage adjustments" discussed in connection with output measures.

Industry detail. In general, the industry classifications shown by Fabricant are employed in this study. Fabricant used the 1929 Census classification involving 326 separate industries because this represented the smallest number of industries covered by the censuses since 1899. Thus, continuous estimates could be presented by combining "subindustries" presented in earlier and later censuses. Since the 1947 Census used a 453-industry classification and the 1954 Census, a 447-industry classification, considerable combination was involved in extending the Fabricant estimates. In a few cases, some of the Fabricant industries had to be combined in order *to* establish continuity with the 1947 industry definitions.

From time to time, in addition to combining or splitting industries, the Census Bureau has changed the definitions of certain industries. Usually overlaps have been provided, making possible the linking of input and output estimates, which then should be interpreted in conjunction with the changed industry definitions. Tables D-V and D-VI indicate the content of the industries in terms of the 1947 Census code numbers, although the Fabricant titles are sometimes retained when the grouping is broader than in 1947. Due to the many changes in definitions in 1947 as compared with earlier censuses, the Fabricant study and the 1947 and 1939 Census volumes should be consulted to determine the precise content of each industry prior to the 1939 overlap with data for that industry as defined in the 1947 Census.[11] In a few cases in the historical series, industry definitions changed without overlaps being given. Although a change would affect both the output and the employment estimates, it could disturb the continuity of the productivity estimates if it were large. Such changes are indicated in footnotes to the Fabricant tables in his Appendix C.

GROUPS OF INDUSTRIES

For purposes of description and analysis, it is helpful to combine the industries of a large segment like manufacturing into groups characterized by at least a broad similarity of primary product. The 1947 Census, following the SIC, combined the various industries into twenty major industry groups. Fabricant employed the fifteen groups distinguished in the 1937 Census plus beverages and tobacco products, which were split off from the food group. In a few cases, he transferred industries from one group to another for the sake of consistency. We used the 1947 Census

---

[11] Appendix D of *Census of Manufactures, 1947*, Vol. I, tabulates the 1939 Census industries equivalent to each of the 453 industry classifications used in the 1947 Census. A similar table is given in Appendix E, Vol. I, of the 1939 *Census of Manufactures* comparing 1939 and 1937 classifications. For the several rearrangements in 1954 of the 1947 industries, see *Census of Manufactures, 1954*, Vol. I, Appendix B.

groups (also used in 1954) plus beverages, a practice that involved the following further breakdown or rearrangement of the 1937 groupings used by Fabricant:

1937 Group	*1947 Group*
Textile products	Textile mill products
	Apparel and related products
Forest products	Lumber and products except furniture
	Furniture and fixtures
Machinery	Machinery except electrical
	Electrical machinery
Iron and steel ⎫	⎧Primary metal industries
Nonferrous metals⎭	⎩Fabricated metal products
Miscellaneous	Instruments and related products
	Miscellaneous manufactures

The 1939 and 1947 Censuses shifted industries among some of the groups as defined by Fabricant after the regrouping described above. The net result of these shifts on the groups relative to the Fabricant (1937) definitions are summarized in Table D-2. The miscellaneous group is not shown as such because all single entries in the table represent transfers to or from the miscellaneous group. Industries are listed here only if they were shifted in their entirety or in major part. In a few instances, minor portions of industries were transferred, as indicated in the 1947 Census, Vol. I, Appendix D.

Since only half the groups were affected by these transfers, and since the transfers were not important in terms of value added except in the miscellaneous group, measures for 1939 and later years in terms of the 1947 classifications were linked to those of Fabricant as expanded. This made it unnecessary to adjust the earlier indexes (1899–1939), but the slight break in continuity in terms of contents of the several industry groups should be kept in mind. Although the expansion of the miscellaneous group has been substantial, measures for this group have an ambiguous meaning in any case because of the product heterogeneity. There were no shifts of industries across group lines between the 1947 and the 1954 censuses. We have combined Major Group 19, Ordnance, with Fabricated metal products for consistency with our employment estimates.

The 1947 Census further divided the major groups into 141 subgroups comprising one or several closely related individual industries. This classification has generally not been used here since it was not necessary for the analysis and output indexes were lacking for many of the component industries. We did, however, use certain subgroupings in order to employ capital estimates that were available for combinations of industries.

TABLE D-2

Industry Shifts among Manufacturing Groups, 1937–1947

Group (1947 classification)	Industries Shifted
Textile products	*Out* Furs, dressed and dyed
Forest products	*Out* Cork products Matches Morticians' goods Billiard tables Fabricated plastics products, n.e.c. Turpentine and rosin (gum naval stores)
Furniture	*In* Mattresses and bedsprings Window shades
Paper products	*In* Wallboard and wall plaster
Chemical products	*Out* Small arms ammunition Fireworks Candles *In* Turpentine and rosin (gum naval stores)
Petroleum and coal products	*In* Paving and roofing materials
Stone, clay, and glass products	*Out* Wallboard and wall plaster Paving and roofing materials *In* Steam and other packing; pipe and boiler covering (gaskets and asbestos insulations)
Fabricated metal products	*Out* Small arms Silverware and plated ware Jewelry Watches and clocks Watch cases Fire extinguishers Needles, pins, and fasteners

(continued)

n.e.c. = not elswhere classified.

TABLE D-2 (concluded)

Industry Shifts among Manufacturing Groups, 1937–1947

Group (1947 classification)	Industries Shifted
Machinery (nonelectric)	*Out* Mechanical measuring instruments
	In Models and patterns
Transportation equipment	*Out* Children's vehicles (carriages and sleds)
Instruments	*In* Watches and clocks Watch cases Mechanical measuring instruments

These subgroups do not necessarily correspond to 1947 Census classifications, but their precise industry content is indicated on Tables D-V and D-VI by Census code numbers.

Current Value Estimates

While our ultimate interest is in physical-volume estimates, it is necessary to examine the nature of the Census current value data. The value estimates are used to adjust partial physical-volume data to full coverage, or they are directly adjusted for price change as an alternative method of estimating real output, as explained in a later section.

VALUE OF PRODUCT

The product value data collected in most census years relate to the value of the quantities of finished commodities produced in factories and to the value of certain services rendered. The values are received or receivable net selling values, f.o.b. plant, after discounts and allowances. The value assigned to products transferred from one establishment to another of a multi-unit enterprise is generally the approximate commercial value.

Reports are obtained on a calendar-year basis from the great majority of firms, regardless of the basis of their own records. In a few industries, such as agricultural machinery and fertilizer, a fiscal year ending prior to December 31 is the reporting basis for value data (but not employment and payrolls). In these cases, the value figures may be somewhat understated during periods of expansion, and overstated during contractions, in comparison with "true" calendar-year totals.

411

In 1929, in lieu of production data, the value of products shipped was collected for the majority of industries; in 1947 and 1954, the shipments basis was general, although data on production were requested whenever it seemed likely that shipments would differ significantly from production. Figures relating to production were used in this study where available. The Census Bureau has stated, however, that shipment values are generally comparable with production values as reported in most of the censuses.

In the first place, it is likely that in previous censuses many manufacturers valued their output in terms of shipments even though value of production was requested. Secondly, the changes in the quantity of finished goods inventories for most industries were of minor importance and there was, therefore, little difference between production and shipments in either 1947 or 1939.[12]

After analyzing the 1929 data for both shipments and production, Fabricant concluded that one-sixth of the industries were appreciably affected by the change in definition.[13] Even if shipment data were reported throughout, however, long-run trends would closely approximate production trends since positive and negative inventory changes tend to cancel out over time. In preparing production indexes for 1947 and 1954, the Census Bureau did adjust the shipments data for estimated changes in inventories of finished goods and goods-in-process.

Ideally, the current value of changes in inventories or goods-in-process should be included as part of the value of production. Acutally, this has been done by Census only in the case of long-lead time items, such as ships and aircraft. If it is assumed that goods-in-process generally tend to fluctuate with output, production trends should not be significantly distorted by the omission prior to 1947. During periods of expansion, however, census production figures would tend to be too small as goods-in-process are accumulated preparatory to and during a rise in output. The reverse would hold true in contractions.

The value of production includes not only commodities, but also certain services: contract work, custom work, repair work, and advertising. Contract work is important in only a few industry divisions, notably printing and apparel, but we deduct payments for contract work throughout in order to avoid duplication in the value-added estimates. Repair work is included by Census only when subsidiary to manufacturing operations. Custom work is reported only when acompanied by own-account work. Excluded are shipments of products that are made from materials owned by others, resold in the same condition as purchased, or returned to an establishment without sale.

[12] *Census of Manufactures, 1947*, Vol. I, p. 18.
[13] Fabricant, *The Output of Manufacturing Industries*, p. 343.

Census value of products does not include the value of research and development on own-account, nor construction undertaken within the establishment by the manufacturer's own force. From an economy viewpoint, additions or major alterations to plant, and possibly research and development as a form of intangible investment, represent final output. To the extent that the proportion of the work force engaged in these activities changes over time, while no allowance is made for the output involved, productivity movements can be distorted. The extent would probably be small in most industries, especially insofar as the investment is an offset to implicit depreciation.

Excise taxes were included in all censuses through 1939. While excluded from the 1947 and 1954 censuses, such taxes were reported separately for tobacco and other industries where important. We have added the excises back into the value of product in these years in order to provide a consistent basis for price deflation. In order to obtain unit factor weights, excise taxes were eliminated along with the value of purchased intermediate products.

In a dozen industries in 1947 and 1954, values of product and materials consumed were not shown. All these were industries in which the proportion of duplication between cost of materials and value of shipments exceeded 10 per cent. To provide continuity in the 1947 value estimates for deflation purposes, unpublished data were obtained from the Census Bureau for some industries; for the others, in which the ratios of cost of materials to value of product has been fairly stable, the 1939 ratio of value of product to value added was applied to the 1947 value added in order to obtain the full complement of value data.

Also to provide continuity, when industry definitions changed and overlapping value-of-product and cost-of-materials estimates were available, these value estimates were linked forward and backwards from 1937. Since the input estimates were similarly linked, consistency between the output and input estimates was maintained.

COST OF MATERIALS

The value of materials consumed represents the net cost, after discounts and allowances (paid or payable), of materials, parts, containers, fuel, and purchased electrical energy actually consumed during the year. Items that represent transfers from other establishments of the same company, or withdrawals from inventories, are included. Excluded are materials for sale in the same form as purchased and materials processed but not owned by the establishment, since these are not included in product.

Since 1935 for some industries, and since 1937 for all industries, the cost of contract work has been included by Census to arrive at a total cost of materials. To provide a consistent series throughout and reduce duplication, we have adjusted cost of materials for all years prior to 1937 to include payments for contract work. To this extent, our value-added estimates for most industries differ slightly from those of Fabricant, who made such adjustments only in the case of industries in which contract work was important.

Excise taxes were included by the Census Bureau in cost of materials for 1931–37, a practice affecting primarily the tobacco and liquor industries. In line with the Fabricant procedure, these taxes were excluded from Census data in order to maintain consistency throughout. Value added and industry gross product for the affected industries thus include excise taxes. Exclusion of excises would make value added closer to factor cost, which as we noted in Appendix A, is to be preferred for weighting purposes. At the group level, national income originating, which excludes excises, was used as an alternative weighting system.

Not all "intermediate products" purchased by establishments for use in the production process are included by the Census Bureau in cost of materials. The omitted items are chiefly business services—insurance, advertising, communications, repair and maintenance by contractors, and purchased professional services. The influence of these omissions on the derived value-added estimates, as compared with factor cost, is noted in the next section.

VALUE ADDED

Value added in manufacturing is generally calculated by the Census Bureau by subtracting the reported cost of materials consumed from the total value of product. The main differences between value added and national income originating stem from the purchased intermediate products not deducted by Census (noted above) and, more importantly, from certain overhead items such as depreciation, rent, labor costs involved in maintenance and repairs, and indirect business taxes. However, a partial offset to the inclusion of these items in value added is provided, particularly since 1937, by the inclusion in income of employer contributions under the social security laws and of other supplements to wages and salaries. Many of the items excluded from national income but not from value added are ones that could only be obtained with difficulty, if at all, on an establishment basis; they are estimated for national income purposes on a company basis.[14]

The national income statisticians also adjust the income estimates for inventory revaluation. That is, inventory profits and losses are deducted from reported income, which includes the positive or negative book profits

---

[14] A rough item reconciliation between value added and national income was attempted by Fabricant for 1929 (*ibid.*, pp. 347–48). Adjusted census value-added estimates by industry, 1899–1937, are shown in the same volume.

estimated to have resulted from the charging of inventories to sales by methods other than replacement price. This puts national income estimates on a current market value basis.

In 1954, national income originating in manufacturing ran about 78 per cent of value added. For the twenty major industrial divisions, the ratios varied considerably around the mean value. Table D-3 shows that the ratio of value added to national income has varied somewhat over short periods, but has displayed little net trend since 1919. The correspondence is less close over the business cycle. Because of the relative inflexibility of overhead items, national income falls more rapidly than value added during business recessions, but advances more sharply during recoveries. If the national income estimates were unadjusted for inventory valuation, the fluctuations of the ratio over the cycle would be even larger.

TABLE D-3

Comparison of Census Value Added and National Income Originating in Manufacturing, Selected Years, 1919–54

	Census Value Added	*National Income*		*Ratio of National Income to Value Added*	
		Kuznets	Commerce	Kuznets	Commerce
	(billions	of dollars)		(per cent)	
1919	23.3	16.2		70	
1925	25.2	16.8		67	
1929	30.1	19.8	21.9	66	73
1937	25.8		19.3		75
1947	74.4		58.7		79
1954	116.9		91.1		78

In weighting industry output measures and adjusting to group coverage, value-added estimates have been used since the theoretically more desirable factor cost estimates were not available. After 1929, in combining group output indexes to arrive at the all-manufacturing index, we tried national income weights based on the Commerce Department estimates. The results, shown later in Table D-7, were so close to those obtained by using value-added weights that we have adhered to the latter for the sake of consistency with the group estimates and of continuity with previous segment estimates.

As the Census Bureau long ago recognized, value added is in many ways preferable to gross value of product as a measure of production. In current prices, value added reflects changes in the relative prices of outputs and intermediate-product inputs, or the "terms of trade" of the industry. After correction for price change (discussed below) value added is a net output measure in that most duplication within and among

415

industries is eliminated. That is, only the processing of products purchased (or transferred) from other plants within the industry, or from other manufacturing or nonmanufacturing industries, is counted as the output of the industry in question. Real net output estimates consistent with national income, rather than value added, would be preferable. Again due to lack of data, we have had to be satisfied with real value-added estimates as a first approximation to the real net measure.

A saving of materials would show up as an increase in net output, but would not be reflected in gross output. An increase in quality due to a greater degree of fabrication would likewise affect the net measure but not the gross. Similarly, greater integration of fabricating activities, and a consequent reduction in materials purchases, would result in a rise in the net output measure along with a rise in inputs, whereas the gross output measure would be unaffected. Conversely, an increase in plant specialization would cause both net output and input to decline, while gross output would not reflect the change. For these reasons, net output measures are considered superior as a basis for productivity comparisons. Further, net, but not gross, industrial output and productivity measures are consistent with national product and productivity estimates.

Output Estimates

In general, the Fabricant indexes of the physical volume of output were used for 1899–1939, when available, and were linked in 1939 to indexes prepared by the Census Bureau in collaboration with the Federal Reserve Board and (in 1954) the Bureau of Labor Statistics (hereafter called the Census indexes) for extension to subsequent years. The methodology employed by Fabricant is summarized below and only significant modifications introduced by Census will be mentioned. Fabricant confined his indexes exclusively to weighted physical units, as did Census for 1947, with one exception. To some extent, we have extended or supplemented the physical-volume indexes wherever reasonably good price indexes were available for the deflation of the value of product. In preparing output indexes for 1954 relative to 1947, Census used price deflation techniques for all industries not covered by quantity data, even though broad imputations were required in some cases. These deflation procedures will be described as well as the broader deflation work necessary to arrive at net output measures, involving the adjustment for price changes of the cost of materials consumed as well as the value of product.

PHYSICAL VOLUME OF GROSS INDUSTRY OUTPUT

The industry indexes were calculated by weighting physical units of the various types of primary products issuing from the industry by their base-period unit values and adjusting for the degree of coverage as measured by the ratio of the value of products entering the index to the total value of product of the industry. The various steps involved in this procedure have implications that will be made explicit.

Physical units and weights. The Census Bureau has long published partial data on the value and number of physical units of various types of goods produced as well as data on the total value of product by industry. Over time, the reporting of physical units has tended to expand, both in terms of the proportion of output covered and, particularly, in the degree of detail given for the various product classes. This may be readily seen in Appendix B of *The Output of Manufacturing Industries*, in which Fabricant presents the detailed data on quantity, value, and net realized price per unit underlying his output indexes as well as percentages of industry coverage—material not reproduced here but that will be of continuing value to the specialist. The corresponding data for 1939 and 1947 are shown in the Census monograph, *Indexes of Production*.[15] Only industry and product index numbers are shown in the more recent Census monograph for 1954.[16]

The continuing expansion of detail is indicated by the fact that the Census indexes for 1954 relative to 1947 are based on data for about 6,000 products, compared with 1,700 products in the 1947-39 comparison and 837 products in Fabricant's indexes for 1937 relative to 1929. The Census products covered 82 per cent of the total value of all manufactured products in 1954 and 60 per cent in 1947, while Fabricant's products covered 51 per cent. Including alternative methods of calculating the production indexes (primarily the use of materials consumed), the percentages of total value of product covered rise to around 66 and 55 for 1939–47 and 1929–37, respectively.[17]

Whenever possible, Census product data were supplemented by statistics from other sources, such as the Bureau of Mines, Department of Agriculture, Internal Revenue Service, and, occasionally, trade associations if their data appeared to be of good quality. In a few cases, non-Census data were used because they appeared superior to available Census data.

The unit in which production is measured was frequently dictated by the way in which the Census Bureau or other agency reported the data. Where a choice existed, the unit was selected which seemed most basic in the sense that the effect on unit value of shifts in the product mix would be minimized. It is important to keep in mind that the units are seldom indivisible. Since the units usually are more or less heterogeneous and comprise several product types or "qualities," each with differing unit

[15] *Census of Manufactures, 1947, Indexes of Production*, Chapter II and Appendix A.
[16] *Census of Manufactures, 1954*, Vol. IV, *Indexes of Production*.
[17] *Census of Manufactures, 1947, Indexes of Production*, p. 8; see also Table D-5, below.

value, shifts in the relative proportion of the various qualities of the product affect the unit values and not the quantity indexes as would be preferable. It is quite possible that over time, as real income rises, a net shift to higher qualities of products takes place, giving rise to a downward bias in the production indexes. Conversely, in contractions, there may be an upward bias as shifts to lower-value types of a product occur. Since the product detail underlying the indexes has gradually increased, this source of bias has diminished over time, although it is still present. In preparing the production index numbers for 1947–54, the Census Bureau substituted deflated value for weighted quantity measures in a number of instances in which comparison of unit value and price index numbers suggested a major degree of product shift.

TABLE D-4

Frequency Distribution of Manufacturing-Industry Indexes, by Percentage of Coverage of Physical-Units Data, Selected Years, 1909–47

Percentage of Coverage	Number of Industries			
	1909	1929	1939	1947
Below 40.0	0	1	6	8
40.0–49.9	3	5	5	10
50.0–59.9	3	4	11	12
60.0–69.9	1	10	16	19
70.0–79.9	8	24	25	28
80.0–89.9	8	28	43	35
90.0–99.9	24	46	67	64
100.0 and over	6	15	30	31
Total number of industries[a]	53	133	203	207

SOURCE: Figures for 1909 and 1929 (as well as for earlier census years not shown here) are contained in Solomon Fabricant, *The Output of Manufacturing Industries in the United States, 1899–1937*, New York (NBER), 1940, Table A-6, p. 353. Figures for 1939 and 1947 are taken from the *Census of Manufactures, 1947, Indexes of Production*, Table 4, p. 9.

[a] Not including industries for which the data necessary to make a coverage adjustment were not available, nor industries for which output indexes were based on methods other than that of weighting of physical units.

The availability of Census product quantity data varies considerably from industry to industry. In some industries, it was not feasible to collect product data; in others, data on most or all primary products were accessible; for most industries coverage varies between these extremes. Fabricant decided to prepare industry output indexes only if the value of the covered products primary to an industry were 40 per cent or more of the total value of industry output in most census years. As shown in Table D-4, a relatively small proportion of all industry indexes was based on coverage of less than 60 per cent. The Census computed several indexes for 1939–47 based on less than the critical ratio in order to fill in group indexes, but these were not separately published. In the 1947–54 indexes, price deflation was used for industries in which the quantity data were inadequate.

The standard procedure used to compute an "unadjusted" production index was to multiply the number of units of each type of commodity by the average unit value for the two years being compared—the Marshall-Edgeworth formula discussed earlier. Fabricant used 1909 as a base with which to compare 1899 and 1904; 1919, to compare 1909 and 1914; and 1929 as the base for the other census years through 1939. Although the Census Bureau computed the indexes for 1947 using 1939 and 1947 weights separately and as cross-weights, we used the latter to maintain consistency with the Marshall-Edgeworth chain for earlier years. Similarly, we used the Census Bureau's indexes based on cross-weights for 1947–54. Interpolation for 1953 and extrapolation to 1957 for the groups were done on the basis of the Federal Reserve Board production indexes.

Coverage adjustment. Adjustment for changes in coverage was needed because, in the various census years, the value of the products entering the raw index often fluctuated as a proportion both of the output of the primary products of the industry and of the total value of industry output including secondary products.

In terms of the following figure, the ideal output index would relate to all products of the given industry $(A + B)$, (where $A = A_1 + A_2$); actual data relate to $A_1 + C_1$, the primary products of the industry, wherever made. In real terms, $A_1 + C_1$ may vary as a proportion of $A + B$ if the coverage of the primary products $(A + C)$ varies; or if, with constant coverage of primary products, the proportion made outside the industry varies (C/A); or if the ratio of secondary products made in the given industry varies in relation to the primary products wherever made, $\left(\dfrac{B}{A_1 + C_1}\right)$. The current value coverage ratio would also vary if the prices of the uncovered-industry production $(A_2 + B)$ varied in relation to the prices of the primary products $(A_1 + C_1)$. It is possible, but unlikely, that the coverage ratio would remain constant as a result of divergent but offsetting price and quantity movements of $A_2 + B$ relative to $A_1 + C_1$.

In the absence of detailed price and quantity information regarding uncovered products $(A_2 + B)$, there are two feasible approaches to converting the product data to an industry basis. One is to assume that the physical volume of total industry output parallels the movement of covered primary production. This would imply that changes in the coverage ratio were due entirely to divergent price movements as between the covered-industry output (A_1) and the rest of the primary and secondary industry output $(A_2 + B + C)$. On this assumption, the unadjusted indexes based on covered primary output would be used as they stand to approximate industry output.

		Given industry	Other industries
Primary products	Data available	A_1	C_1
	Data not available	A_2	C_2
Secondary products		B	

The other approach is based on the assumption that the price movements of total industry output parallel the price movements of the covered primary output. The implication here is that changing coverage ratios are due to divergent quantity movements as between the covered industry output and the other primary plus secondary industry output. This approach necessitates the application of coverage adjustments to the unadjusted indexes.

It seems clear that the second approach yields more accurate results. As Fabricant points out, "prices probably move together within closer limits than do quantities, . . . the dispersion of prices in general is not very large; and within industries we may expect even less dispersion."[18] The Census analysts found that between 1939 and 1947 there was a significantly higher degree of correlation among price changes than among quantity changes as regards pairs of major and minor products for each industry.[19]

Both Fabricant and Census performed tests relating to 1929–37, and to 1939–47. The tests were set up slightly differently, but essentially they involved taking industries with high coverage ratios, deliberately discarding a portion of the quantity data, and then computing new industry

[18] Fabricant, *The Output of Manufacturing Industries*, pp. 364 and 366.
[19] *Census of Manufactures, 1947, Indexes of Production*, p. 97.

indexes on adjusted and unadjusted bases. The tests for both periods showed substantially better results by use of coverage adjustments. That is, the adjusted indexes based on a reduced amount of quantity data were closer to the indexes based on all the available quantity data than were the unadjusted indexes for the sample, in a substantial majority of industries tested.[20]

Instead of dividing industry output values by the weighted average price of covered primary products, a shorter method of adjusting for changing coverage can be used. It consists of computing coverage ratios for the base and given periods, converting the ratio for the given period to an index number relative to the base period, and then dividing the unadjusted index of physical volume by the derived factor. This method, originally developed by Frederick C. Mills, is mathematically equivalent to the deflation procedure[21] and was used by both Fabricant and the Census Bureau.

Obviously, the adjusted index is only an approximation to the true index of the physical volume of industry output. While it might be expected that prices of primary products made outside the given industry (C_1) would parallel the price movements of those made in the home industry, A_1 (and this correspondence would be affected by any differences in the composition of the two groups of primary products), there is less warrant for expecting prices of uncovered primary products (A_2) and particularly secondary products (B) to move with prices of A_1. An argument supporting the adjustment is that since technological advance in an industry tends to affect all branches of that industry, the relative costs and prices of the products involved would probably show less divergence than the prices of products picked at random.

In any case, the 40 per cent cutoff would limit the error. Taking the average true coverage in 1947 as 60 per cent (primary production averages 90 per cent of total value of industry output, and the coverage of primary production averages 66 per cent), a variation of 12 per cent in the average prices of uncovered products relative to the average prices of the covered products would result in an error in the adjusted physical-volume index of no more than 5 per cent.[22] For many industries, the potential accuracy of the indexes is higher, and accuracy should have increased somewhat over time as product coverage has increased. The increasing amount of product detail has also improved the quality of the implicit price deflation for uncovered value of output.

---

[20] For the detailed results of these tests, see Fabricant, *The Output of Manufacturing Industries*, pp. 366–69; and *Census of Manufactures, 1947, Indexes of Production*, pp. 97–98.

[21] The mathematical equivalence is demonstrated in Fabricant, *The Output of Manufacturing Industries*, p. 363. Cf. also *Census of Manufactures, 1947, Indexes of Production*, p. 96.

[22] Cf. Fabricant, *The Output of Manufacturing Industries*, pp. 364—66.

ALTERNATIVE METHODS OF ESTIMATING GROSS OUTPUT

The indexes for some industries, or groups of industries, were constructed by methods that do not use weighted physical units adjusted for coverage. Materials consumption was used for one group by Fabricant and for the same group, plus five other industries, by Census. Deflated value-of-product estimates were not used by Fabricant, and by Census only since 1947. We have used the latter approach up to 1947 to supplement and extend the previously published indexes wherever appropriate price series were available and the results seemed reasonable. The relative importance of the several methods, both before and after the supplementation provided here, is shown in Table D-5, which covers the first and last periods of the Fabricant index and extensions to 1947 and 1954. The substantial coverage, in terms of value added, of the supplementary deflated value series is due largely to the several indexes for 2-digit industry groups. The additional coverage contributed by the deflated value series at the 4-digit level was not large enough to warrant revising the original group indexes. However, these series add to the basis for industry analysis and are used in constructing a segment index for comparison with the previously published all-manufacturing index.

Materials consumption. Indexes of the physical volume of materials consumed are not generally to be recommended as substitutes for indexes of the physical volume of gross output, and even less for net output indexes. Insofar as the ratio of materials consumed to gross output (in real terms) varies, the former measure is biased as an approximation to gross output and is even less accurate as an approximation to net output, since by definition a change in the ratio of materials input to gross output produces a change in the opposite direction in the ratio of net output to gross output. Even when materials input could be readily estimated, this measure has only been used when quantity data or price deflators were completely lacking or seriously defective, and there was no reason to believe that the technical relationship between materials consumption and output had changed to a marked degree.

In printing and publishing, which accounts for most of the value added represented by materials indexes, materials consumption is represented by a few major types of paper, which were measured and weighted separately. As a proportion of total current value of product, the value of materials consumed showed little net change between 1899 and 1947. It can be inferred that the ratio between the real quantities has likewise been stable only if the ratio of final product prices to materials prices has not varied significantly. This cannot be learned directly since time series on average prices or rates in printing and publishing are not available. The fact that total productivity as measured here has increased somewhat

TABLE D-5

Types of Manufacturing Output Indexes: Number and Importance of Represented Industries, Selected Periods, 1899–1954

Method of Representation	*Number of Represented Industries*				*Importance of Represented Industries*			
	1947–54	1939–47	1929–37	1899–1904	1954	1947	1937	1899
					(per cent of value added)			
Total represented by specific indexes								
Excluding deflated value indexes	324	216	143	67	85.6	75.4	60.4	56.8
Including deflated value indexes	435	234	171	93	100.0	89.6	82.4	80.7
Product data	322	210	142	66	82.2	67.6	53.4	50.9
Materials consumed	2	6	1	1	3.4	7.8	7.0	5.9
Deflated value of products[a]	111	18	28	26	14.4	14.2	22.0	23.9
Not represented by								
Indexes other than deflated value					14.4	24.6	39.6	43.2
Any specific index					0	10.4	17.6	19.3
Grand total					100.0	100.0	100.0	100.0

[a] Up to 1947, the deflated value estimates have been prepared for the first time for this study, except for one index, representing 0.1 per cent of value added in 1947, which was used in Bureau of the Census comparisons for 1939–47. The deflated value estimates for 1947–54 were prepared by the Census Bureau and associated agencies. Of the 14.4 per cent of value added in industries so covered, 7.1 per cent was covered by the use of specific price indexes, while 7.3 per cent represents values deflated by group price indexes which involve the same possible errors as the coverage adjustments discussed in the text.

more rapidly in printing and publishing than in paper and paper products (and therefore prices have probably declined relatively) suggests that gross output and real value added may have risen somewhat more than materials consumption over the period. Such a development is not unusual in manufacturing industries, nor is it contrary to the impression that the degree of processing has tended to increase in printing and publishing.

Deflated value of product. Conceptually, deflated value estimates are not inferior to weighted physical output measures. If complete price and quantity data were available, the two approaches would yield identical results provided weighting systems were consistent. The choice between them, other things being equal, depends primarily on the relative degree of coverage of industry output. If different products were covered, the two approaches could be used to supplement each other within the same industry.

Since the coverage of product quantity data in manufacturing was generally higher than the coverage of price indexes and more readily assessable as to quality, Fabricant chose to use this approach consistently for all industries, with the exception of printing and publishing, although by adjusting for coverage he implicitly deflated the value of uncovered products by an average of the available unit value series. We have here accepted all the physical-volume indexes prepared by Fabricant and Census, but have supplemented these by deflated value series as prepared for this study up to 1947 (and as provided by Census since 1947). In some cases, deflated value series were used to represent industries or groups not covered at all by quantity indexes; in other cases, they were used to extend quantity indexes to years not previously covered.

In general, we have prepared deflators only if price series were available that represented types of primary products accounting for at least half the industry output. It should be noted that a considerable degree of imputation is involved in this criterion. It is assumed that the prices of the various unrepresented types of a product move with the price of the type which is specified by the price collection agency. In recent years at least, the Bureau of Labor Statistics, which is the source for most of the price series used, has investigated price movements extensively in order to make reasonable imputations and to shift specifications (with overlapping of the price series) if a given type of product becomes unrepresentative of the broader family. Prices are collected from at least three manufacturers in different areas of the country in an attempt to cover price movements nationally. Annual estimates are averages of monthly or quarterly observations.[23]

[23] For further description of the BLS wholesale price indexes, see *Techniques of Preparing Major BLS Statistical Series*, Bulletin 1168, 1954.

Assuming that the value-of-product estimates are relatively complete and accurate, the validity of the deflated value estimates depends primarily on the representativeness of the price samples underlying the deflators. Since that cannot be determined in the absence of information on average price movements of all the types of products comprising industry output, our selection of industries for which to present deflated value estimates was largely a matter of subjective evaluation. The price indexes comprising the deflators, together with their weights, are listed by industry in a Technical Note to this appendix. The user of the estimates is free to reject those deflated value and derived productivity series which he feels are based on inadequate price information.[24] The Census Bureau in its 1954 *Indexes of Production* used italics for those indexes believed to be of doubtful reliability.

Although the direct coverage of price indexes based on given types of a product is less than that of quantity indexes that are based on units comprising all types of a product, deflated value measures are not necessarily inferior to quantity measures. For if the physical units are relatively undifferentiated and price levels differ substantially among constituent types, the deflated value series has the advantage of reflecting shifts in the quality mix of the product family. Lack of information precludes quantification of these possibilities—they are mentioned to indicate that the degree of direct coverage is not the sole criterion as to the relative validity of deflated value versus physical-volume indexes; representativeness of the price series and homogeneity of the physcial units must also be appraised. In at least one group, food, a weighted average of available price indexes showed approximately the same movements between census years during 1899–1947 as the implicit unit value index. The correspondence could not be expected to be so close in most other groups, however, since both unit value and price data are generally not as adequate as in the food industries.

NET OUTPUT ESTIMATES

Our net output indexes for the food group measure the movement of the difference between Census value of product and cost of materials, etc., after deflation of each (see Table D-6). They thus represent real value added, which is somewhat grosser than real net product originating, as explained above. The estimates were constructed in terms of 4-digit industries or combinations of industries, corresponding, in general, to the

[24] We have presented deflated value series only if the resulting output and derived productivity relations seemed reasonable. As Arthur F. Burns has written: "There is, indeed, no more important check on the validity of conclusions drawn from statistical materials than the reasonableness of the results" (*Production Trends in the United States since 1870*, New York [NBER], 1934, p. 29).

classifications used in the 1947 interindustry study for which materials inputs by industry of origin were available.[25] We had hoped to carry out this approach for all manufacturing, but it proved to be so time consuming that only a pilot study was possible.[26]

TABLE D-6

Manufactured Foods: Gross and Net Output, Key Years, 1899–1947
(1929 = 100)

	Gross Output	Net Output[a]
1899	30.3	34.2
1909	44.9	40.5
1919	65.1	75.3
1929	100.0	100.0
1937	104.2	99.1
1947	158.6	166.4

[a] The net output indexes can be used in conjunction with the input indexes for the food and kindred products group shown in Table D-IV to calculate productivity ratios on this basis (cf. Table 53).

The general procedure followed was to deflate the adjusted value-of-product and value-of-materials series by the available price and unit value series. Thus, the real value-of-product estimates are essentially the counter-part of the physical output series described in the section above, except that in some cases where both were available, price indexes rather than unit value series were used for deflation. This made for consistency with the materials input series, which were usually deflated by components of the industry price deflators. In the case of the industries for which output indexes are not shown in the tables that follow, value of product was deflated either by less adequate price indexes or by an average of the price or unit value indexes used for the covered industries in the group. It was desirable to use full industry detail in order that the price of pur-chased-materials indexes for the group might have changing industry output weights.

Special tabulations from the BLS interindustry study for 1947 showed the purchases of each manufacturing industry, or group of industries, from all the other industries in the economy, exclusive of business services.[27] This

[25] *Industry Classification Manual for the 1947 Interindustry Relations Study*, Bureau of Labor Statistics, mimeo, June 6, 1952, revised March 20, 1953.

[26] Cf. the net output estimates made by the Bureau of Labor Statistics for selected years since 1939: *Trends in Output per Man-Hour and Man-Hours per Unit of Output—Manufacturing, 1939–53*, BLS Report No. 100, 1955.

[27] These tabulations were prepared by the BLS Division of Productivity and Tech-nological Development for the purpose of estimating net output in manufacturing from 1947 to date; unpublished materials from the Interindustry Relations Study, 1947, were loaned to the National Bureau for use in this project.

distribution of materials inputs by industry of origin was necessary in order to obtain weights by which to combine the price indexes appropriate for the deflation of materials costs. In order to economize time, price indexes were not included for materials supplied by those industries which together contributed less than 10 per cent of total materials costs. Fragmentary data contained in earlier Census volumes were consulted so as to determine whether the relative importance of major material inputs had changed significantly over time. When this was the case, the weighting diagram for the materials prices was changed accordingly. Nevertheless, in the majority of industries, constant weights were applied to the price indexes. At the group level, however, changes in input composition due to changes in the relative importance of component industries are reflected in the input estimates and the implicit deflator.

Approximately two-thirds of the materials consumed in manufacturing industries come from within manufacturing. Since the majority of the price or unit value indexes employed to deflate value of product were also used to deflate materials cost, errors in the price deflators would, to a considerable extent, be offsetting for the manufacturing segment as a whole. For that reason, we show the net output indexes only for the segment and for the food group that was deflated in some detail and by price indexes judged to be of good quality. Even in the segment, errors in the price indexes that do not affect both product and materials—that is, prices of final products and of materials purchased from nonmanufacturing industries—will affect the real net output series, although over a broad area offsets are probable. Errors in weighting can also bias the results, but these are less important in the segment than in individual industries since changing industry composition is reflected in the broader segment measures.

OUTPUT ESTIMATES BY INDUSTRY GROUPS

The estimation of output indexes for the major groups and the whole manufacturing sector involved the same steps that underlie the basic industry indexes. The adjusted output indexes (or unadjusted indexes where adjustment is not feasible) are weighted together. Where industry coverage was not complete, but was sufficient to form the basis for a group index, a coverage adjustment was made to yield an adjusted group index. At the group level, the basis for weights and coverage adjustments is value added, instead of the value of product used at the industry level.

Weighting. In combining industry indexes by group, it was possible to employ value-added weights rather than the value-of-product weights, which are a less accurate approximation to factor cost. It should not be thought, however, that the application of value-added weights to gross output indexes yields a net output composite. Movements of the gross and net indexes would be parallel only if the ratio of net to gross remained constant in the component industries, or if changes in the ratios were offsetting.

In combining the industry output indexes, the Marshall-Edgeworth formula may be used, substituting Q (the output index number) for quantities of products, and VA (value added) for prices. A shortcut formula used by Fabricant, and in a slightly different form by the Census Bureau,[28] yields results identical to those obtained by use of the modified Marshall-Edgeworth formula. It may be set down as follows:

$$\frac{\sum (VA_1 + VA_0 Q_1)}{\sum (VA_0 + VA_1/Q_1)}$$

In the Fabricant formula, Q_1 represents the industry output index in the given year, relative to the base year as 100; subscripts $_0$ and $_1$ denote the base and given years, respectively. The cross-weighted indexes are chained together as of the terminal year in each subperiod, as in the case of industry indexes. It was this procedure that we used.

Group coverage adjustment. In several groups, the coverage of the adjusted industry indexes was complete, so further adjustment was not needed. In some groups, the missing industries were primarily those "not elsewhere classified," which generally produce commodities either not important enough to call for separate industry classifications or so highly diverse that the collection of meaningful quantity figures would require an inordinate amount of detail.

While Census had more than 40 per cent value-added coverage of industries in all groups for 1939–47, and full coverage for 1947–54, Fabricant fell short of this percentage in a number of groups and, therefore, did not calculate group indexes. Our supplementation of Fabricant's industry output indexes by deflated value estimates made possible the required coverage for these groups, with the exception of the instruments and miscellaneous group prior to 1929 and of rubber products prior to 1909.

There are more ways of coping with the problem of incomplete coverage at the group level than at the industry level. In addition to assuming that output or price movements in the missing industries are parallel to those in the covered industries, it is also possible to assume that unit value-added or output-per-worker movements are parallel. For the same reasons adduced in the industry discussion, the parallel output assumption may be discarded. As between the assumption of parallel movements of unit value or of unit value added, the latter is preferable. For unit values of industrial

[28] See Fabricant, *The Output of Manufacturing Industries*, p. 370; and *Census of Manufactures, 1947, Indexes of Production*, p. 11.

groups of products to move together, productivity, rates of factor compensation, and prices of intermediate products would have to change synchronously. Parallel movement of unit value added requires only that that the first two of these three elements move in like fashion. There is no reason to expect that prices of the different intermediate products purchased by different industries should move together. On the other hand, there is evidence (see Chapter 7) that factor prices tend to move together, at least over relatively long periods of time. Similarity of productivity movements among industries within a group may be greater than among groups insofar as the industries composing a group have technological similarities that facilitate the spread of particular innovations among their number. The assumption of parallel unit value-added movements was the one adopted by Fabricant. This involves computing coverage adjustment factors based on the ratio of value added in the covered industries to total group value added in the base and the given years.

Census, on the other hand, assumed for the 1939–47 indexes that output per worker in the missing industries of a group changed as it did in the covered industries. Investigation indicated that between 1939 and 1947, changes in output per man as among the industries of a group showed less variation than changes in unit value added. On the other hand, in a test similar to that used for the industry coverage adjustment described above, the two methods gave almost identical results. That is, experimental group indexes, calculated after discarding industry indexes accounting for about one-fourth of value added in the group, approximated the true group index (based on all available industry indexes) to about the same degree regardless of whether they were adjusted on the basis of value added or output per man. In the 1947–54 period, Census found less variation in both unit value and unit value added than in output perman among the industries of a group. For this period, they deflated the value of output of uncovered industries either by selected price deflators, or by the average price of output of the covered industries of the group.

The all-manufacturing index for 1947 relative to 1939 calculated from group indexes, with coverage adjustments based on output per man, is approximately 2 per cent higher than the composite index based on a unit value-added adjustment, and the latter is about 2 per cent higher than a composite of unadjusted group indexes. The differences between the two adjusted indexes are not great in the individual groups, with the exception of electrical machinery, for which the employment-adjusted index is significantly higher.

Since the several types of coverage adjustments are basically similar and yield generally comparable results, the Census indexes have been accepted since 1939 and linked to the Fabricant indexes. For the sake of strict consistency, the value-added adjustments would have been preferable for the recent period. As already implied, however, both adjustments in essence rest on the assumption that productivity changes in the missing industries paralleled those in the covered industries in each group. Each adjustment is only a rough approximation to an application of this assumption. It could be argued that it would be more direct to compute productivity in each group as the weighted average of productivity in the covered industries. Then output changes could be obtained by applying the productivity change to the total group factor inputs. This solution was not feasible, however, since some of the data necessary to compute total factor productivity in the covered industries alone were not available.

ALL-MANUFACTURING OUTPUT

Alternative segment estimates. The output index for the manufacturing segment was calculated by combining the adjusted group indexes, using value-added weights, by the formula used to obtain the group indexes. In the period up to 1939 quantity indexes were lacking for several groups. To handle this problem, Fabricant combined the available group indexes, plus the several available industry indexes in the groups for which coverage was insufficient, and applied a coverage adjustment based on the ratio of value added in the covered groups plus additional industries to total value added in manufacturing. Here the assumption was that unit value added in the missing industries of the uncovered groups moved with unit value added in the rest of manufacturing. Fabricant also computed a segment index based on all available industry indexes and applied a coverage adjustment to this composite. This adjustment was naturally greater, since the group indexes used in the first instance had already been adjusted to cover missing industries. The results of the two approaches were not very different, the group method showing only a slightly lower trend rate of growth. The group method was considered preferable, however, since it is based on the plausible assumption that missing industries are better represented by the other industries of the groups to which they belong than by the covered industries in manufacturing as a whole.

To supplement the Fabricant indexes, we have computed an index for the segment using deflated value estimates for the missing groups through 1939. No coverage adjustment was needed from 1929 forward. Prior to 1929 an adjustment based on value added was used, but it was considerably smaller than Fabricant's. This broader index closely parallels the movements of the Fabricant index; but because of its already wide acceptance, we have employed the Fabricant index in our analyses. The alternative index may be considered as a rough check on the validity of the coverage adjustment employed in the quantity-based index. Another alternative index was computed for the period since 1929, using national income weights for the group indexes instead of value-added weights. Here again, the differences are not large. Despite the theoretical superiority of national income weights, we have worked in terms of the index with value-added weights because of the availability of such weights prior to 1929 and the consistency of this index with the group indexes. The various output indexes just discussed are presented for comparison in Table D-7.

TABLE D-7

Alternative Estimates of Total Manufacturing Output, Selected Years, 1899–1957
(1929 = 100)

	Fabricant Indexes		Fabricant Group Indexes Supplemented by Deflated Value Indexes[a]	
	Average of Industries[b]	Average of Groups[c]	Value-Added Weights	National Income Weights
1899	25.1	27.5	27.3	
1904	31.4	34.2	33.8	
1909	40.3	43.4	43.5	
1914	48.5	51.1	50.8	
1919	60.5	61.0	63.5	
1921	51.9	53.5	52.9	
1923	77.5	76.9	76.7	
1925	81.7	81.9	81.4	
1927	86.5	87.1	86.3	
1929	100.0	100.0	100.0	100.0
1931	71.1	72.0	70.8	70.7
1933	62.3	62.8	61.2	60.9
1935	83.3	82.8	81.7	81.0
1937	104.5	103.3	103.2	102.2
1939		102.5	101.6	100.6
1947		178.3[d]	176.9[d]	175.6
1954		228.2[d]	226.4[d]	228.0
1957		264.6[e]	262.1[e]	260.6

[a] Index derived by combination of Fabricant's group indexes plus adjusted indexes including industry indexes based on deflated value of product where output coverage was not sufficient.

[b] Index derived by combination of adjusted indexes of individual industries. When adjusted indexes were not available, unadjusted industry indexes were used.

[c] Index derived by combination of adjusted indexes of groups plus adjusted indexes (or, if not available, unadjusted indexes) of industries not covered by groups. This is the index used in our study.

[d] 1939–54 extrapolated by output indexes published by Bureau of the Census.

[e] 1954–57 extrapolated by Federal Reserve Board index based on constant 1954 value-added weights.

Estimates prior to 1899. The Fabricant gross output index was extrapolated from 1899 back to 1869 by the index prepared by Edwin Frickey of Harvard University,[29] adjusted to include the output of leather and

[29] *Production in the United States, 1860–1914*, Cambridge, Mass., Harvard University Press, 1947, p. 54.

leather products and of stone, clay, and glass products. Since this index has been exhaustively described by its author, only a brief summary is in order here. Frickey collected quantity data relating to eleven of the fourteen major manufacturing groups, classified as in 1914. His annual interpolators covered ten of the eleven groups for 1899–79, but fewer groups in the earlier decade. Aggregates based on the smaller samples were linked to the larger aggregates to avoid distortion.

Weights were value added in 1899. Coverage adjustments were not used either within the groups or for the segment. Rather, segment weights were distributed proportionately to value added among the covered groups and, within each group, among the covered items. As noted earlier, the assumption of proportional movements of physical volume as between covered and uncovered items is less satisfactory than certain alternative assumptions. While Frickey's indexes have been accepted for the included groups, we have weighted into his index (again based on 1899 value added) the deflated value of product originating in the leather and leather products and the stone, clay, and glass groups, as estimated for census years by Creamer.[30] Frickey also omitted railroad repair shops; but this is desirable from our viewpoint since it is excluded from manufacturing by a later definition and we have excluded the corresponding inputs. The annual Frickey index was used for interpolations between census years.

The coverage of the Frickey index is substantially less than Fabricant's, and thus the estimates prior to 1899 must be considered to have a wider margin of error than those for subsequent years—particularly in view of the absence of coverage adjustments. Even from 1899 to 1914, which is the terminal year of Frickey's index, his coverage is less than that of Fabricant since he deliberately tried to base his index on production items available for the entire period plus items that emerged during the period. Despite the difference in coverage and method, the two indexes are not far apart during the period common to each. On an 1899 base the Frickey index in 1914 is 192, compared with 186 for Fabricant's, and half the gross difference may be explained by Frickey's omission of two major groups covered by Fabricant.

Annual interpolations. Because the Frickey index is more comprehensive than the Mills index used by Fabricant for interpolation of intercensal years from 1899 to 1914, it has been substituted as an interpolator for this period. The Fabricant interpolation based on Warren M. Person's index has been retained for 1914–19. After 1919, intercensal years have been interpolated by means of the Federal Reserve Board index of manufacturing production as revised since its use for the same purpose by Fabricant.

[30] Daniel Creamer, unpublished data prepared for *Capital and Output Trends in Manufacturing Industries, 1880–1948*, Occasional Paper, 41 New York (NBER), 1954.

Input Estimates

For most of the 4-digit industries for which output estimates are available, manhours have been estimated, but capital stock estimates are generally not available. Capital as well as labor input estimates are available for some industry subgroups, although frequently with a gap between 1929 and 1948. At the group level, both manhours and capital stock estimates are available for all our reference years.

In order to combine the two major classes of factor inputs, manhours were weighted by the base-period average hourly labor compensation, and real capital stock by the base-period rate of return on capital. Total input in the manufacturing segment is the sum of weighted factor inputs in the major groups. Because of the lack of complete detail for inputs below the group level, further internal weighting was not feasible.

Due to the various complications involved in estimating both employment and average hours worked, each of these variables is accorded a separate section below. A third section on labor input describes the sources of weights for the manhour estimates. The final section describes the sources of the capital stock estimates and the required weights.

EMPLOYMENT

The employment estimates for industries and groups are all based on data from the *Census of Manufactures* and are consistent with the output estimates as far as industry definitions are concerned. Classification discontinuities, whether adjusted for by linking overlapping estimates or, in some cases, left unadjusted, have been treated in parallel fashion in both the output and employment series. Problems remain to be considered primarily in connection with the comparability over time of the employment data.

Functional coverage. Troublesome questions arise concerning the scope of the employment estimates with respect to functional categories. Ideally, employment should include all persons engaged in the industry whose activity contributes to reported value added. A serious problem affecting continuity of the employment estimates concerns the extent to which distributive "nonfactory" personnel located at manufacturing plants were included in censuses prior to 1935. In 1935, a separate "Manufacturer's Distribution Report" was appended to the usual schedule; 520,000 persons were reported as engaged in distribution ("employees who devote all or the major portion of their time to distribution activities, such as selling, advertising, sales promotion, credit, billing, installing, or servicing goods sold, etc.").[31] Of these, 190,000 had been reported in the manufacturers' schedules. Thus, 330,000 persons, who were engaged in distribution within

[31] Fabricant, *Employment in Manufacturing*, p. 225.

the plant and whose productive activities were presumably included in the value of products, were excluded from the factory employment figures. In 1937 the distributive workers not reported on the manufacturers' schedules were requested. Only 170,000 additional employees were reported, which casts doubt on the comparability of the total figure with that for 1935. There is no reason to believe, however, that the factory employee total for 1937 is not comparable with 1935. In 1939, a separate report was requested for total distributive employees (and certain other categories), and 586,000 were reported. Since this figure is higher than the 520,000 reported in 1935, while the factory employment estimate proper is lower in 1939 than in 1935, it is "likely," as Fabricant pointed out, that employees formerly reported as factory workers were moved into distribution and the other new categories. All distributive workers in the plant were also included in the 1947 and subsequent Census reports, and the more restrictive "factory" worker definition was dropped.

Our procedure has been to treat the factory worker estimates as basically comparable over the entire period through 1937, although there were probably some fluctuations in the proportion of nonfactory workers included.[32] Since, as indicated, the total establishment employment estimates for 1939 and later censuses appear comparable with the 1935 total, we have linked the 1939 total to the 1935 total employment series. (Total employment indexes for the census years 1935–39 are given in the footnotes to Fabricant's tables.)[33] This procedure results in estimates for the groups and segment which are almost identical in movement with those of the Office of Business Economics (OBE) for 1929–39, although a different method of adjustment was used. In essence, OBE used a continuous and consistent series for clerical and administrative employees to extrapolate back the 1939 estimate of all salaried workers, including those engaged in distribution.[34]

Workers engaged in routine maintenance and repair have been included in factory worker data throughout. It is not certain to what extent force-account construction workers engaged in major alterations or additions to plant were included prior to 1939. In 1939 and the subsequent census, these workers were definitely included. The estimates including construction workers for 1939 and later were treated as comparable with those of earlier years. Since the 70,000 workers on force-account construction in 1939 constituted less than 1 per cent of manufacturing employment, possible lack of complete comparability with earlier years is not serious.

[32] See Fabricant's discussion of the various Census questionnaires in this regard (*ibid.*, Appendix A).

[33] *Ibid.*, Table F-1, pp. 264–330.

[34] See "Section on Wages and Salaries and Employment," *Technical Notes, Sources and Methods Used in the Derivation of National Income Statistics*, National Income Division, Office of Business Economics, mimeo, 1948.

Actually, the value of force-account construction work should be counted as capital formation, and included (net of depreciation) in output, if the workers are to be included in employment. To the extent that new construction is merely an offset to depreciation, the inclusion of construction inputs is consistent with output measures gross of depreciation.

Finally, there is the problem of persons employed in central administrative offices (C.A.O.) and other auxiliary establishments. A central administrative office is defined as "an office which operates two or more manufacturing plants, one or more of which are located in cities other than that in which the administrative office is located."[35] Since these workers contribute to the value of product of the associated establishments, they should be included in the employment figures. If all associated establishments were classed in the same industry, total C.A.O. employment could be included; otherwise, a problem of allocation arises. Actually, in all censuses from 1909 through 1925, C.A.O. employees were allocated by the Census Bureau to individual plants, usually on the basis of the relative value of product, and these numbers were included in the salaried-worker figures for the respective industries. In 1929, 1937, and 1939, data were collected but not shown, except for total manufacturing. In 1935 and 1947, data were collected but not tabulated. Since it is impossible to construct estimates of employment including C.A.O. employees by industry and group after 1925, employment in manufacturing establishments proper has been used from 1925 forward, and was linked in 1925 to employment including C.A.O. employees, which goes back to 1909; prior to 1909 employment is again strictly on an establishment basis. In effect, we are assuming that, except for 1909–25, C.A.O. employment is proportional to other industry employment. Since the proportion for all manufacturing changed from 0.94 per cent in 1925 to 1.31 per cent in 1937, any distortion in the secular movement of the total employment series for industries and groups should be minor and may take the form of a slight downward bias.

Employment in other auxiliary establishments is not included in our estimates, and generally this seems proper. The value of the services of sales branches and related warehouses is not included in the industry value data, since values are computed as of the time of shipment from the plant. Establishments producing services, such as power plants or repair and maintenance depots, presumably charge the consuming establishment in the firm accordingly; so the value of the services neither enters into value added nor affects changes in the value of product. Technical and supporting personnel engaged on research and development in separate laboratories should generally not be included in the employment estimates

[35] *Census of Manufactures, 1925,* Chap. IV.

since their work, for the most part, is not immediately related to current output. The 1954 Census was the first to present information on these auxiliary activities.

Class of worker. In line with our principle of taking account of total employment, the indexes are based on the sum of persons engaged in the several classes of work distinguished by the Census: wage earners (or "production workers" after 1939), salaried employees, and proprietors and firm members. Where available, we used the total employment indexes through 1939 prepared and described by Fabricant[36] (with the shift from a factory to a total basis in 1939 linked, as explained above). All series were extended by the total employment estimates presented in subsequent censuses for the same industry or most nearly comparable industry or group, as indicated on the tables to follow.

In the case of the several industries or groupings of industries for which employment indexes are given here but not by Fabricant, we constructed indexes based on his underlying data, published and unpublished.[37] The same adjustments were made as by Fabricant. In connection with the break caused by the exclusion after 1919 of establishments with value of product of $500 to $5,000, Census data made possible an overlap only in the case of wage earners. In this case, the data were linked and the later series extrapolated back by the earlier. The data on salaried personnel were not adjusted since few such persons were employed in small establishments and the series would be little affected by the break. Estimates for 1919 of the number of proprietors of establishments with a value of product over $5,000 were made by Fabricant, and these furnished the basis of our link for this class of worker. It should be noted, however, that since the minimum size of establishment included in censuses was, until 1947, based on value of product, the numbers of establishments and, thus, of proprietors and firm members were affected by significant changes in prices or in scale of operation. This undoubtedly introduced some distortions into the series on proprietors and firm members, but these persons were a small part of total employment in most manufacturing industries.

Although the wage earner classification was always based on the character of work done rather than the basis of compensation, the shift to a production worker definition in 1947 introduced some incomparabilities between the 1939 and 1947 estimates, particularly in certain industries. Since our indexes are based on total employment data, this modification

---

[36] *Employment in Manufacturing*, Appendix F.

[37] *Ibid*; wage earner data by industry are published in Table B-1. Worksheets available at the National Bureau contain the industry estimates for salaried workers, proprietors and firm members, and nonfactory personnel (1935–39) underlying the estimates shown for major groups in Tables B-2, B-3, and B-4.

of the definition of a particular class of worker does not affect the series. Prior to 1947, the employment estimates for wage earners represented annual averages in the sense of an average of monthly figures, each generally relating to the week which included or was closest to the fifteenth of the month. For salaried workers and for proprietors and firm members, the Census presented data relating only to one day, usually December 15. No adjustment was made to the basic data for this; thus, the annual index numbers of total employment may be slightly distorted by cyclical influences.

Because of our exclusive reliance on total employment, we have made some adjustments not needed by Fabricant. For 1899 Fabricant did not show an index number for total employment by industry because the available figures on proprietors and firm members covered hand trades and custom establishments, excluded from later censuses. We have extrapolated the total employment index from 1904 back to 1899 by the movement of the index numbers for wage earners only. Although the two indexes show virtually the same movement for all manufacturing,[38] it should be realized that the movement of the industry total employment series from 1899 to 1904 is not based on complete data and is, therefore, subject to an additional margin of error. In 1931, Census did not collect data on salaried workers. The movement of the total employment index was interpolated between 1929 and 1933 by the movement of the wage earner index; so the same restrictions attach to the 1931 figure as to that for 1899. However, the added margin of error cannot be great in either case because of the preponderant influence of wage earner employment on the total.

Segment totals. Prior to 1947, our output estimates by industry and group are available only for census years, but annual estimates were derived for all manufacturing. Thus, it was desirable also to obtain annual employment estimates for the segment.

From 1929 forward, the carefully prepared OBE series was available. Rather than use it to interpolate our census-year employment estimates, we adopted it as our basic series. It is true that the OBE estimates are a little higher than ours. This is because they are based on comprehensive Social Security data since 1939, which have been extrapolated by Census data and interpolated primarily by BLS estimates, and they thus include small-firm and C.A.O. employment. But the movements are virtually identical, with the exception of those for 1939–47, when the OBE series shows about a 1.5 per cent increase over the Census series. In any case, it is not clear that the Census series is more consistent with the output estimates than are the presumably comprehensive estimates of OBE,

[38] *Ibid.*, Table B-5.

since, for example, C.A.O. employment should be included in an employment series designed to be comparable with output. Rather than have two different series for total manufacturing employment, one purporting to be comprehensive and the other to be more closely comparable to the output series (which is doubtful), the comprehensive series was used for both purposes. It need only be remembered that the series is higher than, and its movements after 1929 slightly different from, the sum of the employment estimates for the twenty groups.

Prior to 1929, we extrapolated the OBE estimates by those of Fabricant. Between census years, the wage earner component was interpolated using BLS estimates for 1929–1939[39] and estimates by Paul Douglas for the intercensal years 1919–1899.[40] The estimates of salaried employees were interpolated between 1929 and 1919 by the Kuznets series,[41] and for earlier years, on the basis of their relationship to wage earners and the ratio of manufacturing employment to labor force for census years 1919–37. The salaried-worker totals for 1929, 1927, 1904, and 1899 were adjusted upward to allow for C.A.O. workers not included in Census data for those years. Proprietors and firm members were interpolated between census years 1929–19 by the estimates of Kuznets,[42] and between census years 1899–1919, on a straight-line basis. At the segment level, the number of proprietors was raised by 10.6 per cent throughout to cover the estimated number of unpaid family workers, based on 1941 economy ratios (see Appendix A).

Independent estimates were made of manufacturing employment for census years prior to 1899 on a basis comparable to those after that date. The chief problem arose from the inclusion of neighborhood industries and "hand trades" in manufacturing prior to 1899. Beginning with the Census of 1905, which covered calendar-year 1904, persons engaged in these establishments were no longer canvassed, and the data for 1899 were adjusted for comparability. We have attempted to make comparable adjustments for 1869, 1879, and 1889.

For wage earners estimation for the early years involved four steps. First, wage earners in industries classified wholly as hand trades were eliminated.[43] Second, an adjustment was made for those industries which included some custom and neighborhood shops. Data for such shops were

[39] *Production-Worker Employment, Payrolls, Hours and Earnings in Manufacturing Industries, 1909, 1914–1938*, Bureau of Labor Statistics, mimeographed release L.S. 53–0902. These estimates are revised as compared with those used by Fabricant for interpolation.

[40] *Real Wages in the United States, 1890–1926*, Boston, Houghton Mifflin, 1930, pp. 438–439.

[41] Simon Kuznets, *National Income and Its Composition, 1919–1938*, New York (NBER), 1941, p. 600.

[42] *Ibid.*, p. 604.

[43] *Census of Manufactures, 1905*, Part I, p. cxv, lists these industries; most form Group 15, "Hand Trades," in *Census of Manufactures, 1900*, Part I, p. cxiv.

available in 1899.[44] The 1899 proportion of wage earners in custom shops to wage earners in all establishments in each industry was assumed to prevail back to 1869, and reported wage earner data were reduced accordingly. Third, wage earners in industries which Fabricant excluded for comparability with later censuses were omitted. Fourth, an adjustment was made to convert employment data to a full-year average basis. In the earlier censuses the average number employed during the time each establishment was in operation was reported, not the average for all months in the year.[45] This resulted in an overstatement of employment, chiefly in seasonal industries. An adjustment factor was derived by computing the ratio of the annual average to the average for months of high employment for industries in which a wide seasonal swing was evident.[46] The ratios for 1899 (the first Census for which monthly employment data were available) were used to step down the reported number of wage earners in seasonal industries in earlier census years. This adjustment is approximate, but 2 per cent or less of reported employment is involved. Table D-8 summarizes the derivation of estimates of the number of wage earners, consistent with the Fabricant estimates, for 1869–99.

The derivation of continuous and consistent estimates for proprietors and salaried workers prior to 1899 presented additional problems. In the Census of 1889 salaried workers were combined with proprietors and firm members. Prior to 1889, data on proprietors were not collected; and salaried workers, if reported at all, were included with wage earners. Furthermore, for proprietors, the 1904 Census did not retabulate 1899 data to exclude hand trades. So for 1899, Fabricant's estimate of proprietors and firm members[47] was accepted, and extrapolated back to 1869 by the number of establishments, a variable which we adjusted in the same manner as wage earners (except for the final seasonal adjustment, which would not affect the count of establishments).

The number of salaried workers for 1889 was estimated indirectly. The reported totals of proprietors and salaried workers in 1889 and in 1899 were available. Also available was the total in 1899 adjusted to exclude hand trades and the several industries excluded by Fabricant. The ratio of the adjusted figure to total reported proprietors and salaried workers in

---

44 *Census of Manufactures, 1905,* Table 1, gives industry data for 1899 excluding custom and neighborhood shops. *Census of Manufactures, 1900,* Table 1, gives data including custom and neighborhood shops.

45 *Census of Manufactures, 1900,* p. cvi.

46 The standard used to determine seasonality in an industry was a doubling of monthly employment at some time during 1899. Consecutive months showing employment above the annual average were taken as the months of high employment, and a ratio (average of twelve months to average of months of high employment) was computed as the adjustment factor to apply to the active-period average employment estimates of earlier censuses.

47 *Employment in Manufacturing,* p. 230.

1899 was extrapolated to 1889 by the change in the ratio of adjusted to unadjusted wage earner data. The 1889 adjustment ratio so obtained was applied to the reported total of proprietors and salaried workers. Salaried workers were computed as the difference between adjusted proprietors plus salaried workers in 1889 less proprietors (as previously estimated). For 1869 and 1879 salaried workers were extrapolated by adjusted wage earners. The extrapolation from 1889 to 1879 was made by industry groups; and from 1879 to 1869, by total wage earners since a group breakdown was not available.

TABLE D-8

Derivation of Estimates of Wage Earners in the Factory System, Decennial, 1869–99
(thousands)

	1899	1889	1879	1869
Wage earners reported in factory system by 1904 Census	4,715			
Wage earners reported in 1899 Census	5,308	4,252	2,733	2,054
Less: Hand-trade industries	623	559	245	234
Custom and neighborhood shops that were part of manufacturing industries	102	74	42	37
Overstatement due to reporting active-period averages		69	43	22
Plus: logging establishments[a]	130	143	68	69
Wage earners after adjustments	4,713[b]	3,693	2,471	1,830
Less: industries omitted by Fabricant	217	131	17	27
Final wage earner estimate	4,496[c]	3,562	2,454	1,803

[a] *Census of Manufactures, 1905*, Part I, p. xxix. Prior to 1904 no provision was made for treating logging operations conducted in connection with sawmill plants as a distinct and complete branch of the lumber industry. In the 1904 Census, data relating to the logging branch were first reported with comparable 1899 data. The ratio of wage earners including logging establishments to wage earners excluding logging establishments was applied to 1869–89 wage earner data in the lumber and timber products industry to estimate data for the logging branch of the industry.

[b] This differs by 0.04 per cent from the published Census figure based on retabulation of 1899 data.

[c] This agrees with Solomon Fabricant's series in his *Employment in Manufacturing*, p. 230.

Annual interpolations in the aggregate for 1889–99 were made on the basis of the Douglas estimates, also used for the subsequent period. Prior to 1889, annual estimates were interpolated on the basis of the relationship between total employment and output for subsequent years, using the Frickey series, which extends back. Since this is obviously a rough expedient, the estimates prior to 1889 are not shown on an annual basis, but only for census years. It is clear that the derived productivity estimates hinge on the estimates for the discrete census years.

AVERAGE HOURS WORKED

A large amount of data is available on the average hours of production workers in manufacturing industries. There are, however, several major problems involved in securing continuous series of actual hours worked; these will become apparent in the following description of sources and methods.

In general, our procedure involved using Census estimates of average actual hours worked per year for 1947 and subsequent years in the various industries, groups, and the segment as a whole. BLS estimates were primarily used in going back from 1947 into the 1930's. Unlike the Census estimates, the BLS series include hours paid for but not worked. This imparts a slight upward bias to the series, since time paid for but not worked increased perceptibly after 1940. Some BLS industry series are continuous back to 1923, and selected series prepared by the National Industrial Conference Board go back to 1914. In 1929 and prior years, however, chief reliance was placed on estimates of standard, or "full-time," hours scheduled in the various industries—based on Census distributions back to 1909, the *Nineteenth Annual Report of the Commissioner of Labor, 1904* and subsequent reports for 1890–1909, and the Aldrich Report (see note 54, below) in earlier years for all manufacturing. An adjustment factor was applied to these estimates to obtain actual hours worked. This factor is obviously a potential source of error. But since it is uniform for years of high-level activity, the trend in actual hours worked per week is determined by the trend in standard hours, which seems reasonable. Shorter-term movements may be affected, but we are chiefly concerned with trend.

The major source of possible error lies in the break in continuity occasioned by the shift from estimates of actual hours worked to the adjusted standard hours estimates. The adjustment factor expressing the ratio of actual to full-time hours is based on the BLS estimate for all manufacturing, which, in effect, is based on data for a sample of industries. Since the ratio undoubtedly varied among industries, some distortion is introduced in the movement of the series between 1929 and the first year of the 1930's for which estimates of actual hours worked were available.

Average actual hours, 1947 forward. Estimates of average hours actually worked per year, covering all manufacturing industries, are available only in the post-World War II period. Production worker manhour data by quarters were collected for the 1947 *Census of Manufactures* and annual totals for all industries were published. Only in the case of small establishments were manhours estimated indirectly. Plant hours worked were requested; excluded were hours paid for vacations, holidays, or sick leave, when the employee was not at the plant. Plant hours inevitably include some idle time, but "stand-by" time is at the disposal of management. Comparable data were collected in the 1954 Census; for years commencing with 1949, the *Annual Survey of Manufactures* provides estimates, which are subject to relatively small sampling errors, for the larger industries and industry groupings.[48]

BLS estimates are also available for a large number of manufacturing industries in the postwar period, based on a sample covering more than 60 per cent of the employees in the industries canvassed. The BLS estimates, while also relating to production or nonsupervisory workers, comprise manhours paid for, whether worked or not. Hours paid for holidays, sick leave, and vacations taken are included. The period reported represents a pay period of one week ending nearest the fifteenth of the month. Since our theoretical objective was to estimate actual hours worked or available at the plant, the Census estimates were preferable, particularly in a period when the trend towards fringe benefits in the form of paid leave was important. The two series are compared in Table D-9.

TABLE D-9

Average Hours of Production Workers in Manufacturing, Comparison of
Census and Bureau of Labor Statistics Estimates, 1947–57

	Census	BLS	Ratio:
	(1947 = 100)		Census to BLS
1947	100.0	100.0	100.0
1948	n.a.	99.3	...
1949	96.9	97.0	99.9
1950	98.7	100.2	98.5
1951	99.0	100.7	98.3
1952	99.0	100.7	98.3
1953	98.5	100.2	98.3
1954	96.4	98.3	98.1
1955	98.2	100.7	97.5
1956	97.4	100.0	97.4
1957	96.4	98.5	97.9

n.a. = not available.

Throughout, the group average hours estimates are weighted industry average hours with production worker weights; the all-manufacturing average comprises the group averages weighted in the same fashion.

Average actual hours prior to 1947. In going from 1947 into the 1930's, the BLS estimates of average hours worked per week were used as the chief means of extrapolation. Fewer industries were covered than in recent

[48] Estimates for 1949–53, showing the standard error, are contained in *Annual Survey of Manufactures, 1953*, Bureau of the Census.

442

years, and the sample was smaller: 55 per cent of employees in 1940, 42 per cent in 1934, and 28 per cent in 1932 (the first year covered by the continuing BLS program). Some industries not covered by BLS were covered by special Census tabulations based on large-industry samples of average hours worked per month: 171 industries were included in 1939, 105 in 1937, 59 in 1935, and 32 in 1933. These estimates were employed in the years for which they were available. For a few industries, use was made of National Industrial Conference Board (NICB) estimates, which embody the same concept of average hours as the BLS series.[49]

In the case of a relatively small number of industries for which hours (as well as output) estimates were available for 1947 and 1929 but not for intervening years, an estimate for our key year, 1937, was obtained through interpolation by the index of average hours for the group. In the few cases in which the change in the group index between 1929 and 1947 was quite different from that of the industry index, the group movement from 1947 to 1937 alone was used. The change in average hours between these latter dates was generally small.

Prior to the BLS permanent program of estimating average hours and earnings, which began in 1932, continuous actual average hours estimates were available for a smaller group of manufacturing industries: 12 industries were covered in a series of special BLS surveys beginning in 1923, and 25 industries were covered by NICB, with the data starting in 1914.[50] In most cases, the BLS series were used where available because the BLS samples were generally more adequate than those of the NICB (southern plants were under-represented in the latter). In a few cases, preference was given the NICB series when these seemed to show trends more consistent with available standard hours estimates.

Adjusted standard hours, 1869–1929. For the majority of industries in 1929 and earlier years, reliance was placed on estimates of standard hours per week, adjusted to approximate actual hours worked. The Censuses of 1909, 1914, 1919, 1921, 1923, and 1929 presented frequency distributions of wage earners by standard-hours classes for all manufacturing industries. We computed averages for each industry, group, and the segment, adjusted to our classifications. In all cases, the midpoints of the hours classes were used. Prior to 1919 the lower open-end class was 48 and under. The midpoint was determined by taking a weighted average of the greater detail available in 1919; the result was 46 hours. Similarly, a weighted average of the 1914 detail for the class intervals over 60 hours yielded an average of about 68 hours, which was used for 1919 and subsequent years.

---

[49] See M. A. Beney, *Wages, Hours, and Employment in the United States, 1914–1936*, New York, National Industrial Conference Board, 1936.

[50] These series are described and shown for the industries for which output estimates also are available in Fabricant, *Employment in Manufacturing*, Table C-2, pp. 236–43.

The assumed midpoint for the interval over 72 hours (74) was unimportant, since even in 1914 less than 1 per cent of wage earners worked more than 72 hours a week. In summary, the mean hours used for each class are shown in parentheses after the indicated class intervals: 44 and under (40); 44–48 (46); 48; 48–54 (51); 54; 54–60 (57); 60–72 (66); 72; over 72 (74).

Our average standard hours are slightly higher than those calculated by Brissenden who, for some reason, used mean values lower than the class midpoints.[51] Investigation of selected industries based on the more detailed BLS prevailing-hours data for 1914 indicated that mean values in these industries are not below the midpoints of the Census frequency distributions; if anything, they tend to be higher. The precise average standard hours figure is not important for our purposes, however, as long as the same method is used for all industries and the segment.

We adjusted the standard hours estimates for the various industries and groups on the basis of the ratio of the BLS actual hours estimates for all manufacturing to the standard hours estimates.

Since the adjustment from 1929 back depends on the BLS estimates of actual hours worked in the manufacturing segment, they will be described briefly.[52] From 1929 to 1923 the BLS estimates were based on the weighted average of estimates for twelve important industries, the industry estimates being obtained by dividing average weekly earnings by average hourly earnings. The ratio of average prevailing hours in these twelve industries to average prevailing hours for all manufacturing was computed from Census data as a basis for level and trend adjustments to the actual hours estimates. The 1929–32 movements were interpolated by the weighted average for the twelve industries. The 1922–20 movements were based on the estimates by W. I. King.

The BLS estimates for 1919, 1914, and 1909 were prepared by essentially the same method. Special studies had been made of average hourly earnings as follows: 27 industries were covered in 1919; 13 industries, in 1914; and in 1909, "several" important industries, with the results supplemented by occupational data for some additional industries. The average hourly earnings estimates were divided into average weekly earnings estimates for all manufacturing, based on Census data, in order to obtain estimates of average hours worked per week. It was felt that the indicated ratios of actual hours worked to prevailing hours were consistent with the relatively high level of scheduled hours then prevailing. Table D-10 shows our averages of prevailing hours in census years from 1929 back for all

[51] Paul F. Brissenden, *Earnings of Factory Workers, 1899–1927*, Census Monograph X, 1929, p. 352.
[52] See Technical Note, "BLS Historical Estimates of Earnings, Wages, and Hours," *Monthly Labor Review*, July 1955, pp. 801–806.

manufacturing and the BLS actual average hours estimates for 1909–29 as well as the further extrapolations described below.[53]

Our estimates would not correctly represent fluctuations in the ratios of actual to prevailing hours in the groups which differ from the sector in this respect. It is believed, however, that the trends of actual average hours based on prevailing-hours estimates are substantially correct. The main possible source of error lies in the movement of the actual hours estimates between 1929, when the adjusted Census average was last employed, and the year of the first available direct actual average hours estimate. That

TABLE D-10

Manufacturing: Prevailing Hours Compared with Estimated Actual Weekly Hours Worked, Selected Years, 1899–1929

	Prevailing Hours	Actual Hours	Ratio: Actual to Prevailing
1899	59.5	52.7	0.886
1904	57.9	51.1	0.883
1909	57.1	51.0	0.893
1914	55.4	49.4	0.892
1919	50.9	46.3	0.910
1921	50.3	43.1	0.857
1923	50.9	45.6	0.896
1929	50.4	44.2	0.877

is, assuming that the actual hours estimates are substantially correct as to level, the adjusted standard hours figures may not be fully comparable since the ratio of actual to prevailing hours may differ considerably among industries. The possible error is reduced for the groups, however, by offsetting errors in the components and by the fact that in most groups the actual average hours estimates for certain industries are based on the continuous BLS or NICB series. Space does not permit showing the industry detail, but the average hours estimates by industry can be calculated from the productivity summary tables. The continuous BLS or NICB series were extrapolated by the adjusted Census estimates from 1923 or 1914 back; if levels differed significantly, the level indicated by the former was preserved through a linking of the series in the earliest overlapping year.

[53] Some recent work that came to our attention after completion of the present study suggests that the BLS estimates of average hours worked in manufacturing may be too low from 1929 back. This is attributed to the fact that the BLS sample was over-weighted with large firms. If this is so, our manufacturing productivity estimates understate the true increase between 1929 and 1933. See Albert Rees, *New Measures of Wage-Earner Compensation in Manufacturing, 1914–57*, Occasional Paper 75, New York (NBER), 1960.

Extrapolation of the prevailing hours estimates from 1909 back to 1890 was accomplished by groups chiefly on the basis of the estimates contained in the *Nineteenth Annual Report of the Commissioner of Labor, 1904* and subsequent BLS reports extending these estimates; and from 1890 to 1869 for the segment, by the estimates contained in the Aldrich Report.[54] Since we are presenting detailed estimates only for the period beginning 1899, average hours by industries were not estimated prior to that date. Average hours were estimated by industry groups back to 1890, however, in order to obtain all-manufacturing estimates using group employment weights. Prior to 1890, the coverage of hours data is not broad enough to warrant the estimation of group averages and the all-manufacturing average is an employment-weighted average of the individual industries included in the Aldrich Report.

The average full-time hours estimates given in the *Nineteenth Annual Report* are unweighted averages of the average hours data for the various component occupational groups constituting the industry labor force. The occupational data were weighted by Leo Wolman's estimates of employment in the various occupations; and his industry averages were used— although, in most cases, they do not differ appreciably in movement from those given in the *Nineteenth Annual Report*.[55]

The use of the *Nineteenth Annual Report* and supplementary materials was somewhat complicated by the fact that whereas full-time hours are presented for 53 industries from 1890 to 1903, data for only 36 industries are continued from 1903 to 1907, and for only 19 industries between 1907 and 1909. The continuous industries presented no problem; if the estimates of the Census Bureau and the Labor Commissioner differed significantly in 1909, the Census level was accepted and the series linked. Even where the Labor series were not continuous, if the absolute levels of full-time hours in 1903 or 1907 appeared reasonable relative to 1909 (the same or higher, but not much higher than indicated by the mean change over the period), the series were accepted as comparable. Where this was not the case, the average movement for the continuous or comparable industries in the same group was used to bridge the gap, and the Labor series was linked to the level of the 1909 Census estimate so extrapolated. The averages for the groups in 1909 were extrapolated by the percentage changes in the averages for the employment-weighted component industries for which hours estimates were continuous or comparable. The extrapolation was done in three stages covering 1909–07, 1907–03,

54 Bureau of Labor Bulletins 59, 65, 71, and 77; and *Report on Wholesale Prices, on Wages, and on Transportation*, Committee on Finance, Senate Report No. 1394, 52d Cong., 2d sess., 1893.

55 We worked from Wolman's unpublished worksheets, at the National Bureau; but his estimates for selected years are published in *Hours of Work in American Industry*, Bulletin 71, New York, (NBER) 1938.

and 1903–1890, in order to make full use of the increasing amount of industry detail in these periods without affecting the level of the series. In the period 1890–1903, the coverage of the miscellaneous group was so small that the all-manufacturing average was substituted for the missing industries. In bridging the gap between 1907 and 1909 in several groups, the average movement for all manufacturing or an industry group which in other periods showed similar levels and movements had to be substituted. The period involved was so short and the average hours movements generally so slight that errors due to this expedient should be minor.

Since the census years 1869 to 1899, with the exception of 1879, were years of relatively good business, the movement of full-time hours for these years relative to 1909 was used to extrapolate the 1909 average actual hours estimates. Although there may have been differences in the ratios of actual to full-time hours in those years compared with 1909 due to trend or cycle factors, they were probably not large. Little or no trend movement is evident in the ratios for 1909–29. Whereas there is a cyclical pattern in the movement of average hours worked relative to full-time hours, the phases of the business cycle in these years were not different enough to warrant rough adjustment.

The situation is different in 1904, a year in which a business cycle trough occurred. For this census year, an adjustment factor was derived from the 1909–26 relationship between the ratio of actual to standard hours and the ratio of employment to labor force. The dependent variable was obtained by using the BLS actual hours series in conjunction with Douglas' annual estimates of full-time hours. The independent variable was obtained by using Fabricant's employment series and Carson's estimates of the manufacturing labor force,[56] 1909, 1914, 1919, and 1929, with straight-line interpolations. The formula is $y = 67.5 + 0.2398x$; $r = +.77$. The computed ratio for 1904 yields an actual hours estimate of 51.1, only 0.1 hour higher than the 1909 figure, whereas estimated full-time average hours were 0.8 hour higher. This estimate is roughly verified by an analysis made by BLS.[57]

Finally, in order to obtain an annual series for output per manhour in the manufacturing segment as a whole, actual average hours worked per week were interpolated between census years prior to 1919 by using the calculated ratios of actual to standard average hours based on the formula

---

[56] Daniel Carson, "Changes in the Industrial Composition of Manpower since the Civil War," *Studies in Income and Wealth*, Vol. 11, New York (NBER), 1949, p. 47.

[57] Technical Note, "BLS Historical Estimates of Earnings, Wages, and Hours," *Monthly Labor Review*, July 1955, pp. 801–806. When Census average weekly earnings in 1904 are divided by the BLS seventeen-industry average of hourly earnings, the implied average weekly hours are 50.4. This figure is not published in the BLS historical average hours series, which begins in 1909, due to the conclusion: "It is probable, however, that the actual average of weekly hours in 1904 was no lower than in 1909. . . ."

given above. These estimates are undoubtedly better approximations to actual average hours than would be estimates based on full-time hours with no allowance for a cyclical factor. They are, however, not presented as an independent series but only as a component of the total manhours estimates for the segment.

TOTAL MANHOURS AND LABOR INPUT

Indexes of average hours worked by production workers, obtained as described above, were multiplied by indexes of total employment (persons engaged) in order to obtain indexes of total manhours worked in the various industries, groups, and the manufacturing segment. This proced-ure involves the assumption that average hours worked by nonproduction workers have moved with those worked by production workers. The assumption does not seem to be unreasonable as far as trends go, although there may be divergences of movement over short periods. It is certainly preferable to make the assumption than to deal with production worker manhours alone. The ratio of production workers to total persons engaged in manufacturing industries has shown a pronounced downward trend, declining from almost 90 per cent in 1900 to 78 per cent in 1953.

Despite the decline in the relative importance of production workers, they still account for the predominant part of manufacturing employment. Thus, some divergence between the average hours worked by production workers and by other persons engaged would not seriously affect the total manhour estimates. As a matter of fact, production workers include some salaried employees; so the latter group is not entirely unrepresented in the average hours estimates. Proprietors were so small a component of the total that no special adjustment was made for their average hours, although this was done in segments where they were an important part of the labor force.

It has been remarked that the BLS estimates of average hours worked in groups of industries are weighted by production worker employment. We have followed this procedure for the group estimates prior to 1929 and for subgroup estimates throughout, since it is simpler, consistent with BLS, and gives approximately the same results as the use of total employ-ment weights.

Labor input was obtained by weighting group manhours worked by average hourly labor compensation. Manhours were computed for all groups in key years. This was done in order to obtain productivity esti-mates by groups, as well as to obtain estimates of labor input for all manufacturing by weighting group manhours. From 1929 forward, the average hourly compensation weights were obtained by dividing group labor compensation as estimated by OBE by OBE estimates of employees multiplied by our average hours worked per year. In the few cases in which regroupings occurred, we had to allocate labor compensation by our standard groupings based on Census wages and salaries for the latter. For 1929 and earlier years, average hourly earnings estimates were derived from the Census estimates of wages and salaries and employment, and our average hours. The earlier figures thus do not take account of supplements to wages and salaries, but these were minor prior to 1929.

TABLE D-11

Manufacturing: Relative Weights of Manhour Indexes,
by Group, Subperiods, 1899–1953
(per cent)

	1899–1909	1909–1919	1919–1929	1929–1937	1937–1948	1948–1953
Foods	10.1	9.7	9.5	9.2	8.9	9.0
Beverages	0.8	0.6	0.6	0.6	0.5	0.5
Tobacco products	1.2	1.0	0.9	0.9	0.9	1.0
Textile mill products	8.8	9.8	9.5	9.3	10.5	10.3
Apparel and related products	6.1	7.0	6.9	6.3	6.0	5.6
Lumber and products except furniture	4.5	4.5	4.5	4.1	4.0	4.3
Furniture and fixtures	3.9	3.7	3.7	3.6	3.6	3.6
Paper and allied products	2.6	2.7	2.7	2.8	3.0	3.1
Printing and publishing	7.7	6.8	7.1	7.7	7.3	7.1
Chemicals and allied products	4.2	4.0	4.0	4.1	4.2	4.4
Petroleum and coal products	1.4	1.5	1.5	1.8	2.1	2.1
Rubber products	1.7	1.8	1.8	1.9	1.9	1.8
Leather and products	3.1	3.3	3.1	2.9	2.9	2.9
Stone, clay, and glass products	3.8	3.5	3.7	3.6	3.4	3.5
Primary metal industries	8.8	9.0	9.0	9.2	9.0	9.2
Fabricated metal products	7.5	7.1	7.3	7.2	7.2	7.4
Machinery, nonelectric	9.4	8.9	8.6	8.9	8.9	9.0
Electric machinery	5.9	5.4	5.2	5.6	5.7	5.6
Transportation equipment	5.8	7.2	7.8	7.7	7.5	7.5
Miscellaneous and instruments	2.7	2.5	2.6	2.6	2.5	2.1
Total	100.0	100.0	100.0	100.0	100.0	100.0

This procedure results in weighting manhours attributed to proprietors by the average hourly compensation or earnings of employees in the various groups. The relative percentage weights applied to the group manhour indexes are shown in Table D-11. The relative stability of the weights reflects the more or less proportionate movement of average hourly earnings in the various groups.

One final adjustment was necessary. The sum of manhours worked in the various groups, which underlies the weighted labor input estimates, is not precisely equal to manhours as estimated directly for all manufacturing.

Small discrepancies in movement occur because (1) from 1929 forward, our employment estimates are those prepared by OBE, which differ slightly from estimates based on Census because of their more comprehensive coverage and to slightly different methods of adjusting the Census employment estimates for consistency from 1939 to 1929, as noted earlier; (2) our weighted average hours series differs slightly from the BLS series because we used total employment weights at the group level. Also, from 1929 back, we used BLS and NICB average hours for available industries plus adjusted standard hours for the other industries in each group. In order not to introduce estimates of employment and average hours for all manufacturing that are slightly different from the presently published ones, we have used the manhours figures for the segment estimated directly and have adjusted our weighted labor input accordingly,

TABLE D-12

Manufacturing:
Labor Input Based on Alternative Methods of Weighting,
Key Years, 1899–1953
(1929 = 100)

	Manhours (unweighted)	Manhours (constant 1929 weights)	Labor Input (changing weights)
1899	60.5	57.2	57.6
1909	83.8	80.7	81.1
1919	105.1	104.8	105.1
1929	100.0	100.0	100.0
1937	88.4	89.5	89.4
1948	132.9	136.9	136.9
1953	148.5	155.8	155.8

i.e., by the ratio of the sum of the underlying manhours to the direct segment estimates of manhours. Thus, the labor input and manhours estimates for the segment are appropriate for the purposes of building up economy estimates, and they are only slightly inconsistent with the sum of the estimates for the major manufacturing groups. The segment manhour estimates were also used to interpolate the labor input estimates (after adjustment) between the census years for which group manhour estimates were made from 1929 back. This merely involves the assumption that the proportions of manhours employed in each group moved in a regular fashion between the census years concerned. The weighted and unweighted manhour estimates for the segment for key years, 1899–1953, are shown in Table D-12. Prior to 1899, labor input was extrapolated by the estimates of manhours worked in manufacturing as a whole.

CAPITAL STOCKS AND INPUT

Our estimates of real capital stocks in manufacturing are based largely on the estimates underlying Creamer's *Capital and Output Trends in Manufacturing Industries*. Since publication of this paper, Creamer has revised the estimates for 1948 and extended them to 1953.[58]

Group estimates. Creamer's estimates for 1919 and prior years are derived from data on the net book value of capital given in the *Census of Manufactures*, combined to achieve industrial comparability over time and adjusted for price change. His estimates for 1929 through 1953 are based on data for corporations, obtained from the Internal Revenue Service, adjusted for industrial comparability, raised to cover noncorporate establishments, and adjusted for price change.

The adjustment for changes in the price of industry fixed capital is made by use of a deflator comprising indexes of building costs and prices of machinery and equipment; inventories are deflated by wholesale prices of the output of the industry. The building costs and the machinery and equipment indexes are each constructed by use of the formula

$$D = \frac{\sum_{t=1}^{n} \left(\frac{t}{n} \times V_t \right)}{\sum_{t=1}^{n} \left(\frac{t}{n} \times V'_t \right)}$$

where D is the deflator; n is the length of life of the capital item; t varies from 1 to n; V_t is the current price value of investment in that item in year t; and V'_t is the value of investment in year t in 1929 prices, derived by deflating V_t by an appropriate price index. The factor t/n assumes that straight-line depreciation has been applied to the original cost of the capital items in deriving net book values. It is assumed that there are no price lags in the book value of working capital.

We have adjusted Creamer's estimates to eliminate financial capital items (cash, receivables, etc.), and to achieve better industrial comparability with our output and employment data. The former adjustment was relatively simple for 1929 through 1953, because the value of inventories were available separately in the Internal Revenue tabulations and could be segregated from other items of working capital. For 1919, the estimates of manufacturing inventories given in Moses Abramovitz' *Inventories and Business Cycles*[59] were used wherever the classification by Abramovitz

---

[58] *Capital in Manufacturing and Mining.*
[59] *Inventories and Business Cycles, with Special Reference to Manufacturers' Inventories*, New York (NBER), 1950.

coincided with our own. Inventories for earlier years were estimated by applying averages of the ratios of inventories to total working capital in 1919–48. Average ratios of fixed capital to total capital in 1904 and 1929 were used as a basis for interpolating the value of fixed capital in 1909, 1914, and 1919, when fixed capital was not reported separately in the *Census of Manufactures*.

The Creamer estimates of real capital stock were adjusted for industry comparability with our output indexes by applying the ratios of Creamer's value of output in current prices to the Census value of production consistent with our output estimates for the various industry groups in each key year.

Segment capital input. Indexes of real capital stock for the manufacturing groups were weighted by the average unit capital compensation in successive pairs of key years beginning with 1929, and the average 1929–37 weights were applied to earlier key years. Capital compensation was derived from the OBE estimates of national income originating by industry by subtracting labor compensation, including an imputed compensation for the labor of proprietors.

There was some difficulty in estimating capital compensation in 1929, since the OBE estimates for that year were based on consolidated corporate income tax returns. To allow for this element of industry incomparability, we estimated the percentage difference in fixed capital for an industry resulting from consolidated tax returns on the basis of data given in *Statistics of Income for 1934* of the Internal Revenue Service, and applied this percentage to the 1929 residual capital compensation figure.

The calculation of a fixed 1929-weighted capital input was a straightforward procedure. To obtain the shifting-weight measure, however, required more ingenuity, because of the changes in industrial classification that took place in the basic data from which OBE computed the national income measures. Adjustments were made to the 1937, 1948, and 1953 capital compensation estimates, based on the percentage deviation between indexes of total employment shown by OBE, which are presumed to be industrially comparable with the industry national income estimates and our own industry employment indexes. These adjusted industry capital compensation estimates were divided by the corresponding capital input indexes in order to obtain measures of changes in unit rates of return.

The industry group capital indexes were then combined, using these modified unit capital compensation estimates, by a variant of the Marshall-Edgeworth formula, in the manner described earlier. The relative weights in the subperiods are shown in Table D-13.

TABLE D-13

Manufacturing: Relative Weight of Real Capital Input, by Group,
Subperiods, 1929–53
(per cent)

	1929–37	1937–48	1948–53
Foods	10.2	10.3	9.5
Beverages	1.3	1.6	1.3
Tobacco products	2.3	1.3	1.2
Textile mill products	7.7	12.4	9.4
Apparel and related products	3.0	2.4	1.9
Lumber and products except furniture	3.1	4.2	3.2
Furniture and fixtures	1.1	2.7	3.1
Paper and allied products	2.1	3.6	4.4
Printing and publishing	4.7	3.6	3.7
Chemicals and allied products	9.3	7.7	7.2
Petroleum and coal products	8.4	7.9	7.6
Rubber products	1.6	1.6	2.1
Leather and products	1.5	2.1	2.2
Stone, clay, and glass products	3.9	4.5	5.3
Primary metal industries	10.8	8.9	11.2
Fabricated metal products	4.2	5.7	5.3
Machinery, nonelectric	9.6	6.9	6.7
Electric machinery	4.6	3.8	4.3
Transportation equipment	7.9	6.6	8.2
Miscellaneous and instruments	2.7	2.2	2.2
Total	100.0	100.0	100.0

TOTAL INPUT

Total factor input in the manufacturing groups and segment was obtained
by weighting the labor and capital input indexes by the average unit
compensation accruing to each, estimated as described above. The relative weights of each factor in the segment as a whole are shown in
Table D-14.

TABLE D-14

Manufacturing: Relative Weights of Labor and Capital Inputs,
Subperiods, 1919–53
(per cent)

	1919–29	1929–37	1937–48	1948–53
Labor	76.8	77.9	75.5	77.0
Capital	23.2	22.1	24.5	23.0

Technical Note to Appendix D

Price Indexes Used to Deflate Value of Output of Manufacturing Industries

Census Code Number	Industry	Period Over Which Price Deflation Is Used[a]	Price Indexes Used (BLS wholesale prices unless otherwise indicated)	Relative Weights
Group 20	*Foods, exluding beverages*			
2042	Prepared animal feeds	1923–14	Bran	29
			Cottonseed meal	25
			Linseed meal	17
			Mill feedings	29
		1914–1899	Cottonseed meal	
2043	Cereal preparations	1925–14	Hominy grits	10
			Corn meal	10
			Oatmeal	30
			Flour, wheat	50
2051	Bread and other baking products	1921–14	Bread, Chicago	29
			Bread, Cincinnati	5
			Bread, New Orleans	5
			Bread, New York	56
			Bread, San Francisco	5
		1914–1899	Bread, Cincinnati	44
			Bread, New York	56
2052	Biscuits, crackers, and pretzels	1921–14	Soda crackers	50
			Sweet crackers	50
		1914–1899	Soda crackers	
2093	Oleomargarine	1923–14	Oleomargarine	
2094	Corn products	1904–1899	Corn meal, white	34
			Corn meal, yellow	34
			Corn starch	32
2096	Vinegar and cider	1939–1899	Vinegar, cider	
2098	Macaroni and spaghetti	1933	Macaroni	
Group 208	*Beverages*	1933–29	The price index for non-alcoholic beverages was used for this period enabling us to compute a 1929-base series	
2081	Beverages, nonalcoholic	1929–27	BLS subgroup, nonalcoholic beverages	
Group 22	*Textile mill products*			
2256⎫ 2259⎭	Knit fabric mills and knitting mills, n.e.c.	1935–33	Imputed unit price of knit goods group	
2281	Hats, fur felt	1933	Hats, fur felt, finished	70
			Hats, fur felt, unfinished	30
2882	Hats, wool felt	1933	Price index for hats, fur felt	
2292	Lace goods	1933	Imputed unit price of cotton group	
2295a	Artificial leather	1933	Artificial leather, heavy	75
			Artificial leather, light	25

(continued)

Technical Note to Appendix D (continued)

Census Code Number	Industry	Period Over Which Price Deflation Is Used[a]	Price Indexes Used (BLS wholesale prices unless otherwise indicated)	Relative Weights
Group 22	(continued)			
2295b	Oilcloth	1933	Oilcloth, shelf	40
			Oilcloth, table	40
			Oilcloth, wall	20
2297a	Jute goods	1904	Jute, raw	
2297b	Linen goods	1904	Linen shoe thread	
2298	Cordage and twine	1904	Manila rope	50
			Cotton yarn	50
Group 23	*Apparel and related products*	1925–19	Creamer's index of BLS clothing prices	
		1919–1899	Shaw's indexes of clothing and personal furnishings	
2325	Hats and caps, cloth	1933	Caps, men's	50
			Caps, boy's	50
2381} 2382}	Gloves, fabric, dress, and work	1933	Gloves (census unit price 1931 and 1935 interpolated by straight line)	
2382	Suspenders and garters	1933	Garters, children's	25
			Garters, men's	25
			Garter's men's, wide	25
			Suspenders, men's	25
2388	Handkerchiefs	1933	Cotton, men's	25
			Cotton, women's	25
			Linen, men's	25
			Linen, women's	25
Group 24	*Lumber products*			
3988	Morticians' goods	1947, 1933	Metal caskets	33
			Wood covered caskets	67
Group 25	*Furniture and related products*	1947–14	BLS group, furniture	
		1914–1899	Bedroom sets	74
			Bedroom chairs	4
			Dining tables	7
			Dining chairs	15
2515	Mattresses and bed springs	1939–27	Mattresses	62
			Bed springs	38
2562	Window shades	1947–27	Window shades	
Group 26	*Paper and allied products*			
264–269	Converted paper products	1939–1899	Imputed unit price of Group 26	

(continued)

Technical Note to Appendix D (continued)

Census Code Number	Industry	Period Over Which Price Deflation Is Used[a]	Price Indexes Used (BLS wholesale prices unless otherwise indicated)	Relative Weights
Group 28	*Chemicals and allied products*			
2841	Soap and glycerine	1899	Export price of soap	
2861 }	Hardwood and softwood	1933	Acetic acid	33
2862 }	distillation		Wood alcohol	34
			Pine oil	33
2882	Linseed oil mills	1933,	Linseed oil	62
		1921–14	Linseed meal	38
		1914–1899	Linseed oil	62
			Flaxseed	38
2886	Grease and Tallow	1947–14	Tallow, edible	10
			Tallow, inedible	70
			Bones, ground	10
			Tankage	10
		1914–1899	Tallow, inedible	
2894	Glue and gelatin	1921–1899	Export price of animal glue	
2895	Carbon black	1909–1899	Lamp black	50
			Bone black	50
			(Prices from *Oil, Paint, and Drug Reporter*)	
Group 30	*Rubber products*	1914–1899	Creamer's index based on BLS price of autos and crude rubber	
3011	Tires and inner tubes	1919	Tires and tubes	75
			Creamer's index of price of other rubber goods	25
3099	Rubber goods other than tires and shoes	1925	Rubber heels and soles	
		1925–21	Unit price of rubber heels, soles, and auto fabrics	
Group 31	*Leather and leather products*			
3121	Industrial leather belting	1947	Leather belting	
		1925–19	Unit price of sole and union leather	50
			Unit price of chrome sole leather	50
		1919–1899	Unit price of belting leather	
3151 }	Leather gloves	1933,	Gloves, men's	75
3152 }		1925–23	Gloves, women's	25
3192	Saddlery, harness, and whips	1947–14	Harness	
		1914–1899	Unit price of harness leather	

(continued)

Technical Note to Appendix D (continued)

Census Code Number	Industry	Period Over Which Price Deflation Is Used[a]	Price Indexes Used (BLS wholesale prices unless otherwise indicated)	Relative Weights
Group 32	*Stone, clay, and glass products*	1923–1899	Combination of industry deflators described below and including the following industries which were not separately presented for industry study: 323, glass products made of purchased glass: 1925–1899, imputed price of glass group. 324, cement: 1899, cement and lime 325, structural clay products: 1909–1899, unit price of four brick series 326, pottery: 1923–1899, two dinner ware series 327, concrete: 1925–04, sewer pipe; 1904–1899, unit prices of four brick series 329, abrasives, etc.: 1909–1899 unit prices of four brick series	
3211 3221 3229	Glass	1923, 1921	Plate glass, 3–5 ft.	10
			Plate glass, 5–10 ft.	10
			Window glass, A	10
			Window glass, B	3
			Milk bottles, quart	9
			Mason jars, quart	9
			Mason jars, quart, self-sealing	8
			Mason jars, pint, self-sealing	8
			Mason jars, pint	8
			Tumblers	9
			Nappies	8
			Pitchers	8
3274	Lime	1933	Lime, common	50
			Lime, hydrated	50
	Wall plaster and board (part of 3272, 3275, 2612 in 1947)	1933	Board, plaster	17
			Board, insulation	50
			Plaster	33

(continued)

457

Technical Note to Appendix D (continued)

Census Code Number	Industry	Period Over Which Price Deflation Is Used[a]	Price Indexes Used (BLS wholesale prices unless otherwise indicated)	Relative Weights
Group 32	(continued)			
2952	Roofing	1933	Roofing, prepared:	
			Individual	25
			Medium	25
			Slate surfaced	25
			Strip shingles	25
3231	Products of purchased glass	1947–27	Mirrors	50
			Glass subgroup (3211, 3221, 3229 above)	50
326	Pottery	1947–25	Dinner sets, semivitreous	13
			Dinner sets, vitreous	25
			Plates	6
			Cups and saucers	6
			Unit price of lavatories	10
			Unit price of water closets	25
			Unit price of flush tanks	15
		1925–14	Plates	50
			Teacups and saucers	50
Group 33	*Primary metal products*			
3341a	Secondary metals, nonprecious	1923–1899	Imputed unit price of Fabricant's subgroup: copper, lead, and zinc	
3341b	Secondary metals, precious	1939–1899	Gold	60
			Silver	10
			Platinum	30
3351 3359 3361	Nonferrous metal products, n.e.c.	1923–14	BLS group, nonferrous metals	
		1914–1899	Unweighted average of nonferrous metals in BLS and Aldrich reports	
3392	Wire drawing	1947–09	Annealed wire	50
			Copper wire	40
			Brass wire	10
3393	Welded and heavy riveted pipe	1947, 1923–14	Black steel pipe	
	Aluminum	1939–14	Aluminum ingot	
Group 34	*Fabricated metal products*	1939–1899	Fabricant's industries with output indexes combined with industries having deflated value indexes described below	

(continued)

Technical Note to Appendix D (continued)

Census Code Number	Industry	Period Over Which Price Deflation Is Used[a]	Price Indexes Used (BLS wholesale prices unless otherwise indicated)	Relative Weights
Group 34	(continued)			
3411	Tin cans and other tinware	1925–14	Tin cans	
		1914–04	Unit price of tinning	
3421⎫ 3422⎬	Cutlery and edge tools	1947	Census output index for cutlery combined with deflated value index for edge tools	
		1939–27	Scissors and shears	50
			Carvers	6
			Knives and forks	6
			Axes	6
			Chisels	6
			Hatchets	6
			Planes	6
			Corn hooks and knives	14
		1927–1899	Carvers	25
			Knives and forks	25
			Chisels	25
			Planes	25
3423⎫ 3424⎬ 3425⎭	Hand tools, n.e.c., files, and saws	1947–27	Angle bars	28
			Augers	5
			Hammers	8
			Vises	11
			Shovels	5
			Rakes	5
			Files	5
			Saws, crosscut	22
			Saws, hand	11
		1927–1899	Augers	8
			Hammers	9
			Vises	17
			Shovels	8
			Files	8
			Saws, crosscut	33
			Saws, hand	17
3431	Plumbers supplies, n.e.c.	1939–27	Water closets	16
			Lavatories	16
			Sinks	28
			Tubs, bath	36
			Tubs, laundry	4
		1927–14	Tubs	50
			Sheet iron	50
3432	Stoves and ranges	1935–1899	Gas stoves	38
			Coal stoves	29
			Oil stoves	31
			Electric stoves	2

(continued)

Technical Note to Appendix D (continued)

Census Code Number	Industry	Period Over Which Price Deflation Is Used[a]	Price Indexes Used (BLS wholesale prices unless otherwise indicated)	Relative Weights
Group 34	(continued)			
3439	Oil burners and heating apparatus	1939–27	Boiler tubes	16
			Boilers, heating	44
			Boilers, range	6
			Radiation	34
		1927–1899	Boiler tubes	
3441	Structural and ornamental products	1937–1899	Structural steel:	
			Pittsburgh	50
			Chicago	50
3444	Sheet metal work	1947–14	Unweighted average of 15 price series	
		1914–1899	Unweighted average of 5 price series	
3481	Nails and spikes	1947–27	Nails	80
			Spikes	20
		1927–1899	Nails	
3489	Wirework, n.e.c.	1937–14	Wire, annealed	36
			Wire, galvanized barbed	14
			Wire, galvanized fence	14
			Wire, woven	36
		1914–09	Wire, barbed	14
			Unit price, wire	86
		1909–1899	Wire, barbed	
3494 } 3495 }	Bolts, nuts, and screw-machine products	1947–27	Wood screws	11
			Stove bolts	16
			Machine bolts	15
			Plow bolts	15
			Track bolts	11
			Rivets, large	16
			Rivets, small	16
		1927–14	Wood screws	45
			Unit price of bolts, nuts, and rods	55
		1914–1899	Wood screws	33
			Unit price of steel bars	67
3497a	Tin foil	1937–25	Unweighted average of aluminum pig, lead pig, and tin plate	
3999a	Fire extinguishers	1939–27	Foam type extinguishers	33
			Soda and acid type extinguishers	67
Group 35	*Machinery, nonelectric*	1947–1899	Sum of 3 subgroups described below	
3522	Agricultural machinery except tractors	1947–14	BLS group index of farm machinery excluding tractors	
		1914–1899	Shaw's index of farm machinery	

(continued)

Technical Note to Appendix D (continued)

Census Code Number	Industry	Period Over Which Price Deflation Is Used[a]	Price Indexes Used (BLS wholesale prices unless otherwise indicated)	Relative Weights
Group 35	(continued)			
357	Office and store machinery	1939–29	OBE deflator for office and store machinery	
		1929–27	Unweighted average of 6 price series	
		1927–1899	Shaw's index for industrial machinery	
	Subgroup: Foundry and machine shop products	1947–1899	Made up of 7 separately deflated industries described below	
351	Engines and tractors		Engines	50
			1947–29: OBE deflator	
			1929–14: BLS prices of 3 engines and ICC index of steam and generating machinery	
			1914–1899: Shaw's industrial machinery index	
			Tractors	50
			1947–14: Three BLS series	
354	Machine tools and accessories		1947–39: BLS standard machine tool index	
			1939–14: ICC metal and wood-working machinery index	
3552	Textile machinery		1947–39: OBE deflator for special industry machinery	
			1939–27: BLS: 7 knitting machines	
			1927–19: Shaw's industrial machinery index	
3491	Steel barrels		1947–39: One BLS series	
			1939–27: Three BLS series	
			1927–14: Steel sheets and iron pails	
3561	Pumps		1947–39: BLS index for pumps (from general and auxiliary machines)	
			1939–27: Three BLS series	
			1927–14: Shaw's industrial machinery index	

(continued)

Technical Note to Appendix D (continued)

Census Code Number	Industry	Period Over Which Price Deflation Is Used[a]	Price Indexes Used (BLS wholesale prices unless otherwise indicated)	Relative Weights
Group 35	(continued)			
358	Service and house-hold machinery		1947–29: OBE deflator for service and house-hold machinery	
			1929–27: BLS: 7 series	
			1927–23: BLS: 3 series; and Shaw's industrial machinery index	
			1923–14: BLS: 2 series; and Shaw's industrial machinery index	
			1914–1899: Shaw's industrial machinery index	
353⎫ 355⎬ 356⎭	Foundry and machine shop products, n.e.c. (residual)		1947–29: OBE deflator for construction machinery, mining machinery, special industrial machinery, and general industrial machinery	
			1929–1899: Shaw's industrial machinery index	
Group 36	*Electric Machinery*	1939–29	OBE deflator for electrical machinery	
		1929–14	Unit price of phonographs	4
			Western Electric's price index for telephone and telegraph apparatus	10
			Shaw's price index for electrical equipment, less phonographs	86
		1914–1899	Shaw's index for electrical equipment	
Group 37	*Transportation equipment*			
372	Aircraft	1947–29	OBE deflator for aircraft based on index of average hourly earnings in aircraft and	50
			BLS price of metal products	50
		1929–19	Hourly earnings in all manufacturing	50
			BLS price of metal products	50
373	Ship and boat building	1947, 1935	OBE deflator for ship and boat building	

(continued)

Technical Note to Appendix D (concluded)

Census Code Number	Industry	Period Over Which Price Deflation Is Used[a]	Price Indexes Used (BLS wholesale prices unless otherwise indicated)	Relative Weights
Group 38	*Instruments and related products[b]*	1939–29	OBE deflator for instruments	85
			Eastman-Kodak price index for instruments excluding photographic supplies	15
3861	Photographic supplies	1939–09	Eastman-Kodak index of prices received for photographic supplies	
Group 39	*Miscellaneous manufacturing[b]*		No group output index was computed prior to 1939 because the industries for which output or deflated value was available did not adequately represent the uncovered industries	
3931	Pianos	1933	Unweighted average of 3 piano series	
3949	Sporting and athletic goods	1933, 1927	Unweighted average of 25 sporting goods series	
3995	Umbrellas, parasols, and canes	1947–27	Umbrellas, women's	50
			Umbrellas, men's	49
			Canes, men's	1

NOTE: This tabulation relates to manufacturing industries for which quantity measures were either lacking or inadequate for the periods indicated, but for which value and price information were available and used to supplement the quantity measures.

[a] Where a single year only is indicated, obviously the price index was available also for adjoining census years, e.g. in the case of 1933, the index was also available for 1931 and 1935.

[b] Groups 38 and 39. Prior to 1939 an output index was constructed for all miscellaneous industries including instruments and related products by combining available quantity indexes for industries in groups 38 and 39 and using, for the uncovered segment, an output index derived by deflating value of product of the total miscellaneous group by the implicit price index for the manufacturing segment. The percentage of value added of the total miscellaneous group represented by industry output indexes was: 1899, 7 per cent; 1909, 16 per cent; 1919, 19 per cent; 1929, 36 per cent; 1929–39, 60 per cent; 1939–54, Census output indexes were available.

TABLE D-I

Manufacturing: Output, Inputs, and Productivity Ratios, Key Years, 1869–1957
(1929 = 100)

	Output	Persons Engaged	Output Per Person	Manhours	Output Per Manhour	Labor Input	Output Per Unit of Labor Input	Capital Input	Output Per Unit of Capital Input	Total Factor Input	Total Factor Productivity
1869	7.1	19.9	35.5	25.1	28.2	23.9	29.6	4.4	158.9	19.4	36.4
1879	10.2	26.6	38.3	32.8	31.1	31.2	32.7	7.6	134.6	25.7	39.7
1889	18.3	38.3	47.8	46.4	39.4	44.2	41.4	17.6	104.0	38.0	48.2
1899	27.5	50.8	54.1	60.5	45.5	57.6	47.7	29.3	93.9	51.0	53.9
1909	43.4	72.7	59.7	83.8	51.8	81.1	53.5	54.4	79.8	74.9	57.9
1919	61.0	100.3	60.8	105.1	58.0	105.1	58.0	92.9	65.7	102.3	59.6
1929	100.0	100.0	100.0	100.0	100.0	100.0	100.0	100.0	100.0	100.0	100.0
1937	103.3	101.2	102.1	88.4	116.9	89.4	115.5	85.4	121.0	88.5	116.7
1948	184.2	146.5	125.7	132.9	138.6	136.9	134.6	120.8	152.5	133.1	138.4
1953	243.4	164.9	147.6	148.5	163.9	155.8	156.2	153.7	158.4	155.2	156.8
1957	264.6	160.9	164.4	141.4	187.1	148.1[a]	178.7	n.a.	...	...	...

n.a. = not available

[a] Calculations made after revised data of the Office of Business Economics became available reveal that a detailed computation of labor input would give an index of 149.0, showing a fall of 4.4 per cent between 1953 and 1957 instead of the 4.9 per cent fall indicated in this table. The difference is so slight we have not corrected for it in the manuscript.

TABLE D-II

Manufacturing: Output, Labor Inputs, and Labor Productivity Ratios, 1869–1957
(1929 = 100)

	Output	Persons Engaged	Output Per Person	Manhours	Output Per Manhour	Labor Input	Output per Unit of Labor Input
1869	7.1	19.9	35.5	25.1	28.2	23.9	29.6
1879	10.2	26.6	38.3	32.8	31.1	31.2	32.7
1889	18.3	38.3	47.8	46.4	39.4	44.2	41.4
1890	19.7	39.9	49.4	48.4	40.7	46.1	42.7
1891	20.2	41.1	49.1	49.5	40.8	47.1	42.9
1892	21.9	43.6	50.2	53.1	41.2	50.6	43.3
1893	19.4	42.1	46.1	50.3	38.6	47.9	40.5
1894	18.8	40.0	47.0	46.4	40.5	44.2	42.5
1895	22.4	43.6	51.4	51.7	43.3	49.2	45.5
1896	20.4	42.7	47.8	49.8	41.0	47.4	43.0
1897	22.0	44.2	49.8	51.5	42.7	49.0	44.9
1898	25.1	45.4	55.3	53.1	47.3	50.6	49.6
1899	27.5	50.8	54.1	60.5	45.5	57.6	47.7
1900	27.7	52.8	52.5	62.8	44.1	59.9	46.2
1901	30.9	55.5	55.7	65.9	46.9	62.9	49.1
1902	35.5	60.4	58.8	72.2	49.2	69.1	51.4
1903	35.4	62.7	56.5	74.4	47.6	71.3	49.6
1904	34.2	59.1	57.9	68.4	50.0	65.6	52.1
1905	39.0	66.1	59.0	77.9	50.1	74.9	52.1
1906	41.6	69.6	59.8	81.9	50.8	78.9	52.7
1907	42.1	72.8	57.8	86.0	49.0	82.9	50.8
1908	33.7	65.2	51.7	73.6	45.8	71.1	47.4
1909	43.4	72.7	59.7	83.8	51.8	81.1	53.5
1910	45.1	76.0	59.3	88.2	51.1	85.6	52.7
1911	42.7	76.0	56.2	87.4	48.9	85.1	50.2
1912	51.3	79.4	64.6	91.3	56.2	89.2	57.5
1913	53.8	80.2	67.1	91.5	58.8	89.7	60.0
1914	51.1	77.4	66.0	86.5	59.1	85.1	60.0
1915	59.9	80.9	74.0	89.8	66.7	88.6	67.6
1916	71.2	95.4	74.6	108.6	65.6	107.5	66.2
1917	70.6	102.0	69.2	115.7	61.0	114.9	61.4
1918	69.8	104.0	67.1	114.6	60.9	114.2	61.1
1919	61.0	100.3	60.8	105.1	58.0	105.1	58.0
1920	66.0	100.1	65.9	107.3	61.5	107.3	61.5
1921	53.5	77.4	69.1	75.4	71.0	75.4	71.0
1922	68.1	84.7	80.4	84.7	80.4	84.7	80.4
1923	76.9	96.2	79.9	99.3	77.4	99.3	77.4
1924	73.4	90.2	81.4	89.2	82.3	89.2	82.3
1925	81.9	92.7	88.3	93.4	87.7	93.4	87.7
1926	86.2	94.7	91.0	96.4	89.4	96.4	89.4
1927	87.1	93.5	93.2	95.2	91.5	95.2	91.5
1928	90.1	93.8	96.1	94.2	95.6	94.2	95.6
1929	100.0	100.0	100.0	100.0	100.0	100.0	100.0

(continued)

TABLE D-II (concluded)

	Output	Persons Engaged	Output Per Person	Manhours	Output Per Manhour	Labor Input	Output per Unit of Labor Input
1930	85.6	89.2	96.0	85.0	100.7	85.1	100.6
1931	72.0	75.6	95.2	69.3	103.9	69.5	103.6
1932	53.8	63.9	84.2	55.4	97.1	55.6	96.8
1933	62.8	68.9	91.1	59.4	105.7	59.7	105.2
1934	69.1	79.9	86.5	62.6	110.4	63.1	109.5
1935	82.8	85.1	97.3	70.4	117.6	71.0	116.6
1936	96.8	92.2	105.0	81.7	118.5	82.5	117.3
1937	103.3	101.2	102.1	88.4	116.9	89.4	115.5
1938	80.9	87.4	92.6	70.4	114.9	71.3	113.5
1939	102.5	95.5	107.3	81.5	125.8	82.7	123.9
1940	118.6	104.3	113.7	89.9	131.9	91.4	129.8
1941	157.9	125.7	125.6	115.5	136.7	117.6	134.3
1942	197.2	146.1	135.0	141.8	139.1	144.6	136.4
1943	238.1	166.3	143.2	168.9	141.0	172.5	138.0
1944	232.5	163.1	142.6	166.8	139.4	170.7	136.2
1945	196.5	145.5	135.1	142.9	137.5	146.5	134.1
1946	160.6	139.1	115.5	127.1	126.4	130.5	123.1
1947	178.3	145.9	122.2	133.3	133.8	137.1	130.1
1948	184.2	146.5	125.7	132.9	138.6	136.9	134.6
1949	173.5	136.1	127.5	120.7	143.7	124.8	139.0
1950	201.1	143.5	140.1	129.5	155.3	134.4	149.6
1951	214.3	154.4	138.8	139.8	153.3	145.6	147.2
1952	223.6	157.2	142.2	142.3	157.1	148.7	150.4
1953	243.4	164.9	147.6	148.5	163.9	155.8	156.2
1954	228.2	153.5	148.7	135.4	168.5	141.9	160.8
1955	255.9	158.6	161.3	142.4	179.7	149.2	171.5
1956	264.3	161.9	163.2	144.3	183.2	151.2	174.8
1957	264.6	160.9	164.4	141.4	187.1	148.1	178.7

TABLE D-III

Manufacturing, Durable and Nondurable: Output, Inputs, and Productivity Ratios, Key Years, 1899–1957

(1929 = 100)

	Output	Persons Engaged	Output Per Person	Manhours	Output Per Manhour	Labor Input	Output Per Unit of Labor Input	Capital Input	Output Per Unit of Capital Input	Total Factor Input	Total Factor Productivity
DURABLE GOODS[a]											
1899	25.0	48.8	51.2	57.5	43.5	53.3	46.9	25.7	97.3	47.0	53.2
1909	39.6	70.3	56.3	79.7	49.7	75.2	52.7	53.5	74.0	70.2	56.4
1919	61.7	102.7	60.1	106.4	58.0	105.9	58.3	90.5	68.2	102.4	60.3
1929	100.0	100.0	100.0	100.0	100.0	100.0	100.0	100.0	100.0	100.0	100.0
1937	92.0	98.0	93.9	86.0	107.0	86.7	106.1	82.9	111.0	85.9	107.1
1948	178.7	155.2	115.1	138.2	129.3	141.7	126.1	117.0	152.7	136.1	131.3
1953	262.9	188.3	139.6	168.6	155.9	176.3	149.1	159.6	164.7	172.5	152.4
1957	270.1	183.4	147.3	160.3	168.5	168.1	160.7	n.a.	...	...	...
NONDURABLE GOODS[b]											
1899	29.6	53.2	55.6	63.4	46.7	61.9	47.8	32.7	90.5	54.1	54.7
1909	47.2	75.8	62.3	85.9	54.9	85.0	55.5	55.2	85.5	77.1	61.2
1919	60.3	99.0	60.9	99.4	60.7	99.6	60.5	95.2	63.3	98.4	61.3
1929	100.0	100.0	100.0	100.0	100.0	100.0	100.0	100.0	100.0	100.0	100.0
1937	113.9	104.5	109.0	85.9	132.6	87.1	130.8	87.7	129.9	87.2	130.6
1948	184.5	133.2	138.5	115.9	159.2	119.6	154.3	124.2	148.6	120.9	152.6
1953	218.1	136.2	160.1	116.1	187.9	121.0	180.2	147.4	148.0	127.8	170.7
1957	246.3	133.4	184.6	112.3	219.3	118.4	208.0	n.a.	...	...	...

n.a. = not available.

[a] The durable subgroup (following the classification of the Board of Governors of the Federal Reserve System) includes nine Census groups: lumber products; furniture; stone, clay, and glass products; primary metals; fabricated metals; machinery; nonelectric; electric machinery; transportation equipment; miscellaneous; including instruments and related products.

[b] The nondurable subgroup includes eleven Census groups: foods; beverages; tobacco products; textile mill products; apparel; paper and products; printing and publishing; chemicals; petroleum and coal products; rubber products; leather and products.

TABLE D-IV

Manufacturing: Output, Inputs, and Productivity Ratios, by Group, Key Years, 1899–1957

(1929 = 100)

	Output	Persons Engaged	Output Per Person	Manhours	Output Per Manhour	Capital Input	Output Per Unit of Capital Input	Total Factor Input	Total Factor Productivity
FOOD AND KINDRED PRODUCTS (excluding beverages)									
1899	30.3	45.1	67.2	54.3	55.8	35.1	86.3	50.3	60.2
1909	44.9	65.3	68.8	76.1	59.0	57.1	78.6	72.1	62.3
1919	65.1	104.6	62.2	110.0	59.2	106.8	61.0	109.3	59.6
1929	100.0	100.0	100.0	100.0	100.0	100.0	100.0	100.0	100.0
1937	104.2	108.7	95.9	96.7	107.8	79.7	130.7	92.6	112.5
1948	154.5	134.6	114.8	122.1	126.5	100.7	153.4	116.9	132.2
1953	170.7	136.0	125.5	119.4	143.0	104.9	162.7	115.9	147.3
1957	188.4	136.6	137.9	119.9	157.1	n.a.	...	...	...
BEVERAGES									
1899	295.9	151.1	195.8	184.6	160.3	170.7	173.3	178.3	166.0
1909	433.6	219.3	197.7	236.6	183.3	239.5	181.0	237.9	182.3
1919	158.9	163.6	97.1	167.7	94.8	140.2	113.3	155.3	102.3
1929	100.0	100.0	100.0	100.0	100.0	100.0	100.0	100.0	100.0
1937	684.9	254.5	269.1	233.1	293.8	200.9	340.9	220.9	310.0
1948	1,342.5	406.4	330.3	389.7	344.5	315.2	425.9	359.0	374.0
1953	1,391.6	395.2	352.1	362.0	384.4	345.1	403.2	356.0	390.9
1957	1,473.7	323.7	455.3	282.4	521.8	n.a.	...	...	...

(continued)

TABLE D-IV (continued)

TOBACCO PRODUCTS

Year									
1899	29.8	113.7	26.2	128.5	23.2	20.9	142.6	83.3	35.8
1909	43.4	144.0	30.1	157.2	27.6	38.1	113.9	107.2	40.5
1919	69.3	133.7	51.8	139.4	49.7	60.7	114.2	106.3	65.2
1929	100.0	100.0	100.0	100.0	100.0	100.0	100.0	100.0	100.0
1937	117.2	77.0	152.2	65.4	179.2	80.0	146.5	71.7	163.5
1948	185.8	64.3	289.0	56.5	328.8	136.6	136.0	83.9	221.5
1953	203.3	66.8	304.3	58.9	345.2	146.4	138.9	88.7	229.2
1957	212.7	59.2	359.3	50.9	417.9	n.a.	...	...	...

TEXTILE MILL PRODUCTS

Year									
1899	40.8	60.8	67.1	70.9	57.5	49.6	82.3	67.1	60.8
1909	60.7	80.9	75.0	91.9	66.1	76.4	79.5	89.1	68.1
1919	71.1	95.5	74.5	90.6	78.5	115.1	61.8	95.0	74.8
1929	100.0	100.0	100.0	100.0	100.0	100.0	100.0	100.0	100.0
1937	108.1	100.3	107.8	76.8	140.8	71.1	152.0	75.7	142.8
1948	161.5	106.7	151.4	89.0	181.5	78.5	205.7	86.6	186.5
1953	168.4	92.9	181.3	76.5	220.1	87.8	191.8	78.9	213.4
1957	168.2	78.7	213.7	64.0	262.8	n.a.	...	...	...

APPAREL AND RELATED PRODUCTS

Year									
1899	30.4	53.8	56.5	68.3	44.5	29.4	103.4	63.2	48.1
1909	50.8	87.2	58.3	104.3	48.7	57.6	88.2	98.2	51.7
1919	64.2	95.0	67.6	94.8	67.7	95.1	67.5	94.8	67.7
1929	100.0	100.0	100.0	100.0	100.0	100.0	100.0	100.0	100.0
1937	103.9	109.1	95.2	87.9	118.2	66.7	155.8	85.3	121.8
1948	154.0	152.9	100.7	137.3	112.2	132.4	116.3	136.5	112.8
1953	171.0	160.7	106.4	140.1	122.1	161.6	105.8	141.8	120.6
1957	180.3	155.7	115.8	133.1	135.5	n.a.	...	...	...

n.a. = not available.

(continued)

469

TABLE D-IV (continued)

Manufacturing: Output, Inputs, and Productivity Ratios, by Group, Key Years, 1899–1957

(1929 = 100)

	Output	Persons Engaged	Output Per Person	Manhours	Output Per Manhour	Capital Input	Output Per Unit of Capital Input	Total Factor Input	Total Factor Productivity
				LUMBER AND PRODUCTS, EXCEPT FURNITURE					
1899	90.6	89.2	101.6	107.8	84.0	43.9	206.4	99.5	91.0
1909	115.6	119.5	96.7	139.9	82.6	78.8	146.7	132.0	87.6
1919	87.7	105.6	83.0	117.5	74.6	79.4	110.5	112.5	78.0
1929	100.0	100.0	100.0	100.0	100.0	100.0	100.0	100.0	100.0
1937	74.7	79.5	94.0	76.0	98.3	54.8	136.3	72.3	103.3
1948	103.2	87.7	117.7	80.9	127.6	64.4	160.2	78.8	131.0
1953	114.0	79.8	142.9	72.1	158.1	66.9	170.4	72.1	158.1
1957	109.0	68.3	159.6	61.3	177.8	n.a.	…	…	…
				FURNITURE AND FIXTURES					
1899	36.7	44.7	82.1	50.4	72.8	29.6	124.0	48.9	75.1
1909	48.9	65.6	74.5	71.9	68.0	52.7	92.8	70.6	69.3
1919	50.6	74.1	68.3	77.4	65.4	66.1	76.6	76.6	66.1
1929	100.0	100.0	100.0	100.0	100.0	100.0	100.0	100.0	100.0
1937	76.6	86.3	88.8	74.9	102.3	62.9	121.8	73.9	103.7
1948	158.4	132.6	119.5	116.2	136.3	64.7	244.8	108.4	146.1
1953	181.3	141.2	128.4	121.1	149.7	73.5	246.7	114.1	158.9
1957	211.8	143.0	148.1	120.6	175.6	n.a.	…	…	…

(continued)

TABLE D-IV (continued)

PAPER AND ALLIED PRODUCTS

Year									
1899	18.3	37.7	48.5	42.5	43.1	20.5	89.3	37.9	48.3
1909	36.7	59.5	61.7	63.4	57.9	45.7	80.3	59.7	61.5
1919	52.8	88.7	59.5	86.6	61.0	70.6	74.8	83.2	63.5
1929	100.0	100.0	100.0	100.0	100.0	100.0	100.0	100.0	100.0
1937	122.0	107.4	113.6	86.1	141.7	90.8	134.4	87.0	140.2
1948	198.2	154.8	128.0	130.2	152.2	122.8	161.4	127.4	155.6
1953	250.1	174.8	143.1	145.4	172.0	156.8	159.5	148.2	168.8
1957	297.4	186.0	159.9	149.8	198.5	n.a.	...	...	...

PRINTING AND PUBLISHING

Year									
1899	17.1	45.1	37.9	50.4	33.9	40.2	42.5	48.6	35.2
1909	35.5	67.7	52.4	70.8	50.1	60.7	58.5	69.0	51.4
1919	54.0	79.3	68.1	78.0	69.2	77.6	69.6	77.9	69.3
1929	100.0	100.0	100.0	100.0	100.0	100.0	100.0	100.0	100.0
1937	101.6	99.0	102.6	82.4	123.3	84.3	120.5	82.7	122.9
1948	146.2	130.8	111.8	112.0	130.5	108.7	134.5	111.5	131.1
1953	168.2	143.1	117.5	120.2	139.9	113.2	148.6	119.1	141.2
1957	195.3	155.4	125.7	127.7	152.9	n.a.	...	...	...

CHEMICALS AND ALLIED PRODUCTS

Year									
1899	18.6	37.9	49.1	45.3	41.1	25.7	72.4	37.8	49.2
1909	31.4	57.4	54.7	67.4	46.6	47.4	66.2	59.8	52.5
1919	51.5	106.0	48.6	113.5	45.4	92.3	55.8	105.4	48.9
1929	100.0	100.0	100.0	100.0	100.0	100.0	100.0	100.0	100.0
1937	123.9	109.0	113.7	97.4	127.2	97.6	126.9	97.5	127.1
1948	309.8	174.7	177.3	160.0	193.6	169.1	183.2	163.5	189.5
1953	470.9	203.3	231.6	181.3	259.7	242.2	194.4	202.9	232.1
1957	612.8	214.8	285.3	190.2	322.2	n.a.	...	...	...

(continued)

n.a. = not available.

TABLE D-IV (continued)

Manufacturing: Output, Inputs, and Productivity Ratios, by Group, Key Years, 1899–1957

(1929 = 100)

	Output	Persons Engaged	Output Per Person	Manhours	Output Per Manhour	Capital Input	Output Per Unit of Capital Input	Total Factor Input	Total Factor Productivity
	PETROLEUM AND COAL PRODUCTS								
1899	8.7	26.5	32.8	33.2	26.2	12.7	68.5	19.1	45.5
1909	16.1	39.6	40.7	45.3	35.5	27.6	58.3	33.1	48.6
1919	39.1	89.4	43.7	92.4	42.3	87.6	44.6	89.1	43.9
1929	100.0	100.0	100.0	100.0	100.0	100.0	100.0	100.0	100.0
1937	113.6	103.1	110.2	73.2	155.2	103.5	109.8	91.6	124.0
1948	201.2	159.8	125.9	127.2	158.2	157.3	127.9	145.7	138.1
1953	254.3	168.3	151.1	127.9	198.8	181.8	139.9	158.8	160.1
1957	278.2	162.4	171.3	120.9	230.1	n.a.	...	...	...
	RUBBER PRODUCTS								
1899	4.3	23.0	18.7	26.2	16.4	8.2	52.4	23.0	18.7
1909	7.7	32.5	23.7	36.6	21.0	16.1	47.8	32.9	23.4
1919	53.7	119.6	44.9	120.1	44.7	78.2	68.7	112.6	47.7
1929	100.0	100.0	100.0	100.0	100.0	100.0	100.0	100.0	100.0
1937	90.6	87.2	103.9	68.9	131.5	55.1	164.4	66.1	137.1
1948	170.2	136.5	124.7	118.9	143.1	97.9	173.9	114.8	148.3
1953	212.9	149.9	142.0	132.8	160.3	114.7	185.6	129.7	164.1
1957	223.7	144.5	154.8	131.4	170.2	n.a.	...	...	...

(continued)

472

TABLE D-IV (continued)

LEATHER AND PRODUCTS

Year									
1899	64.0	76.2	84.0	94.6	67.7	65.2	98.2	89.9	71.2
1909	82.8	96.6	85.7	116.8	70.9	109.8	75.4	115.7	71.6
1919	90.1	111.6	80.7	115.8	77.8	142.6	63.2	120.1	75.0
1929	100.0	100.0	100.0	100.0	100.0	100.0	100.0	100.0	100.0
1937	108.4	101.6	106.7	84.0	129.0	67.5	160.6	81.8	132.5
1948	119.5	106.6	112.1	89.3	133.8	67.7	176.5	86.3	138.5
1953	116.6	101.8	114.5	85.0	137.2	74.7	156.1	84.1	138.6
1957	125.4	98.4	127.4	81.0	154.8	n.a.	...	...	...

STONE, CLAY, AND GLASS PRODUCTS

Year									
1899	29.9	66.2	45.2	80.6	37.1	29.2	102.4	69.8	42.8
1909	56.3	97.8	57.6	115.3	48.8	69.1	81.5	105.6	53.3
1919	55.9	92.4	60.5	103.4	54.1	75.9	73.6	97.6	57.3
1929	100.0	100.0	100.0	100.0	100.0	100.0	100.0	100.0	100.0
1937	99.6	92.7	107.4	87.0	114.5	70.8	140.7	83.3	119.6
1948	177.6	140.9	126.0	134.3	132.2	80.6	220.3	119.4	148.7
1953	214.8	146.7	146.4	137.8	155.9	101.7	211.2	128.4	167.3
1957	242.5	150.1	161.6	138.5	175.1	n.a.	...	...	...

PRIMARY METAL INDUSTRIES

Year									
1899	21.8	45.1	48.3	53.6	40.7	25.7	84.8	46.1	47.3
1909	43.5	61.4	70.8	73.5	59.2	63.1	68.9	70.7	61.5
1919	62.1	98.9	62.8	108.8	57.1	98.9	62.8	106.1	58.5
1929	100.0	100.0	100.0	100.0	100.0	100.0	100.0	100.0	100.0
1937	89.5	113.2	79.1	96.1	93.1	108.5	82.5	99.0	90.4
1948	161.3	150.4	107.2	131.8	122.4	109.9	146.8	126.0	128.0
1953	194.3	163.4	118.9	143.1	135.8	161.6	120.2	147.8	131.5
1957	195.8	160.7	121.8	134.4	145.7	n.a.	...	...	...

n.a. = not available.

(continued)

TABLE D-IV (continued)

Manufacturing: Output, Inputs, and Productivity Ratios, by Group, Key Years, 1899–1957
(1929 = 100)

	Output	Persons Engaged	Output Per Person	Manhours	Output Per Manhour	Capital Input	Output Per Unit of Capital Input	Total Factor Input	Total Factor Productivity
	FABRICATED METAL PRODUCTS								
1899	20.6	45.6	45.2	54.9	37.5	25.8	79.8	48.5	42.5
1909	41.3	73.0	56.6	82.9	49.8	57.6	71.7	77.3	53.4
1919	60.1	94.2	63.8	98.9	60.8	77.8	77.2	94.3	63.7
1929	100.0	100.0	100.0	100.0	100.0	100.0	100.0	100.0	100.0
1937	93.7	99.6	94.1	89.8	104.3	76.5	122.5	86.7	108.1
1948	181.4	159.8	113.5	147.2	123.2	117.1	154.9	140.2	129.4
1953	312.8	212.8	147.0	196.8	158.9	164.7	189.9	188.9	165.6
1957	287.8	194.6	147.9	174.1	165.3	n.a.	...	...	...
	MACHINERY, NONELECTRIC								
1899	28.1	44.5	63.1	48.2	58.3	33.2	84.6	44.5	63.1
1909	44.5	62.2	71.5	63.9	69.6	62.9	70.7	63.6	70.0
1919	73.6	103.3	71.2	98.7	74.6	94.3	78.0	97.6	75.4
1929	100.0	100.0	100.0	100.0	100.0	100.0	100.0	100.0	100.0
1937	100.6	103.0	97.7	86.2	116.7	77.3	130.1	84.1	119.6
1948	218.9	194.1	112.8	162.5	134.7	156.4	140.0	160.8	136.1
1953	287.6	217.5	132.2	185.3	155.2	192.9	149.1	186.0	154.6
1957	281.6	216.9	129.8	178.8	157.5	n.a.	...	...	...

(continued)

TABLE D-IV (concluded)

ELECTRIC MACHINERY

Year									
1899	7.7	11.1	69.4	12.9	59.7	8.3	92.8	11.9	64.7
1909	18.5	25.3	73.1	27.2	68.0	25.1	73.7	26.8	69.0
1919	46.3	69.3	66.8	68.3	67.8	54.4	85.1	65.4	70.8
1929	100.0	100.0	100.0	100.0	100.0	100.0	100.0	100.0	100.0
1937	93.5	89.6	104.4	74.5	125.5	63.8	146.6	72.7	128.6
1948	251.9	185.2	136.0	156.7	160.8	147.2	171.1	155.2	162.3
1953	458.0	258.1	177.5	218.4	209.7	227.6	201.2	220.6	207.6
1957	511.0	261.5	195.4	218.7	233.7	n.a.	...	...	...

TRANSPORTATION EQUIPMENT

Year									
1899	7.3	33.4	21.9	41.4	17.6	19.3	37.8	35.9	20.3
1909	10.7	44.3	24.2	53.6	20.0	28.3	37.8	47.3	22.6
1919	60.8	144.9	42.0	145.6	41.8	107.8	56.4	136.2	44.6
1929	100.0	100.0	100.0	100.0	100.0	100.0	100.0	100.0	100.0
1937	90.7	108.1	83.9	92.2	98.4	97.3	93.2	93.4	97.1
1948	163.7	171.8	95.3	156.2	104.8	139.0	117.8	152.0	107.7
1953	310.8	268.8	115.6	254.8	122.0	198.1	156.9	240.0	129.5
1957	358.2	263.4	136.0	246.1	145.6	n.a.	...	...	...

MISCELLANEOUS AND INSTRUMENTS

Year									
1899	29.3	44.0	66.6	52.4	55.9	25.4	115.4	46.7	62.7
1909	54.7	76.0	72.0	87.7	62.4	53.3	102.6	80.5	68.0
1919	69.5	112.0	62.1	118.5	58.6	72.5	95.9	108.8	63.9
1929	100.0	100.0	100.0	100.0	100.0	100.0	100.0	100.0	100.0
1937	106.2	95.0	111.8	89.0	119.3	70.2	151.3	84.6	125.5
1948	226.4	160.0	141.5	151.8	149.1	120.9	187.3	144.5	156.7
1953	302.1	186.0	162.4	173.7	173.9	141.2	214.0	165.9	182.1
1957	349.4	187.0	186.8	169.6	206.0	n.a.	...	...	...

n.a. = not available.

475

TABLE D-V

Manufacturing: Output and Labor Productivity, by Industry, Key Years,
1899–1954 (1929 = 100)

(These 70 industries represent part of the sample of 80 used for the productivity analyses in Chapters 6 and 7. Seven groups are included in the sample because no representative industry data were obtainable. The 10 remaining industries, for which capital data are available, appear in Table D-VI. O = output; O/E = output per person engaged; O/MH = output per manhour.)

	1899	1909	1919	1937	1947	1954
			DAIRY PRODUCTS (202)			
O	18.5	30.6	64.9	111.3	196.8	179.7
O/E	43.6	48.8	65.4	114.7	139.3	155.0
O/MH	38.5	43.9	59.7	116.5	146.3	176.5
		CANNING, PRESERVING, AND FREEZING: SEAFOOD (2031–32)				
O	52.8	77.8	84.8	103.7	135.5	144.3
O/E	101.5	104.4	90.3	79.6	90.8	129.8
O/MH	83.9	87.6	82.7	97.7	122.1	183.4
	CANNING, PRESERVING, AND FREEZING: FRUITS AND VEGETABLES (2033–35, 2037)					
O	16.9	28.6	54.8	150.8	268.2	402.6
O/E	38.0	54.5	67.4	111.6	163.7	241.5
O/MH	32.3	47.0	62.6	128.6	189.7	288.4
			FLOUR AND MEAL (2041, 2045)			
O	93.7	102.5	113.5	85.8	129.1	109.7
O/E	79.5	64.7	62.4	96.4	130.5	138.0
O/MH	65.0	54.3	56.9	100.5	122.3	140.8
			RICE CLEANING AND POLISHING (2044)			
O	20.6	51.9	88.2	106.2	176.5	233.2
O/E	51.8	62.8	58.3	80.9	94.8	129.6
O/MH	42.0	52.6	51.0	89.5	98.5	140.7
			BAKERY PRODUCTS (205)			
O	22.3[a]	43.9[a]	64.9[a]	97.4	137.7	146.9
O/E	69.5	76.9	81.7	84.8	114.8	117.9
O/MH	55.1	65.1	78.7	91.1	119.5	130.3
			RAW CANE SUGAR (2061)			
O	115.2[b]	167.9	124.7	192.1	190.7	225.0
O/E	64.0	86.9	48.7	108.8	112.3	200.7
O/MH	46.5	67.2	43.8	128.5	127.5	217.6
			CANE-SUGAR REFINING (2062)			
O	44.3[b]	54.8	79.2	89.0	103.4	107.7
O/E	62.4	84.4	60.3	88.6	93.8	105.7
O/MH	47.4	69.8	54.0	103.9	104.0	127.5
			BEET SUGAR (2063)			
O	6.7	45.4	67.4	119.8	163.9	173.5
O/E	26.3	49.9	43.8	98.0	109.6	141.1
O/MH	19.6	40.6	37.9	117.5	129.7	176.5

(continued)

TABLE D-V (continued)

	1899	1909	1919	1937	1947	1954
	CORN PRODUCTS (2094)					
O	43.8[a]	46.8	69.4	84.3	156.0	154.8
O/E	52.5	66.2	65.8	85.2	100.2	90.3
O/MH	37.6	49.0	59.8	92.2	100.0	102.9
	VINEGAR AND CIDER (2096)					
O	101.0[a]	112.5[a]	143.3[a]	85.6[a]	70.4	98.0
O/E	65.5	60.8	71.4	95.9	97.8	113.3
O/MH	56.6	54.3	66.4	109.2	108.8	131.4
	MANUFACTURED ICE (2097)					
O	9.8	29.7	59.8	75.3	105.1	49.2
O/E	44.5	58.0	63.8	118.2	116.0	120.0
O/MH	34.9	46.9	58.0	119.9	118.9	137.9
	BEVERAGES GROUP (208)					
O	295.9	433.6	158.9	684.9	1,325.3	1,365.1
O/E	195.8	197.7	97.1	269.1	334.5	348.1
O/MH	160.3	183.3	94.8	293.8	342.4	396.3
	DISTILLED LIQUORS, EXCEPT BRANDY (2085)					
O	2,573.8[b]	3,365.1[b]	108.3[b]	10,696.3[b]	10,204.2[b]	8,265.4
O/E	949.7	746.8	115.2	1,783.3	1,062.3	1,218.7
O/MH	845.0	691.4	114.7	2,201.8	1,275.2	1,537.2
	CIGARETTES AND CIGARS (2111, 2121)					
O	22.0	32.0	61.0	122.0	200.1	221.5
O/E	22.2	24.2	47.3	162.7	319.1	387.9
O/MH	19.7	22.3	45.4	190.6	361.2	445.7
	CHEWING AND SMOKING TOBACCO (2131)					
O	88.6	129.8	127.5	82.9	82.5	76.3
O/E	34.5	51.3	71.3	87.4	98.2	134.1
O/MH	30.2	45.3	66.7	107.8	113.5	171.8
	WOOLEN AND WORSTED MANUFACTURES (221)					
O	71.3	102.8	97.5	114.4	162.5	99.1
O/E	85.7	95.4	86.7	107.1	143.8	172.3
O/MH	68.1	78.1	84.6	137.7	163.2	199.0
	COTTON GOODS (2223–24, 2233)					
O	49.1	67.5	77.9	98.9	138.0	149.5
O/E	71.0	78.3	77.1	100.1	129.9	165.9
O/MH	61.0	69.3	84.4	130.0	154.2	208.5
	SILK AND RAYON GOODS (2222, 2225, 2234)					
O	22.1	39.6	63.7	135.3	217.4	317.2
O/E	44.8	52.8	65.3	152.9	241.0	389.2
O/MH	40.3	47.7	68.6	203.5	280.9	477.0
	WOOL CARPETS, RUGS, AND CARPET YARN (2271)					
O	60.7	78.3	61.9	92.4	151.6	123.1
O/E	72.3	79.2	89.6	97.9	147.0	159.2
O/MH	60.0	67.6	85.9	123.2	156.3	183.2

(continued)

TABLE D-V (continued)

	1899	1909	1919	1937	1947	1954
	FUR-FELT HATS AND HAT BODIES (2281)					
O	79.3	125.8	94.4	100.0	91.0	45.3
O/E	71.6	85.0	85.0	107.4	130.6	103.7
O/MH	58.7	73.5	86.3	133.9	146.5	123.8
	WOOL-FELT HATS AND HAT BODIES (2282)					
O	135.1	100.8	79.4	256.0	323.4	232.8
O/E	135.1	106.0	107.7	131.9	162.8	295.4
O/MH	122.3	98.7	106.9	180.4	213.7	392.6
	JUTE (EXCEPT FELT) AND LINEN GOODS (2297)					
O	75.5	125.7	109.7	123.9	103.3	103.4
O/E	73.2	91.5	87.9	106.3	143.3	153.6
O/MH	59.4	77.4	84.7	131.0	150.6	178.9
	CORDAGE AND TWINE (2298)					
O	66.8	82.3	92.8	92.1	99.3	91.2
O/E	77.0	84.2	76.8	96.0	104.0	126.7
O/MH	66.3	75.6	74.1	124.6	121.5	154.6
	APPAREL GROUP (23)					
O	30.4[a]	50.8[a]	64.2[a]	103.9	147.9	165.6
O/E	56.5	58.3	67.6	95.2	100.5	108.3
O/MH	44.5	48.7	67.7	118.2	111.6	126.0
	FURNITURE GROUP (25)					
O	36.7[a]	48.9[a]	50.6[a]	76.6[a]	152.6[a]	189.2
O/E	82.1	74.5	68.3	88.8	114.7	144.2
O/MH	72.8	68.0	65.4	102.3	129.2	171.2
	PULP, PAPER, AND PAPER BOARD					
O	19.4	36.5	52.7	119.8	197.9	263.2
O/E	52.9	64.4	60.6	112.0	117.4	142.9
O/MH	47.4	61.0	59.4	143.6	138.5	175.5
	CONVERTED PAPER PRODUCTS (2641–2699)					
O	17.8[a]	35.9[a]	54.1[a]	134.4[a]	205.9	273.8
O/E	45.8	57.4	59.7	124.7	145.7	158.2
O/MH	40.0	53.1	64.3	150.5	172.3	192.7
	PRINTING AND PUBLISHING GROUP (27)					
O	17.1	35.5	54.0	101.6	139.1	175.3
O/E	37.9	52.4	68.1	102.6	108.7	120.6
O/MH	33.9	50.1	69.2	123.3	124.3	145.2
	CHEMICALS, N.E.C., RAYON, AND GASES					
O	6.6	12.5	36.3	171.6	495.9	952.6
O/E	41.8	52.3	48.5	130.4	214.6	301.1
O/MH	33.7	43.0	45.6	143.2	240.3	344.4
	EXPLOSIVES (2826)					
O	25.3	61.6	93.6	92.8	147.7	310.0
O/E	38.4	73.2	50.9	96.6	122.3	82.4
O/MH	29.2	56.7	46.7	99.8	124.1	83.9

(continued)

TABLE D-V (continued)

	1899	1909	1919	1937	1947	1954
	SOAP AND GLYCERINE (2841)					
O	38.0[a]	61.4	89.4	109.0	176.0	192.4
O/E	66.2	67.5	62.6	117.8	130.4	151.6
O/MH	56.4	58.4	61.1	129.0	132.5	175.5
	PAINTS AND ALLIED PRODUCTS (285)					
O	22.2	37.5	52.2	109.0	195.1	208.8
O/E	70.5	74.6	66.8	105.1	135.7	143.0
O/MH	67.7	72.7	71.5	131.5	166.0	186.3
	HARDWOOD AND SOFTWOOD DISTILLATION (2861–62)					
O	28.2	54.1	74.6	101.3	144.0	178.3
O/E	80.3	90.6	68.6	104.8	116.3	153.2
O/MH	66.5	76.5	62.0	118.9	139.9	180.6
	GUM NAVAL STORES (2863)					
O	119.3	90.5	75.6	80.6	39.6	28.4
O/E	110.0	88.2	105.4	97.1	130.5	124.6
O/MH	90.1	74.7	92.8	99.3	141.4	134.6
	NATURAL TANNING AND DYEING MATERIALS, SULFONATED OILS, AND ASSISTANTS (2865, 2843)					
O	25.9	53.7	81.7	101.4	128.9	151.5
O/E	42.7	56.4	49.7	87.0	101.2	131.4
O/MH	37.1	49.9	44.1	98.5	115.5	160.7
	COTTONSEED OIL MILLS (2881)					
O	50.7	73.3	111.0	82.8	77.4	130.0
O/E	72.8	66.0	66.1	81.1	93.4	165.4
O/MH	57.4	53.9	56.5	74.9	93.1	172.4
	LINSEED OIL MILLS (2882)					
O	42.6[a]	42.5[a]	50.5[a]	86.0	59.9	78.8
O/E	87.3	74.2	56.2	88.7	112.2	104.1
O/MH	61.0	51.4	44.5	83.5	117.2	167.7
	GREASE AND TALLOW (2886)					
O	32.8[a]	49.0[a]	62.8[a]	90.9[a]	225.6[a]	333.9
O/E	89.6	60.3	51.4	96.5	120.7	194.4
O/MH	73.2	50.2	46.0	101.6	115.3	188.5
	GLUE AND GELATIN (2894)					
O	28.3[a]	66.8[a]	92.6[a]	138.7	168.0	155.9
O/E	54.7	61.9	67.2	117.9	116.3	125.9
O/MH	45.7	52.6	62.6	127.5	117.8	146.4
	CARBON BLACK (2895)					
O	3.4[a]	8.2[a]	22.9	133.2	316.2	335.4
O/E	68.0	59.4	60.9	118.9	213.4	211.3
O/MH	60.7	54.3	55.9	137.7	253.2	246.1
	SALT (2898)					
O	53.3	67.4	88.2	96.9	112.4	112.6
O/E	62.9	75.3	71.6	118.0	128.8	154.0
O/MH	53.3	65.1	66.0	133.3	144.1	167.6

(continued)

TABLE D-V (continued)

	1899	1909	1919	1937	1947	1954
		COKE OVEN PRODUCTS (293)				
O	18.2	38.3	61.4	87.3	137.1	126.1
O/E	24.1	29.7	45.2	90.4	87.7	81.5
O/MH	18.9	25.6	39.2	123.1	102.2	118.2
		RUBBER PRODUCTS GROUP (30)				
O	4.3[a]	7.7[a]	53.7	90.6	176.4	201.1
O/E	18.7	23.7	44.9	103.9	121.2	147.9
O/MH	16.4	21.0	44.7	131.5	136.4	171.7
		INDUSTRIAL LEATHER BELTING (3121)				
O	47.3[a]	76.3[a]	78.6[a]	86.5	121.4[a]	128.7[a]
O/E	76.4	63.0	70.5	85.6	94.5	111.0
O/MH	66.1	55.8	66.3	100.3	101.7	126.4
		LEATHER GLOVES AND MITTENS (315)				
O	76.0	87.9	94.1	98.0	94.2	66.9
O/E	59.2	82.9	91.4	79.5	82.6	98.5
O/MH	50.6	74.3	89.4	96.5	107.5	132.2
		SADDLERY, HARNESS, AND WHIPS (3192)				
O	539.4[a]	664.8[a]	302.1[a]	59.3[a]	57.2[a]	25.3
O/E	131.4	146.8	88.6	72.7	92.3	87.2
O/MH	106.9	126.7	80.5	79.8	99.1	98.4
		GLASS (3211, 3221, 3229)				
O	24.9	45.0	64.3	162.6	256.9	297.0
O/E	33.3	46.0	57.0	137.2	164.3	189.2
O/MH	29.7	40.4	55.3	160.0	179.5	211.5
		CEMENT, LIME, CONCRETE (324, 327)				
O	9.9	47.8	53.1	82.0	182.9	286.2
O/E	34.5	58.2	68.3	94.6	104.8	138.1
O/MH	28.2	49.5	61.2	114.2	113.8	154.9
		STRUCTURAL CLAY AND POTTERY PRODUCTS (325, 326, 3297)				
O	55.8	79.4	64.0	72.9	108.3	111.9
O/E	67.4	77.0	77.3	96.4	112.7	121.1
O/MH	57.1	68.4	71.6	107.5	127.9	132.6
		BLAST FURNACES (3311, 3313)				
O	32.4	58.1	69.8	87.8	126.9	125.6
O/E	22.3	38.7	41.1	96.4	87.7	84.5
O/MH	15.5	28.1	33.2	107.1	103.8	105.2
		STEEL MILL PRODUCTS (3312, 3323, 3393, 3399)				
O	23.5	43.3	63.2	97.0	152.3	155.3
O/E	52.8	73.1	66.0	80.5	118.4	123.8
O/MH	46.4	60.8	59.5	95.6	138.2	152.9
		PRIMARY NONFERROUS METALS (333)				
O	24.9	48.8	64.2	77.9	115.4	200.8
O/E	33.8	53.9	54.2	81.2	104.3	143.6
O/MH	30.4	48.1	51.2	93.5	121.0	177.9

(continued)

TABLE D-V (continued)

	1899	1909	1919	1937	1947	1954
	NONFERROUS METALS, N.E.C. (3351, 3359, 3361)					
O	13.9[a]	28.3[a]	56.6[a]	88.5	187.1	206.4
O/E	39.6	54.2	57.8	85.4	112.1	118.6
O/MH	36.3	49.3	56.2	99.9	130.4	138.5
	CUTLERY AND EDGE TOOLS (3421–22)					
O	42.6[a]	56.9[a]	84.0[a]	80.2[a]	140.3[a]	133.1
O/E	56.1	52.3	63.6	72.3	84.6	104.0
O/MH	46.0	45.4	58.7	77.3	89.5	116.2
	HAND TOOLS, N.E.C., FILES, HAND SAWS (3423–25)					
O	29.5[a]	51.7[a]	97.0[a]	83.4[u]	214.7[a]	141.9
O/E	84.3	81.0	76.5	91.0	144.6	138.8
O/MH	70.1	71.4	70.5	98.2	153.0	158.2
	OIL BURNERS AND HEATING AND COOKING APPARATUS, N.E.C. (3432, 3439)					
O	15.3[a]	39.1[a]	68.2[a]	93.0[a]	192.6	152.9
O/E	40.2	56.6	72.0	90.4	124.4	153.2
O/MH	33.6	47.9	68.1	98.1	132.4	171.2
	STRUCTURAL AND ORNAMENTAL PRODUCTS (3441)					
O	18.0[a]	39.7[a]	46.7[a]	54.5[a]	91.4	138.0
O/E	43.4	58.3	58.4	78.8	84.4	86.5
O/MH	37.0	52.7	56.7	87.8	93.0	98.6
	SHEET-METAL WORK (3444)					
O	21.3[a]	59.7[a]	54.9[a]	71.2[a]	136.6[a]	178.0[a]
O/E	42.1	63.9	55.6	92.8	124.7	137.0
O/MH	35.4	57.0	54.4	99.2	128.4	146.4
	NAILS AND SPIKES (3481)					
O	127.1[a]	87.6[a]	103.1[a]	87.6[a]	144.2[a]	126.0
O/E	60.8	65.3	63.2	74.8	94.9	103.6
O/MH	49.3	56.1	61.2	88.4	102.9	111.0
	WIREWORK, N.E.C. (3489)					
O	16.6[a]	47.1[a]	50.0[a]	102.3[a]	202.9	227.5
O/E	39.9	82.5	71.5	69.5	94.2	100.2
O/MH	33.2	72.7	67.6	77.1	105.3	115.0
	BOLTS, NUTS, WASHERS, RIVETS, AND SCREW-MACHINE PRODUCTS (3494-95)					
O	10.5[a]	23.6[a]	44.6[a]	85.9[a]	200.7[a]	214.1
O/E	35.0	53.3	49.0	80.7	106.6	99.8
O/MH	29.5	47.5	47.7	100.9	131.3	126.2
	FOUNDRY AND MACHINE SHOP PRODUCTS SUBGROUP (group 35 less farm and office machinery)					
O	26.3[a]	41.1[a]	72.5[a]	102.3[a]	218.8[a]	253.2
O/E	61.7	69.7	71.3	99.1	111.9	128.5
O/MH	57.4	68.4	75.3	118.3	133.5	156.7
	ELECTRIC MACHINERY (36)					
O	7.7[a]	18.5[a]	46.3[a]	93.5[a]	251.1	414.3
O/E	69.4	73.1	66.8	104.4	129.8	179.4
O/MH	59.7	68.0	67.8	125.5	152.6	215.7

(continued)

TABLE D-V (concluded)

	1899	1909	1919	1937	1947	1954
MOTOR VEHICLES AND EQUIPMENT (371)						
O	0.05	1.8	28.2	90.1	115.3	143.0
O/E	10.0	10.5	35.4	84.0	86.2	106.6
O/MH	7.8	8.3	33.0	98.9	94.6	112.5
LOCOMOTIVES AND PARTS (3741)						
O	263.9	282.5	321.2	55.2	134.9	130.9
O/E	170.7	214.2	143.6	64.6	62.7	88.6
O/MH	142.6	187.8	136.6	69.6	74.4	106.8
RAILROAD AND STREET CARS (3742)						
O	119.4	113.7	170.7	93.4	145.3	62.5
O/E	143.9	106.0	130.9	95.8	80.7	68.9
O/MH	119.3	92.1	124.0	110.1	88.4	80.6
TRANSPORTATION EQUIPMENT, N.E.C. (3799)						
O	1,316.6	1,333.2	647.2	71.3	168.6	64.3
O/E	71.1	77.6	117.1	108.0	118.4	125.3
O/MH	61.0	67.1	105.1	126.9	129.4	145.5
INSTRUMENTS AND MISCELLANEOUS MANUFACTURES (38, 39)						
O	29.3[a]	54.7[a]	69.5[a]	106.2[a]	213.2[a]	293.4
O/E	66.6	72.0	62.1	111.8	130.0	164.8
O/MH	55.9	62.4	58.6	119.3	137.0	179.8
PIANOS (3931)						
O	69.2	156.1	188.7	66.0	67.8	71.9
O/E	51.6	61.2	81.7	117.0	109.4	140.4
O/MH	38.7	53.0	77.3	122.4	110.4	158.0

[a] Output is measured by deflated value (see Technical Note to Appendix D for price series used as deflators).

[b] Quantity data used for output index is from a source other than *Census of Manufactures*. For the sugar industries the source is the Department of Agriculture; for the liquor industry the source is the Internal Revenue Service.

TABLE D-VI

Manufacturing: Output and Productivity Ratios, by Industry, Key Years, 1899–1954 (1929 = 100)

(Index numbers for 36 industries for which capital data are available are here summarized. Data for 1947 and 1954 are presented for those 10 industries which are included in the sample of 80 used for analysis in Chapters 6 and 7. Capital data for 8 industries are unavailable for 1929 and 1937, and for 3 industries, unavailable for 1899 through 1919. O = output; O/E = output per person engaged; O/MH = output per manhour; O/C = output per unit of capital input; O/I = total factor productivity.)

	1899	1909	1919	1937	(1947)	1948	(1954)
	MEAT PACKING AND PREPARED MEATS (2011, 2013)						
O	54.1	69.6	90.4	98.0	144.6	134.8	159.3
O/E	106.1	102.8	72.0	91.3	96.7	91.6	101.7
O/MH	95.6	92.9	75.2	114.8	110.6	107.0	123.1
O/C	112.7	88.0	53.2	117.8		104.0	
O/I	97.7	92.2	71.0	115.2		106.6	
	CANNING, PRESERVING, AND FREEZING (203)						
O	19.8	32.7	57.3	145.9		257.2	
O/E	43.6	59.5	69.2	108.5		158.1	
O/MH	37.0	51.2	64.2	124.7		189.1	
O/C	104.2	102.5	81.2	146.5		151.6	
O/I	44.0	58.4	67.7	129.5		178.2	
	GRAIN MILL PRODUCTS EXCEPT CEREALS (2041, 2042, 2044, 2045)						
O	74.7	81.8	90.5	93.7		166.2	
O/E	79.6	64.9	62.6	91.1		103.2	
O/MH	65.4	54.7	57.2	96.4		105.8	
O/C	65.2	47.9	35.3	82.9		104.5	
O/I	65.3	52.6	48.7	92.1		105.4	
	BAKERY PRODUCTS AND CONFECTIONERY AND RELATED PRODUCTS (205, 207)						
O	22.0[a]	44.4[a]	73.6[a]	100.1		144.6	
O/E	64.7	73.8	80.2	93.4		122.5	
O/MH	52.3	62.9	76.5	101.2		129.9	
O/C	128.7	120.3	108.9	136.9		181.0	
O/I	58.2	68.4	80.6	105.9		136.4	
	SUGAR INDUSTRIES (206)						
O	29.7	57.3	76.7	103.7		111.9	
O/E	43.9	66.6	50.8	90.0		95.6	
O/MH	33.7	54.3	44.7	106.2		110.7	
O/C	57.2	96.8	112.8	179.7		197.7	
O/I	37.0	60.0	51.5	116.6		122.4	
	KNITTING MILLS (225)						
O	19.1	33.1	55.4	115.7	176.0	188.8	207.7
O/E	48.7	54.5	66.6	105.4	176.0	182.6	215.2
O/MH	43.8	49.9	68.0	140.1	221.1	231.7	284.1
O/C	78.0	77.7	67.9	192.8		228.3	
O/I	46.9	52.8	68.0	146.1		231.1	

(continued)

	1899	1909	1919	1937	(1947)	1948	(1954)
			CARPETS AND RUGS (227)				
O	50.6	68.6	61.9	94.9		208.1	
O/E	68.6	76.7	86.3	103.2		170.2	
O/MH	58.0	66.7	82.8	132.0		181.0	
O/C	143.3	121.4	96.4	123.2		178.2	
O/I	72.7	78.8	86.9	128.9		180.0	
			LUMBER MILL PRODUCTS (242, 243)				
O	100.5	102.0	91.2	70.4	91.0	95.8	114.3
O/E	110.3	81.5	83.7	93.5	102.8	110.6	141.8
O/MH	91.4	69.6	75.1	98.5	110.3	120.1	164.7
O/C	266.6	156.9	145.9	133.8		184.9	
O/I	99.9	75.1	80.2	102.0		125.7	
			INDUSTRIAL CHEMICALS (281, 282)				
O	9.1	17.5	42.0	160.5		502.8	
O/E	40.8	55.7	49.9	126.3		216.4	
O/MH	33.2	46.2	46.9	139.0		241.0	
O/C	44.2	48.5	55.4	130.3		200.2	
O/I	35.8	46.8	49.1	136.2		227.1	
			ALLIED CHEMICAL SUBSTANCES (283–86, 288–89)				
O	29.3	42.9	59.0	98.5		171.6	
O/E	62.2	59.7	53.2	101.8		114.0	
O/MH	52.3	51.1	49.5	114.3		120.8	
O/C	115.4	91.9	83.3	115.7		93.5	
O/I	69.4	63.8	60.6	114.9		106.8	
			FERTILIZERS (287)				
O	30.4	59.9	80.4	105.9	209.0	215.4	320.8
O/E	60.0	70.7	64.1	108.8	174.7	184.1	270.0
O/MH	53.1	63.9	61.2	132.2	202.7	218.5	311.2
O/C	82.8	89.3	73.6	145.1		202.6	
O/I	58.6	68.9	64.0	135.2		214.1	
			PETROLEUM REFINING (2911)				
O	5.9	11.0	34.0	119.2	191.2	209.3	269.6
O/E	43.4	65.9	46.1	114.3	125.6	132.3	169.0
O/MH	35.1	58.5	46.9	163.7	160.3	168.4	227.3
O/C	54.1	60.1	41.7	113.7		135.8	
O/I	46.5	59.5	43.1	125.6		144.4	
			RUBBER TIRES AND INNER TUBES (3011)				
O			50.9[a]	81.3		136.6	
O/E			41.3	105.4		131.5	
O/MH			40.2	143.9		154.9	
O/C			67.4	166.6		170.3	
O/I			44.2	148.4		158.1	
			RUBBER PRODUCTS OTHER THAN TIRES AND TUBES (302, 303, 309)				
O			71.7	106.7		224.3	
O/E			58.8	106.7		121.4	
O/MH			60.1	126.4		137.8	
O/C			83.5	131.2		120.4	
O/I			62.1	127.0		135.4	

(continued)

	1899	1909	1919	1937	(1947)	1948	(1954)
	LEATHER TANNING AND FINISHING (3111)						
O	69.5	89.3	104.4	112.1	137.8	125.3	112.5
O/E	67.7	72.7	71.9	111.7	142.5	133.2	142.4
O/MH	60.6	66.8	71.3	136.0	166.2	160.0	176.3
O/C	69.9	53.8	59.4	160.1		183.7	
O/I	62.3	63.7	68.6	140.3		164.2	
	FOOTWEAR EXCEPT RUBBER (314)						
O	60.1	78.5	89.2	112.3	128.9	122.7	117.4
O/E	90.1	88.7	85.4	110.0	123.2	116.1	117.2
O/MH	70.2	70.6	82.4	136.1	142.1	140.2	144.2
O/C	143.8	112.3	80.1	156.8		177.3	
O/I	75.5	74.4	82.1	138.6		144.4	
	LEATHER GROUP EXCEPT FOOTWEAR (31 LESS 314)						
O	64.3	85.2	85.9	97.2		107.0	
O/E	69.6	77.0	69.2	96.5		96.4	
O/MH	59.1	67.6	66.5	112.2		112.8	
O/C	81.4	64.5	60.5	149.8		150.5	
O/I	62.4	67.0	65.3	117.8		118.4	
	PRIMARY IRON AND STEEL						
O	23.0	44.4	64.2	93.8		167.5	
O/E	48.8	69.6	64.4	80.9		112.4	
O/MH	40.5	57.3	57.8	95.3		128.5	
O/C	81.3	59.2	55.4	77.1		129.0	
O/I	46.0	57.7	57.2	90.2		128.5	
	PRIMARY NONFERROUS METALS						
O	16.0	32.4	56.5	81.1		171.5	
O/E	42.0	61.1	58.7	77.8		108.8	
O/MH	37.6	54.3	55.8	89.6		124.8	
O/C	82.9	84.6	91.9	90.8		109.2	
O/I	44.3	60.3	62.7	89.9		120.0	
	FABRICATED IRON AND STEEL						
O	20.4	38.8	58.2	91.7		164.8	
O/E	48.1	57.1	62.5	93.7		108.3	
O/MH	39.9	50.3	59.2	104.2		118.1	
O/C	86.4	73.1	75.8	122.8		141.0	
O/I	45.0	53.8	62.0	107.6		122.3	
	FABRICATED NONFERROUS METALS						
O	21.3	46.2	64.5	98.2		197.7	
O/E	41.0	55.2	66.7	95.2		111.8	
O/MH	33.6	48.1	64.0	105.4		120.4	
O/C	61.0	67.8	74.2	117.5		112.6	
O/I	37.9	51.9	66.3	108.1		118.4	
	HEATING AND PLUMBING EQUIPMENT AND STRUCTURAL METAL PRODUCTS (343, 344)						
O	14.2	36.3	51.2	81.0		165.8	
O/E	40.2	55.0	64.3	90.8		142.8	
O/MH	33.3	48.3	61.9	99.5		153.7	
O/C	65.7	63.1	71.4	111.1		136.7	
O/I	37.4	50.9	63.8	101.9		149.6	

(continued)

TABLE D-VI (continued)

	1899	1909	1919	1937	(1947)	1948	(1954)
FARM MACHINERY EXCEPT TRACTORS (3522)							
O	72.2[a]	99.1[a]	99.9[a]	76.7[a]	175.7	222.7	164.6
O/E	64.3	79.4	71.8	87.1	114.9	139.9	135.9
O/MH	57.8	73.7	70.8	108.0	140.3	171.7	175.1
O/C	86.0	72.1	83.9	136.2		164.1	
O/I	65.5	73.1	75.0	116.7		168.8	
OFFICE AND STORE MACHINES (357)							
O	15.6	46.1	67.6	97.2	172.7	181.1	245.4
O/E	64.7	82.5	70.7	84.2	96.9	100.8	133.1
O/MH	55.3	74.6	66.9	92.9	103.4	109.1	151.0
O/C	87.2	88.3	85.6	115.2		86.2	
O/I	64.7	79.5	73.2	100.7		98.6	
MOTOR VEHICLES, MOTORCYCLES, AND BICYCLES (371, 3751)							
O	0.3	2.0	28.9	90.5		123.8	
O/E	6.0	11.2	35.5	84.1		90.2	
O/MH	4.7	8.9	33.1	98.9		100.5	
O/C	12.5	23.0	45.7	96.6		92.0	
O/I	5.7	10.7	35.9	98.3		98.0	
AIRCRAFT AND PARTS (372)							
O			19.1[a]	162.6[a]		1,100.7[a]	
O/E			84.9	95.5		118.0	
O/MH			81.6	96.0		122.3	
O/C			72.3	76.5		89.3	
O/I			79.9	92.2		115.5	
SHIPS AND BOATS (373)							
O	97.0	73.9	551.2	80.5	185.6	165.9	212.0
O/E	119.3	101.2	82.1	70.4	76.5	77.5	103.3
O/MH	99.0	87.5	91.2	82.4	83.3	86.3	117.3
O/C	176.7	114.2	111.1	95.0		80.3	
O/I	106.5	90.9	93.9	84.2		85.3	
RAILROAD EQUIPMENT (374)							
O	149.2	147.0	202.5	82.3		165.3	
O/E	151.9	130.7	134.9	86.7		83.9	
O/MH	126.0	113.6	127.0	98.4		94.8	
O/C	346.2	309.5	226.0	79.7		80.4	
O/I	137.4	123.7	134.7	95.5		92.6	

(continued)

TABLE D-VI (concluded)

	1948 = 100			1948 = 100		
	1899	1909	1919	1899	1909	1919
	PULP, PAPER, AND PAPER-BOARD (261)			CEMENT, LIME, AND CON-CRETE (324, 327)		
O	9.3	17.6	25.3	4.7	22.6	25.1
O/E	44.3	54.3	50.9	30.1	50.7	59.5
O/MH	33.6	43.5	42.1	22.6	39.4	48.8
O/C	55.7	45.7	45.7	28.1	28.9	34.6
O/I	38.6	44.2	43.2	23.7	36.3	44.5
	CONVERTED PAPER PRODUCTS (264–269)			STRUCTURAL CLAY AND POTTERY PRODUCTS (325, 326, 3297)		
O	8.5	17.1	25.7	47.6	67.7	54.6
O/E	30.7	38.4	39.9	58.5	66.9	67.2
O/MH	22.5	29.8	35.9	43.5	52.2	54.7
O/C	72.0	66.5	60.5	56.6	40.2	38.3
O/I	29.0	36.3	41.5	46.0	48.8	49.6
	SOAP AND GLYCERINE, CLEANING AND POLISHING PREPARATIONS (2841–42)			GLASS PRODUCTS (3211, 3221, 3229, 3231)		
O	20.0	32.8	52.5	9.8	18.0	23.7
O/E	57.3	58.8	58.1	20.1	27.2	32.8
O/MH	47.2	49.2	54.6	16.3	21.6	28.8
O/C	90.1	83.7	70.9	36.3	33.0	39.6
O/I	58.7	59.2	60.3	18.7	23.6	30.8
	PAINTS AND ALLIED PRODUCTS (285)			BLAST FURNACES AND STEEL MILLS (331, 3323, 3393, 3399)		
O	11.5	19.4	27.0	15.7	28.7	40.6
O/E	53.7	56.9	50.8	43.1	61.7	56.4
O/MH	42.0	45.2	44.3	29.4	43.6	43.6
O/C	55.3	63.4	60.3	68.0	48.5	44.8
O/I	46.6	51.2	49.7	34.3	44.7	43.8

[a] Output is measured by deflated value (see Technical Note to Appendix D for price series used as deflators).

TABLE D-VII

Manufacturing: Persons Engaged and Manhours, by Group, 1929

Census Code No.		Persons Engaged (thousands)	Manhours (millions)
20	Foods, except beverages	931	2,180
208	Beverages	47	105
21	Tobacco products	138	305
22	Textile mill products	1,296	3,072
23	Apparel and related products	758	1,541
24	Lumber and products except furniture	797	1,809
25	Furniture and fixtures	243	575
26	Paper and allied products	301	773
27	Printing and publishing	627	1,453
28	Chemicals and allied products	378	864
29	Petroleum and coal products	134	346
30	Rubber products	186	420
31	Leather and products	382	856
32	Stone, clay, and glass products	426	922
33	Primary metal industries	754	1,743
34	Fabricated metal products	714	1,589
35	Machinery, nonelectric	1,002	2,487
36	Electric machinery	456	1,089
37	Transportation equipment	704	1,523
38–39	Miscellaneous and instruments	296	638
	Total	10,570	24,290

APPENDIX E
Contract Construction

THIS segment covers new construction (including additions, alterations, and repairs as well as new projects) carried on by (1) general contractors in building construction and in highway, street, and other heavy construction; and (2) special trade contractors, specializing in activities such as plumbing, painting, plastering, and carpentering—either on subcontract from the general contractor or directly for the owner. In the Standard Industrial Classification these categories correspond to Major Groups 15, 16, and 17. Construction performed by force-account workers in establishments primarily engaged in some other business is not included.

Output

The investigator faces at least two major problems in attempting to measure the physical volume of contract construction. One relates to the fact that most buildings and heavy construction projects are not standardized over time but are custom jobs. Thus, numbers of units cannot be weighted to form time series, nor can a sample of units be priced in the ordinary sense to provide indexes for the purpose of deflating value estimates. The other problem is that the available estimates of the value of new construction put in place include more than contract construction, to which the manpower estimates relate. The activity values include also force-account work, which is particularly important in the utility and farm segments and in the category of major alteration and repair.

Our partial solutions of these problems will be discussed in the course of describing the method by which we estimate the real product originating in the construction segment on a basis consistent with the total real national product estimates. These estimates do not purport to be of the same degree of reliability as those made for the segments for which reasonably good physical-unit or price series were available. They are the result of making explicit the implications of the real national product estimates with respect to the portion originating in construction. The output series will be compared with employment and manhours estimates, following a description of the labor series.

SCOPE OF THE ESTIMATES

A solution to the contract versus total construction activity problem is suggested by the availability of estimates of national income originating in the contract construction industry prepared by Kuznets and by the

489

Department of Commerce. The former series begins with 1919; the latter, with 1929. By adding estimates of capital consumption and the contract construction share of indirect business taxes and the other reconciliation items, the national income figures can be expanded to gross national product originating in the industry. Gross national product can then be deflated to provide output estimates relating to contract construction alone.

As we have previously remarked, real gross industry product should be obtained by a "double deflation" procedure. That is, the gross value of output should be deflated by a composite index of output prices, and intermediate products, by a properly weighted index of the prices of the purchased goods and services. Direct deflation of GNP originating can be justified only if intermediate-product purchases are small relative to the value of output, or if prices of intermediate inputs closely parallel prices of output in movement. Materials account for close to half of the value of construction, but input and output prices have moved in unison since World War I, as indicated in Table E-1. We have, therefore, applied the output deflator directly to the industry product estimates for the period since 1919.

TABLE E-1

Contract Construction: Price and Cost Indexes, Key Years, 1915–57
(1929 = 100)

	Construction Costs, Commerce Composite	Wholesale Prices of Building Materials	Average Hourly Wage Rate of Building Trades
1915	53.8	56.1	40.0
1919	100.0	121.1	55.7
1929	100.0	100.0	100.0
1937	98.1	99.8	97.9
1948	200.0	209.3	175.5
1953	234.6	241.2	226.1
1957	263.5	262.8	267.8

SOURCE: *Construction Volume and Costs, 1915-1956*, May 1957, Statistical Supplement to *Construction Review*, Depts. of Labor and Commerce, pp. 54 and 58; *Union Wages and Hours: Building Trades, July 1, 1957*, BLS Bulletin 1227, p. 5.

Prior to 1919, we have extrapolated the real national product originating in contract construction by the deflated value of the new private and public construction components of the real gross national product (described in Appendix A). This procedure involves the implicit assumption that the proportion of total new construction performed by private contractors was constant over the period up to 1919—an assumption avoided by the procedure for the later period. If the output measure prior to 1919 is to be interpreted as "net," the further assumption is involved that the ratio of intermediate input to output was relatively stable. In the construction industry, which has not been noted for rapid technological advance, particularly in the early period, the assumption seems broadly reasonable.

THE PRICE DEFLATORS

The deflator used to convert the current value estimates to physical-volume measures after 1915 is basically the Department of Commerce "composite construction cost" index for private construction, as adjusted from 1929 on by the National Income Division to reflect changing profit margins.[1] The composite is composed of price indexes for different types of construction (Tables E-1 and E-2).

Some of these indexes are so constructed that they reflect changes in the efficiency of the industry. This is accomplished either through adjustment of estimates of labor and materials costs per unit of input for presumed efficiency change or by use of contractor bids over time on standard structures or structural components. Others of these indexes are merely weighted averages of prices of relevant materials and construction wage rates and, sometimes, of certain overhead cost items. The latter "cost indexes" presumably do not reflect changes in efficiency, and insofar as efficiency has increased in the areas for which they are used, they lend a downward bias to the derived output and productivity measures.

Of the more refined types of index, mention should first be made of the residential cost index compiled by E. H. Boeckh and Associates and used by the Commerce Department for deflation of residential building. For brick and frame residences in twenty cities, prices of many types of materials and equipment are weighted by wage rates, adjusted to reflect efficiency of local labor. Despite the presumed adjustment, productivity advance has apparently not been important in residential building. This is suggested by two comparisons.

In their study of residential real estate, Grebler, Blank, and Winnick found that there was a remarkably close correspondence between the long-term movements from 1890 to 1934 of the Boeckh index, extrapolated from 1910 to 1890 by a weighted average of materials and labor costs, and a house price index developed for their study from data contained in the Commerce *Financial Survey of Urban Housing* (1937).[2] Although the price index shows more short-term variability than the cost index (presumably due to more adequate reflection of changing profit margins),

---

[1] *National Income Supplement, 1954, Survey of Current Business*, Dept. of Commerce.

[2] Leo Grebler, David M. Blank, and Louis Winnick, *Capital Formation in Residential Real Estate: Trends and Prospects*, Princeton University Press (for NBER), 1956, Appendix C, pp. 344–58.

the virtual identity of the long-run movements of the two series "argues strongly that the construction cost index measures with quite reasonable accuracy the secular movement of house prices."[3]

The other comparison is between the Boeckh index and the *Engineering News-Record* (ENR) building cost index, which is simply a weighted average of materials and labor costs. Although the product mix underlying the two indexes differs somewhat, the fact that the Boeckh index rises as much as the ENR building cost index between 1913 and 1957 also suggests that productivity advance has not been important in residential building (see Table E-2). There are divergences in shorter periods, notably in

TABLE E-2

Comparison of Three Building-Cost Indexes, Key Years, 1913–57
(1929 = 100)

	Average of 4 Contractor Indexes[a]	*Engineering News-Record*	Boeckh (Residential)
1913	52.1	52.4	51.9
1919	95.8	83.4	92.0
1929	100.0	100.0	100.0
1937	98.4	102.8	93.2
1948	195.3	180.5	209.6
1953	226.0	225.7	242.4
1957	262.0	266.7	263.6

[a] Average of the estimates for building structures, comparable over time, provided by the following contractors: Austin, Fruin-Colnon, Fuller, and Turner; from Miles L. Colean and Robinson Newcomb, *Stabilizing Construction: The Record and Potential*, New York, McGraw-Hill, 1952, p. 248, extended through 1957 by data published in *Engineering News-Record*.

1948–57, when the lesser rise of the Boeckh index suggests some real increases in productivity.

Absence of greater productivity advances in building construction generally, including nonresidential, is also suggested by a comparison of the ENR building cost index with an average of four contractor indexes. The latter indexes are prepared "on the basis of actual estimates for building comparable structures" and should reflect reductions in costs per unit of output as productivity rises.[4] Nevertheless, the ENR and the contractor indexes show much the same long-run trend (Table E-2). Here again, however, there is evidence of significant productivity advance since World War II, which is reflected in the over-all measure of output per manhour shown in Table E-I.

[3] *Ibid.*, p. 352.
[4] See Miles L. Colean and Robinson Newcomb, *Stabilizing Construction: The Record and Potential*, New York, McGraw-Hill, 1952, p. 71 and also Appendix Q.

Among the indexes other than the Boeckh used in the composite deflator, efficiency changes are also purportedly reflected in those prepared by the Turner Construction Company, the George A. Fuller Company, the Interstate Commerce Commission, and the Bureau of Public Roads. The last named index deserves special mention. It is designed to represent the cost of a standard mile of federal-aid and state highway construction. It is based on average bid prices, taken from contract information, for the following items: cubic yards of excavation, square yards of paving, pounds of reinforcing steel and of structural steel, and cubic yards of structural concrete. Over the entire period since its inception in 1922, the index shows substantially less increase than an average of relevant materials and labor prices, reflecting the increased efficiency that has occurred in heavy construction generally as a result of greater mechanization and improved machinery. Table E-3, based on data prepared by the Bureau of Public

TABLE E-3

Highway Construction: Output, Manhours, and Productivity, 1944–55

| | Deflated Construction Expenditures | | Manhours | | Output per Manhour |
	Millions of 1954 Dollars	Index (1948 = 100)	Number of Millions	Index (1948 = 100)	(1948 = 100)
1944	448	24.6	97.6	28.5	86.3
1945	459	25.2	94.3	27.5	91.6
1946	986	54.1	193.4	56.5	95.8
1947	1,590	87.2	305.7	89.3	97.6
1948	1,823	100.0	342.4	100.0	100.0
1949	2,062	113.1	369.2	107.8	104.9
1950	2,263	124.1	374.8	109.5	113.3
1951	2,434	133.5	370.6	108.2	123.4
1952	2,594	142.3	374.9	109.5	130.0
1953	2,908	159.5	399.8	116.8	136.6
1954	3,659	200.7	474.5	138.6	144.8
1955	3,962	217.3	488.8	142.8	152.2

SOURCE: Indexes computed from estimated real highway construction expenditures and manhours employed, presented in *Public Roads*, Bureau of Public Roads, Dept. of Commerce, February 1957, p. 152.

Roads, compares outlays for highway construction deflated by the standard-mile cost index with the corresponding manhours worked. Comparable production and manhour estimates are available only since 1944, but sharply rising movement of output per manhour in highway construction since that date apparently prevailed in earlier periods as well.

The upward productivity trend characteristic of highway construction seems to have prevailed in heavy, engineered construction generally.

This is indicated in a study by Chawner,[5] in which labor-materials cost indexes are compared with indexes for several types of heavy construction based on contractor unit bids. The significantly greater rise in the former indexes between 1915 and 1933 is indicative of important technological advance. The contrast between the Chawner findings and the similarity of movement observed between contractor and cost indexes in building construction led Grebler, Blank, and Winnick to conclude: "A reasonable inference to be drawn is that productivity has increased significantly in heavy construction but much less so in building construction. . . . It is likely that the increases in productivity in building have been concentrated largely in the construction of large buildings, and that residential construction, particularly construction of single-family houses, has shared in this rise, except possibly in the last few years."[6]

The construction cost indexes in the Commerce Department composite deflator that are not contrived so as to make allowance for productivity change are those prepared by W. W. Handy (electric and gas utilities), the Associated General Contractors, the *Engineering News-Record*, the American Appraisal Company, and the farm construction cost indexes of the Department of Agriculture. These indexes are used to deflate types of projects that accounted for around 35 per cent of total new construction activity in 1953—but probably a lesser proportion of contract construction. Assuming that productivity in the areas deflated by cost indexes rose as much as in the areas in which price indexes were used, the over-all productivity increase in the segment would have been about half again as great as that indicated by our calculations in Table E-I. This is probably an overstatement, however, since some of the cost indexes apply to building construction, in which productivity advance has been less than in the industry generally. Even with a substantial upward adjustment, productivity in the construction segment rose significantly less than in the economy as a whole (see last section of this appendix).

Employment and Manhours

The Commerce Department estimates of the average annual number of employees in contract construction from 1929 forward are based on the *Census of Construction* for 1929 and 1935, and on average monthly employment estimates derived from Social Security data for 1938 and subsequent years. Employment in 1929 of salaried workers and of all employees in establishments with an annual volume of business under $25,000 was obtained by dividing the relevant payrolls by average pay. Employment

---

[5] Lowell J. Chawner, "Construction Cost Indexes as Influenced by Technological Change and Other Factors," *Journal of the American Statistical Association*, September 1935. pp. 561–76.

[6] *Op. cit.*, pp. 356–57.

in 1935 was obtained by extrapolation of the 1929 estimate by the average monthly employment of establishments that reported to the censuses of both 1929 and 1935. Annual interpolations for 1929–35 and 1935–38 were made by Commerce on the basis of the deflated volume of construction activity.

The *Census of Construction* data could not be used to estimate the number of proprietors, since they cover only business establishments and not the independently self-employed. The Commerce Department therefore shifted to the *Census of Population* occupational data for 1930, 1940, and 1950. Extrapolation to 1929 and interpolation between 1930 and 1940 were made on the basis of the number of active corporations in the industry as reported annually in *Statistics of Income*, Part I (Internal Revenue Service). Interpolation for 1940–50 and extrapolation since 1950 were made on the basis of the number of operating firms, incorporated and unincorporated, as estimated by Commerce from survey data.

Prior to 1929, our estimates of persons engaged are benchmarked on the gainful-worker estimates of Daniel Carson, adjusted by the estimated ratio of employment to labor force in the economy and further adjusted in 1920 for a probable overcount by Carson of gainful workers in the construction industry.[7] It is Stanley Lebergott's opinion that while Carson's estimates for 1930, 1910, and earlier census years are relatively reliable since they are taken almost directly from reported Census results, the 1920 estimate is high. This is ascribed to the fact that Carson interpolated between his 1910 and 1930 estimates using a series dominated by the movement in numbers of carpenters, painters, builders, and plasterers. Employment in these occupations was affected by the relatively large 1910–20 gain in employment of carpenters and painters by shipbuilding and other nonconstruction industries. Lebergott adjusted for this factor by estimating employment of the affected occupational groups in the other industries on the basis of ratios to operatives. We have accepted his downward adjustment for 1920 and his annual series covering 1920–29.[8]

The number of persons who were self-employed in construction constituted a virtually constant proportion of the total in 1940, 1930, and 1910. The 1910 figure was estimated by Lebergott, from Census lithoprints, as the sum of self-employed carpenters, masons, building contractors, electricians, building painters, paper hangers, plasterers, plumbers, roofers, and structural steel workers. As a test, he used the same procedure in 1940 and obtained a total within 2 per cent of the reported number of

---

[7] Daniel Carson, "Changes in the Industrial Composition of Manpower since the Civil War," *Studies in Income and Wealth, Volume 11*, New York (NBER), 1949.

[8] The Lebergott estimates for this segment, 1919–29, are identical with those published in *Handbook of Labor Statistics, 1950 Edition*, BLS Bulletin 1016, p. 5, which he helped to prepare.

self-employed.[9] On the basis of this evidence, we estimated numbers of proprietors and the self-employed for years prior to 1929 by applying their 1929 ratio to employees to the estimated numbers of employees in the earlier years.

For the period prior to 1920, annual estimates of employment were derived from a regression equation based on the value of new public and private construction in constant dollars and on employment for nine years (four decennial census years from 1890 to 1920, 1929, 1935, and 1938–40). This equation gives a coefficient of correlation of +.98 between real construction and employment.

Average hours worked per week by employees in the contract construction industry as a whole are available from the Bureau of Labor Statistics for 1946 and subsequent years. Estimates of average hours worked by employees in building construction were made by the BLS back to 1934. For 1946–50, the ratio of average hours in the broader group to average hours in building was 1.019. This ratio was applied to the latter series prior to 1946 in order to adjust it to the level of the estimates with broader coverage.

Estimates of average full-time hours in the building trades are available for the entire period since 1869. Leo Wolman's published series covers the years from 1890 to 1937.[10] It can be extended forward by the BLS estimates, and back to 1869 on the basis of estimates of average full-time hours worked per day contained in the Aldrich Report.[11]

In the years since 1934 (excluding 1942–46) there has been a fairly close relation between the ratios of actual to standard hours in building construction and of employment to labor force in the construction industry, using Carson's labor-force estimates for 1930 and 1940, and the 1950 Census estimate for the industry, with linear annual interpolations. The regression equation yields a correlation coefficient of +.94. This relationship was used to derive estimates of average actual hours from the estimates of full-time hours, and the BLS series was extrapolated from 1934 to 1869 by these estimates. The product of average hours, numbers of employees, and weeks per year yielded employee manhours.

The special Census Bureau survey for May 1953 revealed a level of average hours worked per week by proprietors and unpaid family workers that was 14.5 per cent above the BLS estimate of average hours worked by

[9] Stanley Lebergott, "Estimates of Labor Force, Employment, and Unemployment, 1900–50," unpublished MS., p. 42.

[10] *Hours of Work in American Industry*, Bulletin 21, New York (NBER), 1938. It must be noted that Wolman's hours series is based on trade union scales. Since union strength increased over the period, the series probably shows too small a downtrend when used as a measure for the industry as a whole.

[11] *Wholesale Prices, Wages, and Transportation*, Report No. 1394, Senate Committee on Finance, 52d Cong., 2d sess., 1893.

employees in contract construction. To obtain manhours for this group, the employee average hours estimates were raised by the stated percentage throughout, and multiplied by the estimated numbers of proprietors and unpaid family workers. The index of total manhours is shown in Table E-I.

Output-Manhour Comparison

The output-per-manhour series presented in Table E-I should be interpreted less as an independent estimate of the course of productivity in contract construction than as an attempt to spell out the implications of the deflated gross national product estimates in this respect. The trend rate of increase in output per manhour of 0.9 per cent a year between 1889 and 1953 prevailed in the earlier period, 1889–1919, as well as in the later period, 1919–53—so at least the cruder estimates for the earlier period do not result in unreasonable productivity implications as compared with the later period. There is considerable irregularity as among the subperiods, but it will be noted that, generally, the subperiods in which output per manhour fell are those in which the physical volume of construction activity also declined. The one exception to this statement occurred in the subperiod 1889–99, but here the rate of increase in activity decelerated markedly as compared with the two earlier subperiods. Between 1937 and 1948, despite more than a doubling of construction activity, output per manhour increased but little. This was probably associated with the disturbances in the industry resulting from World War II and the reconversion period. The minor gains in productivity of this period were succeeded by a relatively rapid advance in the subperiod 1948–53, which has extended into more recent years.

If, as was suggested earlier, the productivity gains in the construction segment are understated by as much as one-third because of inadequate deflators, the true trend increase in output per manhour is closer to 1.3 per cent than to the 0.9 per cent indicated by Table E-I. But even with so major an upward adjustment, it is apparent that output per manhour in contract construction has increased significantly less, historically, than output per manhour in the private domestic economy as a whole.

TABLE E-I

Contract Construction: Output, Labor Inputs, and Productivity Ratios,
Key Years, 1869–1953
(1929 = 100)

	Output	Persons Engaged[a]	Output per Person	Manhours[a]	Output per Manhour
1869	11.8	24.2	48.8	31.6	37.3
1879	18.4	27.0	68.1	34.8	52.9
1889	33.4	40.3	82.9	48.9	68.3
1899	43.5	55.0	79.1	66.0	65.9
1909	75.7	72.9	103.8	75.4	100.4
1919	56.3	63.4	88.8	62.1	90.7
1929	100.0	100.0	100.0	100.0	100.0
1937	61.4	75.5	81.3	63.7	96.4
1948	132.3	139.0	95.2	129.9	101.8
1953	174.1	155.4	112.0	143.2	121.6

[a] Absolute numbers of persons engaged and manhours are given in Tables A-VII and A-XI.

APPENDIX F

Trade

THIS segment is composed of establishments in both wholesale and retail distribution. In terms of the Standard Industrial Classification, wholesale trade consists of Major Group 50, "Merchant wholesalers," broken down by line of trade, and Major Group 51, comprising other wholesalers, such as sales branches and sales offices of industrial concerns, petroleum bulk stations, agents and brokers, and assemblers (mainly of farm products). The retail trade divisions consist of Major Groups 52 through 59, and we follow the Commerce Department in including also automobile services and garages (Major Group 75). It should be noted that retail trade includes eating and drinking places, such as restaurants and bars, as well as establishments distributing commodities of various types for consumption elsewhere. The basic study upon which we have relied heavily is Harold Barger's *Distribution's Place in the American Economy since 1869*.[1]

Output

We have employed the index of output in wholesale and retail distribution prepared by Barger[2] for 1869–1929, with some minor adjustments, and extended it by similar methods to 1953. Barger's method involved several major steps: the estimation by type of commodity of the physical volume of finished goods for domestic use; the application of ratios representing the portions of each class of goods sold through retail stores in each key year; and the weighting of finished goods sold through retail stores by the gross distributive markup (combined wholesale and retail gross costs of distribution) for each class of commodity.

The estimates of the physical volume of finished goods for domestic use and of construction materials are those of William H. Shaw,[3] together with an allowance by Barger for firewood.[4] The Shaw estimates are in terms of 1913 producer prices; for consistency with the other output indexes we reweighted the Shaw estimates in terms of average prices in each pair of key years. The result of reweighting by the Marshall-Edgeworth formula[5] is to produce a significantly smaller increase in output between 1909 and 1929.

[1] Princeton University Press (for NBER), 1955.
[2] *Ibid.*, Table 10, pp. 22–3.
[3] *Value of Commodity Output since 1869*, New York (NBER), 1947.
[4] *Op. cit.*, pp. 22–23.
[5] *Ibid.*, p. 23, note g.

Ideally, Barger would have liked to have included sales of unfinished goods by wholesalers to industrial consumers, but data were not at hand. Although such sales accounted for possibly one-fourth of the value of goods sold through distributive channels in 1929, they were much less important as a fraction of value added by distribution—possibly one-twentieth or so.[6] Insofar as vertical integration and savings of materials have cut the ratio of the volume of intermediate-product sales to finished-goods sales, the Shaw index may have some upward bias as a basis for the measure of trade throughout.

The fractions of finished-goods output, by type, estimated to be sold through retail stores are shown in Barger.[7] These proportions are based largely on those estimated for 1929 by Simon Kuznets in *Commodity Flow and Capital Formation*.[8] In several cases, changing proportions were used for decennial years back to 1869, based on scattered evidence.[9] Although there was a decline in the proportion of construction materials sold through retail outlets, on net balance the proportion of finished goods passing through the distribution system increased from 1869 to 1929. This development reflects the increased complexity of the economy; and Barger believes that the fraction may have increased more than his calculations show since he changed the ratios prior to 1929 only when evidence supported the change. It should also be noted that sales by wholesalers directly to consumers do not enter the index. These transactions are relatively small.

Barger allocated the various groups of finished commodity output entering trade to thirty-one different types of store and weighted them by the "gross cost of distribution," or margin, in each type of store.[10] Whereas distributive markups generally rose to some extent over the period, it is the relative changes in markups in conjunction with the relative changes in input into distribution that affect the aggregate index. Barger used an average of 1869 and 1929 distributive margins as weights. The later set of weights yields a somewhat smaller rate of increase in the distributive output index after 1909, due in part to the laggard growth in sales of food, on which margins increased relatively, and the dynamic growth in sales of automobiles up to 1929, on which margins were low and relatively stable. Ideally, to fit our weighting scheme, the average of markups in the first and last years of each decade should have been used. Actually, the decennial changes in the markup estimates were not sufficiently precise to warrant frequent changes in weight. But if the accuracy

---

[6] *Ibid.*, p. 25.
[7] *Ibid.*, Table B-2.
[8] New York (NBER), 1938.
[9] Barger, *op. cit.*, Appendix B.
[10] *Ibid.*, Table 26, and discussion of sources in Appendix B.

of the general drift in margins revealed by Barger's researches is assumed, weighting by the bounding years of the longer period seems desirable. The final index of output in distribution appears as the last line in Barger's Table 10, with our revisions for 1919 and 1929 caused by the alternative weighting of finished goods shown there in footnote i.

The Barger procedure is predicated on the assumption that the volume of services rendered per unit of goods handled by wholesale and retail establishments has not changed significantly over time. Barger considered this question in the light of considerable historical evidence bearing on the various types of services rendered by distribution: "We conclude that distribution probably accompanies the handling of commodities with somewhat more service on the average than in 1869 but that, everything considered, the change is not large."[11] In other words, the index of distributive output may be subject to some downward bias on this score, but it is not substantial. In any case, commodity output indexes are also subject to some downward bias insofar as they fail to reflect quality changes.

For the period since 1929, we have changed somewhat the method of estimating output in distribution, although the basic concept remains the same. We have used the deflated values of final purchases of consumer goods and producers' durable equipment, by type, weighted by the corresponding distributive markups, 1929–39 and 1939–48, based on estimates by the Commerce Department. This shift in procedure was dictated by several considerations. Barger himself shifted to the Commerce estimates for 1939–49, but the estimates he used were subsequently revised by the Department. In addition, the Shaw estimates for 1929–39 used by Barger have been reworked by the Department, and the revised real values show a greater increase than the earlier figures.

Further, Barger continued to use the 1929 ratios of goods flowing through distributive channels, the earlier price weights for finished goods, and the 1869–1929 average distributive margins. Based on the detail supplied us for this purpose by Commerce, we were able to use the Marshall-Edgeworth weighting formula both with respect to the prices of the underlying finished goods and the gross margins. The margin weights also reflect changes in the proportions of final goods passing through trade channels, as shown in the *Census of Distribution* for 1929, 1939, and 1948 and used for the Commerce margin estimates.[12]

To the Commerce final purchase series were added real outlays for construction materials. To this series and to the several commodity groups that Commerce estimated by the retail valuation rather than the com-

---

[11] *Ibid.*, pp. 28–36.
[12] The Department's sources and methods are described in *National Income Supplement, 1954, Survey of Current Business*, pp. 103–117 and 126–135.

modity flow method,[13] we have applied Barger's trade ratios of 1929 and his margin estimates for 1929, 1939, and 1948.

Use of the Commerce estimates results in a somewhat broader coverage of trade output than prevails in the Barger estimates. Commerce includes markups for commodities sold directly by wholesalers to final purchasers as well as to retail establishments. This affects primarily producers' durable equipment, which thus has a somewhat greater weight in our index than in Barger's.

Labor Input

EMPLOYMENT

From 1929 forward, establishment employment data are available. The Commerce estimates, which we use, are based primarily on the *Census of Retail Trade* and the *Census of Wholesale Trade* for 1929, 1933, 1935, and 1939, and thereafter on Social Security Administration data. Interpolations prior to 1939 were by Bureau of Labor Statistics indexes based on sample data.

The number of proprietors was estimated on the basis of the Census reports (including the 1948 *Census of Business*), with interpolations and extrapolations by estimates of the number of establishments in the various branches of trade. Both the National Income Division and the Bureau of the Census count proprietors only if they spend a major portion of their time in the industry. Our estimates of unpaid family workers are based on the Census figures.

Prior to 1929, it was necessary to rely for benchmark estimates on occupation data for gainful workers from the decennial population censuses. Barger used this type of series, as prepared for the trade segment by Daniel Carson for the decennial years over the entire period 1870–1940.[14] He lists the chief defects of this series as being (1) its coverage—eating and drinking places and possibly manufacturers' sales branches are excluded, while advertising and miscellaneous business services are included, and (2) the inclusion of unemployed workers attached to the industry.[15] These points are in addition to the difficulties of classifying occupation data according to industry.[16] Barger's conclusion is that the Carson manpower estimates may be subject to some downward bias, particularly since the groups omitted have probably grown in relation to the total.

We extrapolated the OBE estimates of persons engaged, plus unpaid family workers, by Carson's labor force estimates for the segment (including

[13] Cf. *ibid.*, Exhibit 1, p. 104.
[14] Barger, *op. cit.*, Table 1.
[15] *Ibid.*, pp. 7, 43, and 105.
[16] See the discussion by Solomon Fabricant and Daniel Carson in *Studies in Income and Wealth, Volume 11*, New York (NBER), 1949, pp. 3–134.

garages) adjusted to an employment basis. Annual estimates from 1900 to 1929 were interpolated by means of the employment series prepared by Lebergott.[17] Of necessity, the Lebergott estimates are also benchmarked on the occupation statistics of the *Census of Population*. For his annual interpolations, Lebergott rejected the National Industrial Conference Board (NICB) method of interpolating between Census benchmarks by employment in commodity-producing industries, since it produces too volatile a series. He likewise rejected the Kuznets use of state data, since trade employment in the three states chosen by Kuznets did not parallel national employment movements in the segment since 1929. Instead, Lebergott interpolated essentially by real domestic sales of finished commodities by line of trade, which are based on the Shaw estimates. Obviously, the annual employment estimates prior to 1929 cannot be used for productivity analysis in the segment. We therefore show in Table F-I the ratios only for the decennial years in which the employment estimates are independently derived. The annual estimates prior to 1929 are used as part of the economy employment total.

Annual interpolations prior to 1900 were made on the basis of ratios of employment to output (key-year ratios interpolated along a straight line) applied to the output index. Here, again, the annual estimates are used only in obtaining national aggregates.

AVERAGE HOURS AND MANHOURS

In 1929 and earlier years, our estimates of average hours worked per week are essentially those of Barger, but since 1929 we deviate somewhat from his procedure with respect to hours worked by proprietors. The Barger estimates are presented in his Table 5 and explained in the footnotes to that table.[18] Our estimates for key years are included in Table A-IX.

From 1935 forward, BLS estimates of average hours worked per week by nonsupervisory employees in wholesale and retail trade are available. These were weighted together by employment, and extended from 1935 to 1934 by BLS estimates for retail trade alone. Annual interpolations between 1934 and the 1929 estimate of Barger (an extension forward of the King data for 1920–22)[19] were made on the basis of average hours in manufacturing, the indicated change in both segments being close to nine hours a week.

A special tabulation by the Census Bureau of average hours worked by proprietors and unpaid family workers in trade for May 1953 revealed

[17] Stanley Lebergott, "Estimates of Labor Force, Employment, and Unemployment, 1900–1950," unpublished MS., Tables 2 and 3.

[18] *Op. cit.*, pp. 11–12.

[19] Willford I. King, *Employment, Hours and Earnings in Prosperity and Depression, United States, 1920–1922*, 2nd ed., New York (NBER), 1923.

a level approximately 30 per cent above that worked by employees at the same period. In absolute terms, the level of approximately fifty-two hours is significantly below the sixty which had been assumed by Barger for recent decades. We have assumed the same proportionate difference as in 1953 between the average hours worked by employees and self-employed for earlier years back to 1930, when this extrapolation results in an average workweek for proprietors of sixty hours. From 1930 back, we shift to the Barger estimates, according to which the hours of proprietors are held at sixty until the first decade of the century, when hours of both proprietors and employees rise above the sixty mark.

Barger used the King estimates of average actual hours worked per week in 1920–22 to obtain his 1919 figure. He extrapolated this figure of 52.2 hours per week for employees by the average standard workweek, obtained from an intensive survey of available state reports for decennial years back to 1880. He also used the 1880 estimate of sixty-six hours for 1870. Our own survey of state sources strongly suggests that the average workweek in trade establishments was probably higher in 1870 than in 1880; but we have not deviated from the published Barger figures in the early years since the evidence is fragmentary.

In order to arrive at manhours, the average hours worked per week by employees have been multiplied by the average number of full- and part-time employees and by weeks per year. In 1940 the BLS series on average hours, which relates to full- and part-time employees, is substantially below the Census average, which is closer to a full-time hours basis. This is to be expected in view of the large number of part-time workers in this industry.

To employee manhours are added manhours worked by proprietors and unpaid family workers. The average hours estimates, benchmarked on the Census figures, are comparable with the estimates of numbers employed.

Capital Input

Approximately one-half of all real capital employed in wholesale and retail trade in 1929, and a somewhat larger proportion in 1953, consisted of inventories. Estimates of the real stock of inventories were obtained by cumulating real changes in wholesale and retail trade inventories, as estimated by the Commerce Department and converted to a 1929 price base, starting from an estimate of the total current value of trade inventories at the beginning of the base year 1929.

Estimates of the real stock of durable capital were based on book value estimates derived from Internal Revenue Service, *Statistics of Income* data.[20]

[20] Unpublished data collated by Lillian Epstein in connection with the Capital Formation and Financing Study.

The estimates cover 1929–49 and were extended to 1953 using the same source and methods. Data reported for durable depreciable assets, net of depreciation and depletion reserves, from corporate returns with balance sheets, were raised by the ratio of compiled receipts of all corporations to compiled receipts of corporations with balance sheets. The 1931 ratio of 103.5 was used for 1929.

Estimates of net depreciable assets in the noncorporate sector were derived by a somewhat complex procedure. Briefly, for 1939 and 1948, asset ratios to sales were taken from *Statistics of Income* data for corporate groups comparable in size to the noncorporate groups and applied to Census data for noncorporate wholesale and retail sales. The 1939 noncorporate ratio was extrapolated to 1929 by the corporate ratio and applied to 1929 noncorporate sales. Noncorporate durable assets comprise about two-fifths of the total.

Book value deflators are those implicit in the Goldsmith original-cost and constant (1929)-dollar estimates for nonfarm, nonresidential plant and equipment, weighted three and one, respectively.

To cover the real value of site land, the constant-dollar plant and equipment estimates were raised by the ratio 1.282, which represents the 1929 proportions as reported in the corporate returns with balance sheets.

Relative Weights of Capital and Labor

Real labor and capital inputs for key years from 1929 forward were combined by weights based on the Commerce Department national income estimates. Compensation of employees was raised by the ratio of total to employee manhours in order to arrive at total labor compensation, including compensation for the labor of proprietors and unpaid family workers based on the imputation of the same average hourly earnings as received by employees. Capital compensation was obtained by deducting labor compensation from national income originating in trade. Each type of compensation in key years was divided by the real input indexes to obtain unit factor compensations, on the basis of which the percentage weights were computed. The weight of capital was about 13 per cent of the total in each of the subperiods 1937–48 and 1948–53, but was considerably less in 1929–37.

TABLE F-I

Trade: Output, Inputs, and Productivity Ratios, Key Years, 1869–1953

(1929 = 100)

	Output	Persons Engaged[a]	Output per Person	Manhours[a]	Output per Manhour	Capital Input	Output per Unit of Capital Input	Total Factor Input	Total Factor Productivity
1869	7.6	12.8	59.4	15.9	47.8				
1879	15.9	17.1	93.0	21.2	75.0				
1889	23.9	29.1	82.1	36.2	66.0				
1899	36.2	40.0	90.5	49.1	73.7				
1909	53.3	55.9	95.3	62.1	85.8				
1919	66.3	71.6	92.6	74.0	89.6				
1929	100.0	100.0	100.0	100.0	100.0	100.0	100.0	100.0	100.0
1937	104.2	104.4	99.8	91.8	113.5	73.9	141.0	91.1	114.4
1948	167.3	142.9	117.1	116.0	144.2	120.0	139.4	118.6	141.1
1953	190.2	152.8	124.5	120.9	157.3	143.5	132.5	126.0	151.0

[a] Absolute numbers of persons engaged and manhours are given in Tables A-VII and A-XI.

APPENDIX G
Transcription

THE transportation segment is treated largely in terms of the industry groupings used by the Department of Commerce for the national income accounts. These follow the Standard Industrial Classification groupings, with a few exceptions to be noted.

Output and labor input estimates are available for the major groups: railroads, local railways and bus lines, water transportation, pipe lines, and air transport. In the case of highway passenger and freight transportation, output estimates are available only for the intercity portions, and we have tried to split employment accordingly. Included in the residual segment, for which we have employment but not output estimates, are the uncovered parts of highway transportation and the residual Commerce group "services allied to transportation," which is somewhat broader than the SIC group "services incidental to transportation."

For the most part, the output and employment or manhour estimates are based on those of Harold Barger.[1] Real capital estimates, by Melville J. Ulmer,[2] relate only to the railroad and local-transit groups, but may be derived for the segment as a whole. As far as the groups are concerned, then, our total factor productivity estimates are limited to the two mentioned—which accounted for almost four-fifths of national income originating in the segment in 1929, more in earlier years, and less recently. Since estimates of capital and labor inputs are available for the segment as a whole, estimates of output in the segment are derived by means of a coverage adjustment, and segment estimates of total productivity are shown in Table G-I.

Railroads

SIC Major Group 40, Railroads, is composed of three minor groups. Chief of these is Group 401, which includes line-haul operating railroads and electric railroads under the jurisdiction of the Interstate Commerce Commission, and switching and terminal companies (but not urban, suburban, and interurban railways, which are in Major Group 41). Companies having annual operating revenues generally above $1 million

[1] *The Transportation Industries, 1889–1946: A Study of Output, Employment, and Productivity*, New York (NBER), 1951.

[2] *Capital in Transportation, Communications, and Public Utilities: Its Formation and Financing*, Princeton University Press (for NBER), 1960.

are designated as Class I; those below, as Classes II or III. The major group also includes certain services allied to the railroads: Group 402, Sleeping car and other passenger car services; and Group 404, Railway express service.

OUTPUT

The indexes of railroad output, as calculated by Barger for 1890–1946 and extended in this study, are based on weighted averages of freight and passenger traffic. The basic units of measurement for these categories are the ton-mile and the passenger-mile. Unit revenues are used as weights.

In the case of ton-miles, no breakdown by type of commodity or length of haul is possible. The index is, therefore, based on a simple ton-mile aggregate. A weighted aggregate of tons originated, by types of commodities, shows only a slightly larger increase from 1899 to 1940 than an unweighted aggregate; so the absence of internal weights for ton-miles may not be significant.[3]

The basic data on ton-miles, shown in Barger's Appendix B, Table B-1, for 1890–1946, are taken from the Interstate Commerce Commission's annual *Statistics of Railways in the United States*. Barger's estimates were extended by reference to the same source, except in the last two years, for which use was made of the Association of American Railroads, *Statistics of Railways of Class I* (Washington). The ICC data cover Class I, II, and III roads. Coverage for 1911 and later years is substantially complete; Barger adjusted for slight undercoverage in earlier years. He also adjusted for a small discontinuity by eliminating the estimated ton-miles reported by switching and terminal companies before, but not after, 1907.

More detail is available with regard to passenger-miles.[4] For years after 1922, Barger was able to weight separately passenger-miles in three categories: commutation, coach (other than commutation), and parlor and sleeping car. For 1911–22, his index is based on two categories, since data for coach travel then included commutation. Prior to 1911, the index is based on unweighted passenger-miles. The difference in movement between the weighted and unweighted aggregates after 1911 is slight. The Marshall-Edgeworth method of weighting was used, and annual changes were adjusted to changes obtained by use of average unit revenue weights in the first and last years of the following periods: 1911–22, 1922–29, 1929–39, and 1939–47.

The basic data, taken from *Statistics of Railways*, are shown for 1890–1946 in Barger's Appendix B. For 1890–1911, total passenger-miles are for Class I, II, and III roads. The more detailed data for the period since

---

[3] See Barger, *op. cit.*, Table 18.
[4] *Ibid.*, Tables B-1 and B-2, pp. 184–87.

508

1911 relate to Class I roads and the Pullman Company. By means of an adjustment to the output index, described below, uniform coverage is secured throughout. Barger combined the freight and passenger traffic indexes by means of average unit revenue weights for the terminal years of the following subperiods: 1890–99, 1899–1909, 1909–19, 1919–29, 1929–39. Our extension to later years involved the use of average unit revenues in the years 1939 and 1947.

From 1921 on, to achieve comparability with the employment estimates, which are complete for the group, the combined index (which is based on data that do not include switching and terminal companies, express companies, or passenger-miles on Class II and III roads) was multiplied by an index of coverage based on the ratio of operating revenues of all companies to revenues of companies represented in the unadjusted index. The coverage index is quite stable, since the degree of undercoverage did not vary significantly from the 5.9 per cent that prevailed in 1929.

For 1890–1921, Barger has two indexes. One is adjusted to complete coverage and is continuous with the index just described. The other[5] is comparable with his employment estimates, which do not include switching and terminal companies, the Railway Express Company, or the Pullman Company prior to 1911. Table G-III shows the comprehensive index. It is presumably comparable with the capital estimates, and we have built up total employment estimates prior to 1921 correspondingly. That the coverage adjustment ratio for output moves similarly to the ratio of Barger's covered-employment estimates to our total implies that output per worker in the uncovered area moved closely with that in the covered area prior to 1921. Prior to 1916, it was necessary to average fiscal-year estimates in order to convert them roughly to a calendar-year basis.

The Barger index was extrapolated from 1890 to 1880 by the index prepared by Ulmer.[6] Ulmer extrapolated the movement between 1890 and 1880 for ton-miles and passenger-miles by Census data and interpolated by data from Poor's *Manual of the Railroads of the United States* for 1882–90, as extended by Census data covering 1880–82. Ulmer employed average unit revenues in 1880 and 1890 to weight the two components of his index.

The railroad output index was further extrapolated from 1880 to 1869 by means of a weighted aggregate of ton-mile and passenger-mile estimates by Edwin Frickey.[7] Ulmer's unit revenues in 1880 were used as weights.

---

[5] *Ibid.*, Table 23.

[6] *Trends and Cycles in Capital Formation by United States Railroads, 1870–1950*, Occasional Paper 43, New York (NBER), 1954, Table B-2, p. 66.

[7] *Production in the United States, 1860–1914*, Cambridge, Mass., Harvard University Press, 1947, Table 10B, p. 87.

The Frickey estimates were laboriously compiled from the various volumes of Poor's *Manual of the Railroads of the United States*, supplemented to some extent by Census records and annual reports of the railroads themselves.[8] They cover samples of roads representing approximately 50 per cent of gross earnings in each of six geographical regions. Frickey was able to compare total tons and passengers moved by his roads with comprehensive figures for 1871 and 1890. This comparison revealed little bias in his sample for passengers, but a small upward bias with respect to freight tonnage amounting to less than 5 per cent over the two decades. Frickey did not see fit to adjust, or "rectify," the ton-miles estimates, and we have followed his example.

Since no coverage adjustments were made prior to 1890, when Barger's total railroad output index was extrapolated as described, it is assumed that uncovered output moves with the output of the covered line-haul roads. The line-haul roads account for the great bulk of revenue, and the coverage adjustment after 1890 was slight. But the estimates prior to 1890 are of somewhat poorer quality than those based on ICC data.

EMPLOYMENT

Barger's index of employment is presented in his Table 23. The underlying estimates, taken from the same sources as the output estimates, are described in his Appendix B (Table B-1). From 1921 on, the employment estimates are complete for the component groups. For 1911–21, they cover Class I, II, and III line-haul roads and the Pullman Company, and prior to 1911, only the former category.

For the Class I roads, the annual estimates for 1890 to 1914 are based on a single count on June 30; to put these on a more representative basis we have given the current year's count a weight of 2, and the adjacent years, 1 each. The estimate for 1915 is an average of 6 counts; 1916-21, 4 counts; and for the years since 1922, 12 monthly counts have been averaged. For the other categories, the annual estimates are frequently based on less than 12 counts, even in recent years. The total annual estimates of employment from 1929 forward are virtually identical to those contained in the Commerce *National Income Supplement, 1954, Survey of Current Business*, and we have used the latter for consistency with other industries.

In order to estimate total employment from 1890 to 1921, it was first necessary to estimate employment of switching and terminal companies for 1907–21, since in 1908 the ICC stopped collecting employment data for these companies, which were previously included with the Class I, II, and III line-haul roads. Estimates for 1915 and 1916 were available from *Statistics of Railroads*, and interpolations for 1916–21 and 1907–15 were

---

[8] Cf. *Ibid.*, Chapters V and VI.

made on the basis of line-haul employment. Estimates of Railway Express employment had been made back to 1910 by King;[9] and an estimate for 1890 was available from the Census. Interpolation between 1910 and 1890 was done on the basis of line-haul employment. Estimates of Pullman Company employment by Barger were available back to 1912; the 1912 estimate was extrapolated to 1890 by employment on the line-haul roads. As Table G-1 shows, the direct total estimates are quite close

TABLE G-1

Railroad Employment, by Type, 1890, 1910, and 1921
(thousands)

	Line-Haul Roads	Switching and Terminal Companies	Pullman Companies	Express Companies	Total of Direct Estimates	Extrapolated Total, Using Coverage Adjustment
1890	747		7	46	800	801
1910	1,643	29	16	58	1,746	1,768
1921	1,705	59	22	83	1,869	1,869

to those obtained by applying the same coverage adjustment that Barger used for output. It is thus implied that output per worker in the segments for which output estimates are not available moved with output per worker on the line-haul roads.

Estimates of railroad employment for 1870 and 1880 comparable with the estimate for 1890 were taken from Daniel Carson.[10] In 1880 and 1890 the figures are from the *Compendium of the Eleventh Census, 1890*, Part 3, p. 893. The 1870 figure was extrapolated by Carson on the basis of the Census data for steam railroad employment and his projection to 1870 of the ratio between the Census and the broader industry figures. In order to obtain decennial averages, employment for intercensal years prior to 1890 was interpolated on the basis of the output index.

MANHOURS

From 1916 forward, Barger presents estimates of manhours worked on Class I line-haul roads and the Pullman Company. These estimates are based on ICC data and are stated to be "the nearest approach to continuously comparable data on hours actually worked."[11] The estimates were extended from 1946 to 1953 by the sources and methods used by Barger.

[9] Willford I. King, *The National Income and Its Purchasing Power*, New York (NBER), 1930, pp. 57 and 61.
[10] "Changes in the Industrial Composition of Manpower since the Civil War," *Studies in Income and Wealth, Volume 11*, New York (NBER), 1949, p. 127.
[11] Barger, *op. cit.*, Table B-1, n. *e*.

For comparability with the total output index, we have multiplied the manhours estimates by the ratio of employment on Class I roads and the Pullman Company to total employment. This procedure involves an imputation of the average hours worked per year by employees in the covered segment to employees in the uncovered segment. It is a broadly reasonable imputation, and since employment in the covered segment is almost nine-tenths of the total, errors in total manhours because of the imputation are not significant.

It is possible to extend the series to 1915 by an average of ICC estimates of manhours worked for fiscal years 1915 and 1916. From 1915 back, we obtained manhours as the product of employment and estimated average hours worked per year. Leo Wolman has estimated that the standard workweek for steam railroads was 60 hours from 1917 back to 1890, the beginning of the period covered by his study.[12] The Aldrich Report (see Appendix A, note 24), which was the basis of the Wolman estimates, shows 10 hours a day from 1890 to 1869, so we have assumed that the 60-hour standard week applied back to the beginning of our period. Estimates of actual hours worked were obtained from a regression for 1916 to 1941 between the ratio of actual hours to standard hours (using the ICC and Wolman estimates) and the ratio of employment to labor force in the railroad group. The labor force estimates are those prepared by Carson for census years, interpolated linearly, and the employment estimates are those of Barger based on the ICC reports. The coefficient of correlation is +.96, which strongly confirms the presumption that both actual hours worked and employment are sensitive to cyclical movements in output. The average hours-per-week estimates, obtained by applying the ratios from the regression equation to standard hours, were used to extrapolate average hours worked per year from 1915 to 1869.

CAPITAL

The estimates of the value of road and equipment, in 1929 dollars, are based on those developed by Ulmer[13] annually as of January 1 from 1870 to 1951. A two-year moving average was taken in order to approximate more closely calendar-year averages, and the estimates were extended to 1953.

Ulmer's method involved the derivation of estimates of gross capital outlays (excluding land acquisition) and capital consumption in 1929 prices and the application of real net capital outlays to the estimated reproduction cost less depreciation of road and equipment, in 1929 prices, of all railroads on January 1, 1937. The sources, methods, and bases of judgment involved in this complex procedure are described in some

[12] *Hours of Work in American Industry*, Bulletin 71, New York (NBER), 1938.
[13] *Capital in Transportation*, Table C-1.

detail by Ulmer.[14] It is noted that the estimates prior to World War I are subject to larger margins of error than the later estimates, since the capital outlay figures are based on samples, and the construction and equipment cost indexes used for deflation are considerably rougher than those compiled by the ICC for the years since 1910–14.

Theoretically, we should like to include the real value of land and land rights in the capital stock estimates. Ulmer points out that, according to the 1880 Census, land comprised 2.1 per cent of the book value of capital assets. For the period since 1917, the ICC estimates indicate that about 3.7 per cent of gross capital outlays have been for land, but these outlays have been offset to an unknown extent by land sales. The general impression is that the trend of the real capital stock of the railroads, were it possible to include land, would differ little from the trend of the real value of road and equipment alone. Inventories are likewise not included, but these have been relatively unimportant in the transportation industries.

Electric Railways

This group comprises local street and interurban railway systems, including elevated or subway lines and trolley buses, but not the electrified divisions of steam railroads. It is basically SIC Major Group 41, exclusive of local bus lines, whether independent, affiliated, or subsidiary. Output, inputs, and productivity measures are given in Table G-V.

OUTPUT

The traffic indexes from 1902 forward are based on a weighted aggregate of revenue passengers carried and freight car-miles on the electric railways. The indexes and underlying data are presented for 1890–1950 by Ulmer.[15] They represent an expansion and refinement of those contained in Barger.[16] Prior to 1902, the index represents revenue passengers only, a category which accounted for more than 98 per cent of the weighted aggregate in 1902 (using 1939 unit revenues as computed by Barger).[17] We have extended the estimates beyond 1950 using the sources and methods described by Ulmer.

The numbers of revenue passengers less those carried on municipally owned lines were drawn from successive reports of the *Census of Electrical Industries*, 1890, 1902, 1907, 1912, 1917, 1922, 1927, 1932, and 1937. Annual interpolations from 1907 to 1937 and extrapolations since 1937 were made on the basis of numbers of revenue passengers as reported by the American Transit Association (New York) in the annual *Transit Fact*

[14] *Ibid.*, Appendix A.
[15] *Ibid.*, Appendix I.
[16] *Op. cit.*, Chap. 5 and Appendix D.
[17] *Ibid.*, Tables 3 and 4.

513

Book.[18] The Association series includes municipal lines and, after 1917, does not include all pay-transfer passengers; for the extrapolation after 1937, Ulmer adjusted the Association estimates to eliminate passengers carried on municipal lines on the basis of data supplied by the Association relating to all local transit.[19]

Freight car-miles were derived by Ulmer from the Census reports beginning in 1902. Annual interpolations beginning in 1926 and extrapolations after 1937 were made possible by the ICC annual reports, *Transportation Statistics, Electric Railways.*

The passenger and freight traffic indexes were combined on an annual basis from 1926 forward and for the census years from 1922 to 1902. Annual interpolations between 1907 and 1926 were made on the basis of the passenger index. We have interpolated from 1902 to 1890 and extrapolated to earlier years by Frickey's estimates of revenue passengers carried.[20] His series after 1890 is merely an interpolation of Census estimates based on employment estimates and thus does not yield a basis for productivity estimates independent of the 1890 and 1902 figures. Prior to 1890, however, the Frickey series is based on mileage of street-railway lines, the trend of which after 1890 was closely related to numbers of passengers carried. Because of the approximate nature of the output estimates prior to 1890, we do not use them as a basis for industry productivity ratios, but only as a means of deriving the composite output index.

EMPLOYMENT AND HOURS

Employment was estimated by Barger[21] from Census and American Transit Association data for 1890, 1902, 1907, 1912, and annually from 1917 to 1946. We have extended the estimates by data found in Moody's. Annual interpolations for the early years were made on the basis of estimates by Paul H. Douglas,[22] which rely on state data for intercensal years. Extrapolation from 1890 to 1880 and 1870 was based on estimates of gainful workers in the industry, prepared by Alba M. Edwards.[23]

In order to obtain estimates for the privately owned sector of the industry, which is the basis for the output and capital estimates, we have deducted the estimated employment on municipal and state railways. In 1912, there was only one municipal line, employing thirty-three persons. Beginning in 1917, we have computed the ratio of private to total employment in the industry on the basis of data given in the quin-

[18] Reproduced for 1907–46 in *ibid.*, Table D-1.
[19] *Capital in Transportation*, Table I-26.
[20] Frickey, *op. cit.*, Table 15, pp. 108–109, and Appendix C, pp.216–19.
[21] *Op. cit.*, Table D-1.
[22] *Real Wages in the United States, 1890–1926*, Boston, Houghton Mifflin, 1930, p. 440.
[23] *Census of Population, 1940, Comparative Occupation Statistics for the United States, 1870 to 1940.*

quennial censuses through 1937, and interpolated linearly in order to estimate private employment in all years. From 1929 through 1937, however, we have made a further adjustment, using the ratio of the sum of our estimates of private employment in electric railways and local bus lines to the Commerce estimates for the group. The adjustment is minor, but serves the purpose of maintaining all our employment estimates on the Commerce basis from 1929 forward. From 1938 forward, we extrapolated the 1937 adjustment factor for the local-transit industry as a whole by the ratio of the Commerce estimates (private employment) to the American Transit Association estimates (private plus public). This procedure involves the assumption that the ratio for the subgroup moves as does the ratio for the group, which is an assumption parallel to the one made by Ulmer in adjusting the output estimates. Since the adjustment factor for employment moves very closely with that for output, the resulting productivity estimates are virtually the same as would emerge for the industry including the public sector. The employment estimates for private street railways alone after 1937 are less reliable, however, than the employment estimates for the local-transit industry as a whole.

Estimates of average hours worked per week by employees of street railways and bus lines by the Bureau of Labor Statistics are available back to 1932. We have used this series for the street-railway and bus components separately, since the close connection between the two branches of the industry suggests that average hours in each would be similar. Prior to 1953, the BLS series relates to the industry inclusive of municipal lines. The 1953 figure is for the private sector only. An overlap of the two series for the first three months of 1953 indicates that average hours worked in the private component were somewhat higher than in the total industry, but we have not adjusted the earlier figures on this account.

Estimates of average hours actually worked per week for transportation other than steam railroads are available for 1920–22 from the study by King.[24] Data from state sources indicate that in 1920 standard hours were somewhat higher than the 51.8 reported by King (relative to actual hours of 51.0). Also, the hours data in the 1940 Census indicate that average hours worked in the street railway and bus industry were about 1 per cent higher than the average for all transportation other than steam railways. Accordingly, we have adjusted the King estimate for 1920 upward by 1 per cent to 51.5 to approximate average actual hours worked per week in the local-transit industry, as revealed by the state averages which were used for earlier years. A figure of 50 hours for 1929 was arrived at on the assumption that the downward trend of hours in the industry up to 1919 continued, and amounted to the 2-hour drop estimated for all

[24] *Employment, Hours and Earnings in Prosperity and Depression, United States, 1920–22,* New York (NBER), 1923.

manufacturing. We then interpolated linearly between 1929 and 1932, the first year for which BLS presents hours estimates.

Estimates of the value of electric railway plant and equipment, in 1929 dollars, are contained in Ulmer.[25] His estimates are as of January 1, 1870 to 1950; a two-year moving average of the estimates was used to approximate annual averages.

The Ulmer figures start from an estimate of the total net value of plant and equipment on January 1, 1870. Other years are derived by the successive addition of each year's net capital outlays in constant dollars. The estimates exclude publicly-owned facilities and the electric power departments of privately-owned facilities. Inventory change is not taken into account. The value of land and land rights is also excluded. Although land is estimated to have comprised around 8 per cent of the total value of fixed plant in 1890, the data do not permit the estimation of a time series for land.

Local Bus Lines

This industry (SIC Group 415) comprises companies primarily engaged in operating street and suburban passenger bus lines within the confines of a single municipality, contiguous municipalities, or a municipality and its suburban areas. A few bus lines are operated by local railways, but the scope of such operations is small relative to operations of local bus lines not connected with railways. The productivity summary for the group is given in Table G-VI.

The output index is based on the estimated numbers of revenue passengers carried by private bus lines. Following Ulmer, we drew the basic data from the American Transit Association's annual *Transit Fact Book*. The data from 1925 forward relate to numbers of revenue passengers carried on all local bus lines. For 1937 to 1950, Ulmer adjusted this series to exclude the estimated number of passengers carried on publicly owned municipal lines. This adjustment was based on unpublished data furnished by the Association relating to passengers carried by municipal railway and bus lines on the assumption that the municipal proportion of the total is applicable to local railway and bus lines separately.[26] We obtained data to make the adjustment in 1950–1953. For years prior to 1937, it was assumed that the 1937 ratio of municipal to total passengers was constant. From 1922 to 1926, estimates of total bus passengers (including nonrevenue

[25] *Capital in Transportation*, Appendix F.
[26] Ulmer, *Capital in Transportation*, Table I-26.

passengers, who accounted for 11.5 per cent of the total in 1926), were used to extrapolate the revenue passenger index back to 1922. Rough estimates for several earlier years are available from Barger.[27]

EMPLOYMENT AND HOURS

Estimates of employment on all local bus lines (private and public) have been made by the American Transit Association for the years since 1929. Although data relating to motorbus lines were first collected in the *Census of Electrical Industries* for 1922, these related only to companies affiliated with electric railways. The Census for 1937 was the first to collect comprehensive data for the entire industry inclusive of lines operated by companies affiliated with, or subsidiary or successor to, electric railways and independent bus companies. In order to derive employment estimates for the entire industry prior to 1929, the ratio of passengers to employment was extrapolated by that for the affiliated companies and then applied to the total passenger estimates, as shown in Table G-2.

TABLE G-2

Local Bus Lines: Employment in Relation to Revenue Passengers, Selected Years, 1922–53

	1922	1927	1929	1932	1937	1948	1953
Total industry							
Revenue passengers (millions)[a]	357	2,028	2,301	1,862	2,997	8,893	6,593
Employment (thousands)[b]	(10.0)	(40.0)	43.5	39.6	58.4	138.0	126.0
Passenger-employment ratio[c]	(34.8)	(50.8)	52.9	47.0	51.3	64.4	52.3
Companies affiliated with electric railways							
Revenue passengers (millions)	12.41	163.2		749.4	1,306		
Employment (thousands)	0.40	3.6		17.9	26.7		
Passenger-employment ratio	31.0	45.3		41.9	48.9		

NOTE: Includes both public and private lines.

[a] Estimates of the American Transit Association, with the exception of 1922, which was obtained by extrapolating revenue passengers in 1926 by all passengers on local bus lines, 1922–25.

[b] Estimates by the A.T.A., with the exception of 1922 and 1927, which were obtained by dividing numbers of passengers by the passenger-employment ratio.

[c] Numbers of passengers divided by numbers employed, except 1922 and 1927, which were obtained by extrapolating the 1932 ratio by the ratios shown for companies affiliated with electric railways.

This procedure involves the assumption that output per employee in the whole industry moved with that in a relatively small portion of the industry, but it seemed better than alternative expedients. The marked

[27] *Op. cit.*, Table 7.

trend toward bigger buses, which largely accounts for the increase in the productivity ratio, undoubtedly affected the entire industry. An employment estimate of 8,000 is obtained for 1920 if we project the 1922–27 rate of increase in passengers per employee and apply it to estimated output. This compares with an estimate by Barger of 7,000, based on extrapolation of the 1929 estimate by the number of buses. Prior to World War I, the industry did not exist on an organized basis, although public jitney-type operations began around 1912.

According to the 1937 Census, 96.2 per cent of the employees in the industry worked for private companies. In order to retain consistency with Ulmer's treatment of revenue passengers, we have adjusted the employment estimates from 1920 to 1937 by the 1937 ratio of private to total, although the first data on this point for a portion of the industry in 1932 indicate a ratio of 95.2 per cent. A small further adjustment was required for 1929–37 in order to achieve consistency with the Commerce estimates for the transit group. We have likewise used the ratio of private to total employment for the group, discussed in the preceding section, in order to extrapolate the 1937 ratio to more recent years.

The estimates of average hours worked per week on local railways and bus lines, described above, were also used for bus lines alone. Although average hours worked in each of the two types of local-transit operation probably tend to conform to the average for both, it is obvious that man-hours for the two industries in combination should be somewhat more accurate than for each taken separately.

CAPITAL

The capital estimates are based on Ulmer's estimates of the value of plant and equipment in 1929 dollars.[28] A two-year moving average of his January 1 estimates was taken to convert them to a calendar-year basis. His stock estimates are derived by the cumulation of real net capital outlays. The gross capital outlay estimates are largely based on transit industry sources, with adjustments described in Ulmer's Appendixes F and G. Capital consumption is estimated from the capital outlay figures on the basis of a calculated average thirteen-year life.

The Local-Transit Group

A somewhat higher degree of accuracy in the productivity estimates is obtained by combining the output and input estimates for street railways and local bus lines to arrive at estimates for SIC Major Group 41. As implied in the previous discussions, this is desirable since some of the data related to the group as a whole and had to be broken down on the basis of

[28] *Capital in Transportation*, Table G-1.

incomplete information; other data, such as average hours worked and factor cost weights, related to the major group but had been used for the components.

The output indexes were combined on the basis of the relative revenue weights given by Barger for 1939[29] and extrapolated to 1929 by the quantity indexes. The labor and capital inputs in constant dollars were added, and indexes computed. Because the weights used for combining the inputs were based on relative compensation in the industry as a whole, the results are the same as if manhours and real stocks had each been added and weighted.

Summary Table G-IV shows the estimates from 1919 forward. Since the local bus transportation industry was insignificant on an organized basis prior to 1919, the estimates for the major group would be virtually identical with those for street railways (Table G-V) in the early period.

Intercity Bus Lines

Available estimates for intercity bus lines fall within SIC Group 431, Passenger bus lines, except local, which excludes local buses, school buses, sightseeing and other chartered buses, as well as terminal facility operations. Our longer series (Table G-VII) relate to Class I, II, and III carriers, but consistency between the output and employment estimates is not exact. From 1942 forward, more precisely comparable estimates of employment and passenger-miles are available from the ICC for Class I carriers. The latter were defined prior to 1949 in terms of revenues generally in excess of $100,000, whereas from 1949 on the lower limit has been $200,000. Overlapping data in 1949 made possible continuous index numbers.

OUTPUT

Following Barger, we have taken revenue passenger-miles as the measure of the output of intercity bus lines. For the years from 1939 to date, the ICC has prepared estimates of revenue passenger-miles carried by Class I, II, and III intercity bus lines on regular route schedules.[30] These estimates are based on data relating to bus-miles and average revenue passenger loads per bus reported regularly by Class I carriers since 1938, on corresponding data for Class II and III carriers from occasional special surveys beginning in 1939, and on regular annual reports from 1948 to date. The estimates do include intracity traffic of reporting bus lines, but not the relatively small amount of intercity traffic of primarily local carriers. From

---

[29] *Op. cit.*, Tables 3 and 4.

[30] Revised series published in *Transport Economics*, Monthly Comment, Bureau of Transport Economics and Statistics, Interstate Commerce Commission, November 1955, p. 11.

1949 on, the ICC has also estimated intercity revenue passenger-miles by carriers other than these on regular route schedules.[31]

The ICC estimates have been pushed back to 1929.[32] These estimates are quite similar to those prepared by Barger[33] from passenger estimates of the National Association of Motor Bus Operators, multiplied by estimates of the length of the average journey, based on trade opinion. We have used the Barger estimates for 1920–29. Table G-VII also shows estimates by the ICC, from 1943 on, of passenger-miles traveled on Class I intercity buses only and the corresponding employment estimates.

EMPLOYMENT AND HOURS

For some years, the McGraw-Hill Publishing Company has published estimates of employment of intercity and local bus lines based on reports from the carriers. These estimates purport to cover all Class I, II, and III carriers, but not charter and special-service buses. Since the classification of operations is left up to the reporting companies, it is possible that some primarily suburban companies are included with the intercity carriers. Comparability of the employment estimates with the ICC passenger-mile estimates is also not precise because the latter include passenger operations of companies classed as carriers of property. But insofar as the possible discrepancies are not large and maintain a relatively fixed relation to the basic series, the quotient of the two series provides a fair indication of trends in output per worker in the industry, and we have computed it for key years. Estimates by the ICC of employment on Class I intercity motor carriers of passengers for selected years are presented in Table G-3.

TABLE G-3

Class I Intercity Motor Vehicle Passenger Carriers:
Employment in Relation to Numbers of Buses and of Bus-Miles, 1939, 1948, and 1953

	Employment (number)	Buses	Bus-Miles (millions)	Employees Per Bus	Employees Per Million Bus-Miles
1939	22,659	7,263	529.2	3.12	42.8
1948	50,700	16,362	1,200.4	3.10	42.2
1953	40,850	13,500	993.0	3.03	41.1

The McGraw-Hill series is available back to 1947. Since the estimates relate to December 31, we have averaged the year-end figures to approximate average employment during the year. The derived values have been

[31] *Intercity Passenger-Miles*, Statement 5517, File No. 10-D-8, mimeo, July 1955.

[32] See *Bus Facts, 23rd Edition*, Washington, National Association of Motor Bus Operators, 1954, p. 4.

[33] *Op. cit.*, Table E-1.

linked to estimates presented by Barger for 1920, 1929, and 1939.[34] The 1929 and 1939 figures are Commerce estimates which, in turn, are tied to the employment estimate in the 1935 *Census of Business, Motor Bus Transportation* as extrapolated by numbers of intercity buses owned or bus-miles operated. This was the same device used by Barger to obtain the 1920 figure. In order to obtain annual estimates to build up the segment totals, we have interpolated by the number of intercity buses as given in *Motor Bus Transportation*. Table G-3 shows the close relation between buses and employment in years for which both are available. It suggests a slight tendency for employment to fall relative to the number of buses. If this were true in earlier years, the Barger estimate for 1920 may be on the low side.

Estimates of average hours worked per week in the intercity motorbus industry for selected dates during 1933, 1934, and 1935 are contained in a report of the Federal Coordinator of Transportation.[35] We have carried an average of the two survey estimates for October 1935 (covering up to one-third of the industry) of 45.4 hours into 1936 and extrapolated forward by the BLS estimates of average hours worked on street railways and local bus lines. The 1933 average of 50.0 hours is not much below the King estimate for transportation other than steam railroads. Assuming that the King estimate is representative of the intercity bus companies, we have held the estimate for 1922, based on his study, constant until 1929, and between 1929 and the 1933 interpolated averages obtained from the Federal Coordinator's study. These estimates are obviously crude, and we have used them on an annual basis only for building up total manhours in the segment and the economy.

Intercity Motor Trucking

In this section, we are concerned with SIC Industry 4213, Trucking, except local. It includes companies that are preponderantly in the "over-the-road" trucking business, either as common or contract carriers. The large volume of traffic handled by trucks owned by companies classified in other industries is not included. Moreover, the data since 1939 relate to companies subject to the jurisdiction of the Interstate Commerce Commission, which accounted for about three-fourths of the "for-hire" intercity traffic in 1950. Relative to SIC Major Group 42, Trucking and warehousing, the industry covered here accounts for about one-third of income originating in the group. Continuous data are not available relating to the other main components: local trucking and draying, terminal facilities, and warehousing and storage.

[34] *Ibid.*, Table 4.
[35] *Hours, Wages, and Working Conditions in the Intercity Motor Transport Industries, Part I, Motor-Bus Transportation*, 1936.

From 1939 to date, the Interstate Commerce Commission has prepared estimates of intercity freight traffic carried by all agencies as well as by property carriers submitting regular reports. It will be observed in Table G-4 that total ton-miles have increased more than ton-miles carried

TABLE G-4

Ton-Miles of Intercity Motor Vehicle Freight Traffic,
by Type of Carrier, 1939–54
(millions)

	Total Private and "For-Hire"[a]	Class I, II, and III Carriers[b]	Class I Carriers[b]
1939	52,821	19,646	
1940	62,043	20,683	
1941	81,363	26,835	
1942	59,896	28,083	16,000
1943	56,784	28,768	17,184
1944	58,264	27,253	17,901
1945	66,948	27,289	18,143
1946	81,992	30,448	20,480
1947	102,095	37,693	25,512
1948	116,045	46,706	34,070
1949	126,636	47,891	37,880
1950	172,860	65,648	48,749
1951	188,012	72,292	54,145
1952	194,607	70,843	56,188
1953	217,163	76,510	62,873
1954	214,626	69,392	

SOURCE: Interstate Commerce Commission.

[a] Includes all private trucks and for-hire carriers not subject to federal regulation.

[b] Common and contract carriers operating under ICC authority. The reported figures have been raised to full coverage.

by the Class I, II, and III companies. Commission studies indicate that this is not due so much to a change in the relative proportions of private and for-hire carriers as to a substantial rise in the share of for-hire carriers not required to report to the ICC.

It is also evident that Class I carriers have become relatively more important than Classes II and III. This is partly because of rising rates, which have brought an increasing number of smaller carriers above the lower limit of $200,000 gross revenue ($100,000 prior to 1950). Our interest is in the for-hire carriers only. And because reliable employment estimates are available only for the Class I carriers, the output-employment ratios are based on estimates for this class alone (Table G-VIII).

Prior to 1939, we have the estimates of Barger, purporting to cover all for-hire ton-miles.[36] The estimates are admittedly rough, and should be used with this qualification in mind. The absolute level of the Barger estimate for 1939 is somewhat higher than the ICC figure; the difference may be attributed to the fact that Barger included for-hire trucking concerns not reporting to the ICC, as well as to a difference in estimating method. Since the nonreporting for-hire carriers were a relatively small factor in the industry in 1939, we have treated the series as essentially continuous.

EMPLOYMENT AND HOURS

From 1942 to date, estimates by the ICC of employment by the Class I carriers are available. It is from the estimates for the Class I carriers that our basic output-per-worker indexes are calculated. By imputing the same movements in output per worker to the employees of the Class I, II, and III carriers, however, we can estimate the change in employment for the broader category by dividing the index of ton-miles carried by the Class I, II, and III intercity trucking concerns by the index of output per worker for Class I carriers. This we have done in order to narrow the uncovered portion of the motor transport industry.

Following Barger, we have extrapolated employment of the carriers under ICC jurisdiction from 1942 to 1929 by the Commerce estimates for the highway freight transportation industry as a whole. Since this procedure is based on the assumption that the intercity portion of the industry group accounted for a constant proportion of total employment over the period, the estimates are obviously subject to a considerable margin of error. The same is true of the extrapolation from 1929 to 1920, which has been made on the basis of total private-truck registrations, since here the assumption is that a constant proportion of trucks in use have been employed in intercity for-hire trucking. In view of the imprecise nature of the estimates prior to 1942, these have been used only to build up the segment totals, and Table G-VIII shows annual estimates only for the later period. The earlier figures indicate an even greater rate of gain in output per worker than has been the case since 1942.

Information regarding average hours worked per week in motor trucking exists for scattered years. For 1933 and 1935 the results of sample surveys are available.[37] An average for the entire industry can be computed for

---

[36] *Op. cit.*, Tables 8 and F-4, pp. 40 and 242, and the description of sources and methods in Appendix F.

[37] *Hours, Wages, and Working Conditions . . .* , *Part II, Motor Truck Transportation.*

the week of March 24–30, 1940, from a distribution of employment by average hours class intervals.[38] Estimates by the Bureau of Labor Statistics were begun in 1953. The BLS has also published annual estimates of average full-time union hours of truck drivers and helpers going back to 1936. Although these relate to local trucking, it was felt that they could serve to interpolate the trend of hours in the intercity trucking industry between the years in which direct surveys of actual average hours were made. This was done, except for the war period. From 1941 to 1946, the interpolation was made on the basis of the BLS estimates of average hours actually worked per week in the local-transit industry, since a full-time hours series was clearly inappropriate for a period in which actual hours rose substantially in most industries for which records were available.

The result of the field survey for 1933 indicated a level of average hours worked almost precisely the same as that indicated for all nonrailroad transportation operations in 1922 by the survey conducted by King.[39] In the absence of data on hours worked in the trucking industry in early years, we have assumed that the King estimates are representative; and it is worth noting that the 1940 Census shows average hours worked in motor trucking to be close to the average for all nonrail transport. We therefore held average hours worked in intercity trucking at 50.4 per week from 1922 to 1933 and extrapolated to 1920 by the King averages. Obviously, the year-to-year changes in the average hours series have little validity; but the general trend, particularly since 1933, should be reasonably accurate.

Waterways

The estimates of output and employment of United States water transportation companies are built on those presented by Barger.[40] We have broadened the coverage of the output measure to include coastwise and inland passenger traffic, but due to the relatively small weight of this segment our output index is close to Barger's. More important, we have made output and employment estimates for census years between 1889 and 1920, interpolated annually and have extended the estimates to 1953. The results are presented in Table G-IX.

OUTPUT

Separate indexes have been prepared for freight and passenger traffic. These are based on physical-unit data by the several categories shown in Table G-5. The relative 1929 weights were calculated by applying the

---

[38] *Census of Population, 1940*, Vol. III, The Labor Force, Part I, Table 86, p. 259.
[39] *Employment, Hours and Earnings*, Table XXXIII, p. 82.
[40] *Op. cit.* Chapter 7 and Appendix H.

TABLE G-5

Waterway Traffic: Percentage Weights,
by Category, 1929

Freight	86.7
International	38.3
Noncontiguous	6.6
Intercoastal	12.8
Coastwise	14.5
Great Lakes	10.5
Other inland	4.0
Passenger	13.3
International	6.2
Coastwise, intercoastal, and noncontiguous	1.5
Great Lakes, river, and other inland	4.0
Ferry	1.6

1939 revenues per unit[41] to the number of units (ton-miles, passenger-miles, or passengers) carried in 1929.

In terms of the Standard Industrial Classification, it will be noted that we have not explicitly estimated the output of two small components of local water transportation: Industries 4453, Lighterage, and 4454, Towing and tugboat services. Employment in these categories is included in the waterways total employment estimates; we assume that the output of these groups is proportional to the covered traffic. We have likewise not included the output of services incidental to water transportation (SIC Group 446: Piers and docks, stevedoring, canal operation, and water transportation not elsewhere classified). Although shore employment of companies engaged primarily in water transportation is included in our estimates, we follow the Commerce Department in excluding employment of companies engaged primarily in incidental services. Such employment is included in the estimates for the transportation segment as a whole, and the corresponding output is included in the total output of the transportation segment through a coverage adjustment.

Freight traffic. The index of weighted freight ton-miles prepared by Barger[42] has been used for the years available: 1889, and 1920–40 annually. The index number for 1946 required revision; estimates for years since 1946 were prepared by essentially the same sources and methods as those described by Barger.

[41] *Ibid.*, Table 30, p. 128.
[42] *Ibid.*, Table 8, pp. 40–41.

The Barger estimates of ton-miles in 1889 are derived from data given in the *Census Report on Transportation Business in the United States, 1890*, Part II, *Transportation by Water*, and from 1920 on, from various reports of the Maritime Commission, the Army Corps of Engineers, and the Bureau of the Census.[43] Except in the case of inland and Great Lakes traffic, the series are derived from separate tonnage and average haul estimates.[44]

To fill the gap between 1889 and 1920, we first drew estimates of the number of net tons of freight carried by all American vessels and craft (of five tons net register and over) from the Bureau of the Census reports (see Table G-6). These were used to interpolate the years 1906 and 1916 between Barger's index numbers of freight ton-miles for 1926 and 1889.

TABLE G-6

Freight Carried by American Vessels, Selected Years,
1889–1926

	Freight and Harbor Work (million tons)	Freight Carried	
		Tons (millions)	Index (1926 = 100)
1889	129.9		19.4
1906	265.5	177.5	39.6
1916	381.4	258.1	57.6
1926		448.1	100.0

SOURCE: Bureau of the Census, *Water Transportation, 1926*, Table 61, p. 101, and *Transportation by Water, 1916*, Table 1, p. 20. Data cover vessels of five tons net register and over, excluding fishing vessels.

Barger's index of weighted ton-miles increased somewhat more between 1889 and 1926 than the straight tonnage figures. Use of the latter series for interpolation involves the assumption that the implied increase in the average haul of all freight, owing in part to shifts in the composition of trade, occcurred regularly over the period.

Intercensal-year interpolations were made on the basis of a weighted average of the following series: net tonnage capacity of American vessels engaged in carriage of foreign trade entered and cleared at all ports (adjusted where necessary to a calendar-year basis); and the gross tonnage of documented merchant vessels engaged in the coastwise and internal trade of the United States.[45] The index shows much the same trends as the

[43] *Ibid.*, notes to Table H-1, pp. 254–55.

[44] *Ibid.* Illustrative calculations of average hauls are shown in Tables H-3, H-4, H-5, and H-6, pp. 257–62. In some years, it was assumed that the average haul was the same as in a year for which estimates were available.

[45] *Historical Statistics of the United States, 1789–1945*, Dept. of Commerce, 1949, Series K 147, K 153, and K 102.

Census estimates of tons of freight carried, but registers a 20 per cent smaller increase over the period as a whole, reflecting a rise in the ratio of freight tonnage carried to the tonnage capacity or tonnage of the merchant marine. This relationship is itself one aspect of the rising productivity of water transport, reflecting increased speed of voyage and turnaround and, possibly, fuller utilization of capacity. The Barger index was extrapolated back of 1889 on the basis of its relationship to the combined vessel tonnage index between 1889 and 1926.

It will be noted that the Census estimates of harbor work for 1906 and 1916 show a virtually constant ratio to vessel freight carried. This helps support the reasonableness of our assumption of constancy after 1916. From 1906 to 1889, the only aggregate tonnage estimates available include both vessel and harbor carriage.

Passenger traffic. This component was estimated by Barger for 1889 and annually from 1920 to 1940. From 1928 forward, it was based on Maritime Commission estimates of passenger arrivals and departures broken down by intercoastal, noncontiguous, and international categories (including cruises).[46] These estimates, in further detail, were multiplied by estimated average hauls in order to arrive at a passenger-mile total. Prior to 1928, the index numbers were based on data relating to passengers carried in foreign travel only, i.e., arrivals plus departures at United States ports in vessels of all flags, adjusted by changes in the ratio of American-flag vessels to all entrances and clearances.[47] Data on foreign travel after 1940 were not available to Barger.

The series for international travel on American vessels was available on an annual basis for all years and was used to fill the gap between 1920 and 1889, and for extension to earlier years. The Barger series was extrapolated from 1939 to 1946 and subsequent years by the numbers of arrivals and departures from and to foreign countries on American-flag vessels given in the *Annual Report of the Immigration and Naturalization Service*, Department of Justice, Tables 31 and 32, for the relevant years.

Estimates of other passenger travel by American vessels could be obtained for 1929–46 from the annual reports of the Army Chief of Engineers.[48] Indexes based on numbers of passengers carried were prepared by the categories shown earlier. In the case of Atlantic, Gulf, and Pacific ports, it was necessary to subtract the number of arrivals and departures from and to foreign countries, a procedure used by Barger to obtain detailed estimates of coastal and intercoastal passenger traffic for 1939.[49]

[46] Barger, *op. cit.*, Table 33, note a, p. 139; Table H-2, pp. 256–57.

[47] *Overseas Travel and Travel Expenditures*, Bureau of Foreign and Domestic Commerce, Economic Series 4, 1939.

[48] *Annual Report of the Chief of Engineers*, U. S. Army, Part 2, *Commercial Statistics, Water-Borne Commerce of the United States*.

[49] *Op. cit.*, Table 30, pp. 128–9.

Data for 1889, 1906, 1916, and 1926 are given in the censuses of water transportation (see source notes to Tables G-6 and G-7). The classifications are essentially the same as those given by the Army Chief of Engineers from 1929 forward, although there is a somewhat divergent treatment of excursion passengers. Accordingly, we have extended the Census series to 1929, for splicing with the Engineers' data, on the basis of the series on the gross tonnage of vessels engaged in the coastwise and inland trade of the United States, cited above. This series was also used for annual interpolations prior to 1926 and for extrapolation of the Engineers' series after 1946.

Although it is not certain that the several Census estimates (Table G-7)

TABLE G-7

Domestic Waterway Passenger Traffic on American Vessels, by Category,
Selected Years, 1880–1926
(millions of passengers)

	FERRY PASSENGERS	PASSENGERS, EXCLUDING FERRY			
		Atlantic, Gulf and Pacific Ports			Lake, River and Other Inland
		Reported Total	Estimated Overseas[a]	Total Domestic[a]	
1926	445.0	20.9	0.5	20.4	12.1
1916	292.2	26.4	0.3	26.1	13.0
1906	330.7	24.6	0.5	24.1	11.5
1889	182.0	13.0	0.2	12.8	5.6[b]
1880	153.6	11.4	0.1	11.3	3.2[b]

Source: Estimates for 1926, 1916, and 1906 from *Water Transportation, 1926*, Bureau of the Census, Table 73, p. 125; estimates for 1889 and 1880 from *Eleventh Report on Transportation Business in the United States, 1890, Part II, Transportation by Water*, Bureau of the Census, pp. xii, 43, 53, 223, 339, 357, 448–49.

[a] Adjustment to reported Census figures made as described in text.

[b] Census figures for the Great Lakes and St. Lawrence and for rivers of the Mississippi Valley plus our estimates for other inland waterways not reported for 1880 and 1889 (based on extrapolation of the 1906 figure by vessel tonnage on inland waterways).

are entirely comparable, the movements implied do not appear unreasonable. The resulting series should represent total passenger traffic more fully than the foreign travel series alone, used by Barger prior to 1928. It seems reasonable that domestic waterway travel increased less from 1880 to 1926 than foreign waterway travel, as shown by the estimates, due to the rapid growth of competing carriers in the domestic area.

LABOR INPUT

Employment. From 1929 forward, the Office of Business Economics estimates of full- and part-time employees plus proprietors engaged in water transportation are used. These include vessel and shore employees of water transport companies, but not the employees of companies engaged primarily in services incidental to water transportation (such as stevedoring), which are included in Services allied to transportation.

Employment estimates for 1906, 1916, and 1926 are available from the several censuses of water transportation. The movements of our series prior to 1926 differ somewhat from those shown by the Barger series[50] because we attempt to cover total employment in order to be consistent with estimates after 1929, whereas Barger excludes employees on tugs, ferries, and on shore. Estimates of total employment on commercial vessels (including tugs and ferries) for 1926 and 1916 are given in the 1926 Census (p. 24). We assume that shore employment moved with vessel employment, since the numbers employed on shore, given in the Census for 1916 (but not for 1926), comprised approximately 55 per cent of vessel employment, the same percentage as in 1929 according to the OBE estimates for the latter year.

For 1916 and 1906, the 1916 Census gives total employment (p. 20), which is used to obtain the movement over this decade. Some drop in the ratio of shore to vessel employment is indicated by the estimates. From the same source, vessel employment is given for 1906 and for 1889. These figures are used to extrapolate the employment series from 1906 to 1889, a procedure which involves the assumption that the ratio of shore to vessel employment did not change further. The Census employment estimate for 1889 is exclusive of employment on canal boats. We derived a figure of 9,500 for the latter by extrapolating the estimate for 1906 back to 1889 by the estimated change in the gross tonnage of canal boats.[51] An employment estimate for 1880 was based on estimates of employment on steam vessels in 1880 and 1889,[52] to which was added an estimate of employment on sailing vessels, canal boats, and barges, obtained by extrapolating the figures for 1889 back to 1880 by the gross tonnage of these classes of vessels, with allowance for the tendency of employment to decline relative to tonnage. The percentage change in employment so derived is very close to that revealed by statistics of gainful workers in the relevant occupations in 1880 and 1890.[53] The latter approach was used to estimate the percentage change in employment from 1880 to 1870. Annual interpolations between census years were made on the basis of the gross tonnage of documented merchant vessels, excluding those engaged in fisheries.[54]

A final problem was involved in linking the series based on Census data from 1926 back to the OBE estimates from 1929 forward. The

[50] *Ibid.*, Table H-7, p. 263.

[51] Derived from Census data in *Transportation by Water, 1916*, p. 201.

[52] *Report on Transportation Business in the United States, 1890*, Part II, *Transportation by Water*, p. xiii.

[53] See Edwards, *op. cit.*, p. 109.

[54] *Historical Statistics*, p. 207.

estimates used by Barger for 1926–29 are interpolations between the Census and OBE estimates and involve a significant drop in employment. It was our impression that the two estimates were not fully comparable. Accordingly, we extrapolated the OBE estimates to 1926 and linked them to the Census figures. Estimates for the major component of the series, employment on American-flag merchant vessels, were available from Maritime Administration records, and showed an increase from 58,600 in 1926 to 64,500 in 1929. Employment on Great Lakes and Inland vessels was extrapolated back from 1929 to 1926 by its relation to tonnage carried from 1929–39. Change in shore employment was computed to parallel the change in vessel employment, since the ratio of the two in 1929 was practically the same as that in the 1916 Census.

Hours. For 1934, the Interstate Commerce Commission conducted a survey of employment, hours, and compensation on Class A and B carriers under its jurisdiction.[55] The survey covered 20,700 employees out of 34,700 on the regulated carriers (total employment on American-flag commercial vessels was about 152,000). The survey revealed that vessel employees worked an average of 2,625 hours per year, and shore employees of the carriers, an average of 1,660 hours. The average annual hours for all employees, weighted by the relative numbers of the sample, were 2,040.

The 1934 average was very close to the average given in the ICC report *Carriers by Water* for 1947, when regular reporting of hours worked by employees on the Class A and B carriers was begun. This series was used for the years since 1947. The 1934 estimate was held constant to 1941. Vessel employee hours were also held constant from 1941 to 1947, but shore employee average hours were interpolated between 1941 and 1947 on the basis of average hours worked in manufacturing.

In extrapolating to years before 1934, we have also assumed that average hours worked by vessel employees remained at the 2,625 level. This is a relatively high figure, and it suggests that in this occupation average hours worked depend to a large extent on technical factors in the industry. The hours of shore employees, on the other hand, might be expected to change more in line with the hours of workers in other industries. Accordingly, we have extrapolated back the 1934 average hours per year of shore employees by average hours in manufacturing.

Again, the average hours estimates are subject to a considerable margin of error, with the exception of the years for which ICC estimates are available. They are not shown in Table G-IX, but are used in obtaining aggregate manhours in the segment.

[55] *Water Line Statistics, 1920–34*, Statement 364, File No. 48-C-18, mimeo, January 1936.

Airlines

The output and input estimates described in this section relate to scheduled (common carrier) airlines, certified and uncertified (SIC Group 451). Unscheduled (contract) carriers and companies primarily engaged in operating fixed facilities or providing services related to air transportation are included in the residual sector. The estimates in Table G-X begin in 1929; although scheduled airlines were in operation for several years prior to that, the volume of traffic and employment was negligible, and the data pertaining thereto was not sufficiently precise to permit the calculation of output-input ratios.

OUTPUT

The estimates of output are made in terms of the two broad subdivisions: domestic airlines and American-flag international airlines. From 1929 to 1946 the indexes are Barger's,[56] based on data collected by the Civil Aeronautics Administration (CAA) and predecessor agencies. From 1935 forward, the index of domestic traffic is based on a weighted aggregate of revenue passenger-miles, express and freight ton-miles, and mail ton-miles. In earlier years, the index is based on total passenger-miles. The American-flag international component represents passenger traffic throughout: 1937 forward, revenue passenger-miles; 1930–37, all passenger-miles; 1928–30, all passengers. Data for 1946–53 were taken from the 1954 issue of the CAA *Statistical Handbook of Civil Aeronautics.*

Barger weighted the components of domestic traffic by the 1939 revenues per unit of traffic. He assumed the same revenue per passenger-mile on the international as on the domestic lines in order to obtain a weight for the former. We have reweighted the components for the period after 1939 by the average unit revenues in 1939 and 1947.

LABOR INPUT

The annual employment estimates by Barger[57] are averages of year-end data compiled by the CAA. They are virtually identical with the OBE estimates, derived from the same source, through 1941. From 1942 forward, however, the OBE estimates are based on Social Security Administration data. Since these estimates also represent complete coverage of the same segment and are more accurate averages of employment throughout the year, we have shifted to the OBE series for 1942 and subsequent years.

A time series of average hours worked per week by airline employees does not exist. For purposes of obtaining manhours to include in the segment total, we have used the estimate derived from 1940 Census data

---

[56] Barger, *op. cit.*, Table 37, pp. 154–55, for annual indexes. The underlying data are summarized in Table I-1, p. 266.

[57] *Ibid.*, Table I-1, p. 266.

for all peacetime years from 1934 to date. This accords with the general picture of stability of average hours in the other transportation groups during this period. In order to catch the general drop in hours experienced from 1929 to 1933, and the bulge during World War II, we have extrapolated and interpolated for these years by the average hours series for the local-transit industry.

Pipe Lines

This industry (SIC Major Group 46) includes companies engaged primarily in the pipe line transportation of crude petroleum and refined petroleum products. Pipe line transmission of natural gas is classified as part of the the gas utilities.

Barger's estimates of output and employment,[58] 1921–46, which we have extended to earlier and later years, cover interstate trunk lines as reported to the Interstate Commerce Commission. These have comprised a quite stable proportion, around 82 per cent, of total trunk line mileage over the period. Gathering lines are not covered, but the traffic mileage on these is small relative to the trunk lines. The output-input ratios are based on the ICC data. In aggregating for the segment, however, we gave the pipe line output its full weight, including an allowance for trunk line movements on interstate pipe lines.[59] Also, in aggregating employment for the segment, we raised the ICC employment estimates by a constant ratio, to represent full coverage. The adjusting ratio was based on a comparison of OBE estimates for the industry, which are tied into full-coverage Social Security data from 1942 forward, with the ICC estimates; the comparison showed a relatively constant relation between the two series. Our procedure for the segment implies that output-input relationships on the ICC lines are representative of the industry as a whole. The final estimates appear in Table G-XI.

OUTPUT

Since 1936, estimates of billions of ton-miles of crude and refined oil transported over the trunk lines of companies reporting to the ICC have been available in its annual report, *Statistics of Oil Pipe Line Companies*. For 1920–36, Barger estimated ton-miles from ICC data on oil received into the system. He assumed that the 1936 ratio of barrels originated to barrels received into the system held for earlier years. He further estimated the change in the average haul over the period, and by converting barrels into tons for crude and refined separately, was able to derive ton-mile estimates.

For use in an industry output aggregate (Tables A-IV and G-I) we pushed the ton-miles estimates back to 1889 on the basis of estimates of

[58] *Ibid.*, Chapter 6 and Appendix G.
[59] *Ibid.*, Table 4, p. 21, and methodological note, pp. 249–50.

interstate trunk pipe line mileage by Walter Splawn,[60] adjusted by an extrapolation of the trend in the ratio of ton-miles transported to pipe line mileage, 1921–52. The ratio increased at an average annual rate of around 5 per cent, reflecting a gradual increase in the average diameter of pipe, the use of more efficient pumping machinery, and improvements in construction and maintenance. This procedure results in index numbers on 1929 as base of 22 in 1920 (Barger's earliest year), 8 in 1910, 2 in 1900, and less than 0.5 in 1890. While helpful for the purpose indicated, the estimates prior to 1919 are not firm enough to use in direct productivity comparisons.

EMPLOYMENT AND MANHOURS

Estimates of employment are available annually since 1921 in *Statistics of Oil Pipe Line Companies*. While they represent employment by companies engaged primarily in interstate transmission of oil, they are not exactly comparable with the output series since some of the employees work on gathering as well as on trunk lines. Since ICC gathering-line mileage fell somewhat relative to trunk-line mileage, the output-employment ratio is subject to some upward bias, but Barger considers this to be "slight" because of the preponderance of trunk line movement.[61] The level of the ICC estimates has been raised by 7 per cent to correspond with the OBE employment figures in computing the total for the segment. Carson has estimated that gainful workers in the pipe line industry numbered 3,500 in 1910, compared with 11,600 in 1920.[62] Even allowing for some variation in the percentage of gainful workers employed between the two dates, the figures imply virtual stability in output per worker, using the output extrapolation described above. This result does not seem plausible in view of the rapid increase in output per worker since 1920, and reinforces our decision not to present output-employment ratios prior to 1919. We have, however, used Carson's estimates to carry back the employment series for purposes of estimating total employment in the economy.

Estimates of average hours worked per week relating specifically to pipe lines do not exist. In order to build up total manhours in the segment, we have used the estimates of average hours worked in the refining branch of the petroleum industry (see Appendix D).

The Residual and Total Transportation Industries

In the preceding eight sections we have described the output and input estimates for major and minor industry groupings within the transportation segment for which direct output estimates are feasible. This portion of the segment accounted for more than four-fifths of total employment in

[60] *Oil and Gas Journal*, September 27, 1938.
[61] Barger, *op. cit.*, p. 125.
[62] *Op. cit.*, Table 6, p. 54.

1929. Uncovered were parts of SIC Major Group 43: School buses (432), Taxicabs (433), and Motor vehicle transportation not elsewhere classified (439), which includes chartered vehicles, horse-drawn carriages, livery stables, etc.; parts of Group 42: Local trucking and draying (4212), Warehousing and freight terminal facilities (422 through 429); and all of the National Income Division's Services allied to transportation: Fixed facilities for motor vehicle transportation (438 and 4784), Services incidental to water transportation (446), Contract flying (452), Airports and flying fields (458), and Services incidental to transportation (Group 47), such as forwarding, packing and crating, and inspecting and weighing.

Employment figures based on Commerce estimates are available for the residual area since 1929, and can be derived for earlier years (see Table G-8). Direct capital estimates are available only for the steam railroads and local-transit groups, but estimates can be derived for the total segment and, thus, for a residual area broader than that which we have just specified.

OUTPUT

It has not been practical to estimate output directly in the residual sector. It is also not reasonable to assume that uncovered output moved as did covered output. Employment in the residual area increased steadily from about 18 per cent of the total in 1929 to 28 per cent in 1953. Based on labor-force estimates (Table G-8), the proportion in the uncovered area fluctuated between one-fourth and one-third from 1870 to 1900, and fell to about one-fifth between 1910 and 1930 before rising again.

For the purpose of building up aggregate output estimates by industry division, and in order to have figures to compare with capital estimates for the entire transportation division, we have calculated total output for key years by means of coverage adjustments based on the assumption that output per worker in the uncovered area moved with that in the covered. While this procedure suffices to yield rough estimates of total output, it must be held in mind that the output-input ratios are more accurate for the areas in which direct estimates are feasible and for the covered portion of the segment as a whole (Table G-II). The output index for the covered portion of the segment was obtained by weighting together the group output indexes using changing national income weights calculated by the Marshall-Edgeworth formula, as discussed in Appendix A.

EMPLOYMENT AND MANHOURS

The OBE provides estimates of total employment in transportation from 1929 forward. By subtracting estimates for the covered industries (which are consistent with the Commerce estimates) we obtain estimates of employment in the uncovered area. Ratios of total to covered employment are used for the coverage adjustment to the output index. The estimate of employment in the uncovered area in 1930 was used as a base for extrapolation to earlier years in order to be able to build total transportation employment estimates prior to 1929.

The employment extrapolation is based on estimates of the industrial distribution of gainful workers in census years from 1870 to 1930, as shown in Table G-8. The estimates are largely those by Carson, supple-

TABLE G-8

Residual Transportation: Derivation of Employment, Decennial, 1870–1930
(thousands of persons 10 years old and over)

Line No.		1870	1880	1890	1900	1910	1920	1930
1	Total manpower, regulated industries	617	816	1,476	2,034	2,978	3,616	3,886
2	Public utilities and communications	24	38	68	168	394	610	992
3	Transportation	593	778	1,408	1,866	2,584	3,006	2,894
4	Railroads and express companies	274	425	761	1,033	1,675	1,951	1,809
5	Street railways	7	17	54	99	191	232	209
6	Water transport	141	139	126	123	159	195	226
7	Pipe lines and air transportation	...	...	...	1	4	12	43
8	Other	171	197	467	610	555	359	607
9	Adjusted to employment basis	161	186	443	564	536	616	537
10	Other: OBE level	210	243	579	737	701	775	702
11	Of which: intercity motor carriers						57	174

SOURCE

LINE

1 The sum of "transportation and public utilities" and "miscellaneous transportation and communication" less "garages, greasing stations, etc.," as given in Daniel Carson, "Changes in the Industrial Composition of Manpower since the Civil War," *Studies in Income and Wealth, Vol. 11*, New York (NBER), 1949, pp. 47 and 55.

2 The sum of "electric light and power," "gasworks," "telephone and telegraph," and "radio broadcasting," for census years 1910–30, from Carson, pp. 54–55; the 1910 figures were extrapolated back by our estimates of employment derived as described in Appendix H.

3 Line 1 less line 2.

4 The sum of "steam railroads" and "express companies," 1910–30 (Carson, p. 54), extrapolated to 1870 by the Carson (p. 127) estimates of railroad employees.

5 1910–30: Carson, p. 54. The 1910 estimate was extrapolated to 1890 by the employment estimates by Harold Barger, *The Transportation Industries, 1889–1946*, New York (NBER), 1951, p. 216, and from 1890 to 1870 by Alba M. Edwards, *Census of Population, 1940, Comparative Occupation Statistics for the United States, 1870 to 1940*, p. 109.

6 1910–30: Carson, p. 54, extrapolated to 1870 by our estimates, which were tied into Census estimates as described in Appendix G.

7 Carson, pp. 54–55, extrapolated from 1910 to 1900 by pipe line mileage.

8 Line 3 less lines 4–7.

9 Line 8 times the ratio of employment to labor force, as estimated, 1890–1930, by Clarence Long, *The Labor Force under Changing Income and Employment*, Princeton University Press (for NBER), 1958, Table C-1; percentage employment ratios of 94.5 and 94.0 used for 1880 and 1870.

10 From Office of Business Economics; 1930 employment including proprietors extrapolated by line 9.

mented to some extent by the estimates in this appendix and in Appendix H. The residual, line 8, purports to cover SIC Major Groups 42 and 43, and the Services allied to transportation. We have employment estimates for parts of the two former groups for 1920 and 1930 and we subtracted these from the employment estimates extrapolated by line 8 in order to get employment in our residual area. Before extrapolation, however, we changed the index of the residual gainful-workers estimates to an employment basis using an index of the ratio of employment to labor force, as estimated by Clarence D. Long. The procedure is spelled out in Table G-8. The 1930 "other" employment based on the Commerce estimates is considerably higher than the adjusted gainful-workers estimate. As explained in Appendix A, differences in concept can account for some discrepancy. The size of the discrepancy in this case, however, suggests that the coverage of the Carson "other" groups may not be complete. We assume, nevertheless, that the trend is correctly indicated thereby.

It is striking that the trend of "other" employment remained virtually stable from 1900 through 1930. This stability was due to substantial declines in employment in the industries associated with horse-drawn vehicles, offset by substantial increases in employment in the industries associated with motor vehicle transport. Lebergott, in his estimates, assumed no change in the "other" category from 1900 to 1929. Although it yields approximately the same result, we chose this procedure, particularly since we needed to push the estimates back to 1870. It is apparent that there were substantial increases in "other" employment prior to 1900. A particularly sharp increase during the 1880's occurred primarily in the occupational category of draymen, teamsters, and carriage drivers, according to the detailed analysis of Edwards. Despite the general reasonableness of the residual employment estimates, however, it is clear that they are subject to a considerable margin of error.

In building up annual estimates of total employment prior to 1929, we have interpolated the estimates for the residual areas by employment in the covered area. Practically all the proprietors engaged in transportation are associated with the residual industries. This group comprised about 30 per cent of the total number of persons engaged in this area in 1929 according to the Commerce estimates. Although we used the separate Commerce estimates for proprietors from 1929 on, raised by 10.7 per cent to include unpaid family workers, our pre-1929 extrapolations are on the basis of all persons engaged and, thus, include proprietors and unpaid family workers. For the purpose of estimating manhours, however, we have segregated this class of worker in earlier years by assuming the continuance of the 1929 ratio of proprietors to total persons engaged.

536

The movement of average hours worked by employees in the residual area was assumed to be the same as that for the average for all the covered transportation groups back to 1920. We extrapolated the 1920 figure by an average of estimates shown in various state reports for teamsters, hostlers, draymen, carriage drivers, stevedores, and longshoremen. The data have been taken for decennial years and interpolated linearly. The same average hours series was used for the estimated number of proprietors and unpaid family workers, raised by 10 per cent in accordance with the divergence revealed by the special Census Bureau survey in 1953.

Manhours worked in the various groups were weighted by the mean of average hourly earnings in the first and last years of the several subperiods beginning in 1919. The averages for 1919 and 1929 were used for earlier periods. Table G-9 shows the effect of the weighting procedure.

TABLE G-9

Transportation: Labor Input Based on Alternative Methods of Weighting, Key Years, 1869–1953
(1929 = 100)

	Manhours (unweighted aggregate)	Labor Input (weighted aggregate of 8 groups)
1869	23.1	21.7
1879	31.2	30.1
1889	60.4	57.5
1899	79.3	75.8
1909	109.2	108.7
1919	115.2	116.0
1929	100.0	100.0
1937	72.0	70.4
1948	94.1	91.1
1953	85.7	81.9

CAPITAL

Direct capital estimates were made by Ulmer, and used here, only for steam railroads and the local-transit group (electric railways and local bus lines). A total for all "regulated industries" was arrived at by Ulmer through coverage adjustments of capital stock estimates in the base period, and annual net investment estimates were used to obtain stock figures annually. Several manipulations were necessary to obtain the capital stock estimates for total transportation from the broader Ulmer estimates. A residual capital stock series for transportation other than railroads and local transit could be obtained by subtraction. This was done only for purposes of assessing the reasonableness of the total. The probable margin of error attaching to total productivity estimates for the broad residual would be too great for them to be used separately because part of the output series and all of the capital series would hinge on the validity of coverage adjustments; also, part of the employment estimates prior to 1929 are based on gainful-worker estimates. The following paragraphs, therefore, are devoted to describing the capital estimates for the transportation segment as a whole.

Ulmer's estimate of the real value of stocks of plant and equipment for all regulated industries in 1870 was based on his estimates for steam railroads and street railways, inflated by 15.14 per cent to include other transportation, communications, and public utilities.[63] The blow-up factor was derived from his estimates of the book value of the covered groups in relation to a total for the segment. As the first step in cumulating net additions on this base, gross capital outlays of the industries studied by Ulmer in detail were blown up by factors based on the ratio of changes in book values for all industries to book values for covered groups in selected periods to 1919;[64] while total capital outlays were estimated directly in later years.[65] Total real capital consumption estimates were similarly derived,[66] and the resulting real net capital outlays cumulated on the 1870 base.

To get the implied total capital stocks in the transportation segment by subtraction, we estimated total stocks in public utilities and communications as follows. A coverage adjustment was applied to our estimates of real capital stocks for the electric light and power, gas, and telephone industries (see Appendix H, noting that with the exception of the gas industries the estimates are those by Ulmer). The adjustment factors are those applied by Ulmer to the real value of output for the same selected industries; they are based on the ratio of operating revenues of the covered industries to total operating revenues, extrapolated prior to 1922 by the book value of capital estimates for the covered industries relative to the total.

The total transportation capital estimates do not appear to be unreasonable, despite their indirect derivation. Railroad and local-transit capital comprised about 95 per cent of the total in 1889 and about 85 per cent in 1950. While capital in the uncovered segment increased sixfold over the period, compared with a twofold increase in railroad and local-transit capital, this is in relation to percentage increases of 88 and 113 in employment in the covered and uncovered areas, respectively.

[63] *Capital in Transportation*, Tables B-1 and B-9.
[64] *Ibid.*, Tables B-6, B-9.
[65] *Ibid.*, Tables B-2, B-3.
[66] *Ibid.*, Tables B-11, B-12.

The aggregate real capital stock for the segment (unweighted) was combined with real labor input, using the average unit compensation of each factor class in the first and last years of the several subperiods since 1919 as weights (Table G-10). The 1919–29 averages were used for earlier years.

TABLE G-10

Transportation: Relative Weights of Labor and Capital Inputs,
Subperiods, 1919–53
(per cent)

	Labor	Capital
1919–29	78.7	21.3
1929–37	82.9	17.1
1937–48	87.6	12.4
1948–53	88.7	11.3

TABLE G-I

Transportation: Output, Inputs, and Productivity Ratios, Key Years, 1869–1953

(1929 = 100)

	Output	Persons Engaged	Output per Person	Manhours	Output per Manhour	Labor Input	Output per Unit of Labor Input	Capital Input	Output per Unit of Capital Input	Total Factor Input	Total Factor Productivity
1869	4.0	18.6	21.3	23.1	17.1	21.7	18.2	24.5	16.2	22.3	17.8
1879	7.9	25.1	31.7	31.2	25.5	30.1	26.4	36.2	22.0	31.4	25.3
1889	20.2	47.0	43.0	60.4	33.4	57.5	35.1	51.2	39.5	56.2	35.9
1899	35.7	62.5	57.1	79.3	45.0	75.8	47.1	61.6	58.0	72.8	49.0
1909	55.8	88.2	63.3	109.2	51.1	108.7	51.3	77.5	72.0	102.1	54.7
1919	82.2	110.0	74.7	115.2	71.4	116.0	70.9	95.1	86.4	111.5	73.7
1929	100.0	100.0	100.0	100.0	100.0	100.0	100.0	100.0	100.0	100.0	100.0
1937	103.1	77.1	133.7	72.0	143.2	70.4	146.4	97.0	106.3	74.9	137.7
1948	211.8	98.8	214.4	94.1	225.1	91.1	232.5	95.2	222.5	93.1	227.5
1953	228.9	97.5	234.8	85.7	267.1	81.9	279.5	103.5	221.2	85.7	267.1

TABLE G-II

Transportation, Aggregate of Groups Covered by Output Data:[a] Output, Labor Inputs,
and Productivity Ratios, 1869–1953
(1929 = 100)

	Output of Covered Industries	Persons Engaged	Output per Person	Manhours	Output per Manhour	Labor Input	Output per Unit of Labor Input
1869–78[b]	4.7	18.6	25.2	22.7	20.6	23.0	20.3
1879–88[b]	10.3	27.9	36.9	34.5	29.9	35.6	28.9
1889	15.6	36.9	42.3	46.0	33.9	47.6	32.8
1890	17.2	39.3	43.8	49.4	34.8	51.2	33.6
1891	18.5	41.1	45.0	51.8	35.7	53.7	34.5
1892	19.7	43.2	45.6	54.8	35.9	56.9	34.6
1893	19.5	43.9	44.4	55.3	35.3	57.3	34.0
1894	18.7	42.6	43.9	52.3	35.8	54.2	34.5
1895	19.9	42.3	47.0	51.4	38.8	53.2	37.4
1896	20.8	43.6	47.7	52.8	39.4	54.6	38.1
1897	22.2	44.6	49.8	54.0	41.1	55.9	39.7
1898	24.9	46.5	53.5	56.4	44.1	58.5	42.6
1899	27.5	49.3	55.8	60.7	45.3	63.0	43.7
1900	29.7	52.6	56.5	65.6	45.3	68.1	43.6
1901	31.8	56.4	56.4	70.5	45.1	73.3	43.4
1902	34.5	61.0	56.6	77.0	44.8	80.0	43.1
1903	36.6	65.4	56.0	82.9	44.1	86.2	42.5
1904	38.5	68.1	56.5	85.5	45.0	89.0	43.3
1905	42.4	71.8	59.1	90.2	47.0	93.8	45.2
1906	47.0	77.8	60.4	98.9	47.5	103.0	45.6
1907	48.2	80.9	59.6	102.3	47.1	106.5	45.3
1908	47.1	79.4	59.3	97.8	48.2	101.5	46.4
1909	50.5	81.0	62.3	98.9	51.1	102.7	49.2
1910	54.1	86.5	62.5	106.8	50.7	110.9	48.8
1911	55.2	89.4	61.7	110.4	50.0	114.8	48.1
1912	59.2	92.0	64.3	114.1	51.9	118.6	49.9
1913	61.6	94.0	65.5	116.8	52.7	121.5	50.7
1914	59.4	91.0	65.3	110.7	53.7	115.1	51.6
1915	62.9	87.1	72.2	103.9	60.5	107.8	58.3
1916	71.6	91.6	78.2	111.4	64.3	115.7	61.9
1917	78.6	96.1	81.8	116.3	67.6	120.9	65.0
1918	81.0	101.0	80.2	120.8	67.1	125.6	64.5
1919	78.1	106.1	73.6	110.4	70.7	114.3	68.3

(continued)

TABLE G-II (concluded)

	Output of Covered Industries	Persons Engaged	Output per Person	Manhours	Output per Manhour	Labor Input	Output per Unit of Labor Input
1920	86.8	113.9	76.2	120.8	71.9	124.7	69.6
1921	68.4	98.7	69.3	97.0	70.5	99.1	69.0
1922	74.0	97.4	76.0	99.5	74.4	101.3	73.1
1923	86.2	107.3	80.3	110.2	78.2	112.5	76.6
1924	83.4	102.8	81.1	103.3	80.7	104.8	79.6
1925	88.2	102.3	86.2	102.9	85.7	104.3	84.6
1926	94.3	104.1	90.6	105.4	89.5	106.6	88.5
1927	93.6	102.4	91.4	102.9	91.0	103.7	90.3
1928	95.1	99.0	96.1	98.9	96.2	99.2	95.9
1929	100.0	100.0	100.0	100.0	100.0	100.0	100.0
1930	89.3	91.4	97.7	88.5	100.9	88.2	101.2
1931	76.7	79.2	96.8	73.6	104.2	73.0	105.1
1932	63.4	67.1	94.5	59.8	106.0	59.0	107.5
1933	66.7	63.9	104.4	56.8	117.4	55.9	119.3
1934	73.7	66.1	111.5	59.3	124.3	58.6	125.8
1935	78.2	66.6	117.4	60.0	130.3	59.3	131.9
1936	92.7	70.1	132.2	65.2	142.2	64.6	143.5
1937	103.3	73.5	140.5	68.1	151.7	67.6	152.8
1938	90.1	63.9	141.0	58.2	154.8	57.7	156.2
1939	102.7	66.6	154.2	61.6	166.7	61.2	167.8
1940	112.8	68.9	163.7	64.0	176.2	63.6	177.4
1941	140.7	75.1	187.4	71.8	196.0	71.2	197.6
1942	187.6	81.1	231.3	79.7	235.4	78.7	238.4
1943	221.9	88.5	250.7	90.3	245.7	89.5	247.9
1944	227.9	94.1	242.2	95.6	238.4	95.6	238.4
1945	218.3	96.7	225.7	97.2	224.6	97.6	223.7
1946	196.9	95.0	207.3	91.0	216.4	91.2	215.9
1947	208.4	93.1	223.8	88.6	235.2	88.5	235.5
1948	210.5	90.9	231.6	85.4	246.5	84.9	247.9
1949	187.3	83.5	224.3	75.9	246.8	75.7	247.4
1950	211.3	85.5	247.1	74.3	284.4	74.0	285.5
1951	232.4	89.8	258.8	78.2	297.2	78.4	296.4
1952	225.0	88.8	253.4	76.6	293.7	77.0	292.2
1953	226.3	88.6	255.4	76.0	297.8	76.6	295.4

[a] Comprises railroads, electric railways, and waterways throughout; pipe lines beginning 1899; local bus lines, intercity bus lines, and intercity trucking beginning 1919; and airlines beginning 1929. Estimates of persons engaged and manhours for the motor transport groups are exclusive of proprietors.

[b] Annual average for decade.

TABLE G-III

Railroads: Output, Inputs, and Productivity Ratios, 1869–1953

(1929 = 100)

	Output	Persons Engaged	Output per Person	Manhours	Output per Manhour	Capital Input	Output per Unit of Capital Input	Total Factor Input	Total Factor Productivity
1869–78[a]	5.3	18.0	29.4	22.8	23.2	36.4	14.6	26.3	20.2
1879–88[a]	12.6	30.0	42.0	38.0	33.2	49.3	25.6	40.8	30.9
1889	19.2	40.4	47.5	51.3	37.4	57.2	33.6	52.8	36.4
1890	21.1	43.4	48.6	55.7	37.9	58.3	36.2	56.4	37.4
1891	22.7	45.4	50.0	58.4	38.9	59.5	38.2	58.7	38.7
1892	24.1	47.7	50.5	61.9	38.9	61.6	39.1	61.8	39.0
1893	23.6	48.3	48.9	62.3	37.9	64.7	36.5	62.9	37.5
1894	22.4	46.7	48.0	58.5	38.3	66.6	33.6	60.6	37.0
1895	23.7	46.0	51.5	56.8	41.7	66.7	35.5	59.3	40.0
1896	24.7	47.3	52.2	58.3	42.4	65.9	37.5	60.2	41.0
1897	26.5	48.5	54.6	59.6	44.5	65.0	40.8	61.0	43.4
1898	29.9	50.6	59.1	62.6	47.8	64.8	46.1	63.2	47.3
1899	33.2	54.0	61.5	67.8	49.0	64.2	51.7	66.9	49.6
1900	36.0	57.9	62.2	73.9	48.7	64.6	55.7	71.5	50.3
1901	38.4	62.2	61.7	79.6	48.2	65.0	59.1	75.9	50.6
1902	41.7	67.9	61.4	87.7	47.5	65.3	63.9	82.0	50.9
1903	44.0	72.7	60.5	94.4	46.6	65.6	67.1	87.1	50.5
1904	46.0	75.2	61.2	96.8	47.5	66.2	69.5	89.0	51.7
1905	50.8	79.2	64.1	102.0	49.8	67.1	75.7	93.1	54.6
1906	56.6	86.3	65.6	112.7	50.2	68.8	82.3	101.5	55.8
1907	57.6	89.4	64.4	116.3	49.5	71.2	80.9	104.8	55.0
1908	55.9	86.6	64.5	109.4	51.1	73.9	75.6	100.3	55.7
1909	60.2	88.3	68.2	110.5	54.5	76.6	78.6	101.9	59.1

(continued)

543

TABLE G-III (continued)

Railroads: Output, Inputs, and Productivity Ratios, 1869–1953
(1929 = 100)

	Output	Persons Engaged	Output per Person	Manhours	Output per Manhour	Capital Input	Output per Unit of Capital Input	Total Factor Input	Total Factor Productivity
1910	64.5	94.6	68.2	119.9	53.8	79.7	80.9	109.6	58.9
1911	65.5	97.4	67.2	123.8	52.9	82.7	79.2	113.3	57.8
1912	70.3	100.1	70.2	127.9	55.0	85.4	82.3	117.1	60.0
1913	73.0	102.5	71.2	131.4	55.6	88.0	83.0	120.3	60.7
1914	70.1	98.5	71.2	123.6	56.7	89.9	78.0	115.0	61.0
1915	75.0	93.0	80.6	114.2	65.7	90.5	82.9	108.2	69.3
1916	86.3	98.8	87.3	124.0	69.6	90.4	95.5	115.4	74.8
1917	95.1	104.0	91.4	130.0	73.2	90.7	104.9	120.0	79.2
1918	98.0	110.4	88.8	136.1	72.0	90.9	107.8	124.6	78.7
1919	92.8	114.5	81.0	119.9	77.4	90.4	102.7	112.4	82.6
1920	102.2	121.8	83.9	130.7	78.2	89.9	113.7	120.3	85.0
1921	77.7	101.3	76.7	99.1	78.4	89.9	86.4	96.8	80.3
1922	82.9	98.4	84.2	101.0	82.1	90.1	92.0	98.2	84.4
1923	98.0	111.3	88.1	114.7	85.4	91.2	107.5	108.7	90.2
1924	92.4	105.5	87.6	105.9	87.3	93.2	99.1	102.7	90.0
1925	97.2	105.0	92.6	105.7	92.0	94.7	102.6	102.9	94.5
1926	102.4	107.1	95.6	108.3	94.6	96.1	106.6	105.2	97.3
1927	98.4	104.4	94.3	104.7	94.0	97.5	100.9	102.9	95.6
1928	98.1	99.7	98.4	99.4	98.7	98.7	99.4	99.2	98.9
1929	100.0	100.0	100.0	100.0	100.0	100.0	100.0	100.0	100.0

(continued)

TABLE G-III (concluded)

1930	85.7	89.9	95.3	86.7	98.8	101.6	84.4	89.7	95.5
1931	69.2	76.2	90.8	69.8	99.1	102.1	67.8	76.2	90.8
1932	52.4	62.6	83.7	54.6	96.0	101.2	51.8	63.9	82.0
1933	55.0	58.8	93.5	51.3	107.2	99.8	55.1	61.0	90.2
1934	59.7	60.8	98.2	54.7	109.7	98.4	60.7	63.4	94.2
1935	62.6	60.3	103.8	54.9	114.0	97.2	64.4	63.3	98.9
1936	75.5	64.7	116.7	61.3	123.2	96.3	78.4	68.3	110.5
1937	80.9	67.8	119.3	64.2	126.0	96.2	84.1	70.6	114.6
1938	65.9	57.5	114.6	53.3	123.6	95.9	68.7	61.1	107.9
1939	74.8	60.4	123.8	57.1	131.0	95.0	78.7	64.2	116.5
1940	83.0	62.9	132.0	59.9	138.5	94.5	87.8	66.6	124.6
1941	105.5	69.6	151.6	68.6	153.3	94.5	111.6	74.4	141.8
1942	148.0	77.5	191.0	78.2	189.3	94.8	156.1	82.7	179.0
1943	179.3	83.1	215.8	87.6	204.7	94.7	189.3	90.9	197.2
1944	185.0	87.6	211.2	91.7	201.7	94.3	196.2	94.5	195.8
1945	172.4	88.2	195.5	91.0	189.5	94.0	183.4	93.8	183.8
1946	143.3	84.8	169.0	83.2	172.2	93.6	153.1	86.9	164.9
1947	147.2	83.6	176.1	81.8	180.0	93.3	157.8	85.7	171.8
1948	141.8	81.5	174.0	79.4	178.6	93.9	151.0	83.6	169.6
1949	117.4	73.1	160.6	67.1	175.0	94.9	123.7	72.7	161.5
1950	128.6	74.4	172.8	63.5	202.5	95.6	134.5	69.6	184.8
1951	141.2	77.7	181.7	66.0	213.9	96.2	146.8	72.0	196.1
1952	134.5	75.0	179.3	62.9	213.8	96.9	138.8	69.3	194.1
1953	131.6	73.7	178.6	61.4	214.3	97.5	135.0	68.0	193.5

[a] Annual average for decade.

TABLE G-IV

Local Railways and Bus Lines: Output, Inputs, and Productivity Ratios, 1889–1953
(1929 = 100)

	Output	Persons Engaged	Output per Person	Manhours	Output per Manhour	Capital Input	Output per Unit of Capital Input	Total Factor Input	Total Factor Productivity
1889	10.7	25.1	42.6	31.1	34.4	16.9	63.3	28.8	37.2
1899	25.8	45.2	57.1	53.4	48.3	68.9	37.4	56.3	45.8
1909	52.9	86.0	61.5	96.4	54.9	133.9	39.5	103.2	51.3
1919	77.5	107.3	72.2	111.6	69.4	135.1	57.4	116.0	66.8
1920	82.0	111.0	73.9	114.3	71.7	131.5	62.4	117.5	69.8
1921	77.9	103.2	75.5	105.5	73.8	126.7	61.5	109.7	71.0
1922	83.3	107.8	77.3	109.5	76.1	123.0	67.7	112.0	74.4
1923	87.6	109.8	79.8	111.3	78.7	120.6	72.6	113.0	77.5
1924	89.4	107.8	82.9	109.1	81.9	117.7	76.0	110.7	80.8
1925	93.5	106.4	87.9	107.5	87.0	114.0	82.0	108.7	86.0
1926	99.0	106.6	92.9	107.5	92.1	110.1	89.9	108.0	91.7
1927	100.2	104.7	95.7	105.1	95.3	106.4	94.2	105.3	95.2
1928	99.3	101.9	97.4	102.1	97.3	103.1	96.3	102.3	97.1
1929	100.0	100.0	100.0	100.0	100.0	100.0	100.0	100.0	100.0
1930	92.0	93.9	98.0	90.5	101.7	96.9	94.9	91.3	100.8
1931	82.5	85.4	96.6	79.3	104.0	93.6	88.1	81.1	101.7
1932	71.3	76.4	93.3	68.1	104.7	89.5	79.7	70.7	100.8
1933	67.3	71.1	94.7	62.9	107.0	84.6	79.6	65.6	102.6
1934	72.2	71.8	100.6	62.5	115.5	80.3	89.9	64.7	111.6

(continued)

TABLE G-IV (concluded)

1935	73.9	72.1	102.5	63.3	116.7	77.4	95.5	65.0	113.7
1936	81.1	72.9	111.2	65.5	123.8	75.7	107.1	66.8	121.4
1937	81.6	73.9	110.4	66.1	123.4	74.3	109.8	67.1	121.6
1938	77.6	66.8	116.2	58.2	133.3	72.3	107.3	59.4	130.6
1939	81.0	65.7	123.3	58.3	138.9	70.7	114.6	59.4	136.4
1940	84.3	60.7	138.9	54.4	155.0	64.2	131.3	55.4	152.2
1941	76.9	57.5	133.7	52.7	145.9	58.0	132.6	53.5	143.7
1942	106.7	60.4	176.7	57.0	187.2	56.6	188.5	57.5	185.6
1943	131.2	65.8	199.4	63.8	205.6	53.8	243.9	63.9	205.3
1944	139.7	67.1	208.2	66.0	211.7	50.7	275.5	65.8	212.3
1945	142.5	67.5	211.1	67.9	209.9	48.3	295.0	67.5	211.1
1946	143.6	72.5	198.1	69.5	206.6	46.9	306.2	69.0	208.1
1947	138.8	70.7	196.3	66.2	209.7	45.4	305.7	65.8	210.9
1948	120.5	61.1	197.2	56.8	212.1	43.9	274.5	56.7	212.5
1949	106.9	59.3	180.3	53.8	198.7	42.3	252.7	53.7	199.1
1950	96.7	56.1	172.4	50.9	190.0	40.2	240.5	50.8	190.4
1951	86.8	53.9	161.0	49.9	173.9	38.3	226.6	49.8	174.3
1952	84.9	51.4	165.2	47.7	178.0	36.3	233.9	47.5	178.7
1953	76.4	50.0	152.8	45.1	169.4	34.3	222.7	44.9	170.2

TABLE G-V

Local Electric Railways: Output, Inputs, and Productivity Ratios, 1889–1953

(1929 = 100)

	Output	Persons Engaged	Output per Person	Manhours	Output per Manhour	Capital Input	Output per Unit of Capital Input	Total Factor Input	Total Factor Productivity
1889	14.4	28.9	49.8	35.8	40.2	17.5	82.3	32.4	44.4
1899	34.6	52.0	66.5	61.4	56.4	71.5	48.4	63.3	54.7
1902	41.7	59.9	69.6	69.6	59.9	91.0	45.8	73.6	56.7
1903	46.8	66.6	70.3	77.0	60.8	98.1	47.7	80.9	57.8
1904	52.9	75.0	70.5	86.2	61.4	106.0	49.9	89.9	58.8
1905	57.6	81.3	70.8	93.0	61.9	114.4	50.3	97.0	59.4
1906	62.4	87.6	71.2	99.7	62.6	122.8	50.8	104.0	60.0
1907	66.2	92.6	71.5	104.8	63.2	131.1	50.5	109.7	60.3
1908	66.8	96.4	69.3	108.5	61.6	137.1	48.7	113.8	58.7
1909	71.1	98.9	71.9	110.8	64.2	139.0	51.2	116.1	61.2
1910	75.9	106.0	71.6	117.9	64.4	140.3	54.1	122.1	62.2
1911	80.1	112.7	71.1	124.4	64.4	142.1	56.4	127.7	62.7
1912	84.5	118.2	71.5	129.5	65.3	142.3	59.4	131.9	64.1
1913	88.4	119.0	74.3	129.5	68.3	142.1	62.2	131.9	67.0
1914	88.7	117.8	75.3	127.2	69.7	142.6	62.2	130.1	68.2
1915	87.8	118.2	74.3	126.7	69.3	143.0	61.4	129.7	67.7
1916	94.4	118.2	79.9	125.8	75.0	142.7	66.2	129.0	73.2
1917	100.3	123.1	81.5	130.0	77.2	142.1	70.6	132.3	75.8
1918	99.3	119.7	83.0	125.4	79.2	141.8	70.0	128.5	77.3
1919	104.1	123.4	84.4	128.3	81.1	140.2	74.3	130.5	79.8

(continued)

TABLE G-V (continued)

Year									
1920	109.1	127.1	85.8	130.9	83.3	136.4	80.0	131.9	82.7
1921	102.4	117.3	87.3	119.9	85.4	131.6	77.8	122.1	83.9
1922	108.7	122.3	88.9	124.3	87.4	127.5	85.3	124.9	87.0
1923	111.0	122.3	90.8	124.0	89.5	124.5	89.2	124.1	89.4
1924	108.7	117.5	92.5	118.9	91.4	120.8	90.0	119.3	91.1
1925	107.2	113.5	94.4	114.6	93.5	116.5	92.0	115.0	93.2
1926	107.2	111.3	96.3	112.2	95.5	111.9	95.8	112.1	95.6
1927	104.8	106.7	98.2	107.1	97.9	107.6	97.4	107.2	97.8
1928	101.2	102.6	98.6	102.8	98.4	103.7	97.6	103.0	98.3
1929	100.0	100.0	100.0	100.0	100.0	100.0	100.0	100.0	100.0
1930	91.2	93.4	97.6	90.0	101.3	96.5	94.5	91.2	100.0
1931	80.6	84.1	95.8	78.0	103.3	92.9	86.8	80.8	99.8
1932	67.7	73.6	92.0	65.7	103.0	88.5	76.5	70.0	96.7
1933	62.9	67.7	92.9	59.8	105.2	83.4	75.4	64.2	98.0
1934	65.3	68.3	95.6	59.4	109.9	78.7	83.0	63.0	103.7
1935	64.2	66.6	96.4	58.5	109.7	74.9	85.7	61.6	104.2
1936	66.3	64.7	102.5	58.1	114.1	71.9	92.2	60.7	109.2
1937	63.3	62.4	101.4	55.8	113.4	69.4	91.2	58.3	108.6
1938	58.7	54.9	106.9	47.9	122.5	66.9	87.7	51.5	114.0
1939	58.3	50.5	115.4	44.8	130.1	64.8	90.0	48.5	120.2

(continued)

TABLE G-V (concluded)

Local Electric Railways: Output, Inputs, and Productivity Ratios, 1869–1953

(1929 = 100)

	Output	Persons Engaged	Output per Person	Manhours	Output per Manhour	Capital Input	Output per Unit of Capital Input	Total Factor Input	Total Factor Productivity
1940	57.7	44.8	128.8	40.1	143.9	57.1	101.1	43.3	133.3
1941	49.8	39.8	125.1	36.5	136.4	49.2	101.2	38.9	128.0
1942	60.5	39.1	154.7	36.9	164.0	46.6	129.8	38.7	156.3
1943	74.9	44.7	167.6	43.4	172.6	43.7	171.4	43.5	172.2
1944	78.0	45.2	172.6	44.5	175.3	41.1	189.8	43.9	177.7
1945	78.0	44.6	174.9	44.9	173.7	38.7	201.6	43.7	178.5
1946	76.3	43.6	175.0	41.8	182.5	36.8	207.3	40.9	186.6
1947	70.1	40.9	171.4	38.3	183.0	33.7	208.0	37.4	187.4
1948	54.6	34.1	160.1	31.7	172.2	30.8	177.3	31.5	173.3
1949	44.7	31.6	141.5	28.7	155.7	29.4	152.0	28.8	155.2
1950	39.6	29.8	132.9	27.1	146.1	28.2	140.4	27.3	145.1
1951	41.3	27.5	150.2	25.5	162.0	27.2	151.8	25.8	160.1
1952	31.6	28.0	112.9	26.0	121.5	26.1	121.1	26.0	121.5
1953	28.2	26.3	107.2	23.7	119.0	25.0	112.8	23.9	118.0

TABLE G-VI

Local Bus Lines: Output, Inputs, and Productivity Ratios, 1919–53
(1929 = 100)

	Output	Persons Engaged	Output per Person	Manhours	Output per Manhour	Capital Input	Output per Unit of Capital Input	Total Factor Input	Total Factor Productivity
1919	6.8	14.4	47.2	15.0	45.3	2.3	296.9	12.6	54.0
1920	9.7	18.6	52.2	19.2	50.5	2.5	391.1	16.1	60.2
1921	12.6	21.5	58.6	22.0	57.3	2.6	488.4	18.4	68.5
1922	15.5	24.2	64.0	24.6	63.0	7.2	215.3	21.3	72.8
1923	25.4	38.2	66.5	38.7	65.6	20.6	123.3	35.3	72.0
1924	38.0	51.9	73.2	52.5	72.4	35.8	106.1	49.4	76.9
1925	57.1	65.7	86.9	66.4	86.0	48.9	116.8	63.0	90.6
1926	77.2	79.7	96.9	80.3	96.1	63.1	122.3	77.1	100.1
1927	88.1	93.7	94.0	94.1	93.6	75.9	116.1	90.7	97.1
1928	94.4	98.1	96.2	98.3	96.0	88.2	107.0	96.4	97.9
1929	100.0	100.0	100.0	100.0	100.0	100.0	100.0	100.0	100.0
1930	94.3	96.9	97.3	93.4	101.0	107.3	87.9	95.1	99.2
1931	87.7	92.5	94.8	85.8	102.2	112.1	78.2	89.0	98.5
1932	80.9	92.8	87.2	82.8	97.7	114.5	70.7	86.7	93.3
1933	78.9	90.6	87.1	80.1	98.5	116.2	67.9	84.5	93.4
1934	90.4	92.0	98.3	80.0	113.0	122.1	74.0	85.2	106.1
1935	99.8	103.9	96.1	91.2	109.4	140.6	71.0	97.3	102.6
1936	120.6	120.0	100.5	107.8	111.9	173.2	69.6	115.8	104.1
1937	130.2	140.3	92.8	125.4	103.8	200.9	64.8	134.7	96.7
1938	128.1	135.0	94.9	117.7	108.8	211.4	60.6	127.6	100.4
1939	141.6	153.4	92.3	136.2	104.0	222.6	63.6	146.5	96.7

(continued)

TABLE G-VI (concluded)

	Output	Persons Engaged	Output per Person	Manhours	Output per Manhour	Capital Input	Output per Unit of Capital Input	Total Factor Input	Total Factor Productivity
1940	155.2	152.4	101.8	136.6	113.6	247.0	62.8	148.2	104.7
1941	149.0	159.4	93.5	146.0	102.1	283.8	52.5	159.4	93.5
1942	229.7	182.6	125.8	172.4	133.2	315.0	72.9	187.2	122.7
1943	281.0	186.7	150.5	181.1	155.2	312.4	89.9	195.6	143.7
1944	303.9	193.5	157.1	190.4	159.6	297.4	102.2	204.1	148.9
1945	314.3	199.8	157.3	201.0	156.4	294.3	106.8	214.5	146.5
1946	322.9	239.1	135.0	229.1	140.9	306.1	105.5	242.9	132.9
1947	321.9	242.5	132.7	227.0	141.8	347.3	92.7	243.0	132.5
1948	295.9	216.4	136.7	201.3	147.0	381.8	77.5	219.2	135.0
1949	272.4	218.8	124.5	198.7	137.1	374.7	72.7	216.2	126.0
1950	248.7	207.7	119.7	188.6	131.9	348.8	71.3	204.6	121.6
1951	207.9	206.5	100.7	191.2	108.7	322.5	64.5	204.6	101.6
1952	226.7	188.4	120.3	174.8	129.7	298.2	76.0	187.3	121.0
1953	204.6	186.7	109.6	168.4	121.5	274.3	74.6	179.3	114.1

TABLE G-VII

Intercity Passenger Transportation:
Output, Employment, and Output per Employee, 1919–53

	Output	Employment	Output per Employee
	INTERCITY BUS LINES (1929 = 100)		
1919	10.2	25.1	40.8
1929	100.0	100.0	100.0
1937	151.5	76.2	198.8
1948	346.0	164.2	210.7
1953	288.7	141.2	204.5
	CLASS I INTERCITY MOTOR CARRIERS OF PASSENGERS (1947 = 100)		
1943	97.8	83.8	116.7
1944	107.0	89.4	119.7
1945	108.2	94.5	114.5
1946	107.5	103.9	103.5
1947	100.0	100.0	100.0
1948	105.8	100.7	105.1
1949	93.5	95.8	97.6
1950	84.2	87.3	96.4
1951	90.9	87.7	103.6
1952	86.7	85.3	101.6
1953	83.3	85.3	97.7

TABLE G-VIII

Intercity Motor Trucking: Output, Employment, and
Output per Employee, 1919–53
(1947 = 100)

	Output	Employment	Output per Employee
1919	0.7	15.0	4.7
1929	10.4	56.9	18.3
1937	36.0	65.3	55.1
1939	52.1	65.5	79.5
1942	74.5	89.7	83.1
1943	76.3	93.6	81.5
1944	72.3	85.3	84.8
1945	72.4	85.9	84.3
1946	80.8	93.2	86.7
1947	100.0	100.0	100.0
1948	123.9	107.2	115.6
1949	127.1	108.3	117.4
1950	174.2	129.7	134.3
1951	191.8	143.1	134.0
1952	187.9	150.1	125.2
1953	203.0	160.3	126.6

TABLE G-IX

Waterway Transportation:
Output, Persons Engaged, and Output per Person, 1869–1953
(1929 = 100)

	Output	Persons Engaged	Output per Person
1869	11.0	60.7	18.1
1879	11.8	62.4	18.9
1889	16.8	54.5	30.8
1899	24.4	52.2	46.7
1906	39.2	62.3	62.9
1916	54.6	78.3	69.7
1919	77.6	105.1	73.8
1929	100.0	100.0	100.0
1930	89.1	94.9	93.9
1931	74.0	86.4	85.6
1932	60.2	78.0	77.2
1933	68.6	80.2	85.5
1934	73.1	86.4	84.6
1935	76.1	88.7	85.8
1936	84.6	85.3	99.2
1937	95.7	90.4	105.9
1938	78.8	80.8	97.5
1939	86.4	84.7	102.0
1940	99.4	85.9	115.7
1941	n.a.	86.4	...
1942	n.a.	64.4	...
1943	n.a.	83.6	...
1944	n.a.	123.7	...
1945	n.a.	148.6	...
1946	n.a.	120.3	...
1947	175.1	98.3	178.1
1948	163.9	96.0	170.7
1949	150.2	84.2	178.4
1950	160.2	77.4	207.0
1951	189.9	85.3	222.6
1952	176.3	85.3	206.7
1953	169.4	81.9	206.8

n.a. = not available.

TABLE G-X

Airline Transportation:
Output, Persons Engaged, and Output per Person, 1929–53
(1947 = 100)

	Output	Persons Engaged	Output per Person
1929	0.5	2.3	22.6
1930	1.3	3.5	37.1
1931	1.5	5.5	27.3
1932	1.8	6.8	26.5
1933	2.4	7.2	33.3
1934	2.8	7.7	36.4
1935	4.6	8.9	51.7
1936	6.3	11.0	57.3
1937	7.1	13.0	54.6
1938	8.0	15.0	53.3
1939	10.6	17.6	60.2
1940	15.2	22.9	66.4
1941	20.4	29.3	69.6
1942	24.7	41.0	60.2
1943	31.7	55.4	57.2
1944	42.6	56.6	75.3
1945	60.9	63.9	95.3
1946	87.1	98.8	88.2
1947	100.0	100.0	100.0
1948	104.5	96.4	108.4
1949	117.3	95.2	123.2
1950	136.0	95.2	142.9
1951	171.2	108.4	157.9
1952	199.4	124.1	160.7
1953	228.5	132.5	172.5

555

TABLE G-XI

Pipe Line Transportation:
Output, Persons Engaged, and Output per Person,
1919, 1929, and 1937–53
(1929 = 100)

	Output	Persons Engaged	Output per Person
1919	20.7	51.1	40.5
1929	100.0	100.0	100.0
1937	145.6	103.2	141.1
1938	137.5	92.8	148.2
1939	138.9	88.4	157.1
1940	146.8	92.0	159.6
1941	168.5	95.3	176.8
1942	184.0	98.7	186.4
1943	216.3	99.9	216.5
1944	242.1	100.2	241.6
1945	236.0	101.2	233.2
1946	232.6	110.0	211.5
1947	255.5	115.5	221.2
1948	284.6	121.9	233.5
1949	279.8	116.8	239.6
1950	324.7	111.7	290.7
1951	388.0	116.0	334.5
1952	406.1	117.7	345.0
1953	430.3	113.4	379.5

TABLE G-XII

Transportation: Persons Engaged and Manhours, by Group, 1929

	Persons Engaged (thousands)	Manhours (millions)
Railroads	1,845	4,641
Local railways and bus lines		
Electric railways	239	621
Bus lines	41	107
Intercity motor transport		
Bus lines	45	118
Trucking	133	349
Waterways	168	411
Airlines	2	5
Pipe lines	25	67
All other[a]	553	1,630
Total	3,051	7,949

[a] Comprises local motor transport and services allied to transportation.

APPENDIX H

Communications and Public Utilities

THIS segment, as defined by the National Income Division of the Commerce Department, consists of Telephone, telegraph, and communication services not elsewhere classified (SIC Major Group 48); Radio broadcasting and television (Major Group 77); Electric and gas utilities (Groups 491–493); and Local utilities and public services not elsewhere classified (Groups 494–97).

Indexes of output and of total factor inputs have been prepared for the major components: the two communications groups, the two gas utility groups, and the electric utilities. Indexes of output, input, and productivity were computed for the aggregate of the five covered groups and are presented in Table H-II. Indexes of the same variables are shown for the segment as a whole in Table H-I; output and capital estimates for the segments were obtained by means of coverage adjustments.

The magnitude of the uncovered groups is indicated in Table H-1 in terms of the national income estimates used for coverage adjustments after

TABLE H-1

Communications and Public Utilities:
Relative Importance of Covered and Uncovered Groups, 1929 and 1953

	National Income			
	1929		1953	
	millions of dollars	per cent	millions of dollars	per cent
Covered groups	2,756	96.2	9,357	93.5
Telephone, telegraph, and related services	1,125	39.3	4,116	41.1
Gas and electric utilities	1,631	56.9	5,241	52.4
Uncovered groups	108	3.8	650	6.5
Radio broadcasting and television	28	1.0	491	4.9
Local utilities and public services, n.e.c.	80	2.8	159	1.6
Total	2,864	100.0	10,007	100.0

n.e.c. = not elsewhere classified.

557

1929. Coverage adjustments prior to 1929 were based on employment estimates which were prepared for all components throughout. Whereas radio broadcasting was nonexistent before the 1920's, local utilities and public services were of increasing importance going back in time.

The Telephone Industry

The basic data used to obtain output, input, and productivity estimates (Table H-IV) are from the decennial censuses of 1880 and 1890, the quinquennial *Census of Telephones and Telegraph* (in the *Census of Electrical Industries*) 1902-37, and the Federal Communications Commission's *Statistics of the Communications Industry in the United States*, which has been issued annually since 1939 and contains series back to 1926. The data cover only public systems and lines in the continental United States; they do not include lines maintained by companies for their private use or systems operated by federal, state, or municipal governments. The coverage has varied slightly over the years. The decennial censuses of 1880 and 1890 and the *Census of Telephones, 1902* attempted to include data for all systems and lines; those of 1907, 1912, and 1917 covered only systems with an annual income of $5,000 or more; those of 1922 and 1927, systems with $10,000 or more annual income; and those of 1932 and 1937, all systems. The statistics of the Federal Communications Commission are less inclusive than the Census data. Detailed information is compiled for Class A and Class B carriers.[1] The Commission estimates that on the basis of revenues and assets reporting carriers account for more than 95 per cent of the entire industry.[2] Fortunately, all data used, both from Census and FCC sources, could be adjusted to provide continuity since overlapping data are available for years in which coverage changed.

OUTPUT

An output index was obtained by weighting the two categories, local message units and toll and long-distance message units, by average unit revenues in each in the following pairs of years: 1899–1917, 1917–29, 1929–37, 1937–48, 1948–53. Noncensus years during 1899–1926 were interpolated by means of an output index computed by Solomon Fabricant.[3] Fabricant's annual index, 1880–1939, was based on data supplied by the American Telephone & Telegraph Company. The noncensus years during 1880–1902 were obtained by multiplying Fabricant's output

---

[1] Class A carriers are those with annual operating revenues exceeding $100,000; Class B, those with revenues between $50,000 and $100,000.

[2] See *Seventeenth Annual Report for Fiscal Year, 1951*, Federal Communications Commission, p. v.

[3] *Labor Savings in American Industry, 1899–1939*, Occasional Paper 23, New York (NBER), 1945, p. 49.

index for those years by a series obtained as the ratio of our employment index (based on Census) to Fabricant's employment index in census years, interpolated linearly.

There are a number of supplementary elements of production which should be weighted into an over-all telephone industry output index, were it possible to develop adequate physical-unit measures and appropriate weights.

Examples are various types of miscellaneous telephone services such as private-line services, radio and television program transmission, teletypewriter services, and directory service. Even more difficult to evaluate and weight into a telephone output index would be the factor of "readiness to serve." The security and protective features of having communication facilities at hand in case of sudden illness, fire, and other emergencies is another element of telephone service.[4]

MANHOURS WORKED

The employment index is based on the number of employees in the industry as reported in the various censuses and, more recently, by the Federal Communications Commission. The latter series is compiled jointly with the Bureau of Labor Statistics. Coverage adjustments were made to obtain comparability. Noncensus years were interpolated by means of Fabricant's employment index.[5]

Average hours worked per week in the telephone industry for 1937–53 are the estimates of the Bureau of Labor Statistics. This series was extrapolated back to 1914 by average hours worked in the electric utility industry.[6] Extrapolation back from 1914 to 1880 was by means of average hours in the manufactured gas industry, the Aldrich Report series of average daily hours in the gas industry[7] being used to extrapolate from 1890 to 1880.

We were able to test the reasonableness of the figure for average hours worked per week in 1915 as obtained by the above procedure against the findings of an independent study, made by the United States Commission on Industrial Relations,[8] of wages and hours in nine cities throughout the country, and data obtained by communication with the American Telephone & Telegraph Company. Our estimate for 1915 is 45.3 hours

---

[4] Based on communication with John C. Swartley, chief statistician, American Telephone & Telegraph Co.

[5] *Op. cit.*, p. 49.

[6] Jacob M. Gould, *Output and Productivity in the Electric and Gas Utilities, 1889–1942*, New York (NBER), 1946, p. 70, for 1917–37. For 1914–17, see section on electric utilities in this appendix.

[7] *Wholesale Prices, Wages, and Transportation*, Committee on Finance, Senate Report No. 1394, 52d Cong., 2d sess., 1893, Part I, pp. 178–79.

[8] Nelle B. Curry, *Investigation of the Wages and Conditions of Telephone Operating*, 1915.

per week, the Commission's study gives an average of 45 hours, and A.T. & T. data indicate an average 44-hour week.

CAPITAL

The index of constant-dollar capital stock is based on Ulmer's[9] estimates of the value of plant and equipment in 1929 dollars for 1880–1950. A two-year moving average was required in order to center the data, which are as of the end of each year. Ulmer first derived a series on gross capital expenditures in current dollars. Estimates of expenditures for the entire industry for 1913–50 were obtained from the American Telephone & Telegraph Company. For 1880–1912, Census data and data shown in the Federal Communications Commission's *Telephone Investigation*, Exhibits 1360-A and 1366-A, were used. Adjustments were made for write-ups and write-downs and to exclude land. Retirements for 1880–1912 were estimated on the basis of depreciation rates and the average ratio between depreciation and retirements for 1913–17. For 1880 a depreciation rate of 10 per cent was assumed (based on A.T. & T. estimates). The rate for 1950 was obtained as an average of the rates prescribed for ten companies by the Federal Communications Commission. Rates for intervening years were interpolated linearly. Annual capital expenditures for 1880–1912 were obtained as sums of the annual changes in the value of plant and equipment and estimated retirements.

Ulmer obtained a series on gross capital expenditures in constant 1929 dollars by deflating the current-dollar series by an index of construction costs. This index for 1915–50 is a weighted average of indexes for four components: telephone apparatus, wages in the building trades, commercial buildings, and telephone poles in place. For years prior to 1915, the index is based on three series: electrical equipment, construction materials, and wages in the building trades.

Beginning with the assumption of zero physical assets at the end of 1877, Ulmer arrived at his series on the value of physical assets by subtracting from his cumulative gross capital expenditures, cumulative retirements and depreciation, all in constant dollars. We extended Ulmer's series using his methods, and data on the value of plant and annual additions to plant published by the Federal Communications Commission.[10]

TOTAL INPUT

The method used in combining labor and capital inputs to obtain total input is the same as that described in Appendix A. The subperiods used for this group are 1880–90, 1890–1902, 1902–12, 1912–22, 1922–29,

---

[9] Melville J. Ulmer, *Capital in Transportation, Communications, and Public Utilities: Its Formation and Financing*, Princeton University Press (for NBER), 1960.

[10] *Statistics of the Communications Industry in the United States*, annual issues.

1929–37, 1937–48, 1948–53. Estimates of the compensation of labor and capital are from Census data for 1922 and prior years, except that labor compensation for 1880 and 1890 had to be estimated from Census employment figures for those years and wage rates obtained from the Aldrich Report[11] for 1880 and from Douglas[12] for 1890. For subsequent years, labor and capital compensation estimates are based on reports of the Federal Communications Commission, adjusted to the 1929 Commerce Department levels.[13] The relative weights are shown in Table H-2.

TABLE H-2

Telephone Industry:
Relative Weights of Labor and Capital Inputs
Subperiods, 1880–1953
(per cent)

	Labor	Capital
1880–90	55	45
1890–1902	58	42
1902–12	61	39
1912–22	60	40
1922–29	63	37
1929–37	73	27
1937–48	85	15
1948–53	86	14

The Telegraph Industry

The same basic sources (Census and FCC) were used to obtain estimates in both the telegraph and telephone industries. The first telegraph census was taken in 1880 (but included data for 1870), and the second, in 1902, after which they were taken quinqennially to 1937. The statistics relate to commercial systems operated in the continental United States; they exclude government systems, traffic of press associations or newspapers over private or leased wires, and telegraph systems owned and operated by railroads (although supplemental tables are available on the excluded systems). Relevant series for the private industry so defined are presented in Table H-V.

OUTPUT

The measure of output was computed from data on the numbers of message units for the three basic types of transmission—domestic, ocean-cable, and radiotelegraph. Average unit revenues in the terminal years of the follow-

[11] *Op. cit.*, p. 173.
[12] Paul H. Douglas, *Real Wages in the United States, 1890–1926*, Boston, Houghton Mifflin, 1930, p. 334.
[13] *National Income Supplement, 1954, Survey of Current Business*, Dept. of Commerce, p. 176.

561

ing subperiods were used as weights: 1902–12, 1912–22, 1922–29, 1929–37, 1937–48, 1948–53. The 1902 relative weights were used for the earlier periods. Total messages for 1880 were estimated by assuming that the relationship existing between Western Union revenues and total revenues also applied to message units (in 1880 Western Union accounted for 76.6 per cent of the total revenues in the industry). Western Union data were used for interpolations between census years until annual data became available from the FCC reports beginning in 1926.

MANHOURS WORKED

The index of manhours was obtained as the product of the indexes of employment and of average hours worked per employee. Employment estimates before 1927 were based on the censuses; figures for noncensus years prior to 1927 were interpolated by a series on the number of telegraph offices. Estimates of total offices for the industry had to be obtained by interpolating ratios of Western Union offices to the total in census years and applying the ratios to the relevant Western Union data for intercensal years. Employment estimates since 1927 have been published by the Federal Communications Commission.[14]

Average hours worked per week for the period since 1943 are the estimates of the Bureau of Labor Statistics; extrapolation to earlier years was based on hours worked in the telephone industry.

CAPITAL

The index of the stock of capital was constructed in several stages. We started with a series on the gross book value of plant and equipment. For 1880–1922 these data were available for census years. Noncensus years were interpolated by means of data on the value of Western Union plant and equipment. Federal Communications Commission estimates were used for 1927 and subsequent years.

The second step was to estimate accumulated depreciation and thus, by subtraction from gross book values, to obtain net book values. Accumulated depreciation was available for 1927–53 from the Federal Communications Commission's annual publications. For 1880–1922 net book value estimates were extrapolated by gross book value.

The third step was to deflate the net book value of plant and equipment to arrive at a constant (1929)-dollar series. To construct such a deflator, it was necessary to obtain annual estimates of the prices of plant and equipment and to estimate the distribution of each year's net stock by year of acquisition in order to be able to weight the price indexes appropriately. This involved estimates of gross capital outlays and of the average length of life of the fixed assets involved.

[14] *Statistics of the Communications Industry in the United States,* annual issues.

In view of the similarities between the two industries, Ulmer's price index for telephone plant and equipment was used, extrapolated prior to 1879 by construction costs in manufactured gas (see below). *Bulletin "F"* of the Internal Revenue Service[15] gives the average composite useful life for telegraph land-lines as thirty-three years, and that for ocean-cable systems, as sixty-seven years. A weighted average useful life was computed for 1929, 1932, 1937, 1948, and 1953, using as weights the gross book value of plant and equipment for land-lines and for ocean-cable systems. On the basis of such calculations a forty-year composite life was considered reasonable.

Estimates of capital outlays in the telegraph industry, 1915–53, are available from the Department of Commerce.[16] Estimates for 1840–1914 were made by extrapolating back by a series on expenditures in the manufactured gas industry. This is not as farfetched a procedure as it may seem, since the outlay estimates are used merely as a basis for weighting price deflators for the book value of capital in the telegraph industry.

By depreciating each year's capital outlays over a forty-year period and summing in each year the depreciated capital outlays remaining from all previous years, a percentage distribution of the current stock (at original cost) by year of acquisition is obtained. When these percentages are applied to the price index numbers for the current and preceding forty years, the appropriate book value deflator emerges.

TOTAL INPUT

The same methods were used to combine labor and capital inputs as explained in the notes to the electric utility industry (see below). The subperiods are the same as those used in obtaining the weighted output index. The relative returns to labor and capital are from the Commerce Department for 1929–53[17]; from Census data, for 1880–1922. The latter were adjusted to the Commerce level in order to provide a consistent series throughout. The relative weights are shown in Table H-3.

The Communications Group

In order to have a picture of productivity in communications as a whole, the output and input indexes for the telephone and the telegraph industries were combined. Based on the previously described methods and on the sources noted for each component, the relative weights for the various subperiods are shown in Table H-4. The productivity summary for the communications group is presented in Table H-III.

[15] *Bulletin "F": Income Tax Depreciation and Obsolescence, Estimated Useful Lives and Depreciation Rates,* Rev. Ed. (July 1942), 1942, p. 66.
[16] *Construction Volume and Costs, 1915–53,* May 1954, Statistical Supplement, *Construction and Building Materials,* p. 9.
[17] *National Income Supplement, 1954,* p. 176.

TABLE H-3

Telegraph Industry:
Relative Weights of Labor and Capital Inputs,
Subperiods, 1880–1953
(per cent)

	Labor	Capital
1880–90	57	43
1890–1902	64	36
1902–12	74	26
1912–22	78	22
1922–29	77	23
1929–37	84	16
1937–48	96	4
1948–53	91	9

TABLE H-4

Communications: Relative Weights of Industry Output and Inputs,
Subperiods, 1880–1953
(per cent)

	1880–1902	1902–1912	1912–1922	1922–1929	1929–1937	1937–1948	1948–1953
Output							
Telephone	90	85	85	85	86	85	85
Telegraph	10	15	15	15	14	15	15
Total Input							
Telephone	85	83	85	85	86	85	83
Telegraph	15	17	15	15	14	15	17
Labor Input							
Telephone	85	80	82	82	84	83	82
Telegraph	15	20	18	18	16	17	18
Capital Input							
Telephone	86	88	91	90	91	95	89
Telegraph	14	12	9	10	9	5	11

OUTPUT

An index of output for the combined telephone and telegraph industries
was obtained by weighting the output index for each by national income
originating per unit of output, using Marshall-Edgeworth weights for the
subperiods given in Table H-4. The national income originating in each
industry was obtained simply by adding the returns to labor and to capital
for any given year (see notes for the individual industries).

564

The combined indexes of manhours and of capital stock were computed by weighting the individual manhour and capital indexes by compensation per unit of labor and capital input respectively, using the Marshall-Edgeworth formula for the same subperiods as detailed in Table H-4.

The combined index of total input was obtained by weighting the two indexes of total factor input by the average national income originating in each industry per unit of total factor input for the successive pairs of key years.

The Electric Utility Industry

The definition of the electric utility industry employed by the Bureau of the Census in its quinquennial *Census of Electrical Industries* (1902–37) includes privately owned utilities, municipally owned utilities, cooperatives and power districts, federal and state projects, and "other."[18] Although our concern is with the private segment of the industry, this was well over 90 per cent of the total until the early 1930's. Beginning with 1932, we have linked to a series from which public power production was excluded. Indexes of output, inputs, and productivity ratios are presented in Table H-VI.

OUTPUT

For 1904–32, the output estimates are those prepared by Gould and based on the censuses. His output indexes were constructed in two stages. For 1902–17 he first computed an unweighted index for the census years based on the number of kilowatt-hours generated. A true weighted output index could not be obtained for years prior to 1917 since prices charged to the various types of consumer units were not available. Alternative assumptions were then made: (1) that the relative prices for the three basic consuming units (light, power, and rail) were the same in 1902 as in 1917; (2) that the prices in 1902 were the same for all types of consumers. On these assumptions, two separate indexes of kilowatt-hours sold were constructed for 1917 on a 1902 base, using Marshall-Edgeworth price weights. An arithmetic average of the two indexes was used as the weighted output index. For the intervening census years, 1907 and 1912, the weighted index numbers were obtained by multiplying the unweighted output index by the arithmetically interpolated differences between the 1902 and 1917 ratios of weighted to unweighted indexes.[19]

Output indexes for census years 1917, 1922, and 1927 were obtained by weighting (Marshall-Edgeworth formula) kilowatt-hour sales by unit

[18] For a detailed definition, see *Census of Electrical Industries, 1937*, Vol. I, *Electric Light and Power Industry*, pp. 2 and 16.
[19] Gould, *op. cit.*, pp. 20, 26, 145, and 146.

prices for the categories of light, power, and rail. For 1927, 1932, 1937, and 1942 more detailed categories were available for weighting—farm, domestic, small commercial, large commercial, municipal street lighting, street and interurban railroad, street and electrified railroad, and "other."[20]

The weighted output index obtained by linking the chains described above was interpolated as follows to yield an annual series: for 1912–19, an annual series on the output of all public and private agencies in *Electrical World*, September 9, 1922, was used; for 1920–27, Federal Power Commission data were used;[21] for 1926–42, a Marshall-Edgeworth-weighted output index (using the eight categories mentioned above) based on Edison Electric Institute data was used.[22]

Gould's output indexes for 1899–1903 and 1933–42 were not used because a series recently computed by Ulmer was better suited to our needs.[23] Ulmer's series covers 1887–1950. His output index for 1887, 1892, 1897, and 1902 is based on total energy generated less losses as published in *Electrical World*, September 9, 1922. Intervening years were derived by geometric interpolation. Ulmer linked his index to Gould's in 1902, after adjusting the latter's 1902 index from a census-year (June 30, 1902) to a calendar-year basis.

Ulmer's index for 1932–50 is here described. Applying the Marshall-Edgeworth formula with 1932 as a base, he computed an index number for 1937, using sales data from the *Census of Electrical Industries* and a classification of sales into residential, commercial and industrial, and other. Output by government systems was excluded, as it had begun to increase in importance relative to the total. With 1937 as a base and using the same sales categories, Ulmer computed index numbers for 1942, 1947, and 1950 from Federal Power Commission statistics of Class A and Class B utilities. Intervening years 1932–37 were interpolated by Federal Power Commission data on current generated; 1937–50, by the Commission's series on sales to ultimate consumers by Class A and Class B utilities. We extended Ulmer's index to 1953, using his methods and sources.

MANHOURS WORKED

Numbers of wage and salary earners employed in census years 1902–37 were taken from the quinquennial *Census of Electrical Industries*, on a basis comparable with the output measures. In both electric and gas utilities, proprietors of unincorporated enterprises were negligible. Kuznets'

---

[20] *Ibid.*, pp. 146–47.
[21] *Electric Power Statistics, 1920–1940*, FPCS-20, 1941, Appendix, 4.
[22] Gould, *op. cit.*, p. 148.
[23] *Op. cit.*

annual series on employment in private electric utilities, 1917–32, was used to interpolate between census years.[24] The interpolator from 1932 to 1937 was the Bureau of Labor Statistics index of employment in private electric utilities.[25] For subsequent years employment was taken from the Bureau of Labor Statistics. For intercensal years, 1902–17, employment was assumed to grow logarithmically. The 1902–07 annual rate of change in employment was assumed to apply to the three earlier years back to 1899.

Average hours worked per week for 1917–31 were obtained from National Industrial Conference Board publications.[26] The data subsequent to 1931 are from the Bureau of Labor Statistics.[27]. Estimates prior to 1917 were extrapolated by the estimates of average hours worked per week in the manufactured gas industry.

The manhour index is simply the product of the corresponding employment and average hours indexes. Because Gould adjusted output to include electricity produced and sold by electric railways, it was necessary to make a corresponding adjustment to the manhours series since the underlying employment index does not include electric railway employees engaged in producing electricity. To obtain the more inclusive manhour series, we assumed that labor productivity was the same for employees working in electricity-producing departments of electric railways as for regular utility employees. Subsequent to 1926 no adjustment was required since electric departments of electric railways were insignificant in comparison to the total.

CAPITAL

The index of the stock of capital is given by Ulmer. He derived an annual series on gross private capital expenditures back to the inception of the industry, 1880, using Census data, the *Fourteenth Annual Report of the Commissioner of Labor* (1899), Edison Electric Institute data, Federal Power Commission reports, and other supplementary studies. He adjusted the data to exclude land and to eliminate industry write-ups and write-downs of fixed assets.

The gross capital expenditures series was converted to constant 1929 dollars by use of a price index made up of two segments: (1) for 1880–1911, the composite index consisted of (a) an index of the cost of electric equip-

---

[24] Simon Kuznets, *National Income and Its Composition, 1919–38*, New York (NBER), 1941, pp. 676–710.

[25] Gould, *op. cit.*, p. 70.

[26] *The Economic Almanac for 1942–43*, p. 356; and M. A. Beney, *Wages, Hours, and Employment in the United States, 1914–36*, 1936, p. 162.

[27] *Handbook of Labor Statistics, 1947 Edition*, Bulletin 697, p. 126; *Hours and Earnings in the United States, 1932–40*, Bulletin 916, p. 81; *Hours and Earnings*, Annual Supplement Issue, April 1953, pp. 44–45; *Monthly Labor Review*, June 1954.

ment, from Shaw,[28] extrapolated back to 1880 by the Aldrich Report index for metals and implements, excluding pocket knives (weight 5), (b) an index of the cost of construction materials from Shaw (weight 3), and (c) an index of wages in the building trades, from Aldrich Report and Bureau of Labor Statistics series (weight 2); (2) for 1911–53, the Handy index of public utility construction costs was used.[29]

Capital consumption was estimated using a seventeen-year life for equipment installed prior to 1900 and a thirty-seven-year life for equipment installed subsequent to 1919. The average life for the intervening twenty years was obtained by straight-line interpolation.

Ulmer's estimates were extended through 1953, using continuations of his series and following his methods. The series thus computed as the basis for our capital index is one which shows the movement over time of net fixed assets, expressed in constant (1929) dollars. Although inventories are not included, they are so small relative to fixed capital that total real stocks may be assumed to move closely with the latter.

TOTAL INPUT

The manhour and capital stock indexes were combined using the Marshall-Edgeworth formula for six subperiods. The weights used are the relative average unit compensations of the two factors, capital and labor, in the terminal years of each subperiod, as shown in Table H-5.

TABLE H-5

Electric Utilities:
Relative Weights of Labor and Capital Inputs,
Subperiods, 1899–1953
(per cent)

	Labor	Capital
1899–1912	54	46
1912–19	58	42
1919–29	48	52
1929–37	46	54
1937–48	55	45
1948–53	58	42

Unit labor compensation was obtained by dividing total salaries, wages, and supplements for each of the seven key years by the appropriate manhour index. For 1902 and 1912, wage and salary data are from the *Census of Electrical Industries*; for 1919, 1929, and 1937, they are from Kuznets; for 1948 and 1953, they are from Federal Power Commission

[28] William H. Shaw, *Value of Commodity Output since 1869*, New York (NBER), 1947.
[29] *Ulmer, op. cit.*, Table D-19.

data[30] for Class A and B privately owned companies, adjusted first to total coverage and then to the Commerce Department level.

The unit capital compensation estimates were obtained by dividing total capital compensation for each year by the index of the real net stock of capital. Capital compensation was taken to be the sum of net profits and interest paid, reduced by the sum of dividend and interest income received. Sources for obtaining capital compensation are the same as for labor compensation.

Manufactured Gas Utilities

The major sources of data for the productivity estimates for the manufactured gas industry (Table H-VIII) are the various censuses of manufactures (1849 was the first year for which data were given relating to manufactured gas); Gould, for 1899–1929; publications of the American Gas Association (A.G.A.), for 1929–53; and the Bureau of Labor Statistics, for series on average hours worked.

As noted by Gould, the Census attempts to include only gas plants that are predominantly manufacturing establishments. Since 1929, with the increase in sales of mixtures of manufactured and purchased natural gas, the separation of the manufactured from the natural gas industry has become difficult and the use of the Census definition impracticable. In order to provide a more continuous picture of the manufactured gas industry, the American Gas Association generally classifies a plant as manufacturing if about one-quarter or more of the mixture it sells is manufactured gas. Where possible it allocates sales of manufactured and natural gases by the same plant to the separate industries. This is possible where no mixing is involved. In such cases, the corresponding employment and capital data are also allocated.[31]

OUTPUT

In the period 1899–1929 Gould's output index was used. It was extrapolated back by *Census of Manufactures* data on value of product, deflated by Census estimates of the average value per 1000 cubic feet for 1899 and 1889, and extended back to 1869 by index numbers for the price of fuels given in the Aldrich Report.

The Gould index is based on Census data through 1929. The intercensal years, 1899–1929, were interpolated by an A.G.A. annual series on the quantity of gas sold. The index to 1919 was obtained by weighting quantities sold by unit prices for the categories of gas, by-product coke, and by-product tar, using the Marshall-Edgeworth formula, because no analysis of gas sales by type of consumer was available. For 1919–29 the

[30] *Statistics of Electric Utilities in the United States,* annual reports.
[31] For a fuller discussion of industry definition, see Gould, *op. cit.,* pp. 79–80.

categories used for weighting were residential gas sales, industrial-commercial gas sales, miscellaneous gas sales, by-product coke sales, and by-product tar sales.

Although Gould's index includes the period 1929–42 we have not used it subsequent to 1932, since better basic data have become available. The A.G.A. has revised its statistics from 1932 on,[32] stating sales in terms of therms (one therm being defined as a quantity of heat equivalent to 100,000 British thermal units), whereas they had previously been given in terms of cubic feet. (For further discussion of this point see section on the natural gas industry.) We computed a new index for 1932–53, using Marshall-Edgeworth weights and four sales categories (residential, commercial, industrial, and other). The series was adjusted for changing coverage, since miscellaneous by-product sales were not included. The index was linked to Gould's index in 1932.

MANHOURS WORKED

For 1899–1929, the employment estimates are from Gould,[33] who used Census data interpolated by A.G.A. series after 1919. Employment was extrapolated from 1899 to 1869 by the Census data for wage earners only. We interpolated noncensus years prior to 1919 by use of the average relationship of employment to output in census years in order to get segment totals, but productivity indexes are shown only for census years. Employment data for 1929–53 were obtained from A.G.A. *Gas Facts, 1953* and earlier statistical bulletins.

The average hours worked per week per employee are from Gould for 1914 and 1919–42. The years between 1914 and 1919 were interpolated by hours in the electric utility industry. Average hours in 1909 were estimated from *Census of Manufactures* data, using the same ratio of actual to standard as in 1914. The years from 1909 back to 1890 were obtained by extrapolation, using the Bureau of Labor Statistics prevailing hours series. Extrapolation back to 1869 was by the series for the industry from the Aldrich Report. Hours for 1943–48 are from the annual *Economic Almanac* of the National Industrial Conference Board. The BLS series for gas utilities or combined gas and electric utilities was used for 1949–53.

CAPITAL

The same methods were used in computing the index of the stock of capital in the manufactured gas industry as were used for the telegraph industry. A.G.A. data were available for 1929–53. Census data were used for prior years.

[32] See its annual publication, *Gas Facts*.
[33] *Op. cit.*, p. 120.

The price index used for the net book value deflator was the Handy-Whitman index of construction costs,[34] 1911–53, for the gas industry. The Handy-Whitman index was extrapolated back to 1869 by an index obtained by combining Kuznets' construction cost index with Shaw's equipment cost index, using weights of one and three, respectively.[35] These weights are based on the average ratio of the value of land and buildings to machinery and equipment in 1889, 1899, and 1904 (Census data). The Shaw-Kuznets index was extrapolated to 1840 by an average of Kuznets' index and an index of metals prices,[36] again using weights of one and three, respectively.

The series on annual construction expenditures used in computing the deflator was from the A.G.A. for 1945–53. This series was extrapolated to 1929 by means of the Commerce Department series on construction in the gas industry. The annual expenditures for 1915–29 were computed from the same Commerce source. Since the Commerce data include outlays for both natural and manufactured gas, an allocation was made by averaging two series, one obtained by multiplying the combined expenditures by the ratios of value of product in manufactured gas to the combined value of product in manufactured and natural gas, the other obtained by multiplying the combined expenditures by the ratios of physical output in the two industries. The resulting series was raised to the A.G.A. level. Estimates of average annual expenditures prior to 1914 were made using Census data on value of plant and equipment and estimating retirements on the basis of ratios of retirements to property investment that were computed from data published by Handy.[37]

TOTAL INPUT

The indexes of labor and capital were combined by the same methods as those used for the electric utility industry. Compensation of labor was obtained from Census data for 1899 to 1919; from Kuznets[38] for 1929 and 1937 (adjusted to include supplements to wages and salaries); and from the A.G.A. for 1948 and 1953 (also adjusted for supplements). Returns to capital, i.e., the sum of net profit and interest paid, were estimated from the same sources. The compensation estimates were then adjusted to Commerce levels as described in the previous section. Table H-6 gives the weights used to combine labor and capital inputs.

[34] Published currently in *Engineering News-Record* and in *Construction Volume and Costs* (annual) Statistical Supplement, *Construction and Building Materials*. Earlier data are in W. W. Handy, *The Yardstick of Public Utility Operations*, Baltimore, Williams & Wilkins, 1929.
[35] The Kuznets index is from his *National Product since 1869*, New York (NBER), 1946, and unpublished worksheets; Shaw, *op. cit.*, p. 295, col. 25a.
[36] *Wholesale Prices, Wages, and Transportation*, Part I, p. 92.
[37] *Op. cit.*, pp. 26–27.
[38] *National Income*, p. 362

TABLE H-6

Manufactured Gas Utilities:
Relative Weights of Labor and Capital Inputs,
Subperiods, 1899–1953
(per cent)

	Labor	Capital
1899–1909	60	40
1909–19	71	29
1919–29	74	26
1929–37	64	36
1937–48	77	23
1948–53	78	22

Natural Gas Utilities

For purposes of this study, we define the natural gas industry to include companies engaged in the transmission and distribution of natural gas and to exclude companies whose primary function is the production of such gas. The latter activity is classed as a mining operation. According to the SIC Manual, natural gas utilities include industries 4922–24. The productivity summary for this group is shown in Table H-IX.

OUTPUT

Our weighted output index for 1899–1932 is from Gould,[39] his source being successive issues of the *Minerals Yearbook* and *Mineral Resources* of the Bureau of Mines. For 1906–19 only two categories are available for weighting, domestic-commercial and industrial (including gas for field use and carbon black manufacture). For 1919–29 the classifications are domestic-commercial and industrial (excluding field use and carbon black manufacture). For 1929–31, the data are from the American Gas Association;[40] the classifications are domestic, commercial, and industrial. In going back of 1906, the weighted index was extrapolated by unweighted total consumption, including sales for field use and carbon black manufacture. This series was available back to 1882 from Arthur F. Burns.[41] From 1906 forward, the Marshall-Edgeworth formula was used in weighting the different groups.

Although Gould's output series runs to 1942, we recomputed the index for years subsequent to 1931 using the revised data of the American Gas

[39] *Op. cit.*, p. 103.

[40] *Statistical Bulletin 13*, "Comparative Statistics of the Natural Gas Industry, 1929–33," p. 1.

[41] *Production Trends in the United States since 1870*, New York (NBER), 1934, Appendix A, Table 44, col. 45.

Association.[42] An important change was in the unit of measurement of gas quantities. Quantity sold had previously been measured in cubic feet; since the revision it has been measured in therms. The superiority of the therm is that a given volume of gas, so measured, always has the same heat value—in other words, it provides a measure of output of standard quality. The cubic-foot measure, on the other hand, assigns the same output importance to any given volume of gas even though the heat value of two gases of equivalent volume may be considerably different. The difference in movement as a result of the recomputation is shown in Table H-7.

TABLE H-7

Natural Gas Utilities:
Comparison of Weighted Output Indexes, Using Cubic Feet
and Therms, 1932–42
(1929 = 100)

	Therms	Cubic Feet
1932	94.9	94.9
1933	90.8	92.1
1934	96.5	100.0
1935	105.9	107.9
1936	121.6	124.8
1937	131.9	132.1
1938	127.6	126.0
1939	139.3	135.8
1940	153.4	150.0
1941	163.6	159.9
1942	185.5	178.4

The weighted output index, then, for 1932–53 was obtained by combining the thermal values of sales to the four categories of consuming units (residential, commercial, industrial, and other) using Marshall-Edgeworth price weights and adjusting the annual chain index to the 1932–53 change in an index based on end-year weights.

MANHOURS WORKED

The employment figures for 1929–33 are from Gould; for 1934–53, directly from the A.G.A.[43] The employment statistics prior to 1929 are crude. Gould's basic estimate for 1899 is based on several tenuous assumptions; and for 1902, 1907, 1912, 1917, 1919, and 1925, we obtained natural gas employment as the difference between Gould's totals for manufactured and natural gas and his series on manufactured gas alone.[44] We obtained

42 *Gas Facts, 1953.*
43 *Gas Facts, 1953*; Gould, *op. cit.*, p. 123.
44 *Ibid.*, pp. 120, 125, and 136.

an annual series by using the relationship of employment to output for the years in which employment estimates are available. The estimating equation is $y = 5.6828 + 0.6795x$, where y represents computed employment and x, the weighted output index for natural gas.

For 1929–53, average hours worked per employee per year were obtained by dividing total manhours worked by the average number of employees during the year.[45] For years prior to 1929, hours of work were assumed to move in the same manner as in the manufactured gas industry.

CAPITAL

Although there is evidence that natural gas was used commercially as early as 1825 and industrially as early as 1840, investment in plant and equipment was negligible prior to 1880. Estimates of investment in the industry are available for 1880, 1907, and 1914.[46] By assuming geometric rates of growth for 1880–1907 and 1907–14, we computed an annual series on gross expenditures, 1880–1914. A series on construction expenditures in the natural and the manufactured gas industries combined, 1915–29, is contained in *Construction and Building Materials*. The total for the two industries was allocated between them as explained in the notes on the manufactured gas industry. The resulting series for natural gas was raised to the American Gas Association level.

Annual expenditures for 1945–53 are available from the A.G.A. *Gas Facts*. An average was computed of the annual ratios between the A.G.A. series and the Commerce series for 1945–53, and this average was applied to the Commerce series for 1929–44 to raise it to the A.G.A. level. Depreciation was estimated by assuming a fifty-year average composite useful life, the same as that used for manufactured gas.[47] The gross expenditures series thus obtained was converted to constant (1929) dollars using the Handy-Whitman price index (see manufactured gas section for a description). By cumulating gross capital expenditures from the inception of the industry and deducting cumulated depreciation, all in constant (1929) dollars, we arrived at estimates of the annual real net stock of plant and equipment, 1880–1941.

Since firm data on net fixed assets for 1941–53 were available from the A.G.A., these data were used for this period, after being deflated in accordance with the method described in the telegraph industry section. The two series were linked at 1941, thus giving us the continuous series,

[45] Data are from the American Gas Association, *Employee Accident Experience of the Gas Industry, 1954*, and from direct correspondence with the Association.

[46] Federal Trade Commission, TNEC Monograph No. 36, Senate Committee Print, 76th Cong., 3d sess., 1940; *Natural Gas Journal*, June 1915, p. 290; Natural Gas Association, *Proceedings*, 1907, No. 2.

[47] Cf. *Bulletin "F"*, which gives forty-seven years as an average useful life.

1880–1953, from which the capital index was computed and which is shown in Table H-IX beginning with 1899.

Labor and capital input were combined by the same method as that employed in the manufactured gas industry. Labor compensation, 1929–53, was estimated from A.G.A. data and adjusted to the Commerce level. For the key years 1899, 1909, and 1919, labor compensation was estimated by extrapolating the 1929 compensation by an index obtained as the product of the manhour index and an index of average hourly earnings, the latter assumed to be the same as for manufactured gas.

Capital compensation for 1937, 1948, and 1953 are from the A.G.A., adjusted to the Commerce level. The compensation for prior key years was obtained by using estimates of the capital stock in current prices and the 1937 rate of return on capital. Table H-8 gives the weights used in combining the indexes of labor and capital.

TABLE H-8

Natural Gas Utilities:
Relative Weights of Labor and Capital Inputs,
Subperiods, 1899–1953
(per cent)

	Labor	Capital
1899–1909	53	47
1909–19	51	49
1919–29	54	46
1929–37	58	42
1937–48	55	45
1948–53	55	45

Combined Gas Utilities

The separate industry indexes of output, manhours, capital, and total input were combined by the same methods as those used in the combination of the telephone and telegraph industries. Table H-9 gives the weights used; and Table H-VII gives the basic series for the gas industry as a whole.

Other Communications and Public Utilities

The concluding section of this appendix describes the methods used to estimate employment and manhours in radio broadcasting and television and in local utilities and public services not elsewhere classified. As indicated at the outset, these industries are a small part of the segment, and it was not feasible to estimate their output.

TABLE H-9

Gas Utilities: Relative Weights of Industry Output and Inputs,
Subperiods, 1899–1953
(per cent)

	1899–1909	1909–1919	1919–1929	1929–1937	1937–1948	1948–1953
Output						
Manufactured Gas	70	58	49	53	52	46
Natural Gas	30	42	51	47	48	54
Total Input						
Manufactured Gas	50	45	46	51	49	51
Natural Gas	50	55	54	49	51	49
Labor Input						
Manufactured Gas	53	53	53	53	58	60
Natural Gas	47	47	47	47	42	40
Capital Input						
Manufactured Gas	46	32	33	47	33	34
Natural Gas	54	68	67	53	67	66

RADIO BROADCASTING AND TELEVISION

The employment estimates from 1929 forward are those of the Commerce Department. Employment was approximately 4,000 in 1929 and, assuming the same rate of growth before 1929 as after, employment must have been negligible prior to 1926 (i.e., less than 1,000, although the industry was born around 1920). In order to obtain manhours, average hours worked by employees in the telephone and telegraph industry were used.

LOCAL UTILITIES AND PUBLIC SERVICES, NOT ELSEWHERE CLASSIFIED

As defined for national income purposes, this group consists of private water supply systems, sanitary services, steam supply systems, and irrigation systems (SIC Groups 494–97). We have used the Commerce Department estimates of employment from 1929 forward. Little direct information on employment in these groups exists for earlier years. We have broken down the estimated numbers of persons engaged in 1929 (30,000) into major categories, and extrapolated as follows in an effort to approximate, at least roughly, the employment trend in the group.

The category of private water companies, the main component in 1929 (but less important thereafter), was extrapolated by the deflated value of plant and equipment of waterworks as given for selected years from 1880 to 1922 by Kuznets.[48] The figures were extrapolated back to 1869 on the basis of the 1880–1900 trend and forward from 1922 to 1929 on the basis of estimates of the National Industrial Conference Board.[49] Employment on irrigation systems was extrapolated in the same manner. Employment in the remaining category, consisting principally of sanitary systems, was extrapolated on the basis of urban population.

In view of the small size of the group, and the uncertainties attaching to the estimates, annual interpolations were on a straight line. It was assumed that average hours worked per week were the same as in electric and gas utilities.

Segment Totals

Two productivity summaries were made for the segment. One is based on weighted averages of the output and input indexes for the five groups covered by direct estimates of output and capital input (Table H-II). The other purports to cover the segment as a whole (Table H-I); for key years, coverage adjustments were applied to the output indexes. Direct estimates of factor inputs were available for the entire segment.

THE COVERED PORTION OF THE SEGMENT

The output and input indexes for electric utilities, the communications group, and the gas utilities group were combined in order to obtain the productivity summary for the covered part of the segment. The factor compensation estimates, used for weights in successive pairs of key years beginning with 1899, have already been described, with one exception.

Since the censuses of the electric utilities and communications industries were taken quinquennially between 1902 and 1927, it was necessary to interpolate and extrapolate in order to obtain factor compensation estimates for the key years 1899, 1909, and 1919. This was done by computing the ratios of factor compensation estimated from the censuses to compensation estimates prepared by Martin.[50] The ratios were then interpolated linearly and applied to Martin's estimates for the key years. The 1902 ratio was applied to Martin's 1899 compensation estimates. As noted in the preceding sections, the levels of the compensation estimates were adjusted for continuity and consistency with the Commerce figures. The relative weights used to combine the group indexes in the subperiods are shown in Table H-10. The 1899–1909 weights were used for earlier years.

---

[48] *National Product since 1869*, Table IV-12, p. 231.

[49] *Historical Statistics of the United States, 1789–1945*, Dept. of Commerce, 1949, Series A 90, deflated.

[50] Robert F. Martin, *National Income in the United States, 1799–1938*, New York, National Industrial Conference Board, 1939.

TABLE H-10

Communications and Public Utilities, Covered Segment:
Relative Weights of Industry Output and Inputs, Subperiods, 1899–1953
(per cent)

	1899–1909	1909–1919	1919–1929	1929–1937	1937–1948	1948–1953
Output						
Electric	60	49	43	43	33	25
Telephone and telegraph	29	37	43	42	50	59
Gas	11	14	14	15	17	16
Total Input						
Electric	44	41	43	45	42	40
Telephone and telegraph	41	43	42	41	40	40
Gas	15	16	15	14	18	20
Labor Input						
Electric	33	36	36	34	33	33
Telephone and telegraph	51	48	49	51	50	48
Gas	16	16	15	15	17	19
Capital Input						
Electric	48	44	54	60	62	59
Telephone and telegraph	37	40	34	26	18	18
Gas	15	16	12	14	20	23

THE TOTAL SEGMENT

As indicated by Table H-1, five major groups accounted for the great bulk of the national income originating in the segment in 1929, but the proportion has not been stable. In order to adjust our index numbers for the aggregate of the five groups to full coverage in key years after 1929, we have multiplied by index numbers (1929 = 100) of ratios of national income in the segment as a whole to national income originating in the five covered groups. This procedure implies that national income per unit of output has shown the same movements in the uncovered as in the covered parts of the segment.

For key years prior to 1929, the coverage adjustment index was based on the ratios of total persons engaged in the segment to persons engaged in the covered part of the segment. Here the assumption is that output per person engaged moved in parallel fashion in both the covered and uncovered portions of the segment. The coverage adjustment is shown in Table H-11.

The method of estimating employment and manhours in the uncovered part of the segment has already been described. Estimates of real capital

TABLE H-11

Communications and Public Utilities: Adjustment Applied to
Output and Capital Input Indexes of Covered-Industry Aggregate
to Obtain Full-Segment Coverage, Key Years, 1869–1953
(1929 = 100)

	Adjustment Index numbers
1869	147.2
1879	134.3
1889	116.1
1899	109.1
1909	103.5
1919	100.9
1929	100.0
1937	101.1
1948	102.6
1953	102.9

NOTE: Adjustment index based on ratios of total employment in the segment to employment in the covered portion for 1929 and prior years, and on the corresponding national income ratios in 1929 and subsequent years.

stocks in the segment as a whole for 1929 and prior years are contained in Ulmer's study, where they are combined with capital stocks of the transportation segment. Totals for the two segments were segregated as described in Appendix G. After 1929, total capital input in the five groups was adjusted to full coverage by the ratios of total employment to employment in the groups covered by the capital estimates. This ratio showed only a slightly smaller rise between 1929 and 1953 than the index of the national income ratio.

TABLE H-I

Communications and Public Utilities:[a] Output, Inputs and Productivity Ratios, Key Years, 1869–1953
(1929 = 100)

	Output	Persons Engaged	Output per Person	Manhours	Output per Manhour	Labor Input	Output per Unit of Labor Input	Capital Input	Output per Unit of Capital Input	Total Factor Input	Total Factor Productivity
1869	0.9	3.4	26.1	4.7	18.8	4.2	21.0	3.0	29.3	3.6	24.4
1879	1.7	4.8	35.0	6.8	24.7	6.0	28.2	6.4	26.6	6.2	27.3
1889	3.2	9.3	34.9	12.8	25.4	11.4	28.4	10.3	31.5	10.8	30.0
1899	6.7	16.2	41.2	20.0	33.3	17.8	37.4	20.8	32.0	19.3	34.5
1909	22.6	35.6	63.4	42.0	53.8	40.5	55.8	42.8	52.8	41.6	54.3
1919	45.8	60.8	75.3	59.8	76.6	58.3	78.6	59.5	77.0	58.9	77.8
1929	100.0	100.0	100.0	100.0	100.0	100.0	100.0	100.0	100.0	100.0	100.0
1937	115.5	87.1	132.6	74.9	154.2	75.1	153.8	106.6	108.3	89.0	129.8
1948	249.5	124.0	201.2	107.6	231.9	108.9	229.1	130.5	191.2	121.4	205.5
1953	336.0	135.5	248.0	115.5	290.9	117.3	286.4	189.9	176.9	143.3	234.5

[a] Indexes for the sum of five groups (see Table H-II) adjusted for complete coverage of the segment, including radio broadcasting and television, and local utilities and public services not elsewhere classified.

TABLE H-II

Communications and Public Utilities: Output, Inputs, and Productivity Ratios, Aggregate of Five Groups, 1869–1953
(1929 = 100)

	Output	Persons Engaged	Output per Person	Manhours	Output per Manhour	Labor Input	Output per Unit of Labor Input	Capital Input	Output per Unit of Capital Input	Total Factor Input	Total Factor Productivity
1869	0.6	2.3	26.1	3.2	18.8	2.9	20.7	1.2	48.3	2.1	28.2
1879	1.3	3.6	35.0	5.1	24.7	4.6	27.3	2.9	43.6	3.8	33.4
1889	2.8	8.0	34.9	11.0	25.4	10.1	27.6	5.4	51.5	7.9	35.5
1899	6.1	14.8	41.2	18.3	33.3	16.3	37.4	15.8	38.6	15.7	38.9
1909	21.8	34.4	63.4	40.5	53.8	39.3	55.5	40.0	54.5	39.4	55.3
1919	45.4	60.3	75.3	59.3	76.6	57.7	78.7	53.2	85.3	56.4	80.5
1929	100.0	100.0	100.0	100.0	100.0	100.0	100.0	100.0	100.0	100.0	100.0
1930	99.9	99.8	100.1	100.4	99.5	96.1	104.0	108.6	92.0	100.8	99.1
1931	96.8	89.7	107.9	89.8	107.8	88.0	110.0	114.5	84.5	98.2	98.6
1932	87.4	79.7	109.7	74.3	117.6	73.2	119.4	115.4	75.7	89.6	97.5
1933	85.5	75.5	113.2	67.6	126.5	66.6	128.4	113.3	75.5	84.7	100.9
1934	90.0	76.6	117.5	63.7	141.3	63.7	141.3	110.0	81.8	81.7	110.2
1935	96.3	76.9	125.2	64.4	149.5	64.8	148.6	107.1	89.9	81.1	118.7
1936	107.5	81.2	132.4	69.4	154.9	70.4	152.7	105.4	102.0	84.0	128.0
1937	114.2	86.0	132.8	73.9	154.5	74.3	153.7	105.2	108.6	86.3	132.3
1938	111.4	82.4	135.2	70.4	158.2	71.1	156.7	106.0	105.1	84.2	132.3
1939	119.7	82.6	144.9	70.3	170.3	70.7	169.3	106.2	112.7	84.0	142.5
1940	130.3	85.4	152.6	73.2	178.0	74.1	175.8	106.9	121.9	86.7	150.3
1941	145.3	90.5	160.6	78.0	186.3	79.4	183.0	109.3	132.9	91.4	159.0
1942	158.7	89.8	176.7	78.1	203.2	78.0	203.5	110.2	144.0	90.8	174.8

(continued)

TABLE H-II (concluded)

	Output	Persons Engaged	Output per Person	Manhours	Output per Manhour	Labor Input	Output per Unit of Labor Input	Capital Input	Output per Unit of Capital Input	Total Factor Input	Total Factor Productivity
1943	176.2	86.5	203.7	78.1	225.6	78.3	225.0	111.2	158.5	91.3	193.0
1944	183.7	84.1	218.4	77.4	237.3	78.1	235.2	108.6	169.2	90.4	203.2
1945	189.3	86.1	219.9	78.9	239.9	81.6	232.0	108.1	175.1	92.9	203.8
1946	201.7	104.5	193.0	90.3	223.4	95.0	212.3	109.1	184.9	103.2	195.4
1947	224.7	111.6	201.3	94.4	238.0	99.7	225.4	115.7	194.2	108.4	207.3
1948	243.0	120.1	202.3	104.0	233.7	107.1	226.9	126.5	192.1	117.2	207.3
1949	249.6	121.0	206.3	103.2	241.9	104.3	239.3	138.3	180.5	117.7	212.1
1950	272.2	119.6	227.6	102.8	264.8	106.1	256.6	148.9	182.8	121.9	223.3
1951	293.4	123.0	238.5	106.1	276.5	108.9	269.4	160.3	183.0	127.3	230.5
1952	307.8	126.6	243.1	107.6	286.1	111.5	276.1	171.2	179.8	132.2	232.8
1953	326.5	130.2	250.8	110.8	294.7	113.9	286.7	182.6	178.8	137.0	238.3

TABLE H-III

Telephone and Telegraph Industries: Output, Inputs, and Productivity Ratios, 1879–1953
(1929 = 100)

	Output	Persons Engaged	Output per Person	Manhours	Output per Manhour	Labor Input	Output per Unit of Labor Input	Capital Input	Output per Unit of Capital Input	Total Factor Input	Total Factor Productivity
1879	1.3	3.4	39.8	4.9	27.5	3.8	35.3	4.6	29.1	4.0	33.5
1889	3.3	6.5	49.7	9.2	35.4	7.3	44.5	9.3	34.9	7.7	42.2
1899	8.0	12.3	65.4	15.2	52.9	14.1	56.7	22.2	36.0	16.7	47.9
1909	30.8	32.7	94.2	37.9	81.3	37.8	81.5	53.7	57.4	43.2	71.3
1919	48.0	61.7	77.8	60.0	80.0	59.6	80.5	55.7	86.2	58.8	81.6
1929	100.0	100.0	100.0	100.0	100.0	100.0	100.0	100.0	100.0	100.0	100.0
1930	95.8	91.2	105.0	92.1	104.0	91.6	104.6	115.7	82.8	97.0	98.8
1931	90.9	81.9	111.0	82.7	109.9	82.5	110.2	125.8	72.3	92.4	98.4
1932	80.4	73.1	110.0	69.0	116.5	69.1	116.4	127.2	63.2	82.3	97.7
1933	74.4	68.9	108.0	62.0	120.0	62.1	119.8	123.7	60.1	76.1	97.8
1934	76.7	70.0	109.6	58.4	131.3	58.1	132.0	118.3	64.8	71.9	106.7
1935	80.7	69.1	116.8	58.1	138.9	58.1	138.9	113.7	71.0	70.7	114.1
1936	87.8	73.2	119.9	63.0	139.4	62.9	139.6	110.7	79.3	73.8	119.0
1937	92.0	76.8	119.8	66.4	138.6	66.3	138.8	110.0	83.6	76.2	120.7
1938	91.9	72.9	126.1	63.0	145.9	63.2	145.4	111.6	82.3	73.5	125.0
1939	96.2	72.6	132.5	63.1	152.5	63.4	151.7	112.7	85.4	73.8	130.4
1940	102.2	76.6	133.4	67.3	151.9	67.6	151.2	115.4	88.6	78.2	130.7
1941	112.6	86.4	130.3	76.9	146.4	77.5	145.3	122.1	92.2	88.3	127.5
1942	119.7	89.4	133.9	80.3	149.1	81.0	147.8	129.4	92.5	92.7	129.1
1943	127.0	91.5	138.8	85.1	149.2	85.8	148.0	129.6	98.0	97.2	130.7

(continued)

TABLE H-III (concluded)

	Output	Persons Engaged	Output per Person	Manhours	Output per Manhour	Labor Input	Output per Unit of Labor Input	Capital Input	Output per Unit of Capital Input	Total Factor Input	Total Factor Productivity
1944	131.0	89.9	145.7	84.0	156.0	85.0	154.1	126.2	103.8	96.0	136.5
1945	141.4	96.6	146.4	89.1	158.7	90.4	156.4	125.0	113.1	101.0	140.0
1946	161.8	122.8	131.8	107.2	150.9	109.6	147.6	132.7	121.9	120.3	134.5
1947	173.6	128.6	135.0	107.2	161.9	109.8	158.1	153.1	113.4	123.1	141.0
1948	182.7	133.5	136.9	115.7	157.9	119.1	153.4	183.4	99.6	135.8	134.5
1949	185.8	126.6	146.8	107.9	172.2	111.1	167.2	210.0	88.5	130.2	142.7
1950	192.5	127.3	151.2	109.5	175.8	112.9	170.5	225.7	85.3	133.4	144.3
1951	195.7	131.9	148.4	113.9	171.8	117.6	166.4	238.5	82.1	139.3	140.5
1952	198.9	137.7	144.4	116.7	170.4	120.7	164.8	254.5	78.2	143.8	138.3
1953	204.5	139.8	146.3	118.7	172.3	122.9	166.4	273.6	74.7	147.8	138.4

TABLE H-IV

Telephone Industry: Output, Inputs, and Productivity Ratios, 1879–1953
(1929 = 100)

	Output	Persons Engaged	Output per Person	Manhours	Output per Manhour	Capital Input	Output per Unit of Capital Input	Total Factor Input	Total Factor Productivity
1879	0.15	0.6	25.0	0.8	18.8	0.5	31.3	0.6	23.1
1880	0.2	0.7	28.6	0.9	22.2	0.6	33.3	0.8	25.0
1881	0.3	0.8	37.5	1.1	27.3	1.1	27.3	1.1	27.3
1882	0.4	1.0	40.0	1.3	30.8	1.6	25.0	1.4	28.6
1883	0.5	1.1	45.5	1.5	33.3	2.0	25.0	1.6	31.2
1884	0.5	1.2	41.7	1.6	31.2	2.5	20.0	1.9	26.3
1885	0.6	1.2	50.0	1.6	37.5	2.9	20.7	2.0	30.0
1886	0.6	1.2	50.0	1.6	37.5	3.0	20.0	2.1	28.6
1887	0.7	1.4	50.0	1.9	36.8	2.9	24.1	2.2	31.8
1888	0.8	1.5	53.3	2.0	40.0	3.0	26.7	2.3	34.8
1889	0.9	1.6	56.2	2.1	42.9	3.4	26.5	2.5	36.0
1890	1.1	1.8	61.1	2.4	45.8	3.8	28.9	2.9	37.9
1891	1.2	2.0	60.0	2.7	44.4	4.1	29.3	3.2	37.5
1892	1.4	2.3	60.9	3.1	45.2	4.3	32.6	3.5	40.0
1893	1.3	2.5	52.0	3.3	39.4	4.6	28.3	3.8	34.2
1894	1.5	2.7	55.6	3.5	42.9	5.7	26.3	4.3	34.9
1895	1.9	3.2	59.4	4.1	46.3	7.7	24.7	5.4	35.2
1896	2.2	3.8	57.9	5.0	44.0	10.1	21.8	6.9	31.9
1897	2.7	4.8	56.2	6.1	44.3	12.4	21.8	8.4	32.1
1898	3.7	6.1	60.7	7.2	51.4	14.4	25.7	9.9	37.4
1899	5.6	8.3	67.5	10.0	56.0	17.0	32.9	12.6	44.4
1900	6.7	10.8	62.0	12.6	53.2	20.3	33.0	15.4	43.5
1901	9.1	13.5	67.4	16.6	54.8	23.5	38.7	19.2	47.4
1902	11.9	16.2	73.5	18.9	63.0	26.6	44.7	21.7	54.8

(continued)

TABLE H-IV (continued)

Telephone Industry: Output, Inputs, and Productivity Ratios, 1879–1953
(1929 = 100)

	Output	Persons Engaged	Output per Person	Manhours	Output per Manhour	Capital Input	Output per Unit of Capital Input	Total Factor Input	Total Factor Productivity
1903	13.4	17.9	74.9	21.2	63.2	30.5	43.9	24.6	54.5
1904	15.0	19.6	76.5	23.0	65.2	34.5	43.5	27.1	55.4
1905	18.7	24.0	77.9	28.1	66.5	38.8	48.2	31.9	58.6
1906	22.5	28.3	79.5	33.1	68.0	44.8	50.2	37.4	60.2
1907	26.3	30.0	87.7	35.1	74.9	50.1	52.5	40.6	64.8
1908	28.4	31.1	91.3	36.2	78.5	51.8	54.8	41.9	67.8
1909	29.9	32.1	93.1	37.2	80.4	51.3	58.3	42.3	70.7
1910	32.0	35.9	89.1	40.5	79.0	51.5	62.1	44.6	71.7
1911	33.4	39.7	84.1	43.7	76.4	52.5	63.6	47.0	71.1
1912	35.5	41.8	84.9	44.9	79.1	54.1	65.6	48.3	73.5
1913	36.9	45.5	81.1	47.4	77.8	55.4	66.6	50.4	73.2
1914	37.5	45.6	82.2	46.3	81.0	55.4	67.7	49.7	75.5
1915	41.3	45.6	90.6	46.0	89.8	54.2	76.2	49.1	84.1
1916	46.6	50.2	92.8	50.3	92.6	53.4	87.3	51.7	90.1
1917	49.8	55.8	89.2	55.4	89.9	54.3	91.7	55.4	89.9
1918	49.1	57.7	85.1	56.5	86.9	54.4	90.3	56.2	87.4
1919	48.3	59.6	81.0	57.8	83.6	52.8	91.5	56.7	85.2
1920	52.5	65.2	80.5	62.3	84.3	51.7	101.5	59.3	88.5
1921	55.1	67.2	82.0	65.7	83.9	51.4	107.2	61.5	89.6
1922	59.5	68.2	87.2	67.1	88.7	52.6	113.1	62.8	94.7
1923	66.5	73.3	90.7	71.7	92.7	55.9	119.0	67.0	99.3
1924	71.1	78.5	90.6	77.2	92.1	61.2	116.2	72.4	98.2
1925	75.9	80.9	93.8	80.0	94.9	67.4	112.6	76.2	99.6
1926	82.7	83.3	99.3	80.1	103.2	73.7	112.2	78.2	105.8

(continued)

TABLE H-IV (concluded)

Year									
1927	86.6	84.7	102.2	83.2	104.1	80.0	108.2	82.2	105.4
1928	92.7	90.4	102.5	88.4	104.9	87.3	106.2	88.1	105.2
1929	100.0	100.0	100.0	100.0	100.0	100.0	100.0	100.0	100.0
1930	96.5	89.5	107.8	90.3	106.9	116.3	83.0	96.5	100.0
1931	92.9	81.4	114.1	82.1	113.2	127.2	73.0	92.9	100.0
1932	83.3	73.5	113.3	69.4	120.0	129.1	64.5	83.7	99.5
1933	76.3	69.1	110.4	62.2	122.7	125.3	60.9	77.3	98.7
1934	78.5	69.2	113.4	57.6	136.3	119.5	65.7	72.5	108.3
1935	81.8	68.5	119.4	57.7	141.8	114.5	71.4	71.3	114.7
1936	88.8	72.7	122.1	62.5	142.1	111.3	79.8	74.2	119.7
1937	93.1	76.3	122.0	65.9	141.3	111.5	83.5	76.8	121.2
1938	94.0	73.9	127.2	64.0	146.9	113.2	83.0	75.3	124.8
1939	98.9	74.0	133.6	64.5	153.3	114.5	86.4	75.9	130.3
1940	106.1	78.5	135.2	69.1	153.5	117.7	90.1	80.7	131.5
1941	117.2	88.9	131.8	79.4	147.6	125.1	93.7	91.2	128.5
1942	125.3	92.7	135.2	83.6	149.9	132.9	94.3	96.3	130.1
1943	132.9	94.9	140.0	88.5	150.2	133.8	99.3	101.0	131.6
1944	137.3	94.1	145.9	88.6	155.0	130.4	105.3	100.5	136.6
1945	148.2	102.7	144.3	95.4	155.3	129.2	114.7	106.7	138.9
1946	173.5	135.4	128.1	118.9	145.9	137.4	126.3	129.7	133.8
1947	186.9	143.6	130.2	119.6	156.3	159.3	117.3	133.5	140.0
1948	199.2	151.0	131.9	131.8	151.1	191.5	104.0	149.3	133.4
1949	204.0	144.4	141.3	123.8	164.8	220.4	92.6	144.2	141.5
1950	211.5	145.7	145.2	126.2	167.6	237.6	89.0	148.2	142.7
1951	215.1	151.4	142.1	131.9	163.1	251.6	85.5	155.3	138.5
1952	220.7	158.6	139.2	135.9	162.4	268.9	82.1	160.9	137.2
1953	226.7	161.4	140.5	139.1	163.0	289.6	78.3	166.1	136.5

TABLE H-V

Telegraph Industry: Output, Inputs, and Productivity Ratios, 1869–1953

(1929 = 100)

	Output	Persons Engaged	Output per Person	Manhours	Output per Manhour	Capital Input	Output per Unit of Capital Input	Total Factor Input	Total Factor Productivity
1869	4.9	7.2	68.2	9.6	51.1	n.a.	33.7	22.8	47.8
1879	10.9	14.9	73.2	19.9	54.8	32.3	47.2	36.2	60.5
1889	21.9	26.3	83.3	35.1	62.4	46.4	43.3	39.5	63.3
1899	25.0	28.5	87.7	34.2	73.1	57.8	48.0	39.5	71.6
1902	28.3	28.7	98.6	33.5	84.5	59.0	53.5	44.0	90.0
1907	39.6	29.3	135.2	34.3	115.5	74.0	53.5	48.6	73.7
1909	35.8	35.3	101.4	40.9	87.5	73.2	48.9	48.6	73.4
1912	41.3	47.5	86.9	51.0	81.0	74.5	55.4	56.3	83.6
1917	57.8	67.8	85.3	67.4	85.8	74.9	77.2	69.1	65.5
1919	46.4	69.9	66.4	67.8	68.4	80.9	57.4	70.8	97.0
1922	73.2	72.6	100.8	71.4	102.5	89.4	81.9	75.5	104.2
1927	90.2	87.5	103.1	85.9	105.0	88.8	101.6	86.6	
1929	100.0	100.0	100.0	100.0	100.0	100.0	100.0	100.0	100.0
1930	91.3	97.9	93.3	98.7	92.5	109.4	83.5	100.4	90.9
1931	78.6	84.0	93.6	84.7	92.8	111.8	70.3	89.0	88.3
1932	62.5	71.2	87.8	67.3	92.9	108.1	57.8	73.8	84.7
1933	63.0	68.2	92.4	61.3	102.8	107.2	58.8	68.6	91.8
1934	65.9	73.3	89.9	61.0	108.0	106.4	61.9	68.3	96.5
1935	73.8	71.2	103.7	60.0	123.0	105.3	70.1	67.2	109.8

(continued)

TABLE H-V (concluded)

1936	81.3	75.3	108.0	64.8	125.5	104.5	77.8	71.2	114.2
1937	85.4	79.0	108.1	68.3	125.0	94.4	90.5	72.5	117.8
1938	79.0	68.7	115.0	59.5	132.8	92.4	85.5	63.6	124.2
1939	80.4	66.9	120.2	58.2	138.1	90.5	88.8	62.2	129.3
1940	79.4	68.7	115.6	60.5	131.2	83.0	95.7	64.2	123.7
1941	85.8	76.2	112.6	68.0	126.2	79.0	108.6	71.6	119.8
1942	87.4	75.9	115.2	68.5	127.6	76.9	113.7	72.0	121.4
1943	93.0	77.8	119.5	72.6	128.1	63.7	146.0	75.5	123.2
1944	94.4	72.9	129.5	67.7	139.4	61.0	154.8	70.5	133.9
1945	101.3	71.7	141.3	66.0	153.5	59.0	171.7	68.7	147.5
1946	94.2	71.8	131.2	64.3	146.5	58.2	161.9	67.1	140.4
1947	96.8	68.5	141.3	61.9	156.4	50.8	190.6	64.3	150.5
1948	87.7	62.9	139.4	56.9	154.1	50.4	174.0	59.2	148.1
1949	81.1	54.8	148.0	49.6	163.5	48.7	166.5	52.0	156.0
1950	83.4	53.2	156.8	48.1	173.4	46.9	177.8	50.5	165.1
1951	84.6	53.4	158.4	48.2	175.5	44.9	188.4	50.4	167.9
1952	73.9	53.4	138.4	46.9	157.6	44.1	167.6	49.0	150.8
1953	77.6	52.6	147.5	44.4	174.8	43.8	177.2	46.6	166.5

n.a. = not available.

TABLE H-VI

Electric Utilities: Output, Inputs, and Productivity Ratios, 1899–1953

(1929 = 100)

	Output	Persons Engaged	Output per Person	Manhours	Output per Manhour	Capital Input	Output per Unit of Capital Input	Total Factor Input	Total Factor Productivity
1899	2.0	8.8	22.8	10.7	18.6	7.9	25.3	9.4	21.3
1902	3.9	11.3	34.6	13.4	29.0	12.0	32.5	12.9	30.2
1907	7.5	18.0	41.7	21.5	34.9	22.1	33.9	21.9	34.2
1909	9.7	22.0	44.0	26.1	37.1	28.5	34.0	27.3	35.5
1912	13.0	29.9	43.5	32.4	40.1	41.1	31.6	36.6	35.5
1913	13.6	28.1	48.4	29.5	46.0	44.2	30.8	36.2	37.6
1914	15.2	28.9	52.6	29.4	51.8	45.8	33.2	36.8	41.3
1915	16.6	29.5	56.2	29.8	55.7	46.8	35.5	37.4	44.4
1916	21.1	35.6	59.2	35.7	59.1	47.5	44.4	41.2	51.2
1917	24.5	39.6	61.8	39.4	62.1	49.0	50.0	44.0	55.7
1918	31.4	42.8	73.3	41.9	74.9	49.7	63.2	45.8	68.6
1919	36.0	44.8	80.3	43.5	82.7	48.8	73.8	46.3	77.8
1920	39.3	49.1	80.1	47.0	83.6	49.1	80.0	48.1	81.7
1921	36.3	50.6	71.8	49.5	73.4	50.2	72.3	49.9	72.7
1922	41.2	55.4	74.4	54.5	75.6	52.3	78.8	53.4	77.2
1923	50.0	70.7	70.7	69.1	72.3	57.8	86.5	63.2	79.1
1924	54.9	74.7	73.5	73.5	74.7	65.9	83.3	69.5	79.0
1925	63.5	75.5	84.1	74.8	84.9	74.0	85.8	74.4	85.3
1926	73.5	83.8	87.7	80.7	91.1	81.1	90.6	80.9	90.9
1927	81.7	85.9	95.1	84.4	96.8	87.8	93.1	86.2	94.8
1928	89.5	91.9	97.4	90.0	99.4	94.1	95.1	92.1	97.2

(continued)

TABLE H-VI (concluded)

1929	100.0	100.0	100.0	100.0	100.0	100.0	100.0	100.0	100.0
1930	103.5	103.3	100.2	104.2	99.3	106.6	97.1	105.5	98.1
1931	101.9	96.1	106.0	97.2	104.8	111.5	91.4	104.9	97.1
1932	92.7	83.7	110.8	79.0	117.3	112.3	82.5	97.0	95.6
1933	95.4	78.5	121.5	70.8	134.7	110.5	86.3	92.2	103.5
1934	102.2	81.6	125.2	67.9	150.5	107.7	94.9	89.4	114.3
1935	111.2	83.7	132.9	70.6	157.5	105.3	105.6	89.3	124.5
1936	127.3	89.8	141.8	77.2	164.9	104.0	122.4	91.7	138.8
1937	137.5	96.3	142.8	83.2	165.3	104.3	131.8	94.6	145.3
1938	131.0	93.2	140.6	79.8	164.2	105.3	124.4	93.2	140.6
1939	145.0	92.7	156.4	78.8	184.0	105.5	137.4	92.7	156.4
1940	161.4	94.9	170.1	80.9	199.5	105.9	152.4	94.1	171.5
1941	186.5	96.6	193.1	82.5	226.1	107.8	173.0	95.8	194.7
1942	207.3	90.1	230.1	77.5	267.5	109.3	189.7	93.7	221.2
1943	241.1	80.2	300.6	71.5	337.2	108.7	221.8	90.0	267.9
1944	252.7	77.2	327.3	71.4	353.9	106.5	237.3	89.0	283.9
1945	249.1	77.9	319.8	72.8	342.2	104.9	237.5	89.0	279.9
1946	249.4	92.4	269.9	82.4	302.7	105.2	237.1	94.6	263.6
1947	284.4	99.6	285.5	89.5	317.8	108.9	261.2	100.2	283.8
1948	314.8	106.3	296.1	95.7	328.9	116.3	270.7	107.2	293.7
1949	325.5	110.5	294.6	98.3	331.1	125.9	258.5	112.8	288.6
1950	369.8	111.6	331.4	99.4	372.0	135.2	273.5	117.5	314.7
1951	415.8	112.4	369.9	100.7	412.9	143.0	290.8	121.7	341.7
1952	446.1	113.8	392.0	101.3	440.4	151.2	295.0	125.6	355.2
1953	491.0	116.0	423.3	103.1	476.2	160.8	305.3	130.7	375.7

TABLE H-VII

Manufactured and Natural Gas Utilities: Output, Inputs, and Productivity Ratios, 1889–1953

(1929 = 100)

	Output	Persons Engaged	Output per Person	Manhours	Output per Manhour	Labor Input	Ouput per Unit of Labor Input	Capital Input	Output per Unit of Capital Input	Total Factor Input	Total Factor Productivity
1889	11.5	26.6	43.2	34.5	33.3	34.6	33.2	8.9	128.8	23.9	48.1
1899	15.8	35.7	44.3	42.7	37.0	41.6	38.0	23.7	66.7	34.6	45.7
1904	25.4	50.0	50.8	58.3	43.6	57.2	44.4	31.3	81.2	47.1	53.9
1909	37.5	65.6	57.2	75.7	49.5	74.4	50.4	43.2	86.8	62.4	60.1
1914	50.3	80.5	62.5	81.1	62.0	79.4	63.4	59.9	84.0	72.2	69.7
1919	65.9	87.0	75.7	86.4	76.3	85.5	77.1	66.0	99.8	78.3	84.2
1924	75.0	98.1	76.5	91.8	81.7	91.1	82.3	n.a.			
1929	100.0	100.0	100.0	100.0	100.0	100.0	100.0	100.0	100.0	100.0	100.0
1930	101.2	94.4	107.2	94.5	107.1	92.8	109.1	104.0	97.3	97.2	104.1
1931	98.6	90.3	109.2	86.4	114.1	85.6	115.2	106.4	92.7	93.7	105.2
1932	92.1	84.4	109.1	73.0	126.2	74.2	124.1	106.7	86.3	86.9	106.0
1933	88.2	84.4	104.5	72.5	121.7	72.6	121.5	105.9	83.3	85.6	103.0
1934	92.2	90.8	101.5	72.0	128.1	73.1	126.1	104.5	88.2	85.3	108.1
1935	97.5	91.7	106.3	74.1	131.6	74.3	131.2	103.0	94.7	85.5	114.0
1936	105.8	97.8	108.2	77.9	135.8	80.8	130.9	102.0	103.7	89.1	118.7
1937	109.6	98.1	111.7	78.2	140.2	81.2	135.0	100.6	108.9	88.8	123.4
1938	106.7	95.0	112.3	74.7	142.8	77.7	137.3	99.9	106.8	86.2	123.8
1939	113.9	96.0	118.6	73.9	154.1	76.9	148.1	99.4	114.6	85.6	133.1
1940	124.4	100.1	124.3	78.7	158.1	80.6	154.3	99.3	125.3	88.0	141.4
1941	130.3	100.4	129.8	79.2	164.5	79.7	163.5	99.4	131.1	87.4	149.1

(continued)

TABLE H-VII (concluded)

1942	145.1	88.3	164.3	71.2	203.8	70.8	204.9	92.8	156.4	79.2	183.2
1943	156.8	82.3	190.5	68.5	228.9	69.8	224.6	99.6	157.4	80.8	194.1
1944	165.0	81.5	202.5	68.0	242.6	71.1	232.1	96.4	171.2	80.6	204.7
1945	173.1	83.7	206.8	70.7	244.8	73.5	235.5	100.3	172.6	83.5	207.3
1946	183.2	96.2	190.4	75.4	243.0	77.4	236.7	97.6	187.7	85.3	214.8
1947	210.5	111.8	188.3	87.8	239.7	90.6	232.3	100.8	208.8	95.2	221.1
1948	229.3	116.6	196.7	93.8	244.5	94.7	242.1	104.4	219.6	99.1	231.4
1949	238.2	119.3	199.7	94.0	253.4	95.5	249.4	110.5	215.6	101.6	234.4
1950	272.4	122.6	222.2	97.0	280.8	98.3	277.1	120.0	227.0	106.8	255.1
1951	308.8	123.7	249.6	98.8	312.6	98.8	312.6	139.3	221.7	113.6	271.8
1952	330.7	131.5	251.5	102.5	322.6	103.0	321.1	152.8	216.4	120.9	273.5
1953	347.2	135.9	255.5	105.5	329.1	106.5	326.0	162.7	213.4	126.5	274.5

n.a. = not available.

593

TABLE H-VIII

Manufactured Gas Utilities: Output, Inputs, and Productivity Ratios, 1869–1953
(1929 = 100)

	Output	Persons Engaged	Output per Person	Manhours	Output per Manhour	Capital Input	Output per Unit of Capital Input	Total Factor Input	Total Factor Productivity
1869	2.2	16.8	13.2	22.2	10.0	5.6	39.7	15.7	14.1
1879	4.4	20.6	21.2	27.0	16.1	13.0	33.5	21.5	20.3
1889	8.6	25.0	34.2	32.7	26.2	20.9	41.0	28.2	30.4
1899	15.6	43.2	36.1	51.3	30.4	52.3	29.8	52.1	29.9
1904	26.6	60.9	43.7	70.6	37.7	63.7	41.8	68.4	38.9
1909	38.0	77.3	49.2	88.4	43.0	78.9	48.2	85.3	44.5
1914	52.8	97.4	54.2	97.8	54.0	100.8	52.4	98.4	53.7
1919	71.2	96.5	73.8	95.3	74.7	104.9	67.9	97.8	72.8
1924	82.0	105.2	77.9	98.7	83.1	n.a.			
1929	100.0	100.0	100.0	100.0	100.0	100.0	100.0	100.0	100.0
1930	100.2	99.3	100.9	97.7	102.6	101.1	99.1	98.9	101.3
1931	97.5	97.3	100.2	94.1	103.6	103.2	94.5	97.4	100.1
1932	89.7	91.7	97.8	77.6	115.6	103.6	86.6	87.0	103.1
1933	85.8	90.3	95.0	77.8	110.3	102.9	83.4	86.8	98.8
1934	88.4	93.1	95.0	75.7	116.8	101.0	87.5	84.8	104.2
1935	90.1	91.6	98.4	73.3	122.9	98.8	91.2	82.5	109.2
1936	91.9	94.0	97.8	77.2	119.0	95.1	96.6	83.6	109.9
1937	89.9	90.0	99.9	72.8	123.5	91.2	98.6	79.4	113.2
1938	88.4	86.9	101.7	69.7	126.8	89.0	99.3	76.4	115.7
1939	91.5	86.9	105.3	68.7	133.2	88.2	103.7	75.5	121.2

(continued)

594

TABLE H-VIII (concluded)

Year									
1940	98.7	88.8	111.1	70.7	139.6	86.8	113.7	76.7	128.7
1941	100.7	87.6	115.0	69.6	144.7	84.8	118.8	75.4	133.6
1942	109.1	75.1	145.3	60.1	181.5	84.0	129.9	67.6	161.4
1943	116.1	68.9	168.5	58.7	197.8	79.5	146.0	65.5	177.3
1944	119.0	66.0	180.3	58.1	204.8	75.2	158.2	63.9	186.2
1945	125.4	66.0	190.0	58.9	212.9	70.8	177.1	63.5	197.5
1946	133.8	72.5	184.6	58.3	229.5	67.9	197.1	62.4	214.4
1947	150.1	76.9	195.2	62.1	241.7	67.1	223.7	65.2	230.2
1948	146.3	75.7	193.3	61.2	239.1	62.9	232.6	63.5	230.4
1949	137.6	73.4	187.5	59.0	233.2	60.6	227.1	61.2	224.8
1950	138.5	67.7	204.6	54.5	254.1	58.4	237.2	57.1	242.6
1951	137.4	59.6	230.5	48.3	284.5	52.6	261.2	50.7	271.0
1952	133.4	49.8	267.9	40.1	332.7	43.7	305.3	42.2	316.1
1953	131.9	44.4	297.1	35.6	370.5	39.2	336.5	37.5	351.7

n.a. = not available.

TABLE H-IX

Natural Gas Utilities: Output, Inputs, and Productivity Ratios, 1899-1953

(1929 = 100)

	Output	Persons Engaged	Output per Person	Manhours	Output per Manhour	Capital Input	Output per Unit of Capital Input	Total Factor Input	Total Factor Productivity
1899	17.0	25.8	65.9	30.6	55.6	6.5	261.9	19.3	88.1
1900	18.1	28.0	64.6	32.3	56.0	7.5	241.0	20.6	87.9
1901	20.2	31.4	64.3	38.2	52.9	8.7	233.0	24.3	83.1
1902	21.5	33.9	63.4	39.1	55.0	10.1	212.9	25.5	84.3
1903	22.8	35.4	64.4	41.6	54.8	11.6	196.6	27.5	82.9
1904	23.7	36.3	65.3	42.1	56.3	13.4	176.9	28.6	82.9
1905	26.8	39.8	67.3	46.0	58.3	15.5	172.9	31.7	84.5
1906	29.7	43.0	69.1	49.7	59.8	17.8	166.9	34.7	85.6
1907	32.5	46.2	70.3	53.4	60.9	20.5	158.5	37.9	85.8
1908	33.2	46.3	71.7	53.2	62.4	23.2	143.1	39.1	84.9
1909	38.1	51.3	74.3	58.7	64.9	26.0	146.5	43.3	88.0
1910	41.2	54.0	76.3	60.3	68.3	28.8	143.1	45.6	90.4
1911	41.9	54.1	77.4	58.8	71.3	31.6	132.6	46.2	90.7
1912	46.1	57.8	79.8	61.3	75.2	34.3	134.4	48.8	94.5
1913	46.2	57.0	81.1	58.7	78.7	37.1	124.5	48.8	94.7
1914	48.4	58.4	82.9	58.6	82.6	39.9	121.3	50.1	96.6
1915	51.6	60.5	85.3	60.9	84.7	41.9	123.2	52.4	98.5
1916	59.5	67.4	88.3	68.1	87.4	45.2	131.6	57.7	103.1
1917	63.7	70.4	90.5	71.2	89.5	46.2	137.9	59.9	106.3
1918	60.5	71.2	85.0	71.2	85.0	46.1	131.2	59.8	101.2
1919	60.8	75.3	80.7	74.4	81.7	46.9	129.6	61.8	98.4
1920	65.4	81.2	80.5	81.5	80.2	48.2	135.7	66.2	98.8
1921	52.3	67.5	77.5	69.0	75.8	49.1	106.5	59.8	87.5
1922	59.4	76.1	78.1	75.5	78.7	53.5	111.0	65.4	90.8

(continued)

TABLE H-IX (concluded)

Year									
1923	64.7	83.1	77.9	80.1	80.8	57.4	112.7	69.7	92.8
1924	68.2	88.1	77.4	82.5	82.7	63.8	106.9	73.9	92.3
1925	69.2	90.1	76.8	82.1	84.3	69.0	100.3	76.1	90.9
1926	76.4	93.5	81.7	86.3	88.5	77.4	98.7	82.2	92.9
1927	80.2	92.4	86.8	86.0	93.3	86.4	92.8	86.2	93.0
1928	87.3	94.1	92.8	92.0	94.9	93.7	93.2	92.8	94.1
1929	100.0	100.0	100.0	100.0	100.0	100.0	100.0	100.0	100.0
1930	102.3	88.1	116.1	87.2	117.3	106.6	96.0	95.3	107.3
1931	99.9	81.2	123.0	76.0	131.4	109.3	91.4	90.0	111.0
1932	94.9	74.8	126.9	70.3	135.0	109.5	86.7	86.8	109.3
1933	90.8	76.8	118.2	66.8	135.9	108.5	83.7	84.3	107.7
1934	96.5	87.9	109.8	70.1	137.7	107.6	89.7	85.8	112.5
1935	105.9	91.9	115.2	75.4	140.5	106.8	99.2	88.6	119.5
1936	121.6	102.9	118.2	84.9	143.2	108.2	112.4	94.7	128.4
1937	131.9	108.4	121.7	90.6	145.6	109.0	121.0	98.3	134.2
1938	127.6	105.4	121.1	86.5	147.5	109.0	117.1	96.0	132.9
1939	139.3	107.8	129.2	86.0	162.0	108.7	128.2	95.6	145.7
1940	153.4	114.8	133.6	92.1	166.6	109.2	140.5	99.2	154.6
1941	163.6	117.0	139.8	91.6	178.6	110.3	148.3	99.4	164.6
1942	185.5	105.3	176.2	83.7	221.6	100.5	184.6	90.7	204.5
1943	202.3	99.7	202.9	83.2	243.1	113.2	178.7	96.1	210.5
1944	216.3	101.6	212.9	87.1	248.3	110.4	195.9	97.0	223.0
1945	226.5	106.5	212.7	91.7	247.0	118.6	191.0	103.2	219.5
1946	238.4	126.8	188.0	101.6	234.6	115.8	205.9	107.3	222.2
1947	278.1	156.8	177.4	127.5	218.1	121.2	229.5	123.9	224.5
1948	321.3	169.4	189.7	138.6	231.8	128.7	249.7	133.3	241.0
1949	346.2	178.7	193.7	143.9	240.6	139.3	248.5	140.9	245.7
1950	411.8	193.5	212.8	157.5	261.5	155.0	265.7	155.5	264.8
1951	483.5	206.5	234.1	168.1	287.6	187.7	257.6	175.8	275.0
1952	529.6	236.9	223.6	190.7	277.7	213.2	248.4	199.6	265.3
1953	562.8	254.1	221.5	205.8	273.5	230.8	243.8	215.7	260.9

TABLE H-X

Communications and Public Utilities:
Persons Engaged and Manhours, by Group, 1929

	Persons Engaged (thousands)	Manhours (millions)
Telephone	428	998
Telegraph	107	275
Electric	311	756
Manufactured gas	87	231
Natural gas	67	172
Radio broadcasting and television	4	10
Local utilities and public services, n.e.c.	30	75
Total	1,034	2,517

n.e.c. = not elsewhere classified.

APPENDIX J

Finance, Services, and Government Enterprises

Finance and Services

THE segment of finance, insurance, and real estate (which we shall call "finance") comprises SIC Major Groups 60 through 67, with the exception that the National Income Division has shifted Group 654, Title abstract companies, from finance to services. The service segment comprises SIC Major Groups 70 through 89 plus Group 654 with the exception of Major Group 75, Automobile repair services and garages, which the National Income Division includes with trade, and Major Group 77, Radio broadcasting and television, which is included with the utilities. The chief components of the service segment may be broadly characterized as personal services (including hotels and lodging places), domestic service, business and professional services (including private education), commercial amusement and recreation, and nonprofit membership organizations.

Employment and manhours were estimated separately for the finance and services segments, which comprise the great bulk of the "residual" area of the economy for which direct output and capital measures are not available. Output for the two segments combined was estimated indirectly for the period before 1929. Since 1929, real product originating in each of the two segments could be estimated. The output and input indexes and their ratios are shown in Appendix Table J-I.

LABOR INPUT

Employment. In the finance and services segments, the standard procedure was followed of using the Commerce Department estimates for employees and proprietors or self-employed, and inflating the latter to include unpaid family workers. The Commerce estimates of employment after 1939 are tied to Social Security data. Prior to 1939, in the financial segment, there is only one set of comprehensive benchmarks into which the estimates are tied: the 1935 censuses of *Banks, Financial Institutions other than Banks, Insurance,* and *Real Estate Agencies* (all are of the *Census of Business*). The estimates for 1935 were extrapolated to 1929; and interpolations between 1935 and 1939 were made on the basis of unpublished BLS series, National Bureau estimates,[1] and trade data. The proprietor estimates were based

---

[1] Cf. Simon Kuznets, *National Income and Its Composition, 1919–38*, New York (NBER), 1941, Vol. II.

on either the industry censuses or *Census of Population* data. After 1940, extrapolations were generally based on the number of operating firms in the several industries of the segment. Extrapolations to earlier years were not firmly based; in real estate, for example, numbers of proprietors were extrapolated from 1929 to 1939 by the estimated number of full-time equivalent employees.

In the service segment prior to 1939, the employment estimates are largely tied into the *Census of Service Establishments* for 1933, 1935, and 1939, supplemented by censuses for selected service industries in 1929 (hotels, cleaning and dyeing establishments, etc.). The *Biennial Census of Manufactures* was used to obtain employees in motion picture production for 1929–39. Employment estimates for health and legal services were based on special questionnaire surveys conducted by the National Income Division. Employment in educational services was estimated from data contained in the *Biennial Survey of Education*. Employees of religious organizations were estimated from religious directories and the 1926 and 1936 *Census of Religious Bodies*. Employment in other nonprofit organizations was tied into the 1935 *Census of Nonprofit Organizations, Office Buildings, Miscellaneous*. Numbers of proprietors were likewise estimated from the industrial censuses and from data in the *Census of Population*, supplemented by data from trade and professional associations. Employment in domestic service was estimated from the *Census of Population*; and the concept used was that of number of persons engaged, rather than number of jobs.

Prior to 1929, the estimates of employment in finance were extrapolated for census years back to 1870 by the Census manpower estimates for the segment, adjusted to an employment basis. The chief alternative for the 1900–29 period was to use the estimates by Lebergott,[2] but these were based in part on labor force data and involve such broad assumptions that it is not at all certain that they portray the decennial movements more reliably than the Carson estimates for the segment. In any case, Lebergott's figures show practically the same movements for 1900–29, and 1920–29 as the Carson estimates with our adjustments, although Lebergott's 1910 estimate is somewhat lower.

The Lebergott estimates were used, however, to interpolate annually between census years. For banking, Lebergott multiplied annual data on the number of banks by average employment per bank—extrapolated by estimates for national banks made by the Comptroller of the Currency on selected dates and interpolated linearly. Building and loan association employment was extrapolated from 1935 back by using the number of associations and average employment extrapolated by the bank series. Brokerage employment was estimated by multiplying the number of

[2] Stanley Lebergott, "Estimates of Labor Force, Employment, and Unemployment, 1900–1950," unpublished MS., Appendix Tables 2 and 3.

self-employed brokers by the average number of employees per broker, interpolated linearly between 1910 and 1930. The numbers of self-employed stockbrokers were interpolated between census dates by trade information after 1920, and linearly before 1920. The ratio of all brokers to stockbrokers was ascertained for census years, and interpolated linearly. The estimates for brokerage were held constant between 1900 and 1910, since the growth in banking employment alone accounted for the entire growth shown by the Census category of banking and brokerage.

Gainful workers in the insurance industry at census dates were estimated by Lebergott on the basis of insurance agents. Intercensal interpolations were done on the basis of the number of life insurance policies. Self-employment was obtained by interpolating and extrapolating (prior to 1910) the ratios of self-employed to wage earners in years when the breakdown was available. Gainful workers in real estate were interpolated between census dates by the number of available nonfarm housing units, since agents are primarily concerned with the marketing and renting of houses. Ratios of self-employment to total employment were interpolated and extrapolated as in the case of insurance.

For 1900 and prior years, we combined the Census-based estimates of employment in finance and service industries and interpolated intercensal years by the relationship of employment to consumption expenditures for services (which include financial services) in the period from 1900 to 1929. These estimates were used merely for the purpose of obtaining annual employment estimates for the economy, and not for productivity comparisons.

As in finance, estimates of persons engaged in the service industries were extrapolated back from 1929 to 1870 by labor force estimates adjusted to an employment basis. The extrapolation was performed for two broad groups: domestic service, as estimated by Fabricant; and "other services," obtained by subtracting the domestic service estimates from the sum of the Carson estimates of domestic and personal service and of professional service and amusements.[3]

Annual interpolations were made on the basis of Lebergott's estimates plus annual estimates for employment in private education, which were not included by Lebergott in his series. When account is taken of employment in education and in nonprofit institutions, also excluded by Lebergott, the movement of his series is very close to that of the adjusted Carson estimates.

The Lebergott annual estimates were based on a variety of sources: professional directories; data on numbers of hotels and theatres; *Census of Manufactures* data for steam laundries and cleaning and dyeing establishments in part of the period; and interpolations by trade employment in

---

[3] Cf. *Studies in Income and Wealth, Volume 11*, New York (NBER), 1949, pp. 42 and 47.

hand trades, dressmaking, tailoring, and millinery shops. Our estimates of employment in private educational institutions were based on Office of Education data, biennial from 1918 forward and quinquennial from 1915 back, adjusted to a calendar-year basis and interpolated linearly. For domestic service, we followed Lebergott by interpolating linearly (except for 1910–20), on the ground that employment in this area is not affected appreciably by the cycle. Between 1910 and 1920, when employment of domestics declined, we again followed Lebergott by concentrating the decline in the war period, 1914–18, on the basis of the experience of World War II.

Lebergott's division of persons engaged between employees and proprietors was based largely on Census information and on interpolations of the ratios. We have accepted his distribution for 1900–29, making allowance for unpaid family workers as a proportion of proprietors. Prior to 1900, the distribution of total persons engaged by class of worker was based on the 1900 proportions.

Annual interpolation of the total (including domestic service) prior to 1900 was done in conjunction with finance, as described above. Separation of the two divisions was accomplished by applying to the total the ratios of each for census years, interpolated linearly. Estimates for other service were obtained by subtracting from total service the estimates of domestic service employment, which were interpolated linearly between census years.

Average hours and manhours. In the finance, insurance, and real estate segment, estimates of average hours are available for three periods. There are the estimates by King,[4] based on a 7.4 per cent sample for 1920–22; the 1940 Census distribution of all employees in the segment by average hours classes; and special monthly tabulations from 1945 to date by the Census Bureau, based on the current population surveys.

We used averages of the monthly estimates (adjusted for the weeks containing holidays) for the years back to 1945. For 1943 and 1944, the pre-V-J Day figures in 1945 were used. The estimate for 1942 was an interpolation between the 1941 figure of 43.9 (assumed to be the same as the 1940 Census average) and the 1943 figure of 45.0. We also used the 1940 Census average for all years back to 1934, when the hours reductions under the codes of the National Recovery Act took full effect. This assumption of constancy seems more reasonable when it is observed that average hours worked in the financial segment remained remarkably stable after 1946, varying by no more than half an hour between 1947 and 1953. Also, the King estimates for 1920, 1921, and the first quarter of 1922 are virtually constant at 45.5 hours per week. We continued to hold this

---

[4] Willford I. King, *Employment, Hours and Earnings in Prosperity and Depression, United States, 1920–1922*, 2nd ed., New York (NBER), 1923, p. 87.

figure constant for the decade 1922–32. Since the NRA codes affecting average hours in the financial area were approved in the fall of 1933, we reduced the 1932 figure by only one-fourth of the difference between 1932 and 1934 in order to arrive at an average for 1933.

Finance is the area in which our ignorance as to average hours worked prior to 1920 is greatest, and it was necessary to extrapolate the 1920 figure by average hours worked in some other segment. Actually, the reduction of about five hours in the workweek in finance, or somewhat more than 10 per cent, between 1922 and 1953 was very close to that experienced by the private economy as a whole. It was considerably less than the reduction in hours of the service industry, which was at a higher level in 1920, but it was close to the manufacturing change, 1922–53; and the levels of average weekly hours in the two segments were close in 1922. Since it was computationally simpler to extrapolate by manufacturing hours rather than by those for the rest of the private economy as a whole, we have used the former device.

The special Census tabulation for 1953 revealed that average hours worked per week by employees and by the self-employed and unpaid family workers were virtually identical in finance. The same average hours estimates were therefore applied to both classes of workers.

To obtain manhours, the average hours estimates were multiplied by full-time equivalent employees plus self-employed and unpaid family workers and by weeks per year. As noted earlier, the Census average hours estimates are more applicable to full-time equivalents since part-time workers from other industries are not included, and part-time work by industry employees in outside industries would tend to offset part-time workers attached to the given industry. The King sample indicated that the average employee worked 99.6 per cent of full time;[5] so his average hours estimates were taken as applicable to full-time equivalent employees.

Information regarding average hours worked by persons engaged in the service industries is somewhat better than that available for the finance segment, particularly in the early years. From 1920 forward, the sources and methods were much the same as in finance, except that the service segment was broken into two parts: domestic servants, and other than domestic service employees. From the special tabulations provided by the Bureau of the Census, we have annual averages of monthly estimates since 1945 for both divisions. Averages for 1943 and 1944 were assumed to be the same as in the pre-V-J Day part of 1945. For 1940, it was possible to compute average hours worked for each division from the Census hours distributions. In the case of other than domestic service, we held the 1940 figure constant in 1941, then interpolated 1942 linearly between 1941 and

[5] *Ibid.*, Table XIV, p. 49.

1943. Average hours worked by domestic servants were substantially higher in 1940 than in 1945. In this case, we interpolated linearly between the two estimates to obtain figures for the intervening years. The atypical behavior of domestic service with respect to average hours was paralleled by a steady decline in numbers employed during the war period.

From 1940 to 1934, we extrapolated the average hours estimates for both divisions, derived from the 1940 Census, by a weighted average of the BLS average hours estimates for three service industries: laundries, cleaning and dyeing plants, and year-round hotels.

It was then necessary to work forward from the 1920–22 estimates by King. Unfortunately, King's average hours estimates for services are presented in two mixed categories: domestic and personal, and public and professional. On the basis of the available state data, we decided that the approximately 56 hours shown for the former category in 1920 represented an average of about 60 hours for domestic servants (full-time basis) and 52 hours for personal service, with each receiving almost equal employment weights.

The change between 1920 and 1922 in each of these estimates was calculated in proportion to the change in average hours for the total category over the same period. Since our estimates of average hours for government employees were close to those shown by King for public and professional workers, we assumed that average hours for the category also applied to the professional group alone. Accordingly, these estimates were combined with the average hours estimates for personal service, using as weights the relevant manpower estimates of Carson.[6] In going forward, we assumed for both divisions the same reduction of two hours between 1920 and 1929 that was used by Barger for the trade segment. Between 1929 and 1934, the average hours estimates were interpolated linearly.

Prior to 1920, our chief reliance was on reports by eight states which canvassed average hours worked for all or part of the period 1870–1920. In addition to domestic service, information was available for hotels, laundries, barbers, shoemakers, tailors, blacksmiths, cabinet makers, and musicians. We computed unweighted averages of the data by state and by category, using interpolations in some instances, rounding the results for decennial years, and interpolating linearly between the decennial years. The results are obviously not precise, but they should give at least a rough picture of trend in an area in which no estimates are available from secondary sources.

As in finance, the average hours estimates were multiplied by the number of full-time equivalent employees and 52 to obtain manhours.

---

[6] *Op. cit.*, pp. 59–60.

The numbers of proprietors and unpaid family workers (present only in the nondomestic services) were multiplied by the same hours series, raised by 15 per cent. The raising ratio was based on the results of the special Census Bureau tabulation for May 1953.

Within the services segment, manhours worked by domestic servants and by other persons were weighted by average hourly compensation in pairs of key years beginning with 1919 in order to derive labor input. The same procedure was followed in combining labor input in the services segment with manhours in the finance segment in order to get labor input for the two segments in combination (see Table J-I).

OUTPUT

It is possible to spell out approximately the implications of deflated GNP with respect to the real product originating in the finance and service segments. As in construction, for the period since 1929 we added to the Commerce Department industry national income estimates, the finance and service industry portions of depreciation, indirect business taxes, and other (minor) items reconciling income and product. The industry gross national product estimates so obtained were then deflated for each segment by the implicit price deflators for the aggregates of financial and of other consumer services included in GNP.

As discussed elsewhere,[7] this procedure involves two assumptions. One is that the prices of the financial and other services rendered to business move with the prices of services to consumers. Since many of the services performed for individuals and for businesses are of the same type, and since consumer services predominate in any case, the assumption should not produce appreciable distortion. A more important possible source of error is the spotty coverage of the price indexes for consumer services.[8] The other assumption is that the prices of the intermediate inputs into the segments move with the output prices. Since intermediate-product inputs are probably of minor importance in the finance and service segments, this assumption should also not be a source of major error. It is hoped that the several possible sources of error in the real-product estimates tend to be offsetting.

Real-product estimates for the combined finance and service segments for 1889–1929 were derived as a residual by deducting the real-product or gross output estimates (with real-product weights) for the other segments from the total real-product estimates for the private domestic economy.

---

[7] John W. Kendrick, "The Estimation of Real National Product," *A Critique of United States Income and Product Accounts*, Studies in Income and Wealth, Volume 22, Princeton University Press (for NBER), 1958.

[8] See *National Income Supplement, 1954, Survey of Current Business*, Dept. of Commerce, Part IV.

The estimating procedure and possible sources of error involved are discussed in the Appendix A section: "Comparison of Real Product with an Aggregate of Industry Output." Reasons were given there for believing that the residual and total real-product estimates for 1869–89 were not reliable enough for this study; but the estimates for the period since 1889 seem plausible. The fact that the sum of the industry output estimates moves closely with real GNP, 1929–53, is a check for the later period on the accuracy of the computation of real product in finance and services (see Table A-3).

The labor productivity estimates for finance and services shown in Table J-I provide another basis for appraisal of the output estimates. Output per unit of labor input in the combined segments increased at an average annual rate of slightly under 1.5 per cent between 1889 and 1929 and slightly more than 1.5 per cent between 1929 and 1953. Finance and services each showed a 1.5 per cent average annual rate of advance in the later period. These trend rates, which are significantly under the average rates of advance in the private economy as a whole, accord with the general impression that technical advance has not been as strong in the finance and service areas as it has been in the commodity-producing and the utility industry segments. The real-product and productivity estimates for the services segment are probably on the low side, however, since the deflators for domestic service and nonprofit institutions make inadequate allowance for possible efficiency gains in these areas.

There is considerable variability in rates of change in the subperiods, but it is not much greater than in other segments. The variations can be rationalized, but they undoubtedly reflect in part margins of error in the estimates which may affect the subperiod movements to a greater extent than the long-period trends.

Government Enterprises

This section covers those businesslike enterprises, created by governments, which make a direct charge for their services and operate on predominantly commercial principles. They are thus distinguished from "general government" and are treated by the Commerce Department as part of what we call the private economy.

The Post Office Department overshadows the other government enterprises, accounting for approximately 284,000 full-time equivalent employees out of a total of 409,000 in 1929. For the Post Office, we have extended existing estimates of the physical volume of output, as well as of employment and manhours worked. For the other enterprises, employment and manhours were estimated for the purpose of obtaining national aggregates, but output measures were not practicable.

Post Office. For 1896–1948, a series on full-time equivalent numbers of employees in the Post Office Department is available in the Fabricant study.[9] Fabricant excluded temporary employees and certain classes of part-time employees, contractors, and contractors' employees. Temporary employees were unimportant before 1940, but have increased relative to full-time workers in more recent years. This leads to some understatement in the Fabricant series as extended by the same methods, but not enough to affect the secular comparisons for which the employment totals are used. Total employment was reduced to full-time equivalents by reducing by three-fourths the number of fourth-class postmasters and third- and fourth-class clerks. This procedure was based, in part, on the evidence of earnings ratios.

Prior to 1896, full-time equivalent employment was extrapolated by the number of postmasters and city carriers (representing about 45 per cent of employment in 1896). This involves the assumption that the ratio of full-time equivalent employees to total postal employees remained unchanged in the early years.

Postal employees worked a standard 48-hour week until 1931. In 1932 the standard workweek was reduced to 44, and in 1936, further reduced to 40 hours, according to Civil Service Commission reports. Our average hours series is based on these data, and a further adjustment was made to the estimate for 1952 to take account of increased annual holidays and paid sick leave.

Since the average hours series is on a full-time basis, it was multiplied by the index of full-time equivalent employees in order to arrive at the manhours index. In computing the absolute number of manhours for combination with manhours worked in other industries, a deduction was made for the proportion of hours estimated as paid for but taken as leave (see Appendix K for the study on which the deduction was based).

Other government enterprises. From 1929 forward, employment in federal government enterprises other than the Post Office was estimated from the total presented in the *National Income Supplement, 1954,* by subtracting consistent estimates of the number of Post Office employees. Although other enterprise employment grew rapidly during the first years of the "New Deal," and again in World War II and after the Korean outbreak, it was not important prior to 1929. The chief enterprises in the earlier years were the Panama Canal corporations and the War Shipping Board.

---

[9] Solomon Fabricant, *The Trend of Government Activity in the United States since 1900,* New York (NBER), 1952, pp. 176–77 for the years through 1948; 1949–53, extended by methods used in his study.

Employment in such enterprises prior to 1929 was obtained from the annual reports of the Civil Service Commission and was traced back to the formation of the Isthmian Canal Commission in 1904. Prior to this date, federal enterprises other than the Post Office were apparently nonexistent or negligible.[10]

To calculate manhours, it was assumed that hours worked in the other federal enterprises were the same as those worked by employees in federal civilian general government (see Appendix K).

State and local government enterprises consist primarily of water, gas and electric utilities, and, since 1933, state liquor stores. The Commerce Department estimates were used for the years since 1929. These were extrapolated to 1909 by the estimates of King,[11] which were based on Census Bureau data contained in *The Financial Statistics of Cities* and in various state reports. The King estimates check closely with the later Census estimates of state and local government utility and liquor store expenditures,[12] deflated by the average earnings of state and local government nonschool employees (Appendix K) on the assumption that payrolls are a relatively stable proportion of total expenditures. The deflated Census series was used to extrapolate the employment estimates back to 1902.

On the basis of the Census breakdown of expenditures, it was assumed that about 10 per cent of enterprise employment was in publicly owned electric utilities. This portion was extrapolated back to 1889, when the industry virtually began, on the basis of total employment in electric utilities (Appendix H). Most of the remaining employment was in water works, and this was extrapolated from 1900 to 1880 on the basis of Kuznets' estimates of the real value of fixed capital in this category.[13] It was further extended to 1870 on the basis of the 1880–1900 trend. Because of the very small size of the figures in the early period, interpolations between benchmarks from 1870 to 1909 were performed linearly.

It was assumed that average hours worked per week in the state and local government enterprises were the same as in the private electric and gas utilities. Since the number of part-time workers relative to total employment in the private utilities is negligible, the average hours estimates were multiplied by estimated full-time equivalent employees to arrive at total manhours.

[10] *Ibid.*, Table B-16, p. 201.

[11] Willford I. King, *The National Income and Its Purchasing Power*, New York (NBER), 1930, p. 361.

[12] *Historical Statistics on State and Local Government Finances, 1902–53*, Bureau of the Census, Special Studies No. 38, 1955.

[13] Simon Kuznets, *National Product since 1869*, New York (NBER), 1946, p. 231.

POST OFFICE OUTPUT

The initial estimates of the physical volume of services performed by the Post Office were made by Witt Bowden.[14] His estimates for 1908, 1910, 1912, and 1926–31 were incorporated in the work of Fabricant.[15] The extension of the Bowden output index to 1940, shown by Fabricant, was based on estimates in an unpublished study of the National Research Project of the Works Progress Administration, in which the Bowden method was used, and we have likewise followed Bowden in bringing the index up to 1953 (see Table J-II).

Bowden's index represents a weighted aggregate of the number of pieces of mail handled or the number of other transactions performed by the Post Office, by type. The weights are based on the estimated amount of labor involved in performing a unit of each of the various services. Table J-1 shows the types of services for which separate quantity data are

TABLE J-1

Post Office: Relative Weights of Services Included in Bowden Index

Type of Service[a]	Weight
Mail Services	
All matter except fourth class	1.0
Fourth-class matter	8.2
Special Services	
Registration	15.3
Money order transactions	8.1
Special delivery	6.7
C.O.D. transactions	12.5
Insurance	5.2
Postal Savings, depositors	156.0

[a] A broader range of service categories is contained in recent issues of *Annual Report of the Postmaster General* (see Henry D. Lytton, "Recent Productivity Trends in the Federal Government," *The Review of Economics and Statistics*, November 1959).

available and the relative weights used for combining the several series. Labor-time required in handling ordinary letters and circulars per piece is the base upon which the other weights were computed.

Estimates for intervening years, 1908–12, and the years from 1908 back to 1886 were interpolated and extrapolated by the total number of pieces

[14] *Technological Changes and Employment in the United States Postal Service*, BLS Bulletin 574, December 1932, p. 52.
[15] *Op. cit.*, p. 257.

of mail handled.[16] The index for this series was compared with the weighted index from 1933 to 1939, and the maximum difference was 0.5 percentage point. No data were available for "pieces of mail" from 1914 to 1922 and prior to 1886, except for 1847. An estimate for 1919 was interpolated between 1914 and 1922 from the volume of ordinary postage stamps issued, and an estimate for 1879 was obtained from a logarithmic trend line between 1847 and 1886. A two-year moving average of the fiscal-year figures was taken in order to adjust the estimates to a calendar-year basis.

TABLE J-I

Finance and Services:
Output, Labor Inputs, and Productivity Ratios, Key Years, 1889–1953
(1929 = 100)

	Output	Persons Engaged[a]	Output per Person	Manhours[a]	Output per Manhour	Labor Input	Output per Unit of Labor Input
	FINANCE AND SERVICES COMBINED						
1889	17.9	32.3	55.4	42.5	42.1	32.2	55.6
1899	33.6	42.9	78.3	54.4	61.8	44.3	75.8
1909	56.0	59.8	93.6	71.5	78.3	60.8	92.1
1919	71.7	65.9	108.8	69.6	103.0	66.3	108.1
1929	100.0	100.0	100.0	100.0	100.0	100.0	100.0
1937	89.2	98.7	90.4	92.4	96.5	96.1	92.8
1948	132.0	116.7	113.1	93.4	141.3	102.6	128.7
1953	162.6	127.2	127.8	100.4	162.0	111.1	146.4
	FINANCE						
1929	100.0	100.0	100.0	100.0	100.0		
1937	84.4	96.6	87.4	93.2	90.6		
1948	142.1	122.0	116.5	109.1	130.2		
1953	178.1	140.4	126.9	125.2	142.3		
	SERVICES						
1929	100.0	100.0	100.0	100.0	100.0	100.0	100.0
1937	94.6	99.3	95.3	92.2	102.6	97.2	97.3
1948	125.7	115.4	108.9	90.1	139.5	100.5	125.1
1953	152.4	124.0	122.9	95.3	159.9	106.5	143.1

[a] Absolute numbers of persons engaged and of manhours are given in Tables A-VII and A-XI. The services segment is further broken down into two groups; relevant data for the base year, 1929, are (in millions):

	Persons Engaged	Manhours
Domestic service	2.348	7,021
Other service	4.280	11,183

[16] *Statistical Abstract of the United States, 1955,* Dept. of Commerce, p. 518; and earlier volumes.

TABLE J-II

Post Office:
Output, Labor Inputs, and Productivity Ratios, 1879–1953
(1929 = 100)

	Output	Persons Engaged[a]	Manhours[a]	Output Per Manhour
1879	5.8	16.7		34.6
1889	11.3	26.3		43.0
1899	19.8	35.4		55.9
1909	42.3	66.1		64.0
1919	71.8	78.5		91.5
1929	100.0	100.0	100.0	100.0
1930	97.6	100.6	100.6	97.0
1931	89.9	100.3	100.3	89.6
1932	78.1	98.9	90.7	86.1
1933	72.5	95.7	87.8	82.6
1934	76.5	93.7	85.9	89.1
1935	81.8	93.4	85.6	95.6
1936	88.2	99.0	82.5	106.9
1937	92.0	100.8	84.0	109.5
1938	92.9	102.8	85.6	108.5
1939	95.6	103.9	86.5	110.5
1940	100.2	106.3	88.5	113.2
1941	105.4	109.4	91.1	115.7
1942	112.5	111.6	93.0	121.0
1943	120.9	107.6	89.6	134.9
1944	127.5	109.8	91.5	139.3
1945	128.8	112.7	93.9	137.2
1946	130.6	120.3	100.2	130.3
1947	138.7	122.6	102.1	135.8
1948	148.8	134.3	111.9	133.0
1949	155.4	142.9	119.0	130.6
1950	159.8	147.9	123.2	129.7
1951	167.4	143.1	119.2	140.4
1952	172.8	144.6	117.6	146.9
1953	174.4	147.2	119.7	145.7

[a] Number of full-time equivalent employees in 1929 is estimated at 284,000, **and** manhours worked, at 651,000,000.

APPENDIX K

General Government

GENERAL government, as defined by the Commerce Department, comprises those government activities which are financed mainly by tax revenue or debt creation. If direct charges for services rendered are made, these constitute but a nominal part of operating costs, in contrast to the government enterprises whose operations are essentially commercial in character.

Output

The very fact that the services of general government are not sold means that there is no market valuation in the conventional sense and no prices whereby the estimated value of output might be deflated. In many cases it is difficult to visualize and define the many types of real services that are performed by government. Insofar as such services can be defined, it is at least theoretically possible to choose physical-volume measures that approximate the changes in the amount of real services provided—just as the number of pieces of mail handled may be used as a rough measure of Post Office Department services. For example, we might use the number of student days of attendance to approximate the real output of the public school system and the number of vehicle miles traveled as a measure of the output of the public highway system.[1] Work measurement systems in a number of federal agencies with fairly routinized operations, such as the Veterans Administration, Internal Revenue Service, and Social Security Administration, provide raw materials for possible output and productivity indexes.[2] But lack of data for other agencies, and the artificial nature of possible measures, particularly in areas of general administration, have precluded a direct attempt to measure government output, especially since our resources for experimental work were limited.

The Commerce Department estimates of real gross and net government product are patently unsuited for productivity analysis, since they are obtained by multiplying government employment or manhours worked,

[1] See John W. Kendrick, "The Estimation of Real National Product," *A Critique of the United States Income and Product Accounts*, Studies in Income and Wealth, Volume 22, Princeton University Press (for NBER), 1958.

[2] Experimental work along these lines is reported by Henry D. Lytton, "Recent Productivity Trends in Federal Government: An Exploratory Study," *The Review of Economics and Statistics*, November 1959.

by category, by base-period average compensation. Output and input have the same movements, with no allowance for productivity change. Furthermore, the capital factor is completely neglected since the present Commerce concept does not include the value of government capital services in the national product.

The Kuznets estimates of national product do implicitly include government output—in terms of final services to consumers and of intermediate services to business. We do not, however, present the implicit government output series since it is not in itself a satisfactory measure. Kuznets recognizes that his treatment of government is statistically imprecise, and has outlined what he considers a more satisfactory method.[3] As yet, his "product specific" approach has not been translated into quantitative terms.

Employment, Manhours, and Labor Compensation

The general-government estimates have been drawn up in terms of four major components: federal civilian employees and members of the armed forces, and nonschool and school employees of state and local governments. The employment and labor compensation estimates from 1929 forward are those prepared by the Commerce Department, explained and presented in the *National Income Supplement, 1954 Survey of Current Business*. The following section will describe the estimation procedure in earlier years and the derivation of average hours throughout. The employment estimates are presented in Table K-I.

FEDERAL GOVERNMENT

In preparing estimates of real labor input and of the labor compensation part of national income or product originating in the federal government, it is useful analytically as well as statistically to deal with civilian government and armed forces separately. The Commerce Department also treated work relief as a separate category in 1933–43, but in the summary tables we have lumped this with the rest of civilian government.

Employment. Except for work relief, the Commerce Department's estimates of federal employment on a full-time equivalent basis are identical with the full-time and part-time estimates. The 1929 Commerce estimate was extrapolated to 1897 by estimates derived from those of Fabricant,[4] which were based on Civil Service Commission reports. From his estimates of civilian full-time equivalent employment were subtracted estimates of the full-time equivalent number of Post Office Department

[3] Simon Kuznets, "Government Product and National Income," *Income and Wealth*, *Series I*, Cambridge, England, Bowes and Bowes, 1951.

[4] Solomon Fabricant, *The Trend of Government Activity in the United States since 1900*, New York (NBER), 1952, Table B 6, pp. 182–84 and Table B 4, p. 76.

employees. The resulting series is somewhat higher in 1929 than the Commerce estimates, in part because the Fabricant figures include employees of enterprises other than the Post Office. By using his estimates as an extrapolator we are assuming that the enterprise proportion (and discrepancy) remained constant in earlier years. Since the implied proportion is only 10 per cent in 1929, moderate changes in enterprise relative to general-government employment would have little effect on the validity of the Commerce series as extrapolated.

From 1897 back, we have used estimates of paid employees in the executive branch, based on Civil Service Commission records.[5] Since the great bulk of federal civilian government employment is in the executive branch, the omission of estimates for the legislature and judiciary is of no great moment. More serious is the fact that the series, while excluding the armed forces, includes Post Office employment. We have, therefore, deducted the estimates of Post Office employment described in Appendix J and used the residual to extrapolate the Fabricant series. Although we were not in a position to assess the reliability of the estimates prior to 1897, it is reassuring that the figures show much the same upward trend relative to population as shown by the estimates since 1897. Missing years in the earlier period were interpolated on a straight-line basis.

The estimates of the strength of the armed forces are consistent with those of M. Slade Kendrick.[6] His estimates are for fiscal years; by reference to the underlying worksheets we have obtained estimates relating to calendar years. For most years, the estimates are for armed forces strength on June 30. For 1898–1902 and 1917–22, inclusive, the estimates are averages of data for the months of the calendar years; data for a number of missing months had to be interpolated. The estimates are quite close to those given by Fabricant,[7] except for a few of the war years. The Slade Kendrick estimates were based on data which were revised subsequent to the Fabricant volume, however, and in some cases represent more exhaustive investigation of original sources. The estimate for 1929 is between 2 and 3 per cent higher than the Commerce estimate for that year, mainly because nonresidents of the United States are excluded from the Commerce figures. The Commerce series was extrapolated by the National Bureau estimates, a procedure that involves the assumption that the proportion of nonresident members of the armed forces remained constant in the earlier period.

Labor compensation. The compensation of federal civilian employees in years before 1929 was obtained as the product of employment and the

[5] *Historical Statistics of the United States, 1789–1945*, Dept. of Commerce, 1949, Series P 62.
[6] *A Century and a Half of Federal Expenditures*, Occasional Paper 48, New York (NBER), 1955, Table B-3.
[7] *Op. cit.*, Table B 5.

average compensation per employee. The latter series was based on an estimate of average compensation in 1929 derived from the Commerce figures, extrapolated as follows.

Average pay per federal civilian employee (excluding the Post Office) was computed for 1903, 1913, 1923, and 1929, from the worksheet detail underlying the estimates presented in Fabricant,[8] as provided by Robert Lipsey. Fabricant's estimates, in turn, were based on budget payroll data for 1923 and 1929 and on average pay estimates in the earlier years.[9] Annual interpolations and extrapolations to 1892 were based on average wage-salary rates computed from Kuznets[10] for the period from 1919 to 1929 and on estimates of the average annual earnings of government employees in the District of Columbia presented by Douglas.[11] Owing to a lack of information relating to the compensation of federal civilian employees prior to 1892, we have extrapolated compensation back by the average salary of teachers in public elementary schools, based on estimates of the Office of Education as described below.

Average hours and manhours worked. Average hours worked per year by federal civilian employees were estimated separately for "white collar" employees subject to Civil Service Commission regulation, "blue collar" workers under wage board jurisdiction, and work relief employees. Information regarding the length of the workday, number of holidays, and leave privileges was assembled from the various annual volumes of *Civil Service Act and Rules, Statutes, Executive Orders, and Regulations* and was checked against an unpublished list of changes in these variables that is on file at the Employment Statistics Office of the Civil Service Commission. The method is essentially the same as that used by Douglas;[12] a few differences in results reflect the more detailed information available to us.

In computing the number of days worked per year, we assumed that 80 per cent of allowable annual leave and 67 per cent of allowable sick leave were used. These ratios were based on a study of leave for 1947.[13] Sundays and holidays were deducted in full, along with the allowable portion of Saturdays (up until Saturday work was abandoned). The chief influence on average hours worked per year was the number of days worked, since the length of the full workday has been around 7 hours, except in World War II, when it was increased to 8, and prior to 1904, when it seems to have been 6.5.

---

[8] *Ibid.*, Table D 1.

[9] *Ibid.*, pp. 225–226.

[10] Simon Kuznets, *National Income and Its Composition, 1919–1938*, New York (NBER), 1941, Vol. II, Tables G-2 and G-7.

[11] Paul H. Douglas, *Real Wages in the United States, 1890–1926*, Boston, Houghton Mifflin, 1930, p. 375.

[12] *Ibid.*, pp. 191ff.

[13] *Sick and Annual Leave*, Senate Document No. 126, 80th Cong., 2d sess., March 5, 1948.

The situation was somewhat different as regards "wage board" employees. Here, the standard workday has been 8 hours; the workweek was 6 days until 1934, when it was reduced to 5 days. The same adjustments for holidays and leave were used as for Civil Service workers. Total federal civilian employment (except work relief) was roughly divided between the two categories of workers for the purpose of weighting by hours. Weights were determined on the basis of the employment statistics of the Civil Service Commission since World War II, and before then by the ratio of CSC positions to total paid employees in the Executive departments.[14]

Manhours on work relief were calculated simply as the product of full-time equivalent employment, 50.6 weeks per year and 40 hours per week. This is entirely consistent with the Commerce Department series, since "full-time equivalent employment has been computed for all years by use of a 40-hour week as a measure of full-time employment."[15]

As far as the armed forces are concerned, manhours are probably no more significant a measure than is "strength" in terms of numbers of men. That is, much of the security provided by the armed services lies in their readiness for combat in case of necessity, and service men are always on call even when not actually on duty. Yet, in order to provide estimates on a basis comparable with manhours worked in civilian pursuits, we have multiplied armed forces employment by average hours worked by civilian employees of the federal government under Civil Service Commission jurisdiction. Military and civilian government personnel work together in many types of activity and have observed the same hours and holidays. Furthermore, leave privileges have been similar. While use of the same hours series for military as for civilian employees of the federal government is an expedient, it is not basically unreasonable, at least for peacetime.

STATE AND LOCAL GOVERNMENT

In this area the several variables in which we are interested have been estimated in terms of two major groupings: school and nonschool. The basic data of the Governments Division of the Bureau of the Census are available in terms of additional categories: state governments, counties, cities, towns, villages, etc., but we have followed the Commerce Department and worked in terms of the two major categories.

Employment. The Commerce Department estimate of nonschool employment in 1929 was extrapolated to 1900 by the estimates of Fabricant,[16] available for the total for 1900, 1902, and 1910, and on an annual basis from

---

[14] *Historical Statistics*, Series P 65 and P 62.
[15] *National Income Supplement, 1954*, p. 197, n. 7.
[16] *Op. cit.*, Table B 13.

1920 to 1929. His estimates prior to 1929 for state and municipal government employment are based on population-weighted average government employment per capita in a sample of states and cities. Local government employment was estimated independently for 1902, based on Census nonschool expenditures divided by average expenditures per employee in states and cities extrapolated to 1900 by state and city employment. The total nonschool employment figures were interpolated by Fabricant for the years between 1900 and 1929 mentioned above on the basis of the state and municipal employment estimates. We have interpolated the total for 1905 and 1915 by municipal government employment,[17] the remaining intervening years were interpolated on a straight-line basis.

It was noted that in 1900, 1902, 1920, and subsequent years, the ratio between total nonschool and school employment exhibited a remarkably regular upward trend. In order to obtain estimates of nonschool employment from 1899 to 1869, we extrapolated the relationship between nonschool and school employment and applied the calculated ratios to the estimates of school employment, which are available annually throughout the entire period.

The annual estimates of school employment from 1929 to 1909 are those presented by Fabricant,[18] which in turn are extrapolations of the Commerce Department figures, using estimates by Kuznets and King derived from basic data gathered by the Office of Education. From 1911 to 1869, annual estimates of the number of teachers employed in primary and secondary schools were based on Office of Education data.[19] Estimates of the numbers of persons employed in higher educational institutions and in all other schools, were obtained for 1890, 1900, and 1910 from reports of the Office of Education; the proportions of employment assignable to public institutions were calculated from tabulations for 1918 and applied to the estimates for the earlier decennial years. Interpolations were made between decennial figures for employment in higher education on the basis of annual enrollment estimates, and extrapolation back to 1869 was by the number of students graduated from college.[20] The estimated public portion of other school employment was interpolated and extrapolated on a straight-line basis. The effect of the roughness of the estimates of employment in schools other than primary and secondary is mitigated by the fact that this portion accounted for only about 7 per cent of the total in 1910, and less in earlier years. It was considered a gain in accuracy over using the relatively reliable primary and secondary school employment series alone, since a distinct increase in the ratio of employment in

---

[17] *Ibid.*, Table B 19.
[18] *Ibid.*, Table B 11.
[19] *Statistical Abstract of the United States, 1922*, Dept. of Commerce, p. 103.
[20] *Biennial Survey of Education, 1936–38*, Office of Education Bulletin 1940, No. 2, 1942.

higher education to total school employment is evident in the estimates for selected years from 1890 forward.

The estimates from 1910 back were on a school-year basis. We have converted them to a calendar-year basis by the method used by Kuznets, weighting the figures for the school year ending in the given calendar year 2, and those for the following school year 1. The converted estimates were then linked to the Commerce series as extrapolated to 1909 by the calendar-year estimates of Kuznets and King.

Labor compensation. Compensation of state- and local-government non-school employees was obtained in 1929 as the sum of the Commerce Department estimates of wages and salaries and the corresponding proportion of supplements to wages and salaries. Average compensation was computed by dividing total compensation by the corresponding estimates of full-time equivalent employees. This average was extrapolated to 1902 by essentially the same method as that described by Fabricant.[21] From 1929 to 1919, the quotient of the Kuznets payroll and employment estimates was used;[22] from 1919 to 1909, estimates by King were available;[23] and from 1909 to 1903, we employed the Douglas estimates of the average annual earnings of government employees in the District of Columbia.[24] The 1903 estimate was extrapolated to 1869 by the average salary per teacher in primary and secondary schools,[25] converted to a calendar-year basis. Total compensation was then computed as the product of employment and average compensation.

While the average compensation series prior to 1909 are substitute estimates, it is not unreasonable to assume that salaries of public school teachers and other public employees tended to move together. External evidence bearing on the reasonableness of the resulting payroll figures is provided by the fact that "other" state and local purchases, which are computed as a residual by deducting payrolls and construction outlays from an independent total for 1890, 1902, and subsequent years to 1939, show an extremely regular trend when deflated by prices and population.

Total compensation of public school employees in 1929 is the Commerce estimate, after splitting supplements between school and nonschool employees in proportion to their wages and salaries. Total compensation was extrapolated to 1909 by the Kuznets and King estimates of school payrolls, which are consistent with their employment estimates which we used to extrapolate our school employment series. From 1910 back, the estimates of salaries of teachers, supervisors, and principals were raised

[21] Fabricant, *op. cit.*, Appendix D.
[22] Kuznets, *National Income*, Tables G-2 and G-7.
[23] Willford I. King, *The National Income and Its Purchasing Power*, New York (NBER), 1930, Tables CXXII and CXXIII.
[24] Douglas, *op. cit.*, p. 392.
[25] *Statistical Abstract, 1922*, p. 103.

by the ratio of our estimates of public school employment to the employment estimates consistent with the salary estimates. The upward adjustment amounted to 4.6 per cent in 1869 and 7.9 per cent in 1909. We thereby assume that the average earnings of teachers in higher educational institutions and "other" public schools move with those of teachers in public primary and secondary schools. The estimates from 1910 back were converted to a calendar-year basis by the same weighting procedures used to convert the employment estimates and were then linked to the school compensation series for the later years by the 1909 ratio.

Average hours and manhours worked. In the nonschool area of general government on a state and local level, there is no central source of information on average hours worked by public employees such as the Civil Service Commission provides for federal workers. Administrative units are so numerous that a comprehensive survey would be out of the question, even if historical records were available. Because the various government units are in a competitive position vis-à-vis private industry for the employment of most types of worker, it seems likely that, broadly speaking, the trend of average hours worked per year by state and local government nonschool employees would have paralleled the trend of average hours in the private economy generally. This proposition is broadly supported by some figures for several scattered dates. According to the Census Bureau estimates based on the sample surveys underlying the *Monthly Report on the Labor Force*, in 1955 average hours worked per week in public administration (excluding education) were 41.7, compared with an average for all industry of 41.8. On the basis of the 1940 *Census of Population*, Volume 3, Part 1, it can be calculated that government employees worked an average of 44.3 hours in the week of March 24–30, compared with an average for all industry of 43.3. In 1920, according to King,[26] public (and professional) employees worked an average of 48.9 hours a week compared with an average of 49.9 for all industries. It is true that the public administration figures cited include federal as well as state and local employees; but even after allowance for this, the parallelism of trend is quite evident. Accordingly, we have multiplied full-time equivalent employment in state and local governments (nonschool) by our estimates of average hours worked per full-time equivalent employee in the total private economy in order to approximate manhours worked in the former sector.

In the public school segment, we assume that average hours worked per day by the average teacher have not changed significantly over the period. In 1940, the average was 7.75 hours, obtained by dividing the average hours per week given in the 1940 *Census of Population* by 5. This figure

[26] Willford I. King, *Employment, Hours and Earnings in Prosperity and Depression, United States, 1920–22*, New York (NBER), 1923.

allows for total time at school, not just classroom time. We then multiplied this figure by estimates of the average number of school days in each year.[27] The resulting estimate of average hours worked per year was then multiplied by annual estimates of the average number of full-time equivalent teachers.

It will be noted that due to the gradual increase in the number of days worked per year by public school teachers, there has been a corresponding increase in average hours worked per year in teaching. The effect of this on the economy would presumably be counterbalanced by a decline in the hours worked in other industries by persons whose primary occupation was in public education.

State and local work relief employment was treated in the same manner as federal work relief, described above.

TABLE K-I

General-Government Employment, by Type, 1869–1953
(thousands)

| | *Total* | *Federal* | | *State and Local* | |
		Civilian	Military	Nonschool	School
1869–78[a]	458	20	41	142	255
1879–88[a]	618	40	37	208	333
1889	725	50	39	255	381
1890	739	52	37	262	388
1891	754	54	36	270	394
1892	774	56	37	279	402
1893	795	57	38	289	411
1894	819	59	41	299	420
1895	837	60	41	308	428
1896	849	62	40	315	432
1897	866	64	41	323	438
1898	1,028	71	183	331	443
1899	993	83	120	340	450
1900	1,023	88	123	352	460
1901	1,055	94	116	375	470
1902	1,071	96	103	392	480
1903	1,096	93	103	411	489
1904	1,130	99	107	429	495
1905	1,167	115	105	445	502
1906	1,213	128	109	464	512
1907	1,265	139	106	492	528
1908	1,333	144	125	521	543
1909	1,396	154	138	546	558

(continued)

[27] *Biennial Survey of Education*, various volumes.

TABLE K-I (concluded)

	Total	Federal		State and Local	
		Civilian	Military	Nonschool	School
1910	1,453	165	135	578	575
1911	1,506	170	141	604	591
1912	1,565	171	149	635	610
1913	1,611	168	151	665	627
1914	1,688	174	161	702	651
1915	1,753	168	169	740	676
1916	1,794	176	174	746	698
1917	2,527	206	835	758	728
1918	5,060	564	2,968	769	759
1919	3,323	509	1,266	769	779
1920	2,314	380	353	774	807
1921	2,302	286	355	811	850
1922	2,264	258	266	854	886
1923	2,297	244	245	898	910
1924	2,399	240	261	960	938
1925	2,492	244	255	1,017	976
1926	2,553	237	251	1,053	1,012
1927	2,642	233	254	1,121	1,034
1928	2,695	240	256	1,146	1,053
1929[b]	2,775	267	261	1,165	1,082
1937	5,056	2,144[c]	313	1,434[c]	1,165
1948	6,073	1,396	1,468	1,791	1,418
1953	9,139	1,783	3,545	2,079	1,732

[a] Annual average for decade.

[b] Total manhours worked in key years are given in Table A-XI. The 1929 breakdown is as follows (in millions): federal civilian, 525; military, 513; state and local nonschool, 2,918; school, 1,441.

[c] Including work relief employment of 1,627,000 in federal and 33,000 in state totals.

Index

(Page numbers in italics refer to material in tables)